The Rise and Fall of Modern Empires, Vol

The Rise and Fall of Modern Empires
Series Editor: Philippa Levine

Titles in the Series:

The Rise and Fall of Modern Empires, Volume I
Social Organization
Owen White

The Rise and Fall of Modern Empires, Volume II
Colonial Knowledges
Saul Dubow

The Rise and Fall of Modern Empires, Volume III
Economics and Politics
Sarah Stockwell

The Rise and Fall of Modern Empires, Volume IV
Reactions to Colonialism
Martin Shipway

The Rise and Fall of Modern Empires, Volume IV

Reactions to Colonialism

Edited by

Martin Shipway

Birkbeck, University of London, UK

LONDON AND NEW YORK

First published 2013 by Ashgate Publishing

Published 2016 by Routledge
2 Park Square, Milton Park, Abingdon, Oxon OX14 4RN
605 Third Avenue, New York, NY 10017

First issued in paperback 2022

Routledge is an imprint of the Taylor & Francis Group, an informa business

British Library Cataloguing in Publication Data
The rise and fall of modern empires.
Volume IV, Reactions to colonialism.
1. Imperialism–Public opinion–History. 2. Indigenous peoples–Attitudes. 3. Anti-imperialist movements–History. 4. National liberation movements–History.
I. Shipway, Martin.
325.3'2-dc23

The Library of Congress has cataloged the printed edition as follows: 2012953509

ISBN 13: 978-1-4094-3856-4 (hbk)
ISBN 13: 978-1-03-240267-3 (pbk)

DOI: 10.4324/9781315237312

Contents

PART IV MODES OF SOLIDARITY

PART V CRITICAL MODES

PART VI MODES OF REMEMBERING

Acknowledgements

Ashgate would like to thank our researchers and the contributing authors who provided copies, along with the following for their permission to reprint copyright material.

Cambridge University Press for the essays: T.O. Ranger (1968), 'Connexions between "Primary Resistance" Movements and Modern Mass Nationalism in East and Central Africa: Parts I and II', *Journal of African History*, **9**, pp. 437–53, 631–41. Copyright © 1968 Cambridge University Press; Stephen Ellis (1986), 'Conclusion', in *The Rising of the Red Shawls: A Revolt in Madagascar, 1895–1899*, Cambridge: Cambridge University Press, pp. 148–66. Copyright © 1986 Cambridge University Press; John S. Lowry (2006), 'African Resistance and Center Party Recalcitrance in the Reichstag Colonial Debates of 1905/06', *Central European History*, **39**, pp. 244–69. Copyright © 2006 Conference Group for Central European History of the American Historical Association, published by Cambridge University Press, translated with permission; Anil Seal (1973), 'Imperialism and Nationalism in India', *Modern Asian Studies*, **7**, pp. 321–47. Copyright © 1973 Cambridge University Press; Frederick Cooper (1996), '"Our Strike": Equality, Anticolonial Politics and the 1947–48 Railway Strike in French West Africa', *Journal of African History*, **37**, pp. 81–118. Copyright © 1996 Cambridge University Press; Matthew Connelly (2001), 'Rethinking the Cold War and Decolonization: The Grand Strategy of the Algerian War for Independence', *International Journal of Middle East Studies*, **33**, pp. 221–45. Copyright © 2001 Cambridge University Press.

Ohio University Press for the essays: John Lonsdale (2003), 'Authority, Gender & Violence: The War within Mau Mau's Fight for Land & Freedom', in E.S. Atieno Odhiambo and John Lonsdale (eds), *Mau Mau & Nationhood: Arms, Authority & Narration*, Oxford, Nairobi and Athens, OH: James Currey, pp. 46–75. Copyright © 2003 James Currey Ltd; Christopher J. Lee (2009), 'Between a Moment and an Era: The Origins and Afterlives of Bandung', in *Making a World After Empire: The Bandung Moment and its Political Afterlives*, Athens: Ohio University Press, pp. 1–42. Copyright © 2009 by the Center for International Studies, Ohio University. Joanna Lewis (2003), '"Daddy Wouldn't Buy Me a Mau Mau": The British Popular Press & the Demoralization of Empire', in E.S. Atieno Odhiambo and John Lonsdale (eds), *Mau Mau & Nationhood: Arms, Authority & Narration*, Oxford, Nairobi and Athens, OH: James Currey, pp. 227–50. Copyright © 2003 James Currey Ltd.

Oxford University Press for the essays: Antoinette Burton (2000), '"States of Injury": Josephine Butler on Slavery, Citizenship, and the Boer War', in Ian Christopher Fletcher, Laura F. Nym Mayhall and Philippa Levine (eds), *Women's Suffrage in the British Empire: Citizenship, Nation and Race*, London and New York: Routledge, pp. 18–32. Copyright © 2000 Antoinette Burton; Gyan Pandey (1988), 'Peasant Revolt and Indian Nationalism: The Peasant Movement in Awadh, 1919–22', in Ranajit Guha and Gayatri Chakravorty Spivak (eds), *Selected Subaltern Studies*, Oxford and New York: Oxford University Press, pp. 234–81. Copyright © 1988 Oxford University Press; Patrick Wolfe (1997), 'History and Imperialism:

A Century of Theory, from Marx to Postcolonialism', *American Historical Review*, **102**, pp. 388–420.

Polity Press Ltd for the essay: Nigel Gibson (2003), 'Nationalism and a New Humanism', in *Fanon: The Postcolonial Imagination*, Cambridge: Polity, pp. 177–205, 236–38. Copyright © 2003 Nigel Gibson.

Taylor & Francis for the essays: Kevin Grant (2001), 'Christian Critics of Empire: Missionaries, Lantern Lectures, and the Congo Reform Campaign in Britain', *Journal of Imperial and Commonwealth History*, **29**, pp. 27–58; Patrick Chabal (1983), 'People's War, State Formation and Revolution in Africa: A Comparative Analysis of Mozambique, Guinea-Bissau, and Angola', *Journal of Commonwealth and Comparative Politics*, **21**, pp. 104–25; James D. Le Sueur (2001), 'Decolonising "French Universalism": Reconsidering the Impact of the Algerian War on French Intellectuals', *Journal of North African Studies*, **6**, pp. 167–86; James A. Ogude (1997), 'Ngugi's Concept of History and the Post-Colonial Discourses in Kenya', *Canadian Journal of African Studies*, **31**, pp. 86–112. Copyright © 1997 The Canadian Association of African Studies (CAAS)/Association Canadienne des Etudes Africaines (ACEA) reprinted by Taylor & Francis Ltd, http://www.tandfonline.com; James McDougall (2005), 'Savage Wars? Codes of Violence in Algeria, 1830s–1990s', *Third World Quarterly*, **26**, pp. 117–31. Copyright © 2005 Third World Quarterly reprinted by Taylor & Francis Ltd, http://www.tandfonline.com; Jim House (2001), 'Antiracist Memories: The Case of 17 October 1961 in Historical Perspective', *Modern and Contemporary France*, **9**, pp. 355–68. Copyright © 2001 Association for the Study of Modern & Contemporary France reprinted by Taylor & Francis Ltd, http://www.tandfonline.com.

University of California Press for the essay: Pierre Brocheux (2009), 'Cultural Transformations', in Pierre Brocheux and Daniel Hémery, *Indochina: An Ambiguous Colonization, 1858–1954*, Berkeley and Los Angeles: University of California Press, pp. 217–49, 425–28. Copyright © 2009 by the Regents of the University of California. Published by the University of California Press.

Every effort has been made to trace all the copyright holders, but if any have been inadvertently overlooked the publishers will be pleased to make the necessary arrangement at the first opportunity.

Publisher's Note

The material in this volume has been reproduced using the facsimile method. This means we can retain the original pagination to facilitate easy and correct citation of the original essays. It also explains the variety of typefaces, page layouts and numbering.

Series Preface

In the modern world, empires have been a constant and characteristic element of the political landscape. While the fact of colonial conquest is by no means unique to the modern period, the empires of the past three hundred years or so share some fundamental characteristics. These were empires much of whose dominance was based on technological prowess; they were principally the province of Western nations; and they frequently claimed a humanitarian impulse connected to the technology that also helped them succeed in conquering other lands. They were also, for the most part, white empires ruling principally over peoples considered inferior, not least because of their racial difference from their European overlords.

We can trace some critical changes in the nature of empire over time, a shift from colonies of settlement intended to absorb population from Europe to colonies of extraction never intended as sites where large numbers of Europeans would settle permanently. There is no simple linear chronology to this: the two always co-existed but at the same time, there is no doubt that in the nineteenth century there was a growing emphasis on the model of extraction, especially where raw materials for industrial production were available, even while settlement continued.

The colonized adopted a variety of tactics in the face of conquest. Many chose to collaborate, a tactic that could certainly enrich and empower a lucky or canny few. Collaboration came in many forms ranging from enforcement of colonial laws to securing a Western education or converting to Christianity. Just as many, however, adopted the opposite route of resistance, and this, too, had many guises from outright rebellion to slow work routines. We need to remember, too, that many people remained unaware or barely cognisant of a colonial presence, especially in places where colonial officials were sparse on the ground. There was a world of difference between colonies such as French Algeria or British India, where a substantial European population influenced everything from available foodstuffs to architecture, from labour opportunities to town planning, and much of sub-Saharan Africa where a mere handful of colonial officials housed in modest dwellings, and often itinerant, was often the only visible manifestation of colonial rule.

These four volumes are closely concerned with all aspects of modern colonial rule. We have divided the volumes into four broad but inevitably overlapping areas. The four overarching themes that we thought best captured the breadth and depth of this critical historical phenomenon are Social Organization, Colonial Knowledges, Economics and Politics, and Reactions to Colonialism. All four volumes offer analyses of the experience of both the colonized and the colonizer, and pay as much attention to ideas as to events, to the materiality of politics and economics as to the cultures that developed around colonial practice. All take seriously the need to explore the impact of empires locally and globally – that is, in the places which were colonized, in the places responsible for that colonization and in the complex and multiple global ramifications of empire-building. For at every level, the fact of empire shaped political and diplomatic relations, the pursuit of both knowledge and profit, the contours of resistance as well as the quotidian rhythms of life in many parts of the world.

We should recognize, moreover, that while the age of formal imperialism may be over, its consequences have been tenacious. The legacies of colonialism haunt a considerable number of our contemporary political conflicts and have shaped the economics of many locations around the world. Policy debates in the early twenty-first century have been profoundly shaped by a neo-imperialist lobby that argues for a continued relevance for a humanitarian imperialism. These four volumes offer a comprehensive assessment of the impact, effects and legacies of modern imperialism.

PHILIPPA LEVINE
University of Texas at Austin, USA

Introduction

In this fourth and final volume on *The Rise and Fall of Modern Empires*, the brief is to capture and characterize ways in which a variety of actors have reacted to colonialism, and some of the ways in which those reactions have been studied in the scholarly literature. In these pages, therefore, reaction to colonialism encompasses, *inter alia*, resistance to colonial conquest and armed or violent rebellion against colonial rule, both at its zenith and towards its end; elite and 'subaltern' responses to the political and cultural challenges of colonial rule, including those that may be characterized as 'nationalist';[1] preparations for the end of colonial rule and the post-colonial succession; legacies and memories of colonialism; and analyses and critiques of colonialism. Alongside the reactions of the colonized, those of metropolitan actors will be considered, including activists in various causes, political elites and the media; and the picture broadens to include international solidarities with the anti-colonial cause. Helping us to impose some limits on our material, Patrick Wolfe, in Chapter 17 of this volume, usefully reminds us that imperialism is neither synonymous with colonialism nor reducible to the word 'empire', but for these purposes, broadly speaking, both in the selection of essays and in this introduction, colonialism will be taken as a subset of the possible forms of imperialism, characterized by the imposition of alien rule within fixed territorial boundaries, typically ones created (or formalized) for the purpose, administered within the framework of what we may think of as a colonial state. Further, although the colonial period may be seen as a mere 'episode' in the *longue durée* of Asian or African history (J.F. Ade Ajayi, cited in Cooper, 1994, p. 1522), colonialism will be taken here as a historically contingent structural feature of modern colonial empires, mostly from the conquests of the later nineteenth century to the period of post-1945 decolonization.

One conceptual hazard needs to be addressed from the outset. In privileging reactions to colonialism, the binarism implied by our title may end up reproducing (even if reversing) the polarities inherent in colonial ideologies and practices. As Frederick Cooper has argued:

> Both [Indian and African] historiographies wrestle with – but do not quite escape – the dichotomous vision characteristic of colonial ideologies, originating in the opposition of civilized colonizer and primitive colonized. The risk is that in exploring the colonial binarism one reproduces it, either by new variations of the dichotomy (modern versus traditional) or by inversion (the destructive imperialist versus the sustaining community of the victims). The difficulty is to confront the power behind European expansion without assuming it was all-determining and to probe the clash of different forms of social organization without treating them as self-contained and autonomous. (1994, p. 1517)

[1] Associated with the subaltern studies group of radical Indian historians, to whom we return below, the term 'subaltern', although derived from the Italian Marxist Antonio Gramsci, is used following its definition in the *Concise Oxford Dictionary* to mean 'of inferior rank' and hence 'as a name for the general attribute of subordination in South Asian society' (Guha, 1988b, p. 35). We return to nationalism below.

Cooper's binaries of 'colonizer/colonized, Western/non-Western, and domination/resistance' are inescapably reflected in the idea of 'reactions to colonialism', but a further dichotomy prevails in the literature of anti-colonialism even when not explicit. This is the highly charged, but complex, relationship between resistance and 'collaboration'. While it is almost impossible to use the latter term without moral connotation, it covers a range of social and political accommodations with imperial and colonial *force majeure*. Here, the two opposing terms of resistance and collaboration will be viewed as at each end of a scale of possible strategies, rather than as polarized opposites. For imperial historians of the 'Cambridge' school (most notably Ronald Robinson and Jack Gallagher but also Anil Seal, Chapter 7 in this volume), and also for John Breuilly (1993) in his magisterial study of nationalism, collaboration was by far the more interesting strategy.[2] For Robinson and Gallagher, the collaboration of local elites helped explain how the British and other empires were drawn into late nineteenth-century colonial expansion; collaboration was crucial to understanding how British colonial rule could be exercised 'on the cheap', and it provided the basis for an explanation of decolonization, as British colonial governments started to 'run out' of willing collaborators in straitened and ideologically challenging post-1945 circumstances. Correspondingly, Robinson and Gallagher dismissed early resistance movements as 'romantic, reactionary struggles against the facts' (quoted in Chapter 2 by T.O. Ranger, p. 39), while classifying later nationalisms as synthetic, invented creatures of the late colonial imagination (Gallagher, 1982). This lofty rudeness, redolent for Wolfe, in Chapter 17, of 'colonial boys'-club rhetoric' (p. 505), was as nothing, however, compared with Ranajit Guha's invective against the contortions performed in the cause of 'elite' nationalist historiography:

> The modality common to [this historiography] is to uphold Indian nationalism as a phenomenal expression of the goodness of the native elite with the antagonistic aspect of their relation to the colonial regime made, against all evidence, to look larger than its collaborationist aspect, their role as promoters of the cause of the people than that as exploiters and oppressors, their altruism and self-abnegation than their scramble for the modicum of power and privilege granted by their rulers in order to make sure of their support for the Raj. (1988a, p. 38)

Collaboration recurs in the following pages in various guises, including 'loyalists', auxiliaries or 'évolués' (literally, the 'evolved', a singularly revealing term in French and Belgian colonial discourse) effectively taking on the colonial state's dirty work; Fanon's 'national bourgeoisie' class (Fanon, 1965) taking the reins of power from retreating colonial forces, and/or working to head off social revolution; and the 'comprador' acting as intermediary for the maintenance of post-colonial dependency on international capitalism.

The organization of the volume is broadly chronological. We start with two groups of essays relating to the response to repression and conquest in the later nineteenth century. Part I, Modes of Resistance, presents three studies of resistance movements: one in India; a general study of 'primary' resistance in Eastern and Central Africa; and a more focused study of Madagascar. Part II, Modes of 'Civilizing', is devoted to metropolitan responses to colonial expansion, but reveals the ambivalences that accompanied the acquisition and running of empires. The essays in Part III, Modes of Imagining, address the core question

[2] The definitive statement of Gallagher's distinctive view of the British Empire is his *The Decline, Revival and Fall of the British Empire* (1982).

of anti-colonial nationalism. Three are concerned with the earlier twentieth century and with Asia, and three with Africa in the period of decolonization. Part IV, Modes of Solidarity, focuses on the post-1945 period, but widens the field of view to include international and metropolitan responses to decolonization. Part V, Critical Modes, comprises essays dealing with theoretical and literary approaches to empire and to colonialism. And, finally, Part VI, Modes of Remembering, addresses themes of post-colonial violence and memory. Some striking thematic correspondences between the parts may lead the reader to discover further overarching resonances within the volume.

Modes of Resistance

Our first section treats the broad theme of resistance to colonialism in the later nineteenth century. Central to this topic are themes of memories and continuities and, related to this, the question of sources. In Chapter 1, Pankaj Rag raises crucial issues as to how a reliable 'history from below' may be written, given that the archival record is shot through with the presuppositions of the colonial 'official mind'. Rag's topic is the 1857 Sepoy Rebellion (still often known in the post-imperial English imagination as the Indian Mutiny, and referred to by Rag only as '1857') and takes issue with one of the most celebrated interventions of the Subaltern Studies group. In 1983, Ranajit Guha proposed 'inverting' the meaning of official sources in order to capture their underlying sense: 'insurgents' should thus be read as 'peasants', 'fanatic' as 'Islamic puritan', 'daring and wanton attacks on the Inhabitants' as 'resistance to oppression' (1988c, p. 59). For Rag, this approach 'seems to move within a framework of binary opposites which is problematic' (p. 5); and to counter it he proposes a rich and multilayered reading of 1857 based on popular sources including folk tales and folk songs. Rag's approach brings out the eccentricities and ambiguities of local and individual responses to the rebellion; he challenges facile notions of national unity during the rebellion, and elucidates a more nuanced and realistic set of 'intermediary attitudes' ranging from 'stoic indifference' to 'fluctuating vacillations' to outright hostility (p. 31).

In the next two essays, T.O. Ranger and Stephen Ellis explore the connections between 'primary' resistance associated with the response to colonial conquest and later nationalisms. Writing in 1968, Ranger (Chapter 2) challenges traditional historical readings which saw early resisters as reactionary. He synthesizes work on Central Africa, his own area of specialism, and on East Africa to show how early anti-colonial resistance foreshadowed, and was often connected with, later nationalist movements. The similarities, particularly in such cases as the 1896–97 Ndebele-Shona risings in Southern Rhodesia (now Zimbabwe) and the 1905 Maji-Maji rebellion in German East Africa (later Tanganyika, now Tanzania; see Iliffe, 1967, 1979), may be found in the scale of those rebellions, but also in the movements' claims to a broader identity than the merely local. Typically, also, their leadership embraced a millenarian message, as if to re-assert African control in the face of colonial domination. The connections may be direct, through the continuity of resistance, or the link may be an appeal to the memory of primary resistance. Such an appeal can cut both ways: ordinary Africans could be as much deterred as they were mobilized by the memory of defeat. Much depended on whether a satisfactory answer could be found to the question posed by Tanganyikan elders to the nationalist leader Joseph Nyerere: 'How can we win without guns?'

In Chapter 3, Ellis brings some of these issues into sharper focus with respect to the rebellion of the Menalamba (or 'red shawls', so-called as their shawls were ingrained with their native red soil) in Madagascar, 1895–96, but this reading also brings out some contrasts. In particular, this protest was not, in Ellis's view, 'primary' resistance. Although conquered by the French in the 1890s and formally annexed in 1896, Madagascar had effectively been a colonial state since the 1860s, with the Malagasy elite collaborating with the island's rival 'informal' rulers, the British and French. Though the insurgents elude precise characterization, as their social status, aims and outlook differed from region to region, this was essentially a mature nationalist movement which arose on the peripheries of the central Imerina kingdom, led by local dignitaries seeking to expel the French invaders (and indeed any Europeans) and the Malagasy elite who supported them. Paradoxically, they fought in the Queen's name, though her position was also sustained by the French. A strong appeal to a remembered Malagasy past combined with a heady millenarianism in which the British figured as improbable messiahs. Magic too played a part, including a belief, shared with Maji-Maji and revived during the 1947 Insurrection, that bullets could be turned to water – though, as with later Mau Mau oathing in Kenya, this was exaggerated by Europeans keen to emphasize an atavistic primitivism. Defeat forced the Menalamba's patriotic ideals underground, but their memory was dramatically revived in the 1947 Insurrection, an under-studied and ill-understood episode in French decolonization (see Tronchon 1974/1986). When this insurrection was crushed in its turn, the two events were elided, their memory only revived at the time of the 1972 populist revolution against Philibert Tsiranana's pro-French regime. As with Mau Mau (see Lonsdale, Chapter 11 and Ogude, Chapter 19), the memory of defeated resistance or, as in Algeria, the memory of any but the official resistance (see McDougall, Chapter 20), was an uncomfortable one for the eventual post-colonial state.

Modes of 'Civilizing'

Here the perspective shifts to metropolitan responses to conquest and to the often discomfiting realities of colonialism in its ascendancy. The period to 1914 is the age of 'classic' critiques of imperialism, notably J.A. Hobson's *Imperialism, A Study* (1902) and V.I. Lenin's *Imperialism: The Highest Stage of Capitalism* (2010, written 1916) (on which see Wolfe, Chapter 17 and Sarah Stockwell's introduction to Volume III in this series). Yet none of the responses to colonialism surveyed in this section are critiques of colonialism per se; rather, the primary motivation in each case was something else entirely, whether the promotion of Christian evangelism, the cause of women's suffrage or the outcomes of parliamentary politics. At the same time, even while upholding and promoting the colonial endeavour, all sought to improve its execution, while also revealing an acute awareness of its costs, whether counted in lost souls or in monies misspent or misallocated.

European doubts about the colonial enterprise in this period typically crystallized around the so-called Congo Free State, run until 1908 as a private fiefdom by the Belgian king, Leopold II. In Chapter 4, Kevin Grant throws new light on the ultimately successful international campaign against the regime's atrocities by highlighting the role of missionaries in bringing the cause to British public attention through the novel medium of the lantern lecture. If the 'incorruptible *kodak*' revealed truths that perhaps could not have been conveyed more powerfully in another medium, Grant argues that 'the Congo atrocity photographs were incorruptible in the eyes of the British public because missionaries produced them and narrated their significance to promote evangelical reform' (p. 94). Further, Grant seeks to correct a 'secular bias' (p. 116) which has tended to emphasize the influence of radicals such as E.D. Morel over the missionaries' achievements (see Louis, 2006; Porter, 2001).

For missionaries and liberals campaigning against the Congo Free State, it helped that the abuses in question were not being perpetrated within the *British* Empire. British imperialism and liberalism were uneasy allies in this period, provided enough was done to ensure that, as Antoinette Burton puts it in Chapter 5, the British Empire's 'basic goodness, if not greatness' (p. 134) was not compromised. Some of the ideological convolutions to which this position could lead are explored in Burton's study of a tract supporting the British cause in the Boer War by the veteran feminist campaigner Josephine Butler, who saw it as a campaign against Afrikaner ill treatment of Africans. Whereas a younger generation of feminists and other liberal groups opposed the war, and in particular British mistreatment of Boer women and children, Butler recycled older feminist campaigns against slavery, arguing that South Africa be brought more fully under beneficent British control. As Burton argues, this alignment with British imperialism was a means to a wider end, which was to demonstrate women's fitness to participate as citizens in the British polity.

From one perspective, Burton is arguing for the reconnection of imperial and domestic histories. Whereas the two have tended to be pursued along parallel but unconnected historiographical tracks, the 'new imperial history' has re-evaluated the links between empire and metropolitan politics and culture. John Lowry, in Chapter 6, offers an example of how historians have downplayed colonial questions, in this case in the history of imperial Germany to 1918. This is part of a wider project to 'decolonize' German domestic political history, by re-emphasizing the agency of colonized Africans in it. Again the focus is on colonial abuses in the empires before 1914, and on no fewer than six German imperial campaigns against African resistance movements, three in German South-West Africa (now Namibia). These were brutal, but extremely costly, campaigns: sixteen dreadnoughts could have been constructed with the monies spent on South-West Africa alone. What is perhaps surprising is not (as happened in 1908) that this state of affairs should have ended a parliamentary coalition of long standing between the imperial government and the German Catholic Centre party, but that its wider significance has gone unrecognized.

Modes of Imagining

This section takes us to the heart of what it may mean to 'react' to colonialism. In a sequence of more or less discrete case studies, the first three relate to the period of 'high' colonialism in Asia before the Second World War, while the next three treat African cases in the period of decolonization. Although ranging widely in both geographical and thematic scope, the essays revolve around two broad and interlinked sets of questions. The first concerns the response of the colonized to the challenges thrown down by colonial rule, whether those challenges arise from political structures and processes or more broadly from impact on the cultures and identities of the colonized. The second set of questions concerns the futures imagined by the colonized, and the extent to which those imagined futures could be reconciled with the constraints and expectations imposed by imperial domination.

Before proceeding, we need to define nationalism, a term that carries considerable historiographical and theoretical baggage.[3] A brief descriptive account of two influential models of nationalism may help place the following selections in context. The first is John Breuilly's, from his *Nationalism and the State* (1993). Working on a wide comparative basis embracing both European and 'colonial' nationalist movements, Breuilly defines nationalism in terms of its relationship with the (eventual) nation-state, arguing that 'the focus of nationalist movements is upon taking over the state'; it follows that 'not all opposition activity under colonial regimes can be regarded as nationalist' (1993, p. 224; see also Shipway, 2008, pp. 37–38). In Breuilly's model, nationalist movements act along two axes, elite coordination and popular mobilization; a third possible axis is international legitimacy. The second model, widely influential since its first appearance almost thirty years ago, is Benedict Anderson's in *Imagined Communities* (1983). In common with many theorists (Breuilly but see also Gellner, 1993; Hobsbawm, 1990) Anderson sees nationalism as an essentially modern phenomenon, appealing to a shared past situated in the *longue durée*, but accompanying the transition to modernity of American (primarily hispanophone) 'creoles', Europeans and colonized Asians and Africans. In contrast to Breuilly, Anderson is primarily concerned with the cultural sphere, and with the emergence of national consciousness from a community of people 'imagining' themselves as a national unit. In his second edition, Anderson responded to criticisms of his earlier 'oversimplified' treatment of Third World nationalisms with a new chapter, 'Census, Map, Museum', which

> analyses the way in which, quite unconsciously, the nineteenth-century colonial state (and policies that its mindset encouraged) dialectically engendered the grammar of the nationalisms that eventually arose to combat it. Indeed, one might go so far as to say that the state imagined its local adversaries, as in an ominous prophetic dream, well before they came into historical existence. (1991, pp. xiii–xiv; 2006, p. xiv)

His model has been subjected to extensive criticism over the years, not least from the subaltern studies group, notably Partha Chatterjee, whose central objection is that, if 'nationalisms in the rest of the world have to choose their imagined community from certain "modular" forms already made available to them by Europe and the Americas, what do they have left to imagine?' Chatterjee posits an anti-colonial nationalism that grants Western hegemony in the 'material' domain, but maintains sovereignty in an 'inner', purely spiritual domain (1993, pp. 5–6).

The first two essays in this section represent opposite poles in modern Indian historiography. Arguing against an older school of constitutional history focusing on British policy-making, Anil Seal's classic study of the relationship between imperialism and nationalism in India (Chapter 7) shows how the 'collaborator system' developed over time into the full-blown representative system that had emerged by the 1930s. In effect, the Raj 'cut the steps' that nationalist elites ascended from local government to the regions and eventually to national level, and so prepared the transition realized in 1947 from 'British Raj' to 'Congress Raj'. Ranajit Guha may have (somewhat unfairly) had Seal in mind when he wrote that the 'central modality' of 'elitist historiography of the colonialist or neo-colonialist type ... describe[s] Indian nationalism as a sort of "learning process" through which the native elite become

[3] For a useful collection of essays and readings, see Balakrishnan (1996).

involved in politics by trying to negotiate the maze of institutions and the corresponding cultural complex introduced by the colonial authorities in order to govern the country' (1988a, p. 38). Seal shows how representative politics forced Indian elites into the identities suggested by its arbitrary representative categories, much as the colonial census, in Anderson's argument (2006, pp. 164–70), created the subnational or 'ethnic' categories on which later nationalist movements came to rely.

In terms of Breuilly's axes of nationalist action, while Seal focuses on elite coordination at the expense of mass mobilization, Gyan Pandey, representing the subaltern studies group, is concerned chiefly with the peasant masses, but denies that they were mobilized by a nationalist elite. Indeed, he argues in Chapter 8 precisely that the peasant insurgents of Awadh (Oudh), who 'burst onto the national stage' during the 1921–22 Non-Cooperation Movement, were neither 'manipulated' by outside agitators (as the British had it) nor mobilized by the Congress leadership. While he suggests (echoing Rag's concerns) that the peasants' view of the struggle will 'probably never be recovered' (p. 202), Pandey shows how they developed their own vision of what Gandhi stood for (and it was not non-violence), their own ideas of *swaraj* (self-rule) and the robust means by which to achieve it. He also shows how the Congress leadership stepped in, not to mobilize the peasants' struggle within the framework of non-violence, but rather to ensure 'that the struggle be abandoned altogether – in the interests of "unity" in … the "greater" struggle against the British' (p. 211).[4]

Chapter 9, by Pierre Brocheux, is taken from a comprehensive study of French Indochina to 1940, co-authored with Daniel Hémery (2001). Here we see the colonial state apparatus at full steam, intervening not only in the social and economic lives of its colonized subjects but also, decisively, in the cultural sphere. The response of an emergent Vietnamese intelligentsia was one of intense cultural debate and renewal, in which colonial resources were deployed not so much against the colonial state as in spite of it. From a rich weave, one significant strand concerns *quoc ngu*, the transcription of Vietnamese into Latin characters, an enterprise originally undertaken by Jesuits in the seventeenth century and which nineteenth-century French colonizers saw as opening 'a clear path for our civilizing ideas to penetrate' (p. 254). This may have been so, but *quoc ngu* was energetically taken up by the Vietnamese themselves in preference to the unwieldy use of Chinese characters. Its spread promoted literacy and fuelled a veritable explosion of writing and publishing. Not least, *quoc ngu* was a vital vector for the propagation of revolutionary ideas in preparation for the 'opportune moment' of 1945.[5]

The end of the Second World War was a pivotal moment for decolonization, but in contrast to the wave of Asian decolonizations triggered directly by the Japanese occupation of south-east Asian colonies, 1945 arguably marked only the beginning of African decolonization. Indeed, though weakened by the impact of the war, the colonial powers typically sought to renew the bases of colonial rule in Africa. Our next two essays offer careful and nuanced readings of how Africans reacted to, and, more importantly, shaped the dynamics of this African late colonialism. Chapter 10, Frederick Cooper's account of the strike that paralysed the railway system of French West Africa in 1947–48, sits alongside his wider, ground-breaking study

[4] For a contrasting view of the events of 1919–22, see, for example, Brown (1989, pp. 139–75). On 'Gandhi as signifier', see Amin (1988). For a history of modern India sympathetic to subaltern studies positions, see Sarkar (1989).

[5] For a more detailed study, see Marr (1983, esp. chs 4 and 8, pp. 137–89 and 327–67); on 1945, see Marr (1995).

of the labour question in British and French colonial Africa in this period (Cooper, 1996). Cooper shows how the aims of an emerging labour movement were both related to, but also distinct from, and in tension with, wider nationalist politics. The singularity of the strike arose from the ways in which it cut across and complicated categories and identities within the late colonial state. Escaping the usual roles assigned to colonized Africans as either 'peasants' or 'évolués' (assimilated clerks or intellectuals), strikers behaved according to newly learned trade union codes of conduct and, more remarkably, were treated by the French colonial state as strikers engaged in legitimate industrial action. Far from fighting for their freedom, these workers apparently aimed to achieve parity with their French counterparts, in ways that suggested (as it turned out abortively) that the French rhetoric of 'assimilation' might actually have a point. At the same time, paradoxically, the strike's success depended at least in part on the traditional African ways in which the strikers sustained their action by falling back on their rural roots, and on the support of women.

It would be almost unthinkable not to include the work of John Lonsdale on Kenya in a collection of this kind (see also Berman and Lonsdale, 1992; Lonsdale, 1990). Mau Mau has generated a protean historiography, expanding to accommodate every academic and political agenda. While more recent work has focused on the abuses of British counter-insurgency and on the ambiguities of the Gikuyu 'loyalist' position (Anderson, 2005; Elkins, 2005; Branch, 2009), in Chapter 11 Lonsdale situates the movement within the wider Kenyan context, underlining the tensions over land and status within the Gikuyu people which generated Mau Mau, and contrasting these with the factors that spared other Kenyan ethnic groups the full horrors of internecine conflict. He delves into the self-made idiosyncrasy of Mau Mau's culture of insurgency and shows how attempts to build a forest utopia foundered on awareness of what the fighters had lost by isolating themselves from their home culture. Though arguably not directed primarily against the British, Mau Mau acquired a new national awareness, but at best their resistance achieved the 'pyrrhic victory' of forcing the British to rule differently, at the expense of their own morale and cohesion.

Finally in this section, in Chapter 12 Patrick Chabal discusses the prospects for social revolution in the three lusophone African states of Angola, Mozambique and Guinea-Bissau, whose protracted wars of decolonization eventually precipitated the end of the Portuguese Salazarist dictatorship in the 1974 'Revolution of Flowers'. Writing less than a decade after the revolution, and still *in medias res*, Chabal offers a clear-sighted analysis of the parallels and differences between the three cases, as well as the contrasts between these 'late late' decolonizations and those that preceded them. He steers a middle course between scepticism and 'redfoot' revolutionary idealism, to suggest that social revolution was unlikely but not impossible in at least one of the three countries.

Modes of Solidarity

In the first essay in this section, Christopher Lee (Chapter 13) characterizes some of the challenges confronting the historian of decolonization:

> From an empirical standpoint, it [i.e. decolonization] is both a contingent moment *and* a long-standing process with deep roots, at times originating with the act of initial colonization itself. It is an experience that is at once uniquely individual in scope – to people, communities, and nation-states

> alike – and in retrospect seemingly universal: the world witnessed a momentous wave of newly independent nation-states during the second half of the twentieth century, more than doubling the number of members in the United Nations. (p. 381)

So far in this volume, the relationship between colonizer and colonized has largely been explored case by individual case, in ways which, in Lee's terms, tend to privilege long-standing process over contingency, and individual experience over the universal. By contrast, the first two essays in this section situate decolonization within the post-war international system and place it in tension with the other great structuring event of the post-1945 world, the Cold War. Like decolonization, the Cold War was also experienced as domestic conflict at the metropolitan centres of empire; the following two essays remind us that, equally, a process of 'internal decolonization', however imperfect, operated in Paris and London.

Movements of pan-Africanism and pan-Asianism had been around for a long time in September 1945, when the sixth Pan-African Congress met in Manchester, England.[6] The distance travelled between Manchester and the Bandung Conference, hosted by Indonesia's founding President Ahmed Sukarno in April 1955, may be measured with reference to the staging posts of Asian decolonization; uppermost in people's minds still at Bandung was no doubt the catastrophic defeat of the French army by the People's Army of Vietnam at Dien Bien Phu, in May 1954.[7] Dien Bien Phu, of course, is also integral to any narrative of the Cold War (the PAV was equipped by Mao's China, the French army by the US). This ideological ambivalence – anti-colonialism versus anti-'imperialism' – extends in a different way to Bandung itself: to meet under the banner of 'non-alignment' was to define oneself in relation to the two poles of the Cold War, if only by opposition. Similarly, the very concept of a 'Third World' (a term coined only in 1952 by the French demographer Alfred Sauvy) evoked not only the Cold War antagonists (the 'First' and 'Second' Worlds) but also the '*Tiers Etat*' (Third Estate), the French commoners of 1789: the forging of international communities, it would seem, may be every bit as 'modular' as Anderson's 'imagined communities' (Tomlinson, 2003; Wolf-Phillips, 1987). As Lee points out, only three national delegations at Bandung (India, Indonesia and Burma) explicitly supported non-alignment, and the famous 'Bandung Spirit' was soon dissipated by the participants' subsequent regional rivalries and ideological alignments. The Conference itself, then, is largely reducible to its eponymous 'spirit', though it may also be studied in its own right as an innovative example of 'diplomacy as theatre' (see Shimazu, 2011). Lee, conversely, takes Bandung, representing Cold War-era Afro-Asian solidarities, as the launch point for an exploration of several overlapping historical and interdisciplinary fields, taking us beyond the endpoint of decolonization and indeed right up to present-day Sino-African engagement.

If evidence were needed as to the effects of the 'Bandung spirit', in Chapter 14 Matthew Connelly accounts for the immediate, concrete impact it had on the Algerian war of independence, launched on 1 November 1954 and still in its early stages at the time of the Conference. Not only did the Algerian National Liberation Front (FLN) gain vital legitimacy as part of a joint North African delegation alongside Tunisia and Morocco, but the Conference itself inspired an upsurge of insurgent attacks, setting a trend repeated every time the Algerian issue was raised in international fora. Connelly takes this further, showing how the

[6] Lee lists the sequence of pan-African and pan-Asian congresses starting in 1900 (pp. 385–86).

[7] For a recent account, see Logevall (2012).

FLN brought off a 'diplomatic revolution', in which a brilliant Algerian campaign on the international stage transcended the FLN's weaknesses on the Algerian battlefield, where they were dramatically outnumbered, outgunned and outmanoeuvred by a French army that at its peak numbered 450,000 men and deployed a generation of French conscripts and reservists as well as Algerian auxiliaries, the so-called *harkis*, who tragically found themselves on the wrong side at independence (see also Connelly, 2002).[8] The FLN exploited the solidarities of an emerging decolonized bloc at the United Nations, but also played France, the United States and the Soviet Union off against each other. The FLN's legacy may be traced in its grip on power in Algeria even to this day (see McDougall, Chapter 20), but more positively in the inspiration it offered the leaders of other national liberation movements including Nelson Mandela and Yasir Arafat.

Crucially, the Algerian conflict also played out in metropolitan France, in clashes between rival nationalist movements within the Algerian immigrant community, or yet more dramatically between Algerian militants and the French police (see House, Chapter 21), but also in the debates and polemics conducted on the Parisian Left Bank by a self-reflexive French intelligentsia, for whom, as James Le Sueur shows in Chapter 15, Algeria became an essential but fundamentally divisive cause. The Algerian war raised questions as to whom French intellectuals should support – here too the leftist, secularist FLN marshalled intellectual endorsement in preference to the more culturally conservative National Algerian Movement (MNA) of Messali Hadj, though this led to charges that French intellectuals were effectively deciding, in quasi-colonial fashion, who should lead Algeria to freedom. The crisis in the Communist world following Stalin's death split the anti-colonial movement, as much of the French Left, notably a still hegemonic French Communist Party, could not bring itself to condemn violent Soviet repression in Budapest in 1956 – which arguably mirrored French state repression in Algiers. Intellectuals debated the legitimacy of violence; campaigned relentlessly against the use of torture; affirmed the conscript's right to refuse to fight in Algeria; were persistently banned and censored; and, in the case of the Jeanson network of 'suitcase carriers' (*porteurs de valises*) for the FLN, crossed the line into active illegality.[9] More fundamentally, as Le Sueur argues, in supporting the cause of Algerian freedom from France, intellectuals were effectively arguing an end to French culture's post-enlightenment claims to universalism – claims on which French colonialism had been founded. As Todd Shepard (2006) has argued, decolonization for France brought a retreat into the 'hexagon' of metropolitan France, but also a fundamental refashioning of French identity.

British intellectual responses to the end of empire or to South African apartheid may seem pallid in comparison with their French equivalents (Howe, 1993). Conversely, studies of French media representations of decolonization tend to be considerably less lively than Joanna Lewis's account of Mau Mau's treatment in the British popular press (Chapter 16) (but see Rioux, 1990).[10] Mau Mau was of course a gift to racy, populist journalism as practised by the

[8] Although research on Algeria has burgeoned, recent narrative accounts of the war have not surpassed Alistair Horne's classic *A Savage War of Peace: Algeria, 1954-1962* (2006); but see Evans (2011) and, in French, Thénault (2005); on historiography, Branche (2005).

[9] For a more detailed discussion, see Le Sueur (2001).

[10] The popular photo-magazine, *Paris-Match*, 6–13 November 1954, reported the launching of the FLN's insurrection as 'The Terrorist Wave has Crossed the Algerian Frontier', against a full-cover portrait of the Italian screen icon Gina Lollobrigida.

Daily Mail and *Daily Mirror*, with its prurient rumours of bloodthirsty oathing ceremonies, tales of plucky, revolver-toting Englishwomen in sunglasses and headscarves, and horrific images of *panga* attacks on white settlers (more of whom were killed in traffic accidents in Nairobi than at the hands of Mau Mau) (Lonsdale, 1990) and their pets. However, Lewis charts a gradual shift as the Emergency wore on, masked by prolonged periods of a more characteristic indifference to imperial affairs which neglected even the Hola camp massacre in 1959 (to say nothing of the horrors of the Kenyan 'pipeline' of detention camps). By the turn of the 1960s, not only the Labour-leaning *Mirror* but also the right-wing *Mail* were revealing a 'class-driven distrust for the bearers of imperial power in colonial Africa' (p. 465), and urging the renunciation of an increasingly burdensome empire.[11]

Critical Modes

Frantz Fanon has become an almost legendary figure, an exemplary activist in the Algerian cause and an indispensable theorist of anti-colonial revolution, more recently enjoying, as Patrick Wolfe states in Chapter 17, 'foundational status in postcolonialism' (p. 511). He was also, quite simply, a writer and critic; had leukaemia not claimed him aged 36 in 1961 he might have lived into ripe old age to critique 9/11 or its disastrous consequences. Even without Fanon's activism, writing about colonialism may itself be a reaction to colonialism, whether it springs from a priori ideological positioning or simply from sympathy with the 'subaltern'. Considering only the contributors to this volume, first, it was always likely that Africanist historians writing in the wake of decolonization, including Ranger, Lonsdale and (rather later) Chabal, would constitute themselves, as Lonsdale puts it, '[in] our anxious middle class way ... into a Committee of Concerned Scholars for a Free Africa' (1981, p. 143). Second, Ranajit Guha's de facto manifesto for the subaltern studies group (1988a) declares an agenda that transcends the historiographical, in which the relative status of 'subaltern' and 'elite' reflects more than purely historical concerns. Third, French intellectual commitment to the Algerian cause has inspired the involvement of a younger generation of historians, whose work has become possible with the gradual opening of the archives, but who have also engaged in a wider 'war of memories' surrounding the war (see Branche, 2005; Stora, 2007).

Chapter 17, the first essay in this section, is a case in point, as Patrick Wolfe's concluding sentence starts with a modest premise that colours the whole essay: 'If we wish to produce histories that tell us enough about imperialism to suggest ways of resisting it...' (p. 523). Though his interest in Aboriginal/European encounters in Australia is otherwise unrepresented in this series, this selection has been made for the comprehensive survey he offers of theoretical approaches to imperialism over much of the twentieth century. He also adopts a useful analytical framework, organizing his material around 'two oppositions that, though misleading, have demonstrably structured debates about imperialism' (p. 492). First, his distinction between the internal and the external has been followed here in the opposition of the 'colonial' and the 'imperial' and in a focus on the colonial 'periphery', while allowing that the poles of 'centre' and 'periphery' may sometimes be reversed. Second, he opposes the ideal and the material, 'whose alternatives include ideological versus practical, cultural versus

[11] On the camps, see Elkins (2005); on British popular responses to the end of Empire, see Ward (2001) and Howe (2005).

economic, discursive versus instrumental, etc.' (p. 492). This Cartesian distinction is of course an artificial one in practice, though it helpfully distinguishes the cultural from the economic, but, as Wolfe notes, most theories 'stress one at the expense of the other' (p. 492). As becomes clear, this refers to the Marxian emphasis on the material versus the more recent focus on discursive power derived from Michel Foucault. This 'cultural turn' may be discerned, for example, in the shift within the subaltern studies group from a broadly Marxian perspective (with a possibly Maoist insistence on the peasant over the worker as agent of revolution) to a more Foucauldian idea of all-pervading cultural domination (see Spivak, 1988). Conversely, Wolfe acknowledges Edward Said's sleight of hand in *Orientalism* (1978), a primordial post-colonial text, in yoking 'Foucault's concept of discourse ... to Antonio Gramsci's thoroughly Marxist concept of hegemony', as not to do so would have 'entailed an erasure of subjecthood that would have taken the colonizer out of colonialism' (pp. 511–12).

Aside from Fanon's actual life and work, there are also the posthumous, semi-fictional Fanons, not least the prophet of violence espoused by movements such as the Black Panthers and the Basque separatist movement, ETA; this latter persona may be owed in some measure to Jean-Paul Sartre's self-indulgent preface to *Wretched of the Earth*:

> The rebel's weapon is the proof of his humanity. For in the first days of the revolt you must kill: to shoot down a European is to kill two birds with one stone, to destroy an oppressor and the man he oppresses at the same time: there remain a dead man, and a free man; the survivor, for the first time, feels a national soil under his feet. (Fanon, 1965, p. 19)

Nigel Gibson, in Chapter 18, does Fanon the service of treating him as a serious political philosopher, analysing his model of post-colonial nationalism, as presented in *Wretched of the Earth*, both as it appears in an African decolonization that Fanon could already see going sour around him and as an unattained ideal. Gibson posits three possible nationalisms: a 'moderate and conformist' 'nationalism$_1$', in which an emergent, kleptocratic, 'nationalist bourgeoisie' gratefully takes over the state from its former colonial rulers; a more militant 'nationalism$_2$', loosely modelled on the Algerian FLN, which favours modernization, but without engaging the people, unless by exhorting them to further sacrifices; and a utopian 'nationalism$_3$', which seeks to harness the people's efforts by educating them towards a new humanism (p. 527). Perhaps the saving grace of Fanon's premature death was that it spared him further disillusionment.[12]

To switch tracks from history to literature can be a jarring manoeuvre, though it has been practised with ease in both directions by many critics in the post-colonial field. In the case of the Kenyan novelist Ngugi wa Thiong'o, the shift is facilitated by Ngugi's position; he sees literature and history as closely intertwined, and, as James Ogude notes in Chapter 19, considers his novels a 'part of Kenya's historiography' (p. 577). At the heart of Ngugi's Gikuyu-centred fictional world is the conflict between the haves and have-nots or, more precisely, between Ogot's 'loyalist crowd' (1972) and the dispossessed who turned to Mau Mau. However, Ngugi's polarized opposition between the two sides is at odds with a more subtle exposition of the collaboration/resistance dyad, as expounded at the outset of this introduction, and as carried in a strand of Kenyan historiography running from Ogot to Daniel Branch (2009). Although it is already central to his early writings up to his seminal *A Grain of*

[12] For a comprehensive biography, see Macey (2000).

Wheat (1966), Ngugi's concern with the wrong direction taken by post-independence Kenya was confirmed by his study of Marx, Fanon *et al.*, but became increasingly wedded to the emerging arguments of the dependency theorists in the 1970s.[13] As Ogude argues, the headline thesis of dependency applied to Africa, 'how Europe underdeveloped Africa', coupled with Fanon's denunciation of the 'national bourgeoisie' (Gibson's 'nationalism$_1$'), trapped Ngugi in a stark exposition of Kenyan and Gikuyu realities, forcing him to suppress more complex realities in various narrative 'ellipses', notably in his portrayal of Mau Mau as 'a monolithic nationalist movement devoid of any contradictions' (p. 568). A further paradox of Ngugi's writing explored by Ogude opposes his not unwarranted view of modern African ethnicity as 'a product of the colonial history of divide and rule' (p. 573), on the one hand, with his radical decision to switch from writing in English to his native Gikuyu, thus arguably contributing to the 'reinvention of Gikuyu ethnic consciousness' (p. 574) on the other.

Modes of Remembering

The final section of this collection addresses aspects of post-colonial memory and commemoration, and especially ways in which memories of colonialism have been distorted or occluded by 'official versions' of national history, or by the direct interference of the state. The section comprises two complementary readings, both concerned with memories of the Algerian war of independence (1954–62), viewed, as it were, from opposing sides of the Mediterranean.

First, in Chapter 20, James MacDougall addresses a central theme in Algerian history, which is the apparent continuity of intense violence, from the sustained brutalities of the French conquest after 1830, right through the colonial period, culminating in the war of independence, and reaching forward to embrace Algeria's civil war, the 'dark decade' of the 1990s. The violence is undeniable, but McDougall questions whether this has any explanatory force in Algerian culture, either 'by some particularly perverse streak of "national character", [or] by inculcation through a long colonial oppression' (pp. 588–89). He argues, first, that, in a move characteristic of imperial ideology, the French colonial state and settlers projected their own 'savagery' onto the colonized, justifying their own violence as 'defensive, preventive – even, already, as pre-emptive' (p. 591). This 'alterity of violence' is reflected, albeit distantly, in Albert Camus's novels from *The Outsider* (1942, whose plot turns on the motiveless killing of an unnamed Arab) to his final, unfinished manuscript, *The First Man* (published 1994). It also helps explain the disproportionate violence of the armed forces and settler vigilantes in the Sétif and Philippeville massacres (1945, 1955) and of the settlers' last-ditch terrorist organization, the OAS (*Organisation Armée Secrète*). Second, McDougall argues that colonial rule generated the nationalist view that violence was the only legitimate response to 'inflexible, unreformable, total oppression' (p. 592). Other, more moderate responses to colonial oppression, in particular the efforts of francophone intellectuals and 'moderate' nationalists to bring about reform of the colonial system from within, were written out of the nationalist narrative of necessary violence leading to victory in 1962.[14] Third, he explores the consequences of this nationalist narrative for post-independence Algeria, notably the

[13] On dependency theory, see Wolfe, Chapter 17 in this volume, pp. 496–500.

[14] On Algerian nationalism before the Second World War, see McDougall (2006).

mismatch between the near-mythical figure of the *mujahid* (FLN fighter) and the experience of most Algerians, who endured the war and the violence done to them, rather than actively fighting. The war became a reference point for both the state and Islamic militants in the troubles of the 1990s, but only through reinvention of 'the nationalist register of legitimacy' (p. 598), further enhanced by imported elements from elsewhere in the Middle East and the Islamic world.

The contrast provided by Jim House in Chapter 21 arises not so much from his metropolitan French – and indeed Parisian – perspective, as from the focus on one very precise event, the massacre of 17 October 1961, which has come to stand as a forceful symbol of a long and bloody conflict, but which also, as House suggests, 'fulfils a metonymic function, representing, in condensed form, many of the aspects of racism in contemporary France' (p. 610). Its significance here arises from the event's erasure from public memory, and from painstaking reinstatement of that memory undertaken according to a '*devoir de mémoire*' (duty of memory). House offers many reasons why the events were quickly forgotten or obscured. Not least, the police were good at covering their tracks: we will never know how many unarmed Algerians were killed that night. Within a few months, in March 1962, a ceasefire was declared in Algeria, and France acquiesced with apparent readiness to President Charles de Gaulle's urging to 'turn the page'. House traces the ways in which memory 'went underground' but was kept alive by victims' families and survivors, and increasingly by anti-racist organizations. More recently, memory has revived as part of an 'Algerian syndrome' succeeding the 'Vichy syndrome' with which French society gradually came to confront the 'dark years' of occupation during the Second World War (Rousso, 1994). As House suggests, the relationship between Vichy and Algeria is close but ambivalent. Vichy, and the 'syndrome' around it, offers precedents for the confrontation of memory – even the idea of a '*devoir de mémoire*' is associated with memories of the Shoah. Obvious institutional continuities between Vichy and Algeria were brought out at Maurice Papon's 1997 trial for crimes against humanity in occupied France, though his responsibility as Prefect of Police for the 1961 massacre was arguably more palpable. Indeed, it may appear that the French can best confront their colonial past, or implications for present-day issues of immigration and race, through the filter of older events whose memories have lost some of their urgency. Although the fiftieth anniversary of the events of 17 October 1961 was not marked officially, a year later the new Socialist President, François Hollande, acknowledged the killing of Algerian demonstrators in a 'bloody repression', and accorded the French Republic's 'lucid recognition' of the massacre, albeit to predictable protests from the right and far right.[15]

***

As several readings in this collection make clear, not only those in the final section, the legacy of colonialism continues to be felt more than half a century after the bulk of the colonial empires dissolved in a wholesale and apparently triumphant reconfiguration of the

---

[15] 'Hollande reconnaît la répression du 17 octobre 1961, critiques à droite', *Le Monde*, 17 October 2012. For a more extensive account, see House and MacMaster (2006). The massacre has become an essential point of reference for numerous recent films, including *Nuit noire 17 octobre 1961* (Alain Tasma, 2005), *Caché* (*Hidden*, Michael Haneke, 2005), *Hors-la-loi* (*Outlaws*, Rachid Bouchareb, 2010) and *Ici on noie des Algériens* (Yasmina Adi, 2011).

international system. As historians we can readily appreciate the resonances of the ways in which nationalists, rebels, freedom-fighters, activists – alongside the unnumbered legions of the colonized – reacted to colonialism, fought against it or simply endured it. Often the task of the historian is to uncover and acknowledge the abuses of the colonial past. Not only in France, but even in Britain, which still congratulates itself on a relatively 'peaceful' retreat from empire, the state and its (former) agents have had to face up to a possible 'war of memories', as ex-Mau Mau fighters prepare to sue the British government over their alleged torture at the hands of the Kenyan colonial state (Anderson, 2011). Equally historians have a responsibility to study the colonial past in all its complexity, even (and indeed especially) if that involves correcting or nuancing the received ideas and half-truths sustained by both the former colonizer and the colonized. Frederick Cooper suggests that the problem with the history of decolonization, and, by extension, with that of the modern colonial empires, is that 'we know the end of the story' (1996, p. 6). Few if any of the essays presented here confirm a straightforward narrative of 'inevitable' nationalist triumph against a 'dying colonialism', or indeed of a simple, Manichaean struggle between domination and resistance, or between resistance and collaboration. Indeed, where such narratives are presented as part of a post-colonial founding myth, as is arguably the case for Algeria, India or Kenya, those myths tend to be the object of internal as well as external challenge and critique. If the deeper stories are more complex, more ambivalent and more human, this must partly be because colonialism was more than an external or alien 'other' to which people simply reacted (though it was that too, and conquest must certainly have appeared that way), but an inextricable part of men's and women's lives. Equally, people's lives became insinuated into a colonial system which drew them in, and which offered opportunities as well as threats and violence, an enlargement of horizons as well as oppression and the entrenchment of privilege. Finally, in this, as in the preceding volumes in this series, it is to be hoped that the reader will be offered an insight into the multifaceted richness of a vibrant and expanding historical field; as the references here and in the essays will also suggest, the volume could have been filled many times over.

References

Amin, Shahid (1988), 'Gandhi as Mahatma: Gorakhpur District, Eastern U.P. 1921–2', in Ranajit Guha and Gayatri Chakravorty Spivak (eds), *Selected Subaltern Studies*, Oxford and New York: Oxford University Press, pp. 288–348.

Anderson, Benedict (1991), *Imagined Communities: Reflections on the Origins and Spread of Nationalism* (2nd edn), London and New York: Verso; first published 1983.

Anderson, Benedict (2006), *Imagined Communities: Reflections on the Origins and Spread of Nationalism* (3rd edn), London: Verso; first published 1983

Anderson, David M. (2005), *Histories of the Hanged: Britain's Dirty War in Kenya and the End of the Empire*, London: Weidenfeld & Nicolson.

Anderson, David (2011), 'Mau Mau in the High Court and the "Lost" British Empire Archives: Colonial Conspiracy or Bureaucratic Bungle?', *Journal of Imperial and Commonwealth History*, **39**, 5, pp. 699–716.

Balakrishnan, Gopal (ed.) (1996), *Mapping the Nation*, London: Verso.

Berman, Bruce and Lonsdale, John (1992), *Unhappy Valley: Conflict in Kenya and Africa*, 2 vols, London: J. Currey.

Branch, Daniel (2009), *Defeating Mau Mau, Creating Kenya: Counterinsurgency, Civil War and Decolonization*, Cambridge and New York: Cambridge University Press.

Branche, Raphaëlle (2005), *La guerre d'Algérie: une histoire apaisée?*, Paris: Seuil.

Breuilly, John (1993), *Nationalism and the State* (2nd edn), Manchester: Manchester University Press.

Brocheux, Pierre and Hémery, Daniel (1995), *L'Indochine: Une Colonisation ambiguë*, Paris: La Découverte.

Brocheux, Pierre and Hémery, Daniel (2001), *L'Indochine: Une Colonisation ambiguë* (new edn), Paris: La Découverte.

Brown, Judith M. (1989), *Gandhi: Prisoner of Hope*, New Haven, CT and London: Yale University Press.

Chatterjee, Partha (1993), *The Nation and its Fragments: Colonial and Postcolonial Histories*, Princeton: Princeton University Press.

Connelly, Matthew (2002), *A Diplomatic Revolution: Algeria's Fight for Independence and the Origins of the Post-Cold War Era*, Oxford: Oxford University Press.

Cooper, Frederick (1994), 'Conflict and Connection: Rethinking Colonial African History', *American Historical Review*, **99**, 5, pp. 1516–45.

Cooper, Frederick (1996), *Decolonization and African Society: The Labor Question in French and British Africa*, Cambridge: Cambridge University Press.

Elkins, Caroline (2005), *Britain's Gulag: The Brutal End of Empire in Kenya*, London: Jonathan Cape.

Evans, Martin (2010), *Algeria: France's Undeclared War*, Oxford: Oxford University Press.

Fanon, Frantz (1965), *The Wretched of the Earth*, Harmondsworth: Penguin; originally published 1961.

Gallagher, Jack (1982), *The Decline, Revival and Fall of the British Empire*, Cambridge: Cambridge University Press.

Gellner, Ernest (1983), *Nations and Nationalism*, Oxford: Blackwell.

Guha, Ranajit (1988a), 'On Some Aspects of the Historiography of Colonial India', in Ranajit Guha and Gayatri Chakravorty Spivak (eds), *Selected Subaltern Studies*, Oxford and New York: Oxford University Press, pp. 37–44.

Guha, Ranajit (1988b), 'Preface', in Ranajit Guha and Gayatri Chakravorty Spivak (eds), *Selected Subaltern Studies*, Oxford and New York: Oxford University Press, pp. 35–36.

Guha, Ranajit (1988c), 'The Prose of Counter-insurgency', in Ranajit Guha and Gayatri Chakravorty Spivak (eds), *Selected Subaltern Studies*, Oxford and New York: Oxford University Press, pp. 45–86; originally published in R. Guha (ed.) (1983), *Subaltern Studies II*, New Delhi: Oxford University Press.

Hobsbawm, Eric (1990), *Nations and Nationalism since 1780: Programme, Myth, Reality*, Cambridge: Cambridge University Press.

Hobson, J.A. (1902), *Imperialism: A Study*, London: George Allen & Unwin.

Horne, Alistair (2006), *A Savage War of Peace: Algeria, 1954–1962* (rev. edn).

House, Jim and MacMaster, Neil (2006), *Paris 1961: Algerians, State Terror, and Memory*, Oxford: Oxford University Press.

Howe, Stephen (1993), *Anti-Colonialism in British Politics: The Left and the End of Empire*, Oxford: Clarendon Press.

Howe, Stephen (2005), 'When if Ever did Empire End? Internal Decolonization in British Culture since the 1950s', in Martin Lynn (ed.), *The British Empire in the 1950s: Retreat or Revival?*, Basingstoke: Palgrave Macmillan.

Iliffe, John (1967), 'The Organization of the Maji Maji Rebellion', *Journal of African History*, **8**, 3, pp. 495–512.

Iliffe, John (1979), *A Modern History of Tanganyika*, Cambridge: Cambridge University Press.

Lenin, V.I. ([1916] 2010), *Imperialism: The Highest Stage of Capitalism*, London: Penguin; originally written 1916, and published in pamphlet form, 1917.

Le Sueur, James D. (2001), *Uncivil War: Intellectuals and Identity Politics during the Decolonization of Algeria*, Philadelphia: University of Pennsylvania Press.

Logevall, Fredrik (2012), *Embers of War: The Fall of an Empire and the Making of America's Vietnam*, New York: Random House.

Lonsdale, John (1981), 'States and Social Processes in Africa: A Historiographical Survey', *African Studies Review*, **24**, 2/3, pp. 139–225.

Lonsdale, John (1990), 'Mau Maus of the Mind: Making Mau Mau and Remaking Kenya', *Journal of African History*, **31**, 3, pp. 393–421.

Louis, Wm Roger (2006), 'E.D. Morel and the Triumph of the Congo Reform Association', in *Ends of British Imperialism: The Scramble for Empire, Suez and Decolonization*, London: Palgrave Macmillan, pp. 153–82; originally published in J. Butler (ed.) (1966), *Boston University Papers on Africa*, Vol. II: *African History*, Boston: Boston University Press.

McDougall, James (2006), *History and the Culture of Nationalism in Algeria*, Cambridge: Cambridge University Press.

Macey, David (2000), *Fanon: A Life*, London: Granta.

Marr, David (1983), *Vietnamese Tradition on Trial, 1920–1945*, Berkeley: University of California Press.

Marr, David (1995), *Vietnam 1945: The Quest for Power*, Berkeley: University of California Press.

Ogot, Bethwell A. (1972), 'Revolt of the Elders: An Anatomy of the Loyalist Crowd in the Mau Mau Uprising', in Bethwell A. Ogot (ed.), *Politics and Nationalism in Colonial Kenya*, Nairobi: East African Publishing House, pp. 134–48.

Porter, Andrew (2001), 'Sir Roger Casement and the International Humanitarian Movement', *Journal of Imperial and Commonwealth History*, **29**, 2, pp. 59–74.

Rioux, Jean-Pierre (ed.) (1990), *La Guerre d'Algérie et les Français*, Paris: Fayard.

Rousso, Henry (1994), *The Vichy Syndrome: History and Memory in France since 1944* (new edn), Cambridge, MA: Harvard University Press; originally published 1987.

Said, Edward (1978), *Orientalism*, London: Routledge & Kegan Paul.

Sarkar, Sumit (1989), *Modern India, 1885–1947* (2nd edn), New Delhi: Macmillan.

Shepard, Todd (2006), *The Invention of Decolonization: The Algerian War and the Remaking of France*, Ithaca: Cornell University Press.

Shimazu, Naoko (2011), '"Diplomacy as Theatre": Recasting the Bandung Conference of 1955 as Cultural History', ARI working paper series 164, Asia Research Institute, National University of Singapore.

Shipway, Martin (2008), *Decolonization and its Impact: A Comparative Approach to the End of the Colonial Empires*, Oxford: Blackwell.

Spivak, Gayatri Chakravorty (1988), 'Subaltern Studies: Deconstructing Historiography', in Ranajit Guha and Gayatri Chakravorty Spivak (eds), *Selected Subaltern Studies*, Oxford and New York: Oxford University Press, pp. 3–32.

Stora, Benjamin (2007), *La Guerre des mémoires: La France face à son passé colonial*, Paris: Editions de l'Aube.

Thénault, Sylvie (2005), *Histoire de la Guerre d'indépendance algérienne*, Paris: Flammarion.

Tomlinson, B.R. (2003), 'What was the Third World?', *Journal of Contemporary History*, **38**, 2, pp. 307–21.

Tronchon, Jacques (1974/1986), *L'Insurrection malgache de 1947*, Fianarantsoa and Paris: Karthala and Ambozontany.

Ward, Stuart (ed.) (2001), *British Culture and the End of Empire*, Manchester: Manchester University Press.

Wolf-Phillips, Leslie (1987), 'Why "Third World": Origin, Definition and Usage"', *Third World Quarterly*, **9**,/4, pp. 131–-27.

Part I
Modes of Resistance

[1]

1857: Need for Alternative Sources

PANKAJ RAG*

There has often been a tendency on the part of historians of 1857 to argue about its character in terms of certain specific labels - whether it was a 'conspiracy' or was it 'spontaneous' ; whether it was 'feudal reaction' , a 'restorative' movement or was it a religious war; whether people were primarily driven by 'economic' concerns or were civil 'outbursts' mere consequences of the political vacuum?[1] As has been increasingly realised in recent years, 1857 was too complex a movement to be adequately explained in terms of general labels of universal application and such labels no longer occupy an unquestioned status. In the last two decades or so, as an integral part of world historiographical shift, regional variations in the nature of causes and organization have been increasingly highlighted. The trend can be said to have begun with Eric Stokes who concentrated on the districts of western Uttar Pradesh to show how the response to the uprising was worked out in these areas in terms of agrarian conditions and organizational factors.[2] Similarly, Brodkin analyzed the tracts of western Rohilkhand to argue about the patterns and dynamics of the Revolt in the region.[3] Other works centering on specific regions have also appeared from time to time.[4]

However, even in all these works, what has been emphasised is the 'elitist' level of Indian society. The Revolt for long has been studied in terms of a given goal and elaborated in terms of the role of 'glorious' leaders like Nana Peshwa, Rani of Jhansi, Tatya Tope, Kunwar Singh and to on, towards achieving that goal. Even the Marxian approach of P.C. Joshi and others explains its failure in terms of limited retrogressive aims of the leadership and betrayal by the landed elements. Whether the leaders mobilised or betrayed; the leaders remain as the crucial actors on the stage.

Even in Stoke' s rigorous work, diversity of response is explained purely in terms of magnate or 'village elite' . In *The Peasant and the Raj* the leaders and the aristocracy seem to react to the political vacuum within broadly defined caste and communal groups. Though in *The Peasant Armed* (published after his death) Stokes seems to move away from caste as the basic unit of analysis to 'dharra' (multi-caste faction); even here the tendency to explain the Revolt remains in terms of the economic impact of British rule on the magnates and elites of the 'dharras' .[5] There has been little attempt to understand the thoughts and actions of thousands of ordinary non-elite villagers who rose on such a considerable scale. Even in the works, for instance, that of S.B. Chaudhuri, where people do come into the picture, there is a tendency to treat them as automatic responders to the objective changes brought about by British rule, or as a passive or semi-passive mass that was activated by the mobilization efforts of the leaders. There was no real attempt to study the vital elements of popular perception of grievances and of the ways in which people worked out such perceptions and gave meanings to them in terms of their own cultural codes, symbols and value systems.

Only in the last decade or so, as a part of the world wide trend of 'history from below' , there has been a true shift in perspective and as a result aspects of autonomous popular consciousness and action during the Revolt of 1857 has started receiving greater attention. Rudrangshu Mukherjee in his work on 1857 in Awadh has shown how the influx of colonialist policies upset the moral economy of the peasant world; how the complementarity of the taluqdar-presant relationships, where inequality was 'circumscribed by custom and mediated by various forms of beneficience' , was disrupted by alien colonialist operations with shocking repercussions on the ethical and normative visions of the peasants; and how the Awadh issue acquired the status of an ideology in the eyes of the inhabitants of the region - all of this underlining his vital conclusion that the issue was 'created in the minds of various sections of population in terms of notions of traditional loyalty and prestige' .[6] Ranajit Guha in his pathbreaking work on peasant insurgency has discussed 1857 in some detail to show how the peasants could often act as the subjects and makers of their own history, how they could exhibit an autonomy in perception and action divorced from the aims and interests of their leaders of the ruling class, and how they worked out their response in terms of their own language and ideas of solidarity, transmission and mobilization.[7]

However, even in the works which have attempted to study 1857 from a perspective of 'history from below' ; the sources used to construct rebel mentality are primarily elitist official sources (the minutes, dispatches, correspondence, reports and narrative of events written by British officials and generals) which have very little to say about rebel mentality. Rather, these sources speak of the overriding concern on the part of the colonialist state to preserve law and order and the common rebel is totally denied a mind and rationality of his own. The Rebellion is treated either as a conspiracy by some ill-willed men or as a mishap or disease —something akin to an epidemic. Such official sources prefer to treat 1857 as an uprising without an issue wherever possible, and where it was not possible the issues are termed as unreasonable, irrational and steeped in obscurantism and fanaticism.

The term 'rebel' , 'badmash' , 'dacoit' , all seem to overlap one another. Wherever an uprising occurred it led to 'anarchy' or 'disorganization' in the eyes of the British; by the same logic wherever it was suppressed the place was 'fast settling down' - as if the Rebellion was just a freak wave and an abnormal mishap in the smooth course of sedentary life under the beneficial British rule.[8] The solution advocated and practised by historians like Ranajit Guha to 'invert' these official sources in order to arrive at the rebel mentality seems to move within a framework of binary opposites which is problematic. Such an approach misses out on a whole range of nuances and shades of intermediary attitudes and interpretations that various groups of rebels manifested through their actions and perceptions. It gives us little idea of the separate cultural domain that the groups of common men had tried to preserve against the onslaught of the colonialist regime. There is very little help from the official sources in trying to construct the various constituents of popular culture - its notions of 'dharma' and life, its meaningful symbolism and ritual significance within polity and society arrived at by different groups of rebels - all of which are essential to truly grasp and understand the modalities and idioms of popular grievances and actions in 1857 with the casual and characteristic inter-relations and spatial variations. It is here that the importance of sources of oral and popular history like folk songs, folk tales, etc., as a primary source material for constructing the history of 1857 from the point of view of a common rebel acquires relevance. A serious criticism of the historians of the so-called 'subaltern' school is that unfortunately, their 'new' writing is still largely based on the old elitist sources. Despite realising the significance of sources of oral and popular history and giving some indications to their possible use for the writing of an alternative history from below, the actual use of this vast store of source material is still largely lacking.[9]

Though historians have made use of the proclamations and letters of rebel leaders of note to comment on the particularities of the ideological inclinations, aims and interests of the Rajas and chieftains, for a deeper insight into the ideological predelictions, mental make-up and the arena of realities of the common rebels during 1857, it is high time that one woke up to the necessity of using 'non-elitist' sources. One understands that this is a task that has to be undertaken with caution - the sources of oral history are not always historically correct in so far as correctness in chronology is concerned; the bravery of the rebels is often exaggerated and outcomes of battles distorted, and there is always a possibility of aberrations and interpolations over time resulting in a question mark over the 'purity' of the source. Yet, despite these limitations, if proper care is exercised in analysing them, their value is immense as the repository of the mental, physical and cultural world of the common men who participated in 1857.

The area chosen here to illustrate the utility of such sources in constructing different facets of the Rebellion is one that abounds in folk songs and local literature on the theme, but has been relatively ignored in serious regional historiography of 1857; namely eastern Uttar Pradesh and the adjoining areas of western Bihar, especially Shahabad. These were areas of great rural revolts during 1857 and provide an ideal arena to study the various aspects of the physical and mental world of the ordinary rebel with all its virtues and pitfalls. It has been the practice of many historians to dismiss folklore as conservative simply because the customs and beliefs do not conform to the accepted ideas about post-enlightenment rationality and innovation. However, common men and women of mid-19th century India had their own notions of rationality, propriety and utility; all of which informed their stand in 1857 to a large extent, and which can be properly appreciated through a rigorous study of folklore. It is not my contention here to use folklore and contemporary local or regional plebeian literature in isolation; nor is it simply to be used as a gap filler. It can both affirm and contradict what is known, but more importantly can provide alternative shades to the same truths or half-truths from a different perspective.

II

The common rebels saw in the Raj an entity and structure that unwantedly and repeatedly interfered in their way of life and they rebelled by attacking and obliterating everything that they perceived as symbolising that structure. The boast of Jodhu Singh in Jahanabad that he would destroy every public building between the Soane and Monghyr is typical of many of the rebels of the period. Such destructions were not always the momentous byproducts of rampant frenzy. In Allahabad, hundreds of men were 'systematically engaged for many days' in wanton destruction of a railway storehouse - the undertaking of 'systematic destruction' for a long period clearly underlining the deep filtration of hatred for any symbol of colonial power.[10] Destruction for the rebels had its own joy. It signified a triumph of liberation from perpetual exploitation and oppression under the colonialist institutions. An extract from a 'panwara' in the area of Shahabad makes an interesting study in this regard:

> They are up now at Masaurhi, and Masaurhi thana smashed/The *sipahees* all gain freedom/and now Punpun too they raid/and Punpun *thana* smashed/now a siege in Patna laid/The prisoners all gain freedom/and they are up now at Maner[11]

The *sipahees* too gain freedom from the shackle of the British *thana* in the same way as the prisoners gain freedom from jails. The identification of *thanas* and jails as one in the mind of the common rebel and the equation of both as oppressive symbols of colonial bondage is noteworthy. The liberation of *sipahees* from one is identical with the liberation of convicts from the other. The British sense of justice; British concepts of discipline, law, order and punishment are all denied in popular perception which hails their destruction as freedom - a powerful statement attacking the whole system through its semiological and linguistic structure of articulation. Though much has been written in historiography on the impact of the British revenue and legal policies on the agrarian system in the first half of the 19th century, the trend has mainly been to objectively outline the causes and draw a straight line between cause and effect, the latter reflected in the uprising of 1857. Such an approach tends to ignore the vital factor of popular perception of such changes which differed over different social groups and regions - a factor which can provide a richness of variety to the known, and a repertoire of knowledge about the unknown facets of

1857. The pathos and helplessness of the common villagers can only be captured truly if one moves to alternative sources, for they can help in illuminating the hitherto hidden domain of popular feeling in historiography - a domain which through its subjectivity and intensity can provide a much more realistic and logical correlation with the spirit and vigour of popular action during 1857. The exploitation under the British legal system, where the trap of the grinding wheel of litigation meant for the peasants wastage of cultivation days, indebtedness and incessant milking of their resources, is aptly expressed in a near contemporary poem by Sukhdevji - an obscure Bhojpuri saint poet writing sometime in mid-nineteenth century where accountability in hell is expressed through the punitive metaphor of courts underlining the perception of the new legal system as an afflicting curse by the common man :

> *Samujhi pari jab jaeb kachhari*
> *.....Khael peeal lel del kagaj baki sab niksi*
> *Dharmaraj jab lekha leehan loha ke sotwar mar paree*
> *age peechhe chopdar dhai bi mugdar jam ke phans pari*
> *agin khamb men bandhi ke rakhihen, Hajri jamini koi na kari*

> (You will understand once you go to the court. Whatever you have eaten or drunk will all come out - only papers would be left with you, i.e., all your riches will go and they shall be replaced by tons of useless paper. Being called to account by Dharmaraj (here, judge) is like being beaten by an iron rod; the court-retainers would not let you escape from the strangulation that you will face. No one will come forward to bail you out, and you will feel as if you have been tied to the pillars of the court for ever).[12]

For an ordinary Indian, used to custom-bound relationships based on words of honour and ties of obligation and duty, the whole British legal system based on written contracts and documents and drawn out on tons of 'useless' paper was alien and extortionist. In this moving poem, paper symbolizes the unwanted inroad of an alien system that takes away the sustaining items of an ordinary man' s life and yet justifies it as legal. In fact, the anguish at the complexities and unfamiliarity of this alien 'paper based' justice with no recognition of the norms of tradition-based political and cultural order has become a part of folk ethos. A Magadhi saying defines the new politico-legal system by using the same metaphor of paper as 'kagaz ke raj hona' (rule of paper) and a Bhojpuri folk song equates the expensive and ruinous court cases with the curse of having a marriageable daughter in traditional community life.

Chik baheli soom dhan, au beti ke badhi
Ehu ke dhan na ghate takar badan se rari[13]

Courts and magistracy would thus prove the prime targets of rebels at all places. Though all symbols of colonial power and authority were attacked, the ultimate triumph for the people seems to have been the capture or destruction of the court or the bungalow of the magistrate. In the following extract from a folk song describing the capture of the Arrah court the use of the word 'adhikar' to emphasise the symbolical eclipse of British authority in a township is noteworthy.

Rama Arra par kaile chadhaiya re na
Rama Kutchhery ke uparwa re na
Rama Kunwar Singh Karle adhikarwa re na

(O Rama, the forces of Kunwar Singh invaded Arrah and captured the court)[14]

The credit for translating these aspirations of the people into action is indeed given to Kunwar Singh in most of the folk songs of the region.

Buxar se jo chale Kunwar Singh Patna aa kar teek
Patna ke magister bole karo Kunwar ko theek
Atuna baat jab sune Kunwar Singh dee bungala phunkwaee
gali gali magister roee, lat gae ghabdai

(Kunwar Singh started from Buxar and arrived in Patna. The magistrate of Patna announced that he would teach Kunwar Singh a lesson. As soon as Kunwar Singh heard this, he got the magistrate' s bungalow burnt. The magistrate is now weeping in the streets and even the governor has panicked)[15]

However, even in such folk songs, he is not presented as a leader who has enforced his own wishes on the people of his community. Rather, as we shall discuss later, in many of the folk songs and folk tales he is shown as carrying out the wishes of the community. In fact, folklore has a valuable advantage in that it denotes the voice of feelings of a community rather than the individual. Even if they are seen as hailing the glories of an individual leader; the language, the semiology and the choice of words and their presentation often provide us with a significant insight into the mental domain of the community, its normative structure, its systems of deference to tradition or resistance to forces of change and the trajectories through which such attitudes moved during 1857-59 in different areas. In some folk songs the reasons given for Kunwar Singh' s rebellion indicate less of his actual motivations than the fact that people created images of Kunwar Singh based on their own miseries and hopes.

Kailas des par julum jor firangiya
Julum Kahani Suni tadpe Kunwar Singh
Ban ke lutera utral fauj firangiya
Sahar gaon looti phunki, dihlas firangiya
Sun sun Kunwar ke hirday lagal agia

(The 'firangi' forcibly oppressed the country and Kunwar Singh was deeply moved when he heard the tales of their atrocities. The 'firangi' army arrived to loot and it looted and burnt cities and villages. When he came to know of all this, Kunwar Singh was enraged.)[16]

It is true that the impact of British policies in the first half of the 19th century, and the changes affecting various sections of the population provide us with a proper perspective to study 1857. However, as Bayly has pointed out, the actual level of land revenue or the specific degree of penetration by moneylenders in particular areas may have been much less of the 'bania' and the infidel had grown to subvert the whole moral economy and value system of society. It is no wonder that the 'bania' is often a subject of ridicule and mockery in village popular culture. *Bania reejhe to hans de* is a pertinent and much experienced folk description of a miser 'bania' who does not share his prosperity with the community through ties of beneficience unlike the traditional feudal gentry.[17] There exists a typical folk song in which the rebel sepoys are refused food and fuel by a liar 'bania' while they are shown as being welcome with open arms by Kunwar Singh:

Mark, Bania, our plight/we' ve had no bite/for full four nights and days/seen us some ration and fuelwood; some or Khassi - goat;/some ghee, some atta seen as! But a Bania' s answer note; 'Sipahee, trust my word; at all/no ghee, nor atta is here; nor fuel, nor ration, possible/no succour hence, I fear/......while at Jagdishpur, 'the baboo did incline/ to order a jajam to be spread;/And the men all squat to dine.[18]

In fact, it is remarkable to note in the popular saying '*Shehar Sikhaya Kotwali*' (man learns from experience) that the idiom of 'Shehar' (city) as the centre for the new trends in commerce and commercial ways is supplemented by that of 'Kotwali' (another symbol of the new colonial system in the field of law and order).[19] The new experiences of commerce and law under the colonial dispensation which now define the parameters of determining worldliness, are in the eyes of the common villager, mutually inclusive and both are parts of the same unfamiliar and impersonal system that had invaded their lives. This new system was both intimidating and perplexing - something strange was happening all around. It is no coincidence that in Bhojpuri folk songs 'opium' cultivation and trade are always depicted in the strange metaphor of a pregnant and/or blind cow whose dairy products are being sold in the market even as she is much pregnant and unmilked.

Pehle dahi jamai ke, pachhe duhni gai
Bachhwa okar pet men ki dwåre laynu bikai
Pet men bacha anhar gai
Jekar makhan Bengala jai.[20]

Is the creation of this strange, uncustomary (something that is not done) metaphor in popular mentality for 'opium' cultivation and trade simply a literal depiction of the physical anatomy of the poppy plant or does it through its linguistic irony indicate the way in which the common villagers of eastern United Provinces and adjoining areas perceived the expansion of opium by the Europeans on a large scale (especially in poorer areas like Ghazipur where the government opium agency pumped advances and forced cultivation) as something alien, foreign, abnormal and outlandish? The metaphors of cow and calf again seem quite distinctively selective - these were the sacred symbols of the village religious and cultural ethos and the colonial regime was invading the norms and beliefs worth being maintained in this sacred regime by its own ridiculous notions of livelihood and economy (here symbolised by opium) that was as unacceptable, blind to sensitivities (hence opium equated with 'anhar' or blind cow) and laughable as the idea of milk products from a much pregnant cow. After all grain crops were much more lucrative than this outlandish, costly and polluting cash crop which was facing from the 1840s increased competition from the cheaper Chinese product and was surviving, decidedly to the utter resentment of the poor cultivator in Gorakhpur and Ghazipur, simply due to the pressure from the government by forcibly extending cultivation and pulling down prices.[21] It is from folk culture and folk memory that one can trace many unexplained details of day to day resentment felt by the common man whose norms of dignity and ideas about livelihood, and propriety were assaulted by the new regime. Opium merchants and indigo planters would be the principal targets of popular fury, besides auction purchasers, in the countryside in both Ghazipur and Gorakhpur during 1857. The village inhabitants of Chaura in Ghazipur would herald the uprising by attacking an indigo planter named Mathews 'who barely escaped with his life, all his property being plundered and burnt' .[22] It is again no coincidence that after the treasure of the collectorate at Ghazipur had been safely shifted, the British would employ the whole force of the newly arrived Madras Fusiliers at the opium factory which was 'put into a state of defence' .[23]

Plundering the rich is a familiar expression of popular discontent. This sort of plunder in the context of 1857, acquires a logic of its own if one examines the composition of the crowd of plunderers in most cases. Apart from the sepoys, it was made up of, what the British termed in a derogatory sense as, the 'rabble' of the population which in reality comprised the marginal groups - the out of work artisans and craftsmen, destitutes and beggars, retrenched soldiers, impoverished petty gentry, labourers and so on. Though there is no reason to develop a systematic causal relationship behind every act of plunder by these marginal groups who were constantly on the lookout for booty in peace or war, yet there are certain indications that the memory of better days predisposed them to plunder. Bayly has argued that day labourers from marginal groups who participated in the unstable export economy were especially vulnerable to its fluctuations, and hence one explanation of the nature of plundering during 1857 can be that such people were trying to secure themselves for future by looting bullion, ornaments and other negotiable items.[24]

At this point one needs to stress that the contexts of power and status in colonial India - worked out within its own semiology of authority and ritual status - were reinforced by the flux that the onset of colonialism produced in the social, political and economic realms. For instance, in major centres of cloth production such as Lucknow, Banaras, Mau and Mubarakpur (in Azamgarh), the weavers and spinners faced violent fluctuations in their trade and a progressive erosion of their markets - a tendency that was the combined result of the British policy of importing machine made goods as well as that of a decline in demand following the erosion in power and influence of military and royal establishments along with that of their avenues of patronage and employment. Shift to weaving coarser, cheaper cloth as well as to unfamiliar vocations like agricultural labour seemed the only alternatives for the weavers and spinners in a fast changing ambience. Such weavers, artisans and craftsmen who had seen better, honourable days, and who had been rendered jobless under the new colonial regime were the main participants in the popular upsurge in cities, towns and *qasbas*. It was not only a question of material deprivation - this was overdetermined by a sense of loss of pride, honour and prestige in day to day life.[25] The proverb *Julha dhuniya samjhul* (Do you think I am as lowly as a *julaha* or a *dhuniya*) in this belt starkly reminds us of the downward slide of such communities on the scale of social prestige and vanity.

1857 saw an eruption of such grievances of these marginal groups in the form of numerous attacks on commercial men and rich *mahajans*. In Banaras city itself, where the town population remained remarkably quiet, Muslim weavers 'temporarily raised the green flag of holy war'.[26] In Allahabad the weavers joined Liaqat Ali - himself a weaver by birth - in total revolt and it was this groundswell and its triumph that succeeded in 'driving many sympathisers with government... into seclusion'.[27] Kanpur, a 'rootless city' with a preponderance of labourers and destitutes, saw the merchants hastily trying to bring about some sort of 'order' under Nana's regime in order to prevent this groundswell from getting out of bounds.[28] In Gaya again, the Hindu *mahajans* were the chief sufferers 'preyed upon at once by the Mohammedan rabble of the lower town and by the priests of the upper' - the former most decidedly dominated by the weavers and artisans of Gaya fame.[29] In fact, for thirteen days no rebel leader came forward to organise a government in Gaya - a testimony to the triumph of the ordinary people in the city.[30] In Arrah, in a unique trial after the suppression of the Revolt, the 'townspeople of Arrah' as a whole were accused of rebellion against the British.[31] Craftsmen like the local blacksmiths were instrumental in Arrah in actively helping the rebel sepoys through manufacture and supply of cannon shots.[32] Similar help by local artisans was also rendered in

Shahabad where thousands of village 'lohars' made swords for the peasant rebels, and in Kanpur where skilled artisans were used by Nanhe Nawab to make cannon shots for the tanks.[33]

It would be overstretching a point if we conclude that all the artisans, weavers and craftsmen who played a significant role in the upsurge did possess a clear cut idea about the structure of the colonial authority and policies that had led to their impoverishment and social degradation and therefore knowingly and purposefully they attacked the merchants because they symbolised that structure. However, though vague and nebulous - their perception could at least identify the immediate oppressor, and since the latter had usually benefited under the colonial regime, an attack on him did acquire - by implication - the relevance of a challenge to the British authority in the context of 1857. This is not to conclude that plunderers were always objectively discriminate and that only British loyalists were plundered. It is true that villages were often looted indiscriminately and mercilessly by rebel magnates, sepoys as well as by the common population. At the same time, it would not be wrong to say that 1857 gave an opportunity to the sufferers under the colonial regime to take out their wrath at those whom they considered relatively prosperous. To the extent that the latter consisted of a number of sympathisers of the government, their outburst worked in an anti-British direction.

Official sources however do not provide us with a complete picture of 'loot' and 'plunder'. In the various descriptions of such incidents in the official discourse, missing are the elements of glee, vitality and a sense of legitimacy from the point of view of the plunderers. On the contrary, plunder is never lamented in folk songs. In this Bhojpuri folk song (which is a variant of Gujar folk song on the same theme of plunder in the Meerut bazar) what is lamented, instead, is the fact of missing out on plunder:

> *Log sab lutle sal dusala/hamar saiyanji lutle rumal/Meerath ke sadar bazaar ba/hamar saiyanji lute na jane...*
>
> (People looted expensive shawls and wraps while my husband looted just a little handkerchief. Oh my husband is a fool - he does not know how to loot the Meerut Sadar bazar).[34]

Plunder thus is an act of masculanity - it is considered by the common women folk as an essential legitimate act by the men in order to gain honour and prestige. It has its political implication too, which sometimes comes out clearly as the following Braj folk song on the same theme suggests:

> *Firangi lut gayo re Hathus Ke bazar men/Top luti gayo, ghoda luti gayo/Tamancha luti gayo re Jako chalte bazar men.*[35]

Thus plunder here becomes a purposeful act - it is the public demeaning of the Englishman and his symbols of status like tank, pistol and horse in an open bazar that adds to the joy of the plunderer.

It is remarkable that the folk song in Mirzapur depicting the avenge of Udwant Singh' s death by Jhoori Singh (who, it is said, beheaded Jt. Commissioner Moore and brought his head to Udwant Singh' s mourning widow) is expressed through a teasing, joyous dialogue between *devar* (brother-in-law, here Jhoori Singh) and *bhabhi* (sister-in-law, here Udwant Singh' s wife) - perhaps underlining the festive mood in which the people had celebrated this insult of an Englishman being behaded by a countryman.

> *Ghodwa par chaddhi ke parai gawa Moorwa/Kaise le aain bhauji tore age mundwa*
>
> (Jhoori Singh teases his *bhabhi* that Moore has fled away on his horse, so how could he now bring his severed head to her?)
>
> *Hamara devar jujharu ho bhauji bali bali jae/laike chale jab bhalwa ho parlay mach jae/Moorwa ke kawan bisatiya ho der kurwa lagaye/ achraj hamen bad hol.s ho binu hate kauni aaye.*
>
> (Udwant Singh' s wife replies that she knows and admires her *devar* as a brave fighter; when he walks with his spear it is like a catastrophe on earth. Moore, thus, is no match for her *devar* and it is surprising howhe has come back without fulfilling his promise of beheading the Englishman).[36]

Such *devar-bhabhi* dialogues are extremely common in eastern Uttar Pradesh during times like Holi - an occasion which provides license and liberty to break traditional norms of deference, and this structuring of the episode of Moore' s death in the form of a *devar-bhabhi* dialogue is perhaps an indication of the comprehension of and rejoining in this incident by the common people of this region as a symbol of a cataclysmic moment of triumph (use of word '*pralaya*' is noteworthy) when the traditional fear and awe inspired by the Englishman had been inverted and the Englishman had been reduced to a laughable beheaded caricature of himself. Underlying this apparent teasing of Jhoori Singh and the taunt of his *bhabhi*, thus, lies a much more meaningful ultimate ridicule - that of the invincible Englishman.

A regional poet Sakhawat Rai, who was an eyewitness to the uprising of 1857, has similarly celebrated the killing of the English soldiers as a moment of extreme indignity of the invincible race by describing them as falling in the battlefield like trunkless elephants (a symbol of ultimate disgrace in popular language) and being feasted upon by vultures, jackals and dogs:

> *Gidh medrai swan syar anand chhaye*
> *Kahin gire gora kahin hathi bina soondh ke*[37]

1857 provided people with a situation in which they could attempt to defy the authority of the Englishman in day to day life. There were instances of *bhishtis* refusing water to Englishmen, cooks standing half-naked before guests in the house deliberately and messenger boys being impudent and indifferent to orders.[38] Verbal abuse, scorn and insult were levied at the Englishmen through cultural idioms, symbols and a language of popular usage. Peter Burke has illustrated that the active force of language is the insult, 'a form of aggression in which adjectives and nouns are used not so much to describe another person as to strike that person' in order to bring about his social destruction.[39] Shirer, in his *Daily Life during the Indian Mutiny* has described a similar situation in a Banda village where two peons sat alongside a magistrate - something they would never have dared to do in normal times - and after playfully assessing the value of a peon as four annas, scornfully questioned the value of the '*sarkar*' (government). Here the equation of the colonial regime with a low valued commodity - perhaps even lower than the lowly peons - exemplifies the way in which linguistic symbolism, gaining strength from traditional cultural idioms of comparison, succeeds in subverting the aura of colonialist authority.

Verbal defiance, insolent behaviour and symbolical fulmination often preceded or accompanied the upsurge. At Azamgarh, the 17th N.I. first openly declared that they would not allow the treasure to leave for Banaras, as was the British plan. Then, soon after the treasure left the station, they in a mutinous mood, left their ranks; and on being threatened by one sergeant Lewis that they would be hanged or transported if they rebelled, every man of the regiment commenced to yell, and some rushing down to the sergeant cut him down, crying out - 'if we are to be hanged at all events we' ll kill you first'.[40] In Banaras, Lt. Col. Spottiswoode, mistakenly convinced that he had calmed down the agitated sepoys of the 13th Irregular Cavalry, was surprised when he received a volley of fire from the same sepoy he was talking to. His pleadings that the English were friends had no impact on the sepoy as 'the reply was another volley'.[41] A distinct attitude of deliberate defiance seems to have replaced the customary disciplined behaviour that the English officers had been used to from the sepoys. Rather than obedience and servility, the prevalent attitude was one of hostility aiming to misguide the British through lies and chicanery. P. Walker, the Deputy Collector of Mirzapur, on inquiry from the zamindars of the neighbouring villages near Chunar - with whom he was personally acquainted - about reports of the firing heard in the vicinity was misinformed that 'it had been consequent on a marriage procession'.[42] Similarly Major Burroughs commanding the 17th N.I. at Azamgarh had been lulled into a false sense of security by the sepoys and after the outbreak 'could therefore hardly believe that all the men said and promised was false'.[43] In Gorakhpur, the magistrate Bird was openly insulted and the jail guards refused his order to destroy the bridge of boats.[44] The normal tendencies of fear and subordination had given way to a confident sense of power and command. The Commissioner of Patna reported his resentment that the rebels behave 'as if they were gentlemen and we were thieves'.[45]

We have indicated earlier in our discussion how people visualized the Revolt in terms of their grievances, expectations, desires and hopes. Needless to say, different sets of people had different aspirations from the Revolt, and they reacted to it in varied ways. Again, the same issue could be interpreted differently by different sets of people depending on social outlook, political inclinations, region-specific situations or cultural traditions.

The overriding concern of all the rebel leaders seems to have been a restoration of their earlier power and status which had been eroded by the British Raj and its interfering policies. On a broad general ideological plane, it could mean for many the restoration of the Mughal empire and the provincial kingdoms; while for many dispossessed zamindars and landholders at a local level it could simply mean the ouster of auction-purchasers, recapture of their lands and restoration of their lost fortunes. For rebel leaders like Mohammed Hasan - the *nazim* of Gorakhpur - loyalty to Awadh and commitment to its cause was the dominant theme of Revolt. That even the landholders under him were fighting for a restoration of conditions under the 18th century Nawabi is clear from the fact that many of them objected to the retention of *thanedars* by Mohammed Hasan on his assumption of power on the ground that '*thanedars* were unknown under the Nawabee'.[46] It is evident from the immediate ouster of auction-purchasers and re-entry of their lands by such dispossessed landholders that for them restoration of Nawabee meant, above all, restoration and unhindered enjoyment of their lands. Loyalty to Awadh never became an emotive issue for the landed magnates of Gorakhpur. Restoration of Nawabee for them, unlike Mohammed Hasan, simply meant restoration of their own personal or clan fortunes.

However, in regions of Jaunpur adjoining the Awadh border, where the Rajkumar chieftains even had blood-ties with the taluqdars of Awadh, the issue of loyalty to Awadh acquired a much more emotive colour than in other regions of eastern Uttar Pradesh. Here there would be no later day collective conciliation by the British unlike the Palwars of Azamgarh. The Awadh issue entered the Allahabad parganas north of the Ganga too, where the Awadh taluqdars had formerly ruled and staked their claims in 1857. Thus while in June and July 1857 it was 'ousted zamindars versus auction-purchasers', in September, 1857 it became 'Awadh and ousted zamindars' versus British government'.[47] The ideology of the rebels could have many components interpenetrating each other with variations in intensity over time and space.

What exactly did the Awadh issue mean to a rebel with a certain ideological commitment to the cause of Awadh? A study of the mental attitudes and ideology of a leader like Mohammed Hasan, with the help of the set of letters discovered by the British in his captured *palki*, provides a revealing answer.

His letter to the Deputy Magistrate of Gorakhpur, Khairuddeen, reveals that the moral sustenance to keep the fight on against the British is drawn from God. If the British are mighty, God is 'Almighty' Insurgent violence thus acquires, in the eyes of such rebels, the status of a religious service. At the same time, loyalty to Awadh is the recurring sentiment for Mohammad Hasan throughout his letters. He is ready to negotiate with the British only on the condition that the British undo their treachery to Awadh by restoring it in accordance with the treaty signed with Shujauddaulah. For him the rebellion of 1857 'arose solely out of the annexation of Oudh', for in his eyes the British 'had no right to establish themselves in Oudh'. A promise was a very important ethical and social notion in mid-19th century India; and the British by exceeding 'all bounds in their breaking of promises' were violaters of a legitimate social norm and hence were illegitimate tresspassers.

Restoration of Awadh to Mohammad Hasan, on one hand decidedly meant the restoration of his own honour and prestige, for he ends the letter to Khairuddeen by asserting that in a restored Awadh he would act as *Vakeel* to 'see that the treaty signed with Shujauddaulah was properly executed'. But along with this dream of material prosperity in this world, loyalty to the kingdom of Awadh was also his religion, his *dharma* — the fulfilment of which would bring him prosperity in the other world.[48] It should be kept in mind here that *dharma* should not be seen simply as a narrow sectarian outlook. 'Religious war' in this light, is hardly a suitable description of 1857. It was more a war in defence of a whole system of moral and social values, principles and ideas - all that the broad term 'religion' or *dharma* stood for - that had been endangered by British policies.

Defence of this *dharma* and its constituents like honour was not only the prime ideal of the chieftains and ex-rulers; even an ordinary rebel had his own perceptions of it. The decline of the ideals of honour and prestige at all levels was keenly understood by him as honour and self-respect were significant components of the cultural environment in which he lived. In popular mind kingship had been symbolically associated with authority, splendour and prosperity, and therefore erosion of such symbols was considered provocation sufficient for revolt in many places. Thus the pain felt at the end of the glorious Awadh kingdom is expressed both by the famous poet Ameer Meenai and the people in the Awadhi speaking belt in similar terms of lamentation at the loss of pomp and show of the Kaiserbagh melas:

> *'Ameer afsurda ho kar guncha-e-dil sookh jata hai*
> *woh mele ham ko Kaiser Bagh ke jab yad ate hain'*.[49]

> Sripati Maharaj,/this calamity avert!/O, when shall his majesty, Our King regain his own state?/....The artillery lies abandoned in the dumps/And the elephants are left uncared for in their stables,/ Chargers and swift horses wander groomless in the city,/And all my comrades too are lost/ In the Kaiser Bagh now the Begums

weep and wail/Their hairs hanging loose in disorder.

(Awadhi and Bhojpuri folk song)[50]

The following folk-song reveals vividly how keenly even the common people of Shahabad had grasped this reality with a faultless political instinct:

> *Babua, marle maratha jujhal sikhwa ho na/ Babua, peshwa ke putwa gulamwa ho na/ Babua, Dillipati bhai le kangalwa ho na/ babua, manglo par mile nahin bhikhwa ho na/ Babua, ohe din dada leli taruaria ho na*
>
> (Oh Babua, when the Marathas and the Sikhs were gone fighting, and the sons of Peshwas had been reduced to slaves; Oh Babua, when the Emperor of Delhi too had become a pauper and they were reduced to the status of beggars in vain; Oh Babua, that day our grandpa took up his sword)[51]

It is interesting to note that kingship and authority here are not localized, but encompass all regions of north India. Thus their local hero Kunwar Singh does not take up arms simply for his own personal cause, but, on the contrary, he does so for a much wider political issue in which all - the Sikhs, Marathas, Pathans - join together. Such folk-songs disprove the oft-held claim that for an ordinary rebel, the issue was a narrow, localized one. He had an acute perception of political realities much beyond his local territory. Many folk-songs in Shahabad are elegies on the deplorable conditions of the Begums of Awadh under the Company rule.

For the people of Bhojpur, erosion of pride and honour were deeply felt sentiments. It was humiliating for the traditional warrior community of Bhojpur, employed under chieftains, to lose their proud and valiant occupation and be forced to take up cultivation as a result of the British regime:

> *Oh Babua, scorpions bred in our cannons/ Oh Babua, the barrels of our guns have rusted/ Oh Babua, we have made sickles out of the steel of our swords/ Oh Babua, the Bhojpuris had even thrown their lathis aside/ Oh Babua, that day our grandpa took up his sword*[52]

Kunwar Singh here is a symbol of these proud warriors fighting to redeem the infringement on their honour. For the people Kunwar Singh is not a remote ruler on the throne; he is a community leader attached to the commoners through ties of blood and kinship. In popular perception, Kunwar Singh seems to be fighting less for his personal jagirdari privileges and much more *'to keep safe our pride and our plenty/ Our religion, our cows!/ Oh Babua, to protect the rent-free lands of our widows!/ And to protect our mothers and sisters from disgrace/ Oh Babua, to defend the fair name of our fathers and grandfathers'* [53]

The song shows that the narrow definition of Kunwar Singh as a defender of Hinduism in Bihar is not an adequate description. *Dharma* in popular mind stood for a whole range of political and social values that their hero sought to defend. The notions of *dharma*, honour and prosperity intermingle with each other in popular consciousness, which is political enough to argue for the resumption of rent-free grants of widows. This political articulation derives its legitimacy from a cultural code where traditions and customs of the past are venerated, and where changes brought about by the British are resented as they tarnish these traditions which are symbolized by the 'fair names of our fathers and grandfathers' . Thus it is not only material deprivation, but politics of a particular kind-rooted in cultural traditions and articulated through cultural symbols - that instigated and signified the broad sweep of rebellion in Shahabad. In fact, a comparison of the folk songs of Awadh heartland with that of Shahabad reveals that while in the case of Awadh heartland such concerns as outlined above, though present, are often overdetermined and overshadowed by the images of pathos for the nawab and his lost kingly splendour and opulence, in the case of Shahabad, community concerns occupy a pride of place. It is for this reason that Shahabad and the adjoining Bhojpuri belt provide us with perhaps the best domain to study popular mentalities during 1857. A popular Bhojpuri folktale even goes to the extent of giving the credit for the taking up of arms by Kunwar Singh to a call by the people of the region. Popular memory in the Bhojpuri region even recalls one Bansuria Baba as the 'guru' and adviser of Kunwar Singh.[54] What is also noteworthy is that though Kunwar Singh is highlighted in the folk-songs, the role of an ordinary rebel sepoy is not altogether forgotten:

> *Pahli laraiya Kunwar Singh jeetle/ Doosri Amar Singhbhai/ Ahe teesri laraiya sipahi sab jeetle/ Uthe lat ghabrai.*

(The first battle was won by Kunwar Singh and the second by his brother Amar Singh. But the third battle was won by all the sepoys together and this alarmed the British General).[55]

The notion of the whole Rajput community and all family members taking up the fight recurs again and again in the folk-songs, as the fight is for the defence of the ancestral honour of the total community of Rajput warriors of Bhojpur. Thus, if Kunwar Singh is old, it is deemed to be the duty of his younger brother Amar Singh to take over his role:

Jeera aisa dant ho jaye, a San aisa bar hojaye/Jul-Jul mans latkat jaye, banh men koobat mile jaye/Kaise tega pakroon main, kaise Money ko maroon main/Tab le Amarsingh bole ka, sun bhaiya meri bat/ Baithal bhaiya pan chabao, main angrezon ko dekhloonga.

(Kunwar Singh laments - 'my teeth and hair my flesh and the strength in my arms have all dissipated. How shall I now lift my arms and kill Money, the Collector? To which Amar Singh replies - 'O brother, listen to me. Don' t you worry, you rest enjoying your betel-leaf for I shall deal with the British).[56]

The territory of mobilization of rebellion extended much beyond the *mauza* and deep into the adjoining areas. Connections of kith and kin were forged with Kunwar Singh and his men even much beyond the borders of Shahabad. Pursued by the British forces in April 1858 and eager to cross back into Bihar at Muneahar in Ghazipur Kunwar Singh 'found himself among friends and the wants of his troops were voluntarily supplied by the villagers' who were of the same caste and 'almost universally in his favour' .[57] Again at Sheopur Ghat in Balia, the police, the 'mallahas' and zamindars 'friendly to Kunwar Singh were all instrumental in deceiving the officers responsible for the withdrawal of the boats and furnishing them to the rebels' .[58] The strong ties of brotherhood that the zamindars of Sheopur Ghat had with Kunwar Singh can be ascertained from the following folk song, that is still sung in Sheopur Ghat, in which the Zamindar brothers Sidha Singh and Nidha Singh assured the emissary from Kunwar Singh that they were ready to bring a smile to their clan brother Kunwar Singh' s face by selling their elephants and horses and feeding the sepoys from this income:

Larbi na ta ka harbi, bhain ke hansaibi/hathi ghora benchi ke, sipahin ke khiyayibi[59]

It is important to note here that the symbols of feudal honour like the horses and the elephants could be sacrificed for a more important question of honour that 1857 signified - the honour of the traditions and pride of at least the clan, if not the community. Such subtle nuances in the perception and conception of honour can be evident only by recourse to sources of oral history. Clan and caste linkages were one of the primary modes of mobilization of large sections of the community, though traditional inter and intra clan rivalaries could also dilute the spirit of rebellion at times.

Caste solidarity and aspirations directly related to a sense of loss on the part of a rebel community. It could be a loss of ancestral lands to moneylenders and auction-purchasers; expulsion from what it considered to be its traditional homeland, or a decline in wealth and status of its elite group which had lowered its prestige and standing both in its own eyes and in that of others. These issues often overlapped each other and combined in various ways to create a community sense of loss and deprivation. Ranajit Guha has argued against terming of such losses as purely 'economic' in nature; in fact 'there was no loss, whatever its cause, that was not felt to be a loss of power', and hence such grievances had a strong political character.[60] The Palwars of Azamgarh entered Mahul pargana in June 1857 and claimed the villages of the pargana to have been theirs.[61] Similarly, the Mona Rajputs of Bhadohi in Mirzapur had not forgotten that before passing into the hands of the Raja of Banaras in 1746-47, the large estates of Bhadohi were totally and solely their own.[62]

The notion of community was thus not merely a geographical notion. It was also a part of collective consciousness, clan memory and history. Thus the Srinet Rajputs of the ruling family of Sattasi in Gorakhpur had a recurrent memory of the 12th century division of lands of a common ancestor Bhagwant Singh into Unwal, Bansi (comprising Ratanpur Mugher) and Haveli Gorakhpur. The latter, consisting of Haveli Gorakhpur, Bhauapar and Sylhet was equal in area to eighty-seven ('sattasi' in Hindi) kos, giving the name 'Sattasi' to the area which the ruling family of Sattasi had in possession originally. Over the centuries and largely under the British revenue settlements, the territory of the Sattasi Raja had shrunk much below eighty-seven kos. It was this rightful claim over the original 'sattasi kos' that got revived from clan memory by the Raja and his kinsmen in 1857 and it was this claim that was used as a legitimate mobilising cause in the war against the alien British trespassers.[63]

The notion of 'Chowrasee Des' provides us with another clue to clan solidarity seeking its basis in history. 'Chowrasee' or 'eighty-four' refers to a tract of country containing the number of settlements or villages in the occupation of a particular clan which got spread, some time in history, from original villages.[64] That this notion of a common territorial homeland was vibrant among the Jat and the Rajput communities of North West Provinces had been testified by Elliot in the 1830s.[65] Even this notion was revived in 1857 from clan memory to mobilise against the British who had tresspassed upon and violated the sanctity of 'Chowrasee Des' , for we hear of the Chowrasee zamindars of Khyragarh pargana in Allahabad attacking government servants employed in collecting revenue in the area that they rightly claimed as their own.[66] Sources of oral history are rich in providing an insight into such notions of collective consciousness that were revived during 1857 for mobilisation. In Gonda (Awadh) we have folk songs underlining the notion of 'Chowrasee Des' in regard to Raja Devi Baksh Singh:

Raja Devi Bakas as sunder
Unke hath sone ka mundar
Unke aage sab lage chhuchhundar
Unke Chowrasee kos man rahe raj[67]

Similarly, ethnic bonds and traditional instruments like panchayats and assemblies to mobilise for rebellion were extensively used as can be seen in the case of Mewatis of Allahabad where the crucial decision to rebel was taken in mauza Samadabad in a 'panchayat of Mewatis held on 5 June 1857 at the house of Saif Khan Mewati and all, excepting Saif Khan, decided to rebel the same day.' [68] The Mewati landed and military gentry which had been rendered marginal and desperate following the crisis of the 1830s and whose life-style had been cramped by the growth of colonial bureaucracy and the commercial economy under the Company, found in 1857 an ideal opportunity to rebel. That they were not simply motivated by plunder, despite having been branded a 'criminal tribe' by the British, is clear not only from their lengthy deliberations in the panchayat before deciding to rebel, but also from the fact that in Allahabad, they were 'the real contrivers of the rebellion of the sepoys and the Risala' [69]. The ties of geographical vicinity represented by the Mewatis of all villages near Allahabad-Samadabad, Rasulpur, mauza Beli, Baghara, Shadiabad, Jonhol, Shevri, Fatehpur Bichhua, Katra, Karnal Ganj, Mahadpuri, Bakhtiara, Bakhtvari, Rasulpur (village), Minhajpur and others - again helped them here to rise as a community against the British.[70]

Sources of oral history also reveal - perhaps with greater feeling - the various ways in which the connections of kith and kin were forged for mobilisation in 1857. In this moving folk song Kunwar Singh is shown as desperately sending messages to all his clan chieftains in adjoining areas for help against the British:

Sone Kalam hathon men le likh paruana bheje ka
Ja Tekari dakhil hua, ja Dumraon dakhil hua,
Ja Dalippur dakhil hua, Ja Ramgarh dakhil hua;
Sun to Babu meri baat, Gotia bhai aap kahete
Meri madad par aao kam, main angrezom se bigda hoom
Meri madad par aao kaam.[71]

Badrinarayan has indicated how sentiments like challenge, pathos and notions of virtue and sin (intermingled with warnings about next birth) were used to enlist people for the rebel cause.

Je na dihee Kunwar Singh ke sath
U agila janam men hoi suar

(One who shall not join Kunwar Singh shall be a pig in his next birth)[72]

According to accepted social norms of 19th century Uttar Pradesh and Bihar, the ties of kinship and blood were very strong obligations and it was expected of other kinsmen to join and aid their 'brothers' fighting in defence of their ancestral honour and traditions. Failure to do so was treachery in the eyes of the people who still recall the perfidy of the Raja of Dumraon who, though a relative of Kunwar Singh, did not come to his aid when the situation so demanded:

Ek to main aas kailin Raja Dumrao ke
who bhagi chalele jaise ban men ke kharha
Kulhi gumalka Rama, matiya men mili gaile
nahi lebe pavalia hum Suraj

(Kunwar Singh in first person - 'I had relied upon the Raja of Dumraon but he too ran away like a hare in the forest. Whatever I had thought of has been ruined to dust - I could not attain my Raj').[73]

It is interesting to note that sometimes even persons like Harkishan Singh (the chief lieutenant of Kunwar Singh) who were on the rebel side are branded as traitors in oral historical tradition.[74] Does the oral tradition here indicate those subtle facets and nuances of conflict within the rebel community which are totally hidden in official sources of 1857? It is again remarkable that the *wazir* Ali Naqi Khan of Lucknow too enjoys the dubious reputation of a traitor, so much so that the saying *'nakki ho jaana'* has come into vogue in Awadh as a term for going back on one' s word.[75]

The use of the term *'nevta'* (traditionally used for invitation class and community members to for ritual festivities like birth, marriage, *shraddha* and so on) was also given a new meaning in the context of 1857.

Gaon gaon men duggi bajal, Babu ke phiral duhai
Loha chabvai ke nevta ba, sab saj apan dal badal
Ba jan gavankai ke nevta, choori phorvai ke nevta
Sindoor ponchhvai ke nevta ba, Rand kahvar ke nevta
Jei no hamar te math dei, jei ho hamar te sat dei
Ba ehan na nauka Samjhaike, ba een na nauka boojhai ke
Keeto phairo nevta hamar kee to taiyyar ho juijhike[76]

In this moment of crisis, *nevta* is redefined as an invitation to fight at all costs - even at the cost of life and widowhood to the womenfolk. It is a call to forget all notions of self interest and dutifully join together in the quest for the protection of the community. In fact, in the context of 1857 initial mobilization on clan or caste lines could easily extend itself to include people from other castes and merge into the wider issues that 1857 stood for.

Joining in the rebel cause in popular mentality, was no less an essential *dharma* than participating in the other rituals of life and death. Numerous folk songs describe how Kunwar Singh and Amar Singh always began the preparation for battle against the British with a ritual bath and embalming of body with sandalwood paste.

Sir se gosul kia banai
Chanan lagaulan atho ang
Vardi peti le mangao
Jhalam jhar le mangao[77]

In fact, in the context of 1857, the notion of *dharma* could acquire different meanings for different people with spatial variations. As indicated earlier, *dharma* in mid-19th century India was an all embracing term for a whole matrix of ethical and social values, it provided a normative structure of practices and customs according to which life should be governed; therefore defence of religion in a way stood for the defence of a whole way of life which, in the ambience of 1857, could very well mean a way of conflict with the offenders.

Aspects of masculinity and valour got linked with the notion of defence of this way of life in popular consciousness. Those who hide in their houses and refuse to opt for the path of struggle are worth ridicule and disrespect, as the following taunt by the womenfolk at such cowards reveals:

> *Lage saram laj ghar men baith jahu/Marad se bani ke lugaiya ae hari,/Pahirke Sari; choori; munhwa chhipai lehu/Rakhi eebi tohri pagariya ae hari.*
>
> (If you feel shy like a woman, then hide in the house. O husband, wear a sari and bangles and hide your face. We women would save your *pagdi* (honour)[78]

Cultural identities of masculinity and valour are invoked in this war of honour to gain strength. The expression of the fight against the British through culturally rooted idioms and symbols is, perhaps, an affirmation of that separate cultural domain that the rebels were trying to preserve from British encroachment. Thus the defeat of Kunwar Singh is expressed by the ordinary rebels in terms of the loss of desire to play Holi any longer.

> *Babu Kunwar Singh, tohre raj bina/Ab na rangaibo kesaria.*
>
> (O Babu Kunwar Singh, we shall dye no more our garments in sacred saffron/till your raj comes again).[79]

Holi, in cultural traditions, has often allowed a temporary reversal of social order through *swangs*, acting and dramas enacted by the people. 1857 was fought with aims of reverting back to the old order. However, since Kunwar Singh has been defeated, the chances of such reversal are very dim and hence its symbolical expression in the form of Holi no longer seems relevant. Further, '*kesariya*' or saffron has always been associated in Indian cultural tradition as the colour of both happiness as well as bravery and valour. Thus in this mood of defeat, when valour has been proved futile, dyeing of the garments in saffron is no longer proper. It shall be proper only when its symbolical status would get vindicated by the restoration of Kunwar Singh' s Raj.

It is however, remarkable, that even in this song of 'despair' the atmosphere is revitalized by ending with a '*phaag*' recalling those few, but significant, moments of victory and merriment that the community enjoyed when the red '*abeer*' of struggle had engulfed the bungalows due to Kunwar Singh' s might with the sword.

Bangla pe udela abeer ho lala, bangla pe udela abeer
Ho Babu, aho Babu Kunwar Singh Tegwa bahadur
Bangla pe udela abeer[80]

The significance of the uprising and the hope for a restoration some day in future thus lives on in popular memory. It shall be given a new dimension in the mass movement against the British in the 20th century when songs on Gandhi would emerge and indicate the various shades of meaning and imagery that Gandhi and his struggle acquired in popular perception. The deep rooted impact of this tradition of resistance on popular consciousness can be gauged from the following folk song in the Bhojpuri belt, in which the women remember and treasure the heroes of the community struggles as fondly as the ornaments that adorn their bodies.

Kanphulwa par Kunwar Singh, gardania par Gandhi ke
Eeranwa par tahra Arjun ke teer dhanush

(The earstuds are decorated with the figure of Kunwar Singh, the necklace with that of Gandhi while your earrings match the bow-arrow of Arjun).[81]

The articulation of revolt through culturally rooted symbols is evident in the identification of the inner world with the physical environment outside that had resisted the forces of the change which the colonial regime had ushered. Thus the equation of the determination to stand up for a cultural world with the strength of the resolute and plucky hills is a constant theme of the folk songs of the region in which the tenacity of Kunwar Singh and his dedication to the ideology he is thought to have rebelled for are juxtaposed against the backdrop of the unyielding Kaimur and Sasaram hills.

Similarly, it is interesting to note that, in popular imagery, the antidote to the mechanized tanks of the British are their own much respected, long befriended and customarily venerated domains of the naturally growing forests.

> *Sun journel meri bat, tumhara top mata hai/Mera jangal pita hai, main jangal chhoroonga nahin.*
>
> (O general listen to me; if your tank is your mother, my jungle is my father and I will never abandon it)[82]

In the context of 1857 the age old tradition of veneration of forests by the community is given a new interpretation both as a protector against the British and as an abettor to sustain community struggle in the form of their own brand of guerilla warfare against the open, tank aided battle by the British.

It is interesting to note that while the symbols like Khilats, *nazranas*, flags and proclamations through drums used by the rebel leaders emphasized display and opulence to underline power and authority, those of the ordinary rebel population (as evident in such folk songs) were made up of festivals, forests, rivers and other objects of common participation. This is especially true of the folk songs in the Bhojpuri belt of Bihar and eastern Uttar Pradesh where though not denying the role of Kunwar Singh as leader, his feelings are expressed in popular folk songs more through common symbols like Holi, the deer of the forests, and colts; all of which are shown as participating with everything on stake and with all their heart in the war that their hero had continued to wage despite being betrayed by his relatives:

> *Babu Kunwar Singh ke neel ka bachherwa*
> *Peeala katorwan doodh*
> *Hali hali dudhwa piain ae Kunwar Singh*
> *Rain jae ke badue door*
> *Abki rainia jitao neela bachherwa*
> *Sonwe madhaibo chado khur*
>
> (Babu Kunwar Singh's blue colt is drinking bowls of milk. O Kunwar Singh, make him drink fast for he has a long way to travel to the battle front. O blue colt, if you shall make us win this battle, we shall cover and adorn all your hooves with gold)[83]
>
> *Babu banwa khele le sikarwa*

Roweli banwa ke hiraniya
Pahil ladai Babu Hetampur bhaili
Rajwa bahelia dihlasi na
Satrah sau satasi mauza kuchhua na bujhle
Garh lutwa dihle na,
Rajwa dehlas dhokha na.

(From jungle to jungle Babu gave fight
and deer of the forest wept at sight
The first battle he fought at Hetampur
where Raja gave gumman to Britisher
He cared nothing for seventeen
hundred eighty seven villages
And had his fortress battered
Alas! the Raja treacherous one)[84]

One cannot escape concluding thus, that his actual motivations notwithstanding, Kunwar Singh was perceived more as a leader from within the community rather than one who is distant and impersonal. Such perceptions perhaps helped Kunwar Singh to enjoy a wider popular support than any other rebel leader.

Gajra ka gajreet banaya, murai ke darwaza
Sarkand ka je top banaya, lade Kunwar Singh Raja

(Of carrots he made a palace, and of radish he could contrive a door. Of sweet potatoes he made cannons - thus fought Raja Kunwar Singh)[85]

In this extract the comparison of the symbols of power and struggle with common vegetables that grow 'under the ground' is perhaps the most moving tribute by the people to the strategy of 'guerilla' warfare that was adopted by Kunwar Singh and his men to fight the British. As against the open warfare practiced by larger loftier armies, 'guerilla' warfare was a strategy that had been practised in the Indian tradition for ages by smaller caste or village based organizations which in the context of 1857 in Shahabad proved as strongly rooted in and linked with the soil as the vegetables growing under it.

III

Much has been written in historiography about the rumours regarding adulterated flour, the greased cartridges and polluted ghee that contributed to the sense of outrage among the soldiers and the civilian population. Ranajit Guha has pointed out that both the opposition between the British and Indians, and the unity of all Indians were expressed in terms of a single theme - that of ritual pollution - phrased as a rumour in 'many portentious shapes'.[86]

However, this unity of Indians was not always perfect. We must move away from the traditional assertion in nationalist historiography that 1857 saw everywhere a unity of all castes and communities against the British. Though it is true that the wide range of issues that 1857 stood for could often mean that the issues would themselves emerge as crucial mobilising factors transcending clan or dynastic rivalaries and personal interests or gains, however this was not the case everywhere. In fact 1857 is too complex a movement to be explained in terms of unilinear models. Even within the region under study, there were variations in the intensity and pattern of mobilisation and action depending on a host of factors ranging from the interaction of traditional local power structure with the forces unleashed by the colonial regime to the extent of networks of caste and clan and their mutual relations, and from the factors of a region's specific grievances and benefits to the extent of popular initiative and participation.

Thus in Gorakhpur region, the Majhauli Raja - despite having clan ties with the rebel Rajas of Narharpur - had an ancestral history of harassment by the Awadh nawabs and their amils which had forced his ancestor to seek refuge in Saran in Bihar, and hence for him there was no question of siding with Mohammad Hasan with strong pro-Awadh sentiments.[87] On the contrary, for the Gautam Rajput family of Nagar whose estates at Ganeshpur had been given to the Pindarah by the British, the resentment was too recent to be forgotten and hence they were openly rebelleous[88]. The zamindars of Amroha similarly had a history of conflict with the British from the days of their ancestor Zalim Singh in the 18th century and hence thanas Eloea and Dumreeganj in the pargana of Amroha were one of the most 'disturbed' areas in the district.[89]

Nor is the binary model of total opposition or total loyalty to the Raj of universal application. A variety of intermediary attitudes ranging from stoic indifference to fluctuating vacillations also affected the shape of mobilisation in 1857. Thus in Azamgarh, mobilisation for the rebel cause would reverse its course after a time to turn into a conference of alliance with the British. The question of survival after shaken self-confidence due to constant defeats became more important than the ideology of 1857 for many like Palwars for whom, in any case, the issue was largely limited to restoration of their lands. In Jaunpur, by contrast, ideology played a much more important role due to the blood-relations the Rajkumars had with a number of Awadh taluqdars. Here anti-British stance was prolonged and more ferocious. Apart from the ideological commitment to Awadh, the preponderance of auction sales and the embitterment of the gentry were important contributory factors for the intensity of the Rebellion. Yet, even here not all were affected by this sentiment - despite hardships at the hands of auction purchasers and calls of clan loyaltv, one-fifth of taluqdars in Jaunpur remained loyal to the British.

Even among the lower castes cases of both loyalty to the rebel cause as well as indifference or hostility to it can be seen. Polarization and divisions within Indian society based on the hierarchical system of ritual pollution were not always or altogether submerged within the cohesive whole of unity against the '*firanghi*' . Thus Jhuri Singh, after avenging the death of Udwant Singh by severing the head of Moore, did not carry it to the widow of Udwant Singh himself, but 'forced Munai chamar to carry it' , as recalled in his deposition during the trial by Ujahil Chamar in a tone of unconcealed resentment at the forcible treatment of his fellow casteman.[90] In an uprising with strong overtones of religion and ritual pollution it is not surprising that those sections of Indian society that had traditionally been regarded as lowly or 'polluting' found themselves often untouched by the forces of solidarity that the movement generated. In the social and political order that 1857 was seeking to defend, the sweeper, scavengers and other such lowly castes were outside the scheme of things. In many Bhojpuri folktales and songs the otherwise 'ideal' heroes Lorik and Sorthi are also shown as hating the untouchables:

> *'Jab chheri deehen chamain hamri sharirea ho/hamaro dharmva chali jai...'*[91]

The untouchables were considered as much of defilers by the rebels as the British, and were supposed to remain outcastes continuing their lowly functions once the 'puritan' traditional order was re-established. Even Nanak Singh' s 'Jangnama' , a near contemporary account (which was discovered by Amrit Lal Nagar during his creditworthy tour of Awadh to collect material on 1857) of the fierce battle between Thakur Balbhadra Singh of Chahlari and the British does not have a single untouchable figuring in the list of ninety commoner warriors mentioned there.[92]

Even Kunwar Singh' s rebel government, which underlined its popular base by having a *mali* and a *goala* within its ranks, has no reference to any untouchable.

It is interesting to note how the two pollutes - the British and the Indian untouchables/lowly castes - seem to have allied together in most parts of eastern Uttar Pradesh and Bihar against the Rebellion. We find them aiding the British in large numbers, and the British seem to have attempted to utilize this to their advantage. Thus captain Bruce at Kanpur, on anticipating rebel invasion, raised a police force consisting solely of men of lower caste *mehtars*.[93] This 'Sweepers Police' was helpful in re-establishing British authority at Bithoor and also in capturing the fort of Sul Kynee on the Kalpee road.[94] Even in Banda, the collector, Mayne, raised a foot-levy of *Khangari* and *Bhungees*.[95] That the British had realized the advantage of this scheme as an expedient policy is evident from the instructions given by the Commissioner of Patna division to magistrates of all districts for recruitment of men of only lower caste - '*Dusadh*' and '*Chamar*' - in the extra police force.[96] Again, near Jaunpur, where most of the Rajput zamindars and their kindred had forced the British to run for shelter from one place to another, it were some *chamars* who carried the ailing father of George Matthews (an army officer) to a place of safety.[97] Similarly, an English lady imprisoned in Bibighar, of all persons, could only find a *bhangin* ready to carry her letter to the English at Allahabad. The letter was caught and the *bhangin* whipped.[98] as a fitting sequel to the turn of events, once Kanpur was recaptured by the British, the rebels were asked to perform the lowly task of cleaning the blood stains of Bibighar, and on their refusal, they were whipped by *mehtars*.[99]

Although it is true that many zamindars did succeed in mobilizing their lower caste retainers in their attacks on auction-purchasers and in Allahabad 'a sort of enthusiasm' was prevalent among the lower classes in Kunwar Singh' s favour, it is nevertheless evident from the examples cited above that, if not everywhere, at many places the lower caste groups and especially the 'untouchables' showed a remarkable autonomy of action quite different from the general trend of rebellion within the upper caste groups. The extent to which and the ways in which these examples relate to the perception by the lowest castes of the relations of subordination and domination within Indian society and to their resentment against the vindication of such relations in rebel ideology are important questions in the context of 1857 that must be examined by historians in greater detail. Such high/low caste tensions have so far been little noted in the historiography of 1857 due to the hegemony of the nationalist framework. In fact, even a sophisticated historian like Ranajit Guha is not really immune from it. He too has not been always able to avoid the language of 'collaboration' and 'betrayal' and hardly focusses upon the high-low caste tensions within Indian society. In fact, a 'subaltern' like a high caste ordinary peasant rebel could very well be an 'elite' in the eyes of the low caste sweepers and labourers of the countryside. Anti-colonialism of the 1857 type was not necessarily liberating in an unproblematic sense for the subordinate groups like low castes and women.

NOTES

The author is grateful to Pt. Ganesh Chowbe of Motihari, Bihar for making available some rare copies of Bhojpuri journal.

1. For these approaches, see S.B. Chaudhuri; *Civil Rebellion in the Indian Mutinies*, Calcutta 1957; R.C. Majumdar; *The Sepoy Mutiny and the Revolt of 1857*, Calcutta, 1957; S.N. Sen; *Eighteen Fifty Seven*, Delhi 1957; J.W. Kay; *A History of the Sepoy War in India, 1857-58*, 6 vols, London, 1876; V.D. Savarkar, *Indian War of Independence, 1857*, Bombay, 1947 (first published 1909); P.C. Joshi (ed) *Rebellion 1857 - A Symposium*, Delhi 1957.
2. Eric Stokes, *The Peasant and The Raj*, Cambridge 1978.
3. E.I. Brodkin, *The Struggle For Succession: Rebels and Loyalists in 1857*, Modern Asian Studies, Vol. VI, 11972, pp.277-90.
4. See for instance, R. Devi: *Indian Mutiny: 1857 in Bihar*, Delhi, 1977; Shyam Narain Sinha; *The Revolt of 1857 in Bundelkhand*, Lucknow, 1982; K.L. Shrivastava, *The Revolt of 1857 in Central India - Malwa*, Bombay, 1966; N.K. Nigam, *Delhi in 1857*, Delhi, 1957; K.K. Dutta, *Biography of Kunwar Singh and Amar Singh*, Patna 1957.
5. Eric Stokes, *The Peasant Armed*, Oxford, 1986.
6. R. Mukherjee, *Awadh in Revolt*, 1857-58, OUP, 1984.
7. R. Guha, *Elementary Aspects of Peasant Insurgency in Colonial India*, OUP, 1983.
8. S.A.A. Rizwi(ed), *Freedom Struggle in Uttar Pradesh, Vol. IV* p.73 (hereafter FSUP IV)
9. Even a recent book by Tapti Ray, *The politics of a popular uprising: Bundelkhand in 1857*, Delhi, 1994, prefers to rely on official sources and the letters and proclamations of soldiers to construct the moments of Rebellion. The vast repertoire of folk songs in Bundelkhand are totally glossed over.
10. C.E. Buckland, *Bengal under Lt. Governors, Vol. I*, Calcutta, 1901, p.93.
11. Extract from the 'The Ballad of Kunwar Singh' available in translated form in P.C. Joshi, *1857 in Folk Songs*, Delhi, 1994 p.129.
12. Quoted in D.P. Singh, *Bhojpuri ke Kavi aur Kavya*, Patna 1958, p.159, Translation

mine.

13. The source for the saying is Dr. Sampathi Aryani, *Magahi Lok Sahitya*, Delhi 1965 p.58 and for the folk song is Dr. Shridhar Mishra, *Bhojpuri Loksahitya - Sanskritik Adhyayan*, Allahabad, 1971, p.161.
14. Shridhar Mishra: op. cit. pp.368-69. Translation mine.
15. Extract taken from Shri Rasbiharilal, *Lokgeetan men Babu Kunwar Singh*, Bhojpuri, Arrah; year 3, No.7 April 1955, p.34. Translation mine.
16. Source - Compiled in Badrinarayan, *Lok Sanskriti men Rashtrawad*, Delhi, 1996, p.94.
17. Source of the saying is Aryani: op. cit. p.180.
18. Extract from the 'The Ballad of Kunwar Singh' compiled in translated form in P.C. Joshi, *1857 in Folk Songs*, Delhi 1994 pp.109-110.
19. Source of the saying is Aryani, op. cit. p.184.
20. Source: Shridhar Mishra, op. cit. p.168, 179.
21. C.A. Bayly: *Rulers, Townsmen and Bazaars, North Indian Society in the age of British expansion, 1770-1870*, Cambridge, 1983 p.290. Bayly points out that despite forcible intervention by the State, the benefits to the cultivator appear to have been limited to a small area, particularly the Padrauna tahsil of Ghazipur district. Even in Padrauna tahsil the 'major cultivaters took the first opportunity of the coming of the railway to move into much more lucrative grain production, leaving the difficult, costly and polluting drug to their poorer neighbours'.
22. District Gazetteer of Ghazipur (1903-05) p.173.
23. Ibid. p.172.
24. Bayly: op. cit. p.364.
25. For an excellent analysis of the impact of the new social and economic forces unleashed by the colonialist regime on the position of the weavers of eastern Uttar Pradesh see Gyanendra Pandey: 'Encounters and Calamities: The History of a North Indian Qasba in the 19th Century' in R. Guha(ed) *Subaltern studies III*, Delhi, 1984.
26. *FSUP IV*, p.20.
27. District Gazetteer of Allahabad (1903-05) p.182.
28. *FSUP IV*, p.526.
29. District Gazetteer of Gaya (1906) compiled by L.S.S.O' Malley. Italics mine.
30. S.B. Singh: 'Gaya in 1857-58' in Proceedings of Indian History Congress, Mysore, 1966.
31. Q. Ahmad, 'The Unique Trial of Arrah Town', *Journal of Bihar Research Society*, Vol.XLVI, 1960.
32. Ibid. p.159.
33. Ram Vilas Sharma, *San Sattavan ki Rajya Kranti* Agra, 1957.
34. Source of the folk song - Krishnadev Upadhyaya, 'Bhojpuri Lokgeeton men 57 ki Kranti ke swar', *Tripathga* Year 2, August 1957, p.60.
35. Quoted in Dr. Bhagwan Das Mahaur, *1857 ke Swadheenta Sangram ka Hindi Sahitya par Prabhav*, Ajmer 1976, p.426.
36. Quoted in op. cit. p.417.
37. Quoted in Shyamanand Singh, *Kavi Shekhawat an unhakar Kuchh pad* in Bhojpuri, year 4, Vol. 3-6, January 1956, p.79.
38. Srinivas Balaji Hardikar: *Nanasheb Peshwa*, Delhi 1969, p.84.
39. Peter Burke: *The Art of Conversation*, Oxford, 1993, p.27.
40. *FSUP IV*, pp.22, 84.
41. Ibid, p.40.

42. Ibid, p.48.
43. Ibid, p.114.
44. District Gazetteer of Gorakhpur (1903-05).
45. K.K. Dutta: *Biography of Kunwar Singh and Amar Singh*, Patna, 1957, p.173.
46. FSUP IV, p.157.
47. Ibid. p.654.
48. Ibid. pp.377-394.
49. Quoted in Dr. Vinaymohan Sharma(ed), *Hindi Sahitya Ka Brihat Itihas*, Vol.VIII', Kashi 1957.
50. Extract taken from P.C. Joshi, *1857 in Folk Songs*, Delhi, 1994, p.29.
51. Extract taken from Shridhar Mishra, op. cit., Translation mine.
52. Source of folk song in translated form from P.C. Joshi: 'Folk Songs of 1857', in P.C. Joshi(ed) *Rebellion 1857 - A Symposium*, Delhi, 1957, pp. 280-281.
53. Ibid. p.280.
54. Badrinarayan: op. cit., p.33.
55. Source of folk song - Shridhar Mishra: op. cit. p.160.
56. Source of the extract is the 'Nonidih ki ladai' from folk ballad. Durgashankar Prasad Singh, 'Kunwar Singh ke Panwara' in Bhojpuri, Arrah, year 3, No. 7, April 1955, p.43.
57. *FSUP IV*, p.446.
58. Ibid, p.447.
59. Source of folk song: S. Mishra, *Bhojpuri Lok geet ke vividh roop*. Translation mine.
60. Guha: op, cit, p.317.
61. *FSUP IV*, pp.102, 410.
62. District Gazetteer of Mirzapur (1903-05).
63. In details of history of Sattasi, see S.N.R. Rizwi, *Attartvin Sadi ke Zamindar*, PPH, 1988.
64. For a recent discussion on the notion of 'Chowrasee Des' in western Uttar Pradesh see Gautam Bhadra, 'Four Rebels of Eighteen Fifty Seven' in R. Guha(ed) *Subaltern Studies IV*, Delhi, 1985.
65. Quote.' in Bhadra: op, cit.
66. *FSUP IV*, p.783.
67. Quoted in Amritlal Nagar, *Ghadar ke phool*, Delhi edition, 1991, p.80.
68. *FSUP IV*, p.549.
69. Ibid. p.548.
70. Ibid. p.550.
71. Source of folk song: 'Dulaur ki ladai' compiled in Durgashankar Prasad Singh, op, cit, p.40.
72. Badrinarayan: op, cit, p.35. Translation mine.
73. Source of the folk song - S. Mishra: op, cit, p.144. Translation mine.
74. For instance, in the folk ballad 'Nonidih ki ladai' or the 'Battle of Nonidih'.
75. Nagar, op, cit. p.131.
76. Source of folk song - Badrinarayan: op, cit. p.36.
77. Source of folk ballads compiled in Durgashankar Prasad Singh, op. cit. pp.41, 43.
78. Source of folk song - Shridhar Mishra: op, cit, p.158.
79. Ibid. Translation by P.C. Joshi in his *1857 in Folk Songs*, p.97.
80. Source of folk song - Mahaur: op. cit. p.415.
81. Source of folk song - Shridhar Mishra: op. cit. p.146. Translation mine.

82. Source of this extract is the folk ballad 'Nonidih ki Ladai' compiled in Durgashankar Prasad Singh: op. cit. p.43.
83. Source of folk song - Shri Rasbiharilal, op. cit. p.34. Translation mine.
84. Ibid. p.34. Translation in P.C. Joshi: *1857 in Folk Songs*, p.79.
85. This jogira folk song is taken from Mahaur: op. cit. p.148. Translation in P.C. Joshi, *1857 in Folk Songs*, p.83.
86. Guha, op. cit. p.264.
87. Lala Khadgbahadur Mall, *Bishwen Vansh Vatika*, Bankipur, 1887, pp.70-71.
88. *FSUP IV*, p.328.
89. Rizwi, op. cit. p.64.
90. *FSUP IV*, p.83.
91. Shridhar Mishra; op. cit. p.156.
92. Nagar; op. cit. p.99.
93. *FSUP IV.*
94. Ibid.
95. Ibid. p.839.
96. Letter No. 324, dated 12.06.1857 from Commissioner of Patna, quoted in S.B. Singh, op. cit.
97. *FSUP IV*, p.129.
98. Vishnubhat Godase, *Majha Pravas*, Poona, 1907, quoted in Hardikar, op. cit. p.151.
99. Ibid. p.151.

[2]

CONNEXIONS BETWEEN 'PRIMARY RESISTANCE' MOVEMENTS AND MODERN MASS NATIONALISM IN EAST AND CENTRAL AFRICA. PART I

BY T. O. RANGER

A recent authoritative review of developments in African historiography pointed to one 'kind of synthesis which has always seemed worthwhile undertaking', the attempt to trace 'an historic connexion between the last-ditch resisters, the earliest organisers of armed risings, the messianic prophets and preachers, the first strike-leaders, the promoters of the first cautious and respectful associations of the intelligentsia, and the modern political parties which (initially at least) have been the inheritors of European power'.[1]

The 'historic connexions' between prophets and preachers, trade-union leaders and rural radicals, the founders of the Native and Welfare Associations and the organizers of mass nationalism, are now beginning to emerge from the very interesting work being done on the political history of East and Central Africa. But it cannot be said that the 'last-ditch resisters' and the 'earliest organisers of armed risings' have so far been placed very satisfactorily in this general context.

On this particular question, indeed, there has been very considerable scholarly disagreement. One school of thought would emphatically differentiate these initial violent reactions from later manifestations of opposition and particularly from nationalism. Nationalist movements, they contend, are essentially modernist in outlook and directed towards the concept of a territorial loyalty. Primary resistance movements, on the other hand, were inherently backward-looking and traditional; not only tribal but emphasizing the most 'reactionary' elements in tribal life. Such movements, it is held, repudiated those within African societies who wished to come to terms with modernization and to accept education, the missionary influence, and the new commercial and technical opportunities. Resistance movements of the early colonial period, write Robinson and Gallagher, were 'romantic, reactionary struggles against the facts, the passionate protest of societies which were shocked by a new age of change and would not be comforted'. Primary resistances, so Coleman tells us, were 'impulsive negative retorts', striving vainly to recapture the past and looking in no sense to the future.[2]

Such movements are contrasted with 'the defter nationalisms' which planned 'to reform their personalities and regain their powers by operating

[1] 'African syntheses', *The Times Literary Supplement*, 28 July 1966.

[2] R. E. Robinson and J. Gallagher, 'The partition of Africa', in *The New Cambridge Modern History*, XI (Cambridge, 1962), chap. 23, p. 640; J. S. Coleman, *Nigeria: Background to Nationalism* (Berkeley, 1963), 172.

in the idiom of the Westernisers'. It was, so the argument continues, often the men and societies that chose not to resist at all in the first instance that provided the leaders of the 'defter nationalisms' which are the obvious parents of the modern mass movements. Such men, or such societies, through their initial acquiescence or co-operation, gained privileged access to education and economic opportunity and thus learnt the new skills of opposition. Resistant societies on the other hand are generally believed to have suffered the fate sketched by Oliver and Fage:

> If African leaders...were less far-sighted, less fortunate, or less well advised, they would see their traditional enemies siding with the invader and would themselves assume an attitude of resistance, which could all too often end in military defeat, the deposition of chiefs, the loss of land to the native allies of the occupying power, possibly even to the political fragmentation of the society and state.

Societies so roughly handled fell into a sullen passivity in which meaningful political activity was impossible until the old war leader could be replaced by the man with modern skills and outlooks. There was thus, especially in resistant societies, a sharp hiatus between the primary and secondary manifestations of opposition to European rule. In any real sense 'an historic connexion' did not exist.[3]

This view is not necessarily the result of lack of sympathy for pre-colonial African societies or for African grievances in the early colonial period. In essence it is the view put forward in 1924 by the famous protagonist of the Kenyan African cause, Norman Leys.

> Tribal risings ceased [wrote Leys] because they were always hopeless failures. Naked spearmen fall in swathes before machine-guns, without inflicting a single casualty in return. Meanwhile the troops burn all the huts and collect all the live-stock within reach. Resistance once at an end, the leaders of the rebellion are surrendered for imprisonment...Risings that followed such a course could hardly be repeated. A period of calm followed. And when unrest again appeared it was with other leaders...and other motives.[4]

The nationalist and anti-colonial tendency in modern African historiography has tended to dispute this view of a hiatus between primary and secondary resistance, though so far without really demonstrating a continuity. The most interesting expression of this counter-view has been the paper given by Professor A. B. Davidson of Moscow to the International Congress of African History, held in Dar es Salaam in September 1965. So far from seeing primary resistance movements as cut off from modern nationalism, Davidson holds that

> it is impossible to understand the African past without the re-establishment of the truth about this resistance...and without making a study of what was the answer of one people or another to the establishment of colonial rule it is difficult to

[3] R. Oliver and J. D. Fage, *A Short History of Africa* (London, 1962), p. 203.

[4] N. Leys, *Kenya*, 1924.

understand not only the past of that people but its present as well. It is difficult to comprehend the character of the liberation movement in the recent revolutionary years. Many things in this struggle and even in its demands...were defined by long-standing traditions of resistance. An attentive study of the history of popular resistance in Africa will inevitably prove that this struggle acted as one of the most important stimuli to historical development for the African peoples... Resistance left its mark on the most important internal processes of the development of the African peoples; in the course of resistance tendencies to change developed more quickly.[5]

Recent work on West Africa, particularly Francophone West Africa, has tended to substantiate Davidson's view, or at least greatly to qualify the views expressed by Coleman or Robinson and Gallagher. Thomas Hodgkin and Ruth Schachter Morgenthau have demonstrated for Mali and Guinea the continuing importance for the modern period of the resistance offered to the French by Samory and the heirs of Al Hajj Umar; showing how an alternative prestigious leadership remained available for mass discontent, and how such discontent could be channelled by the survivors or heirs of the resisters against the 'loyalist' and collaborating African authorities set up by the French; showing how this alternative leadership succeeded to the radical and reformist traditions of the nineteenth-century Islamic movements and was able to make the transition fairly readily to the notions of modern mass nationalism; and showing how not only the memory but also the surviving structural alliances of the resistant Samory and Al Hajj Umar systems could be used as the foundation of radical mass parties in the modern period. Professor Ajayi has recently suggested that the legacy of these fighting Islamic theocracies, doomed in Robinson and Gallagher's version to 'romantic, reactionary struggles against the facts', is of immediate significance to the nationalist reformer.

The over-riding interest of the colonial regime...was the maintenance of law and order, not reform. The result has been, therefore, that many of the nationalist governments of today are finding that on a number of issues they have to pick up the threads of social and political reform from the point where the radical Muslim and Christian reformers of the nineteenth century left off at the coming of colonial rule.[6]

No such argument has yet been propounded for East and Central Africa, and probably no argument in the same sort of terms can be propounded. But it seems worth while to see if it is not possible to challenge the assumption of hiatus in East and Central Africa also, and to establish some 'historic connexions' between primary and secondary resistance. This paper is an initial exploration of such possibilities.

[5] A. B. Davidson, 'African resistance and rebellion against the imposition of colonial rule', in *Emerging Themes in African History*, ed. T. O. Ranger (Nairobi, 1968).

[6] J. F. Ajayi, 'The continuity of African institutions under colonialism', ibid.; T. Hodgkin and R. Schachter, *French-Speaking West Africa in Transition* (New York, 1960).

The argument for East and Central Africa has to begin, I think, by establishing what is perhaps an obvious but yet insufficiently appreciated fact; namely that the environment in which later African politics developed was shaped not only by European initiatives and policy or by African co-operation and passivity, but also by African resistance. In this sense at least there is certainly an important connexion between resistance and later political developments.

In some cases the environment of later politics was shaped by the consequences of the total defeat of attempted resistance. We have seen above the stress placed by Oliver and Fage on the inevitable defeat of primary resistance movements. Yet there has been a curious failure to appreciate the wide significance of such defeats as a psychological factor. Let us take the case of Kenya as an example. British rule was established in Kenya with few spectacular or large-scale displays of force. For this reason it was possible to write about the 'pacification' of Kenya in the terms employed by A. T. Matson in 1962: 'Except in abnormal cases... the amount of force used was minimal, with the result that the pacification of the Protectorate and the settlement of its tribes were accomplished with astonishingly little loss of life... Most of the operations were carried through by local forces acting more as police than conquerors.' But such a view overlooked the fact that, for each Kenyan African society that suffered what Matson would describe as a police action, the experience of rapid and total defeat could be traumatic. The point is well brought out by Professor Low. 'It was force and military prowess which in the main effected the critical submissions to British authority of the peoples' of the Kenya uplands, he tells us.

> Any map which outlined the operational theatres of the many small British military expeditions during the first fifteen years of British rule...would exhibit few interstices...And for all the exiguousness of these expeditions in European terms, they were often vastly greater, more lethal demonstrations of force than any which the defeated tribes had experienced from any quarter in the past, since they almost invariably took the form of a wholly unequal encounter between guns upon the British side and spears upon the African.

The Embu people provide an admirable example of the long-lasting impact that could be made by one of these rapid suppressions of primary resistance. For all their intransigence and for all their war-like reputation, Embu resistance was broken within two weeks when British forces entered the area in 1906; thereafter all arms were surrendered at a place called Ngoiri, and the Embu forbidden to carry offensive weapons.

> Ever since the tribe has been as law-abiding as its neighbours [an Embu historian tells us], although the memories of 1906 still remain fresh... In fact, at the feeder road leading to Ngoiri Primary School, built on the scene of the surrender of the weapons, there is a sign board on which is written the words: 'RETURN OUR SHIELDS AND OUR SPEARS'. The sign board was planted there in 1963 on Kenya's

Independence Day, and demanded the return by the Wazungu of the weapons burnt at Ngoiri in 1906.[7]

And if the memory of a two-week humiliation could dominate 'the fireside stories told by the grandmothers and grandfathers' of Embu, it goes without saying that the impact of more spectacular defeats was more profound and important. Julius Nyerere tells us that memories of the suppression of primary resistance were among the factors which

> determined the strategy of Tanganyika's independence struggle...Memories of the Hehe and Maji Maji wars against the German colonialists, and of their ruthless suppression, were deeply ingrained in the minds of our people. So, too, was the fact that our conquerors had themselves been defeated in battle by the British who governed the territory. The people, particularly the elders, asked, 'How can we win without guns? How can we make sure that there is not going to be a repetition of the Hehe and Maji-Maji wars?' It was therefore necessary for TANU to start by making the people understand that peaceful methods of struggle for independence were possible and could succeed. This does not mean that the people of this country were cowardly, or particularly fond of non-violence; no, they knew fighting; they had been badly defeated and ruthlessly suppressed. As realists, therefore, they wanted to know why TANU thought we could win even without guns. [This] determined the initial emphasis on the United Nations.[8]

Yet, having made this point of the continuing significance of memories of defeat, it is at once necessary to go on to say that not all resistances were doomed to total failure and crushing suppression. Some of them preserved liberties, wrung concessions or preserved pride. In so doing they made their own very important contributions to the creation of the environment in which later politics developed. I have argued this case in more detail elsewhere and will content myself here with some illustrations.[9]

Let us take the Basuto, for example. The Basuto demonstrate the invalidity of many of the generalizations usually made about resistant societies. They were certainly not backward-looking. Their leaders desired missionary education, a fruitful economic contact with the outside world, and British protection. These were things that some co-operative African societies also desired. A co-operative society like Barotseland, for example, was able to obtain them by accommodation with the colonial power. The

[7] A. T. Matson, 'The pacification of Kenya', *Kenya Weekly News*, 14 Sept. 1962; D. A. Low, 'British East Africa: The establishment of British rule, 1895–1912', in *History of East Africa*, II, ed. V. Harlow and E. M. Chilver (Oxford, 1965), 31, 32; D. Namu, 'Primary resistance amongst the Embu' and 'Background to Mau Mau amongst the Embu', Research Seminar Papers (Dar es Salaam, Oct. 1965 and Nov. 1966).

[8] J. K. Nyerere, *Freedom and Unity* (Dar es Salaam, 1966), 2–3.

[9] These themes and others in this paper are treated at greater length in T. O. Ranger, 'African reaction to the imposition of colonial rule in East and Central Africa', in *History and Politics of Modern Imperialism in Africa*, ed. L. H. Gann and P. Duignan (Stanford, forthcoming). Although the two papers are distinct in theme, some parts of the argument are necessarily the same, and there is some repetition in this paper of passages also included in the Stanford chapter.

Basuto, on the other hand, resisted; not because they were less well informed or less well advised than the Lozi, but because resistance was the only way of protecting themselves from the Afrikaners or the Cape, from total disarmament and probable dispossession. They were much closer to the dynamic frontier of white expansion than Barotseland. Nor was their resistance in vain. The so-called Gun War of 1880–1 between the Basuto and the Cape ended in a solid political victory for the Basuto. They won protection against white settlement and effective retention of their guns. And the direct consequence of the war was the surrender by the Cape of all responsibility with respect to Basutoland, and the establishment of the British Protectorate in March 1884. It hardly needs to be said that this hard-won Protectorate became the essential environment for all later Basuto political activity.[10]

Not many African societies were able to gain as much as this from resistance. But even those which suffered military defeat and failed to keep out white settlement or to preserve their institutions sometimes had something to gain by resisting. An example of this which I have elaborated elsewhere is that of the Ndebele of Southern Rhodesia. Their uprising in 1896 was defeated but they came out of it with some political gains. Before 1896 the Ndebele state had been in ruins; its white rulers had broken up all its institutions; confiscated all Ndebele land and nearly all Ndebele cattle; disregarded every Ndebele political authority. The 1896 rising at least showed the whites that this had been unwise. The Ndebele were still a formidable military foe; it took many men and much money to defeat their rising; and even then it had not been convincingly defeated by the end of the 1896 dry season. Rhodes faced a long-drawn-out war of attrition in which the authority of the British South Africa Company might well have collapsed through bankruptcy or British political intervention. So he negotiated with the Ndebele. They thus won in 1896 what they had not had in 1893—a voice in the settlement. The policy of the British South Africa Company was now defined as being to restore to the Ndebele *indunas* as much of the powers they had possessed under Lobengula as was possible; they received official salaries. So was struck an alliance between the Ndebele chiefs and the Rhodesian administration which still has important political consequences today.[11]

Even a much more complete defeat than this could still leave an African people with something positive to carry into the future. The Hehe of Tanzania, for example, were shattered in war by the Germans. Here there was no question of negotiations or concessions won by resistance. But military defeat did not break up the Hehe system. Out of their long resistance to the Germans the Hehe carried self-respect. Oliver and Fage have told us that 'for the African peoples the most important factor at this stage

[10] J. Halpern, *South Africa's Hostages* (London, 1965), chap. 3; I am also indebted to Mr A. E. Atmore for my understanding of the significance of the Gun War.

[11] T. O. Ranger, *Revolt in Southern Rhodesia, 1896–7* (London, 1967), chaps. 7 and 10.

of colonial history...was the intangible psychological issue of whether any given society or group was left feeling it had turned the early colonial occupation to its own advantage, or alternatively that it had been humiliated'. Their assumption in this passage is that defeated resistances led to humiliation, and this is an assumption which had been made by a good many of the writers, for instance, on Southern Rhodesia nationalism, who frequently depict the Ndebele and the Shona as consciously 'conquered people', and hence less politically assertive than peoples in Zambia and Malawi who do not have memories of humiliation. But this is an assumption that the Hehe and other instances challenge. The Hehe did not turn the early colonial situation to their own advantage, but they retained pride. 'Today all Wahehe idealize Mkwawa', wrote a British district officer in the 1920s. 'This may be because he actually beat the white man in battle.' Alison Redmayne, who has made a detailed study of Hehe political history, sees this pride as one of its determining influences.[12]

Resistances also helped to shape the environment of later African politics because of their impact upon the thinking and action of the colonial authorities. Thus actual or potential resistance brought about the collapse of the commercial companies which were at first employed by the Germans and the British to open up their East African spheres of influence, and forced the two governments to assume direct responsibility. Moreover, both under company and colonial office rule, the possibility and actuality of resistance was a main factor in bringing about those alliances between the colonial administration and co-operating African societies which are generally agreed to have been so important to later political activity. Despite their technological superiority, the new colonial regimes were weak in men and finance and needed allies to deal with resistance or rebellion. Finally, African rebellions did much to shatter the early European attitude of masterful complacency. The thinking of administrators and settlers, especially in Tanganyika after Maji-Maji and in Rhodesia after the Ndebele and Shona risings of 1896–7, was dominated by the fear of the repetition of such outbreaks. This fear had many and complex effects, but among other things it led to certain concessions to anticipated African discontent as well as to military and police contingency-planning. If Africans in Tanganyika wanted at all costs to avoid another Maji-Maji rising, so also did administrative officers.[13]

But it was not only the attitudes of defeated African societies and those of apprehensive white settlers which were affected by resistance and rebellion. There was a complex interplay between so-called 'primary' resistance and manifestations of 'secondary' opposition. We have seen above that many scholars have employed a rather rigid periodization in

[12] A. H. Redmayne, 'The Wahehe people of Tanganyika'. Oxford University D. Phil. thesis, 1964. See also her article in this number of *J. Afr. Hist.*

[13] J. Iliffe, 'The effects of the Maji-Maji rebellion on German occupation policy in East Africa', *British and German Colonialism in Africa*, ed. P. Gifford and W. R. Louis (Yale, 1968); Ranger, *Revolt in Southern Rhodesia.*

their approach to African nationalist historiography. The period of resistance is followed by hiatus; then arises the new leadership. But we must remember that the effective establishment of colonial rule throughout southern, central and eastern Africa took a very long time to achieve. 'Primary' resistance to it was still going on in some areas while 'secondary' movements were developing elsewhere. Independent churches, trade unions, welfare associations, Pan-Africanist movements all existed at the same time as expressions of tribal or pan-tribal resistance. This fact was important in forming the attitudes of the more radical 'secondary' politicians.

In another paper I have given two examples of this. One concerns the interaction of the career of the South African leader, Tengo Jabavu, and the fact and memories of the Ndebele rising. The second example is the fascinating one recorded in Shepperson and Price's account of the contacts between Nyasaland and Zululand. In 1896 Booth, the radical missionary, travelled from Nyasaland, taking with him one Gordon Mathaka, because the Yao wished 'to send a messenger to the other tribes in the south who had known the white man a long time to find out what they thought'. Mathaka heard the opinion of the Zulu Christian *élite*. 'No matter what the Yao thought', they told him, 'no living white man, whether carrying guns or not, would in the end be the friend of the black men.' And when Booth himself gathered together some 120 African intellectuals to discuss his projected African Christian Union, 'after a twenty six and a half hour session they rejected his scheme on the simple grounds that no white man was fit to be trusted, not even Booth himself...No trust or reliance at all could be placed in any representative of "the blood-stained white men, who had slain scores of thousands of Zulus and their Matabele relations".' These Zulu intellectuals did not perceive as sharply as some modern historians the gulf between primary and secondary resistance.[14]

Nor, indeed, did the men who met in London in 1900 for the first Pan-African Conference. These Afro-Americans, West Indians, West Africans, and so on, stated that they were meeting partly because of their concern over the wave of violent conflict between black and white which appeared to be sweeping Africa, instancing the Sierra Leone tax revolt and the Ndebele rising of 1896 as examples. Partly as a result of the impact made by the Ndebele rising, this first Conference appealed to Queen Victoria for reforms in Rhodesia.[15]

This sort of interaction lasted into the 1920s. One example, again a Rhodesian one which refers back to Ndebele resistance, must suffice. In June 1929 the first militant African trade union was holding its meetings in Bulawayo; weekend after weekend it hammered away on the theme of

[14] Ranger, 'African reaction to the imposition of colonial rule', loc. cit.; G. Shepperson and T. Price, *Independent African* (Edinburgh, 1958), 70, 71, 76.

[15] I. Geiss, 'The development of Pan-Africanism in the twentieth century', Lauterbach conference paper, June 1966.

African unity, appealing not only to the pan-tribal union movements of South Africa but also to successful examples of continuing armed resistance. 'If Lobengula had wanted to he could have called every nation to help him. He did not. That is why he was conquered. In Somaliland they are still fighting. That is because they are united. Let us be united.'[16]

It will be seen therefore that there is a long ancestry behind the attention currently paid by nationalist leaders to the heroic myths of primary resistance. When a man like Nelson Mandela seeks inspiration in tales 'of the wars fought by our ancestors in defence of the fatherland' and sees them not as part merely of tribal history, but 'as the pride and glory of the entire African nation', he is echoing the response of many of his predecessors.[17]

In all these ways, then, resistances formed part of the complex interaction of events which produced the environment for modern nationalist politics. I now want to turn to a more complex and interesting argument. This argument runs that during the course of the resistances, or some of them, types of political organization or inspiration emerged which looked in important ways to the future, which in some cases are directly, and in others indirectly, linked with later manifestations of African opposition.

The best way into this argument is by returning for a moment to the views of Robinson and Gallagher, and their contrast between the passionate backward-looking resistances and the defter manipulations of Western ideas which led to modern nationalist politics. As noted above, it is often argued that the leading co-operating societies played a key role in the initial stages of this process of adaptation of Westernism and in so doing looked in important ways to the nationalist future. In particular it can be argued that, in a series of so-called 'Christian Revolutions', the key collaborators sought to solve some of the weaknesses of nineteenth-century African state systems; to make their bureaucracy more efficient through literacy; to liberate the central political power from traditional sanctions and limitations and to break away from dependence on kinship or regional groupings. All this was to be done through an alliance with the missionary aspects of the colonial presence in particular. This concept of 'modernizing autocracy', of the king or the aristocracy introducing internal readjustments designed to modernize 'traditional' political systems in order to allow for modernization in other ways, can be applied with force to Buganda; to Barotseland, especially after the accession of Yeta III; to Bechuanaland, where the example of Khama was of great importance to other societies; to Ankole; and so on. The cases are not, of course, identical, but in all of them internal changes of great importance were going on which can be seen, in Low's terminology, as attempts to solve the problem of effective *scale* by making use of the Christian Great Tradition.[18]

[16] John Mphamba's speech, 29 June 1929, C.I.D. report, National Archives, Salisbury, S 84/A/300. [17] N. Mandela, *No Easy Walk to Freedom* (London, 1965), 147.

[18] Ranger, 'African reaction to the imposition of colonial rule', loc. cit.

We can hardly doubt that these changes were indeed an important pointer to the future, even if the scale proved inadequate and there had to be a further movement to territorial nationalism with which these older nationality units were sometimes in conflict. But these movements had major weaknesses from the first. The answer and opportunity provided by these Christian Revolutions was by definition a minority one, requiring alien sanctions for a relatively long time and not able to depend upon mass commitment. The breach with traditional restraints, indeed, often involved a serious weakening of the mass sense of belonging. Now, the modern nationalist movements of East and Central Africa are certainly characterized by an attempt to create effective bureaucratic and other institutions for a territorial state; but they also have to try to modernize at a more profound level by achieving mass commitment to these new institutions. Not all nationalist parties succeed in this by any means. But there can be little doubt that the 'ideal' nationalist movement consists of bringing together the urge to centralize and modernize institutions with an upsurge of mass enthusiasm. It can be argued that if the Christian Revolutions provide a fascinating early example of *élite* innovation, some of the 'primary resistances' provide equally fascinating examples of attempted answers to the problem of how to commit the masses to an effective enlargement of scale.

Here I am thinking mainly of those primary resistances which for one reason or another were unusually protracted—like the Nandi experience—or the so-called rebellions. I distinguish these two categories from other primary resistances or wars because in these cases the problem of organization, in fact the problem of scale, becomes most urgent. In many instances the initial war was fought in terms of the traditional military system, and there was little attempt to modify it or to involve more of the people within the state or to involve other peoples outside it. But a long-drawn-out struggle or a rising is a different matter. The question then arises as to how a society can effectively resist, having been beaten the first time or having initially been incapable of putting up a resistance at all. The distinction made by Iliffe between the initial tribal wars fought by the Germans in Tanganyika and the Maji-Maji rising is of the greatest importance. Maji-Maji, he says, was a 'post-pacification revolt, quite different from the early resistance... That had been local and professional, soldiers against soldiers, whereas Maji-Maji affected almost everyone in Tanganyika. It was a great crisis of commitment.'[19]

The point can be well illustrated in the cases of the two greatest rebellions in East and Central Africa, the Ndebele–Shona risings of 1896–7 and the Maji-Maji rising of 1905. The main problem about these risings is not so much *why* they happened as *how* they happened. How was it possible for the Ndebele and their subject peoples to rise together in 1896, when

[19] J. Iliffe, 'The German administration of Tanganyika, 1906–11', Cambridge University Ph.D. thesis, 1965.

in the 1893 war the subject peoples had abandoned their overlords? How was it possible for the Ndebele and the western and central Shona to co-operate in the risings in view of their long history of hostility? How was it possible for the Shona groups to co-operate among themselves in view of their nineteenth-century history of disunity? How was it possible for the very diverse peoples of southern Tanzania to become involved in a single resistance to the Germans? Finally, how was it that these apparently odd and patch-work alliances offered to the whites a more formidable challenge than had the disciplined professional armies of 1893 or the Hehe wars?

In the Rhodesian case part of the answer certainly lies in the appeal back to traditions of past political centralization. But both in Rhodesia and in Tanzania the main answer lies in the emergence of a leadership which was charismatic and revolutionary rather than hereditary or bureaucratic.

The African societies of East and Central Africa could draw in times of emergency upon a number of traditions of such charismatic leadership. Two emerge as particularly important in connexion with the sort of large-scale resistance we are discussing. The first of these is the prophetic tradition. Many African societies of East and Central Africa had religious systems in which specialist officers played an institutionalized prophetic role, speaking with the voice of the divine either through possession or through dream or oracular interpretation. Such prophet officers have usually been regarded by scholars, in common with 'traditional religion' as a whole, as conservative and normative forces. The prophet has been thought of as the ally of the established political order and as the guardian of its customary moral norms. But, as I have argued in a recent paper, the prophetic authority could not be so confined; the claim to speak with the voice of the divine was always potentially a revolutionary one, and if the prophet could invest the ordinary operations of a society with divine sanction he could also introduce new commandments. In his brilliant Malinowski Lecture for 1966, I. M. Lewis has suggested a typology and spectrum of possession and prophetic movements which throws a good deal of light on the point I am trying to make. His spectrum ranges from hysterical possession cults on the periphery of religious practice, to fully institutionalized tribal religions at the centre, in which the Messianic revelations of moral teaching shrink into creation myths and myth charters of the establishment. Lewis goes on to discuss the complex relationship of such establishment religions, 'which celebrate an accepted code of public morality', with the Messianic tradition. Establishment religions, he suggests, may have sprung from or may precede a Messianic movement; there are nearly always within them 'undercurrents' of Messianism and nearly always also opportunities for the rise of 'revitalizing prophets'; and often, where the establishment religion itself seems incapable of revitalization, it is surrounded by peripheral cults in which the innovatory vitality of prophetism is still present. 'It seems probable', he writes, 'that such displaced and peripherally relegated cults may provide the kind of institutional and inspirational continuity which, in appropriate historical circumstances, enables new messianic cults to develop.'[20]

The second tradition of charismatic innovating leadership is that of the witchcraft-eradication movements. Mary Douglas has a fascinating account of Lele religious ideas which brings out very clearly the radical potential of such movements. The 'normal' religious beliefs and activities of the Lele present a balance between a general emphasis upon order and simplicity and the insight of esoteric cults into complexity and sorrow. But death and disease create tensions within the Lele system which cannot be dealt with adequately either by the routine protective devices of popular religion or the insights of the cults.

For the Lele, [she writes] evil is not to be included in the total system of the world, but to be expunged without compromise. All evil is caused by sorcery. They can clearly visualize what reality would be like without sorcery and they continually strive to achieve it by eliminating sorcerers. A strong millenarian tendency is implicit in the way of thinking of any people whose metaphysics push evil out of the world of reality. Among the Lele the millenarian tendency bursts into flame in their recurrent anti-sorcery cults. When a new cult arrives it burns up for the time being the whole apparatus of their traditional religion... the latest anti-sorcery cult is nothing less than an attempt to introduce the millennium at once.[21]

In the various resistances to the establishment of colonial rule, there is no question that religious leadership played an important part. The character of this leadership varied greatly, however. Sometimes the establishment religion of an existing unit committed itself to resistance alongside the established political and military system. Sometimes the established religious officers resisted the movement of the established political authorities into a 'Christian Revolution'. But sometimes, in the great movements of rebellion and resistance that we are now particularly discussing, innovating religious leadership sprang up to revitalize or to challenge the established religious structure as well as the whites and, where necessary, the African political authorities. Such innovating religious leadership sprang out of either the prophetic or the witchcraft-eradication traditions. In their different ways both called for the creation of a new order in which neither sorcery nor colonial pressures nor the tensions of small-scale society would exist; both offered protection and invulnerability to those who observed their new commandments. They thus offered solutions, on however temporary a basis, to the problem of morale, to the problem of the combination of different groups, and to the problem of co-ordination.

The operation of this sort of leadership, and its interaction, can be seen

[20] T. O. Ranger, 'Towards a historical study of traditional religion in East and Central Africa', East African Academy Symposium paper, Kampala, 1966; I. M. Lewis, 'Spirit possession and deprivation cults', *Man*, I, no. 3, Sept. 1966.

[21] Mary Douglas, *Purity and Danger* (London, 1966), chap. 10.

in the movements we are now discussing. In the Congo, a number of scholars have described the various prophetic and witchcraft-eradication movements which stimulated primary resistance to the whites and which brought together far-flung coalitions. Such movements, in Doutreloux's analysis, sprang mainly from the weaknesses of Congolese societies, which could find no permanent solution to the problem of fragmentation and instability. What stability existed was given by religions of the ancestors or cults of the land and fertility, but these were by definition always operative on too small a scale, and they were constantly undermined, moreover, by the disintegrative effect of witchcraft belief. Prophet movements and witchcraft eradication cults arose in an attempt to remedy this situation. They assaulted witchcraft and also traditional limitations; the prophet movements proclaimed themselves as a church or creed for all Africans and imposed new regulations and prohibitions upon believers: they endeavoured to create an indigenous Great Tradition to rival that alien Great Tradition which the Christian revolutionaries used.[22]

Something of the same pattern can be seen for the most striking mass primary resistances of East and Central Africa. Certainly it seems to hold for the two great risings already discussed—the Shona–Ndebele and the Maji-Maji rebellions. I have argued at length elsewhere that what I described as the 'traditional' religious authorities were the main co-ordinators, and in a real sense leaders, of the risings in Matabeleland and Mashonaland, and that the priests of the Mwari cult in the first province, and the spirit mediums of the Chaminuka–Nehanda hierarchies in the second, were the main vehicles of co-operation between the various elements engaged. Perhaps in these articles I have emphasized the 'traditional' character of this religious leadership too much. Certainly it was important that they presented themselves as survivors from the imperial past of the Shona—the one cult so intimately identified with the old Rozwi empire and the other with the Mutapa dynasty and its outriders. But at the same time the emergence of these religious leaders as leaders also of a widespread rebellion constituted what Gann has described as 'a theological revolution'. Contemporary white observers stressed that the Mwari cult had previously been concerned with matters of peace and fertility and its militant, authoritarian character in 1896 took them by surprise; no doubt there was both ignorance and *naïveté* in their idea of its earlier total severance from politics, but there seems no question that the power and the nature of the authority of the Mwari priesthood underwent significant development in 1896. Nor does there seem much question that this 'theological revolution' took the form ascribed by Doutreloux to the prophet movements. The Mwari priests and the spirit mediums imposed new regulations and prohibitions upon their followers; to enter the rebellion was to enter a new society and to become subject to a new 'law'; the rebels were brought into the fellow-

[22] M. A. Doutreloux, 'Prophétisme et culture', in *African Systems of Thought*, ed. Fortes and Dieterlin (London, 1965).

ship of the faithful by the dispensation of 'medicine' and promised immunity from bullets; they were promised success in this world and a return from death to enjoy it. (When the religious leaders were attempting in 1897 to bring into being a Rozwi 'front' in all the areas of Mashonaland as a means of co-ordinating the secular side of the rising after the withdrawal of the Ndebele aristocracy, they promised that all Rozwi who were killed should be resurrected and participate in the coming golden age.) The religious leaders move out of the limitations which, as well as the advantages, were implied by their connexion with specific past political systems, and speak to all black men. And they are to an extent successful. For a time the charismatic leadership of the prophets brings together Ndebele aristocrats, subject peoples, deposed Rozwi chiefs, Shona paramounts; as Gann puts it, 'the proud Matabele chieftains now agreed to operate under the supreme direction of an ex-serf, a remarkable man who in "normal" times would hardly have acquired much political influence'.[23]

In the case of the Maji-Maji rising, the evidence presented by Iliffe suggests a possible combination of both the prophetic and the witchcraft-eradication elements in the inspiration and co-ordination of the rising. Clearly the Kolelo cult played an important part. It 'was influential over a wide area and...provided centres to which large numbers of people went to receive medicine and instructions which they distributed on return ...The evidence is perhaps sufficient to conclude that the Kolelo cult provided a machinery which could reach the peoples of the Rufiji complex and perhaps further afield'. Like the Mwari cult, the Kolelo belief involved priest-interpreters of the oracle; like the Mwari cult also, its normal preoccupation was with fertility and the land. And, as Iliffe tells us, some evidence suggests that 'in the period before the rebellion the Kolelo cult was transformed from its normal preoccupation with the land to a more radical and prophetic belief in a reversal of the existing order by direct divine intervention'. The prophets of the new development commanded revolt in the name of 'the new God, who would come to live in the land'. 'He will change this world and it will be new...His rule will be one of marvels.' They provided protective medicine; prescribed a new form of dress and imposed new prohibitions; they promised invulnerability or resurrection. The drinking of the holy water was a sign of entry into a rebel communion. The appeal was to all Africans. 'Be not afraid,' the message ran, 'Kolelo spares his black children.'[24]

At the same time there seems evidence to suggest that the innovatory potentialities of witchcraft-eradication movements were also being used. 'The Vidunda understood the *maji* in the context of an attack on sorcery', Iliffe tells us. In southern Ubena 'a series of anti-sorcery movements had

[23] T. O. Ranger, 'The role of the Ndebele and Shona religious authorities in the rebellions of 1896 and 1897', in *The Zambesian Past*, ed. E. T. Stokes and R. Brown (Manchester, 1966) L. H. Gann, *A History of Southern Rhodesia* (London, 1965).

[24] J. Iliffe, 'The organization of the Maji-Maji Rebellion', *J. Afr. Hist.* VIII, no. 3 (1967).

entered from the east, from Ungindo and the Kilombero... Maji-Maji was also brought by Ngindo, and it seems that the pattern of Bena response followed that normal with a *mwavi* medicine, the *hongo* administering the *maji* to the assembled people in the presence of the chief'. 'It seems very probable', he concludes, 'that both the rebellion...and subsequent movements were drawing on an established pattern of indigenous millenarianism. Just as the rising in the Rufiji complex became associated with the cult of Kolelo, so its expansion appears to have taken place within the context of recurrent movements to eradicate sorcery.' My own work on subsequent witchcraft eradication cults in the Rufiji complex and in the Maji-Maji area generally, leads me to suppose that the ability of such movements to pass rapidly across clan and tribal boundaries, and to sweep people into a unity which overrides suspicions and allegations of sorcery, was indeed an important element in the 1905 rising.[25]

The Maji-Maji and the Shona-Ndebele risings were, of course, exceptional affairs, resistances on a grander scale than anything else in East and Central Africa. There were, however, other examples of attempts to come to terms with the problem of scale. There is the Nandi case, for example, where the pressures of the nineteenth century produced a steady increase in the power of the Nandi prophet figure, the *Orkoiyot*, until at last the Nandi operated for the first time as a united military power in a 'rebellion' against British rule under the prophet's command. There were somewhat similar developments among the Kipsigis and perhaps the Meru. Or there is the very interesting example of the Nyabingi movement.[26]

The Nyabingi movement presented itself as a challenge to white occupation and administration in the northern areas of Rwanda, in parts of the Congo, and in Kigezi district. During the First World War, Nyabingi forces attacked British, Belgian and German troops impartially. Especially among the much-fragmented Kiga people, the cult promised to play an important integrative role. 'Just prior to the coming of the British', so a student of the Kiga tells us, 'a spirit possession cult which might have contained the seeds of a larger-scale political organisation was breaking out all over the district.' The cult involved mediumship, promised immunity to its adherents and appeared not so much as a pan-African as a pan-Bantu movement. European observers contrasted it with the stable and conservative official religion of the Rwanda monarchy. 'It has everywhere proved itself revolutionary in method and anarchic in effect', wrote the Assistant District Commissioner, Kigezi, in 1919. 'Fanaticism and terror are everywhere inculcated...The whole appeal is to fear and to the lower instincts, to the masses, Bahutu, against the classes, Batussi...The whole aspect of the Nabingi is of a fanatic anarchic sect as

[25] Iliffe, op. cit.; T. O. Ranger, 'Witchcraft eradication movements in Central and Southern Tanzania and their connection with the Maji-Maji rising', Research Seminar Paper, Dar es Salaam, November 1966.

[26] S. Arap' Ngeny, 'Nandi Resistance to the establishment of British administration, 1893–1906', Research Seminar Paper, Dar es Salaam, November 1965.

opposed to the liberal and religious principles of the indigenous Kubandwa cult.'[27]

It would be possible to multiply these examples on a smaller scale—a list of risings or resistances allegedly led by prophets or 'witch-doctors' in East and Central Africa amounts to some forty instances, in some of which, at least, the same sort of radical religious leadership was involved.

Almost everywhere this kind of leadership was seen by the Europeans as profoundly reactionary, as endeavouring merely to preserve the tribal past and to exclude all innovation. In fact it was often revolutionary in method and in purpose and sought to transcend tribal limitations. Prophet leaders were often men able at one and the same time to appeal to past notions of unity—even the Nyabingi cult appears to have celebrated the spirit of a Bantu queen, deposed in myth by a pastoralist invader—and also to attempt to restructure society. Thus they appealed to a wider unity than had been achieved in the past and they were not afraid in its service to challenge the authority of secular leaders.[28]

There are striking examples of this challenge to reluctant secular authority both in the 1896–7 Rhodesian risings and in Maji-Maji. Thus the Mwari priesthood in 1896 dismissed Ndebele *indunas* and replaced them with more militant supporters of the rising, while the leading spirit medium in Mashonaland also announced the dismissal, and tried to procure the assassination, of 'loyalist' paramounts. Thus, as Iliffe tells us, when Chief Ngwira of Vidunda attempted to prevent his people following the *hongo*, or Maji-Maji messenger, 'Hongo appointed himself chief of the district'. On the strength of this and other instances he writes that beyond the original Rufiji complex 'Maji-Maji spread as a millenarian revolt which threatened established authority. Only the strongest could reject it.'[29]

Moreover, in addition to the implied criticism of the inadequacies in scale of tribal societies and to the explicit challenges offered to some of their political leaders, risings of this sort often gave scope for the emergence of 'new men' with some acquaintance with modernizing skills. Owners and

[27] Report by Captain J. E. T. Phillips, A.D.C., Kigezi, 31 July 1919, National Archives, Dar es Salaam, Secretariat 0910. See also M. J. Bessell, 'Nyabingi', *Uganda Journal*, 6, no. 2 (Oct 1938); P. W. T. Baxter, 'The Kiga', in *East African Chiefs*, ed. A. Richards (London, 1959); M. M. Edel, *The Chiga of Western Uganda* (Oxford, 1957). Since this article was written I have been able to read a detailed appraisal of the political implications of the Nyabingi cult by Mr F. S. Brazier of Makerere University College, 'The Nyabingi cult: religion and political scale in Kigezi, 1900–1930'. Mr Brazier finds that in Kigezi Nyabingi was, indeed, 'a cult of resistance' and suggests that 'it attained its near-monopoly status among the cults which had a Kiga following just because it answered best to the political needs of the time—a rallying point against the incursions of the Ruanda and Twa', and later of the British and their Ganda agents. He notes that Nyabingi priests were involved in a series of incidents of resistance widely scattered in time and place. But he also remarks that at any single time the Nyabingi priesthood was not able to bring about widespread and co-ordinated resistance. The cult was an important focus of resistance and covered a wide area but was itself too individualistic and loosely structured to succeed in any very extensive enlargement of scale.

[28] For specific examples of religious leaders urging wider unity see Ranger, 'African reaction to the imposition of colonial rule', loc. cit.

[29] Iliffe, op. cit.

skilled users of guns were, of course, important figures in contests of this kind, and perhaps also men who were believed to understand the enemy. At any rate, as Gann has pointed out, among the personal bodyguard of the leading Shona spirit medium in 1896 were men 'who had been in touch with Europeans and picked up some of their skills'. I have myself described elsewhere how, in the 1917 Makombe rising in Portuguese East Africa, a classic 'primary resistance' despite its late date, there was a return to the new opportunities of leadership by men who had gone to seek their fortunes in the colonial economy, producing a leadership of paramounts and spirit mediums, returned waiters and ex-policemen.[30]

Finally, one can detect in some of these resistances the same ambiguity of attitude towards the world of the whites which characterized later mass movements. Thus in Rhodesia we have the Chaminuka medium's prophecy that the Shona would be able to preserve their independence only if they could resist the temptation to acquire the goods of the whites; we have the Nehanda medium's instructions to the rebels to fight only with traditional weapons. Yet we also have the promises made by the chief Mwari priest, Mkwati, that his followers had only 'to wait until all the whites are dead or fled and then they will enjoy the good things of the town and live in palaces of corrugated iron'. 'Directly the white men are killed', a police inspector was told in 1903 during another rebellion scare, 'we will occupy all your houses; all these nice things will be ours.'[31]

Resistances of this sort, then, can hardly be adequately defined as 'reactionary' or as essentially backward-looking, however passionate and romantic they may have been. In many ways they were tackling the problems which more recent proto-nationalist and nationalist movements have faced. But there still remains a key question. The great 'primary resistance' movements may have been *similar* to later expressions of opposition to colonial rule but were they *connected*? They may not have looked to the fragmented tribal past and attempted to preserve it, but did they look to the future and provide the basis for, and tradition of, the mass political movements of the twentieth century? It is to this question that the second part of this article will be devoted.

[30] T. O. Ranger, 'Revolt in Portuguese East Africa: the Makombe rising of 1917', *St Antony's Papers*, no. 15, ed. K. Kirkwood (London, 1963).

[31] *The Daily Chronicle*, 13 July and 10 Sept. 1896; intelligence reports, Inyanga, 26 Mar. 1904, National Archives, Salisbury, A/11/2/12/12; Ranger, *Revolt in Southern Rhodesia*, chap. 10.

631

CONNEXIONS BETWEEN 'PRIMARY RESISTANCE' MOVEMENTS AND MODERN MASS NATIONALISM IN EAST AND CENTRAL AFRICA: II

BY T. O. RANGER

IN the first part of this article a number of possible connexions between 'the last-ditch resisters' and the 'earliest organizers of armed risings', and later leaders of opposition to colonial rule in East and Central Africa, were explored. It was argued that African 'primary' resistance shaped the environment in which later politics developed; it was argued that resistance had profound effects upon white policies and attitudes; it was argued that there was a complicated interplay between manifestations of 'primary' and of 'secondary' opposition, which often overlapped with and were conscious of each other. Then the argument turned to a more ambitious proposition, namely that 'during the course of the resistances, or some of them, types of political organization or inspiration emerged which looked in important ways to the future; which in some cases are directly and in others indirectly linked with later manifestations of African opposition'.

Half of the case for this assertion was set out in the first article, and the character of the organization and aspirations of the great resistance movements was discussed. It was argued that they attempted to create a larger effective scale of action; that they endeavoured to appeal to a sense of African-ness; that they displayed an ambiguous attitude to the material aspects of white colonial society, often desiring to possess them without at the same time abandoning the values of their own communities; that they attempted to assert African ability to retain control of the world by means of a millenarian message. In all these ways, it was asserted, they were *similar* to later mass movements. But the first part of this article ended by posing, rather than answering, the key question of whether they were also *connected* with later mass movements. It is to this question that we must now turn.

It has most often been argued, of course, that 'primary' resistances were *not* connected, either directly or indirectly, with later forms of opposition. Resistances were followed, it was held, by 'a period of calm', out of which emerged 'other leaders and other motives'. And it is unquestionably true that after, say, 1920 there were very few 'tribal' risings and that different sorts of political organization were developed by new men. To that extent periodization of African nationalist history is legitimate enough. But, as I suggested in the first part of this article, we need to look for continuity in mass emotion as well as for continuity in *élite* leadership, if we are to establish a satisfactory historiography of nationalism. It is obviously important to ask whether there was any continuity in terms of mass emotion between the sort of risings I have been discussing and modern nationalism.

The first part of an answer is that there is undoubtedly a link between these resistances and later mass movements of a millenarian character. Nor is this link merely a matter of *comparing* the Shona-Ndebele or Maji-Maji risings with later prophet movements or witchcraft eradication cults. There is often a quite direct connexion. The millenarian movements of the twentieth century in East and Central Africa varied widely in character. Sometimes they remained frankly 'pagan', and are hard to distinguish from the Nyabingi type of movement. (Nyabingi itself, long enduring as it was, continued to operate into the 'secondary' opposition period, and gave the British administration in Kigezi, right up until the end of the 1920s and beyond, the same sort of bother that was being provided elsewhere by 'new' pagan cults or by semi-Christian or Christian-independent movements.) In other cases Christian elements entered to a greater or lesser degree, but this does not prevent direct or indirect connexions with primary resistance movements, as we shall see.[1]

The most direct connexions, of course, are provided by examples like that of Nyabingi, which provided the basis both of 'primary resistance' and of persistent twentieth-century millenarian manifestations. Next come movements like that of the Mumbo cult in Nyanza province, Kenya. The Mumbo cult has recently been examined in a very interesting paper by Audrey Wipper. It arose among the Gusii, apparently around 1913, after the defeat of various 'primary resistances'. It reached peaks of activity in 1919, in 1933, and to a lesser extent in 1938 and 1947; it was one of the movements banned in 1954. Thus in point of time it bridged the period between the suppression of the Gusii risings of 1904, 1908 and 1916 and the emergence of modern mass nationalism. In character it was strikingly similar to the sort of movement we have already discussed. Although arising among the Gusii, it was 'a pan-tribal pagan sect', creating its own society of true believers, whom it bound by its own codes of conduct and to whom it promised eventual triumph and reward. The colonial period, in its mythology, was merely a testing period devised by the God of Africa to sort out the true believers from the faint-hearted; before long those who remained true would enter into the wealth and power of the whites. Mumbo had the most direct links with the period of primary resistance. 'The Gusii's most venerated warriors and prophets, noted for their militant anti-British stance, were claimed by the movement,' Miss Wipper tells us. 'Zakawa, the great prophet, Bogonko, the mighty chief, and Maraa, the *laibon* responsible for the 1908 rebellion, became its symbols, infusing into the living the courage and strength of past heroes... Leaders bolstered up their own legitimacy by claiming to be the mouth-piece of these deceased prophets.'

Indeed, if Miss Wipper is right, we are close here to the idea of an 'alternative leadership', stemming from traditions of resistance and opposed

[1] Bessell, op. cit. 'Nyabingi' *Uganda Journal*, 6, no. 2 (1938).

to officially recognized authority. 'Especially successful in effecting such claims were the descendants' of the prophets and chiefs concerned. 'Thus, with the progency of the Gusii heroes supporting the sect, a physical as well as a symbolic link with the past was established. Here was a powerful symbolic group whose prestige and authority could well be used to arouse, strengthen and weld the various disunited cults into a solid anti-British opposition.' Miss Wipper makes the important point that the cult looked back only to those figures who themselves stood out from and tried to transform traditional small-scale society; 'it looks to the past for inspiration and to the future for living'. 'Its goals', she tells us, 'are Utopian and innovative rather than traditional and regressive', involving attacks upon small-scale traditional values as well as upon European values. It would seem that Professor Ogot has considerable justification for applying the word 'radical' to the cult, and in claiming that 'the history of African nationalism in the district must be traced back' to its emergence.[2]

An interesting later example of a movement in the same western district of Kenya in which the continuity with the tradition of primary resistance was 'symbolic' rather than 'physical' is provided by the Dini Ya Msambwa cult, of Elijah Masinde. Through this cult Masinde called for Bukusu and for wider African unity, meeting together with cult representatives from Uganda, Suk, North Nyanza and Kiambu to resolve 'that since they have similar traditional religions they must unite in Dini Ya Msambwa'. Masinde also made a millenarian appeal, and referred back emphatically to the heroic and traumatic experience of the resistances. Mr Welime tells us that

> In September 1947 he led about 5,000 followers to Chetambe's, where in 1895 many Bukusu died in their campaign against Hobley. He wanted his followers to remember the dead in their prayers. One interesting thing about this meeting is that they were dressed as in readiness for the 1895 war. At this meeting it is alleged that he unearthed a skull in which a bullet was found buried in the mouth... The crowd became very emotional and destructive.[3]

Similar examples of direct 'physical' and indirect 'symbolic' connexion with primary resistances can be given for Christian independent church movements. In the first category comes, for instance, Shembe's Nazarite Church in Zululand, so vividly described by Professor Sundkler. This impressive manifestation of Zulu, rather than South African, nationalism referred back to 'one of the most dramatic occasions in the history of Zulu nationalism', the Bambata rising of 1906. It was physically linked to this rising through the person of Messen Qwabe, one of its leaders. Shembe himself proclaimed: 'I am going to revive the bones of Messen and of the people who were killed in Bambata's rebellion.' All five sons of Messen

[2] A. Wipper, 'The cult of Mumbo', East African Institute Conference paper, January 1966; B. A. Ogot, 'British administration in the Central Nyanza district of Kenya', *J. Afr. Hist.* IV, no. 2 (1963).

[3] J. D. Welime, 'Dini ya Msambwa', Research Seminar Paper, Dar es Salaam (1965).

have joined the church, which was given posthumous spiritual approval by their dead father, and it is taken for granted that all members of the Qwabe clan will be members of it. In the second category comes Matthew Zwimba's Church of the White Bird, established in 1915 in the Zwimba Reserve in Mashonaland, which appealed to the memory of the 1896–7 rising by regarding all those who died in the fighting in the Zwimba area as the saints and martyrs of the new church. It is important to note also that Zwimba regarded himself as very much a modernizer and succeeded, at least for a time, in establishing himself as the intermediary between the chiefs and people of Zwimba and representatives of the modern world.[4]

It can be shown, then, that some at least of the intermediary opposition movements of a millenarian character, which are usually by common consent given a place in the history of the emergence of nationalism, were closely linked, as well as essentially similar, to some movements of primary resistance. Can we go further than this? It would be possible to argue, after all, that whatever may be the interest of such millenarian movements in the history of African politics, they have not in fact run into the main-stream of modern nationalism and in some instances have clashed with it. A movement like Dini Ya Msambwa might be cultivated for short-term purposes by a political party—as KANU is said to have cultivated it in order to find support in an otherwise KADU area—but it can hardly be thought to have had much future within the context of modern Kenyan nationalism.

It seems to me that there are a number of things to be said at this stage. I have argued that modern nationalism, if it is to be fully successful, has to discover how to combine mass enthusiasm with central focus and organization. This does not mean that it needs to *ally* itself with movements of the sort I have been describing which succeeded, on however limited a scale, in arousing mass enthusiasm. Indeed, it will obviously be in most ways a rival to them, seeking to arouse mass enthusiasm for its own ends and not for theirs. But it would be possible to present a triple argument at this stage. In the first place, one could argue, where nationalist movements *do* succeed in achieving mass emotional commitment, they will often do it partly by use of something of the same methods, and by appealing to something of the same memories as the movements we have been discussing. In the second place, where nationalist movements are faced with strong settler regimes, as in southern Africa, they will tend to move towards a strategy of violence which is seen by them as springing out of the traditions of 'primary resistance'. And in the third place, where nationalist movements fail, either generally or in particular areas, to capture mass enthusiasm, they may find themselves opposed by movements of this old millenarian kind, some of which will still preserve symbolic connexions at least with the primary resistances.

[4] B. G. M. Sundkler, *Bantu Prophets in South Africa* (London, 1961); T. O. Ranger, 'The early history of independency in Southern Rhodesia', *Religion in Africa*, ed. W. Montgomery Watt (Edinburgh, 1964), 54–7.

Let us turn first to the question of the methods by which nationalist parties achieve mass emotional involvement. Here Dr Lonsdale's comments on the history of politics in Nyanza Province—the home of both the Mumbo cult and of Dini Ya Msambwa—are pertinent. Having described how Christian independency in the Province had its roots in pre-colonial religious phenomena, and how the first and second generations of the *élite* could not come to terms with it, he notes that 'only after the start of popular, mass nationalism did the politicians court the independents'. In a sense, he suggests, the values of the independents triumphed in mass nationalism rather than those of the *élite* welfare associations and proto-nationalist parties. 'The independents' selective approach to Western culture has triumphed over the early politician's desire to be accepted by and participate in the colonial world. It is symbolic of the victory of the mass party over the intellectual and occupational *élite* of the inter-war years.'[5]

The new mass party in East and Central Africa, as it spreads to the rural districts, comes to embody much of the attitude which has hitherto been expressed in less articulate movements of rural unrest. It often appears in a charismatic, almost millenarian role—the current phrase, 'a crisis of expectations', which politicians from Kenya to Zambia employ to describe their relations with their mass constituents, is not a bad description of the explosive force behind all the movements we have described. Often the party locally—and nationally—appeals to the memories of primary resistance, and for the same reason as the millenarian cults did; because it is the one 'traditional' memory that can be appealed to which transcends 'tribalism' and which can quite logically be appealed to at the same time as tribal authorities are being attacked and undermined. My own experience of nationalist politics in Southern Rhodesia certainly bears out these generalizations. It was the National Democratic Party of 1960–1 which first really penetrated the rural areas and began to link the radical leadership of the towns with rural discontent. As it did so, the themes and memories of the rebellions flowed back into nationalism. 'In rural areas', writes Mr Shamuyarira of this period, 'meetings became political gatherings and more ... the past heritage was revived through prayers and traditional singing, ancestral spirits were evoked to guide and lead the new nation. Christianity and civilization took a back seat and new forms of worship and new attitudes were thrust forward dramatically...the spirit pervading the meetings was African and the desire was to put the twentieth century in an African context.' So Mr George Nyandoro, grandson of a rebel leader killed in 1897, and nephew of a chief deposed for opposition to rural regulations in the 1930s, appealed in his speeches to the memory of the great prophet Chaminuka round whom the Shona rallied in the nineteenth century; so Mr Nkomo, returning home in 1962, was met at the airport by a survivor of the rebellions of 1896–7, who presented him with a spirit axe as a symbol of the apostolic succession of

[5] J. M. Lonsdale, 'A political history of Nyanza, 1883–1945', Cambridge University Ph.D. thesis (1964), chaps. 11 and 12.

resistance; so the militant songs copied from Ghana were replaced by the old tunes belonging to spirit mediums and rebel leaders.[6]

Again there are senses in which the Tanganyika African Peoples Union appeared to the people of southern Tanzania as the direct successor of the Maji-Maji movement. 'Many people took the water', runs an oral account of the spread of Maji-Maji collected in 1966.

You know this is how the water spread very quickly. Take for example the struggle for independence in Tanganyika. If you did not buy a TANU card you were considered as an enemy to Independence by those around you...The same thing with the 'maji', although this was more serious. If your wife took the water and you did not, you were considered an enemy to your fellow Africans, so you had to be removed. For how can anyone allow the life of one man who is dangerous to hazard the lives of the whole people.[7]

At any rate the continuity between Maji-Maji and TANU is a theme of some importance in contemporary Tanzanian politics.

The people fought [so Julius Nyerere told the Fourth Committee of the United Nations in December 1956] because they did not believe in the white man's right to govern and civilize the black. They rose in a great rebellion, not through fear of a terrorist movement or a superstitious oath, but in response to a natural call, a call of the spirit, ringing in the hearts of all men, and of all times, educated and uneducated, to rebel against foreign domination. It is important to bear this in mind in order to understand the nature of a Nationalist movement like mine. Its function is not to create the spirit of rebellion but to articulate it and show it a new technique.

Today, as TANU strives to retain and to develop its character as a radical mass movement, the appeal back to Maji-Maji has become more frequent. 'On the ashes of Maji-Maji' writes the *Nationalist*, 'our new nation was founded.'[8]

A caution and clarification is perhaps in order here. Obviously the *Nationalist* writer quoted above is being very selective in his use of the pre-TANU political tradition. In this paper I am anxious to show that in some ways the radical, millenarian tradition of mass protest *does* run into modern nationalism, but I certainly do not wish to claim that it is the *only* tradition that runs into modern nationalism. TANU has as its background not only Maji-Maji and the Hehe wars, but also the centralizing *élite* associations—the Tanganyika African Civil Servants Association; the Tanganyika African Association—led by the men of what Dr Iliffe has called 'the Age of Improvement'. There is obviously a danger in the nationalist historiography which sees an exclusive line of ancestry running from one episode of violent resistance to another, excluding the accommodators and the pioneers of modern political organization. Yet the fact that today Maji-Maji is seen in

[6] N. S. Shamuyarira, *Crisis in Rhodesia* (London, 1965), 68–9.

[7] Interview between Mr G. C. K. Gwassa and Mzee Hassan Mkape, Kilwa Kivinje, June 1966.

[8] Speech by J. K. Nyerere, 20 December 1956 to the 578th meeting of the Fourth Committee of the United Nations; editorial comment, *The Nationalist*, 18 September 1967.

this way as the most significant predecessor to TANU, even if this is a myth in some respects, is in itself a fact which influences contemporary nationalist politics in Tanzania.

This brings us to the second point. It is natural that a nationalist movement which is still engaged in an increasingly violent struggle for independence will turn even more exclusively to the tradition of resistance. This has certainly happened in Southern Rhodesia, for example. The present phase of guerrilla activity in Rhodesia is called by the nationalists 'Chimurenga', the name given by the Shona to the 1896 risings. 'What course of action will lead to the liberation of Zimbabwe?' asks a Zimbabwe African National Union writer. 'It is not the path of appeasement. It is not the path of reformism. It is not the path of blocking thirds. It is the path of outright fearless defiance of the settler Smith fascist regime and fighting the current war for national liberation. It is the path of direct confrontation. It is the path of Chimurenga.' Here, within the Rhodesian movement, there is not only an attempt to stress the mass, radical characteristics of the nationalist parties as with TANU, but in many ways a repudiation of the party as an organizational form in favour of a return to the older tradition.

> The nationalist movement has failed to mobilize these disparate Africans of Rhodesia into an effective revolutionary force [writes Davis Mugabe] because it has moved uncertainly from one European model to another, without ever sinking its roots deep into the African soil...For almost three decades, the nationalist leaders based their operations and their pronouncements on the myth that they spoke for an integrated political community. Although we tried to paper over the differences for the sake of appearances, no real attempt was made to build bridges between the vaShona, the amaNdebele, and the immigrant groups, or even between the city politicians and the peasant farmer. In the anger and bitterness of the past year, however, a new sense of unity can be detected. It has little connexion with the personality feuds of earlier times, for the old game of constitutional politics has run its fruitless course ...From now on the only political leaders who will matter are those who are working 24 hours a day with the people in the countryside—not those in city offices with party names on the door, or in jail, or manning governments in exile. Somewhere in Rhodesia is our Mao or our Castro. His ideology and past affiliations are unimportant; but he must be a man who can become one with the people of the village and with the guerrillas preparing for war in the mountains. Bridges will fall into place between Rhodesia's divergent peoples when they are organized to fight acre by acre for what is most important to them—'the land on the hill'.[9]

Once again it is time for a caution. Mr Mugabe is appealing back to Chimurenga, 'the first war of independence', as an example of a war fought for the things people understand—land and cattle—and as an example of how best to unite the African people of Rhodesia. I have written about the 1896–7 uprisings in terms of the attempts then made to find such a basis of action and unity. To the extent that the risings took place and presented so

[9] 'Spotlight on Zimbabwe', *The Nationalist*, 18 July 1967; Davis Mugabe, 'Rhodesia's African majority', *Africa Report*, February 1967.

formidable a challenge, this attempt was successful. But one should not forget that the success of the leaders of the 1896–7 movement did not last long. Defeat broke up unity; it remains an unproven question whether unity would have survived victory. In the event it was probably true of 1896–7, as Dr Iliffe has written of Maji-Maji, that the collapse of all the high hopes resulted immediately in greater disunity and tensions. The Ndebele and the Shona joined together for a time under the leadership of the prophets; but the Ndebele, or most of them, made a separate peace while the Shona fought on. The unity gave way to Shona attacks on surrendering Ndebele. After 1896 the whites managed Ndebele society by playing upon the triple division into 'loyalists', rebels who negotiated, and rebels who vainly opposed negotiation. After 1897 Shona society was divided in a similar way. These great movements of mass resistance are important as *attempts* at unity.

It is time to move to the third point—that these traditions of resistance can sometimes be used *against* nationalist movements as well as *by* them. Indeed the whole question of African resistance to *African* pressures is one which urgently needs investigation before we can obtain a balanced view of the significance of resistance as a whole.

A number of preliminary points, however, can already be made. In the first place, of course, the extension of the concept of resistance to include African resistance to African pressures reminds us that historical discussion of the role of resistance as a force for change cannot be restricted to the period of the Scramble and the Pacification. This is true even if we limit the idea of resistance to European–African confrontations: the Shona, for instance, had a long tradition of rebellion against the Portuguese which served as the background to their rebellion against the British. But it is even more importantly true if we consider African resistance to African pressures. During the nineteenth century, East and Central Africa were exposed to a number of powerful African intrusions which threatened the very existence of certain societies. Partly in response to these intrusions, the existing secular authorities in some African societies attempted to build up new powers; sometimes this attempt also provoked resentment and resistance within the society.

Some at least of these resistances to external African invaders or to the expansion of internal central authority took the form of the reactions to European rule which I have described above. The prophetic and witchcraft eradication traditions were as available to movements of this kind as to later movements of protest against the whites; certain features of the later movements which historians have felt to be characteristic of response to colonialism as such were almost certainly present in these earlier manifestations. Thus the Nyabingi movement, which we have seen already as a focus of integrative opposition to colonial rule and as a continuing messianic cult in the twentieth century, originated as a movement of opposition to Tutsi control of northern Rwanda and served as a rallying point for Hutu resistance from the middle years of the nineteenth century onwards. Thus the hierarchy of Shona spirit mediums, which we have seen involved in the 1896 risings, also provided a focus for Shona reactions to earlier Ndebele raids; the hero-figures of nineteenth-century central Shona history are the two great mediums of the Chaminuka spirit who rallied the western and central Shona and who were killed at Lobengula's orders.

Then again, during the colonial period itself, a good deal of what we can properly call African resistance, in the sense of movements similar to those categorized as 'primary resistance' movements, has taken the form of protest against dominance or sub-imperialism by other African peoples. A few examples may be given. The violent opposition, once more using the Nyabingi cult as its vehicle, of the Kiga clans to the control of the Ganda agents of British over-rule; the rebellion in 1916 of the Konjo people against Toro control, which is being followed up at the present time by a second rebellion of the Konjo for the same reasons; the disturbances in Balovale and elsewhere against the control of local government by the Lozi; these are all instances of resistance which clearly have to be fitted into any general discussion of the topic.

Finally there is the problem of African resistance, again in the same sense of violent 'primary' style reaction, to African governments after the attainment of territorial independence. I am thinking here of events like the clashes between the followers of Alice Lenshina and members of UNIP in Zambia; of the upheavals organized by the Parmehutu association in Rwanda; above all of the Congo rebellions, particularly of the Kwilu rising. The atmosphere of these events is very similar in many ways to that of the 'primary resistances'.[10]

Let us take the Kwilu example. The Kwilu rebellion seems to fit neatly enough into the category already mentioned, in which the nationalist movement fails to retain the confidence of the mass and is faced with a millenarian style resistance. In a recent study of the Kwilu rising, a convincing argument is stated for the thesis that the inspiration for resistance came not from alien ideas but from 'frustations profoundly Congolese'. What was being aimed at, so the authors hold, was 'an inherently Congolese social revolution' which must be seen in the long line of millenarian integrative attempts so characteristic of Congolese history in the nineteenth and twentieth centuries. The Kwilu rising must be seen in the context of preceding movements in that area: the Bapende revolt of 1931, in which, 'the Bapende reached a magico-religious belief in their own invulnerability'; The Great Serpent sect of 1932, which predicted 'the collective rising of the dead, the eclipse of the sun, and the coming of a Man, part white and part black' who would institute a new order; the Nzambi Malembe movement of 1945,

[10] Andrew Roberts, 'The Lumpa Church of Alice Lenshina and its antecedents', mimeo. (Dar es Salaam, 1967). Dr Roberts argues that the clash between the Lumpa Church and the United National Independence Party arose because both organizations were making claims to exclusive emotional commitment in the same area. The Church reacted against the loss of many of its numbers to the later secular mass movement.

which appealed to the memory of the old empire of the Kongo and which outlawed all fetishes and witchcraft; the Dieudonne movement of the 1950s, which again ordered the destruction of all fetishes and general baptism in its own holy water.

Into this background modern nationalism arrived in 1959 with the creation of the Parti Solidaire Africain, which promised in its election campaign 'total reduction of unemployment, work for all, multiplication of schools, free primary and secondary education, a rise in salaries for all, improvement in housing, free medical care'. 'Independence', the tribesmen were told, 'would be an era of leisure, plenty and happiness.' They found it instead a time of firm government by the progressive *élite* of the moderate P.S.A., and the authors quote what they hold to be a typical reaction. 'Before independence we dreamed that it would bring us masses of marvellous things. All of that was to descend from the sky... Deliverance and Salvation... But here it is, more than two years we have been waiting, and nothing has come. On the contrary our life is more difficult, we are more poor than before.' And so, the argument concludes, the masses turned to a 'this-worldly-oriented messianic movement, headed by a compelling leader-saviour', Mulele.

This analysis may be greeted with some scepticism, but it rests on more than an easy comparison of Socialist idealism with millenarian panaceas. Mulele, it is generally accepted, has acquired the characteristics of previous prophet figures in the minds of his followers—he is regarded as invulnerable to bullets; his followers hope to share his invulnerability and explain death in battle as punishment for 'having transgressed certain norms and practices of the movement'. Rebels take *mai Mulele*, the water of the rebellion, as a sign of commitment and guarantee of invulnerability. Mulele lays down new rules of conduct for his fighters as strict as, and strikingly similar to, the prohibitions of the Shona mediums in 1896—his followers must live communally, must not loot, must not use European goods. As the authors comment, these rules, in addition to creating the sense of the new society, are as essential in 1966 as they were in 1896 to preserve discipline among irregular rebel forces. According to the authors, many of those who support the movement draw a quite conscious parallel between the colonial rule against which their fathers revolted in 1931 and the present regime in Kwilu province. But the authors, also make the point that, like Miss Wipper's followers of Mumbo, the rebels look to the past for inspiration and to the future for living. The revolt is no rejection of modern goods and advantages, but rather an attempt to obtain them on a 'just' basis and within a 'good' society defined in African communalist terms. 'The new society is conceived of as a gigantic village made up of thousands of small villages in which the people find their own authenticity.'[11]

[11] R. C. Fox, W. de Cramer and J. M. Ribeaucourt, 'The second independence: a case study of the Kwilu Rebellion in the Congo', *Comparative Studies in Society and History*, VIII, no. 1 (October 1965).

I should perhaps say in conclusion about the Mulelist movement something which applies to all the others discussed in this paper. I have no intention of maligning or mocking the Mulelist movement by stressing its character as a successor to other millenarian Congolese cults. However strange their mythologies and structures may appear to us, these movements require to be taken seriously and with sympathy as consistent expressions of aspirations which in the end have to be met in one way or another by the rulers of East and Central Africa, whether white or black. The aspiration to 'put the twentieth century in an African context'; the aspiration towards a new society 'conceived of as a gigantic village made up of thousands of small villages in which the people find their own authenticity'; the aspiration towards gaining control of their own world without surrendering its values; all these are still characteristic of the rural masses of East and Central Africa. It is, of course, true that these movements have not offered lasting or effective solutions; to extend the already cited description of Nyabingi to all of them, they have been 'revolutionary in method' but also 'anarchic in effect'. It is the task of the nationalist movements of East and Central Africa, therefore, to maintain mass enthusiasm for their own solutions. It is their task to demonstrate that they can institutionalize and make permanent their answers to the problem of how to increase effective scale without destroying African communalist values more successfully than the primary resistance leaders or the millenarian cults.

[3]

Conclusion

Stephen Ellis

The shades of Rabezavana and Rabozaka are looking down upon us.
Proclamation by the nationalist secret society PANAMA, 1947

THE NATURE AND CAUSES OF THE *MENALAMBA* MOVEMENT

In this book the terms 'rebel' and 'rebellion' have been used to describe the *menalamba* movement. The rising was directed against a government which the insurgents held to be illegitimate in every respect except that of the queen's right to reign. She was on the side of the French. The *menalamba* therefore took great pains to excuse their revolt by claiming that Queen Ranavalona III and her leading counsellors were on their side. They even went as far to say that it was those who served the queen's real government, and thereby the French, who were rebels. The *menalamba* considered themselves to be the guarantors of the true royal heritage, and those who served France to represent a corrupt form of it. The kingdom was split into two camps, each claiming, with considerable support, to be the sole legitimate government of the state. This is one definition of a civil war.

It was a war in which society was split less vertically than horizontally. That is, it did not divide the state into two geographical units, although it is possible to distinguish certain regions as particularly ardent for or against the *menalamba*. The crucial division was between the top and the bottom of the scale of power measured by the standard which had been in force since 1869. Almost everyone possessing a certain wealth, or above a certain grade in the hierarchy of the royal government, and almost all orthodox Christians, were on the side which supported the French. The collaborators were therefore those Malagasy who continued to serve or to obey the rump of the old royal government after 1895, and the colonial government after the abolition of the monarchy in 1897. The resisters were those who subscribed to the *menalamba* programme, who swore the oaths of loyalty to the old kings, revered the talismans, or took up weapons against the French and the royal government. It was simultaneously a rebellion and a war of national resistance.

It was also a war of religion. Imerina had become accustomed to the conduct of politics through religious channels and the Christian government had thus assumed an important function of the sovereign, which was to ensure the harmony of society, nature and the cosmic order. People attributed any disaster on a large scale to a failure in royal power. When the government became unable to ensure stability, which was so in the later nineteenth century, and when it could not guard the nation's independence, which was the case in 1895, then it followed that the system of government must be to blame. The worse conditions of life became, the more the Merina suspected a massive disruption of the social order to be traced back to the queen's conversion to Christianity. They turned to the outlawed cults of the talismans, which formed an organized opposition, prevented from expression until 1895 by the Church persecution and by the guilty knowledge that the queen had herself rejected the cult. The forces which caused the failure of the Christian government lie deep in Merina history. It was never considered wholly legitimate because of the upstart origin of its Andafy-Avaratra prime ministers, because of the foreign influence represented by its Christian rituals, and because it presided over an economy hampered by adverse conditions of trade.

The revolution in government and economy in the early nineteenth century had produced a dynamic which sent Merina settlers as far afield as Betsileo-land and the east coast at the same time as wealth and labour were sucked towards the capital. The process by which Antananarivo exploited the provinces had already produced clear patterns in the earlier nineteenth century. Each centre of provincial power had essentially reached its own collaborative bargains with the central government at the time of Andrianampoinimerina's political settlement or in subsequent reigns. The reactions encountered by the French were dictated largely by these earlier bargains.

The first distinction among these reactions is to be found in the aims of the revolts of 1895–9. Whether discontent took the form of an anti-Merina movement, as among the Betsimisaraka, or whether the response was a call to re-establish an acceptable Merina government, as in the case of the *menalamba*, depended on the degree to which the population in question had accepted the idea that it formed part of the kingdom of Madagascar. All *menalamba*, Merina or not, considered themselves subjects of the kingdom of Imerina, alias the kingdom of Madagascar; they form the centrepiece of this book. They came from the margins of the Christian kingdom, in every sense. Inside these margins there were striking differences in the type and intensity of response to French invasion, which depended upon the tacit political bargains already existing between Antananarivo and its provinces.

The variety of relations between Antananarivo and its periphery meant that it was possible to detect the same category of official or the same social group playing an opposite role in different provinces. One may take the example of the great marcher-lords, men who had acquired private armies and the command of large districts during the campaigns against outlaws before 1895. They existed only in areas too remote from the capital to have been utterly drained of resources in earlier times. Rainijaonary, the military commander of Vakinankaratra, was a most valuable ally of the French. His family had governed the province for generations, an instance of a provincial élite which had reached an understanding with the magnates of Antananarivo and enjoyed a local power-base. His ancestors had helped to repress the popular insurrection of 1863–4. Rabezavana, on the other hand, the leading warlord of Marofotsy-land, was perhaps the most powerful of the *menalamba*. He had risen to power in his home country mostly by his own efforts. He was often reprimanded for his disregard of orders from the central government.[1] Rabezavana, whose authority derived from his ability to rule where centrally appointed officials had failed, fought with the *menalamba*. Rainijaonary, whose status depended upon working with the government in Antananarivo, sided with the French.

The same almost perverse opposites of response occur in many ways. In Vakinankaratra, the *menalamba* finished by recruiting Catholics to attack the Lutheran Church. In the north it was the other way round: the *menalamba* moved closer to the Protestants. Once more the explanation is concerned with views of central government. In the south the Catholics often represented freedom from the tyranny of the state as it was seen in the Lutheran Church. In the north the Protestant Church, for all its past faults, was seen as an institution both more authentically Malagasy and less oppressive than the colonial government.

The same sort of approach is useful in discussing the opinion frequently given by French observers that the rising was some sort of feudal reaction. The view is a valid one only if the analogy with Europe is not pressed too far, as it invariably was by French officials. Imerina had indeed been subjected for several decades to an assault on local structures of power of the sort which occurred in France in the seventeenth and eighteenth centuries. In some parts of Imerina hereditary fief-holders or other notables had managed to retain their privileges and power by reaching an understanding with the central government. In Voromahery, local notables had been left in place because of the physical distance of their province from Antananarivo. Prime Minister Rainilaiarivony found them useful as allies in a province which he could not otherwise grasp. The leaders of the Voromahery turned out to be French collaborators as soon as the French understood the autonomous constitution of the province. In parts of Vakinisisaony close to the capital many fief-holders had successfully defended their position by alliance with the noble faction at court. They were able to do this because their power to recognize the government's legitimacy was essential to the prime minister. They used French influence after 1896 with great success, aided by the fact that their patron Prince Ramahatra was one of Gallieni's closest collaborators. However, in Vonizongo, where local power structures had suffered longer and more effective persecution at the hands of the old government, traditional fief-holders formed the backbone of the *menalamba*. It may be said that where fief-holders had been degraded by the old government they were often prominent among the *menalamba*. Where they had successfully resisted or compromised with the government, they frequently worked with the French.

The issue was further complicated because one of the most common mistakes of administrators arriving from France was to assume that nobles and fief-holders were one and the same thing, and that they were the natural enemies of republican France. They could point to the fact that certain noble groups were especially important among the *menalamba*, notably the Zanadralambo and the Zafimamy (if the latter are to be considered noble, which is not always the case). It is worth repeating that the nobles of Imerina were different from those of medieval France. They formed perhaps a quarter of the free population.[2] A few were fief-holders. Fewer still had great power. The majority were peasants who lived exactly like their neighbours, and might have a lower standard of living than many slaves. There was absolutely 'no cohesion among the *andrianas* as a body', one missionary wrote, of the sort which bound European aristocrats in the face of a rising bourgeoisie.[3] Just as much or as little as the commoner demes, some noble groups had prospered by association with the government of the Andafy-Avaratra while others had not.

The noble groups which supported the *menalamba* most fully were those which had declined in ritual status since their foundation. In the case of the Zafimamy they had declined so far that some said they were not noble at all. Those which collaborated with the French, like the Andriantompokoindrindra of Ambohimalaza, were those which had shared to a larger extent in the spoils of Rainilaiarivony's government. Thus the same criterion broadly applies to nobles as to fief-holders. The more closely a group was identified with the old government, the more it had succeeded in maintaining its status, the less likely it was to join the *menalamba*.

It is also possible to speculate that the distribution of the *menalamba* bore some relation to the patterns of earlier administrative changes. On the largest scale this is certainly untrue. That is to say there was no correlation between the degree to which a province participated in the rising and the extent to which it had been penetrated by centrally appointed officials. One has only to look at the very different histories of Avaradrano and eastern Vakinankaratra, which both played a conspicuous part in the *menalamba* movement. The main effect of administrative reforms of the Christian era was simply to shape the resistance which emerged. The *menalamba* in each province were cast in the mould of the government they knew best. The most modern provinces produced the most modern rebels.

To judge from the evidence on fief-holders, it seems that the response to administrative reforms of an earlier period determined the reactions of certain types of office-holders, but rarely entire provinces. The same may be said of the incidence of forced labour, which had fallen unevenly on various sections of the community. There is no evidence that it was decisive in turning regions for or against the *menalamba*. Western Vakinankaratra for example, which suffered from heavy labour-dues under both the old regime and under the French, was quiet throughout. This was perhaps because under its military commandant Rainijaonary it was ruled by a strong indigenous élite which had itself been strengthened, not weakened, by the techniques of modern government. The political status of western Vakinankaratra had apparently prevented it from being bled by the capital to the same extent as other provinces.

It may well be that such analyses of the impact of administrative reforms or of forced labour would be most useful in the detailed study of a small area. The implication of case-studies in earlier chapters is that pastors and governors appointed from outside a given village tended to collaborate with the French, at least in the sense that they urged people to remain calm. Officials who served in their native village tended to side with the *menalamba* or to look on helplessly, unless they were very unpopular for some reason. These suggestions could be tested only by further research. In any case the *menalamba* were a product of anarchy, and the first rule of anarchy is that there are no rules. It is possible to find many examples which do not conform to the general pattern because of local conditions. It is also important to note that the appeal of nationalism was strong enough to combine Malagasy of every conceivable origin in a common cause, in defiance of any sociological scheme.

In what ways can one describe the *menalamba* other than as insurgents and patriots? It is fair to say that they sprang from the periphery of Imerina and that, in the early days at least, they were staunchly anti-Christian and anti-foreign. The French usually saw them in terms of economic and political classes, the British missionaries in terms of religion. These two points of view are not irreconcilable. Many provinces had been so drained of their wealth by the government in Antananarivo as to have become almost a waste land; hence the extraordinary bitterness with which the *menalamba* spoke of the corrupting influence of money. The provinces contained refugees and malcontents of every sort, who had consistently rejected Christianity as the tool of a government of usurpers. Impoverished groups were equally likely to be nobles or commoners, for neither category suggested a certain level of wealth. They were less likely to include household slaves, because these had generally benefited from economic changes of the previous quarter century. This economic analysis is unsatisfactory in the sense that there were many groups of Malagasy who had suffered from economic changes but who neither joined the *menalamba* nor resisted the French. Conversely in the far north Rainitavy tended to recruit for the *menalamba* among the richer part of the population.

Slaves, in fact, are worthy of further discussion. The *menalamba* were strangely reticent on the subject of slavery which is interesting in itself since it was both a respectable Malagasy institution and one which was economically viable in the fringes of Imerina from where most of the *menalamba* sprang. One would therefore expect them to have had clear views on slaves and slavery. One prominent rebel leader, Rainijirika, was himself a slave.

Gallieni thought the slaves among the insurgents sufficiently numerous as to be worth splitting from the freemen and wooing to the French cause. But there is some evidence that the *menalamba* drew a disproportionately large amount of support from the free castes and from the slave-demes, who were not slaves in any economic sense.[4] It was only after the emancipation decree of September 1896 that slaves joined the *menalamba* on a large scale in some regions, in order to escape total destitution.

If relatively few slaves joined the insurrection until late 1896, then one may seek an explanation in the extent to which slaves had maintained or even increased their living standards in the late nineteenth century compared with freemen. The available statistics suggest that freemen decreased as a proportion of the total population during the nineteenth century. Their numbers may even have declined in absolute terms at certain periods.[5] The fall in the numbers of freemen relative to the population as a whole is so striking that it cannot simply be explained by the fact that slaves were imported in large numbers or by speculation that slaves had a higher birthrate. It was freemen who bore the brunt of government oppression under Queen Ranavalona I and in later years for reasons which are very complex. Free demes have been very resistant to many aspects of central control throughout Merina history. They have stubbornly guarded their solidarity, their group identity and their ancestral land in the face of often heavy odds. The Andafy-Avaratra disliked that independence and coveted the ancestral land. The rising of the *menalamba* was an expression of the despair of the freemen, and in that sense a study of its origins involves contemplation of the relationship between autonomous demes and ambitious sovereigns or prime ministers through a long period.

The Merina define freemen and demes by reference to ancestral tombs. All fugitives, all who had left their tombs and their homelands, were held to have declined in status. The *menalamba* were created when fugitives of all types sought ritual leadership, which their outlaw-chiefs were unqualified to give them. They found this spiritual reassurance in the cults of the talismans, openly displayed once more in 1895. Thus the outlaws of yesteryear became patriots again. The talismans permitted them to return within the pale of respectable society according to the customs of the ancestors. Hence the leaders of the religious revival were generally old, settled demes which had been excluded from the Christian hierarchy for one reason or another and had clung to their talismans as reminders of better days. The Zanadralambo and Zafimamy again are good examples. The resulting union of bandits and deprived demes was cemented by nationalism, which was enunciated notably by those lapsed Christians who were such prominent leaders.[6]

This does not mean that the *menalamba* came from the lowliest or poorest class of society, only that they all were convinced that they had been cheated of their birthright. In the case of the fugitives the reasons for this are obvious. In some of the settled groups and adherents of the revival of the talismans the reasons are more complex. They might be families or demes who had lost status and political power in the face of recent political reforms; or individual pastors who had been deprived of their office by a rival, perhaps for adultery or rum-drinking. They might equally be demes which had suffered from the political settlement made in the days of King Andrianampoinimerina, who died in 1810. Ritual leadership of the *menalamba* bands tended to go to those who had fallen from the highest point. The more recently a group had joined the opposition to the central government, the more it would seek reassurance from a group of great antiquity or of high or once-high status. Some of the most distinguished of the ritual leaders were groups of fallen nobility, who formed a ready-made alternative to the existing government. *Menalamba* alliances therefore often worked in pairs, a group of relatively low status seeking one of higher status to which it had traditional affiliations. Examples can be found in the combinations of Manendy and Zanadralambo; of Mandiavato and Zafimamy; of Marofotsy and Tsimahafotsy. This is probably not an innovation of the *menalamba* but represents a revival of a traditional concept of ritual rank which had been neglected by recent governments.

The search for status was also a search for greater wealth and power. But the *menalamba* did not call for a redistribution of wealth. They prided themselves on their scorn of money and hated the plutocrats because their money had corrupted the constitution. The *menalamba* wanted to throw out the foreigners and to restore their own rightful place in the affairs of their homeland or province. To some extent this involved a rejection of the degree to which government had become centralized, but above all it was a rejection of the people who had carried out this policy, the Andafy-Avaratra and their allies.

The *menalamba*, then, included those whose golden age had been centuries before, and those who considered it to have passed only recently. The more distant the ideal, the more archaic were the forms of ritual and organization adopted by the *menalamba* contingent in question. The Mandiavato looked no further back than the early nineteenth century, for that was when they enjoyed the position to which Andrianampoinimerina had raised them. The followers of Rafiringa in Vakinisisaony referred to a much older time and a more antique concept of society, for their great days had gone even before Andrianampoinimerina. All were bound by the appeal to the sacred earth and homeland of Madagascar, ancient concepts influenced by a new, imported nationalism.

In this context it is useful to observe what some authors have discerned in protest movements which aspire to restore old orders. Millenarian activity is said to be characteristic of deprived groups, that is of those whose expectations have been most bitterly disappointed.[7] Insurrections whose programme consists of comprehensive and backward-looking demands are said to be associated with social groups which have been disappointed by the rise of new classes.[8] Further clues to the nature of the *menalamba* may be found in the instances of fanatical bravery on the part of insurgents who thought that garments blessed by a talisman would protect them against bullets, which is a belief recorded in many other revolts in Africa and elsewhere.[9] It is sometimes, but not always, a symptom of a millenarian movement. Other features commonly found in millenarian ideologies have interesting parallels in the *menalamba*,[10] but it is impossible to escape the impression that this was not a typical or fully fledged millenarian movement. Its leaders were somehow too calculating and had too firm a grasp of political reality to be placed in the same bracket as the millenarian leaders of other places and times.

The reports of religious ecstasy among the *menalamba*, or of fanatical charges in the face of bullets, were often exaggerated by Europeans who saw in the rising an irrational manifestation of the dark and diabolic. Furthermore the instances occurred mainly in the earliest or most isolated movements, especially the rising at Amboanana in 1895. The *menalamba* never believed that they were destined to build a paradise on earth, which is the principle of any millenarian movement. But syncretic or millenarian ideas were circulating before and after 1895 in Betsileo-land, which was hardly touched by the insurrection, and in Imerina during and after 1899.

The *menalamba* did not believe in a messiah. To some extent they believed in a messianic agency, in the sense that the northerners in particular thought that they might acquire the power of the old kings if they could capture the holy town of Ambohimanga. They made the greatest effort to do so only towards the end of the rising, in November 1896. Another element which might be considered evidence of millenarian belief was the curious assertion that the real leaders of the rising were not in the *menalamba* camps, but somewhere in Antananarivo. In the same way the belief in forthcoming British intervention took real hold only when the monarchy was abolished, and reached its height at the time of the Fashoda crisis in 1898. It may originally have been based on a shrewd political calculation, but it came to assume the proportions of a *deus ex machina*.

All this suggests that millenarianism was not far below the surface in the Malagasy response to invasion in areas like Imerina and Betsileo-land which had been heavily evangelized. It further suggests that this aspect of the movement was most in evidence when the insurgents lacked sophisticated leaders of the sort which they had in 1896. Hence the evidence of a millenarian movement is fairly persuasive in the Amboanana rising of 1895, and overwhelming only in the agitation of 1899. The fact that the leaders of the *menalamba* were of a very different type from their followers has already been mentioned in various contexts. On the whole they were more likely to be literate, to have travelled, to have been churchmen, and to have been employed in government service. In a word they were more like Europeans. These leaders knew that Ratsitiavola and Ratiatanindrazana, Mr Does-not-love-money and Mr Patriot, were fictitious characters. Whether they thought there was a real chance of British intervention is less clear. They exploited both myths for their own purposes, just as Gallieni did for his.

The Rising of the Red Shawls

It is often suggested that millenarian movements occur at a specific point in the introduction of western and Christian ideas into a foreign country, the stage at which an attempt is made to adapt old ideologies to the needs of the modern world.[11] Imerina had seen this sort of response on an ideological level in the earlier nineteenth century. This had certainly been the case in the syncretic movement of 1834, and probably in the cult surrounding King Radama II.[12] Both movements were forward-looking. The *menalamba*, on the other hand, were comparatively unconcerned to blend old with new in the world of abstract ideas. They had no Christian eschatology. It would seem that popular culture had already decided, before 1895, which aspects of Christianity to assimilate, and which to reject. The *menalamba* represented a rather more advanced stage in coming to terms with the European world. For twenty-five years Imerina had been ruled by a westernized government which bullied its citizens to give, to pay, to buy, to sell, as a part of this new regime. The *menalamba* put to the test the acceptability of European and Christian organs of government and all that they implied in economics. In so doing they came to accept many imported institutions as authentically Malagasy.

Imerina after 1869 closely resembled a colonial society. It was ruled by an indigenous élite, but one so far distant from its citizens in taste, means of subsistence, and religion, as to be quite foreign. It was committed to encouraging the economic development of its subjects and to improving their morals, both attitudes being more usually associated with colonial governments. The *menalamba* movement was in many respects a revolt against this colonization from within. It therefore displayed features more often associated with modern nationalist movements than with the sort of campaigns of primary resistance analysed by Terence Ranger.[13]

This leads to consideration of a point made by Georges Balandier in writing about the anti-colonial or nationalist risings of the Mau Mau and of the Malagasy of 1947. He has tried to explain why both these risings were seen by their protagonists almost as dramas acted in the realm of myth.[14] The reason, he writes, is that the effective banning of indigenous politics in a colonial state frustrated normal expressions of discontent and the process by which fact is turned into myth or history. Grievances were instead translated into spiritual or ritual areas of thought and behaviour. This is true of Imerina after 1869. The Christian government did far more than outlaw the old talismans; it silenced the political and religious expression of a large part of society, the part which was most conservative in morals and politics and which was employed in the most backward sectors of the economy.

Traditional religion was a part of the mechanism by which recent events are explained, remembered and take their place in history. The great oral histories, the highest form of art developed in old Imerina, were charged with political significance. A whole generation after 1869 was afraid even to recite its histories,[15] because their local traditions disagreed with the official versions and could be interpreted as subversive. The traditional feasts at which they were recited had in some cases been forbidden. Little which occurred in the world could be incorporated into the historical and political schema by non-Christians. For twenty-five years all innovation was relegated to the domain of the anti-social and of the sorcerer. This is what Balandier wrote of the Mau Mau:[16]

> This insurrection failed not only because of its material weakness, but also because it was not conceived in terms of modern political subversion. It remained a force directed towards an idealized past, that of the pre-colonial period, more than a force directed towards a precisely defined future. In a manner of speaking – and here one may see the reasons for its failure – this revolt . . . was rooted in a mythological time-scale and was not situated in the context of a historical period which had been consciously studied and assimilated.

This is applicable to the *menalamba*. They believed certain things of the French and of their rulers which were obviously untrue. Even in 1895 there were rumours that the French were going to massacre or enslave all the Malagasy, whereas at this stage the invading army had behaved very correctly. Most Merina believed quite firmly that the queen was on the side of the *menalamba*, despite everything she said and did to the contrary, and that Great Britain was too. In many respects the *menalamba* were re-enacting a whole period of history which had not been allowed to take its place in the popular ideology. They sometimes appeared to be more concerned with probing old internal wounds and investigating Imerina's past than with fighting the French. Gallieni, not known as a whimsical man, grasped this very quickly. He realized that it was more effective and less expensive to open the royal tombs at Ambohimanga than to try and destroy the enemy in a pitched battle, as his predecessors had done. It is not of purely intellectual interest to comment on the *menalamba* obsession with history. Tradition, for the Merina, was the point of reference for all social organization and the legitimization of rule. The oligarchy of the nineteenth century had sought to confirm its power by a distortion of tradition, or so its opponents felt, and the *menalamba* sought to remake this history as it should have been. This helps to explain why the *menalamba*, in common with some other insurgents produced by basically oral cultures, were so concerned with rhetoric, myths, and constructs of the imagination.

The movement was most effective in terms of modern political subversion when it had strong Europeanized leaders who had assimilated ideas of European origin. A minority of *menalamba*, many of them lapsed Christians, used the rhetoric of nationalism and their familiarity with European techniques of warfare and organization as a way of uniting diverse grievances in one movement. They were leaders, and might be called nationalists according to almost any definition of that word. So the movement was notably most modern and most efficient in opposing the French in the north, where Christianity had taken the deepest root.

As is so often the case, it was not those who had suffered the most who rebelled the most. The peoples who had been most vilely oppressed by the old Merina government were probably the Betsileo and Betsimisaraka, neither of whom joined the *menalamba* or resisted the French in significant numbers. If the same question is put to the history of Imerina, the question of the relation between hardship and revolt, the reply is similar. Probably the most bloody government known to old Imerina was that exercised in the middle years of Ranavalona I, say from 1836 to 1857. But the kingdom came closest to civil war slightly before and after these dates, in 1828–32 and 1863–4. In each case the main cause of unrest was a reshuffling of factions at court, and a rupture in the system of religion by which local government was conducted, order upheld and witchcraft averted. These conditions applied once more in 1895.

THE LEGACY OF THE *MENALAMBA*

During colonial times people who wrote about the African past – Europeans especially – tended to assume that anyone who had resisted the imposition of colonial rule was by definition a reactionary. It seemed self-evident that the true progressives, those Africans who were most in harmony with the spirit of the age, were the ones who collaborated with colonial governments and who served a colonial apprenticeship in the techniques of running a nation-state. Generally speaking it was the collaborators in Africa who formed new élites, or breathed new life into old ones, and who inherited the apparatus of the state when independence came to Africa. Since about 1963, by which time much of Africa had achieved political independence, a school of historiography has begun to question these assumptions in trying to define more thoughtfully the traditions established by the resisters of colonial rule and in estimating their contribution to modern African nationalism.[17]

Madagascar's experience was an unusual one. It has already been noted that the Merina kingdom after about 1810 was imposing a new national identity on most of Madagascar, and that after 1869 it bore a close structural resemblance to a colonial state. A form of Malagasy nationalism was already established when central Madagascar was plunged into civil war in 1895, dividing the population roughly into supporters and resisters of colonial rule. The *menalamba* leaders may have had a clearer and more sophisticated concept of that ideal than the majority of their followers, but the fact that the appeal to nationalism was the most powerful unifying force known to them says a great deal for its popularity. The collaborators in 1895–9, for obvious reasons, were not able to play the nationalist card. It was only after the defeat of the *menalamba* that those who had collaborated with the French took up the argument that they were working for the national unity of Madagascar by helping to submit the whole island to a central government committed to modernization. Indeed, Gallieni himself sometimes claimed to be one in a line of unifiers of the island starting with Andrianampoinimerina.[18]

Conclusion

The principal method by which historians have sought to understand better the significance and effects of collaboration and resistance to European conquest in Africa has been by examining the relation, in sociological or structural terms, between the primary resisters and later generations of nationalists. They have for example studied whether groups which were militarily defeated by European invaders nevertheless succeeded in creating institutions or symbols which were to be at the heart of later nationalist movements. It has been demonstrated that in some parts of the African continent the resisters had a modernizing effect in surmounting former tribal units, in producing leaders of a new kind, in inventing or popularizing proto-nationalist ideas, or in negotiating special terms with the colonial power which, in its anxiety to make peace, may have granted concessions to former resisters.[19]

One of the main problems in following such an approach in the case of Madagascar has been the reluctance of historians and politicians of every type to contemplate the legacy of the *menalamba* until very recent times. Gallieni tried deliberately to falsify the history of the *menalamba*, and his fiction was reproduced by almost all the French officials who were his contemporaries and who had the wherewithal to have written a more penetrating analysis of the rising.[20] No other European has written at length on the subject since that generation wrote its memoirs. As for the Malagasy, they have been extremely reticent about the *menalamba*. Many Malagasy historians have been members of the Protestant Church, itself a later vehicle for nationalism, and quite a few have been direct descendants of the Merina churchmen who occupied a no man's land in 1896. And yet of the Malagasy Protestant authors with access to both oral and written sources only Maurice Rasamuel tried to answer the question of the *menalamba* directly.[21] The silence of other Protestants is partly because the *menalamba* have posed a dilemma for them, one very similar to that faced by thousands of Christians in 1895–6: if the *menalamba* were really patriots, as they claimed, then why did they burn churches? Similarly the oral traditions which have been collected in Imerina since 1896 rarely mention the *menalamba*, despite the fact – or more likely because of the fact – that the movement was so crucial in the destruction of those good old days of which the traditions are so fond. The secrecy surrounding the *menalamba* for most of the twentieth century has been so complete that many Malagasy came to understand the word *menalamba* as a general term meaning 'bandit'.[22] Even after the creation of an independent Malagasy state in 1960 no one at first wished to claim the inheritance of the *menalamba*. It would have called into question too sharply the nature of the state at that time and its continuing dependence upon collaboration with France. The nationalist rising of 1947 was still too recent and too painful to mention such a subject. The nationalism of the *menalamba* made the government uneasy. Only with the installation of a government proclaiming itself revolutionary after 1972 were the *menalamba* hailed as the direct ancestors of a modern radical nationalism.

The Rising of the Red Shawls

The only visible exception to this general neglect occurred during the nationalist insurrection of 1947. The insurgents of that year sometimes referred to *menalamba* leaders by name in their proclamations. Like the *menalamba* they claimed to have central leaders who were in fact fulfilling an imaginary role assigned to them by the insurgents but who were vital to the cohesion of the movement. The rising was likewise aimed at a restoration of traditional values in an independent Madagascar. In 1947 as in 1896 the main weapon employed by the insurgents was the conviction that a united people would possess supernatural power. Again, this belief was associated with the expectation of help from a foreign ally whose role was quasi-mystical. In 1896 that help was supposed to come from Britain, in 1947 from the United States of America or the United Nations. There can be no doubt that the 1947 rising was in many ways consciously modelled on that of the *menalamba* and that in other respects it was inadvertently so. But whether the resisters of 1947 were direct descendants of the *menalamba* in a literal sense is a question which cannot yet be answered for lack of research. Despite Jacques Tronchon's major study,[23] we still do not know exactly who they were. Suffice it to say that the insurrection was strongest on the east coast. One of the major groups of insurgents of 1947, the Vorimo, were quite well disposed towards the French in 1895 but may have fought against them in the Tanala risings of 1897. Others, like the Zafimamy of Imerina, were insurgents in both risings.

Nowadays there are many different components to Malagasy nationalism. Not all of them fall within the scope of this study, which examines only the *menalamba*. Of those elements which were tempered in the crucible of 1895–9, the easiest to trace is that associated with the Protestant Church. Even during the year of 1896 *menalamba* ideas about the Church, and churchmen's feelings about the *menalamba*, changed dramatically. In some cases the Protestant Church ceased to be popularly regarded as an alien institution, to become one which could be used to oppose the French and to uphold true Malagasy values. Protestantism came to be accepted because it had formed part of the old monarchy and because it was known to be sponsored by Britain, an enemy of France. These notions were reinforced by the execution of Rainandriamampandry and the persecution of Protestants in 1896–7. The former LMS churches in particular came to be regarded as both genuinely Malagasy and yet a part of the twentieth century. The same cannot be said of the old talismans, which never recovered their popular appeal after 1896.

The modern Protestant Church is still closely associated with the bourgeoisie of Antananarivo whose ancestors controlled it before the French conquest. Many Protestant leaders of this century in fact could trace their ancestry directly to magnates of the old government. In shooting Rainandriamampandry and rejecting the Protestant élite which he represented, the French alienated a network of influential families allied by marriage and tradition. They were the core of the nationalist secret society known as the Vy, Vato, Sakelika (VVS) – Iron, Stone, Branch – [24] which is generally considered the first nationalist movement after the conquest. The VVS was suppressed in 1915. The tradition of Protestant nationalism was represented during the 1930s by leading city pastors like Rabary and Ravelojaona, who were also historians. It passed to the leaders of the Mouvement démocratique de la rénovation malgache (MDRM), such as Albert Rakoto-Ratsimamanga and Joseph Ravoahangy, who were respectively the grandson of the Prince Ratsimamanga executed with Rainandriamampandry and the nephew of the last queen of Madagascar. These and others of their background sustained the nationalist agitation of 1947 but, like many leading Protestants before and since, they were at heart partisans of peaceful change. Here we encounter another reason for long Protestant silence concerning the *menalamba*: a real popular insurrection threatened the status of Merina Protestants within Madagascar. This was true in 1896, in 1947, and in more recent times.

Independence has not greatly changed the nature of Protestant nationalism. It still produces leaders from the same tradition, like Richard Andriamanjato – a biographer of Rainandriamampandry – or Roland Rabetafika, a great-grandson of the queen's pastor exiled in 1897. Moreover the rift caused in Antananarivo's oligarchy by the French conquest and by the feuding between prominent families which resulted in Rainandriamampandry's death has long since been resolved. For a generation or more the descendants of collaborators like Rasanjy, Ramahatra or Rainianjanoro were the bitterest enemies of the descendants of the Protestant magnates. Now they mix easily, their fundamental community of interest being greater than the fading memory of old divisions.

The legacy of the true *menalamba*, of those who lived in the rebel camps and occupied the countryside, is less easy to trace or to define. It is rarely seen in the politics of modern Antananarivo. It is largely a tradition of rural resistance to central government, of tax revolts, of a return to an idealized past. The *menalamba* were not the first to launch a peasant rising in Imerina. There are records of similar risings in earlier times, notably in western Imerina in 1863–4. Modern accounts of rural banditry have a distinct resemblance to those written over a century ago. Banditry still occurs in the very same margins where outlaws habitually gathered under the royal government and whence the *menalamba* drew some of their support, like the remote areas around Anjozorobe. But the *menalamba* were far more than rural malcontents, since they aimed not at the removal of specific grievances but at the reordering of society. They intended a social revolution of a type unrecorded in previous Merina history except perhaps in the distant times when the *hova* replaced the Vazimba as the rulers of Imerina. The means which they developed to express their aspirations have become part of an insurrectionary tradition most fully felt in 1947 and which again surfaced in 1972–5. One modern politician, Richard Ratsimandrava, attempted to harness his government to that tradition with a programme of radical rural reform. There are apparently some people who believe that Ratsimandrava was not really assassinated in 1975.[25] This is surely another echo of the rural dissident tradition by which fictitious or resurrected leaders are created in the popular imagination.

The *menalamba* made Malagasy nationalism into a creed so popular that it may be used by the people against the central government on occasion. Almost every Malagasy knows that there existed before the French conquest a state which claimed to be the sole government of Madagascar and whose capital was at Antananarivo. Before 1895 there had been many who resisted this claim and others, even Merina, who admitted it but detested its spokesmen. With the abolition of the monarchy much of the former unpopularity of this government faded, and left only the vague memory of a time when Madagascar belonged to the Malagasy. Regional jealousies continued to exist and were exploited by the French. But as early as 1896 there were former opponents of Merina hegemony who were willing to fight in the name of the queen and of the royal government because this was the factor most likely to unite all Malagasy against the French invaders. The *menalamba* were instrumental in putting the Merina royal tradition at the service of the whole people. When General de Gaulle came to Antananarivo in 1958 and made a famous speech promising independence, he was able to use the queen's palace as a symbol of Malagasy independence.[26] Similarly the protesters of 1972 in Antananarivo used the old royal colours of red and white as an emblem, while General Ramanantsoa, who restored peace after the troubles of that year, derived much of his authority from the fact that he was a descendant of Madagascar's last queen.[27] These symbols may have been appreciated by the Merina of Antananarivo more than by the other peoples of the island, but they show how an old royal tradition has been incorporated into modern, island-wide nationalism.

The memory of the *menalamba* is here to stay. In the past decade it has been popularized through newspapers and the radio as a means of restoring to the Malagasy that proper pride in their own past which the colonialists tried to remove. But in many respects the exact legacy of the *menalamba* is one of permanent opposition. The *menalamba* indeed reinforced and spread the nationalist idea but they did so in the context of creating or strengthening channels of resistance which still form a potential threat to a government of any ideological colour. Malagasy nationalism is sufficiently rich and diverse for both government and popular opposition to claim to incarnate older traditions. But the claim of governments since 1972 that they represent the radical tradition of the *menalamba* looks suspiciously like a revival of the old practice of manipulating genealogies to enhance current claims for power.

CAPITALISM AND RESISTANCE

One of the most striking claims made by the *menalamba* was that their rulers had been seduced by foreign silver. It was true in a metaphorical sense. Although few of Imerina's ruling class actively desired colonization they had been prepared for it economically and culturally by several decades of European influence. To put it crudely, they knew that they could flourish in the French colony of Madagascar more easily than they could have done in the sort of kingdom which the *menalamba* aimed to establish.

This raises the question of the extent to which the *menalamba* were protesting against the intrusion of certain forms of capitalist relations rather than against the imposition of foreign rule in itself.[28] That is not to deny that patriotism was crucial to the articulation of the *menalamba* movement. But close examination of the rising shows the importance of their revolt against what they felt to be an improper use of, and demand for, money. Many leaders of the rising came not from that section of the community which lived as far as possible from farming but from the ranks of small traders. We know that Rainijirika and Rafanenitra for example were former traders. Rabozaka and Randriamisaodray, to judge from their administrative grades, probably had some commercial interests too. Rainitavy actually acquired most of his followers from among traders who felt threatened by the influx of European, Indian and creole merchants into inland markets. A disproportionately large number of minor leaders came from the class of itinerant petty traders and rum-sellers, some of whom were also Christian lay-preachers, who had abandoned the life of sedentary agriculture without ever moving into the big league of wholesale merchants, urban landlords and money-lenders. All of these small traders felt their livelihood to be threatened by Europeans or by those Malagasy traders and capitalists who enjoyed political power.

Moreover although the rank-and-file of the *menalamba* were usually farmers rather than traders, they too were in revolt against an unacceptable economic order. The taxes which they were obliged to pay were levied by rulers who could no longer raise sufficient cash from customs receipts or from trade. When the magnates required them to do forced labour for blatantly private and commercial uses rather than for the public good, it was partly because forced labour gave Merina grandees a competitive edge over Europeans. The island's richest people were not themselves adversely affected either by the creeping colonization of European traders and creditors who intruded into inland markets from the 1860s, or by formal colonial rule. Many of the Merina magnates ceased to compete directly against Europeans in the last quarter of the nineteenth century, preferring to invest their money in property or in money-lending. In the long run they were not damaged even by the emancipation of slaves, either because they had had sufficient foresight to draw their investment out of slaves in time, or because they could continue to exploit freed slaves in new ways.[29]

The Rising of the Red Shawls

By the late nineteenth century Imerina's rulers were caught between European demands – backed by force after 1883 – and popular intransigence. It is possible to identify three principal elements in the series of political equations which characterized the age of imperialism.[30] The imperial power had to have a working relationship with the indigenous élite, which in turn needed the acquiescence of the people whom it ruled. Every time that the imperial power made a heavier demand upon the indigenous élite of an African or Asian state, the local rulers had either to refuse the demand, which provoked the wrath of the imperial power, or to impose the demand on their subjects and constituents by force if necessary. European economic penetration after the mid-nineteenth century changed the balance of power between Europeans and various groups of Malagasy to the extent that some of the equations which defined their previous relationship ceased to hold good. French conquest was therefore, as it were, a process of rewriting those equations. France invaded because the prime minister of Imerina was unable to give the guarantees of security, freedom of trade and control of foreign policy which Paris demanded. When the French government did eventually impose first a protectorate and then a colony, on terms satisfactory to itself, the arrangement proved unacceptable to the mass of the people represented by the *menalamba*.

European demands upon Madagascar became overwhelming only after 1861 when Britain and France insisted on free trade, the right to evangelize and the right to hold property in the island. The rulers of Imerina, unable to resist these demands without the risk of a war which they could not afford and could not win, in turn required of their people forced labour, military service, taxes and the consumption of imported goods. But a glance at the main causes of popular discontent on the eve of the French conquest reveals that they date back to a period before European governments were demanding radical change. Military service was a burden for the Merina even in the 1820s. Forced labour was heavy and destructive of harmony in many villages by the middle of the century. Even the pace and mode of Christian conversion were dictated more by the enthusiasm of the Merina government than by the endeavour of the missionaries. Throughout the century the adoption of institutions of a European type or on an enlarged scale of operation pressed ahead faster than any European government demanded. This is even true of the period of Queen Ranavalona I, despite what the missionaries wrote about her. The changes enforced by the government of Imerina before 1861 were intended to have a modernizing effect in strengthening central government, especially by creating a literate civil service and a standing army. Although many of these innovations were inspired by European models they were done at the behest of an indigenous ruling class which saw in them a means of constructing a nation-state under its own control. A new type of state was arising in Imerina and colonizing Madagascar from within from about 1810. The considerable changes in the structure and scale of Merina government which occurred in the earlier nineteenth century derived from policies initiated in Antananarivo, not in Paris or London. They were the result of an internal dynamic.

But Merina society, rapidly changing though it was, was unsuited to the demands put upon it first by Imerina's rulers and later by the French. Its character was such that certain aspects of the modernization carried out in the nineteenth century were self-destructive, notably in regard to labour. It was a civilization based on the intensive cultivation of rice without machinery or significant capital investment, but with a great investment of time and labour by generations of freemen who had built the irrigation works. Kings before 1810 had encouraged the development of a society which consisted as nearly as possible of free demes fixed on the land of their ancestors. The kings thus promoted prosperity by establishing strong government over the settled and hard-working population which maintained dykes and canals. It is a measure of the success of royal government that Imerina has maintained the highest concentration of population in Madagascar for several centuries although it does not have the most fertile land in the island.

The innovations of the nineteenth century were paradoxical in the sense that mobility of labour was destructive of the fabric of this society and of its agricultural system. Freemen were the cultural and economic backbone of old Imerina. But they were also the people least disposed to accept the principle of labour mobility which threatened the way of life which had been evolved by their ancestors and which had ensured their collective survival in the face of hardships natural and man-made. The freemen would submit to almost any imposition except leaving their land and their ancestral tombs. For their part the magnates of the kingdom could not accept the introduction of wage labour which, though a vital component of economic development, would have undermined their own authority. Freemen had to travel to work, but they also identified with their ancestral villages. They had to work for others, but they were not to be paid.

Strangely enough, the defeat of the *menalamba* and the establishment of a colonial state which tried to create a modern labour force by taxes, education and a dozen other means have not destroyed what the Merina call the customs of the ancestors. The way of life which was normal in old Imerina has become an abstraction for the many who are nowadays obliged to earn their living other than in their ancestral villages. But far from becoming less important, the cult of the ancestors has become the means by which demes retain their identity in changed circumstances.[31] Merina villages are physically dominated more than ever by the large stone-built tombs where the forefathers of their inhabitants lie.

Some Europeans allowed themselves a moment of sentimentality when they saw a colonial government attempt the systematic destruction of the society of the ancestors. 'Today this curious Malagasy society lies in the dust', wrote a French administrator. 'We have destroyed it as a child breaks a toy, for pleasure, and, on the place where it stood, we have constructed a house of paper, all façade and with no foundations.'[32] The thousands of Merina who followed Andrianampoinimerina's coffin from Ambohimanga to Antananarivo one March night in 1897 were obsessesd with the same thought, from a real terror of what the future would bring in a world where the customs of the ancestors were no longer respected. But if Andrianampoinimerina were to rise from his tomb in the citadel at Antananarivo, and to walk once more through the villages of Imerina, he might be surprised at how much was familiar to him in the lives of the inhabitants.

Part II
Modes of ‘Civilizing’

[4]

Christian Critics of Empire: Missionaries, Lantern Lectures, and the Congo Reform Campaign in Britain

KEVIN GRANT

Alice Harris was at the Congo Balolo Mission station at Baringa, 1,200 miles inland from the west coast of Africa, in the territory of the Congo Free State. She and her husband, the Reverend John Harris, had established the station as a mission outpost on the Upper Congo in September 1900, and they had been recently joined by a medical missionary, the Reverend Edgar Stannard. John Harris was attending a missionary meeting down river on this particular day, 14 May 1904, when two African boys arrived suddenly at the station and attempted to convey some pressing news. Alice Harris and Stannard surmised that a detail of African 'sentries' of the Anglo-Belgian India Rubber Company (ABIR) had attacked a village in the vicinity for failing to provide the company with rubber in accordance with its assigned tax. Shortly thereafter, Harris and Stannard encountered two men from the village who were proceeding to the local ABIR agent to protest against the attack, bearing the proof of their claims in a small bundle of leaves. At the missionaries' request, one of the men, who identified himself as Nsala, opened the bundle and displayed the freshly cut hand and foot of a small child. Harris gathered from Nsala's explanation that the sentries had killed his wife and daughter, then devoured them, leaving behind only the daughter's hand and foot. Appalled by this revelation, Harris persuaded the man to pose with the child's remains for a photograph.[1]

Harris framed the photograph on the veranda of her home, with the child's hand and foot upon the floor and Nsala gazing at them in profile. When John Harris returned to Baringa on the following day, Alice told him about the massacre and showed him the photograph, which she had developed. John wrote to the Director of the Congo Balolo Mission (CBM), Dr Harry Guinness: 'The photograph is most telling, and as a slide will rouse any audience to an outburst of rage, the expression on the father's face the horror of the by-standers the mute appeal of the hand and foot will speak to the most skeptical.'[2]

FIGURE 1
NSALA WITH CHILD'S REMAINS

Source: Reprinted from E.D. Morel, *King Leopold's Rule in Africa* (William Heinemann, London, 1904).

The 'slide' to which John Harris referred was a lantern slide, a popular feature of missionary lectures in Britain since the early 1890s. The prospective audience for this slide would be composed of local missionary auxiliaries, chapel congregations, working men's meetings, and, in the broadest sense, the British public. The Harrises had already participated in the missionary lecture circuits in Britain, the private and public forums of missionary publicity known among missionaries as 'deputation meetings'. Photographs, projected as lantern slides, had become powerful instruments of missionary propaganda, and the Harrises now proposed to use photography to serve their mission and, in turn, the peoples of the Upper Congo by exposing the atrocities of the Congo Free State.

Missionaries played a central role in mobilizing popular support for the Congo reform campaign in Britain, the largest humanitarian movement in British imperial politics during the late Victorian and Edwardian eras. The twenty years preceding the Great War witnessed a remarkable revival of humanitarian protest in British imperial politics, recalling the legendary activism of abolitionists in the mid-nineteenth century. In addressing latter-day debates over issues such as the South African War, historians have identified the Edwardian critics of empire as advocates of a secular, liberal ideology based upon natural rights and a radical critique of capital, distancing them from the evangelical tradition of Victorian philanthropy.[3] For almost fifty years, historians have argued that a radical, Edmund Dene Morel, drove the Congo reform campaign to defend the rights and cultures of African societies, while promoting free trade on the Congo on behalf of British merchants. This essay demonstrates, by contrast, that the Congo reform campaign achieved popular support in Britain only after missionaries, and especially the Reverend John and Alice Harris, popularized the lantern lecture as a mode of protest and transformed the campaign into an evangelical crusade.[4] The success of missionaries in the Congo reform campaign suggests that evangelical Christianity, rather than radicalism, remained the predominant force in the humanitarian politics of empire in Britain in the early twentieth century.

Humanitarianism was and is a contested political field shaped by political economy and disparate philanthropic ideologies. British missionaries supported the creation of the Congo Free State to further their own expansion into central Africa, and they withdrew their support only after the state's policies on property rights and commerce stifled their work of proselytization. In this respect, it is significant that British missionaries did not attempt to end European expansion on the Congo, but rather to correct the evils of 'imperialism' as a particular, malignant form of overseas rule. Missionaries shared to a significant extent in the economic critique of European expansion espoused by radicals such as John Hobson, who published the most well-known statement of this critique, *Imperialism*, in 1902. This radical critique defined 'imperialism' as a product of industrial capitalism, driven by international financiers who manipulated European governments to establish coercive monopolies for their own profit, rather than for the benefit of the general populace at home or abroad.[5] Like Hobson, E.D. Morel and other radicals, missionaries condemned 'imperialism' as a betrayal of the principle of free trade, which had been a tenet of the Victorian 'civilizing mission' of empire. In contrast to radicals, missionaries supported free trade in the service of a distinctly evangelical project of expansion.[6]

Missionaries were well positioned in British imperial culture and politics to take a leading role in the Congo reform campaign. The embodiment of British moral authority in Africa was the missionary and explorer, David Livingstone, who had been instrumental in constructing Britain's conception of the 'Dark Continent'.[7] Moreover, missionary societies had become formidable organizers and fund raisers among all classes of British society, enjoying the support of prominent ministers and politicians who reached the apogee of their political power in the 1906 general election, following more than fifteen years of participation in anti-imperialist campaigns.[8]

In articulating their evangelical agenda, missionaries capitalized upon decades of experience as photographers and, more recently, as presenters of lantern lectures in church halls and theatres.[9] There is, as yet, no significant body of scholarship on missionaries' use of photographic propaganda in Britain, though the works of James Ryan and Annie Coombes have set the stage for further study.[10] The missionaries of the Congo reform campaign relied upon their previous, standard lantern lectures as models for their subsequent 'Congo atrocity meetings', but they also departed from standard procedure by using photography and lantern lectures to mobilize international protest against an imperialist regime. While it is reasonable, in the latter regard, to see the Congo atrocity photographs as precursors of the broader genre of atrocity photography and humanitarian protest in the later twentieth century, one must also bear in mind that these photographs were framed in historically particular ways to achieve historically specific, religious objectives.

'To many Victorians', James Ryan explains, 'photography seemed to be a perfect marriage between science and art: a mechanical means of allowing nature to copy herself with total accuracy and intricate exactitude.'[11] Missionaries exploited this 'evidential force' of photography to render the suffering of Africans 'real' to British audiences.[12] In Samuel Clemens' satire, *King Leopold's Soliloquy*, the vilified ruler of the Congo Free State declares, 'The kodak has been a sore calamity to us ... I was looked up to as the benefactor of a down-trodden and friendless people. Then all of a sudden came the crash! That is to say, the incorruptible *kodak* ...'[13] Looking beyond the mechanics of visualization and realization, this essay suggests that the Congo atrocity photographs were incorruptible in the eyes of the British public because missionaries produced them and narrated their significance to promote evangelical reform.[14] On the strength of their lantern lectures, missionaries transformed the Congo reform campaign into a national movement, manifesting the central role of Christianity in defining popular views toward the moral authority of empire in Edwardian Britain.

I

British missionaries participated in the earliest stages of the European occupation of the Congo river basin. As Henry Stanley tracked the Livingstone river (as the Congo was then known) for over 2,000 miles to the west coast of Africa in 1877, the Baptist Missionary Society (BMS) and the Livingstone Inland Mission (LIM) were preparing to expand inland from the mouth of the river at Boma. The British missions had allied themselves in this venture with King Leopold II of Belgium, who had his own, as yet veiled, interests in acquiring the Congo as an imperial territory. Towards this end, Leopold supported the initial explorations of the BMS and LIM in 1878, even before he hired Stanley to go back up the Congo in the following year.[15] King Leopold cultivated relations with British missionaries, merchants, and abolitionists in the hope that they would lobby the British government to support his interests in the Congo against those of his European rivals, France and Portugal. Leopold's British allies were convinced that a French or Portuguese regime would be hostile to their proselytization, trade, and campaigns against slavery. They were therefore receptive to Leopold's promises to promote free trade, sponsor the expansion of all Christian missions – whether Catholic or Protestant – and to fight against the slave trade on the Congo. When the European powers gathered to discuss the partition of west and central Africa at the Berlin Conference of 1884–85, Leopold used these same promises to secure the backing of the British government, which was pleased to avoid a new administrative role in central Africa even as it exploited the conference's humanitarian rhetoric.[16]

British missionaries celebrated their good fortune when, in February 1885, the Berlin Act placed the Congo under the authority of the *Association Internationale du Congo* (AIC), which was itself under the control of King Leopold. Five months later, Leopold unilaterally dissolved the AIC and met no opposition when he declared his personal sovereignty over a vast African territory which he named *l'État Indépendant du Congo* – known commonly in Britain as the Congo Free State. The philanthropic declarations of the Berlin Conference were subsequently ignored by Congo State officials, who negotiated with slave traders and launched punitive expeditions to compel African villages to provide them with labour or supplies under the pretence of taxation. In 1891 the state issued a decree that arrogated to itself all 'vacant lands' on the Congo, as well as the produce of those lands which now fell under its ownership. Leopold then gave tens of thousands of acres of land to concessionaire companies in which he held major investments, thus expanding his exploitation of the Congo without incurring the cost of a large imperial administration. Captain Guy Burrows, a former Commissioner of the Aruwimi District, estimated that by the mid-1890s there were only 670 Europeans in the region of the Upper Congo, of whom about half were state officials. 'These white officials', Burrows remarked, 'are stationed in some fifty Government posts, each ... the administrative centre, so to speak, of 14,000 square miles more or less. To properly administer such a country under existing conditions is clearly a physical impossibility.'[17]

Members of the two British missions on the Upper Congo, the Baptist Missionary Society and the Congo Balolo Mission, had witnessed state-sanctioned slavery and seen or heard about atrocities by the mid-1890s.[18]

The missions tolerated these practices due to their dependence upon the state for security, transportation services, and African labour, which they received in exchange for taxes. Moreover, although the British missions made occasional protests to the Congo State, they generally declined to protest publicly in Europe for fear that the state would expel them from the river.[19] In June 1890, for example, the Reverend George Grenfell of the BMS reported to its Secretary, Alfred Baynes, that he had seen slaves chained neck to neck at the Congo State station at Npoto, and he further observed that officials regularly abducted women as hostages to be held until their men performed assigned tasks or paid ransom in kind or in the local currency of brass rods. Grenfell cautioned Baynes that this information was 'strictly private and confidential. For altho' I think it right that you should know our circumstances yet I do not feel called upon to publicly question the action of the State – our difficulties are serious enough without having the whole weight of officialdom against us.'[20] Thirteen years later, Grenfell commented to Baynes that he regretted 'the wrong doings of officials and the sufferings of the people', but he believed that the conditions of Africans would eventually be improved by 'the opening up of the country and the letting in of the light'.[21]

It was, in fact, not slavery or atrocities *per se* that pushed missionaries to convey their protests to the British government and public, but other state practices which threatened their work of conversion. The missions' problems intensified at the turn of the century on two fronts. Firstly, the rubber industry on the Congo grew rapidly after the mid-1890s, and the increasing labour demands of the state and concessionaire companies interfered with the missionaries' access to African communities. More importantly, the state refused to grant new stations to British Protestant missions, at the same time as it encouraged the growth of Belgian and French Catholic missions which took a more circumspect view toward its brutal practices.[22] It is noteworthy that even under these circumstances the Protestant missions did not establish a closely united front of opposition to the state's policies, nor did the majority of members in any given mission participate actively in public protests against the regime. It was only after years of failed attempts to expand inland that the executive of the Congo Balolo Mission condemned the Congo State in the British press in April 1903, with the Baptist Missionary Society following suit in October 1905.[23]

The Reverend John and Alice Harris had arrived on the Congo in this increasingly charged atmosphere in 1898. As members of the Congo Balolo Mission, they were initially stationed 1,000 miles up-river at Ikau, where John managed the mission station and Alice taught English to local children. Four years later, the Harrises moved two hundred miles farther inland to Baringa, in the concession of the Anglo-Belgian India Rubber

Company, described by Robert Harms as 'a plundering and tribute-collecting empire of the crudest sort'.[24] The Harrises' relations with local traders and officials became strained as the company's demands for African labour undermined the evangelical work of the mission. The company then turned decisively against the missionaries in the months after the CBM Home Council condemned the Congo State, and after a British consular official, Roger Casement, completed a damning investigation of atrocities on the upper river in September 1903. Although Casement had not travelled as far as the Baringa mission station, he had received crucial assistance from British missionaries at every stage of his journey. Brethren of the CBM and the BMS provided Casement with guidance and translation services, arranged meetings with informants and even handled his correspondence with the Foreign Office.[25] In the wake of Casement's investigation, John Harris explained in a letter to the CBM Director, Dr Guinness, 'We have been repeatedly given to understand that the continuance of missionary work, even to a limited extent, depends upon our silence regarding the outcome of the methods of administration.'[26] When the Harrises subsequently complained to local officials about the 'native policy' at Baringa, the ABIR Director, Albert Longtain, forbade the neighbouring villages to sell food or labour to the mission station. By June 1904 the Harrises were subsisting on tinned foods and goats' milk. John Harris observed to a Congo State official in July, 'I must say ... that the treatment permitted to us for trying to help the State carry out its laws is such as tends to close our mouths here and drive us to the public in Europe.'[27] A month later, the local company agent, Raoul Van Calcken, ordered his sentries to torment the Harrises by 'firing ... guns across and in the vicinity of the mission at all hours'.[28] It was under these circumstances that Alice Harris sent her first atrocity photographs to Britain.

Roger Casement's investigation established precedents for Alice Harris' photographic representation of atrocity. One of the missionaries who accompanied Casement, the Reverend W.D. Armstrong of the Congo Balolo Mission, took photographs of mutilated African boys and men, treating the mutilated bodies of Africans as definitive proofs of alleged and unseen acts of atrocity. Missionaries reported that Congo State officials required their African sentries to produce one hand for every shot fired, in order to insure that cartridges were spent upon people, rather than wild game.[29] The victims whom Armstrong photographed were simultaneously to embody the humanity of the Congo people and the inhumanity of a regime that literally consumed them in its accounting. In arranging his portraits of atrocity, Armstrong instructed each of his subjects to wrap a white cloth around himself to create a backdrop against which his mutilated limb or limbs would stand in stark relief. In a subsequent interview with a Congo State official, a boy named Epondo, pictured below, said that the white men had instructed him to hold the stump of his arm in clear view for the camera.[30] Armstrong asked Casement to deliver this and several other photographs to the Director of the CBM in London. As discussed below, the cause of Epondo's mutilation, and the reliability of this photograph as evidence, would be subsequently challenged by defenders of the Congo regime.

It is not clear that Alice Harris knew about Armstrong's atrocity photographs before she took her own. Nonetheless, several months later, Harris also privileged the body as evidence of atrocity. After taking the

FIGURE 2

EPONDO

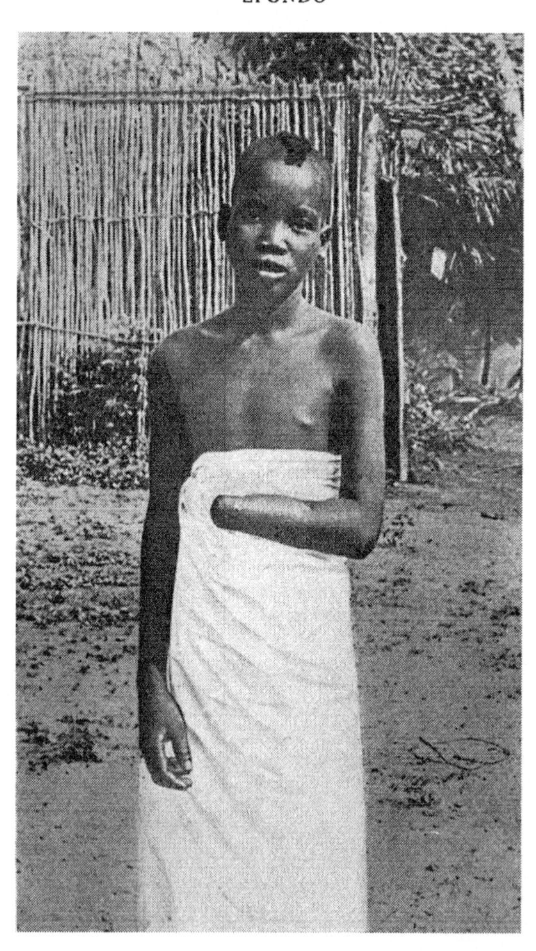

Source: Reprinted from Samuel Clemens, *King Leopold's Soliloquy* (T. Fisher Unwin, London, 1907).

photograph of Nsala and the child's remains, Harris wrote to the company agent, Van Calcken, protesting against the alleged massacre of the previous day. In proving her accusations, Harris stated, 'We have seen the hand and foot of the child, Boali, who with her mother was eaten by the sentries or their servants.'[31]

The Harrises experienced some relief from their hardship later in the year, following an investigation by a state-sponsored Commission of Inquiry.[32] In a subsequent letter to the CBM Home Council, John Harris articulated the direct connection between his decision to protest and his goal of conversion. Reflecting upon the damning evidence that he and Alice Harris had presented to the Commission, he concluded, 'When this is made public it will without doubt create the profoundest sensation. One effect will be a greater confidence in Missionaries and in missionary enterprise ... Do you not think it highly probable that the near future will demand a considerable advance in missionary effort on the Congo?'[33]

II

Reports of atrocities on the Congo had reached Britain since the early 1890s, arriving from consular officials, British employees of the Congo State, merchants, and brethren of the American Baptist Missionary Union.[34] Toward the end of the decade, a British lobby assembled against the Congo Free State under the leadership of H.R. Fox Bourne, the Secretary of the Aborigines' Protection Society (APS), and members of the Liverpool, Manchester, and London Chambers of Commerce. These groups protested initially against the Congo State's violation of their rights to trade on the Congo under the terms of the Berlin Act. Fox Bourne and his merchant allies advocated, by contrast, free trade as an ethical means of colonial development which was mutually beneficial to Europeans and Africans. The issue of the state's exploitation of Africans was a secondary concern, one which would be presumably alleviated by eliminating the monopolies of the Congo State and the concessionaire companies.

Edmund Dene Morel entered the Congo controversy in these years as an aspiring journalist and an employee of a Liverpool shipping company that did business with the Congo State. Morel eventually emerged as the primary spokesman for the merchant lobby, arguing, like Fox Bourne, that Africans should have property rights and be permitted to trade freely with British merchants. He asserted, moreover, that these rights to free trade, coupled with the self-interest of merchants, would insure Africans' freedom:

> The right of the native to his land and to the fruits of his land; his right to sell those fruits to whomsoever he will; his right as a free man to

> his freedom – those are the real principles at stake. The British merchant, in fighting primarily for himself, is indirectly fighting the new form of slavery which has been introduced into Africa with such fatal results by the Sovereign of the Congo State, and in taking the stand he has done the British merchant is rendering a great service to humanity.[35]

Fox Bourne and Morel shared an aversion to missionary 'enthusiasm', and they regarded missionaries as unreliable allies in the reform of the Congo State. They were wary of them primarily because they believed that missionaries would invariably compromise the work of merchants and the welfare of Africans in the interest of conversion. Morel had received this critical view of missionaries from his two mentors in African affairs, the explorer and ethnographer, Mary Kingsley, and the Liverpool merchant, John Holt.[36] Incensed by the reluctance of the British missions to join British merchants in criticizing the Congo regime, Morel declared in the *Manchester Guardian* of 13 September 1901: 'Missionaries who shut their eyes to the nameless atrocities and excesses which the system...daily entails may, if they wish, continue to endeavor to influence public opinion; but, if so, they must be prepared for the protests of others who interpret differently the teachings of the religion of which such missionaries are the professed followers and expounders.'

Nonetheless, Morel and Fox Bourne realized that they needed British missionaries to testify against the Congo State in order to persuade the British public and, in turn, the government to take up their cause. Morel approached the Baptist Missionary Society in 1901 and was rebuffed in the light of the mission's efforts to win approval from the Congo State for further expansion into the Congo interior.[37] In 1902 he approached Dr Guinness of the Congo Balolo Mission who confirmed that slavery and atrocities were occurring in the Congo State. Yet Guinness explained that the British government was not likely to intervene, so that any public protest by his missionaries would only undermine their long-term evangelical goals. Within a year, however, the CBM had given up hope that the Congo State would permit its expansion, and Guinness allied himself with Morel despite their ideological differences.[38]

Morel believed that the nascent Congo reform campaign would 'grow into a movement as big as the Anti Slave Trade movement', but neither he nor Fox Bourne had experience in grass-roots, political mobilization.[39] They advocated 'rights' and 'free trade' for Africans, but their rallying cry moved only a small, if influential, clique of merchants, journalists and politicians. Missionaries, by contrast, believed that they could rally the British public to the cause of Congo reform in evangelical terms. Dr Guinness wrote to

Morel: 'I am anxious that you may not mistake where your real supporters will be. Believe me that they will largely be found amongst those who are pronounced Christian men and women.'[40] Morel responded, 'We want to convert not only the religious people, but hard-headed men of the world. Now nothing, rightly or wrongly, acts upon such men as a greater deterrent than the feeling that "religious fervor" or missionary enthusiasm is the controlling motive.'[41]

Guinness, the son of a prominent evangelical family, was a dynamic and well-known Baptist minister. In the early 1890s he had begun giving lantern slide lectures to promote the work of his mission, having previously operated a photography studio while serving as a missionary in South America.[42] On the basis of this experience, Guinness developed a lecture entitled, 'A Reign of Terror on the Congo', which he began to deliver in a series of 'Congo atrocity meetings' in Scotland in November 1903, drawing thousands of people with the promise of lantern slides. The strong evangelical tone of the lecture was established at the outset, as Guinness began with organ music and a hymn, 'Thou whose almighty word – chaos and darkness heard', followed by a simple prayer. He then delivered an hour-long presentation, weaving a story of promise, betrayal and redemption. In setting the stage for his story, Guinness opened with an overview of the geography, environment and peoples of the Congo. He then presented a standard, heroic account of the era of European exploration and King Leopold's philanthropic pronouncements. In a regular lecture, Guinness would then have focused upon the savagery of the Congo people, highlighting practices of slavery, polygamy and cannibalism which would be ended by Christian conversion. However, in the pivotal stage of the 'Reign of Terror on the Congo', Guinness concentrated instead upon the savagery of the Congo Free State, realizing its betrayal of humanity through the display of atrocity photographs.[43] These photographs were contextualized with what missionaries later called 'horror narratives': descriptions of the events that preceded and caused the alleged atrocity, the process through which the atrocity was committed, and the aftermath of the event. As Guinness commented to Morel, 'Some of the slides are immensely effective ...'[44] With images of atrocity still clear in the minds of his audience, Guinness concluded his lecture in customary fashion with a glowing account of the Congo Balolo Mission. He promised a bright future for Africans with the assistance of missionaries whose good works depended upon generous donations, which he duly received.

Looking towards the publication of Roger Casement's damning consular report on the Congo State in early 1904, Guinness conducted a series of mass meetings in eleven town halls in Scotland, beginning at Aberdeen on 17 January and concluding at Greenock on 19 February. Meanwhile, a deputation secretary of the CBM, the Reverend Peter Whytock, spoke on the Congo question in smaller towns around Glasgow and Edinburgh. Whytock had been a missionary on the Congo from 1889 to 1892, and he was the first of more than a dozen former Congo missionaries to play an instrumental role in condemning the Congo State before the British public. Employing a standard mode of advertising for missionary deputation meetings, Guinness and Whytock arranged for local ministers to announce their lectures during Sunday sermons. Guinness spoke to an audience of 3,000 in Aberdeen, another 3,000 in Dundee, 2,000 in Edinburgh and 4,000 at St Andrew's Hall in Glasgow, the largest hall in Scotland. 'I am having a grand time ...', Guinness wrote to Morel, 'everywhere crammed to the door – and greatest enthusiasm!'[45]

Guinness' evangelical representation of the Congo crisis, replete with hymns and prayers, troubled E.D. Morel and his allies. Lady J.A. Chalmers, a friend of Morel, attended Guinness' meeting in Edinburgh and reported, 'The lecture was admirable and most convincing but, between ourselves, I must say I was personally repelled rather by the sensational and emotional character attempted to be given to it by the singing, etc.' Morel concurred with Chalmers' impression and confided, 'For my part, I am so constituted that the very talk of religion in a matter of this kind sets my teeth on edge.'[46] Morel and Fox Bourne were particularly worried that Guinness would promote divisive sectarian politics on the international level and alienate support for their campaign among Catholics in Britain.[47] Morel's apprehensions were later realized by the strident criticism which the CRA would receive from Irish Catholics in the House of Commons and the Catholic Press in England. Most importantly, King Leopold was initially able to exploit the Protestant character of the Congo reform campaign to rally support in Catholic Belgium.[48]

The success of Guinness' lectures brought tensions to a head within the Congo reform lobby. Fox Bourne withdrew the endorsement of the Aborigines' Protection Society from Guinness' meetings, asserting that he was using them to advertize and finance the religious work of his mission, rather than the sufferings and rights of Africans.[49] Roger Casement, however, believed that Guinness' evangelical approach could serve the Congo reform campaign immensely.[50] He negotiated a settlement between Guinness, Fox Bourne and Morel, extracting an empty promise from Guinness that he would henceforth present his lectures on 'non-sectarian' lines.[51] Casement recognized that Guinness could reach a broader spectrum of British society than Morel and Fox-Bourne in their efforts to gather support for Congo reform. Morel and Fox Bourne had focused their attention upon a small, elite group of men in trade, politics, and the professions. Acknowledging the limitations of his personal contacts, Morel conceded to Lady Chalmers, 'the advantages of co-operating with Guinness are that he can tap a lot of religious philanthropic people for the Association, which I cannot tap'.[52]

Roger Casement proposed the creation of a 'Congo Reform Association' (CRA) in January 1904, and he persuaded Morel to serve as the Honorary Secretary. After the publication of Casement's parliamentary white paper on the Congo in February, the Congo reform lobby began to make arrangements for the inaugural meeting in Liverpool. The organization of the meeting was handled by the Reverend W.G. Pope, a deputation secretary of the Regions Beyond Missionary Union (RBMU), of which the Congo Balolo Mission was a subsidiary. The RBMU put up a portion of the funding for the meeting, and Pope enlisted numerous local ministers to publicize the event from their pulpits.[53]

Approximately 2,000 people attended the first meeting of the CRA, which was held on 23 March 1904 at Liverpool's Philharmonic Hall. The Association came into existence before a boisterous house, though its leadership did not have a definite plan for future action. As the secretary, Morel dictated that the 'Programme of the Congo Reform Association' should be 'to secure for the natives inhabiting the Congo State territories the just and humane treatment which was guaranteed to them under the Berlin and Brussels Acts'.[54] This just and humane treatment would be insured, 'By the restoration of their rights in land, and in the produce of the soil, of which preexisting rights they have been deprived by the legislation and procedure of the Congo State.'[55]

The Preliminary Committee of the CRA determined that its central task was to disseminate information about the Congo Free State through meetings and publications. The committee also proposed to form auxiliaries in Britain and establish alliances with humanitarian groups overseas. These were heady days for the CRA, as it coasted on its initial momentum. Guinness and Morel spoke to an audience of over 2,000 at Exeter Hall, and Guinness continued to give lantern lectures in Scotland and London. Morel, a prolific writer, published a number of exposés, including the book, *King Leopold's Rule in Africa*, featuring several of Alice Harris' photographs.[56] In September, Morel went to the United States, met with President Roosevelt and convinced Samuel Clemens to lend his pen to Congo reform by writing a satire, *King Leopold's Soliloquy*, which featured atrocity photographs by the Reverend W.D. Armstrong, Alice Harris, and the Reverend Henry Whiteside – all of the Congo Balolo Mission.

The lists of the CRA's subscribers and public supporters in its first year of operation provide a general perspective upon the group's strengths and limitations. It is noteworthy that it did not keep a systematic account of funds-received until 1907, so that the following figures are merely suggestive.[57] These figures, which cover the period from March 1904 to January 1905, are drawn from 128 subscriptions and donations gathered from a partial list of donors and from acknowledgements of gifts in Morel's correspondence files.

British merchants who traded with West Africa provided a significant portion of the CRA's initial funding. This group provided more than a third of its budget of approximately £895 between March 1904 and January 1905. Moreover, most of the budget in this period was comprised of large donations: only five people donated a total of £400.0.0, and less than a third of subscribers gave under £1.0.0, although the basic subscription rate was 10 shillings. These relatively large donations suggest that the CRA gathered much of its funding from a wealthy and middle-class constituency. Smaller donations from the working-class were so rare that, two years later, Morel would remark in a letter to his patron, William Cadbury, that the CRA had received 'five shillings from a working man with a very touching letter'.[58] At least half of the CRA's early financial supporters resided in Liverpool or London, and it appears that most CRA funding was initially drawn from these cities. Finally, only 21 – or about 17 per cent – of the 128 gifts were attributed to women by name, a percentage which would increase in later years under the influence of missionaries.

Turning to the published list of CRA supporters, one sees that as a parliamentary lobby the organization could cross party lines, winning endorsements from equal numbers of Liberal and Conservative Members of Parliament.[59] Dr Guinness exerted his influence by recruiting several prominent non-conformist ministers, including four past-presidents of the National Council of Evangelical Free Churches.[60] There were also some conspicuous absences from the CRA's list of supporters. For instance, it did not have public endorsements from labour leaders.[61] It is also remarkable that the supporters included only a few members of the Society of Friends, given that several prominent Friends had already joined the Congo reform campaign under the auspices of the Aborigines' Protection Society. Finally, the CRA recruited only one Catholic, Lord ffrench, and no representatives of the Baptist Missionary Society, the largest British mission on the Congo.

Despite a promising start, the Congo reform campaign began to falter in Britain in the autumn of 1904. By 6 July the CRA had gathered a respectable £653.17.11, but subscriptions had then diminished significantly. It received just over £6 in October 1904, and Morel discovered to his dismay that his wealthy merchant sponsors would not relieve the current financial distress. In assessing the attitude of the general public in December, Roger Casement declared: 'Interest in the Congo question is practically dead. No one cares a d--n about it.'[62] Morel did not know how to raise funds outside of his personal circle of commercial contacts, and he did not know how to overcome the public's apathy. Surveying the remnants of the Congo reform campaign at the end of the year, Morel remarked to his friend, Alice Stopford Green, 'Things look very black.'[63]

III

The Congo reform campaign drifted in a state of limbo until the summer of 1905, when Morel found a powerful patron in William Cadbury of the cocoa company, Cadbury Brothers, Ltd. Cadbury was instrumental in bringing the Society of Friends into the Congo reform campaign, and in June 1905 he stunned Morel by donating £1,000 to the CRA.[64] One month later, the Reverend John and Alice Harris arrived home on furlough from the Congo, proposing to conduct a speaking tour of Britain in order to rally support for the creation of CRA auxiliaries. Although Morel hesitated to embrace this initiative, perhaps in the light of his difficulties with Guinness, he quickly bowed to pressure from Cadbury and Roger Casement.[65]

John and Alice Harris changed the discourse of the Congo reform campaign. Embracing Morel's radical views on property, free trade and rights, the Harrises incorporated Christian morality and the principle of duty into their call for reform. John Harris explained to Morel, 'You appeal to the more educated classes and politicians, what I want to do is to appeal to the popular mind'. Harris advocated property rights and free trade for Africans, but, he added, 'the ordinary Englishman is quite in ignorance of this subject and therefore we want to be careful to hit his intellect on the right spot'.[66] The 'right spot' was Britain's Christian conscience, and the tool for hitting that spot, as John and Alice Harris understood, was the lantern slide image of atrocity.

The lantern lectures of the Congo reform campaign were initially financed by a missionary society, they were generally staged in religious institutions, and, most importantly, they were narrated by missionaries. As employees and representatives of the Regions Beyond Missionary Union, the Harrises took advantage of the mission's relations with numerous nonconformist ministers to arrange local meetings throughout England. Meanwhile, William Cadbury gave them access to the Society of Friends, enabling John Harris to address the Society of Friends' Meeting for Sufferings in October 1905.[67] On the bases of these contacts, the Harrises and other missionaries would hold the largest number of their 'atrocity meetings' in Baptist and Congregationalist chapels and at Friends' meetings. Moreover, John Harris spoke regularly to Pleasant Sunday Afternoon Society Brotherhoods, as on 1 October 1905, when he addressed a PSA meeting of over 1,000 working men at Christ Church in London.[68]

Like Dr Guinness, the Harrises framed the image of atrocity within a narrative of promise, betrayal and redemption. The civilizing mission had been betrayed by the Congo State, and, by extension, the British government which had naively supported King Leopold some twenty years earlier at the Berlin Conference. Invoking their faith in the essential morality of Britain and their shame over Britain's complicity in the creation of the Congo regime, the Harrises rallied their audiences to protest as an act of Christian duty. The display of lantern slides was timed to realize King Leopold's act of betrayal and drive home the missionary's call for redemption. In the middle of a standard, hour-long presentation of some sixty images, there were twelve 'atrocity photographs'.[69] The images were often complemented by 'Congo hymns', from which the following stanza is drawn:

> Britons awake! Let righteous ire
> kindle within your soul a fire,
> let indignation's sacred flame
> burn for the Congo's wrongs and shame.[70]

The prospect of the redemption of 'civilization' on the Congo was closely identified with missionaries. In the course of a standard lecture, the accounts of atrocities were followed by an image of the Reverend John Harris and a chief of Baringa. 'Ladies and Gentlemen', the speaker would declare, 'amid all these tales of darkness there is just one ray of light' – that was, the missionary. The next slide displayed 'natives at a Missionary's house', accompanied by the statement, 'The villagers know that the missionary is their friend.'[71] Contrary to the claims of the Congo State that the 'native' was lazy and incapable of improvement, the speaker displayed images of Africans making bricks and palm oil. 'He is willing to learn', the speaker asserted. 'He listens to the white missionary and yields to the influence of love.'[72] Yet the missionary's work was undermined by the state, which treated the natives as slaves and drove them from the mission stations.[73] 'Are the Churches of Christ to remain silent?', asked the speaker. 'Will the heart of civilisation remain unmoved? Surely not.' The speaker then concluded his or her call for reform by declaring, 'Let us demand that suitable sites shall be granted for the erection of mission stations. And if our legal and reasonable requests are refused, then let us send a man-of-war to the mouth of the Lower Congo, with orders to prohibit the entry or departure of steamers or craft of any kind until they are granted.'[74]

There is not adequate space here to discuss the critics of the Congo reformers at length, but it is important to note that the declarations and photographic evidence of the Congo reform campaign did not go unchallenged. In the summer of 1903 the Congo State organized the

Federation for the Defence of Belgian Interests Abroad, which published the first number of its monthly organ, 'The Truth about the Congo', in July. This periodical presented its accounts and commentaries in three columns of English, French and German, and it was distributed in Britain and other countries through news vendors and upon the seats of trains. In waging its propaganda war on behalf of the Congo State, 'The Truth about the Congo' attempted to refute the photographic evidence upon which the Congo reform campaign depended. In the case of Epondo, cited above, the advocates of the Congo State asserted that his hand had not been cut off by a state sentry, but had been bitten off by a wild boar. This assertion produced various conflicting testimonies that threatened to undermine the veracity of the missionary narrative. Moreover, the Congo State attempted to provoke doubt about the authenticity of the photograph of Epondo by publishing a satirical, doctored photograph that featured the Secretary of the Congo Reform Assocation, E.D. Morel. The photograph below, which appeared in 'The Truth About the Congo' on 15 November 1905, is captioned: 'A photographic proof. – Mr. MOREL has just killed Epondo's wild boar.'[75] While this photograph demonstrates that the 'reality' of Congo atrocity photographs was subject to dispute, there is no indication that the Congo State's propaganda campaign could compete in Britain with missionary authority.

The Congo atrocity meetings, arranged and led by missionaries, raised the profile of Congo reform in Britain, riding the wave of evangelical politics which brought an unprecedented number of nonconformists into Parliament in the general election of 1906. The election finally persuaded Morel of the potential power of religion in British politics. In February he wrote to a prominent minister and member of the RBMU, the Reverend F.B. Meyer, regarding the Congo campaign: 'You will have been busy with election fury up to now. Is there any chance of pushing a bit now, through Nonconformist Bodies throughout the country? ... If Nonconformity is in earnest in this matter, it can MAKE the Government take action.'[76] Morel continued to develop his strategic alliance with Nonconformists through John Harris' mediation, and by January 1907 he was personally distributing CRA subscription forms to ministers to place upon the seats in their chapels.[77]

Following the general election, the Congo reform campaign experienced a dramatic increase in requests from chapel congregations for missionary lantern lectures. In an effort to manage this emerging reform movement, John and Alice Harris became the Joint-Organizing Secretaries of the newly formed London auxiliary of the Congo Reform Association in May 1906. The Regions Beyond Missionary Union continued to pay their salaries, and their service to the CRA was defined as a 'loan'.[78] The RBMU would finance

FIGURE 3

DOCTORED PHOTOGRAPH OF MOREL WITH WILD BOAR

Source: Reprinted from the periodical, *La vérité sur le congo*, 15 Nov. 1905. Note that this photograph was originally published in the periodical, *Petit Bleu*, 17 Oct. 1905.

the Harrises' work until the CRA began to pay their salaries in September 1908.[79]

John and Alice Harris gave over 300 lectures and arranged many others in the London auxiliary's first year of operation. The auxiliary then sponsored almost 300 more meetings in its second year. Despite the Harrises' best efforts, they were overwhelmed by requests from chapel congregations for lantern lectures, and so they recruited other Congo missionaries to join them as speakers, including members of the Baptist Missionary Society.[80] When requests for speakers continued to exceed their capacity, the Harrises distributed standard lectures, accompanied by slides, for ministers to use in their sermons.[81] Recognizing the importance of lantern lectures in its propaganda campaign, the CRA formed its first Finance Committee in March 1907 to acquire and manage the funds necessary for the increasing number of 'atrocity meetings'.

E.D. Morel had initially recorded the missionary lectures in the 'CRA Official Organ', but by the middle of 1906 he could not provide enough space to list the many meetings which were taking place. Morel's correspondence indicates, furthermore, that missionaries and ministers regularly neglected to notify him of meetings, suggesting that the lists of hundreds of meetings in the 'Official Organ' are far from complete. There is, nevertheless, a discrete group of meetings, known as 'Town Meetings', which offer some perspective upon the scope of the revival of the Congo reform campaign under the Harrises' management.

John and Alice Harris organized Town Meetings as forums for the establishment of CRA auxiliaries. They laid the foundation for town meetings by mobilizing support among chapels, Friends' meetings and, to a lesser extent, trade unions. These groups, in turn, submitted memorials to their mayors, who then convened and chaired the 53 Town Meetings mapped below. After the Harrises and other lecturers had set the stage for a Town Meeting, E.D. Morel would often attend as the official representative of the CRA.[82] The Town Meetings represent areas of particularly strong support within a reform campaign that extended from Devon to lowland Scotland. The first town meeting occurred in Liverpool on 4 January 1906, followed by a meeting at Sheffield on 29 May. It was in December 1906, however, that the meetings began to increase rapidly, proliferating throughout 1907 on the basis of hundreds of local lantern lectures by missionaries and ministers (see figures 4–6).

Missionaries used their lantern slide lectures to transform the Congo reform campaign in two important ways. Firstly, the 'atrocity meetings' served as catalysts for the creation of CRA auxiliaries after 1906. These auxiliaries lobbied local government officials, raised funds and disseminated information. The first auxiliary was established in Liverpool

FIGURE 4

TOWN MEETINGS OF THE CONGO REFORM CAMPAIGN, 1906

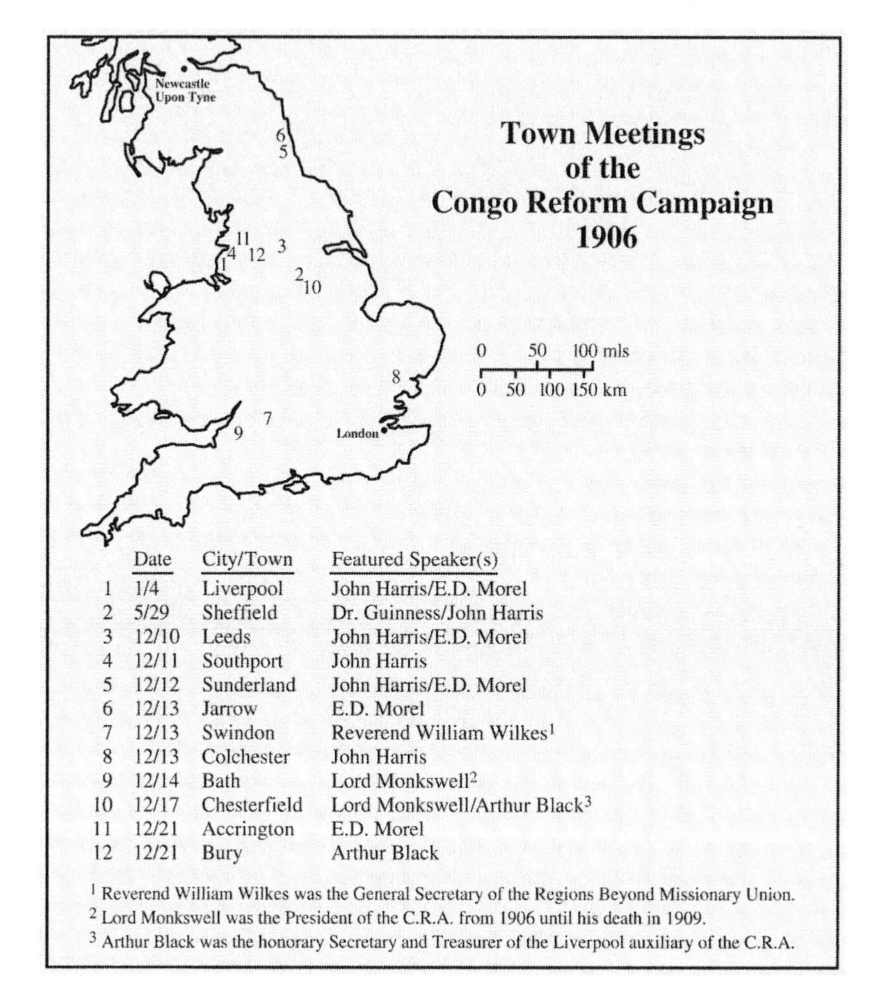

	Date	City/Town	Featured Speaker(s)
1	1/4	Liverpool	John Harris/E.D. Morel
2	5/29	Sheffield	Dr. Guinness/John Harris
3	12/10	Leeds	John Harris/E.D. Morel
4	12/11	Southport	John Harris
5	12/12	Sunderland	John Harris/E.D. Morel
6	12/13	Jarrow	E.D. Morel
7	12/13	Swindon	Reverend William Wilkes[1]
8	12/13	Colchester	John Harris
9	12/14	Bath	Lord Monkswell[2]
10	12/17	Chesterfield	Lord Monkswell/Arthur Black[3]
11	12/21	Accrington	E.D. Morel
12	12/21	Bury	Arthur Black

[1] Reverend William Wilkes was the General Secretary of the Regions Beyond Missionary Union.

[2] Lord Monkswell was the President of the C.R.A. from 1906 until his death in 1909.

[3] Arthur Black was the honorary Secretary and Treasurer of the Liverpool auxiliary of the C.R.A.

FIGURE 5

TOWN MEETINGS OF THE CONGO REFORM CAMPAIGN, 1907

	Date	City/Town	Featured Speaker(s)
13	1/05	Taunton	Lord Monkswell
14	1/11	York	John Harris/Lord Monkswell
15	1/17	Newcastle	John Harris/E.D. Morel
16	1/24	Nottingham	E.D. Morel
17	1/25	Oldham	John Harris/E.D. Morel
18	1/29	Scarborough	(unknown)
19	2/07	Bamsley	Aurthur Black
20	2/8	Birmingham	John Harris/E.D. Morel/Bishop of Birmingham
21	2/11	Plymouth	John Harris/E.D. Morel
22	2/16	Ilford	John Harris/Lord Monkswell
23	2/19	Exeter	E.D. Morel
24	2/20	Devonport	John Harris/E.D. Morel
25	2/25	Barrow in Furness	E.D. Morel
26	2/26	Newport	E.D. Morel
27	3/12	Stafford	John Harris/E.D. Morel
28	3/13	Oxford	E.D. Morel/T. Fowell Buxton
29	4/?	Grantham	John Harris
30	4/?	Ossett	John Harris
31	4/8	Huddersfield	E.D. Morel
32	4/11	Leamington Spa	John Harris
33	4/13	Sandbach	Aurthur Black
34	4/15	Stonehouse	(unknown)
35	4/25	Yeovil	John Harris
36	5/?	Conventry	Reverend Charles Padfield[1]
37	5/2	Bideford	John Harris
38	5/3	Bristol	John Harris/E.D. Morel/Lord Monkswell
39	5/15	Exeter	John Harris/E.D. Morel/Bishop of Exeter
40	6/18	Tunbridge Wells	E.D. Morel
41	10/3	Birkenhead	John Harris/E.D. Morel/Lord Monkswell
42	10/28	Yarmouth	E.D. Morel
43	12/2	Hartlepool	John Harris/E.D. Morel

[1]Member of the Congo Balolo Mission.

FIGURE 6

TOWN MEETINGS OF THE CONGO REFORM CAMPAIGN, 1908

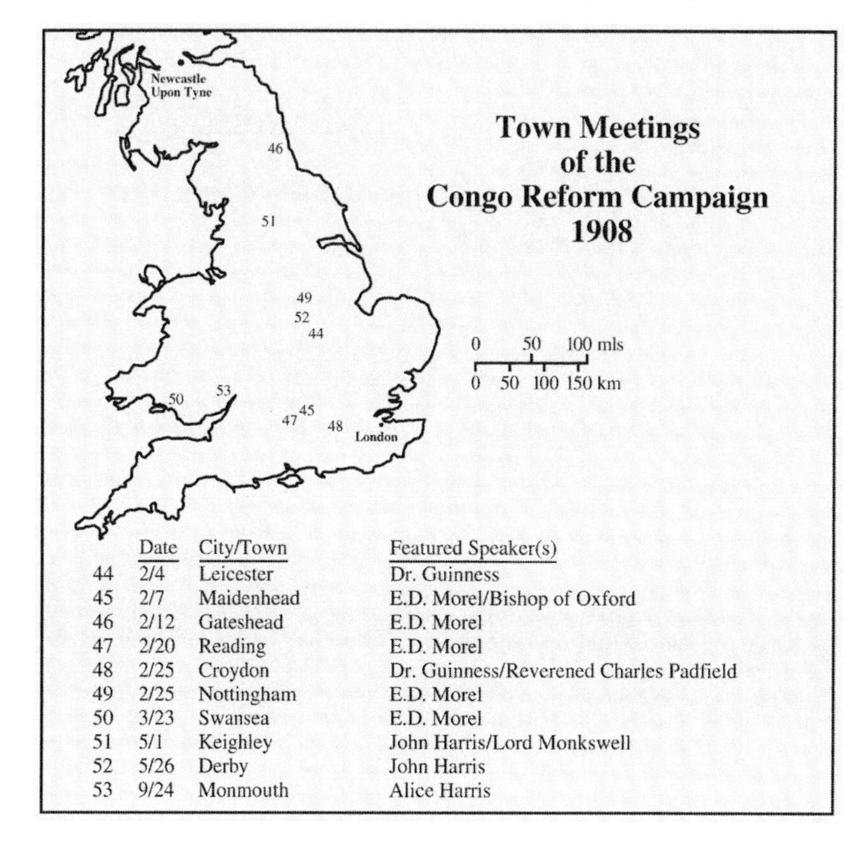

	Date	City/Town	Featured Speaker(s)
44	2/4	Leicester	Dr. Guinness
45	2/7	Maidenhead	E.D. Morel/Bishop of Oxford
46	2/12	Gateshead	E.D. Morel
47	2/20	Reading	E.D. Morel
48	2/25	Croydon	Dr. Guinness/Reverened Charles Padfield
49	2/25	Nottingham	E.D. Morel
50	3/23	Swansea	E.D. Morel
51	5/1	Keighley	John Harris/Lord Monkswell
52	5/26	Derby	John Harris
53	9/24	Monmouth	Alice Harris

in March 1906, but it was the London auxiliary, formed in May 1906 under the management of John and Alice Harris, that was designated as the main fund raising and propaganda agency of the CRA. In addition to producing lantern lectures, the London auxiliary managed the distribution of CRA literature, including tens of thousands of free pamphlets and leaflets. There were approximately two dozen auxiliaries established after 1906, most upon the occasion of a town meeting. Several of these disappeared after brief flurries of activity, but nineteen survived to stir up local interest in Congo reform in the next several years. Few records remain for these groups, but it is possible to give a chronological and geographical overview of their development (see figure 7).

Nonconformist ministers were the backbone of the new CRA auxiliary network. The importance of ministers is apparent in a published list of auxiliary committees in October 1907. Of 210 committee members, more than a quarter (58) were ministers. This strong religious influence had been manifested earlier in 1907, when the National Council of Evangelical Free Churches declared 14 April to be 'Congo Sunday', instructing its affiliated ministers to preach on the 'Congo crime'.

The growth of CRA auxiliaries had a major impact upon funding. The group's income leapt from £815.0.3 in the fiscal year 1906–07 to £1720.7.0 in 1907–08. This increase reflects the input of at least nine auxiliaries established after February 1907 and a rise in funds generated by 'passing the hat' at lantern lectures.[83] This year proved to be the first in which the CRA operated in the black, and it would stay in the black until it wound-up in 1913. This is remarkable in view of the finances of two comparable philanthropic organizations, the Aborigines' Protection Society and the British and Foreign Anti-Slavery Society, which laboured under perpetual deficits, with meagre budgets of several hundred pounds.

The growth of auxiliaries shifted the main sources of CRA funding away from businessmen in the African trade. In 1907–08 the Association recorded 474 gifts, aside from small donations in 'atrocity meetings', for a total of £1057.7.5. There were twenty gifts of £10 or more for a total of £575.0.0, and among these larger donations only two came from businessmen with prominent commercial interests in Africa.[84] E.D. Morel observed in this period that approximately one half of the CRA's funding had come from the Society of Friends.[85] Also, of these 474 gifts, 136 were attributed to women by name, indicating a more open approach to women which missionaries brought to the Congo reform campaign.[86]

Despite the success of the missionaries' reorganization of the CRA, E.D. Morel was by no means reconciled to permitting the campaign to assume a religious character. In April 1906 both the Baptist Missionary Society and the Regions Beyond Missionary Union suggested that they might break

FIGURE 7

FOUNDING OF CONGO REFORM ASSOCIATION AUXILIARIES

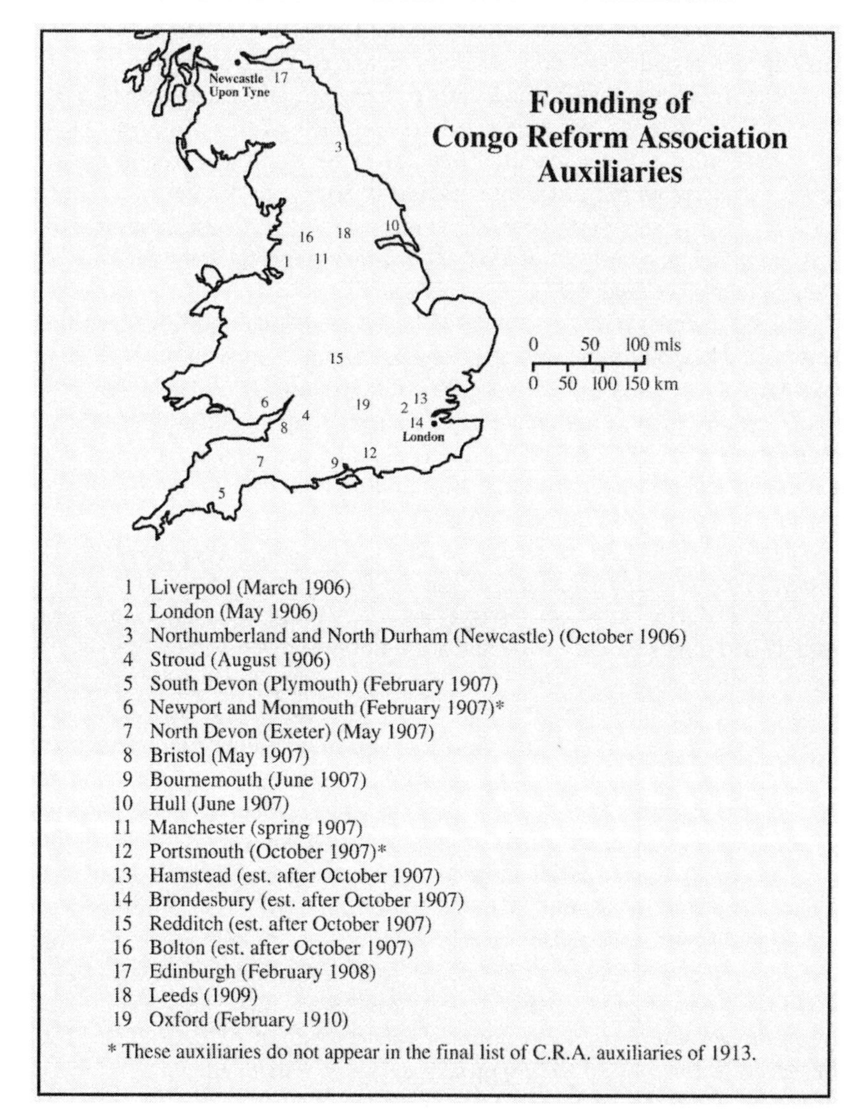

away from the Association and conduct independent campaigns. Morel responded aggressively: 'The idea that the Baptist Society or Guinness are going to dictate to me, shows if they entertain it, that they don't know who they have to deal with ... It would be a fatal mistake for the CRA to allow itself to be swamped by any denomination; this would never do.'[87] By February 1907 the Congo Balolo Mission attempted to prevent its missionaries from sending information directly to Morel, creating a rift in allegiances between Morel and John and Alice Harris.[88] Morel perceived that the missions had allied themselves with the Congo Reform Association in order to win administrative reforms that would permit them to expand their evangelical work, rather than secure Africans' property rights and trade with British merchants. In fact, the RBMU and the BMS had never ceased to appeal to the Congo State through the British Foreign Office for new station sites.

As dissension split the ranks of the Congo reformers, their campaign gathered momentum throughout 1908. In November of that year, King Leopold bowed to international and domestic pressure and sold the Congo Free State to Belgium. This was a turning point in the life of the CRA. The organization's goal had been partially achieved, but, by general consensus, its officers opted to continue its work until practical reforms on the Congo had been completed. 'Atrocity meetings' continued in Britain and monies poured into the CRA treasury.[89] Morel's scepticism of missionaries was substantiated in 1909. The Congo State, now under Belgian national authority, offered new stations to the Congo Balolo Mission, and the mission's brethren in the field began to report a decrease in state violence. As a result, the CBM Home Council expressed public support for the new regime and instructed its missionaries to stop publicizing their evidence of continuing abuses. E.D. Morel criticized the mission for caving in to the Congo State, which had not yet given guarantees that it would abolish its oppressive system. Morel wrote to the Secretary of the Congo Balolo Mission in August 1909: 'The Belgian Government is doing its utmost to undermine the British movement for a radical alteration of this fundamental iniquity by throwing sops to the British Missionary Societies, and by other traditional manoeuvres.'[90] Morel's remonstrations and appeals had no effect. In May 1911 he commented: 'The Baptist Missionary Society are still kept out of their stations, and are getting cross. The Congo Balolo Mission people are dumb.'[91]

In 1910, John and Alice Harris left the Congo Reform Association due to personal conflicts with Morel and became the Joint-Organizing Secretaries of the recently amalgamated British and Foreign Anti-Slavery and Aborigines' Protection Society.[92] Lantern lectures and donations decreased precipitously in the Harrises' absence, and Morel turned his attention toward administrative policy in Nigeria and 'secret diplomacy' over Morocco.[93] By 1913 it was apparent that British popular interest in the Congo had dissipated, and that the Foreign Office would soon recognize the Belgian regime. The CRA thus chose by default to declare victory, although it continued to receive reports of misgovernment on the Congo. Its leaders believed that they had waged a battle of historical significance, and they voted to use their surplus funds to enable Morel to write a history of the Congo reform movement.[94]

The perspective of this history was presaged in the final, celebratory meeting of the CRA, held in London in June 1913. Morel was lionized by his allies, but John and Alice Harris and the other missionaries who had mobilized popular support for the Congo campaign in Britain were absent from the stage. 'In point of fact', John Harris remarked two years later, 'none of those who had borne the heat and burden of the day were even invited on to the platform when the meeting was held for closing up the work of Congo Reform!'[95]

IV

Religion is conspicuous by its absence from most of the major scholarship on British popular politics and empire in the late Victorian and Edwardian eras.[96] This revisionist history of the Congo reform campaign suggests that there has been a secular bias in the historiography of humanitarian protest in the age of 'imperialism', a bias which has, arguably, overstated the public influence of radicals such as E.D. Morel. The historian's attraction to Morel might be attributed to political affinity, and it might also be attributed to the rhetorical strength of his published corpus. Yet the original context in which a corpus was read is not easily preserved, and thus one must question the extent to which the author's views were representative of his or her society. Visual texts such as photographs and lantern lectures – like exhibitions and music halls – provide valuable sources through which to test the currency of an ideology. Towards this end, one must attempt to discern the political contexts and the specific narratives in which the visual texts were situated. Looking beyond the Congo atrocity photographs, a great deal of work remains to be done on the general development, and the distinctive, denominational narratives, of missionary lantern lectures and other forms of proselytization in Britain. Historians have yet to illuminate the local 'deputation' work and the ubiquitous auxiliary networks through which missions played an influential role in promoting and mediating the British public's relation to Europe's overseas empires.

Missionary lantern lectures and grass roots organization made the Congo reform campaign into the largest sustained protest against imperialism in the decades before the Great War. In 1908, the Foreign Secretary, Sir Edward Grey, observed: 'No external question for at least thirty years has moved the country so strongly and so vehemently as this in regard to the Congo.' Although historians have commonly identified the campaign with the radical politics of E.D. Morel, Grey's statement belies this impression. Grey alludes to the controversy over the Bulgarian atrocities, which William Gladstone mobilized as an evangelical crusade, laying the groundwork for his famous Midlothian campaign. This was an apt precedent for the Congo reform movement, which was characterized by evangelical politics, as articulated by British missionaries who returned from the Congo to carry their protests through Britain's chapels. In joining the public protest in Britain, missionaries employed the discourses of 'free trade' and 'rights' which Morel advocated through his publications. However, in the context of their 'atrocity meetings,' missionaries refigured these discourses in terms of their own evangelical goals of expansion and conversion. John Harris had observed to Morel in 1905 that he and Alice Harris would transform the Congo reform campaign by hitting the intellect of the 'ordinary Englishman' on 'the right spot'. As Sir Edward Grey recognized in 1908, this spot marked the British public's understanding of imperialism as a civilizing mission based upon both commerce and Christianity.

Hamilton College, New York

NOTES

This essay has developed through a series of papers delivered at the Anglo-American Conference of Historians, the North American Conference on British Studies, the North Atlantic Missiology Project's conference on 'The Imperial Horizons of British Protestant Missions', and the Princeton Theological Seminary. I am pleased to thank Thomas Metcalf, who chaired the dissertation from which this essay is drawn, and Andrew Porter, who oversaw my archival research in Britain. I also wish to thank the following individuals who provided critical insights at various stages of this project: Antoinette Burton, Tabitha Kanogo, Thomas Laqueur, Philippa Levine, David Lieberman, Lisa Trivedi, and Andrew Walls. Finally, I gratefully acknowledge that the Fulbright Commission and the Mellon Foundation funded the archival research for this project.

1. The above sequence of events is conveyed in the following correspondence: Alice Harris to Mons. Van Calcken, 15 May 1904, Mss. Brit. Emp. S19, D5/10; John Harris to Dr Harry Guinness, 19 May 1904, Mss. Brit. Emp. S19, D5/9, Papers of the British and Foreign Anti-Slavery and Aborigines' Protection Society, Rhodes House, Oxford University (hereafter Anti-Slavery Papers); Edgar Stannard to Dr Harry Guinness, 21 May 1904, reproduced in the appendix of E.D. Morel, *King Leopold's Rule in Africa* (London, 1904), 442–47. It is noteworthy that Alice Harris had only a basic knowledge of the local Mongo. She probably relied upon an African translator, perhaps drawn from her students at the mission's school.
2. John Harris to Dr Harry Guinness, 19 May 1904, Anti-Slavery Papers, Mss. Brit. Emp. S19, D5/9.
3. See, for example, Miles Taylor, 'Patriotism, History and the Left in Twentieth-Century Britain', *Historical Journal*, 33, 4 (1990), 971–87.

4. The following studies treat E.D. Morel as the driving force behind the Congo reform campaign in Britain. These same studies overlook or significantly underestimate the importance of missionaries in mobilizing support in Britain: Robert Wuliger, 'The Idea of Economic Imperialism, with special reference to the life and work of E.D. Morel' (Ph.D. Dissertation, University of London, 1953); A.J.P. Taylor, *The Troublemakers* (London, 1957); Ruth Slade, *English-Speaking Missions in the Congo Independent State (1878–1908)* (Bruxelles, 1959); Wm. Roger Louis, 'The Triumph of the Congo Reform Movement, 1905–1908', in Jeffrey Butler (ed.), *Boston University Papers on Africa, Vol. II* (Boston, 1966); Kingsley Nworah, 'Humanitarian Pressure-Groups and British Attitudes to West Africa, 1895–1915', (Ph.D. dissertation, University of London, 1966); Wm. Roger Louis and Jean Stengers (eds), *E.D. Morel's History of the Congo Reform Movement* (Oxford, 1968); S.J.S. Cookey, *Britain and the Congo Question, 1885–1913* (London, 1968); Bernard Porter, *Critics of Empire* (New York, 1968); Catherine Anne Cline, *E.D. Morel, 1873–1924: The Strategies of Protest* (Belfast, 1980); Jules Marchal, *E.D. Morel contre Léopold II: L'Histoire du Congo, 1900–1910*, Vols. 1 and 2 (Paris, 1996); Adam Hochschild, *King Leopold's Ghost* (Boston, 1998).
5. Richard Koebner and Helmut Dan Schmidt, *Imperialism: The Story and Significance of a Political Word* (Cambridge, 1964); Bernard Semmel, *The Liberal Ideal and the Demons of Empire* (Baltimore, 1993).
6. Regarding free trade politics, see Bernard Semmel, *The Rise of Free Trade Imperialism* (Cambridge, 1970); Anthony Howe, *Free Trade and Liberal England, 1846–1946* (Oxford, 1997); Frank Trentmann, 'The Strange Death of Free Trade: The Erosion of the "Liberal Consensus" in Britain, c.1903–32', Eugenio Biagini (ed.), *Citizenship and Community* (Cambridge, 1996), 219–250.
7. Patrick Brantlinger, *Rule of Darkness* (Ithaca, 1988), 179–82; National Portrait Gallery, *David Livingstone and the Victorian Encounter with Africa* (London, 1996).
8. Andrew Porter notes that British charitable giving to overseas missions was surpassed only by donations to education and church building. See Andrew Porter, 'Religion and Empire: British Expansion in the Long Nineteenth Century, 1780–1914', *Journal of Imperial and Commonwealth History*, 20, 3 (Sept. 1992), 370–90. Regarding nonconformity and politics, see Stephen Koss, *Nonconformity in Modern British Politics* (Hamden, 1975); David Bebbington, *The Nonconformist Conscience: Chapel and Politics, 1870–1914* (London, 1982).
9. John MacKenzie, *Propaganda and Empire* (Manchester, 1984), 32.
10. James Ryan, *Picturing Empire: Photography and the Visualization of the British Empire* (Chicago, 1997); Annie E. Coombes, *Reinventing Africa* (New Haven, 1994). Victorian missionaries were quick to bring the new, and cumbersome, technology of photography into the field. When, for example, David Livingstone made his expedition from the mouth of the Zambesi to Victoria Falls in 1858–63, he was accompanied by the photographic team of his brother, Charles, and Dr John Kirk. Although this pioneering photography was regarded as scientific, missionaries soon constructed overtly propagandistic images through studio sets and, with technological advancements, photographs taken 'on the spot' in Africa and around the world. For a discussion of photography and the Zambesi expedition, see James R. Ryan, *Picturing Empire*, 28–44. Also see David Killingray and Andrew Roberts, 'An Outline History of Photography in Africa to ca. 1940', *History in Africa*, 16 (1989), 197–208; Elizabeth Edwards, *Anthropology & Photography, 1860–1920* (New Haven, 1992).
11. Ryan, *Picturing Empire*, 17.
12. I borrow the term 'evidential force' from Roland Barthes, *Camera Lucida: Reflections on Photography* (New York, 1981), 88–89.
13. Samuel Clemens, *King Leopold's Soliloquy* (Orginally published by P.R. Warren & Co., Boston, 1905. Reprinted by T. Fisher Unwin, London, 1907), 65–66.
14. James Ryan provides a general discussion of the photograph's relation to particular imperial ideologies and political contexts. Ryan briefly addresses the work of the Reverend John and Alice Harris, acknowledging the need for further treatment of photography and humanitarian protest. See Ryan, *Picturing Empire*, 11–20, 222–24.

15. David Lagergren, *Mission and State in the Congo* (Uppsala, 1970); Roger Anstey, *Britain and the Congo in the Nineteenth Century* (Oxford, 1962).
16. Suzanne Miers, 'Humanitarianism at Berlin: Myth or Reality?', in Stig Förster, Wolfgang Mommsen and Ronald Robinson (eds.), *Bismarck, Europe and Africa: The Berlin Conference, 1884–1885 and the Onset of Partition* (Oxford, 1988), 333–45. Also see Neal Ascherson, *The King Incorporated* (New York, 1964), and S.E. Crowe, *The Berlin West Africa Conference, 1884–1885* (London, 1942).
17. Capt. Guy Burrows, *The Curse of Central Africa* (London, 1903), 205.
18. The stations of the Livingstone Inland Mission had been turned over to the American Baptist Missionary Union in 1884. The Congo Balolo Mission had then been established in 1888 by the same group of British missionaries and patrons who had organized the LIM.
19. In a related vein, Paul Lovejoy notes that missionaries were commonly reluctant to prioritize abolition over conversion in nineteenth-century Africa. See Paul Lovejoy, *Transformations in Slavery: A History of Slavery in Africa* (Cambridge, 1993), 253–54.
20. Grenfell to Baynes, 23 June 1890, Baptist Missionary Society Archive, Angus Library, Regent's Park College, Oxford (hereafter BMS Papers), Grenfell and Baynes Correspondence, Box A19.
21. Grenfell to Baynes, 31 Aug. 1903, BMS Papers, Grenfell and Baynes Correspondence, Box A/20.
22. Jules Marchal, *L'Etat Libre du Congo: Paradis Perdu. L'histoire du Congo, 1876–1900*, 2 (Borgloon, 1996), 141–349; Samuel Nelson, *Colonialism in the Congo Basin, 1880–1940* (Athens, 1994), 79–102.
23. Lagergren, *Mission and State*, provides the most thorough discussion of the experiences and policies of the British missions, as well as the best overview of the various denominations and nationalities of Protestant missions on the Congo. Regarding conflicts and negotiations between the British missions and the Congo State, also see Kevin Grant, 'A Civilised Savagery: British Humanitarian Politics and European Imperialism in Africa, 1884–1926' (Ph.D. dissertation, U.C. Berkeley, 1997). For further discussion of American missions on the Congo, see Robert Benedetto (ed.), *Presbyterian Reformers in Central Africa* (Leiden, 1996).
24. Robert Harms, 'The World ABIR Made: The Maringa-Lopori Basin, 1885–1903', *African Economic History*, 22 (1983), 125.
25. Marchal, *E.D. Morel contre Léopold II*, I, 192–202.
26. John Harris to Dr Harry Guinness, 20 March 1904, London School of Economics, E.D. Morel collection (hereafter Morel Papers), F8, File 74.
27. John Harris to Judge Bosco, 2 July 1904, Anti-Slavery Papers, Mss. Brit. Emp. S19, D5/10.
28. John Harris to F.B. Meyer, 20 Aug. 1904, Anti-Slavery Papers, Mss. Brit. Emp. S19, D5/10.
29. Grant, 'A Civilised Savagery', 47–49.
30. *Accounts and Papers of the British Parliament*, 1904, 62, Cd. 2097, 'Further Correspondence Respecting the Administration of the Independent State of the Congo', 16, 34.
31. Alice Harris to Mons. Van Calcken, 15 May 1904, Anti-Slavery Papers, Mss. Brit. Emp. S19, D5/10.
32. Jean Stengers, 'Le rôle de la Commission d'Enquête de 1904–1905 au Congo', *Annuaire de l'Institut de Philologie et d'Histoire Orientales et Slaves*, 10 (Bruxelles, 1950), 701–26.
33. John Harris to the Council of the CBM, 18 Dec. 1904, Anti-Slavery Papers, Mss. Brit. Emp., S19, D5/11.
34. Cookey, *Britain and the Congo Question*, 22–55; John Hope Franklin, *George Washington Williams: A Biography* (Chicago, 1985), 180–279; Felix Driver, 'Henry Morton Stanley and His Critics: Geography, Exploration and Empire', *Past and Present*, 133, (Nov. 1991), 134–66.
35. *Liverpool Daily Post*, 4 April 1902.
36. For a summary of Morel's politics, see Paul Rich, *Race and Empire in British Politics* (Cambridge, 1986), 27–49.

37. Grant, 'A Civilised Savagery', 56–57.
38. Guinness marked his new alliance with Morel by publishing an article, 'The Congo Evil: How to Deal with It', in Morel's publication, *West African Mail*, 17 April 1903.
39. E.D. Morel to Alfred Emmott, 28 Jan. 1904, Morel Papers, F4, CRA, 1903–08.
40. Guinness to Morel, 2 Feb. 1904, Morel Papers, F4, CRA, 1903–1908.
41. Morel to Guinness, 5 Feb. 1904, cited in Slade, *English-Speaking Missions*, 280.
42. I am pleased to thank Professor Andrew Walls for informing me about Guinness' earlier work in the photography studio.
43. I have not found a list of the specific images which Guinness used in this lecture series, but it is probable that he displayed the photos by the Reverend W.D. Armstrong which Roger Casement had brought back to London.
44. Guinness to Morel, 2 Feb.1904, Morel Papers, F4, CRA 1903–08.
45. Guinness to Morel, 8 Feb. 1904, Morel Papers, F4, CRA, 1903–08.
46. Lady J.A. Chalmers to Morel, 8 March 1904, Morel Papers, File 9; Morel to Lady J.A. Chalmers, 10 March, Morel Papers, Copybook, Jan.–May 1904.
47. E.D. Morel to John Holt, 19 Jan. 1904, cited in Slade, *English-Speaking Missions*, 300, fn. 2.
48. Ruth Slade, 'King Leopold II and the Attitude of English and American Catholics towards the Anti-Congolese Campaign', *Zaire*, 11 (June 1957), 593–612; Jean Stengers, 'Morel and Belgium', in Louis and Stengers (eds.), *E.D. Morel's History*, 221–51.
49. H.R. Fox Bourne to E.D. Morel, 29 Dec. 1903, Morel Papers, F8, File 67.
50. Casement to Morel, 25 Jan. 1904, Morel Papers, F8, File 16.
51. E.D. Morel to Alfred Emmott, 26 Jan. 1904, Morel Papers, F4, 1903–08.
52. Morel to Lady J.A. Chalmers, 10 March 1904, Morel Papers, Copybook, Jan.–May 1904.
53. Morel to Alfred Emmott, 31 May 1904, Morel Papers, Copybook, May 1904–March 1905; Morel to Edward Russell, 9 March 1904, Morel Papers, Copybook, Jan.–May 1904.
54. Regarding the Brussells Conference on the slave trade and liquor traffic, see Suzanne Miers, *Britain and the Ending of the Slave Trade* (New York, 1975).
55. 'Programme of the C.R.A.', Supplement published in *West African Mail*, May 1904.
56. E.D. Morel, *King Leopold's Rule in Africa* (London, 1904)
57. The CRA established a Finance Committee in March 1907 to raise funds to meet the overwhelming number of requests for lantern lectures and pamphlet literature. It was not until November 1908, however, that the CRA centralized its collection of funds in London by requiring auxiliaries to forward their gifts. Until that time, treasury duties were divided between London and Liverpool. To make matters more obscure, Morel did not publish registered lists of subscribers until 1907 because he did not want to reveal the meagre basis of the organization's funding. The CRA began keeping certified accounts in 1907 only to refute charges that it was a lobby funded entirely by merchant interests. By this time, missionaries had shifted the focus of funding away from merchants, as will be demonstrated below.
58. E.D. Morel to William Cadbury, no date (but references within the letter indicate that it was written in the first week of April 1905), Morel Papers, Copybook, March 1905–Nov. 1905.
59. CRA supporters included six Liberal MPs, six Conservative MPs, and one independent MP.
60. The past-presidents were the Reverends John Clifford, R.F. Horton, J. Munro Gibson and F.B. Meyer.
61. Although E.D. Morel would join the Labour Party in 1918, he did not have connections to the British labour movement in 1904. See E.D. Morel, *The Black Man's Burden* (London, 1920), 153.
62. Roger Casement to E.D. Morel, 14 Dec. 1904, Morel Papers, F8, File 17.
63. E.D. Morel to Alice Stopford Green, 28 Dec. 1904, Morel Papers, Copybook, Feb. 1904–Jan. 1905.
64. With Cadbury's influence, the Congo scandal was raised for the first time at the Yearly Meeting of the Society of Friends in June 1905. See correspondence between Morel and Cadbury in Morel Papers, F8, File 11, and *The Friend*, XLV, 23, 9 June 1905, 378–79.

Regarding Cadbury's donation to the CRA, see E.D. Morel to William Cadbury, 26 June 1905, Morel Papers, F8, File 11.

65. Roger Casement to E.D. Morel, 28 Aug. 1905, Morel Papers, F8, File 20.
66. John Harris to Morel, 19 Aug. 1905, Morel Papers, F8, File 75.
67. *The Friend*, XLV, 41, 13 Oct. 1905, 670–72.
68. 'C.R.A. Organ', Oct. 1905, 402.
69. 'The Congo Atrocities. A Lecture to Accompany a Series of 60 Photographic Slides for the Optical Lantern'. Morel Papers, Section A (hereafter Congo Atrocities Lecture).
70. Quoted in Wm. Roger Louis, 'Morel and the Congo Reform Association, 1904–13', in Louis and Stengers (eds.), *E.D. Morel's History*, 210.
71. Congo Atrocities Lecture, 24.
72. Ibid., 29.
73. Ibid., 17, 30.
74. Ibid., 31.
75. *La Vérité sur le Congo*, 15 Nov. 1905, 455. This photograph was reprinted from the publication *Petit Bleu*, 17 Oct. 1905.
76. Morel to F.B. Meyer, 1 Feb. 1906, Morel Papers, Copybook, Nov. 1905–May 1906.
77. Morel to Reverend W.H. Haden, 17 Oct. 1906, Morel Papers, File 1, Box 'Morel Cuttings'.
78. *Regions Beyond*, May 1906, 113–14.
79. Marchal, *E.D. Morel contre Léopold II*, 2, 362–63.
80. The following is a list of other missionaries, returned from the Congo, who lectured on behalf of the Congo reform campaign. This list is drawn from notices of lantern lectures in the 'CRA Official Organ'. Brethren of the Congo Balolo Mission: Rev. Arthur Bowen, Rev. C.E. Franck, Rev. Herbert Frost, Rev. Somerville Gilchrist, Rev. B.J. Lower, Rev. Charles Padfield, Rev. William Wilkes, Rev. John Whitehead, Rev. Peter Whytock; brethren of the Baptist Missionary Society: Rev. John Howell, Rev. Kenred Smith, Rev. J.R.M. Stephens; brethren of the American Baptist Missionary Union: Emily Banks, Joseph Clark.
81. See note 69 above.
82. Regarding the organization and role of town meetings, see Morel to F.B. Meyer, 27 Nov. 1905, Morel Papers, Copybook, Nov. 1905–May 1906; Morel to Mrs. Emmott, 1 Oct. 1906 and Morel to John Harris, 17 Dec. 1906, Morel Papers, File 1, Box 'Morel Cuttings', volume of out correspondence; Morel to Robert Emmett, 5 Nov. 1909, Morel Papers, F9.
83. In the fiscal year 1907–08, the London auxiliary turned a profit on 86 lectures, collecting numerous small donations for a total of £346.19.3.
84. Arnold Rowntree gave £10 and Barrow Cadbury gave £50. By this time, William Cadbury had begun to finance E.D. Morel personally, rather than through gifts to the CRA.
85. E.D. Morel, 'The Congo Reform Association and Mr. Belloc', *The New Age*, 21 Dec. 1907. Press clipping in Morel Papers, File I, vol. 1907–08.
86. For evidence of women's significant contributions to British overseas missions at the turn of the century, see F.K. Prochaska, *Women and Philanthropy in Nineteenth-Century England* (Oxford, 1980), 231–35.
87. Morel to John Harris, 26 April 1906, Morel Papers, Copybook Nov. 1905–May 1906.
88. Morel to John Harris, 28 Feb. 1907, Morel Papers, Copybook, Jan.–Oct. 1907.
89. The CRA attempted to systematize and then centralize its accounts in 1907–08, but the extant records of finances are haphazard and incomplete. I present below a rough profile of funding between 1904 and 1913, with irregularities in chronology determined by the archival records: 25 Jan. 1904 to 6 Jan. 1905: £895.19.7; 7 Jan. 1905 to 19 April 1906: more than £1200, but precise figures unavailable; 20 April 1906 to 31 March 1907: £815.0.3; 1 April 1907 to 31 March 1908: £1720.7.0; April 1908 to Nov. 1908: unavailable; 3 Nov. 1908 to 31 Dec. 1908: £461.15.5; 1 Jan. 1909 to 31 Oct. 1909: £1955.1.6; 1 Nov. 1909 to 31 Oct. 1910: £1899.4.8; 1 Nov. 1910 to 31 Oct. 1911: £879.19.10; 1 Nov. 1911 to 30 Sept. 1912: £683.14.5; 1 Oct. 1912 to 13 June 1913: unavailable.
90. Morel to Reverend William Wilkes, 25 Aug. 1909, Emmott Papers, II, Mss. Emmott 4.

91. Morel to John Harris, 23 May 1911, Morel Papers, F8, File 77.
92. Regarding conflicts over authority within the CRA between Morel and John Harris, see Marchal, *E.D. Morel contre Léopold II*, 2, 359–63, 437.
93. See note 89.
94. See Louis and Stengers, *E.D. Morel's History*.
95. John Harris to Miss C.W. Mackintosh, 6 Dec.1915, Anti-Slavery Papers, D3/13.
96. See, for example, the series published by Manchester University Press, 'Studies in Imperialism'.

[5]

"States of injury"

Josephine Butler on slavery, citizenship and the Boer War[1]

Antoinette Burton

In her recent collection of essays, *States of Injury: Power and Freedom in Late Modernity* (1995), Wendy Brown argues that Western liberal political constituencies, feminists among them, have often protested against exclusion from the universal category of citizen by insisting on their "wounded attachments" to the nation-state as the basis for civic participation. In this tradition, it is not simply powerlessness but the pain of marginalization and disenfranchisement which has served as the foundation for critiques of universalism *and* claims to justice in the public sphere.[2] Brown's thoughtful reading of how power, freedom and resistance are imagined in late modernity (and especially under liberal bureaucratic regimes) insists not just that modern feminism is part of the western liberal tradition, but that some of its strategies for political inclusion are characteristic, if not constituent, of that tradition – thus re-establishing feminism in the domain of politics rather than relegating it to the sphere of the social or even the cultural, and suggesting its complicity with normalizing regimes of power like the patriarchal nation-state. What remains underexplored in Brown's theoretical framework is the extent to which ostensibly autonomous political communities and actors have historically relied on the injuries of "others" to (re-)focus the attention of the state on their own desire for inclusion in the body politic. This is perhaps because for Brown, the genealogy of modern Western liberalism and its affiliates is only implicitly, rather than expressly, colonial – a limitation I would like to take advantage of in order to lend some historical depth to her argument and contribute to ongoing conversations about how and under what specific historical and cultural conditions British feminists used the opportunities provided by empire to seek citizenship in the Victorian polity.

As a number of scholars have suggested, Victorian middle-class feminism depended on a variety of colonized bodies, black and brown, for its moral claims on the domestic body politic. English women from Elizabeth Heyrick to Josephine Butler to Millicent Garrett Fawcett argued that British women deserved the vote – or at the very least, representation in the public sphere – because of their capacity to sympathize with and represent the interests of

Afro-Caribbean slaves, Indian prostitutes and non-western women more generally from the 1860s to the First World War.[3] When Brown's "states of injury" argument is viewed in this long historical context – one which makes visible the impact of colonial ideologies on Western feminist movements – it enables us more fully to appreciate why many late-Victorian feminists tried to negotiate discourses of imperialism which excluded them from formal political participation in the imperial state even as they legitimated women's social and above all racial contributions to the colonial enterprise. For with its twin emphases on the subjection of "native" peoples and the investment of British feminists in their pathetic plight, imperial feminism in the last decades of the nineteenth century was characterized by a rhetoric of pathos and suffering which, for all its righteous concern about the need for reform and uplift, did little to critique British colonialism or to distance The Cause from it. Indeed, it might be said that Victorian feminists were at pains to announce their own "wounded attachments" to the Empire through their sympathy for its colonial subjects – an identification which signaled their commitments to the *colonial* nation-state as well.

Feminist discourses on slavery were crucial to this ideological project, since ideologies of slavery, whether pro or anti, were premised on the notion that the slave, even when capable of resistance, was most often helpless in the face of either natural incapacity or culturally-sanctioned constraint. To be sure, idioms of slavery had a long history in British political culture, dating from the early working-class radicals through the Chartists and beyond. Victorian feminists' strategic use of anti-slavery rhetoric and abolitionist imagery was at once derived from and transformative of these tropes, even as it highlighted slavery's historically specific intersection with colonial policy and imperial expansion.[4] But examination of the rhetorical accomplishments of feminist anti-slavery discourse has so far been largely limited to the context of the transatlantic anti-slavery campaigns of the early-Victorian period, when in fact metaphors of slavery, freedom and abolition persisted throughout the nineteenth-century women's movement in Britain, taking on new life and serving a variety of political purposes. As Laura Mayhall has shown, even twentieth-century suffragists consistently read and quoted from texts like Mill's *The Subjection of Women* and Giuseppe Mazzini's *The Duties of Man*, both of whom made parallels between slavery and white women's status available to their readers in order to further their arguments about the nature of political representation and citizenship in modern democratic culture.[5]

The persistence of slavery in feminist discourse beyond the most self-evident context of the early anti-slavery movement is an important if heretofore neglected historical phenomenon, not least because it reveals the extent to which many in the first generation of Western feminists seeking entrance into the public sphere relied upon a fundamentally gendered identification with suffering "others" to legitimate their quest to be counted as political subjects. In order to understand how feminists made use of slavery to fashion arguments about women's participation in the imperial civilizing mission beyond the anti-slavery period, this essay will examine a discrete example of Victorian feminist production, Josephine Butler's *Native Races and the War* (1900). In her tract – which was a defense of British military aggression in South Africa as well as of its imperial interests there – Butler mobilized the discourse of anti-slavery to justify Britain's involvement in the war as well as to foreground the "pathetic" plight of African men under Afrikaner rule. More specifically, in a narrative that echoed and refigured British feminists' attachments to the sentimentalized discourses of anti-slavery, Butler foregrounded the "states of injury" to which black South Africans had been subject in order to make an argument for the necessity not just of British imperial rule, but of British women's suffrage as well. She made black South Africans her special cause, producing an apologia for "native" rights and, in the end, a justification for Britain's worldwide imperial power which required its commitment to a colonial war. *Native Races and the War* demonstrates how reliant late nineteenth-century feminist discourse *could* be on the narrative of abolition which underpinned Britain's national/imperial identity.[6] It is also evidence of how invested this prominent imperial feminist was in the injuries done to colonial Others as the basis of her case for the indispensability of white women's political emancipation.

At this juncture it is important to underscore that women's anti-slavery efforts, like the British anti-slavery movement as a whole, did not directly threaten the colonial enterprise, but shored it up instead by making the putatively "free labor" of emancipated blacks and the indentured labor of colonial subjects the basis of post-emancipation imperial economy – thus re-attaching the capitalist state to a more just (if entirely self-interested) imperial mission now purged of an institution which had become the cultural embodiment of evil and corruption for an influential stratum of the metropolitan middle class.[7] At stake here is not, therefore, Butler's resistance to colonialism but her defense of it – and, more particularly, her recurrent use of the rhetoric of abolition, more than half a century after formal emancipation, to make her case for an imperial war.

Even at this late date, slavery (with its implicit evocation of black, and most often African, bodies) remained one of the most evocative signs of social and political injustice for Victorian feminists – more powerful perhaps even than the (brown) body of the Indian woman which tended to preoccupy bourgeois female reformers of the period. Aided by campaigns against the white slave trade and the crusade to repeal the Contagious Diseases Acts, the trope of slavery remained common currency among feminists until the First World War. Indeed, the latter was called the "Abolitionist" movement by participants and their contemporaries, of whom Josephine Butler was the celebrated leader.[8] The discursive familiarity of slavery and its poignancy as an irrefutable sign of an injury which had to be prevented or, at the very least, assuaged, undoubtedly shaped the terms through which Butler applied the theme of abolition to the South African scene on the eve of the twentieth century.[9] She relied on slavery also because she hoped that by evoking the "wounded attachments" of an earlier generation of feminists she might persuade her contemporaries and fellow-reformers, if not the government itself, to see the benefits of an imperial war which she believed should be dedicated to the eradication of slavery and protection of "native" peoples. The fact that she was virtually alone among her feminist and progressive allies in her support of the Boer War suggests that hers was not a typical feminist, or even a typically gendered, position. Her contemporary Millicent Garrett Fawcett supported the war, while Emily Hobhouse criticized it – though unlike Butler, neither of them made "native races" their special concern, focusing on the plight of Afrikaner women and children instead.[10] And yet *Native Races and War* is a fundamentally liberal feminist text, and the peculiarity of its arguments should not distract us from the continuities it exhibits between nineteenth-century colonialism and contemporary feminist dilemmas about political representation, its potential violences and its often vexing contradictions.

When *Native Races and the War* was published in 1900, the Boer War had scarcely been going on for a year and had not even entered its most controversial phase (the sieges of Kimberly and Ladysmith were lifted early in the new year; Mafeking was relieved in May 1900). The writing of it most likely predated Lord Kitchener's farm-burning policies (March 1900), the "Khaki Election" (October 1900) and the creation of the concentration camps for captured Afrikaner women and children, their families and dependents (December 1900). Butler's inattention to the camps, which was *the* point of intervention for those few British women who did get involved in debates about the war, may be ascribed to the fact that the book was in print well before 1901, when Emily Hobhouse brought them before the British public.[11] *Native Races and the War* should be understood first and foremost as a vestige, however peculiar, of the "frenzy of jingoism" which the war inspired from its beginning in late 1899, when negotiations between Paul Kruger, president of the Transvaal, and the British government, led by Joseph Chamberlain as Colonial Secretary, failed to satisfy Westminster.[12] As such, it ought to take its place alongside the pamphlets, speeches and other ephemera which testify to the popular enthusiasm of a fin-de-siècle war which was, according to one contemporary, "the biggest thing since the Mutiny."[13]

Despite the ways in which the London press polarized the fighting as "Anglo-Boer," and insisted on framing popular and high political responses as either pro- or anti-Boer, the war can be read in such bald terms only by ignoring the contradictory connections between and among the combatants and reducing a many-sided contest to a facile binary. For in addition to occluding the complex relationship which British Uitlanders had to Afrikaner rule, metropolitan preoccupation with the Anglo-Boer axis eclipsed the role played by African Christians, peoples of mixed race, Indian laborers and traders and educated, enfranchised "natives" in South African society and political economy before, during and after the outbreak of war. There were times, especially in private correspondence, when Butler herself succumbed to this tendency to reduce the struggle in question to a Briton-versus-Boer proposition. Before *Native Races* was in print, Butler expressed her opinions on the subject privately, as for example in a letter to a correspondent in 1899:

> I pray constantly for England, our dear country . . . she has her faults, her sins, great ones too, as well as great virtues and high qualities. Her heart is sound. There is no nation on earth that fears God as she does . . . what one must hope for in the present war is that it may be soon over – that the Boers may be sufficiently beaten to be induced to lay down their arms, and that we may offer them *peace* on just and reasonable terms, and that they will settle down under British rule.[14]

Evangelical language and conviction about Britain's manifest destiny continued to characterize her descriptions of what was going on in South Africa into the new century. In letters to friends she described Kruger as "an old Devil"[15] and the British military maneuvers as "the work of the Holy Spirit."[16] Such rhetoric had been typical of Butler's speech, both public and private, since the early days of the first repeal campaigns of the 1860s.[17] As has been documented, it became intensified in the context of colonial campaigns such as the crusade against regulated prostitution in India in the 1880s, where Butler imagined that the rescue of Indian women from the hands of government inspectors was the work of providence making itself known through British feminists.[18] But the Boer War called forth what may be said to be the most religiously charged imperial rhetoric Butler ever articulated. For her, South Africa was nothing less than Britain's rightful possession, its divinely given property. As she put it when she wrote to her assistant Miss Forsaith in July of 1902, the forces of good:

> will kindle (please God) the holy fire, and carry the fiery Cross into . . . our Empire – that fire which alone will prevail over the Satanic devices and the powers of hell which are arising to dispute with us the true possession of S. Africa.[19]

In contrast to the tack she took in personal correspondence, the arguments put forward in *Native Races and the War* appear to unsettle the manichean dichotomies articulated privately by Butler and popularized by pressmen like W.T. Stead because they focus on the suffering and injustice visited on black South Africans under Afrikaner rule.[20] Butler insisted in her book that the war was not about gold or territory or British–Boer conflicts or even divine right, but about the fact of Africans' continued enslavement instead.[21] For Butler – veteran feminist, Contagious Diseases Acts repeal campaigner and, in her own words, "an old abolitionist" – slavery was "one of the direct causes" of the hostilities. Invoking the Abolition Act (passed by the British parliament in 1833 and implemented in the colonies in 1834), she claimed that "wherever British rule is established, slavery is abolished." In her view, therefore, only the re-establishment of "peace under the principles of British rule" would settle the South African question.[22] The right of self-possession under the law and, more specifically, the right of labourers to "their [own] hire" – two of the most important principles behind the anti-slavery campaigns of the early-Victorian period – were her chief concerns here. Now, as before, the concept of slave-versus-free rested on liberal utopian presumptions about the benefits of imperial capitalism, presumptions which Butler did not evidently question. Her invocation of the right to free labor in *Native Races* is superficial and even naïve, but it enabled the book to do the political work she intended: namely, to present the dangers of slaveocratic practices for black South Africans as the grounds of her anti-Boer sentiment and in turn, of her commitment to the British war effort.

Butler's sense of identification with African slaves as laboring bodies worthy of the sympathy of the metropolitan public was the cornerstone of her argument in favor of the war – much as workhouse women picking oakum and Indian prostitutes had been to the domestic and imperial repeal campaigns she had led in the 1870s and 1880s respectively. As in the Indian repeal debate, Butler was keen to provide the testimony of experts and local witnesses to authorize her claims about the exploitation of "natives" ostensibly under the protection of British colonial power and, above all, to underscore the righteousness of British military action against the Boers.[23] Hence *Native Races* is brimming with quotations from missionaries, writers and prominent African leaders, all affirming the persistence of slavery and detailing countless instances of violence, brutality and inhumanity inflicted on black bodies by Afrikaner civilians and military alike. Not content to rely on either newspaper accounts or hearsay, and never having been to South Africa herself, she quoted from a Royal Commission undertaken in the Transvaal in 1881 in which a variety of native chiefs and other informants had testified to the practice of slavery in the South African Republic. In response to Sir H. de Villiers' question, "What did the Boers do with you when they caught you?" one Frederick Molepo replied "they sold me." "How much did they sell you for? – One cow and a big pot." Another unidentified headman testified that blacks were routinely "put up to auction" by the Boers and that he himself had been purchased by Frederick Botha, then *veldt cornet*, or justice of the peace – thus signifying that such practices occurred even among Boer officials.[24] "Many more of such extracts might be quoted," Butler informed her readers, "but it is not my motive to multiply horrors. These are given exactly as they stand in the original, which may all be found in Blue Books presented to Parliament."[25]

Butler's manipulation of "authentic" and authoritative voices to speak about the atrocities and humiliations of slavery signifies how canny she was when it came to manipulating political conventions like the quintessentially British Blue Book. Her ventriloquism also indicates how determined she was to make the question of African slavery, its history and its newly emergent historical forms in contemporary South Africa central to the justification for war she was producing. For in an important sense, what *Native Races* offered was an alternative account of the whys and wherefores of the Boer War – one which insisted on the injured black South African male as the pivotal figure upon whom the justness of the military cause relied. As a history of the events leading up to the war of 1899 which privileged the ongoing effects of a slave system, *Native Races* is evidently an attempt to challenge other accounts, to criticize British government leadership, and especially to deplore the ways in which South Africa had long been and remained "a costly sacrifice made on the Altar of Party."[26] Despite her attempts to enable the "native races" to speak for themselves, by constructing a counter-history which placed slavery at its center, Butler offered up images of blacks as the unfortunate victims of Afrikaner primitiveness and their enslavement as the direct effect of the Boers' fatally flawed national character. In doing so she effectively represented Africans to her readers not only primarily as slaves, but as objects of humanitarian identification and sympathy: as subjects heretofore largely unseen as part of the war's rationale but in fact attached politically and above all, morally, to the British body politic – precisely because of the pathos she hoped and believed their plight elicited.

The question of *Native Races* as an act of representation is something I will return to. But first it bears emphasizing that as a rhetorical maneuver, Butler's attempt to re-orient the debate about the Boer War so that it focused on blacks and slavery did not ultimately destabilize the Anglo-Boer axis that characterized other accounts, but in fact re-established that axis on new and firmer ground. For if Butler viewed the war as a conflict over slavery, she also saw it as the triumph of a superior civilization over a retrograde and inferior culture, with the injury done to Africans serving as the most powerful evidence of Afrikaner unfitness for rule. In her opinion, Afrikaans and its speakers were an example of "arrested development," occupying a place on the scale somewhere between African slaves and free Britons.[27] Evidence of Afrikaner barbarity, a staple of newspaper coverage and pro-war commentary, did not appear much in *Native Races*, again possibly because Butler wrote the book relatively early on in the war. But she did discuss the customs of the enemy privately, commenting to Millicent Garrett Fawcett that she was glad to hear that an Afrikaner had been convicted under British law for murdering a black man – "for them to kill a native has been little more than killing a rabbit or a hare."[28] Slavery and a capacity for brutal practices were, in Butler's view, as deeply and essentially "engraved in the minds of Dutch settlers"[29] as anti-slavery was part of the British constitution – so that the battle was not just between Briton and Boer, but between two nationally competitive destinies as well. The attachment of blacks to the metropolitan body politic, then, was not merely a matter for humanitarian reform through voluntary association but justified, in her view, active and sustained military intervention as well.

Butler's views on "the Boer" were by no means untypical in the late-Victorian metropole. English images of the oppressive, uncouth Afrikaner dated back to the eighteenth century and, as Todd Lee has shown, the war in South Africa brought these images before the public in quite dramatic ways through fiction and the political cartoon, genres which caricatured the Boer male as criminal, dull-witted, and brutal.[30] Queen Victoria, for her part, likened Afrikaners to the slave owners in *Uncle Tom's Cabin*.[31] In Butler's view, simply because the Boers continued to embrace slavery despite its abolition, whatever havoc was wreaked on them was therefore merely rightful "historic vengeance."[32] The specter of Germany was all but invisible in her account, thus enabling Butler to read British involvement as righteous and historically fated – a triumph of the strong over the weak, and of the righteous over the damned – rather than the more complex geopolitical struggle it also undoubtedly was. For her the litmus test of national strength was, moreover, explicitly defined by the level of commitment to abolition demonstrated by any people. Her choice of narrative strategy required her to construct the "native races" not just as dependent on British intervention, but as chattel who had been "handed" back to their Boer masters under the Pretoria Convention of 1881, rather than as active participants in the fighting and the negotiations ostensibly "between" Boers and British at every stage.

As the work of Peter Warwick and others on black people and the war suggests, South African blacks were in fact actively involved – as propagandists, journalists, trench drivers, wagoneers, scouts and saboteurs – and were in no sense simply the passive spectators of military events and operations. Nor had they been in the decades leading up to 1899, when African constituency organizations were growing in number and black electors, though still the minority of Africans, had begun to exercise local and regional political influence.[33] In contrast, Butler's account represented "native races" chiefly as moveable property in a colonial game in which, again, they had no ostensibly autonomous role to play, except as living proof of the injuries inflicted on them by savage Afrikaner customs and practices. Indeed, the testimony which Butler so scrupulously materialized in the book functions as an affirmation of blacks' true loyalties and as evidence of the binaries of good and evil which the British and the Boers represent respectively. As she had in the case of Indian women's voices in the C.D. Acts repeal campaign of the 1880s, Butler used the voices of "native races" to demonstrate the true success of British imperial power: the willingness of colonial subjects to choose British rule over that of all others. As a Zoutpansberg chief, Umgombarie, is reported to have said to the Royal Commission: "I have fought with the Boers, and have many wounds . . . [but] I will never consent to place myself under their rule. I belong to the English Government. I am not a man who eats with both sides of his jaw at once; I use only one side. I am English." Or as another said more bluntly, "I belong to the English. I will never return to the Boers."[34]

Clearly Butler's representation of Africans as slaves irrevocably "wounded" by Afrikaner rule is not borne out by powerful, self-possessed testimony such as this – a contradiction which suggests how unstable and how misrepresentative her account finally is. As importantly, Butler's defense of British imperial interests appears to be an idiosyncratic and unconventional argument unless we understand it in the context of women's campaigns against slavery and the feminist crusade against the C.D. Acts – organized social movements in which Victorian middle-class women assailed government policy but rarely if ever criticized the larger imperial civilizing mission which motivated it on both counts. What distinguishes *Native Races* from these earlier critiques, of course, is the call to war which it endorses. Butler's defense of British military aggression is intriguing precisely because it reveals how national allegiances underlay imperial commitments – because it demonstrates, in other words, the difficulties which embracing war for the sake of preserving the Empire might pose to a liberal imperial feminist. For despite her frustration over what she viewed as the British government's inability to understand that slavery was what was really at stake in the war, Butler did not particularly relish the idea that Britain was being viewed as the aggressor in the conflict either. As she reminded her readers, England was not the invader of the Transvaal, Kruger was – an interesting spin on the Great Trek (the movement of Dutch settlers from the Cape to the east and north, 1837–44) and its aftermath.[35] Nor did she wish to see British imperial interests held responsible for the outbreak of hostilities, even though she admitted that "England is now suffering for her past errors, extending over many years."

> The blood of her sons is being poured out like water on the soil of South Africa. Wounded hearts and desolated families at home are counted by tens of thousands. But it needs to be courageously stated by those who have looked a little below the surface that her faults have not been those which are attributed to her by a large proportion of European countries, and by a portion of her own people . . . these appear to attribute this war to a sudden impulse on her part of Imperial ambition and greed . . . there will have to be revision of this Verdict . . . the great error of England appears to have been a strange neglect, from time to time, of the true interests of her South African subjects, English, Dutch and Natives. There have been in her management of this great Colony alternations of apathy and inaction, with interference which was sometimes unwise and hasty. Some of her acts have been the result of ignorance, indifference, or superciliousness on the part of our rulers.[36]

In this passage, Butler offered a critique of British imperial action not by attacking its use of naked force or military pressure, but by pointing to its neglect of its colonial subjects in South Africa. This was, in the end, the great injury upon which her complaint was based; the nation's responsibility for down-trodden "native races" was, in turn, the wounded attachment which bound Britain inexorably to the black population there.

There is some hint that Britain was experiencing the vengeance of history in this war, but ultimately it was the Empire's responsibilities and not its failures that Butler emphasized, here as elsewhere in the narrative. Most remarkable perhaps is the way Butler subtly but surely imagined that the Dutch ought properly to be sheltered under the protective wing of English colonial "subjecthood" – thus indicating her belief that blacks, Afrikaners and poor whites should all submit to the strong but beneficent arm of British imperial sovereignty. Whether this was because she believed, as Todd Lee has argued about many novelists/writers of the period who wrote adventure stories about the war, that the Afrikaners had been corrupted by over a century of intimate contact with Africans in South Africa, is not clear from *Native Races*.[37] For Butler, it was the historical fact and cultural possession of the British Constitution which licensed the United Kingdom's rule over a variety of peoples and territories; any breach of its principles legitimated British intervention, especially where slavery was concerned. It might even be argued that it was their unabashed embrace of slavery which, for Butler, merited the Afrikaners' colonization by the British. Butler did not deny that there might be unfair, discriminatory or exploitative individual Britons in the Transvaal; thus she insisted, wherever Englishmen in South Africa had "denied to native labourers their hire (which is the essence of slavery), they have acted on their own, and illegally."[38] But her real and consistent purpose throughout *Native Races* was to draw attention *away* from the unsightly particulars of British rule so that the public's eye might be focused on the Afrikaners' slaveocratic practices – and so that Britons might better understand why Afrikaners and blacks alike should be subject to English law.

If Butler suggested that blacks and Boers should occupy the same status as colonial subjects in the eyes of imperial Britons, she did not envision that "native races" either would or should have social equality in the new, post-war South Africa. For her, equality was limited to "equality of all before the law" and did not extend to the social realm – "which belongs to another region of political ideas altogether."[39] There was not, in other words, to be compensation to blacks for the injuries suffered by their enslavement – except possibly through the redemptive act of political emancipation for British women, which would guarantee those same women a voice in parliament so that they could, presumably, stand up against slavery and other bodily injuries in the most important House in the Empire. In her discussion of what kinds of political rights natives might eventually be awarded, Butler revealed the liberal, evolutionary lens through which she viewed South African blacks, and how readily she turned them to objects of political shuffleboard when the question of their citizen/subject status was at issue.

Toward the end of *Native Races* she argued that natives did not want the franchise and in any event "it does not seem desirable that they should too early become 'full fledged voters'."[40] Besides, she observed, "in their hearts they hope for and desire simple legal justice." She was evidently unaware that growing numbers of Cape blacks had the vote, or else she chose to gloss this fact in order to make more sweeping observations about the democratization of the "native" electorate. In the meantime, her recommendation that an education test be applied, or "some proof of a certain amount of civilization and instruction attained" before they should be permitted to vote, foreshadowed later developments under what Shula Marks and Stanley Trapido have called the "conquest state" that emerged after the war.[41]

Butler was, in any event, deeply invested in the classic English liberal argument where political representation was concerned:

> to have to wait a little while for that does not seem from the English woman's point of view at least, a great hardship, when it is remembered how hard our agricultural labourers had to wait for that privilege, and that for more than fifty years English women have petitioned for it, and have not yet obtained it, although they are not, I believe, wholly uncivilized or uneducated.[42]

Of course, not even liberals and missionaries in nineteenth-century South Africa believed that the natives were "by nature either intelligent or law-abiding," much less that they should receive political rights.[43] Nonetheless Butler's reasoning, which invoked the gradual democratization of the British electorate through extra-parliamentary reform and liberal/elite accommodation (via the Reform Acts of 1832, 1867 and 1884), made her commitments to the promise of gradual evolution quite plain. Blacks in South Africa could not be allowed to gain the vote before British women because this would mean that the natural order of parliamentary enfranchisement as Butler and a number of Victorian feminists understood it – white women first, black men next – might be interrupted. Such rationales were to be used with increasing frequency in the first decades of the twentieth century as the question of votes for women took on a more imperial cast and as the possibility of enfranchising black men in white settler colonies became a more pressing question.[44] That Butler should use these arguments here, in defense not just of Britain's colonial power but of a war of colonial aggression, suggests how powerful the narrative of progress and the promise of liberal inclusion could be to those on the outside of parliamentary political power in fin-de-siècle Britain – particularly when imperial destiny was perceived to be at stake.

Butler's biographers have puzzled over the position she took on the Boer War, arguing that it was so out of step with both her lifelong commitments *and* her relations with those to whom she was otherwise politically sympathetic that it almost defies explanation.[45] Barbara Caine has recently argued that in the course of her work for the Abolitionist (i.e. the anti-Contagious Diseases Acts) Federation, Butler had encountered so much European anti-British feeling in the 1890s that she was driven into a defense of the war out of a long-frustrated patriotism.[46] Butler's private correspondence bears this reading out: one letter in particular suggests that she might have taken up the stance she did to signal to the membership that her views and theirs were diverging on a number of important subjects.[47] Butler also saw South Africa as an "opening" offered to her by God in her old age: "He seems to want this old skeleton to buckle on her armour again, and the armour rattles rusty on the old fleshless ribs."[48] But even these interpretations are insufficient in light of the very public traditions of anti-slavery and colonial sympathy through which Butler, if not the middle-class Victorian women's movement in general, tried to articulate feminism's special, historical place in British imperial culture across the long nineteenth century – traditions through which some of them argued, with increasing enthusiasm in the first two decades of the twentieth century, for representation as a reward for the wounded attachments which bound them, however tenuously, to the British imperial state.

In this sense Butler's position was not really peculiar, but was instead the rather predictable outcome of her personal experience of forty years of abolitionist campaigning for the good of the imperial nation-state which she wished to reform, but in whose basic goodness, if not greatness, she passionately believed. By staking a position that was simultaneously anti-slavery and pro-empire, Butler was, quite simply, remaking early slavery idioms so that they served the variety of causes (nation, race, empire, progress) to which Victorian feminists had traditionally been dedicated. The extent to which her embrace of empire was typical of late-Victorian culture more generally should not be overlooked either. For despite an active Stop-the-War pamphlet campaign and the commitment of two major metropolitan newspapers to the pro-Boer effort, there was a decided lack of anti-imperial opposition to the war – a phenomenon that places Butler squarely in the late-Victorian mainstream, even if her position ended up seeming peculiar in the eyes of her lifelong, mostly liberal and Liberal party fellows. Nor should we underestimate the ways in which the war split the Liberals and the Victorian left, in complex ways and along a variety of ideological lines that were not easily reconciled and in fact contributed to the refashioning of liberal politics in the first two decades of the twentieth century.[49] Butler's insistence on the "wounded attachments" created by black slaves was decidedly at odds with many liberals' equally evocative attachment to "white" women and children – thus signaling a shift in fin-de-siècle liberal values which anticipated the post-war period with its emphasis on eugenic citizenship, national fitness, and racial motherhood.[50]

If Butler was out of step with these ideological currents, it was because she represented a kind of liberal feminist politics which was becoming obsolete by century's end. Her insistence on the trope of abolition to advance the cause of war in South Africa is evidence both of the passing of her brand of rights politics *and* of anti-slavery's lingering rhetorical purchase – especially for a woman like Butler who was devoted to reforming the kind of "singular iniquity" against personhood that slavery represented. It also reminds us of how easily political discourses can mobilize violence – feminist discourses included – when they are motivated by the kind of liberal protectionist ethos that requires persistent "states of injury" for its own legitimation. Butler's willingness to invoke the injuries of slavery, and what's more, her insistence upon them as a justification for war and a pretext for white women's citizenship, makes clear the kinds of political affiliations that might be claimed from the state through reference to the suffering of others. This classically liberal/imperialist maneuver appealed to the conscience of the imperial nation. As Wendy Brown has observed for late modernity more generally, such an appeal required that someone in Butler's position share the nation's political ideals and hence too that she reproduce some of "the mechanisms and configurations of power" it stood for as she sought identification with it.[51] Considering that Butler had devoted her life to liberal crusades to keep the state out of the lives of women and the poor, her commitment to British intervention in South Africa is a fruitful example of how imperial commitments could complicate political loyalties, rendering historical subjects at times unrecognizable, though culturally intelligible nonetheless. To be sure, Butler's petition fell on deaf ears. Nor did the "states of injury" argument in all its twentieth-century variation end up securing British women the vote in either 1918 or a decade later. At the same time, Josephine Butler's defense of "native races" and the Boer War is a reminder that the tension between feminists' longing to share in power and their desire to transform its very bases has a rich and vexed past – a past shaped not just by the historical coincidence of the women's movement with modern liberalism but also by its particular collision, and its peculiar collusion, with Western imperial ideologies and their regimes.

Notes

1 This essay was originally published as "States of Injury: Josephine Butler on Slavery, Citizenship, and the Boer War" in *Social Politics*, 1998, vol. 5, no. 3, pp. 338–61 and is reprinted with the permission of Oxford University Press. It has benefited from close readings by Judith Allen, Leora Auslander, Frances Gouda, Rob Gregg, Nicoletta Gullace, Madhavi Kale, Ian Fletcher, Todd Lee, Philippa Levine, Laura Mayhall and Doug Peers.

In keeping with late twentieth-century standards, and at the suggestion of a number of scholars, I use the term "Afrikaner" instead of "Boer" – except in reference to the "Boer War" itself, and in those instances where changing contemporary usage would significantly alter its historically-specific cultural meaning(s).

2 W. Brown, *States of Injury: Power and Freedom in Late Modernity*, Princeton, Princeton University Press, 1995, p. 1 and p. 75.

3 I distinguish between "English" women and "British" women's suffrage here in order to gesture towards the complex relationship between London-based feminists and their Scots, Irish and Welsh "sisters." See C. Midgley, *Women Against Slavery: The British Campaigns*, New York, Routledge, 1992; V. Ware, *Beyond the Pale: White Women, Racism and History*, London, Verso, 1992; A. Burton, *Burdens of History: British Feminists, Indian Women and Imperial Culture, 1865–1915*, Chapel Hill, University of North Carolina Press, 1994; L. Leneman, *A Guid Cause: The Women's Suffrage Movement in Scotland*, Aberdeen, Aberdeen University Press, 1991; and R. Owens, *Smashing Times: A History of the Irish Women's Suffrage Movement, 1889–1922*, Dublin, Attic Press, 1992.

4 E.P. Thompson, *The Making of the English Working-Class*, New York, Vintage, 1966 and R. Gregg and M. Kale, "The Empire and Mr Thompson," *Economic and Political Weekly*, 1997, vol. 32, no. 36 (September 6), pp. 2273–88.

5 L. Mayhall, "Family, State, and Citizenship: Suffragist Discourse and Canonical Texts, 1869–1914," unpublished paper provided courtesy of the author.

6 I underscore "could" here because I am not suggesting these connections are universal or ineluctable, simply that Butler's text represents one articulation of them.

7 See E. Williams, *Capitalism and Slavery*, Chapel Hill, University of North Carolina Press, 1944/1994; and M. Kale, *Fragments of Empire, Capital, Anti-slavery and Indian Indentured Labor Migration*, Philadelphia, University of Pennsylvania Press, 1999.

8 See M. Valverde, *The Age of Light, Soap and Water, Moral Reform in English Canada 1885–1925*, Toronto, McLelland and Stewart, 1991 and P. Levine, "The White Slave Trade and the British Empire," forthcoming in vol. 18, *Criminal Justice History*.

9 See Burton, op. cit., ch. 5.

10 See P. Krebs, "'The Last of the Gentlemen's Wars', Women in the Boer War Concentration Camp Controversy," *History Workshop Journal*, 1992, vol. 33, pp. 38–56 and E. Hobhouse, *The Brunt of the War and Where it Fell*, London, Methuen, 1902.

11 See Krebs, op. cit.; B. Roberts, *Those Bloody Women, Three Heroines of the Boer War*, London, John Murray, 1991; and R. van Reenen Rykie (ed.), *Emily Hobhouse, Boer War Letters*. Cape Town, Human and Rousseau, 1984.

12 Krebs, op. cit., p. 38 and R. Price, *An Imperial War and the British Working Class, Working-Class Attitudes and Reactions to the Boer War, 1899–1902*, London, Routledge and Kegan Paul, 1972, ch. 4.

13 Quoted in B. Farwell, *The Great Anglo-Boer War*, New York, W.W. Norton, 1990, p. xi.

14 Josephine Butler Autograph Letter Collection (JBALC), Butler to ? October ? 1899 (letter fragment).

15 JBALC, Butler to Miss Forsaith, January 17, 1900.

16 JBALC, Butler to Miss Forsaith, February 12, 1901.

17 See J. R. Walkowitz, *Prostitution and Victorian Society*, Cambridge, Cambridge University Press, 1980.

18 Burton, op. cit., ch. 5.

19 JBALC, Butler to Miss Forsaith, July 1, 1902.

20 See S. Koss (ed.), *The Pro-Boers, Anatomy of an Anti-War Movement*, Chicago, University of Chicago Press, 1973, pp. 32–3 and J. S. Galbraith, "The Pamphlet Campaign on the Boer War," *Journal of Modern History*, 1952, vol. 24, pp. 111–26.

21 For debates about what causes to privilege in accounting for the outbreak of war see A.N. Porter, *The Origins of the South African War, Joseph Chamberlain and the Diplomacy of Imperialism 1895–99*, Manchester, Manchester University Press, 1980, and his essay, "The South African War (1899–1902), Context and Motive Reconsidered," *Journal of African History*, 1990, vol. 31, pp. 43–57.
22 J. Butler, *Native Races and the War*, London, Gay and Bird, 1900, p. 1.
23 Burton, op. cit., ch. 5.
24 Butler, *Native Races*, p. 12.
25 Ibid.
26 Butler, op. cit., p. 108; see also p. 151.
27 Butler, op. cit., p. 63. See also T. Lee, "Imperial Imaginings, British Stereotypes of Afrikaners during the South African War," *Southern African Historical Journal*, conference proceedings, forthcoming, and provided courtesy of the author.
28 JBALC, Butler to Millicent Garrett Fawcett, July 13, 1900.
29 Butler, op. cit., p. 32.
30 Lee, op. cit. and "The Image of the Enemy, British Stereotypes of the Afrikaner during the South African War, 1899–1902," M.A. Thesis, Georgia State University, 1993, provided courtesy of the author. See also M. Streak, *The Afrikaner as Viewed by the English , 1795–1854*, Cape Town, C. Struik, Ltd., 1974.
31 S.B. Spies, "Women and the War," in Peter Warwick (ed.), *The South African War, The Anglo-Boer War, 1899–1902*, London, Longman, 1980, p. 177.
32 Butler, op. cit., p. 32.
33 P. Warwick, "Black People and the War," in Warwick, op. cit., pp. 186–209; his *Black People and the South African War*, Cambridge University Press, 1983; B. Willan, *Sol Plaatje, South African Nationalist, 1876–1932*, Berkeley, University of California Press, 1984; and S. Trapido, "African Divisional Politics in the Cape Colony, 1884 to 1910," *Journal of African History*, 1968, vol. 9, pp. 79–98.
34 Butler, op. cit., p. 9.
35 Ibid. p. 129.
36 Ibid. p. 21.
37 Lee, "Imperial Imaginings."
38 Butler, op. cit., p. 2.
39 Ibid. p. 132.
40 Ibid. p. 134.
41 S. Marks and S. Trapido, "Lord Milner and the South African State," *History Workshop*, 1979, vol. 8, p. 72.
42 Butler, op. cit., p. 134.
43 See Farwell, op. cit., p. 23, n. 1.
44 Burton, op. cit., ch. 6.
45 See G. Petrie, *A Singular Iniquity, The Campaigns of Josephine Butler*, New York, Viking Press, 1971, pp. 283–4.
46 B. Caine, *Victorian Feminists*, New York, Oxford University Press, 1992, pp. 173–5.
47 JBALC, Butler to Millicent Garrett Fawcett, June 20, 1899.
48 JBALC, Butler to Miss Forsaith, July 1, 1902.
49 See Price, op. cit., especially chapter 1; and Koss, op. cit., p. xxxii and following.
50 See A. Davin, "Imperialism and Motherhood," *History Workshop Journal*, 1978, vol. 5, pp. 9–65.
51 Brown, op. cit., p. 1.

[6]

African Resistance and Center Party Recalcitrance in the Reichstag Colonial Debates of 1905/06

John S. Lowry

On May 26, 1906, as German chancellor Bernhard von Bülow rested on the North Sea coast recuperating from a recent physical collapse, his administration suffered a resounding triple defeat in the Reichstag at the hands of his hitherto indispensable Catholic political partners in the Center party. In the course of a single day, the Centrists rejected the military justification for a railroad in wartorn Southwest Africa, ruled out further government compensation for settler losses in the Herero and Nama Uprisings, and then blocked the elevation of the Colonial Department of the Foreign Office to the status of an independent imperial office. Moreover, the intense interest of Kaiser Wilhelm II in the passage of each of these colonial measures rendered the Center's decisive contribution to the rout acutely embarrassing for the chancellor. Faced seven months later with a similar Centrist refusal to authorize more than twenty of the latest twenty-nine million marks toward suppression of the Nama, Bülow would then dissolve the Reichstag, putting a definitive end to nearly a decade of government-Center parliamentary cooperation.

This latter decision by the chancellor has correctly been attributed in large measure to his need to regain his dwindling credibility with the Kaiser.[1] Preoccupation with this fact, however, has long tended to lead to broad generalizations minimizing the pertinence of colonial issues to the parliamentary clash even as the colonial crisis itself has often been causally dissociated from African actions and ascribed rather to Matthias Erzberger's investigative

[1]Berckheim to Marschall von Bieberstein, Dec. 14, 1906, Report 31, Großherzogliche Badische Gesandtschaft Berlin (BdGB), Abt. 49/2039, Generallandesarchiv Karlsruhe (GLAK). Karl Bachem, Dec. 20, 1906, Note, Nachlaß Bachem, 259: 8, Historisches Archiv der Stadt Köln (HASK). Joachim Haferkorn, *Bülows Kampf um das Reichskanzleramt im Jahre 1906* (Würzburg-Aumühle: Druckerei und Verlag wissenschaftlicher Werke, 1939), passim. George Crothers, *The German Elections of 1907* (New York: Columbia University Press, 1941), 97 f. Wilfried Loth, *Katholiken im Kaiserreich. Der politische Katholizismus in der Krise des wilhelminischen Deutschlands* (Düsseldorf: Droste, 1984), 118 f. Katharine Anne Lerman, *The Chancellor as Courtier: Bernhard von Bülow and the Governance of Germany, 1900–1909* (New York: Cambridge University Press, 1990), 127–166.

initiative.[2] First to challenge the problematic Eurocentricity of such an interpretation, Wolfgang Reinhard attempted in 1978 to reconcile his subscription to Hans-Ulrich Wehler's likewise Eurocentric thesis of social imperialism with his own intent to recognize Africans "not as raw material, but as active agents of German history."[3] Unfortunately, despite Reinhard's call for a "decolonization" of the history of the crisis, the most recent domestic political histories directly concerned with this period have continued to portray the African contribution to the government-Center breach as at most contextual.[4] While

[2]An early explicit statement of this traditional view of the dissolution may be found in Hans Pehl's 1934 dissertation: "[T]he ultimate and decisive reason for the dissolution was not the conflict in the colonial question; rather, this was only the external occasion for things that lay far deeper," which Pehl proceeds to identify as Bülow's own weakened position as chancellor. Hans Pehl, "Die deutsche Kolonialpolitik und das Zentrum (1884–1914)" (Ph.D. diss., Johann Wolfgang Goethe-Universität Frankfurt a.M., 1934), 86. Unlike Pehl, George Crothers acknowledges the link between the weakening of Bülow's position with the Kaiser and the Center's struggle with the colonial administration, but he makes no association of the latter with reverberations from African resistance. Crothers, *German Elections*, 98. Klaus Epstein essentially ascribes the entire colonial crisis to Erzberger's political acumen and moral enthusiasm. Klaus Epstein, "Erzberger and the German Colonial Scandals, 1905–1910," *English Historical Review* 74 (1959): 637. John Zeender is somewhat more attentive to the impact of the Southwest and East African uprisings upon government-Center relations, yet he is inconsistent in his recognition of the enormity of the costs involved. John Zeender, *The German Center Party, 1890–1906* (Philadelphia: American Philosophical Society, 1976), 99.

[3]Wolfgang Reinhard, "'Sozialimperialismus' oder 'Entkolonisierung der Historie'? Kolonialkrise und 'Hottentottenwahlen,' 1904–1907," *Historisches Jahrbuch* 97/98 (1978): 391. Reinhard aims to correct Wehler's one-sided emphasis upon Eckart Kehr's thesis of the "primacy of domestic politics" and the associated concept of "social imperialism." The latter theory attributes imperialism to a manipulative strategy of domestic control by a nation's ruling elite through "the diversion outwards of internal tensions and forces of change in order to preserve the social and political status quo" at home. Hans-Ulrich Wehler, *Bismarck und der Imperialismus* (Cologne: Kiepenheuer und Witsch, 1969), 115, quoted in English translation in Geoff Eley, "Defining social imperialism: use and abuse of an idea," *Social History* 3 (October 1976): 265. Reinhard, "'Sozialimperialismus' oder 'Entkolonisierung'?," 384–389. Generally averse to theories of imperialism underscoring the contributions of actors on the colonial periphery, Wehler has preferred to see the colonial controversy of late 1906 as the key nationalist diversionary "opportunity" seized by Bülow to facilitate the electoral integration of his awkward new bloc of parties. From this premise, it has been implicitly necessary that the colonial issue not also constitute a substantive *cause* of the domestic political crisis from which the chancellor was attempting to escape by social imperialist means. Hans-Ulrich Wehler, *Deutsche Gesellschaftsgeschichte*, 3. Band, *Von der "Deutschen Doppelrevolution" bis zum Beginn des Ersten Weltkrieges 1849–1914* (Munich: C. H. Beck, 1995), 985–989, 1009, 1137–1140. Wehler, "Bismarcks Imperialismus 1862–1890," in *Krisenherde des Kaiserreichs 1871–1918. Studien zur deutschen Sozial- und Verfassungsgeschichte* (Göttingen: Vandenhoeck & Ruprecht, 1970), 138, 149–161. Wehler, *The German Empire 1871–1918*, trans. Kim Traynor (New York: Berg, 1997), 171–179. Dirk Stegmann, *Die Erben Bismarcks. Parteien und Verbände in der Spätphase des Wilhelminischen Deutschlands—Sammlungspolitik 1897–1918* (Köln: Kiepenheuer & Witsch, 1970), 105–113. Reinhard's own attempt to reconcile peripheral and social imperialist interpretations falters on the logical incompatibility of the two models. He soon returns to his original social imperialist predilection, stranding most of his carefully marshaled African causes without clearly defined German effects. Reinhard, "'Sozialimperialismus' oder 'Entkolonisierung'?," 402–412.

[4]Katharine Anne Lerman, for example, correctly emphasizes the importance of the defeat of the Colonial Office and the Podbielski-Fischer Affair in the erosion of the chancellor's position with the Kaiser, but makes scant connection between these factors and events in the colonies. Lerman, *Chancellor as Courtier*, 127–166, esp. 145 ff., 153–157, 163 ff. Christian Leitzbach looks to Bülow's

German social, cultural, and literary historians have more recently been making substantial advances in an analogous "decolonization" project within their disciplines, discussion of the agency of colonial populations in German domestic political history *per se* has remained largely dormant for twenty years.[5]

This paper therefore re-initiates exploration of the question of the role played by African resistance in driving a wedge between the Bülow administration and the Catholic Center party. In particular, I would argue that already by early 1906 African resistance movements had called attention to such a wide array of enormously expensive and morally repugnant issues that Centrists of all persuasions felt compelled to challenge Berlin with a resolutely independent colonial political line. Naturally, in this challenge the Centrists did not all tack at the same angle. Indeed, the strain of the colonial crisis also exposed internal party discord between the chiefly Prussian bourgeois and aristocratic party elders on the one hand, and the delegation's generally more South German populist wing on the

---

quite questionable memoirs for confirmation of the speculations of Friedrich Naumann and Karl Bachem about the origins of the dissolution. On this basis he concurs with Pehl: "It has thereby been established beyond doubt that the colonial scandals and the rejection of the supplementary budget were only a pretext for von Bülow to part with a troublesome Reichstag majority." Christian Leitzbach, *Matthias Erzberger. Ein kritischer Beobachter des Wilhelminischen Reiches 1895–1914* (Frankfurt a.M.: Peter Lang, 1998), 358–360, 363 f. Likewise, in a work that otherwise leans heavily toward the anti-Kehrite thesis of "creeping parliamentarization," Volker Schulte sees the Reichstag dissolution as a social imperialist diversionary tactic and the colonial issue as correspondingly incidental. Volker Schulte, "Die Reichstagswahlen 1907. Parlamentarierungsforderungen [*sic*] und interfraktionelle Allianzen von Zentrum und Sozialdemokratie" (Ph.D. diss., Universität Göttingen, 1989), 135. In one noteworthy exception to this pattern, Winfried Becker recognizes a vital African contribution to the German domestic crisis in the serious fiscal disruption that the Herero and Nama Uprisings unleashed upon the Reich; however, he does not integrate the role of any other Africans. Winfried Becker, "Kulturkampf als Vorwand. Die Kolonialwahlen von 1907 und das Problem der Parlamentarisierung des Reiches," *Historisches Jahrbuch* 106 (1986): 59–84, especially 61 ff., 83. Also reprinted in Johannes Horstmann, ed., *Die Verschränkung von Innen-, Konfessions- und Kolonialpolitik im Deutschen Reich vor 1914* (Paderborn: Katholische Akademie Schwerte, 1987). In a recent essay on the Reichstag dissolution and the elections of 1907, Ulrich van der Heyden has likewise endorsed Reinhard's argument that Africans had become "active agents" in German history through provocation of the colonial crisis. Still, van der Heyden does not bolster this point with further evidence, and, at times, his account even appears to be leaning in the opposite direction. Ulrich van der Heyden, "Die 'Hottentottenwahlen' von 1907" in *Völkermord in Deutsch-Südwestafrika. Der Kolonialkrieg (1904–1908) in Namibia und seine Folgen*, ed. Jürgen Zimmerer and Joachim Zeller (Berlin: Christoph Links Verlag, 2003), 97–102.

[5] Notable works in this vein in social, cultural, and literary history include Sara Friedrichsmeyer, Sara Lennox, and Susanne Zantop, eds., *The Imperialist Imagination: German Colonialism and Its Legacy* (Ann Arbor: University of Michigan Press, 1998); Lora Wildenthal, *German Women for Empire, 1884–1945* (Durham: Duke University Press, 2001); Pascal Grosse, *Kolonialismus, Eugenik und bürgerliche Gesellschaft in Deutschland 1850–1918* (Frankfurt a.M./New York: Campus, 2000); Andrew Zimmerman, *Anthropology and Antihumanism in Imperial Germany* (Chicago: University of Chicago Press, 2001); Daniel Walther, *Creating Germans Abroad: Cultural Policies and National Identity in Namibia* (Athens: Ohio University Press, 2002); Krista O'Donnell, Renate Bridenthal, and Nancy Reagin, eds., *The Heimat Abroad: The Boundaries of Germanness* (Ann Arbor: University of Michigan Press, 2005); and Bradley D. Naranch, "'Colonized Body,' 'Oriental Machine': Debating Race, Railroads, and the Politics of Reconstruction in Germany and East Africa, 1906–1910," *Central European History* 33 (2000): 299–338.

other, comprised largely of farmers and lesser clergy yet enhanced by two smaller elements, artisans and trade union activists.[6] At times the more governmental party leaders, many of them judges or lawyers, would take the administration's part against the insistence of the populists on the protection and expansion of the Reichstag's parliamentary and colonial legislative prerogatives. Moreover, these jurist leaders were far more concerned than the populists by the ominous surge of anticlericalism in Germany since the partial repeal of the Anti-Jesuit Law in March 1904. While the young Swabian newspaper editor and union activist Matthias Erzberger led the populists in unrestrained attacks upon the Colonial Department, the overworked and ailing senior Centrists warned in vain that an overly conspicuous exertion of Catholic parliamentary muscle would fan the flames of anticlericalism to new heights. This in turn might well endanger the party's strategic position by undermining the chancellor's credibility with the Kaiser.[7]

Notwithstanding such instances of internal party friction, however, Centrists of all persuasions still displayed remarkable consistency in their determination in late 1905 and early 1906 to secure greater fiscal responsibility in colonial spending and in their efforts to preclude further costly rebellions by limiting administrative excesses in the colonies through the establishment of direct parliamentary oversight and legal safeguards protecting the civil rights of non-Europeans. This far-reaching Centrist campaign to assert parliamentary authority in colonial affairs was driven chiefly by the fiscal and political consequences of widespread African resistance movements. The considerable momentum this dynamic had achieved by May 1906 sheds light on the similarly implacable stance the Center would subsequently adopt the following December, an intransigence without which Chancellor von Bülow would have had neither motive nor occasion to dissolve the Reichstag.[8]

* * *

[6]Loth, *Katholiken im Kaiserreich*, 39–51, 81–113. Max Schwarz, *MdR: Biographisches Handbuch der Reichstage* (Hannover: Verlag für Literatur und Zeitgeschehen, 1965). Bernd Haunfelder, *Reichstagsabgeordnete der deutschen Zentrumspartei 1871–1933. Biographisches Handbuch und historische Photographien* (Düsseldorf: Droste Verlag, 1999).

[7]Bachem to [Franz Bachem?], Dec. 4, 1905, Nachlaß Bachem, 239, HASK. Bachem, Mar. 21, 1906, Note, Nachlaß Bachem, 238, HASK. Bachem, Dec. 15, 20, 1906, Notes, Nachlaß Bachem, 259: 8–9, HASK. Hertling to Anna von Hertling, Apr. 4, 1906, Nachlaß Hertling, 17: 51, Bundesarchiv Koblenz (BAK). "Parlamentarisches—Die Krankheit des Abgeordneten Prinz Arenberg," *Germania*, Mar. 1, 1906, Nr. 48. Karl Bachem, *Vorgeschichte, Geschichte und Politik der deutschen Zentrumspartei* (Köln: Verlag J. P. Bachem, 1929–1932), 6: 318–330, 337, 342–350. Rolf Kiefer, *Karl Bachem, 1858–1945. Politiker und Historiker des Zentrums* (Mainz: Matthias-Grünewald-Verlag, 1989), 171–174. Helmut Walser Smith, *German Nationalism and Religious Conflict: Culture, Ideology, Politics, 1870–1914* (Princeton: Princeton University Press, 1995), 139 f.

[8]The parameters of the present essay are limited to the impact of African resistance upon government-Center relations during the 1905/06 parliamentary season. Accordingly, I will not venture here beyond May 1906 into an account of the Reichstag dissolution itself, nor will the present space permit delving much into the critical relationship between Bülow and Wilhelm II. For a discussion of the impact of African resistance movements upon these latter questions, please refer to the

No fewer than six distinct insurrections broke out in German-occupied Africa during the period from late 1903 to mid-1905, and several of these were tenacious enough to persist even into 1907. Three of the six erupted upon Southwest African soil alone. In the extreme southeast of that colony, the Bondelswart Nama rose in October 1903 to protest German territorial encroachment and to defend their captain's jurisdiction from an overzealous district official.[9] With the colonial troops thus engaged in the distant south, the Herero in the region around Windhoek forswore their prior toleration of encroachment, expropriation, and brutality and carried out a massacre of 123 whites in January 1904.[10] Third, similar grievances in the south, along with the fear of imminent disarmament, precipitated the inauguration of a general Nama uprising the following October.[11] Although by late 1904 the German colonial troops had condemned most of the Herero to death by dehydration in the Omaheke desert, the costs they had imposed on Berlin would survive as a matter of public debate into 1905/06.[12] Meanwhile, the Nama guerrillas long eluded defeat, regularly attacking the German supply lines that extended hundreds of kilometers over mountains and deserts back to Lüderitzbucht, Windhoek, and the Cape colony. Indeed, this vulnerability kept the ratio of German support troops to front-line soldiers at three

final chapter of my forthcoming book: John S. Lowry, *Big Swords, Jesuits, and Bondelswarts: Wilhelmine Imperialism, Overseas Resistance, and German Political Catholicism, 1897–1906* (Boston: Brill Academic Publishers, 2013).

[9]Leutwein to Colonial Department, Sept. 28, 1904, Report 917, Enclosure III, Akten des Reichskolonialamts (RKA), 2116: 149, Bundesarchiv Potsdam, collections now at the Bundesarchiv Lichterfelde (BAP/L). König to Solf, Jan. 26, 1904, Nachlaß Solf, 25: 9 f., BAK. Horst Drechsler, *Südwestafrika unter deutscher Kolonialherrschaft. Der Kampf der Herero und Nama gegen den deutschen Imperialismus (1884–1915)*, 2d ed. (Berlin—East: Akademie Verlag, 1984), 115–119.

[10]Leutwein to Colonial Department, Mar. 14, 1904, Report 153, RKA, 2114: 107–111, BAP/L; and May 17, 1904, Report 395; Rohrbach to Leutwein, May 28, 1904, RKA, 2115: 63, 65 f., 69, 109 ff., BAP/L. Leutwein to Colonial Department, Sept. 28, 1904, Report 917, Enclosure III; Leutwein, "Verzeichnis derjenigen Weißen, gegen welche in den Jahren 1902, 1903 und 1904 ein Verfahren wegen Gewalttätigkeit gegen Eingeborene vor dem kaiserlichen Bezirksgericht Swakopmund eingeleitet wurde," Sept. 30, 1904, RKA, 2116: 147–149, 171–174, BAP/L. Stuebel, Jan. 30, 1905, *Stenographische Berichte über die Verhandlungen des Deutschen Reichstags* (RTSB), 4110A. Theodor Leutwein, *Elf Jahre Gouverneur in Deutsch-Südwestafrika*, 2nd ed. (Berlin: Ernst Siegfried Mittler und Sohn, 1907), 465–484. Drechsler, *Südwestafrika*, 131–171.

[11]Leutwein, *Elf Jahre*, 454–464. Drechsler, *Südwestafrika*, 171–220.

[12]Großer Generalstab, Kriegsgeschichtliche Abteilung, *Die Kämpfe der deutschen Schutztruppe in Südwestafrika* (Berlin 1906, 1907), 1: 199, 204 f., 208, 210, 214. Conrad Rust, *Krieg und Frieden in Hereroland. Aufzeichnungen aus dem Kriegsjahre 1904* (Leipzig: L. A. Kittler, 1905), 385. Kurd Schwabe, *Im deutschen Diamantenlande. Deutsch-Südwestafrika von der Errichtung der deutschen Herrschaft bis zur Gegenwart (1884–1910)* (Berlin: Ernst Siegfried Mittler und Sohn, 1910), 243, 320 f., 329, 336, 343 f. Bernhard Fürst von Bülow, *Denkwürdigkeiten*, ed. Franz von Stockhammern (Berlin: Ullstein, 1930), 2: 21. Drechsler, *Südwestafrika*, 156, 158 f., 163 ff., 167, 188–193, 197 f., 213 f.

to one even as the Nama gradually surrendered.[13] As a result, by December 1906 the total of past and immediately foreseeable expenses involved in suppressing the Herero and Nama Uprisings would reach 456 million marks, the mathematical equivalent in 1906 of the cost of constructing twelve German dreadnoughts.[14]

Contemporary uprisings elsewhere in the German colonial empire were far less expensive, but nevertheless substantial. Within ten days of the outbreak of war with the Herero, the Anyang of northwest Cameroon decimated an armed expedition directed against their rubber trade monopoly and began a successful offensive against German positions in the Cross valley.[15] Likewise, isolated armed resistance to the Gesellschaft Süd-Kamerun in the Njong and Dscha valleys in late 1904 swelled by spring 1905 into an arc of multiethnic insurgency extending across southern Cameroon from Jukaduma to Lolodorf.[16] Finally, in July 1905 embitterment over extensive forced labor, taxation, and

[13]Budget for Southwest Africa (BSWA), 1906; Draft bill (DB), Second Supplementary Budget (SupB) 1905, Nov. 28, 1905, *Reichstags-Drucksachen* (RDS) 24; Arenberg, Deimling, Seitz, Dec. 12, 1905, *Protokolle der Kommission für den Reichshaushalts-Etat* (ProtBc); Deimling, Dec. 13, 1905, ProtBc; DB, Fourth SupB 1905, Dec. 20, 1905, RDS 152, Akten des Reichstags (RTA), 1097: 198 f., 208 f., 245, 250, 280, BAP/L. Hohenlohe-Langenburg, Dec. 2, 1905, RTSB, 79D–80B. Hohenlohe-Langenburg, May 26, 1906, RTSB, 3527C–3528A. Deimling, Dec. 2, 1905, RTSB, 87B/D. Deimling, May 26, 1906, RTSB, 3538B/C. Paasche, Report from Subcommittee, Feb. 23, 1906, ProtBc; Seitz, Jacobs, May 23, 1906, ProtBc, RTA, 1098: 107, 258 f., BAP/L. "Denkschrift über den Verlauf des Aufstands in Südwestafrika (Fortsetzung)," Nov. 24, 1905, RDS 5; ibid., Feb. 2, 1906, RDS 202; DB, Complementary Budget (ComB) 1906, May 19, 1906, RDS 474, Appendix II, MA 95403, Bayrisches Hauptstaatsarchiv (ByHSA). "Kubub-Keetmannshop [*sic*]," Colonial Department to Bülow, Oct. 22, 1906, Memorandum, Akten der Reichskanzlei (RKzA), 926: 132–135, BAP/L. Drechsler, *Südwestafrika*, 187–193.

[14]The Reichstag had authorized all 4.6 million marks requested for the Southwest African campaign for budget year 1903, 106.8 of 109.3 million for 1904, and 117.1 of 118.7 million for 1905. As of June 1, 1906, however, it had approved only 84 of the 119.3 million that the government had thus far requested for that budget year. To the total of all the funds actually authorized as of June (312.5 million) was then added the government's December 1906 estimates of its budget overruns for 1904 and 1905 (30 million) along with the funds requested in the two supplementary budgets for 1906 (38.1 million), the budget for 1907 (66.6 million), and the anticipated complementary budget for 1907 (8.6 million). Space prohibits the listing here of each of the relevant budgets for Southwest Africa, but the collection may be found in RTA, 1095–1099, BAP/L. See also Stengel, Dec. 5, 1906, ProtBc; Quade, Dec. 6, 1906, Statement, Enclosure to the Protocol of the 67th Session of the Budget Committee, RTA, 1099: 39, 41, 43 f., BAP/L. Stengel, Nov. 30, 1906, RTSB, 4044C–4045A. Schaedler, Nov. 28, 1906, RTSB, 3974C. Erzberger, Nov. 30, 1906, RTSB, 4038A/B. Spahn, Reporter, Dec. 13, 1906, RTSB, 4358D. Peter-Christian Witt gives the estimated construction costs of a dreadnought in the 1906 naval budget as 36.5 million marks. Peter-Christian Witt, *Die Finanzpolitik des Deutschen Reiches von 1903 bis 1913. Eine Studie zur Innenpolitik des Wilhelminischen Deutschland* (Lübeck und Hamburg: Matthiesen Verlag, 1970), 143.

[15]Johanda Ballhaus, "Die Landkonzessionsgesellschaften," in *Kamerun unter deutscher Kolonialherrschaft. Studien*, ed. Helmuth Stoecker (Berlin—East: VEB Deutscher Verlag der Wissenschaften, 1968), 2: 150–161.

[16]Rudi Kaeselitz, "Kolonialeroberung und Widerstandskampf in Südkamerun (1884–1907)," in ibid., 2: 46–54. Adolf Rüger, "Die Duala und die Kolonialmacht 1884–1914. Eine Studie über die historischen Ursprünge des afrikanischen Antikolonialismus," in ibid., 2: 201 f.

brutality culminated in the outbreak of the millenarian Maji Maji Uprising in East Africa among the Matumbi and Ngindo, whose call to arms was answered by many peoples throughout the southern third of the colony.[17] As a consequence of the remarkable coincidence and extent of these colonial insurrections from 1903 to 1905, both the financial burden of imperialism and the political stakes surrounding German colonial policy increased by leaps and bounds.

The escalating importance of colonial issues in German politics after 1903 was likewise fueled by the more peaceful efforts of West Africans to improve their lot. Beginning in late 1902, Anago and Dahomey villagers in Togo sought to make District Official Geo Schmidt of Atakpamẽ accountable for overworking the populace, levying excessive fines, unduly confiscating livestock, flogging men raw, and sexually abusing a minor. Catholic missionary championship of this cause then precipitated an explosive confrontation with the anticlerical Lome administration, including a 1903 nocturnal police raid on the Atakpame mission station of the Societas Verbi Divini (SVD) and the imprisonment for three weeks of both of its priests. As the details of the affair finally emerged in Germany in 1906, the combination of the original grievous crimes against the Togolese with the injustices committed against their German Catholic advocates would render the so-called "*Kulturkampf in Togo*" a major source of Centrist implacability vis-à-vis the government.[18]

The party's obduracy was then only reinforced by the harsh response of the Cameroon administration to the 1905 Reichstag petition of the Bonambela Duala. King Dika Akwa and two dozen other Bonambela Duala chieftains organized a petition to the Reichstag in June 1905, demanding the recall of the entire regime of Governor Jesko von Puttkamer. Basing this appeal upon some two dozen grievances against German officials, the petition sought an investigation of the Buea administration's razing of Duala homes, its imposition of the head tax, its failure to remunerate forced labor, and cases of officially condoned murder, cruel floggings, and abuses of office in securing concubines.[19] The

[17]John Iliffe, *Tanganyika under German Rule, 1905–1912* (Cambridge: Cambridge University Press, 1969), 9–29. G. C. K. Gwassa and John Iliffe, eds., *Records of the Maji Maji Rising* (Dar es Salaam: East African Publishing House, 1968). Judith Listowel, *The Making of Tanganyika* (London: Chatto & Windus, 1965), 34–44.

[18]The Reichskolonialamt collection now at the Bundesarchiv Lichterfelde holds six bound volumes of documents solely concerned with this controversy. RKA, 3915–3920, BAP/L. Karl Müller, *Geschichte der katholischen Kirche in Togo* (Kaldenkirchen: Steyler Verlagsbuchhandlung, 1958), 160–177. Karl Rivinius, "Akten zur katholischen Togo-Mission. Auseinandersetzung zwischen Mitgliedern der Steyler Missionsgesellschaft und deutschen Kolonialbeamten in den Jahren 1903–1907," *Neue Zeitschrift für Missionswissenschaft* 35 (1979): 58–69, 108–32, 171–90.

[19]"Beschwerdeschrift der Akwa-Häuptlinge an den Deutschen Reichstag," June 19, 1905, RDS 21, RKA, 7238: 25–29, BAP/L. Rüger, "Die Duala und die Kolonialmacht," in *Kamerun*, ed. Stoecker, 2: 201–215. Andreas Eckert, *Die Duala und die Kolonialmächte. Eine Untersuchung zu Widerstand, Protest und Protonationalismus in Kamerun vor dem Zweiten Weltkrieg* (Münster: Lit, 1991), 145–159.

draconic sentences of multiple years of hard labor meted out for the allegedly libelous petition would inflame both Centrist moral indignation and fiscal fears that such a despotic regime might yet provoke Cameroon's third uprising. As these civil remonstrations from the colonies coincided precisely with the aforementioned intense period of revolts, a dishearteningly long catalog of embarrassing and costly imbroglios resulted, and these proceeded to drive a large wedge between the Bülow government and the Catholic Center party.

* * *

The Kaiser's appointment in November 1905 of an anticlerical relative as acting Colonial Director and presumptive Colonial Secretary provides a prime illustration of the African impact upon German politics. The thoroughly unqualified Ernst Erbprinz zu Hohenlohe-Langenburg would never have replaced Director Oskar Stuebel in the Colonial Department had not the Matumbi unleashed the Maji Maji Uprising in southern East Africa several months earlier. The governor of that colony, Gustav Graf von Götzen, had long since agreed to his own appointment as colonial director when word of violent disturbances around Kilwa reached him on August 1, just six days before his scheduled departure for Berlin to relieve Stuebel. Götzen's assumption of the directorship of the Colonial Department was thereby first delayed and then revoked at his own request as populations rebelled across southern East Africa.[20]

By detaining Götzen indefinitely, the Maji Maji deprived the Bülow administration of the opportunity of appointing a director with firsthand colonial experience who simultaneously enjoyed the favor of the Center party.[21] Moreover, anticipation of the Reichstag's reaction to this latest rebellion on top of those raging in Southwest Africa and Cameroon rendered the colonial directorship still less desirable, even with the prospect of the department's elevation to an

[20]Götzen to Bülow, July 16, 1905, Telegram 38; Götzen to Foreign Office, July 24, 1905, Telegram 39; Götzen to Richthofen, Aug. 5, 1905, Telegram 44, Nachlaß Richthofen, 17: 170 f., 90, BAK. Richthofen to Below, July 19, 1905; Stuebel to Richthofen, Aug. 30, Sept. 1, 1905, Nachlaß Richthofen, 14: 146, 129–133, BAK. Richthofen to Bülow, Oct. 23, [1905], Nachlaß Richthofen, 4: 42, BAK. Götzen to Hutten-Czapski, May 25, June 4, 1906, Nachlaß Hutten-Czapski, 84: 5–8, BAP/L. P. [Deputy Envoy] to Podewils, Sept. 17, 1905, Report 485, ByGB, 1077, ByHSA. Lerchenfeld to Luitpold, June 27, 1906, Report 359, Königliche Bayrische Gesandtschaft Berlin (ByGB), 1078, ByHSA. Gustav Graf von Götzen, *Deutsch-Ostafrika im Aufstand 1905/06* (Berlin: Dietrich Reimer, 1909), 54.

[21]Indeed, Matthias Erzberger, soon to be the nemesis of the Colonial Department, had just lauded the count's administration of East Africa in the Reichstag in March 1905, and the Centrist would still be expressing a thoroughly positive opinion of Götzen long after one might have expected the Maji Maji Uprising to have tarnished the governor's record. Erzberger, Mar. 18, 1905, RTSB, 5372D. Erzberger, Dec. 14, 1905, RTSB, 323A. Erzberger, Mar. 17, 1906, RTSB, 2114C/D. [Erzberger], "Die Systemlosigkeit der Kolonialpolitik," *Kölnische Volkszeitung* (*KVZ*), Sept. 1, 1905, Nachlaß Richthofen, 14: 130, BAK. [Erzberger], "Ein Kolonialministerium?" *KVZ*, Sept. 4, 1905, Nachlaß Bachem, 428: 1, HASK. Götzen to Hutten-Czapski, June 4, 1906, Nachlaß Hutten-Czapski, 84: 7 f., BAP/L.

Imperial Colonial Office. The Centrist colonial enthusiast and Bülow's personal friend Franz Prinz von Arenberg was uninterested in the post and could suggest no suitable candidates.[22] Director Heinrich Wiegand of the Norddeutscher Lloyd declined to accept Bülow's overtures in early November, as did at least two other Hanseatic businessmen and the Bavarian foreign minister, Hermann von Pfaff.[23] Having hastened Stuebel's departure and blocked Götzen's candidacy, the East Africans had created a vacuum at the head of the Colonial Department which, after a delay of more than three months, positively invited the Kaiser to exercise his predilection for unusual personnel appointments. Wilhelm's choice for presumptive Colonial Secretary then fell upon Ernst Erbprinz zu Hohenlohe-Langenburg, a blood relative of the Kaiserin Auguste Viktoria and husband of the Kaiser's own first cousin, Princess Alexandra of Sachsen-Koburg-Gotha. The coming of age of the princess' nephew had terminated Hohenlohe-Langenburg's ducal regency in July, and Wilhelm perceived the problematic vacancy at the head of the proposed Colonial Office as the ideal opportunity to relieve "Erni" of his unemployment.[24]

Unlike Götzen, however, Hohenlohe-Langenburg lacked relevant experience beyond membership in the German Colonial Society, and this rendered the new acting colonial director highly dependent for advice upon his own departmental subordinates.[25] Indeed, initially in December 1905 not even the more governmental Centrists would consider approving the creation of an Imperial Colonial Office as it meant promoting such an "unimpressive" candidate who, in Karl Bachem's words, "understands nothing of colonial matters."[26]

[22]Arenberg to Julius Bachem, Dec. 2, 1905, cited in Bachem, *Vorgeschichte, Geschichte*, 6: 339. Klehmet to Zimmermann, Mar. 6, 1905, Nachlaß Zimmermann, 32: 15, BAP/L. *Berliner Lokalanzeiger*, Mar. 25, 1907, Nr. 154, Biographie 61, Papiers Arenberg (36/13), Nekrologe: 4, Archief van Arenberg, Edingen, Belgium.

[23]Hammann to Bülow, Nov. 6, 7, 1905, Memoranda, Nachlaß Hammann, 10: 54 f., BAP/L. Bachem, Mar. 21, 1906, Note, Nachlaß Bachem, 244: 7, HASK. Werner Schiefel, *Bernhard Dernburg, 1865–1937. Kolonialpolitiker und Bankier im wilhelminischen Deutschland* (Zürich: Atlantis Verlag, 1974), 37. Lerman, *Chancellor as Courtier*, 136. For the attitude of a leading Hanseatic businessman toward the trials of the colonial directorship, see Bülow, Nov. 28, 1906, RTSB, 3959A.

[24]Richthofen to Bülow, Nov. 13, 1905, Note, Nachlaß Richthofen, 14: 144, BAK. Wilhelm II to Hohenlohe-Langenburg, Nov. 14, 1905, Open Telegram 150, Nachlaß Ernst Fürst zu Hohenlohe-Langenburg, Übernahme der Leitung der Kolonialverwaltung, Hohenlohe Zentralarchiv Neuenstein (HZAN). Lerchenfeld to Podewils, Mar. 22, 1906; Lerchenfeld to Luitpold, June 27, 1906, Report 359, ByGB, 1078, ByHSA. Bachem, *Vorgeschichte, Geschichte*, 6: 334–337. Bülow, *Denkwürdigkeiten*, 2: 185 f.

[25]Hohenlohe-Langenburg to Stuebel, Nov. 20, 1905, Nachlaß Ernst Fürst zu Hohenlohe-Langenburg, Übernahme der Leitung, HZAN. Hohenlohe-Langenburg to Hermann Fürst zu Hohenlohe-Langenburg, Dec. 10, 1905, Nachlaß Hermann Fürst zu Hohenlohe-Langenburg, 70, HZAN. Bachem to [Franz Bachem?], Dec. 4, 1905, Nachlaß Bachem, 239: 7, HASK. Bachem, *Vorgeschichte, Geschichte*, 6: 335 f. "Der neue Kolonialdirektor," *Germania*, Nov. 17, 1905, Nr. 265. "Mißstände in der Kolonialverwaltung," ibid., Mar. 28, 1906, Nr. 71. Lerchenfeld to Podewils, Mar. 22, 1906, ByGB, 1078, ByHSA.

[26]Bachem to [Franz Bachem?], Dec. 4, 1905, Nachlaß Bachem, 239: 7, HASK.

Moreover, whereas Götzen as colonial director might have reasonably anticipated Centrist goodwill, the prince's confessional record ensured that the influential Catholic party would receive his appointment with suspicion. Not only was Hohenlohe-Langenburg a prominent member of the virulently anticlerical Protestant League co-founded by his father, but, as regent of Sachsen-Koburg-Gotha, his had also been one of the Bundesrat votes cast against the repeal of Article 2 of the Anti-Jesuit Law in 1904.[27] On the other hand, the would-be Colonial Secretary stood so high in the Kaiser's favor that there were widespread reports in spring 1906 that he might soon replace Bülow as chancellor. Given then the latter's longstanding policy of courting the Center, the prospect in early 1906 that the Catholic party would deny Hohenlohe-Langenburg the colonial secretariat placed a particularly heavy burden upon the chancellor.[28] Hence, it is fair to conclude that, if the East Africans had not scuttled Götzen's candidacy, the Colonial Office debates would have proved much less heated than they actually did in the wake of Hohenlohe-Langenburg's appointment.

Meanwhile, shortly after Hohenlohe's appointment Bülow authorized a preliminary Colonial Department investigation into the recent indiscretions of Emanuel Wistuba, the Togo administration's furloughed German Catholic chief clerk. Best known for having provided advice to the SVD mission in 1903 regarding his immediate superiors' conspiracy against the Afro-clerical defensive partnership at Atakpame, the clerk had also been approached directly by the Togolese translator Wilhelm Mensah, a horrified witness of a porter's lethal flogging at the hands of the leading anticlerical conspirator Judge Werner von Rotberg. Having therefore taken Mensah's deposition on his own authority, Wistuba eventually entrusted public pursuit of the matter to the SVD after internal channels had ignored the accusation.[29] Subjected as a

[27]Lerchenfeld to Podewils, Mar. 22, 1906, ByGB, 1078, ByHSA. "Ein Zeichen der Zeit," *Deutsche Zeitung*, Nov. 24, 1905, Nr. 276, RKA, 6907, BAP/L. "Zentrumsintrigen gegen den Erbprinzen Hohenlohe," *Königsberger Allgemeine Zeitung*, Mar. 6, 1906, RKzA, 1662: 44 f., BAP/L. "Kanzlerkrisis?" *Ostpreußische Zeitung*, Mar. 11, 1906, Nachlaß Hammann, 6: 36, BAP/L. Hohenlohe-Langenburg to Hermann Fürst zu Hohenlohe-Langenburg, Feb. 11, Mar. 22, 1906, Nachlaß Hermann Fürst zu Hohenlohe-Langenburg, 71, HZAN. Bülow, *Denkwürdigkeiten*, 2: 186.

[28]"Kanzlerkrisis?" *Ostpreußische Zeitung*, Mar. 11, 1906; "Unglaubhafte Krisengerüchte," *KVZ*, Mar. 14, 1906, Nachlaß Hammann, 6: 36 f., BAP/L. Bülow to Hammann, May 27, 1906, Secret, and June 30, 1906, "Nur für Sie!" Nachlaß Hammann, 12: 21, 30 f., BAP/L. Hohenlohe-Langenburg to Hermann Fürst zu Hohenlohe-Langenburg, Mar. 22, 1906, Nachlaß Hermann Fürst zu Hohenlohe-Langenburg, 71, HZAN. e. [Erzberger], "Sturz des Reichskanzlers?" *Schlesische Volkszeitung*, Mar. 20, 1906, Nachlaß Bachem, 242, HASK. Bachem, Mar. 21, 1906, Note; "Die Genesung des Fürsten Bülows," *KVZ*, May 22, 1906, Nachlaß Bachem, 244: 7, D6, HASK. "Politische Nachrichten," *Reichsbote*, Mar. 31, 1906, Nr. 76, RKzA, 1662: 48, 86, 90, BAP/L. Bülow, *Denkwürdigkeiten*, 2: 186. Lerman, *Chancellor as Courtier*, 128–132, 137.

[29]Bücking to Stuebel, Aug. 7, 1903; Bücking to District Court Lome, Aug. 10, 1903, Denunciation of Rotberg; Graef to König, Colonial Department, Sept. 14, 1903, Report, RKA, 3915: 220, 228 f., 251–261, 265–269, 300–303, BAP/L. Tietz to Colonial Department, Apr. 21, 1904, Report, RKA, 3918: 132, BAP/L. Bücking to Stuebel, Sept. 4, 1904, including Enclosures 4 and 5; König to Stuebel, Oct. 8, 1904, Memorandum, RKA, 3919: 116 (9 ff., Anlagen 4/5),

result of his actions to preliminary disciplinary interrogation during his 1904 furlough and declared mentally unfit for continued colonial service, the desperate Wistuba had then secured through the SVD the patronage of Saarburg's outspoken Center populist, the maverick Superior Court Judge Hermann Roeren.[30] Impressed with Wistuba's courageous piety and appalled by the revolting malfeasance in Togo, Roeren failed to discourage his distraught protégé from threatening the Colonial Department with publicity and from pooling documentary materials with another disaffected official.[31]

It was for these latest transgressions that Bülow ordered the preliminary investigation in December 1905. In response, Roeren himself threatened to expose the entire Togo Affair in hopes of discouraging an actual referral of Wistuba's case to the Disciplinary Chamber.[32] Accordingly, by mid-January 1906 at the latest, Roeren had described the "Kulturkampf in Togo" to the Center caucus and secured that body's permission to unleash the scandal of child molestation, bloody floggings, and imprisoned priests at the colonial budget's second reading in March.[33] As a result, although Roeren refrained from actually making the speech that spring, his mere intention of doing so had released the appalling Togo Affair from the purview of a small handful of party negotiators to spark the anger of the Center delegation as a whole.[34] Thus, even as the Maji Maji Uprising brought about the appointment of an anticlerical and ill-equipped colonial

119–124, BAP/L. Schmitz to SVD Brethren, May 17, 1903, RKA, 3920: 177 f., BAP/L. Colonial Department to [Loebell], "Fall Wistuba," [early February] 1906, Memorandum, RKzA, 945: 22, BAP/L. Roeren, Dec. 3, 1906, RTSB, 4090A/B.

[30]Bücking to Stuebel, Sept. 4, 1904, including Enclosures 4 and 5; König to Stuebel, Oct. 8, 1904, Memorandum, RKA, 3919: 116 (9 ff., Anlagen 4/5), 119–124, BAP/L. Colonial Department to [Loebell], "Fall Wistuba," [early February] 1906, Memorandum, RKzA, 945: 22, 24, BAP/L. Tietz to Zech, Dec. 9, 1903; Zech to Colonial Department, Dec. 11, 1903, Report 719, RKA, 3916: 145 ff., BAP/L. Roeren, Dec. 3, 1906, RTSB, 4085D–4086C. For more on Roeren, see Ronald J. Ross, *The Beleaguered Tower: The Dilemma of Political Catholicism in Wilhelmine Germany* (Notre Dame: University of Notre Dame Press, 1976), 66–68, 73–77. Loth, *Katholiken im Kaiserreich*, 117.

[31]König to Stuebel, Oct. 8, 1904, Memorandum, and "Gutachten in der Missionsangelegenheit Togo," Nov. 8, 1904; König, Nov. 25, 1904, Memorandum, RKA, 3919: 119–124, 159, 197 f., BAP/L. Colonial Department to [Loebell], "Fall Wistuba," [early February] 1906, Memorandum; Rose to Loebell, Apr. 24, 1906; Loebell to Roeren, June 13, 1906, R2409, RKzA, 945: 22 ff., 34 f., 49, BAP/L. König to Colonial Department, Nov. 7, 1906; Wistuba to Poeplau, Oct. 14, 22, 1904, Nachlaß König, 7: 26, 95 f., BAP/L.

[32]Colonial Department to [Loebell], "Fall Wistuba," [early February] 1906, Memorandum; Schnee, "Aufzeichnung betreffend den Bürovorstand Wistuba," Sept. 20, 1906, RKzA, 945: 22, 71 f., BAP/L. König, [1906], Memorandum, Nachlaß König, 8: 21, BAP/L. Dernburg, Dec. 3, 1906, RTSB, 4101C/D, 4102B, 4116B. Roeren, Dec. 3, 1906, RTSB, 4114D–4115A.

[33]Erzberger, Jan. 19, 1906, RTSB, 668A. Bachem, Dec. 20, 1906, Note, Nachlaß Bachem, 259: 8, HASK.

[34]Roeren to Loebell, June 8, 1906; Loebell to Roeren, June 9, 1906, R2387; Schnee, "Aufzeichnung betreffend den Bürovorstand Wistuba," Sept. 20, 1906; Dernburg to Bülow, Mar. 20, 1907, CB1155/24322; Loebell to Bülow, Mar. 22, 1907, Secret memorandum, RKzA,

director in Berlin, Anago and Dahomey civilian resistance lifted the curtain for the Center on the apparently chronic anticlericalism and malfeasance in the middle and lower ranks of the colonial bureaucracy overseas, a distasteful insight that tended to intensify German Catholic recalcitrance on other colonial issues.

* * *

In the meantime, African armed resistance had also exposed the administration's undiminished disdain for Reichstag prerogatives. This disregard in turn provoked considerable exasperation within the ranks of the Center party. As the Catholic jurists and aristocrats were more easily appeased, however, Berlin could sometimes enlist them to disclaim their populist colleagues' indignation and thereby transform the conflict somewhat into an internal party disagreement. Still, on several important occasions precipitated by the Nama and Maji Maji wars, the party elders considered it impossible to exculpate the government for parliamentary transgressions, whereupon they reproached Berlin as resolutely as the populists.

Just as in 1904, a key parliamentary grievance in late 1905 involved the government's failure to summon the Reichstag during the summer to authorize expenditures for wars waged overseas. This time the Reichstag was not convened until November 28 although both the Southwest and East African wars had already precipitated substantial extrabudgetary spending several months earlier. This aroused discord within the Center between the party leaders and the populists over the seriousness of Berlin's transgressions.

Less governmental than his jurist brother in the Reichstag, the co-editor of the *Kölnische Volkszeitung* Franz Bachem began to write provocative articles on colonial issues in early August 1905 and publish them along with similar ones by the young Swabian populist Matthias Erzberger. For five weeks, the Catholic newspaper repeatedly cast doubt upon the constitutionality of the recent dispatch of troops to fight the Nama in Southwest Africa.[35] Rather than summon the Reichstag at the height of the Moroccan crisis, however, Bülow simply secured Prince von Arenberg's cooperation in an unsuccessful

945: 42 f., 45 f., 72, 237, 240, BAP/L. Bachem, Dec. 20, 1906, Note, Nachlaß Bachem, 259: 8, HASK. Bachem, Mar. 21, 1906, Note, Nachlaß Bachem, 244: 7, HASK.

[35]The *Kölnische Volkszeitung* ran eleven articles in this series, including [Erzberger], "Abermals eine Verletzung des Budgetrechts?" *KVZ*, Aug. 2, 1905, Nr. 632. [Franz Bachem], "Eine neue Verletzung des Budgetrechts des Reichstags?" *KVZ*, Aug. 5, 1905, Nr. 641. [F. Bachem], "Die Einberufung einer außerordentlichen Reichstagssession," *KVZ*, Aug. 7, 1905, Nr. 647. [F. Bachem], "Die Erörterung über die Truppennachschübe nach Südwestafrika," *KVZ*, Aug. 10, 1905, Nr. 656. [F. Bachem], "Zur Verletzung des Budgetrechts," *KVZ*, Aug. 17, 1905, Nr. 676. [Erzberger], "Die Verwirrung im Kolonialamt!" *KVZ*, Sept. 6, 1905, Nr. 737. See also Lerchenfeld to Podewils, Aug. 6, 1905, Report 435, ByGB, 1077, ByHSA. The moderately populist Hessian textile manufacturer Richard Müller-Fulda likewise supported this press campaign (cf. Müller-Fulda to Karl Bachem, Aug. 10, 1905, Nachlaß Karl Bachem, 228, HASK).

attempt to persuade Bachem to temper the rhetoric of his publication.[36] Erzberger raised the issue again in the Reichstag in December, but the party leadership evidently subscribed to Berlin's computational formula since the matter was not pursued further.[37]

In a similar case, the Maji Maji Uprising in East Africa had cost the Reich close to a million marks in just over four months before the Reichstag was summoned in late November.[38] While this sum was but a small fraction of the previous unauthorized overseas expenditures of the summers of 1900 and 1904, the government recognized that the Chinese and Herero precedents of those years greatly increased the likelihood of Reichstag insistence upon satisfaction for the unsanctioned measures. In private consultations, the Bülow administration then established that, in fact, the leaders of the Center, National Liberal, and Conservative parties expected a request for indemnity in advance of their authorization of the two million marks needed for the war through March 1906. Consequently, from the outset the Third Supplementary Budget of 1905 included an article requesting parliamentary exemption for those funds already spent without consultation with the Reichstag.[39]

Whereas this concession appeased the senior Centrists, Erzberger protested in a plenary session of the Reichstag in mid-January 1906 that the Bülow administration's frequent requests for indemnity had become "cheaper than blackberries."[40] In the Budget Committee, the Swabian populist further argued that the government must have known by August or September 1905 that increasing transportation costs in the Nama War would necessitate a fourth supplementary budget of thirty-one million marks to provision the troops in Southwest Africa from January through March 1906. Therefore, the Reichstag should have been summoned at least two months earlier to authorize both additional budgets. Erzberger consequently urged the committee to refuse to grant indemnity on the East African bill. Center leader and Prussian jurist Peter Spahn, however, defended the Bülow administration on the basis of wartime exigencies and the government's readiness to seek the exemption. Prince von Arenberg likewise admonished Erzberger that the letter of the law was not dead, but rather had to

[36]Helfferich to Richthofen, Aug. 14, 18, 1905; Helfferich to Bülow, Aug. [24,] 1905; Richthofen to Bülow, Aug. 30, 1905, Nachlaß Richthofen, 14: 86–97, 79–85, 102–105, BAK.

[37]Erzberger, Dec. 2, 1905, RTSB, 80D–81A. BSWA 1906; DB, Fourth SupB 1905, Dec. 20, 1905, RDS 152, RTA, 1097: 187 f., 280, BAP/L.

[38]Seitz, Feb. 1, 1906, ProtBc; DB, Third SupB 1905, Dec. 7, 1905, RDS 136, RTA, 1058: 44, 30, BAP/L.

[39]Nieberding to Bülow, Nov. 16, 1905; Stengel to Bülow, Nov. 11, 1905, Memorandum; Posadowsky to Bülow, Nov. 23, 1905, I.A. 6996; Bülow to Loebell, Nov. 24, 1905, R4546; Reich Chancellery to Loebell, Nov. 29, 1905, Secret Memorandum, R4637, RKzA, 924: 53–60, 63 f., 75, BAP/L. DB, Third SupB 1905, Dec. 7, 1905, RDS 136, RTA, 1058: 29 f., BAP/L. Richthofen to Bülow, Aug. 30, 1905, with enclosure, Nachlaß Richthofen, 14: 102–105, 112–120, BAK.

[40]Erzberger, Jan. 16, 1906, RTSB, 589B. "*[D]ie Gesuche um Indemnität werden nachgerade im Deutschen Reiche billiger als die Brombeeren.*"

be interpreted.[41] Hence, both the Nama and the Maji Maji Uprisings generated significant disagreement between the Center populists and the party elders over whether the government's unilateral military spending and tardy summoning of the Reichstag had placed it in violation of the German constitution.

Nonetheless, African struggles also gave rise to parliamentary issues that prompted the Center's jurist leaders as well as their populist colleagues to take a strong stand against Berlin. For example, by late 1905 the government had still not properly justified unauthorized preliminary railroad work that had been initiated in July 1904 in anticipation of the supposedly unexpected Nama Uprising, but that had then been rejected by the Reichstag in January 1905. Rather than submitting a separate bill with due substantiation and a renewed request for indemnity, the government merely annotated the 1906 budget for Southwest Africa with passing reference to an extrabudgetary expenditure of 200,000 marks for the Windhoek-Rehoboth line. To make matters worse, the construction company involved had also been paid the balance of its contract even after the obligatory retraction of the original budget line. Accordingly, by the winter of 1905/06 senior Centrists Karl Bachem and Peter Spahn were as vexed as Erzberger with the government's disdain for the express wishes of the Reichstag, and this irritation likely contributed to the Budget Committee's unanimous opposition to authorization of the first four million marks for the actual construction of the railroad.[42]

Even more disturbing for the Center, scrutiny of the fall of the East African military station at Liwale exposed a misappropriation of Reich funds that distressed the jurists as much as the populist elements within the party. The Maji Maji under Ngameya and Abdulla Mpanda had been able to take Liwale by setting fire to the station in August 1905 despite the fact that the original German budget had specified that its roofs be constructed of tin, not highly flammable thatch. Indeed, evidence even suggested a diversion of the relevant funds to construction of luxury buildings in the colonial capital at Dar-es-Salaam. Such reports were of particular significance because news of the early Maji Maji victory at Liwale had facilitated the rapid spread of that movement throughout southern East Africa.[43] After three separate Centrist

[41]DB, Fourth SupB 1905, Dec. 20, 1905, RDS 152, RTA, 1097: 279 f., BAP/L. Erzberger, Spahn, Arenberg, Feb. 1, 1906, ProtBc; Report of the Budget Committee, Feb. 8, 1906, RDS 120a, RTA, 1058: 44, 46, 57, 59 f., BAP/L. "Die Budgetcommission des Reichstags," *Germania*, Feb. 2, 1906, Nr. 26. Bülow, *Denkwürdigkeiten*, 2: 186. Bachem, *Vorgeschichte, Geschichte*, 6: 219 f.

[42]BSWA 1906, RTA, 1097: 187 f., 198 ff., BAP/L. Bachem to [Franz Bachem?], Dec. 4, 1905, Nachlaß Bachem, 239, HASK. Erzberger, Dec. 14, 1905, RTSB, 325C/D. Erzberger, Reporter, Mar. 24, 1906, RTSB, 2285A. Erzberger, Südekum, Spahn, Feb. 23, 1906, ProtBc, RTA, 1098: 107 f., BAP/L.

[43]Bachem, Mar. 16, 1906, RTSB, 2078A–2079A. Bachem, Mar. 17, 1906, RTSB, 2117C/D. Spahn, Mar. 15, 1906, RTSB, 2028B/C. Götzen, *Deutsch-Ostafrika im Aufstand*, 66 f., 74. Joseph F. Safari, "Grundlagen und Auswirkungen des Maji-Maji-Aufstands von 1905. Kulturgeschichtliche

interpellations by Bachem, Erzberger, and Spahn over the course of six weeks, the government finally declared in March 1906 that it could not determine whether the East African government had misappropriated construction funds, but that the inordinately swift loss of Liwale was undoubtedly attributable to its flammability.[44] An indignant Bachem thereupon warned that the government's sluggish reply undermined parliamentary confidence in the colonial administration, while the Swabian jurist Adolf Gröber likewise rebuked the government for its inability to ascertain whether the diversion had occurred.[45]

That same spring, the immense costs imposed upon the Reich by the Herero and Nama Uprisings engendered an increased willingness on the part of the Center party elders to confront the issue of government favoritism toward capitalist war profiteers. Bachem, for example, argued vociferously in favor of Erzberger's motion of December 1905 to make passage of the Lüderitzbucht-Kubub Railroad conditional upon Berlin's consent to revoke all land and mining concessions in Southwest Africa not exercised by April 1909. Accusing the giant land corporations of being the sole beneficiaries of the costly suppression of the Nama, the Rhenish lawyer contested the government's presumption that German taxpayers should now finance the railroad that a British firm had neglected to build into that company's own domain. Given Berlin's failure to create the mandated parliamentary commission to investigate such concessions, both Bachem and Erzberger went so far as to threaten a Centrist rejection of all further colonial requests until the government presented a fundamentally reformed program for its overseas empire.[46]

Similarly, whereas Erzberger had been the only Centrist attacking the Tippelskirch Company the previous year, by early 1906 many of the party's bourgeois professionals had also come out in opposition to that firm's long-standing near-monopoly in the equipping of Germany's colonial troops.[47] Now leading the campaign for the majority of the Center, Erzberger accused the firm of charging inflated prices averaging thirty percent over market

---

Betrachtungen zu einer Heilserwartungsbewegung in Tansania" (Ph.D. diss., Universität Köln, 1972), 69–75.

[44]Bachem, Erzberger, Feb. 7, 1906, ProtBc, RTA, 1058: 52, BAP/L. Spahn, Mar. 15, 1906, RTSB, 2028B/C. Bachem, Mar. 16, 1906, RTSB, 2078A–2079A. Seitz, Mar. 16, 1906, RTSB, 2079A/D.

[45]Bachem, Mar. 16, 1906, RTSB, 2079C–2080A. Gröber, Mar. 16, 1906, RTSB, 2080C.

[46]Bachem, Müller-Fulda, Golinelli, Motion Erzberger, Dec. 13, 1905, ProtBc; Erzberger, Dec. 12, 1905, ProtBc; Erzberger, Müller-Fulda, Dec. 14, 1905, ProtBc, RTA, 1097: 250 f., 246, 255, BAP/L. Erzberger, Dec. 2, 1905, RTSB, 83D–84A.

[47]Erzberger, Jan. 13, 1905, ProtBc; Erzberger, Spahn, Arenberg, Jan. 17, 1905, ProtBc, RTA, 1096: 236, 244 ff., BAP/L. Erzberger, Dahlem, Motion Erzberger, Feb. 16, 1906, ProtBc, RTA, 1098: 56 ff., BAP/L. Erzberger, Mar. 23, 1906, RTSB, 2234D–2238C. Motion Hompesch, Resolution for the Second Reading of the Colonial Budget, Mar. 12, 1906, RDS 282, RKA, 7257: 84, BAP/L.

value. He likewise indicted the Colonial Department itself for having repeatedly renewed contracts with this firm and a handful of other North German corporations, thereby quashing competition at the expense of artisans, small manufacturers, the South German economy, and the debt-ridden Imperial Treasury.[48] Indeed, an eight-year contract extension with Tippelskirch had scarcely been signed in 1903 before the wave of African armed resistance compelled Berlin to an elevenfold increase in its yearly purchases under a price-list entirely lacking in volume-discount provisions.[49] Erzberger accordingly estimated that fully twenty-five percent of the eight million marks now paid annually to Tippelskirch amounted to sheer profit.[50]

Within the Center party, Erzberger enjoyed significant bourgeois professional support in this campaign against capitalist war profiteering. In February 1906 Professor Georg Freiherr von Hertling, Karl Bachem, and three other Center jurists co-sponsored Erzberger's motion calling upon Bülow to issue colonial supply contract guidelines that presupposed the dissolution of the arrangement with Tippelskirch.[51] A month later, Karl Trimborn, Hugo Am Zehnhoff, and four other prominent Catholic jurists joined the populists around Erzberger in demanding the immediate cancellation of unfavorable long-term colonial contracts with such corporations as Tippelskirch, Jordan, Oranien Apothecary, and Woermann Shipping. Moreover, support for such precipitous contract termination was so widespread within the party that the Center's venerable aristocratic chairman Alfred Graf von Hompesch-Rurich lent his name to the subsequently successful resolution.[52] Hence, the high costs of African military success against Germany contributed directly to Centrist estrangement from the Bülow administration by fanning the flames of Catholic economic resentment toward colonial interests enjoying undue government favor.

[48]Erzberger, Motion Erzberger, Feb. 16, 1906, ProtBc; Erzberger, Mar. 27, 1906, ProtBc, RTA, 1098: 56, 58, 187, BAP/L. Erzberger, Mar. 23, 1906, RTSB, 2235A–2236D. Erzberger, Mar. 24, 1906, RTSB, 2258D–2259B.

[49]Erzberger, Mar. 23, 1906, RTSB, 2235D–2236A. Seitz, Mar. 23, 1906, RTSB, 2240C/D. Seitz, Fischer, Gamp, Feb. 16, 1906, ProtBc; Fischer, Mar. 27, 1906, ProtBc, RTA, 1098: 57 f., 186, BAP/L. "Denkschrift betreffend die Entwicklung der Geschäftsverbindung der Kolonial-Abteilung mit der Firma v. Tippelskirch," Feb. 2, 1906, *Kommissions-Drucksachen* (KDS) 20, RKzA, 944: 45, BAP/L.

[50]Erzberger, Mar. 23, 1906, RTSB, 2235C/D, 2236D. Erzberger, Mar. 24, 1906, RTSB, 2257C. Erzberger, Mar. 26, 1906, RTSB, 2309A. Erzberger, Mar. 27, 1906, ProtBc, RTA, 1098: 187, BAP/L.

[51]Erzberger, Dahlem, Motion Erzberger, Feb. 16, 1906, ProtBc, RTA, 1098: 57 f., BAP/L. Erzberger, Mar. 23, 1906, RTSB, 2235A/B. Erzberger, Mar. 24, 1906, RTSB, 2259A/B.

[52]Motion Hompesch, Resolution for the Second Reading of the Colonial Budget, Mar. 12, 1906, RDS 282; Oral report of the Budget Committee regarding... the Resolution Hompesch, Mar. 28, 1906, RDS 333, RKA, 7257: 84, 111, BAP/L. Erzberger, Mar. 23, 1906, RTSB, 2234D–2235A, 2235C, 2237. Erzberger, Mar. 24, 1906, RTSB, 2257B–2258C. Erzberger, Mar. 26, 1906, RTSB, 2309A. Erzberger, Spahn, Mar. 27, 1906, ProtBc, RTA, 1098: 187 f., BAP/L. Memoranda, Feb. 2, 1906, KDS 20, RKzA, 944: 45, BAP/L.

In much the same way, the Center's bourgeois party elders as well as its populists objected to government economic favoritism toward the species of ruthless colonial traders and overindulged settlers whose misconduct was reaping such an expensive and deadly harvest all across Africa. For example, just as Erzberger regularly censured the trading companies of southern Cameroon for driving the populace to rebel, the conservative Centrist judge Wilhelm Schwarze-Lippstadt warned in March 1906 that the continued sanctioning of that colony's lucrative arms trade could cost the Reich millions in a general uprising on the Southwest African model.[53] Similarly, in late 1905 both the generally governmental Judge Gröber and his outspoken populist protégé Erzberger indicted the German settlers of Southwest Africa for exploiting and abusing the indigenous population to the point of revolt.[54]

Nonetheless, the Bülow administration presented the Reichstag with a proposal in May 1906 that went well beyond even full compensation of the settlers' losses at Herero and Nama hands although the Center as a whole had previously declared forty-percent restitution more than adequate recompense. Had it been approved, the complementary budget title would have provided the settlers not only with total reimbursement for the remaining 7.5 million marks of direct Herero and Nama damage, but also with an additional three million for estimated losses in unrealized cattle profits.[55] The entire Center party resisted this narrow colonial favoritism at taxpayer expense. From the bourgeois professionals Spahn, Gröber, and Hertling to the populists Erzberger and Speck, Centrists refused even so much as to consider further compensation of any kind because the Reichstag had still not received an accounting of the five million already authorized and distributed.[56] As for the restitution of the settlers' unrealized profits, the jurist Karl Bachem considered this the most foolish of the Reich's proposals.[57] Centrists of all persuasions therefore helped send both segments of this budget title to an unequivocal parliamentary defeat on May 26, 1906, this being the second of the three blows to the administration that day.[58]

[53]Schwarze-Lippstadt, Mar. 16, 1906, RTSB, 2058B/C. Erzberger, Dec. 14, 1905, RTSB, 322D–323A. Erzberger, Jan. 18, 1906, RTSB, 636C/D. Erzberger, Mar. 20, 1906, RTSB, 2174A. [Erzberger], "Allerlei zur Kolonialpolitik," *KVZ*, Sept. 8, 1905, Nr. 743. [Erzberger], "Die Gesellschaft Südkamerun," *KVZ*, Sept. 14, 1905, Nr. 762.

[54]Gröber, Dec. 13, 1905, RTSB, 277B. For Erzberger citations, see the previous footnote.

[55]Bachem, Spahn, Erzberger, Jan. 20, 1905, ProtBc, RTA, 1096: 259 f., BAP/L. Erzberger, Jan. 31, 1905, RTSB, 4147D, 4148C/D. Erzberger, Reporter, May 26, 1906, RTSB, 3543C/D. ComB 1906, May 19, 1906, RDS 474, Appendix I, MA 95403, ByHSA.

[56]Motion Müller-Fulda, May 23, 1906, KDS 107, RKA, 2224: 210, BAP/L. Müller-Fulda, Gröber, May 26, 1906, ProtBc, RTA, 1098: 265 f., BAP/L. Spahn, May 26, 1906, RTSB, 3532D. Erzberger, Reporter, May 26, 1906, RTSB, 3543C–3544A. Erzberger, May 28, 1906, RTSB, 3577C/D.

[57]Bachem, May 27, 1906, Note, Nachlaß Bachem, 242, HASK.

[58]See in addition to the previous two footnotes Paasche, Vice President, May 26, 1906, RTSB, 3548A/B.

Meanwhile, despite the dwindling number of Nama guerrillas in late 1905 and early 1906, their continued successes and increasing geographic inaccessibility had forced the German government to request another 155 million marks, a sum that threatened to swallow at least three-quarters of the entire first year of revenue from that spring's arduously pursued tax reform.[59] Convinced in March that recent major surrenders meant that subjugation was nearly complete, the Center joined the parliamentary left in refusing to entertain the requested increase from 78 to 93 million marks for the maintenance of more than 14,000 troops in the colony.[60] By May further capitulations left only several hundred Nama in the field, yet the military in Southwest Africa admitted having already spent 34 of the 78 million just authorized and meant to last yet another ten months.[61] By this point, even leading Catholic conservatives such as Bachem and Spahn had begun to advocate the previously unthinkable, namely, that the complete evacuation of southern Southwest Africa would be preferable to any further continuation of this fiscal debacle.[62] Accordingly, as the proposed Keetmanshoop extension of the Lüderitzbucht-Kubub Railroad could not be completed before May 1908, indignant Center populists, jurists, and even aristocrats rejected its military justification and sent the line to an overwhelming defeat in the Reichstag plenum of May 26, not long before the aforementioned rejection of full compensation for Southwest Africa's war-ravaged settlers.[63]

[59]Budget for the Expedition to Southwest Africa, 1906; BSWA, 1906; DB, Second SupB 1905, Nov. 28, 1905, RDS 24; DB, Fourth SupB 1905, Dec. 20, 1905, RDS 152, RTA, 1097: 165–200, 206–209, 279 f., BAP/L. DB, Third SupB 1905, Dec. 7, 1905, RDS 136, RTA, 1058: 30 f., BAP/L. DB, ComB 1906, May 19, 1906, RDS 474; DB, Second ComB 1906, May 19, 1906, RDS 473, MA 95403, ByHSA. Witt, *Finanzpolitik*, 126 f., 131 n. 490.

[60]BSWA, 1906, RTA, 1097: 181–186, BAP/L. Paasche, Report from Subcommittee, Feb. 23, 1906, ProtBc, RTA, 1098: 107, BAP/L. Erzberger, Reporter, Mar. 24, 1906, RTSB, 2279C–2280A. Ballestrem, President, Mar. 24, 1906, RTSB, 2284B.

[61]Drechsler, *Südwestafrika*, 190–193, 197 f. Chancellery to Bülow, Mar. 3, 1906, Secret Memorandum, Eo R991, RKzA, 937: 254, BAP/L. "Denkschrift über den Verlauf des Aufstands in Südwestafrika (Fortsetzung)," Nov. 24, 1905, RDS 5; ibid., Feb. 2, 1906, RDS 202, MA 95403, ByHSA. Deimling, "Von der alten in die neue Zeit," 1929, Manuscript, Nachlaß Deimling, 2: 92, 104, Bundesarchiv-Militärarchiv Freiburg. Schwabe, *Diamantenlande*, 243, 329, 336, 343 f. Seitz, Erzberger, May 23, 1906, ProtBc, RTA, 1058: 108, BAP/L. Erzberger, Reporter, May 26, 1906, RTSB, 3526B. Bachem, May 27, 1906, Note, Nachlaß Bachem, 242, HASK. Spahn to Martin Spahn, May 22, 1906, Nachlaß Martin Spahn, 318, BAK.

[62]"Abgeordneter Dr. Spahn zur politischen Lage," *Germania*, Sept. 26, 1905, Nr. 221. Bachem, Dec. 13, 1905, ProtBc; Erzberger, Dec. 12, 1905, ProtBc; Müller-Sagan, Dec. 14, 1905, ProtBc, RTA, 1097: 250, 246, 255 f., BAP/L. Gröber, Müller-Fulda, May 23, 1906, ProtBc; Erzberger, May 25, 1906, ProtBc; Gröber, Erzberger, May 26, 1906, ProtBc, RTA, 1098: 259, 262, 266, BAP/L. Spahn, May 26, 1906, RTSB, 3533A/B. Erzberger, Reporter, May 26, 1906, RTSB, 3526B/D. "Die Budgetcommission des Reichstags," *Germania*, May 26, 1906, Nr. 119.

[63]DB, ComB 1906, May 19, 1906, RDS 474, MA 95403, ByHSA. Gröber, Müller-Fulda, Erzberger, May 23, 1906, ProtBc; Müller-Fulda, May 25, 1906, ProtBc, RTA, 1098: 259, 262, BAP/L. Bachem, May 27, 1906, Note, Nachlaß Bachem, 242, HASK. Erzberger, Reporter, May 26, 1906, RTSB, 3526B–3527A. Spahn, May 26, 1906, RTSB, 3533B. Spahn, May 28, 1906, RTSB, 3565C. Gröber, May 26, 1906, RTSB, 3540B/D. "Die Budgetcommission des Reichstags," *Germania*, May 26, 1906, Nr. 119. Roll Call Vote, ComB 1906, Chapter 2, Item 10,

Finally, on the same fateful day, the Center delegation demolished government hopes for an Imperial Colonial Office.[64] As a rueful Karl Bachem had already explained to Bülow in March, his party's sharp opposition to creation of a Colonial Office arose from aggravation over "the duel declaration, the arrest of the missionaries in Togo, over everything which has come to light in Cameroon and the rest of the colonial administration."[65] Thus, even as the Maji Maji warriors had delivered the helm of the German colonial administration into the impotent hand of the anticlerical Hohenlohe-Langenburg, the civilian initiatives of the Anago and Dahomey of Togo and the Duala of Cameroon resulted in the Center's realization that this administration was perpetrating terrible abuses all across Africa. For many Centrists, the establishment of a Colonial Office under Hohenlohe would have therefore been tantamount not only to condoning the anticlerical attitudes in the colonial administration, but also to promoting the very senior bureaucrats responsible for the atrocious and costly state of affairs overseas.[66] On the other hand, the humiliation of the Kaiser's favorite deeply offended the monarch, who thereupon openly faulted Bülow for having conceded the principle of Reichstag per diems without first securing the secretary's office for Hohenlohe-Langenburg.[67] Similarly incensed by the Reichstag's rejection of the Kubub-Keetmanshoop railroad extension, the Kaiser even ordered Colonel Berthold von Deimling to proceed with its construction in direct defiance of the parliament, a command the monarch ultimately revoked only under sustained pressure from the chancellor.[68]

* * *

[Kubub-Keetmanshoop Railroad], May 26, 1906, RTSB, 3560 ff. Among Centrists the railroad extension failed by a vote of 2–72.

[64]Roll Call Vote, Budget 1906, Chapter 69a, Item 1, State Secretary, May 26, 1906, RTSB, 3560 ff.

[65]Bachem, Mar. 21, 1906, Note, Nachlaß Bachem, 244: 7, HASK.

[66]Lerchenfeld to Podewils, Mar. 22, 1906; Podewils to Lerchenfeld, Mar. 23, 1906; Lerchenfeld to Luitpold, June 27, 1906, Report 359, ByGB, 1078, ByHSA. "Mißstände in der Kolonialverwaltung," *Germania*, Mar. 28, 1906, Nr. 71. Bachem, May 27, 1906, Note, Nachlaß Bachem, 242, HASK. Posadowsky to Bülow, May 28, 1906, RKzA, 1662: 128, BAP/L. "Ein Zeichen der Zeit," *Deutsche Zeitung*, Nov. 24, 1905, Nr. 276, RKA, 6907, BAP/L. "Zentrumsintrigen gegen den Erbprinzen Hohenlohe," *Königsberger Allgemeine Zeitung*, Mar. 6, 1906; Posadowsky to Bülow, May 28, 1906, RKzA, 1662: 44 f., 128, BAP/L. Bülow, *Denkwürdigkeiten*, 2: 186.

[67]Varnbüler to Weizsäcker, Nov. 3, 1906, Report 5, Württembergisches Ministerium der Auswärtigen Angelegenheiten, E50/03, 200, Hauptstaatsarchiv Stuttgart. Wilhelm II to Bülow, May 28, 1906, Telegram, cited by Bülow, [circa 1910], Note, Nachlaß Bülow, 153: 10, BAK. Bülow to Wilhelm II, May 30, 1906, Telegram 2, RKzA, 1663: 10, BAP/L.

[68]Below to Tschirschky, June 12, 1906, Nachlaß Tschirschky, Politisches Archiv des Auswärtigen Amts, Bonn. Lerchenfeld to Luitpold, June 27, 1906, Report 359, ByGB, 1078, ByHSA. Hohenlohe-Langenburg to Bülow, Aug. 1, 1906; Bülow to Tschirschky, Aug. 3, 6, 1906, Zu R3105, Eo R3160; Bülow to Loebell, Aug. 13, 1906, Eo R3262, Secret; Loebell to Bülow, Sept. 3, 1906, Telegram 31, RKzA, 926: 78–84, 91 ff., 108, BAP/L. Dernburg to Loebell, "Kurze

Besides prompting the Bülow government to pursue political, military, and fiscal policies that alienated a thoroughly exasperated Center, the far-reaching consequences of African resistance impelled the Catholic party to seek a more active role for the Reichstag in colonial affairs. Ascribing the rebellions and the filing of grievances to government complicity in the abuse and exploitation of Africans, the Center hoped to preclude future costly uprisings through the promotion of justice for colonized populations. Accordingly, the Center populists and, to no small extent, its jurists demanded that the government concede the restriction of the executive right of decree, the separation of the colonial judicial system from the administration, and the expansion of parliamentary jurisdiction in colonial affairs in order to guarantee certain basic human rights to the Reich's non-European subjects. Here again, however, Catholic populists and jurists also at times found themselves at odds over the appropriate measure of criticism to be leveled against the Bülow administration.

As undoubtedly the most outspoken Centrist proponent of these demands, the Swabian populist Matthias Erzberger linked a significant portion of the Reich's fiscal woes to the administration's abuses of its executive and judicial powers over colonized peoples. In the East African case, he repeatedly cited reports from the colony tracing the Maji Maji Uprising to resentment over the introduction and inequitability of official forced labor since the imposition of the hut tax in 1897. More recently, the district officials at Kilwa and Lindi had unilaterally introduced communal cottonfields in which all East Africans in those districts had been obliged to work at preposterously low wages for twenty-four days during their own annual harvest. Erzberger attributed the uprising primarily to these two policy blunders of a colonial administration that had exceeded the stipulations regulating its exercise of the Kaiser's right of decree.[69]

Where East Africa was concerned, however, Erzberger found little support from the Center party elders for his attacks upon Berlin's record. Rather than criticize the imposition of communal cottonfields, Arenberg and Schwarze-Lippstadt faulted only the despotism and greed of the Arab and African overseers. While Erzberger focused upon the evils of forced labor, the Rhenish prince and the Westphalian judge alleged in February and March 1906 that

---

Zusammenstellung der von der Schutztruppe erstatteten Berichte," Jan. 12, 1907, OK14 G. J. Pers., Memorandum; Dernburg to Loebell, Jan. 11, 1907, OK18 G. J. Pers, RKzA, 937: 308 f., 315, BAP/ L. Haferkorn, *Bülows Kampf*, 108.

[69][Erzberger], "Zwangsarbeit in Deutsch-Ostafrika," *KVZ*, Nov. 7, 1905, Nr. 921. Erzberger, Dec. 14, 1905, RTSB, 324D–325A. Erzberger, Jan. 16, 1906, RTSB, 590C–591C, 605C. Erzberger, Mar. 19, 1906, RTSB, 2132B, 2134D. Erzberger, Feb. 1, 1906, ProtBc; Erzberger, Feb. 7, 1906, ProtBc; Erzberger, Feb. 8, 1906, ProtBc; Erzberger, Feb. 15, 1906, ProtBc, RTA, 1058: 44, 52 ff., 73, BAP/L.

the inherent laziness of Africans necessitated the application of some measure of force to induce them to work. Moreover, far from finding the three-rupee hut tax excessively high, Schwarze-Lippstadt believed the error lay solely in the introduction of that tax in regions where the Reich's dominion was not yet secure.[70]

Nonetheless, the bourgeois professional Centrists otherwise often appeared to share Erzberger's dismay at the widespread colonial maladministration that had already resulted in serious German losses and might do so again at any moment. Thus, in early December 1905, even as jurists Alois Fritzen and Karl Bachem sought to temper opposition within the party to the governmental line, they concurred with the populists that the extremely expensive uprisings could largely be traced to abuses perpetrated by colonial officials against African populations. Not only did Bachem privately ascribe the rebellions to "the filthy mismanagement [*Schweinewirtschaft*] of some officials," but Fritzen also publicly charged that the brutality and incompetence of German colonial administrators had provoked the conflicts.[71]

A week after Fritzen's speech, Judge Adolf Gröber elaborated upon the same accusation. The Swabian jurist called upon Berlin to respond to the assertion of Prussian Supreme Court Justice Felix Meyer that the attempt by Warmbad's District Chief Jobst in October 1903 to exercise judicial authority over the Bondelswart captain Albrecht Christian had violated Germany's "protection treaty" with that clan. The understandable resistance of the Bondelswarts had then proved to be the first domino of the Herero and Nama Wars. Gröber likewise cited Meyer's contention that the German installation of High Chief Samuel Maharero in 1890 had been inconsistent with Herero hereditary custom and that the ensuing land purchases by whites had ignored the fact that Herero law did not give a high chief authority to sell communal land. Finally, the prominent Centrist presented Justice Meyer's evidence that it had been the outrageously inadequate size of the reservations created by the colonial administration that had driven the Herero to take up arms.[72]

Like Erzberger, Center jurists were also outraged by the draconic libel sentences that the colonial administration meted out to the Bonambela Duala chieftains of Cameroon in early December 1905. Within the week, word reached the German press that King Dika Akwa, Chief Muange Mukuri, and

[70]Arenberg, Feb. 7, 1906, ProtBc; Arenberg, Feb. 8, 1906, ProtBc, RTA, 1058: 53 f., BAP/L. Schwarze-Lippstadt, Mar. 16, 1906, RTSB, 2061B/C. It is worth noting, however, that Erzberger also believed that Africans were intrinsically lazy (Erzberger, Dec. 14, 1905, RTSB, 325B).

[71]Bachem to [Franz Bachem?], Dec. 4, 1905, Nachlaß Bachem, 239: 7, HASK. Fritzen, Dec. 6, 1905, RTSB, 135B/C.

[72]Gröber, Dec. 13, 1905, RTSB, 276C–277B. Leutwein to Colonial Department, Sept. 28, 1904, Report 917, Enclosure III, RKA, 2116: 149, BAP/L. König to Solf, Jan. 26, 1904, Nachlaß Solf, 25: 9 f., BAK. Drechsler, *Südwestafrika*, 65, 115–119. Otto von Weber, *Geschichte des Schutzgebietes Deutsch-Südwest-Afrika* (Windhoek: Verlag der S.W.A. Wissenschaftlichen Gesellschaft, n.d.), 124.

Georg Njo a Dibonge had been sentenced to nine, seven, and three years of hard labor, respectively, for their unprecedented and refreshingly peaceful appeal to the Reichstag and chancellor.[73] An incredulous Judge Gröber protested that, regardless of possible flaws in the chieftains' claims, the grievances of Africans unfamiliar with German legal practice had to be handled more diplomatically than would inadequately substantiated complaints leveled by Reich citizens.[74] Similarly, testifying to the great indignation the sentences had aroused throughout Germany, Erzberger observed in January that even a wholly groundless complaint could not possibly warrant nine years in prison.[75] Particularly shocked by the "horrendous" sentences, the Bavarian judge Richard Kalkhoff took the colonial administration to task in March for having both preempted Reichstag consideration of the petition and violated the German penal code in seven different ways.[76]

From the outset, this intense Centrist reaction to the sentencing of the Duala had been linked to pervasive Catholic fears of yet another expensive colonial insurrection. Thus, in his December speech before the Reichstag, Gröber warned the government that its harsh treatment of the petitioners was "the correct way to occasion further uprisings."[77] While sufficiently embarrassed to withhold legal confirmation from the sentencing, Acting Colonial Director Hohenlohe-Langenburg still refused in January 1906 to consider ordering the release of the Duala from investigative custody during the new probe, claiming that the resulting loss of authority would jeopardize German rule in that troubled colony. Erzberger, however, found his suspicions of imminent catastrophe confirmed by Hohenlohe's remarks. He therefore urged the government to free the Bonambela Duala leadership precisely to avert disaster in Cameroon since miserable prison conditions had already played an important role in the outbreak of the Herero War.[78]

Nor was such Centrist apprehension of impending costly uprisings limited to Cameroon. Erzberger was quite concerned that the government of Southwest

[73]Colonial Department to Puttkamer, Sept. 12, 1905, Order 861; Hohenlohe-Langenburg to Puttkamer, Dec. 2, 1905, Telegram 69; Puttkamer to Foreign Office, Dec. 6, 1905, Telegram; Puttkamer to Colonial Department, Nov. 22, 1905, Report 1310, Secret; Lämmermann to Puttkamer, Dec. 6, 1905, Judgment, RKA, 4435: 3, 13 f., 20 (8–14), 23–39, BAP/L. Hohenlohe-Langenburg, Jan. 18, 1906, RTSB, 630A/C.

[74]Gröber, Dec. 13, 1905, RTSB, 276C.

[75]Erzberger, Jan. 16, 1906, RTSB, 592A. Erzberger, Jan. 18, 1906, RTSB, 632C/D. Erzberger, Mar. 13, 1906, RTSB, 1979C.

[76]Kalkhoff, Mar. 2, 1906, ProtBc, MA 76195, ByHSA.

[77]Gröber, Dec. 13, 1905, RTSB, 276C.

[78]Hohenlohe-Langenburg, Jan. 18, 1906, RTSB, 630C/D. Erzberger, Jan. 18, 1906, RTSB, 632D–633A, 636C–637A. Erzberger, Mar. 20, 1906, RTSB, 2174C/D. Erzberger, Semler, Feb. 6, 1906, ProtBc, RTA, 1058: 51, BAP/L. Erzberger, Mar. 5, 1906, ProtBc, MA 76195, ByHSA. Erzberger revealed the limits of his own concept of justice, however, when he suggested in the Budget Committee that, if the Buea government would only drop the charges against the Bonambela, it might still save face by "deporting the guilty to Togo."

Africa might recklessly attempt to expropriate the land of the hitherto neutral but militarily powerful Ovambo in the north.[79] Even colonial enthusiast Judge Schwarze-Lippstadt emphasized the perils of the misguided attempt of a district official in East Africa to promote the breeding of imported German bulls into the local stock. With the folly of an autocrat, the official had simply rounded up and castrated all the indigenous bulls in the region. The Westphalian jurist admonished the government that precisely this kind of facile despotism in the colonies could "immediately give rise . . . to an uprising that [could] cost us millions."[80]

Accordingly, although tempering Erzberger's interpretation of the Maji Maji Uprising, the Center party leaders otherwise shared his assessment that the Reichstag had to exercise far more control over the colonial administration than it had hitherto. The jurists therefore co-sponsored the drive for an expansion of parliamentary jurisdiction overseas in hopes that greater justice for non-Europeans would yield a peaceful, and thereby less expensive, colonial empire. Arguing in concert that the common root of the uprisings lay in the arbitrary measures of German officialdom, Judge Gröber and Erzberger both promoted their party's resolution of December 1905 calling for legislation to expand the Reichstag's colonial authority at the expense of the much abused executive right of decree.[81] In addition, given that the Southwest African catastrophe had first erupted over an overextended administration's unlawful intrusion into indigenous affairs, Erzberger, Arenberg, and Spahn led the Budget Committee in slowing the Reich's all-too-rapid expansion in East Africa by eliminating personnel authorizations for four of eight proposed new administrative districts in February 1906.[82]

Finally, the Bonambela Duala grievances and the administration's harsh reaction thereto underlined for Catholic professionals and populists alike the necessity of separating the judicial system from the colonial administration and establishing legal safeguards to protect the civil rights of indigenous peoples. Therefore, in March 1906, Centrists of all persuasions responded to the Duala petition with the successful Kalkhoff Motion. Sponsored by three Catholic judges, Professor Hertling, and Erzberger, the proposal called upon the Reich not only to appoint an impartial judge to investigate the Duala grievances, but also to

[79]Erzberger, Jan. 18, 1906, RTSB, 637A. Erzberger, Mar. 23, 1906, RTSB, 2234A. Erzberger, Feb. 20, 1906, ProtBc, RTA, 1098: 70, BAP/L.

[80]Schwarze-Lippstadt, Mar. 16, 1906, RTSB, 2058D.

[81]Gröber, Dec. 13, 1905, RTSB, 276C–277C. Erzberger, Dec. 14, 1905, RTSB, 324D–325A, 331A/B. Erzberger, Jan. 16, 1906, RTSB, 590C–591C, 605C. Erzberger, Mar. 19, 1906, RTSB, 2129B–2136A. Erzberger, Mar. 20, 1906, RTSB, 2173D–2174A.

[82]Erzberger, Jan. 16, 1906, RTSB, 594B. Erzberger, Mar. 13, 1906, RTSB, 1975C. Arenberg, Erzberger, Feb. 8, 1906, ProtBc; Arenberg, Erzberger, Spahn, Feb. 9, 1906, ProtBc, RTA, 1058: 55, 62 f., BAP/L. "Parlamentarisches: Die Budgetcommission des Reichstags," *Germania*, Feb. 10, 1906, Nr. 32. Erzberger in fact wished to eliminate all eight.

guarantee civil rights to all non-Europeans appearing before criminal and disciplinary courts and, in the meantime, to protect those merely in investigative custody from subjection to corporal punishment, forced labor, and shackling.[83] In short, African resistance movements had created such a crisis in Berlin that the Reichstag was moving with uncharacteristic firmness toward asserting authority in an area where it had previously deferred to the government.

* * *

Nevertheless, while agreeing that the irresponsible actions of colonial officials had inflicted terrible losses upon the Reich, Center populists and jurists undoubtedly differed significantly in the manner in which they approached discussion of colonial personnel policy. On the one hand, guarding the party's strategic political position, the party elders largely spared Berlin mention of official misconduct not itself linked to a major indigenous initiative. Instead, they focused upon the proposal of policy changes to improve the caliber of German officials in the overseas empire. The Center leaders recommended, for example, that government agents entering colonial service receive special preparatory education, preferably within the context of a self-contained career bureaucracy for the colonies. Likewise, they proposed that, contrary to prevailing practice, alcoholism ought to render a man ineligible for colonial appointment, whereas the state of matrimony should not.[84] As these and other jurist suggestions were generally uncontroversial, they were received graciously by Director Hohenlohe-Langenburg.[85]

Erzberger, by contrast, brandished scandalous official conduct ignored by his senior colleagues and accused the Colonial Department of condoning the maltreatment of colonized populations by neglecting to investigate serious charges of abuse and then hounding lesser officials who had dared to object to such corruption.[86] Fearful that the young Swabian was giving the Kaiser ever

[83]Erzberger, Dec. 14, 1905, RTSB, 324D–325A, 331B/C. Erzberger, Jan. 16, 1906, RTSB, 591C, 592A. Erzberger, Mar. 19, 1906, RTSB, 2133D–2134B, 2135A–2136A. Erzberger, Mar. 20, 1906, RTSB, 2174C/D. Motion Kalkhoff, Mar. 5, 1906, KDS 26, RTA, 1074: 259, BAP/L. Kalkhoff, Mar. 2, 1906, ProtBc; Kalkhoff, Erzberger, Mar. 5, 1906, ProtBc, MA 76195, ByHSA. Kalkhoff, Reporter, Mar. 20, 1906, RTSB, 2163A/B, 2179D.

[84]Schwarze-Lippstadt, Mar. 16, 1906, RTSB, 2059A/D. Bachem, Mar. 17, 1906, RTSB, 2093B–2094C. Bachem, Mar. 16, 1906, RTSB, 2077D–2078A. Bachem, Arenberg, Feb. 7, 1906, ProtBc, RTA, 1058: 52 f., BAP/L. "Parlamentarisches: In der Budgetcommission des Reichstags," *Germania*, Feb. 22, 1906, Nr. 42.

[85]Hohenlohe-Langenburg, Jan. 18, 1906, RTSB, 632A/B. Hohenlohe-Langenburg, Mar. 16, 1906, RTSB, 2062D–2063A. Hohenlohe-Langenburg, Ohnesorge, Feb. 7, 1906, ProtBc, RTA, 1058: 52 f., BAP/L. Ohnesorge, Mar. 17, 1906, RTSB, 2094C–2095A.

[86]Erzberger, Dec. 14, 1905, RTSB, 323B–324B, 326C/D. Erzberger, Mar. 13, 1906, RTSB, 1976B–1978A. Erzberger, Mar. 15, 1906, RTSB, 2047C–2048C. Erzberger, Mar. 20, 1906, RTSB, 2175B. Erzberger, Mar. 26, 1906, RTSB, 2291B–2293D, 2300B–2301A. Erzberger, Ohnesorge, Feb. 14, 1906, ProtBc, RTA, 1058: 70 f., BAP/L. Justizrat Dr. Löwenstein, *Der Prozeß*

more reason to heed the rising tide of anticlerical sentiment, the Center jurists had been privately urging Erzberger for months to exercise more restraint in his attacks upon the integrity of the Colonial Department. These warnings proved to no avail, however, and it was in this connection that some party elders deemed it necessary to take more active measures against the outspoken populist.[87]

Thus, although afflicted by a chronic neurological illness, Karl Bachem forced himself to participate more regularly in the committee and plenary Reichstag colonial debates of early 1906 in order to provide Berlin with a somewhat more governmental counterweight to Erzberger. Twice Bachem even appealed to the party's Executive Committee to remove Erzberger from the Reichstag Budget Committee, but the youthful Swabian enjoyed protection on the former body from his mentor Judge Adolf Gröber and from the Hessian textile manufacturer Richard Müller-Fulda.[88] Likewise in March, with the approval of most of the Executive Committee, Spahn disavowed Erzberger sharply before the entire Reichstag for attempting to dictate personnel policy to the administration in the case of two of his colonial informants. Perceiving the majority of the delegation behind him, however, Erzberger simply shrugged off Spahn's rebuke in condescending fashion, and populists from across southern Germany swiftly rallied around the insubordinate young Swabian.[89]

While Bachem and Spahn thus obviously shared a deep concern regarding the potential perils of the Center's colonial campaign, it has already been demonstrated above that the jurist party leadership nevertheless regularly placed itself at the forefront of the same movement. In the end, as the wave of African resistance propagated and aggravated numerous conflicts between the government

---

Erzberger-Helfferich. Ein Rechtsgutachten mit einem Begleitwort von Justizrat Dr. Löwenstein (Ulm: Süddeutsche Verlagsanstalt, 1921), 84–87, in Nachlaß Erzberger, 31, BAK.

[87]Bachem, Mar. 21, 1906, Note, Nachlaß Bachem, 238, HASK. Bachem to [Franz Bachem?], Dec. 4, 1905, Nachlaß Bachem, 239: 7, HASK. Bachem, Dec. 20, 1906, Note; Bachem, Dec. 15, 1906, Confidential; Bachem to Otto, May 18, 1907, Nachlaß Bachem, 259: 8–9, 12, HASK. Hertling to Julius Bachem, Apr. 10, 1906; Hertling to Bäumker, Apr. 26, 1906, cited in Karl von Hertling, "Manuskript," Nachlaß Hertling, 56: 73 f., 77, BAK. Hertling to Anna von Hertling, Apr. 4, 1906, Nachlaß Hertling, 17: 51, BAK. Bachem, *Vorgeschichte, Geschichte*, 6: 343 ff.

[88]In addition to the sources in the Karl Bachem papers cited in the preceding note, see also Bachem, *Vorgeschichte, Geschichte*, 6: 347 f. Epstein, "German Colonial Scandals," 653. Kiefer, *Bachem*, 172 ff.

[89]Spahn, Mar. 15, 1906, RTSB, 2029A/B. Erzberger, Mar. 15, 1906, RTSB, 2049C/D. [Julius Bachem], "Eine parlamentarische Auseinandersetzung," *KVZ*, Mar. 17, 1906, Nr. 224; [Julius Bachem, citing a letter Karl Bachem credited to Müller-Fulda], "Zu dem Zwischenfall Spahn-Erzberger," *KVZ*, Mar. 20, 1906, Nr. 233; "Spahn-Erzberger," *Tägliche Rundschau*, Mar. 30, 1906, Nr. 151; Bachem, Mar. 21, 1906, Note, Nachlaß Bachem, 238, HASK. "Aus Württemberg," *Augsburger Postzeitung*, Mar. 24, 1906, Nr. 67; "Norddeutsches und Süddeutsches Zentrum," *Hannoverscher Courier*, Apr. 11, 1906, Nachlaß Heim, 109, Stadtarchiv Regensburg. Bachem, *Vorgeschichte, Geschichte*, 6: 344–348. Epstein, "German Colonial Scandals," 652 f. Zeender, *German Center Party*, 108 f.

and the party, the widening gulf between official impenitence and populist outrage left the more conservative Center leaders swinging to and fro between sharp castigation of the Bülow administration and futile admonitions toward their own incensed colleagues.

* * *

In sum, by early 1906 numerous African military and civilian initiatives had generated intense exasperation with the Bülow administration among Centrists of all persuasions, even among bourgeois party leaders otherwise more disposed to caution and compromise. First, the Maji Maji Uprising prevented an experienced governor admired by the Center from succeeding Stuebel as colonial director and rendered the post still less attractive to other qualified candidates. The East African uprising thereby contributed to the politically and professionally imprudent appointment of an imperial favorite whose liabilities from the Centrist standpoint included both his anticlerical views and an utter lack of qualifications for the post. Second, the considerable military challenges presented by the peoples of Southwest and East Africa encouraged Berlin to handle inconvenient Reichstag prerogatives with contempt and thus to provoke parliamentary conflicts not only with the Center populists, but also at times with the party leadership. Third, the tremendous costs of particularly the Nama War brought the entire Catholic party to the limit of its deference to the Reich in military affairs and to the end of its tolerance for government favoritism toward colonial economic interests. Fourth, Anago, Dahomey, and Duala civilian resistance exposed to the Center as a whole the apparently endemic malfeasance and anticlericalism among German colonial officials, an insight that greatly exacerbated the party's increasing recalcitrance in colonial affairs.

Finally, the pathos of the widespread African grievances evoked forceful Centrist accusations against the brutality and incompetence of colonial officials, whom even the bourgeois professionals held largely responsible for the devastating losses to the Reich. Indeed, the disturbing frequency and enormous expense of the uprisings engendered a pervasive fear among Centrists of further imminent disasters that only rigorous Reichstag oversight, expanded legislative powers at executive expense, and legal safeguards guaranteeing the civil rights of non-Europeans might hope to avert. Thus incessantly agitated by the consequences of a wide array of violent and peaceful African resistance movements, an indignant Center party threw down the gauntlet in May 1906, dealing the Bülow administration a stunning triple parliamentary defeat in colonial affairs, a provocation that would soon meet its rebuttal in the Reichstag dissolution the following December.

EASTERN KENTUCKY UNIVERSITY

Part III
Modes of Imagining

[7]

Imperialism and Nationalism in India

ANIL SEAL

AMONG the dominant themes of world history during the nineteenth and twentieth centuries have been the imperialism of the west and the nationalism of its colonial subjects. Nowhere were these themes developed more spectacularly than in South Asia; its history quite naturally came to be viewed as a gigantic clash between these two large forces. The subject then was held together by a set of assumptions about the imperialism of the British and the reactions of the Indians against it. That imperialism, so it was thought, had engineered great effects on the territories where it ruled. Those who held the power could make the policy, and they could see that it became the practice. Sometimes that policy might be formulated ineptly or might fall on stony ground or even smash against the hard facts of colonial life. But for good or ill, imperial policy seemed to be the main force affecting colonial conditions. It emerged from an identifiable source, the official mind of Whitehall or the contrivances of pro-consuls; and so the study of policy-making made a framework for investigations into colonial history.

These assumptions were convenient, but historians of colony after colony have knocked them down. The emphasis has shifted from the elegant exchanges between London and colonial capitals to the brutal clashes between colonial politicians struggling at the more humdrum levels where the pickings lay. No longer will it do to exalt the work of Mr Mothercountry, cobbling together constitutions for dependencies, above the inescapable constraints inside them. The old assumption that direct imperial power was strong has been replaced by the new doctrine that it was hobbled at every turn. It depended on local allies. Local conditions might buckle its policies. Often it did not know what it was doing. Assumptions about the irresistible power of imperialism were always slippery notions;[1] now they are refuted notions. Once the study of policy-making lay in the mainstream; now it has retreated into

[1] Perhaps the most devoted advocate of imperial power was Curzon, but bitter experience led him to conclude that 'The Government of India is a mighty and miraculous machine for doing nothing'. Curzon to Hamilton, 9 April 1902. Curzon Papers, Mss Eur F 111/161, India Office Library.

backwaters. The effect upon the study of modern Indian history is plain. Historians have switched their attention from imperial fiats to Indian facts, from the rambling generalizations of the Raj to the concreteness of local studies, from large imprecision to minute exactitude. In so doing, they have demolished part of the framework of the subject.

At the same time they have cracked the other casing which helped to hold it together. However tentative its beginnings, nationalism in India used to be seen as a general movement which voiced the interests of large sections of the Indian people. Just as imperial policies were thought to lead to imperial practice, so nationalist programmes were thought to emerge from national movements. But much the same findings which have been fatal to the old views about imperialism have also destroyed the view that nationalism was a force working generally inside a nation. As its provincial, and then its local roots have been laid bare, what looked like an all-India movement appears as nothing of the sort. Programmes proclaimed from above were at odds with the way politicians worked lower down. What held true in one part of India was not true in another. It is no longer credible to write about a movement grounded in common aims, led by men with similar backgrounds, and recruited from widening groups with compatible interests. That movement now looks more like a ramshackle coalition throughout its long career. Its unity seems a figment. Its power appears as hollow as that of the imperial authority it was supposedly challenging. Its history was the rivalry between Indian and Indian, its relationship with imperialism that of the mutual clinging of two unsteady men of straw. Consequently, it now seems impossible to organize modern Indian history around the old notions of imperialism and nationalism. But their disappearance has had awkward results.

Having failed to discover unities in the politics of all-India, historians cut their losses by turning to the study of the regions, whether defined as the old provinces of British India or as areas with a common language. There they hoped to find unities to help them regulate these new fields of study: caste seemed to explain much about the politics of Bengal and Madras, as did religious allegiance in the Punjab, kinship in the United Provinces and language in Orissa or the Karnatak. In turning to the regions, and to the solidarities within them, these scholars were in fact falling back on positions prepared long ago by the British administrators. Over and over again the Old India Hands had stressed that India was not a nation but a congeries of countries,[2] each of which

[2] According to Sir John Strachey, '... the first and most essential thing to learn about India—[is] that there is not, and never was an India, or even any country of

contained large groups of people who were held together by bonds such as caste and kin, community and language, and who could be classed under these tidy heads for the convenience of the administrators. Here were sets of ready-made uniformities around which the historian of the region could crystallize his explanations. For a time it seemed as though the truisms of the Raj were to become the dogmas of the historians.[3] But the roots of politics turned out to lie lower still. Other workers have dug below the province and the region, into the district, the municipality, even the village. Mining at such deep levels had led to the caving-in of beliefs that there were regional uniformities cementing Indian politics. What seems to have decided political choices in the localities was the race for influence, status and resources. In the pursuit of these aims, patrons regimented their clients into factions which jockeyed for position. Rather than partnerships between fellows, these were usually associations of bigwigs and followers. In other words they were vertical alliances, not horizontal alliances. Local struggles were seldom marked by the alliance of landlord with landlord, peasant with peasant, educated with educated, Muslim with Muslim and Brahmin with Brahmin. More frequently, Hindus worked with Muslims, Brahmins were hand in glove with non-Brahmins; and notables organized their dependents as supporters, commissioned professional men as spokesmen and turned government servants into aides. In the everyday decisions of life as they were taken in many localities, the social dockets devised by the administrator and adopted by the historian had little meaning.

As knowledge has increased, so has confusion. Politics at the base seem different in kind from politics in the province or in the nation. Whatever forces may have brought men into partnership at these higher levels, they can hardly have been the same as those which made men work together in the neighbourhoods. However persuasive the slogans from the top, they can have made little impact upon the unabashed scramblers for advantage at the bottom. Indeed there seems no necessary reason why the politics of these localities should have become enmeshed with the larger processes at all. It is not obvious why bosses

India, possessing according to European ideas, any sort of unity....' It is interesting that this classic apology for British rule stressed its centralizing and unifying impact, but denied that 'such bonds of union can in any way lead towards the growth of a single Indian nationality'. John Strachey, *India* (London, 1888), pp. 5, 8.

[3] The officials of the Raj provided many of the data upon which studies of the political arithmetic of the regions are based, and administrative practice rested on their categories. That is another reason why their arguments have powerfully influenced the new wave among historians of India.

in Tanjore or Belgaum should have sought allies in Madras or Bombay, still less in all-India circles. But there is no denying that such linkages existed, and that they came to exert a vast influence over the country's politics. The Indian Association and the Unionist party each spanned a province; the Hindu Mahasabha, the anti-untouchability league, the movements for sanatanadharma and cow-protection worked across several provinces; the Home Rule Leagues, the National Liberal Federation, the Indian National Social Conference, the all-India Scheduled Castes Federation, the Khilafat Party and the Muslim Conference claimed to be national bodies; while the Congress and the Muslim League were undeniably all-India organizations. Non-cooperation, civil disobedience, and the movements for Quit India and for Pakistan were not the products of the village green. It would be a sterile historiography which resigned itself to declaring that these were the products of linkages whose nature is unknown. The result would be the disintegration of the subject.

One of the main tasks in its reintegration must be to identify the forces which drove Indian politics upwards and outwards from the oddities of the locality, or downwards from the hollow generalities of all-India, which bonded their political activities together, and which determined the nature of the relations between them. This work of reconstruction must also find an explanation for the extraordinary volatility and discontinuity of political behaviour in so much of India, as well as for the palpable gap between what politicians claimed to represent and what they really stood for. The priorities of politicians, the roles they played, the principles they claimed to support, seem to have varied as they moved between one arena and another; in each and every sphere, the alliances they made showed extreme shifts and turns. Members of the Justice Party in the nineteen-twenties were the Congressmen of the nineteen-thirties. Cooperators became non-cooperators. The gaolbirds of civil disobedience came out for council entry. Congress Muslims turned round and supported Pakistan. These are large problems, and they call for large solutions. It is not good enough for the historian to set up an explanation of the workings of politics at one level and then cast around for a few supporting examples at another, higher or lower, conveniently forgetting that most of these cases actually cut across the grain of his argument. In the analysis of a political system which worked at different levels, models appropriate for one of them cannot simply be transposed to the others. Local, provincial and national politics worked as they did because they were interconnected; it is the connections which must be elucidated. The problem is central to the history of all colonial nationalisms in modern times. Formed out of disparate aspirations and grievances, they were somehow generalized into unities stronger than their own contradictions. In the Indian context, the problem takes this form. A great deal of local Indian politics (although, as we shall see, not all) was organized into factions by the influence of the strong upon the weak, and into systems apparently insulated from each other. Lateral connections and solidarities which might have united them were few. Yet they came to be linked with other systems, thereby producing large movements. What was the nature of those linkages?

Several explanations have been suggested. One line of argument has stressed the enduring importance of traditional forces throughout all the changes in modern India. Webs of kinship and of clan, solidarities of community and ritual might be seen as conserving or regenerating supra-local unities. Another argument asserts that the development of the economy drove the localities into larger and larger systems of production and exchange. Admittedly there was no national economy: development was far too patchy for that. But in some parts of India the increase in cash crops, the growth of trading communities and the development of the professions stimulated both town and country, encouraging the spread of social groups, whether they were rich peasants in the Andhra delta, traders along the Ganges, the western-educated in Calcutta or businessmen in Bombay. There is merit in both arguments. Certainly there were cases in most regions where the emergence of larger groupings can best be explained by linkages which were the result of traditional or economic forces. It is still more suggestive that some of these groupings tended to stick together through thick and thin, an atypical trait which was to give them great importance in Indian politics. However, these cases of horizontal connection cannot explain how linkages were forged between the host of factions that did not possess solidarities of this sort. Yet it was precisely these factions that were the stuff of most Indian politics. On the unsteady base of local squabbles for spoils rested the larger political systems of India: the Justice and Unionist parties, and the Congress itself, were largely built out of this rubble. Both types of politics need to be explained, but the arguments mentioned so far can apply only to the loyalties of horizontal connection and not to the vast mass of political systems which lacked them. In order to provide a more general explanation, we propose an alternative approach.

This entails reopening the study of government, although not along the old lines. The argument that the rule of strangers in India goaded their subjects into organizing against it is not our concern. The suggestion that government prepared its own destruction by fostering an intellectual elite is not relevant.[4] The fact that the power of imperialism was far from irresistible can readily be admitted. What is important about the role of government is the structure which the British created for ruling their Indian empire. However much they may have relied on Indian collaborators, their government was organized for the power and profit of their imperial system throughout the world. In the pursuit of this aim, they needed to treat their Indian possessions as a whole. Though they were the successors of nawabs and maharajahs galore, they were in India not as partitioners but as unifiers. Essentially, the Indian empire was meant to be indivisible.[5] Hence it was ruled through a chain of command stretching from London to the districts and townships of India; hence too, the government of India held sway over all-India, so that even the pettiest official intervention in a locality issued from a general authority. These administrative lines formed a grid which at first rested loosely upon the base. Later it was pressed down more firmly by the heavier intervention of the Raj in local matters and by the growth of representative institutions. Indians needed to treat with the Raj, and increasingly they came to do so by exploiting its structure of control and the forms in which its commands were cast. This called for a political structure of their own which could match the administrative and representative structure of the Raj, and was in time to inherit its functions. In this way we may help to explain the nature of the linkages which were to bind together the very different activities of Indians in arenas large and small.

II

We shall begin by looking afresh at the interplay between imperialism and Indian political society. It is our hypothesis that the structure of imperial government can provide a clue to the way Indian politics developed. This structure in India cannot be explained by Indian considerations alone. It is obvious that the development of the Raj moved widdershins to the tendencies prevalent in the British empire as

[4] Graduates and professional men in the presidencies undoubtedly had a large part to play in the politics of province and nation. But they were not quite as important as they once appeared. Some of the suggestions in Anil Seal, *The Emergence of Indian Nationalism* (Cambridge, 1968), have dropped through the trapdoor of historiography.

[5] Of course the presidencies liked to recall their separate historical pasts. So did the princes. But the Supreme Goverment eroded these little local vanities.

a whole. When the British were relying upon the techniques of informal empire to better their world position, their Indian possessions stood out as a huge exception, as a formal empire on the grand scale. At the very time they were slackening control over many of their colonies, they were tightening London's hold over India. Incongruities of this sort continued into the twentieth century, when the administrative diversities in the new African colonies contrasted with the uniformities of the Raj, and when imperial control over defence and foreign policy, splintered throughout much of the empire, remained as firm as ever in India. Most of the essential aspects of the connection between Britain and India remained substantially unchanged until 1947. Why should this have been so? The reasons for these incongruities lie in the permanent importance of India to the position of Britain in the world and the permanent difficulties of maintaining the British position in India.

India's worth was clear to Pitt and Dundas; the establishment of British power in India was matched by her growing importance as a base for further expansion in the Indian Ocean and the Yellow Sea. During the nineteenth century India became a good customer for British manufactures; she was to become a useful supplier of raw materials, a crucial element in the British balance of payments and a field for large capital investment. But the balance sheets of imperialism do not reveal the full importance of the Raj to the British Empire. Imperialism is a system of formal or informal expansion, driven by impulses of profit and of power, each of which feeds on the other. India's growing foreign trade helped to push the influence of the British deeper into west and east Asia alike. Her growing military power underwrote the informal influence they were developing in those regions, as well as the formal empire which they built in Burma, Malaya and East Africa. India became the second centre for the extension of British power and influence in the world; and when she dropped this role after 1947, the British empire did not take long to disappear.

Throughout the century and a half of British rule, the Raj was being worked in the service of interests far larger than India herself, since they bore upon the British position in the world. That is why the control of the Raj as a system of profit and power had to lie in London. And that is why London's control over India had to be matched by the increasingly tight grip of the Governor-General over his subordinate administrations. These imperial aims combined with the circumstances in India itself to determine the structure of government and the nature of its administration. The British wanted to pull resources out of India, not to put their own into India. Therefore the administrative and military system had to pay for itself with Indian revenues. At the top, this called for a skilled bureaucracy capable of handling large issues bearing upon the economy and the army. But at lower levels this control had to be looser. There, imperial ends had to be satisfied by more modest programmes. The chief source of Indian revenue lay in land, and it had to be collected from millions of payers. In the localities the main tasks were to secure the cheap and regular collection of revenue and to see to it that the districts remained quiet. But these tasks were beyond the unaided capacity of the British administrators on the spot.[6] British agents were costly. Happily, Indian collaborators were not, and for much of the business of extracting tribute and keeping the peace, the British were content to follow the precepts of Clive and Cornwallis by relying on the help of influential Indians prepared to work with the regime. It was in the administration of the localities that the vital economies in ruling had to be made. There, governance had to be pursued by simpler arrangements, such as the frontier methods of Nikel Seyn in the Punjab or the lonely patrols of Cross Beames in the wilds of Orissa, or by enlisting the cooperation of zemindars, mirasidars, talukdars, and urban rais.

By accepting such men as their local collaborators, the British were in fact striking a political bargain. Its terms were that they could depend on the collection of revenue, provided that they did not ask too officiously who paid it; and that they might take public order for granted, provided that they themselves did not play too obtrusive a part in enforcing it. The British built the framework; the Indians fitted into it. Local bargains of this sort were of great advantage to the British because they reduced Indian politics to the level of haggles between the Raj and small pockets of its subjects, a system which kept them satisfactorily divided. These were solid gains, but they had to be paid for. In return, the British had to acquiesce in an arrangement where strong local intermediaries could block them from meddling in the affairs of those who owned land, or controlling the others who tilled it. This meant in practice that the British were winking at the existence of a legal underworld where the private justice of faction settled conflicts with the blows of lathis, or where, at the best, the strong could get their own way in the courts. In the mythology of empire, the age of Elphinstone, Munro and Thomason seems one of heroic social engineering; but under the pinnacles of their Raj lay a ground-floor reality where Indians battled with Indians, sometimes for the favours of the district officer, sometimes to do each other down without reference to him and

[6] White settlers, once prohibited, later were never more than a handful.

his book of rules. At these levels, it might be the British who governed, but it was Indians who ruled.

This is not to suggest that at any period the Raj was merely a night-watchman and receiver of tribute;[7] or that its systems of collaboration simply meant confirming things as they were. Even under John Company, government ratified, or upset, social and economic arrangements which extended far beyond the localities. In this rupturing of the autonomy of regions and localities lies one of the chief innovations of British rule. The Raj defined the forms and established the categories even in matters where its subjects were allowed a free hand. Already in this period Indian response had to take note of British regulation. After 1843 men from Sind, Gujarat, Maharashtra and the Karnatak had to vie with each other for the favours of an administration run from Bombay city. Once men had been classed as zemindars or ryots in the settlements, they had to accept these classifications when they treated with government.

But the irruption of government into the regions and localities went much further in the second half of the nineteenth century. As imperial interests expanded, so did their demands upon India. Indian revenues had to pay for an army liable to defend British interests outside India;[8] they had to meet the growing overheads of administration; they had to guarantee loans for the railways. These demands were harder to meet. In 1858 the Crown inherited from the Company a regime crippled by poverty, and until the end of the century the reorganized government was never to escape from financial weakness. A costly dash in and out of Afghanistan, a fall in silver or a bad monsoon could tip Indian finances into deficit. Crises were likelier than windfalls. Direct taxes yielded little.[9] Locked in these fetters, the Raj had to create more resources and

[7] Many of the land settlements of the Raj were also designed to stimulate agrarian improvement; its canals brought new land under cultivation; its improvements to transport linked cities which it had done so much to create. It sent Indians to school, partly to train cheap clerks for its offices, but also to create economic men. But to judge the Raj as an immensely powerful system of government makes sense only in terms of policy-making. In practice, many of its efforts were buckled by the hard facts of Indian society.

[8] About a third of the total expenditure of the Indian government in the four decades before World War I was on its army. Statistical tables on government's finances (and on many other aspects of Indian society and economy) are being prepared, with the help of C. Emery, by the modern Indian history project at Cambridge, financed by a grant from the Social Sciences Research Council. It is hoped to publish these results soon.

[9] Expanding its revenues was a difficult task for a government which relied upon so regressive a system of taxation. Income tax was obstructed by Indian interests, customs duties were kept low by imperial interests, opium was threatened by humani-

take its cut. Tribute from the lease of franchises to local notables was no longer enough to meet the bill. Loose controls by London of Calcutta, by Calcutta of its provinces, by provincial capitals of the districts had all to be tightened. Raising revenues meant a greater administrative intervention in the affairs of Indian society, going deeper than the previous system had done. But such an intervention was exposed to the perennial dilemma of the Raj. If the administrative cost of intervening was not to overtake the returns and the security of the state not to be put at risk, Indian collaboration would have to be much extended. So the Raj mitigated its administrative drive by devising new methods of winning the cooperation of a larger number of Indians. Systems of nomination, representation and election were all means of enlisting Indians to work for imperial ends.

The Government of India Act of 1858 had created a Secretary of State whose powers stretched far beyond those of his predecessor, the President of the Board of Control. He was in continuous touch with policy-making; before long he had won 'abundant power in one way or another of enforcing his views';[10] and he could demand due obedience from all British authorities in India. Thus the constitutional principle became established that '. . . the final control and direction of affairs of India rest with the Home Government, and not with the authorities . . . in India itself'.[11] Even the Acts of 1919 and 1935 kept London in command of the centre, and until 1947 the vital attributes of sovereignty remained there.[12] London did what it pleased with India's army; it took her to war, and it brought her to peace; London alone could alter her constitution. It was London that took the decisions about the siphoning-off of Indian revenues, the pace of Indian development, and the deployment of Indian power; and these controls were kept intact until London decided to divide and quit.

Not only did the nature of imperial aims call for London's control

tarian interests. Until the beginning of the twentieth century, government finances continued to be propped up by the peasants, since receipts from land revenue were greater than receipts from all other taxes put together.

[10] Sir Charles Wood quoted in R. J. Moore, *Sir Charles Wood's Indian Policy 1853–66* (Manchester, 1966), p. 39.

[11] A. C. Banerjee, *Indian Constitutional Documents 1757–1947* (Calcutta, 1961, third edition), II, 319.

[12] Control over defence and foreign policy was not even mentioned in the Montagu–Chelmsford report; the Government of India Act of 1935 stated that this control was to remain in British hands (26 Geo. V, c. 2, section 11). London also kept the true underpinnings of profit. It was from London that Indian loans came; London manipulated the exchange rate of the rupee as it saw fit and knocked India off the gold standard when that suited its purpose. Even the granting of tariff autonomy to India meant less in practice than in publicity.

over India; it also called for control over its subordinate administrations to keep them in line with British purposes. The Charter Act of 1833, which brought the Supreme Government into being, had also granted the Governor-General in Council control over the entire revenues of all the territories in British India. Point by point, the government in Calcutta hammered home these advantages, strengthening its managerial services, framing a central budget, and regulating finances so that the provinces had to live on whatever doles the centre saw fit to allow them. One by one, the old freedoms of the Presidencies were mopped up by Calcutta. In 1893 the Bombay and Madras military commands were abolished; during the early twentieth century the central government gradually wrested from the provinces their control over relations with the princely states. It became the orthodoxy of constitutional lawyers that, whatever the rights and the duties of the provinces in running their affairs, yet '. . . in all of them the Government of India exercise an unquestioned right of entry . . .'[13] During the nineteenth century the provinces had been degraded into mere agents of the centre. In the twentieth century administrative necessity might demand decentralization and political pressures might call for devolution, but even the Acts of 1919 and 1935 were not permitted by the rulers of India to threaten central control over matters that crucially affected imperial purposes in India.[14] In terms of formal constitutional history these Acts may have altered the working arrangements of the Raj; but in terms of power they were simply changes in the methods by which the British pursued their essential aims.

But managers need agents, and in the Indian empire these had to be the provincial administrations. The general principles of legislation and administration were laid down from above, but the execution of both had to be undertaken in the provinces. In the later nineteenth century London and Calcutta decided that more needed to be done with their Indian empire: tenancy legislation, new laws about contract and transfer of land, public works, irrigation, public health, forest conservancy, famine codes, takkavi loans, education both primary and secondary, all

[13] *Report on Indian Constitutional Reforms* (Calcutta, 1918), para. 49, p. 33.

[14] After 1919 the provinces had assured monies of their own; but the central government took a firmer grip than before in auditing their accounts. Again, the provincial governments administered the Criminal Investigation Departments founded between 1905 and 1907; but important intelligence work was always left to officers from the central CID after 1919, and the reforms of 1935 led to the appointment in the province of a Central Intelligence Officer who was responsible to the Intelligence Bureau in New Delhi. Sir Percival Griffiths, *To Guard My People. The History of the Indian Police* (London, 1971), pp. 342–54.

came to be in the day's work for this improving government. Much of the legislation was framed in the provinces. Most of the actual work was done in the provinces. Provincial secretariats and district officers had new duties piled upon them. The local arms of all the central departments, whether forestry or agriculture, commerce or industry, excise or education, were jerked into a new activity. The hordes of petty officials who had been government servants more in name than in deed, now had to respond more efficiently to orders from above.

But these developments had to be paid for. Since government needed to squeeze the last rupee out of its territories, this in turn could only mean more thorough intervention on its part. In pulling up the slack at the base of the system, the Raj called upon its provinces and their agents to meddle more actively below. The easy-going collaboration which had guided affairs in so many localities was no longer adequate for those purposes. Hence there were bound to be big upsets in old franchises. But here was the rub. Even under the old system, there had been plenty of upsets. After the rising of 1857, the British became preoccupied with the stability of their rule, more sensitive to Indian pressures, more alert to Indian opinion. They were well aware that they had to soothe discontents and, wherever possible, deflect them against other Indians. The new situation complicated that task: the heavier the intervention, the higher the risk.

Between the pressures of imperial demands and of Indian discontents, the Raj negotiated uneasily. In obedience to the former, there had to be more rule-making and general instructions from headquarters, and the power of the bureaucracies had to smack harder upon Indian society. On the other hand, these new intrusions into old immunities were balanced by the development of a system of representation, designed to make administrative pressures more acceptable, the rule-making process less arbitrary, and the recruitment of Indian assistants at the levels where they were needed less difficult. This system was set to work particularly at the points of execution rather than of command.

To begin with, there were strong pragmatic grounds for granting Indians a limited say in the conduct of local affairs.[15] These were not in the main the reasons that appealed to Ripon in his famous resolution, nor have they been emphasized by historians who see local self-government as the first stage in the political education of Indians. As Lawrence

[15] But leading Indian politicians, concerned to change the structure of the Legislative Councils, quickly lost interest in local self-government when they saw that it was to begin and end in the localities; only when it came to be tied more firmly to the structure of rule above, did their interest in the municipalities and rural boards revive.

and Mayo were acutely aware, financial stringency made good sense of changes which successfully loaded the new municipalities with police and conservancy charges. When municipal and local boards were formed in most of the provinces after 1882, economy was again the clue. These local institutions also aided the Raj in its search for resources. Their powers were small, but the sums they raised and disbursed steadily increased. They had another useful role to play. They enabled government to associate interests in the localities more widely, and balance them more finely, than had the old rule of thumb methods of the Collector.[16]

Beyond these pragmatic considerations, the widening of the representative system carried political advantages of a different sort. It brought more Indians into consultation about the management of their affairs; yet it kept them at work inside a framework which safeguarded British interests. In other words, the new system was casting wider nets to find collaborators. Conversations in the dak bungalow or on the Collector's verandah were no longer a satisfactory means for selecting them. Nomination based on the representation of interests was one way of finding them; elections found even more. Both methods worked to keep them in equipoise. In this way, representation became one of the vehicles for driving deeper into local society.

But these modest representative bodies were to become important for another reason. Once the British extended municipal and district boards into most of the provinces, they went on to use them for purposes beyond the limited spheres of local taxation and administration. The British found them convenient as a way of adding, first a representative, and later an elective, veneer to the superior councils which they were now developing. After the India Councils Act of 1861, provincial legislative councils were set up in Madras, Bombay and Bengal; the North-western Provinces obtained a council in 1886, and the Punjab in 1897. The Act of 1892 increased the number of nominated members on these councils; but it also admitted the elective principle by the back door, since nominations might now be recommended by specific Indian organizations. In practice, this came to mean that district boards and municipalities, together with landlords, chambers of commerce and universities, nominated a few members. In 1909 the Morley–Minto reforms extended the links between higher and lower councils and

[16] Thus, for example, the membership of the rural boards in the Central Provinces was intended to represent the interests of landlords and traders; during the eighteen-eighties some towns in the Punjab began to reserve seats for communities. Much the same process can be seen in the municipalities of the United Provinces before 1916.

enlarged the role of local men. Twelve of the twenty-seven members of the Legislative Council of the Governor-General were to be chosen by the non-official members of the provincial councils; and in each of the provincial councils a number of members were to be elected by the municipalities and district boards. At the same time, special interests such as landlords, Muslims and businessmen had the right to elect members to both provincial councils and the council of the Governor-General.

Throughout this evolution two processes were at work. First, it is evident that Government was now balancing interests by separating them into categories of its own defining. Who were 'the Mohammadan Community in the Presidency of Bengal' or the 'Landholders in the United Provinces', each of whom was to elect one member to the Governor-General's Council? Neither of these bland categories made any sense at the local level in Bengal and the United Provinces; both of them ignored the different interests and rivalries among those groups whom the British bundled together in a phrase.

In the second place, the spread of representation had now produced a legislative system which extended from the lowest to the highest level in India. In one sense the system formed a sort of representative pyramid. In most provinces the sub-district boards acted as electoral colleges for part of the membership of district boards. Together with the municipalities, these boards elected members to the provincial councils, which in turn elected members to the imperial council. But in a wider sense the British had now constructed a representative and legislative structure which complemented their administrative structure. Together these two systems created bonds between the localities and the higher arenas of politics and administration.

While the reforms of 1919 upset the pyramid, they greatly strengthened these bonds. Local bodies no longer elected to provincial councils, but they were bolted much more firmly into provincial politics. As part of the bargain of dyarchy, local self-government became the responsibility of ministers who were appointed from among non-official members. They used their influence over local affairs to reward their friends and punish their critics. But there was another side to the coin. Members of local boards and of provincial councils alike were now elected on a much wider franchise. Hence a wider range of local interests had to be cajoled. Members of the new provincial councils found that their constituents were much more disposed to re-elect them when the lives of these voters had been sweetened by tit-bits flung to them by the ministers. Charity in the locality now began in the province.

The hierarchy of British rule through Indian collaboration survived the reforms of 1935. The centre still kept a firm grip over sovereign authority, reserving important powers over the provinces and giving its Indian collaborators little say in these safeguards; by granting the provinces the substance of self-government, by widening the electorate, the British ensured that their provincial successors had also to take account of far larger numbers of Indians who had the vote. While shooting Niagara, the British saw to it that their central powers remained intact and that India was still ruled by an interconnected system of government. The federal provisions of the 1935 Act never came into operation. The uncertainty that flowed from this, together with the outbreak of war, meant that this Act was only a temporary settlement. The proposals from the Viceroy, the missions from London, and the talks at Delhi were preludes for transfer of power at the centre which the Raj had guarded so jealously for so long.

As preparations to concession, whether interim or final, the British stuck to their old strategy of thrusting their subjects into broad categories and divisions. The Hindus, Muslims, Sikhs and Depressed Classes defined by the Communal Award of 1932 were the penultimate classifications in a policy which ended in Partition. By the federal arrangements of 1935 an even more improbable category, the Indian Princes, was brought into the game. This was part and parcel of a process which can be seen both in the administrative and the representative systems of the Raj in India. As government intervened more, as its regulations became more uniform, its rules more Olympian, the categories which defined Indian diversity had to become more and more abstract and rough-hewn. What remained true from first to last was that Indians could not afford to ignore them in their political response.

III

In this section, the emphasis will lie on the forces which brought together the politics of small and larger arenas in India. By scrutinizing linkages, perhaps some of the puzzles of modern Indian history will be resolved: Why have good arguments about the nature of politics at one level lost cogency when applied to another? Why have Indian politicians played such apparently inconsistent roles in different spheres? Why have they claimed to stand for one interest when in fact they were pursuing another? How have the politics of constitutionalism and agitation been connected? What has governed the timing of outbursts of activity and of relapses into quiescence?

A straightforward hypothesis provides a way into the problem. Government was intervening in the local affairs of its subjects. These interventions took place inside a system of rule stretching from London to the Indian village. Government was pressing upon the uneven and disjointed societies of its subjects; they reacted, and their reactions differed. Indian diversity ensured endless variations in their response to government pressure, normally uniform, but they all had to devise systems of politics which enabled them to react at the points where that pressure was applied. In responding to government Indians had to be adaptable, and here one pliancy met another. However much it may have blustered to the contrary, the Raj was designed to respond to some pressures from its subjects, who were thus encouraged to organize to treat with it. Some saw advantage in doing so. Others saw it as necessary insurance against disadvantages. Either way, their efforts to exploit the network of government constitute one of the forces linking the arenas of Indian politics.

But the argument must go beyond this simple hypothesis. Government intervention might be on the increase; but it never gained exclusive possession of the lives of its subjects. Indians stood firmly by their own essentials, whether these were matters of ritual, family feuds or local standing. The Raj, plastic in many matters but unbending in some, maintained its reserved topics. So too did its subjects.[17] Neither side cared much about the other's.[18] Hence many of the Indian responses to government's initiatives were for limited purposes and at limited periods.

There is another qualification to the hypothesis. It would be convenient if Indian political action had been simply a response to British initiative; but it would be too convenient to be true. Admittedly, there were parts of the country with few interests beyond those of the locality; and here kinship spun small webs, buying and selling were done in tiny marts, and religious horizons seldom lay beyond the nearby temple or mosque. In the arid Madras Deccan, for example, common interests

[17] One consequence of the reforms was the growing intervention by Indians in matters where the Raj had always feared to tread: the Hindu Religious Endowments Act of 1926 was not a measure that the Madras Government would have passed before devolution.

[18] Of course, when the British retreated upon the centre, their concern with the details of the religious and social prejudices of their subjects became more remote than ever, while Indian interest in the powers which the British retained became much keener.

were narrow, and government institutions provided the chief impulse for bringing village and firkar into wider systems. But other regions had more powerful solidarities. Whatever moved the rich peasants such as the jotedars of Midnapore, the patidars of Gujarat and the ryots of the Andhra deltas, the Agarwal enthusiasts who traded along the Ganges, or the Khilafatists of Hindustan, it was not merely a desire to parley with their rulers. Granted, they could not ignore the Raj, since it had helped to widen the opportunities for trade and to heighten the resentments of Muslims. But they possessed a community of interest which did not simply arise from the behest of the Raj. Cases such as these make it clear that the bald hypothesis with which we began cannot provide a total explanation of the problem of linkages.

Early in the nineteenth century Indian politicians were already anxious to negotiate with London. That is evidence of the logic of the interconnection. Over high policy, such as the constitution or fiscal issues or the employment of covenanted civilians, it was not Calcutta which could satisfy them, but only the ultimate authority. From the time of Rammohan Roy's passage to England, every reconsideration of India's constitution by parliament led to a rush of Indian petitions to Westminster, and the setting-up of organizations to back them. The Bombay Association, the Deccan Sabha, and the Madras Native Association owed their existence to the Charter revision of 1853. In the eighteen-eighties, hopes for constitutional crumbs created several new associations in the presidency capitals and then in 1885 joined them together into the Indian National Congress. At first this mendicancy by the nation led to little more than annual festivals, where provincial delegates met, orated and dispersed.

Their provincial organizations might seem hollow, with nothing to lose but their prospectuses; but they had an operational part to play. As officials and legislatures in the provinces took more of the decisions and made more of the rules, butting into local sanctuaries, shuffling the standing of men and their share of the booty, they gave district bosses reasons for negotiating with the administration at heights to which they had not previously been minded to climb. It was through the provinces that government intervened; hence it was through provincial politics that local men hoped to influence it. Searching for credentials, coteries in the capitals sought supporters up country; needing a forum, mofussil men sometimes turned to the magniloquently named bodies in the cities.

The Raj itself had cut the steps which these petitioners had to mount; it had also defined the tests they had to pass. Its administration had carved its peoples into large administrative blocks;[19] and it had set up a system of representing them. In effect Indians were now being invited to voice the interests of others, if they could show credentials as the spokesmen of a block. This amounted to a licence, almost a command, to form associations intelligible to government. For the ambitious politician the entrance fee was to assert or pretend affinities with those who had been bundled into the same category.[20] Some of these associations were small, claiming to speak for parochial interests; but others, such as the National Muhammadan Association of Calcutta and the British Indian Association of Bengal, bravely claimed wider constituencies.

As the British extended their representative systems, the growth of these associations became self-sustaining. As a promoter successfully asserted his claim to speak with government, he might hope for nomination to the higher councils, for greater influence over the regulations and useful contacts among the bureaucrats at the top. But the promoter's gain was likely to mean his competitor's loss; and the best hope for the loser was to adopt the same tactics as the winner for whom they worked so well. The result was often an organizational tit-for-tat where the forming of one association provoked the forming of a rival. At least this might prevent one's case from going by default; it might cast doubt on the credibility of his opponents; and at best it might pluck from them the coveted accolade of official recognition. But competitiveness led to more than that. Rivalry forced opponents to search for supporters at lower levels. The Indian Association did so in Bengal, and so did Tilak in Bombay, when he wooed city labourers for his Home Rule League. It compelled defeated groups to look for allies at their own level elsewhere, as the Ghose brothers, Bipin Chandra Pal and Aurobindo were doing when they approached Tilak in Poona during the swadeshi and boycott agitations. It might compel them to seek help at higher levels, as the Hindu zealots had in mind when they formed an all-India Hindu Mahasabha in 1909. Associations looking

[19] It suited the administrative convenience of the British to deem that throughout India, a landlord was a landlord and that a Muslim was a Muslim. Deeming is always dangerous, and many historians have been misled by this example of it. Sir Herbert Risley was responsible for much of the category-making behind the Morley–Minto reforms; but we need not suppose that such a distinguished ethnographer, with thousands of castes to his credit, believed that Indians could really be shut into such large boxes.

[20] In the towns and villages, men of different religions, castes and occupations worked promiscuously together, heedless of the categories of the census and legislation. Indians had to don new caps to fit the rules. Cornwallis's zemindars and Munro's ryots had done much the same.

for support above, below, and at their side proliferated greatly. Now, they required politicians whose profession was to act as intermediaries and spokesmen, men at home with the governmental grid and the matching structure of politics, able to shuttle between arenas. Sometimes they had no base of their own, and this very freedom from the webs of local interest gave them a role that went beyond the localities. The careers of Dadabhai, Gokhale, the Ali brothers, the Nehrus, Jinnah and Gandhi himself show the increasing importance of the profession of politics.[21] Associations, like cricket, were British innovations, and, like cricket, became an Indian craze.

This explanation has been baldly stated because the purpose of an introduction is to introduce and the range of cases is immense. But the visit to India of the Secretary of State at the end of 1917 provided striking illustrations of the process that had been at work. As soon as Montagu arrived, deputations and memoranda cascaded upon him. 222 associations addressed representations to him. They were just the tip. Many other groups would have approached him had they not been turned away. Still others left their cases in the hands of larger bodies.[22] The 112 deputations which won an audience with Montagu had clearly been organized in terms of the categories devised by the British. Nineteen claimed to represent landowners; eleven, businessmen; twenty-three, Muslims; five, high-caste Hindus and eight, the 'depressed classes'. Again, the fact that ninety-four of them limited their membership to one or other of the British provinces, shows how truly the lines for Indian political organization traced the administrative boundaries of the Raj.[23] That many of these classifications existed only in the thinking of the Raj is plain from the rivalries which now came into the open. Forty-four representations in all had been received from Muslim bodies; they showed divisions so glaring as to cast doubt on the existence of a Muslim community at all. In the Punjab the provincial branch of the Muslim League, having seceded from the all-India body in protest

[21] These are examples of political brokers (and in due course managers) at the top; they had innumerable counterparts, who performed much the same function at lower levels: Rafi Ahmed Kidwai of the United Provinces, Rangaswami Iyengar and Satyamurti in Madras, and Anugraha Narayan Sinha in Bihar are middlemen of this sort.

[22] 'Addresses presented in India to . . . the Viceroy and . . . the Secretary of State for India', *Parliamentary Papers*, 1918, XVIII, 469–587.

[23] Their membership also illustrates that a politician might be forced to play many roles. As Montagu's advisers recognized, 'One individual might, and often did, appear as a member of several deputations, which represented, for instance, his religious community, his social class or professional interest, and his individual political views'. *Ibid.*, 472.

against the Congress-League scheme, now led a cat-and-dog existence with the new provincial body which had been improvised to take its place. There was also the Punjab Muslim Association, which had been founded by landlords and claimed to speak for 'humbler agriculturists, the great bulk of the population of this province'[24]—a memorable example of how categories could be profitably confused. But for a community to split, it did not have to be large. The Ahmadiya sect of dissident Muslims might have seemed small enough to see the virtues of unity; but while their chief spokesman rejected the Congress-League scheme for demanding too much, its 'immediate adoption' was demanded by the Ahmadiya Anjuman Ishaat-i-Islam, a 'body of about 50 persons established at Lahore'.[25] In the United Provinces, again, Muslim opinion was sharply divided. Here the provincial branch of the League supported the joint scheme, while the UP Muslim Defence Association rejected it. Less concerned with constitutional formulae, the ulema of the provinces held more antique views. At the Deoband seminary the maulvis called for an alim on every council, while the Majlis Muid-ul-Islam of Lucknow simply demanded that the Jewish Secretary of State should bring India under the rule of the true principles of the Koran.

The exploitation of community for political rivalry was matched by the exploitation of the caste categories of the census. Montagu met several deputations which each claimed to speak for all the forty million non-Brahmins of the Madras Presidency. They split along the usual lines, the Madras Presidency Association supporting the Congress-League scheme, the others repudiating it. But another deputation, from the Adi Dravida Jana Sabha, raised the spectre of six million untouchables in the south, harassed by Brahmins and non-Brahmins alike, for whom the only hope lay in special representation. This indeed was the prize the southern politicians yearned for, especially those whom Montagu was spared from seeing. The alleged unity of the non-Brahmins could not hold firm against such a prospect: Nadukottai Chetties, Tiyyas, Nadars, Marawars, Lingayats, Visva Brahmins,[26] Adi Andhras and Panchamas all called for it.[27] Orthodox Brahmins, Jains,

[24] *Ibid.*, 478.

[25] *Ibid.*, 479, 486.

[26] These pretentious pot-makers, the Visva Brahmins, managed to split into five separate associations, with three distinct demands.

[27] Solomon's problem was child's play compared to Montagu's; the Governor of Madras, who had to work the minister's solutions by balancing these claims inside dyarchy, bitterly complained: 'Oh, this communal business. I am being bombarded by all sorts of sub-castes of the non-Brahmins for special representation and as I

Buddhists and Christians all joined in the rush, and in all some thirty-eight groups in Madras demanded special consideration and special rights. Madras was the extreme example of the general trend throughout India. In every province, at every level and inside every category, political associations were formed as the expression of claim and counter-claim, of group and counter-group, of competitors vying for the favour of the Raj by playing politics couched in its own formulae.

The Secretary of State made his way to these rancorous caravanserais in the period before his new constitution devolved powers to the provinces and gave Indians a share of them. Until then many local politicians did not keep a continuous line open to the province. Associations were, of course, one of the ways of doing so, but they were not enough to ensure success in the everyday affairs of localities. There, the old arts were still the best. No amount of bombinating in the British Indian Association could by itself give a zemindar control over his neighbourhood; the man who walked tall in the Sarvajanik Sabha might be without a shred of power in Poona; there were earthier and surer ways of pursuing interests. These associations were such imperfect indications of men's real priorities in the localities that we cannot assert that their expansion completely explains the growing linkages in Indian politics apparent in Montagu's time.

Yet nearly all localities were being pulled into larger worlds. Two political forces drew them upwards, the one constitutional, the other agitational. The pressure of provincial bureaucracies upon the little sanctuaries continued to grow, and to interfere more with their lives. The Madras government, for example, raised its revenues from eight crores of rupees to twenty-four between 1880 and 1920. Some part was redistributed within the province. To share these golden showers, the men in the localities had to surrender some of their isolation. The twin instruments of nomination and election made it easier to influence provincial decisions after 1909. The Act of 1919 greatly extended representation, and it also gave a smattering of power in the provinces themselves to Indian politicians, not least the power of spending money in their localities. This brought a heightened reality into elections; and, as we have seen, it made the politicians both of the centre and of the locality more dependent on each other.

But another motor for driving local affairs up to higher arenas was

believe there are some 250 of these, I am not likely to satisfy many in a council of 127. You're a nice fellow to have given me this job!' Willingdon to Montagu, 20 February 1920. Willingdon Papers, India Office Library. David Washbrook dug out this gem.

provided by the development of Indian politics. The forming of the Home Rule Leagues and the alliance between the Congress and the Muslim League in 1916 were portents of agitations which could now be set in motion by bodies claiming to stand for all-India interests. By 1920, these agitations were dominating politics.[28] Gandhi shouldered aside the old Congress hands who had previously claimed to speak for the movement. His own agitation, fortified by his alliance with the Khilafatists, emerged as the non-cooperation campaign of 1920–22. In practice the campaign was a series of interconnected district battles, fought by men from the localities. The hillmen of Kumaon, the coolies of Assam, the headmen of Oudh, the turbulent peasantries of Midnapore and Guntur, Kaira and Bhagalpur, were all using what were allegedly national issues to express their local complaints. Local grievances were chronic and narrow, but they put the stuffing into campaigns which were intermittent and wide. It was not possible for the localities to reject the linkages of agitation. For the provincial and national leaderships to press the British at the top, they had to cause the base to fulminate, and so they did all they could to bring the localities into the movement. Many localities welcomed a wider agitation as a means of paying off old scores against the administration and those who sided with it. But in any case, had they ignored the movement, they would have risked losing all influence upon what was clearly a growing power in their province.

Some of the supporters from the localities made awkward allies for the leadership. National and provincial campaigners with large interests to watch had to be more prudent than men whose local grievances were not assuaged by all-India strategies. When Gandhi wanted to cool his campaign in 1922, the men of Bardoli and Guntur were spoiling for a fight; his efforts to observe the armistice in 1931 meant nothing to the peasants of Rae Bareli or Bara Banki. But these difficulties in controlling agitation were balanced by its success in bringing ever more local politicians into the ambit of the provinces.

During the quiescent period between 1922 and 1928, many of these agitational links snapped, and provincial parties almost closed down shop in the districts. But it was business as usual in the political exchanges of the provincial capitals, where jobbers organized factions to enter and break the councils, or to work them. It mattered little to these

[28] Constitutional politics and agitation rode in unsteady tandem throughout this period. The defeat of the constitutionalists in 1920 was more tactical than strategic. By December 1920 when the Nagpur Congress met, the first elections under the reforms had come and gone. By the time of the next elections in 1923, the Swaraj party was in the front seat, and Gandhi was back-pedalling from gaol.

groupings whether they retained formal allegiance to the Congress or not; they did so only when it suited their convenience, and when it did not, they left the Congress to their rivals. They stepped nimbly in and out of the all-India organizations, like so many cabs for hire. From local torpor and national insignificance, Indian politics were rescued by constitutional changes. The Award had settled the share of the communities. By extending the electorate, the imperial croupier had summoned more players to his table. By transferring political power to politicians in the provinces, he made them the main agencies of intervention in the localities. Now there was no help for it. Local men were forced into connections with those who claimed to represent the big battalions and would control their destinies in the future. At last the localities were soldered to the provinces.

But the agitations and negotiations which led to the Act of 1935 had also given a new importance to organizations claiming to represent all-India interests. Gandhi returned to take control of civil disobedience; Congress spoke with one voice at the Second Round Table Conference. Once power in the provinces was up for bids, interests outside the Congress also needed their national spokesmen. So the Muslims reorganized under Jinnah in 1934–5, and groups with even shakier all-India connections, such as the Depressed Classes, found it necessary to have a negotiator of their own. All these spokesmen grew in stature by being recognized, even if reluctantly, by Delhi and London, as the plenipotentiaries of constituents in the provinces. But just as the Raj had to counter-balance provincial devolution by strengthening its centre, so Indian politicians at the centre had to confront an analogous problem, since provinces controlled by Indians might go their own way. The only safeguard open to the leaders of Congress and League against provincial autonomy was to construct central controls strong enough to tie their provincial satraps to them. In this difficult task they were helped by two trends. Although the 1935 Act was intended by the British to contain Indian politics within the provinces, they could not be checked at that level. Some factions, such as those led by Pant in the United Provinces, Rajagopalachari in Madras and Kher in Bombay, cheerfully glutted themselves with power in the provinces between 1937 and 1939. But plenty of others had no power to enjoy. Hence the Congress High Command could arbitrate between the 'ins' and 'outs' of the provinces, and in the Central Provinces went to the length of breaking a ministry.[29] Provincial leaders whose hopes had been permanently blasted by the

[29] Once war came, Vallabhbhai ordered all the Congress ministers to quit office. Reluctantly they obeyed.

Communal Award had every reason to cling to their centre. In this way, the adhesion of the Muslims of the United Provinces helped to keep the League alive during the two lean years before the war.

The other trend strengthening the centres was the steady raising of the constitutional stakes. The offers of Linlithgow in 1940 and of Cripps in 1942 promised an immediate share in the central government and a post-dated cheque for its control after the war. These were matters beyond the provincial politicians. They could whip their own dogs, but no one else's. Only men claiming to take all the nation's interests into account, and having the all-India organizations to back these claims, could work at such altitudes. In the deadly end-game played with Wavell, the Cabinet Mission and Mountbatten, these politicians claimed to be custodians of all the sets of interests crammed into the Pandora's boxes of the Congress and the League. Now there was everything to play for: the prize was the mastery of the subcontinent. Those who competed for it had to provide a firm leadership to their followers. The size of the stake let Jinnah break at last the independence of the Muslim bosses in the Punjab. Just as the agitations of the twenties and thirties had swung the localities behind the provincial leaderships, so the crisis of the last days of the Raj swung the provinces behind the national leaderships. The parallel went further. Just as civil disobedience had been complicated by *enragés* who went further than their leaders had wished, now on the eve of independence there were pressures from below which reduced the leaders' freedom of manœuvre. Jinnah was hoist with his own petard of Pakistan, and Nehru was harassed by the Sikhs and the Hindu Mahasabha. But in the outcome, Nehru, Jinnah and Vallabhbhai Patel settled the fate of the provinces over their heads, and all but one of them[30] marched obediently into one or other of the new nations of India and Pakistan. At last the province had been soldered to the centre.

* * *

These interpretations arise from two main arguments. Simply put, Indian politics were an interconnected system working at several levels; and government had much to do with the linking of those levels. When these arguments are applied to modern Indian history, some of its conundrums look less intractable. In the first place, we need not be dismayed if some of the hard facts which have been revealed at the base of the system seem to run counter to the ways in which politics worked at

[30] The North-West Frontier Province.

other points. Once Indian politicians were pressed into treating with government and their fellow subjects at several levels, they played several roles, each of which might seem to make nonsense of the others. But those who varied their tunes between bucolic patter and urban suavity were not brazen impostors. To make use of the system, they had no choice but to play those contradictory roles. In catching them out at their tricks and dwelling on their inconsistencies, historians are simply playing a game at which the administrators used to excel. But to demonstrate that Indian politicians were not always what they claimed to be is not to describe what they were. Moral judgment is easy; functional analysis is hard. Perhaps our approach will help to make the one more difficult and the other less arduous.

Secondly, the part played by ideology in the growth of Indian politics can now be re-assessed. Those who have convinced themselves that India is the home of spiritual values have found them everywhere in her politics; others have seen nothing but *homo homini lupus*. The truth seems to lie in between. Whatever held together the gimcrack coalitions of province and nation, it was not passion for a common doctrine. It was lower down that ideology was important. Illustrating the wit and wisdom of Mohamed Ali would be unprofitable as well as painful; but there is no gainsaying the Hindu zealotry in the localities of Hindustan, or the Muslim resentments against it which lent that adventurer an improbable fame. Ideology provides a good tool for fine carving, but it does not make big buildings.

We can make some inroads into a third question. Many historians have argued that the timing of Indian agitation was governed by the imminence of British concession. The point is a simple one; it was made by Simon; and it is demonstrated by the landmarks of constitutional change from 1853 until 1947. Yet at the lower levels these simplicities melt into a more revealing complexity. There, government intervention helped to create the agitations over cow protection in 1893, the partition of Bengal in 1905, the canal colonies of the Punjab in 1907, the municipalities of the United Provinces before 1916, the coolies of Assam in 1921–22, the rights of village officers in the Kistna and Godaveri deltas in 1922, and the agrarian grievances of Gujarat, Oudh and Andhra during the Depression. Agitations of this sort fed into the larger movements, helping to start and sustain them, often surviving them and remaining at hand for the next all-India campaign.

This conclusion alters our ideas about the nature of these large campaigns. Many local grievances dragged on, whether the leaderships were militant or not. When the malcontents of the neighbourhood aligned themselves with the provincial and national campaigns which arose from time to time, they hoped to exploit these issues for their own causes. The small issues, which historians used to neglect, moved on different clocks from the large issues on which study has been concentrated. Small discontents existed before they were caught up by the agglutinative tendencies of larger campaigns and they went on simmering after the large agitations had cooled. Many localities had their irreconcilables, men whose interests could not be patted smoothly into the prudences of provincial politics, and who turned into permanent 'outs'. This held good at higher levels too. After their position had been exploded by the Communal Award and by the silent consent to it of the all-India Congress, Bengalis, who had hitherto been among its leaders, now became malcontents at the national level, willing to make common cause with the mavericks of other provinces. Subhas's Forward Bloc looked backwards to the old triangle of Lal, Bal and Pal, to the Home Rule Leagues or the Hindu Mahasabha of Bhai Parmanand. All of them were coalitions of 'outs'.

In turn, this helps to explain the relations between the constitutional and the agitational sides of Indian politics. For many historians, Indian politics kept on making clean breaks from one to the other; the smooth formulations which Sapru penned at Albert Road in Allahabad went unheard every time the trouble-makers escaped from their cages. This was not the way matters went. As we have seen, the roots of political activity in the localities twisted in many directions. Local grievances always looked for the best outlets. We cannot make a simple distinction between the constitutionalists, who scampered from board to council, and the agitators from less accommodating areas who shunned such opportunism. Local studies reveal that there was much interaction between them. Even the most uncooperative areas had to work through government institutions; even the dacoits could not disregard them.[31] Gandhi freely allowed satyagrahis to hold posts in local government, and the president of the Ahmedabad municipality in the mid-twenties was a not unknown agitator named Vallabhbhai Patel. The converse was true as well. Constitutionalists readily became agitators when local conditions forced them to do so. The law-abiding municipality of Nagpur organized one satyagraha over flags, and the time-servers of Jubbulpore were swept into another over forests. Many local men were dual-purpose politicians, switching their bets between constitutionalism and agitation according to the temper of their sup-

[31] Many villages hired their chowkidars from the criminal tribes, following the old adage.

porters and the calculation of their interest. These ambiguities were shared by men at all levels.

These conclusions suggest that some of the difficulties in Indian history can be met by putting new life into old factors, and that the subject can be reintegrated by seeing the roles of imperialism and nationalism in a different light. Imperialism built a system which interlocked its rule in locality, province and nation; nationalism emerged as a matching structure of politics. The study of local situations, the components of these larger wholes, cannot by itself identify a bedrock reality. The Raj had smashed the autonomy of localities; the historian of British rule cannot put it together again. Indian politics have to be studied at each and every level; none of them can be a complete field of study on its own. Each of them reveals only that part of social action which did not depend upon interconnection. As that part became caught up by the linking forces of Indian history, it steadily shrank.

In no colonial situation can government's part be ignored. We have suggested that much of the crucial work of connecting one level with another came from its impulses. This hypothesis can explain many of the problems of linkage. Others still elude us. We need more facts about such bonds as kinship patterns, urban ties, professional and educational interests. All that can be said at present about arguments built upon them is that they are probably significant, possibly crucial, but certainly not general. In the meantime, the range of cases which can be explained by looking at imperialism and nationalism in the new way suggests that their importance has been too hastily marked down. Perhaps this volume will do something to bring them back into their own.

[8]

Peasant Revolt and Indian Nationalism: The Peasant Movement in Awadh, 1919-22

GYAN PANDEY

In January 1921 the peasants of Awadh burst onto the national stage in India. Huge peasant demonstrations at Fursatganj and Munshiganj bazars in Rae Bareli district led to police firing on 6 and 7 January. At other places in Rae Bareli, Faizabad and Sultanpur districts, peasant violence—the looting of bazars (as at Fursatganj), attacks on landlords, and battles with the police—broke out around this time. For some weeks, indeed, many a landlord was too scared to appear anywhere on his estate. 'You have seen in three districts in southern Oudh [Awadh] the beginnings of something like revolution', Harcourt Butler, the Governor of UP (the United Provinces of Agra and Awadh, modern Uttar Pradesh), observed in March 1921.[1] The peasants' actions received wide publicity in the nationalist press, too, especially after Jawaharlal Nehru had been drawn into the Munshiganj events of 7 January.

Virtually for the first time since 1857 the Awadh peasant had forced himself on the attention of the elites in colonial India. The debate was quickly joined. The leaders of the major nationalist party, the Congress, who had been involved in some of the peasant meetings and demonstrations of the preceding months, now stepped forward to defend the peasants in the courts and to prevent further violence. Colonial administrators rushed to consider remedial legislation: 'It has for long been obvious', as one of them put it, 'that the Oudh Rent Act requires amendment.'[2] The Liberals, moderate nationalists who were moving away from the

[1]Harcourt Butler Colln., Mss. Eur. F. 116 (India Office Library, London), vol. 80: Note of Butler's interview with taluqdars, 6 March 1921.

[2]Uttar Pradesh State Archives, Lucknow (hereafter UPSA), U.P. General Administration Dept. (hereafter GAD), File 50/1921, Kw: Commissioner, Lucknow Division to Chief Sec., U.P., 14 Jan. 1921.

Congress as it adopted a more militant posture at this time, shared something of both the Congress and the Government positions. With local Congressmen, some of them had supported the initial organizational efforts and demands of the tenants. After January 1921, they were foremost in pressing for legislation to improve their conditions.

The underlying causes of the peasant protest that brought forth these reactions lay in a pattern of agrarian relations that had evolved over a long period. In 1856 Awadh was brought under direct British rule in order, it was said, to rescue the province from the effects of misrule and anarchy. The mutiny and civil rebellion of 1857-9, which brought some of the fiercest fighting and severest reprisals of the century, formed, from that point of view, an unfortunate interlude. After that the benefits of Pax Britannica flowed freely, towards some. Chief among the beneficiaries were the two hundred and eighty or so taluqdars who, for their part in the recent uprising, were now held up as the 'natural leaders' of the people. The taluqdars were mostly local rajas and heads of clans, officials and tax-farmers who had secured an independent position in the land before the British annexation, plus a handful of 'deserving chiefs' who were given estates confiscated from the most notorious of the rebels. On this motley crowd the new rulers formally conferred many of the rights of the landowning gentry of Britain. Three-fifths of the cultivated area of Awadh was settled with them in return for the regular payment of revenue and assistance in maintaining order in the countryside. And British policy was now directed towards ensuring the taluqdars the wealth, status and security necessary to fulfil this role. The extent of the British commitment to the taluqdars was indicated by Harcourt Butler when he wrote, in the 1890s, that for political purposes 'the Taluqdars are Oudh'.[3] By the Encumbered Estates Act of 1870 and subsequent measures, the colonial administrators even agreed to bale out any insolvent taluqdari estate by taking over its management for as long as twenty years—although this ran counter to all their principles of political economy.

Some effort was made to secure the intermediary rights of other traditionally privileged groups: village proprietors, coparcenary

[3]T.R. Metcalf, *Land, Landlords and the British Raj: Northern India in the Nineteenth Century* (Delhi, 1979), p. 198; see also Metcalf in R.E. Frykenberg, (ed.), *Land Control and Social Structure in Indian History* (Madison, 1969), p. 147.

communities controlling various plots of land and privileged tenants of several categories. This was necessitated in part by the prolonged resistance of many of these inferior right holders, such as the Barwar Rajputs of Amsin Pargana and the under-proprietors on the Raja of Pirpur's estate (both in Faizabad district).[4] Legally and in terms of actual power, these intermediary groups retained something of their earlier position in the taluqdari as well as the non-taluqdari areas of Awadh.[5] Yet Pax Britannica and the compromise sub-settlements of the 1860s tended to work against the interests of the lower classes.

Generally it was laid down that under-proprietors would pay the Government revenue plus a further 10 to 50 per cent. Thus they bore the entire burden of any enhancement of revenue while the taluqdars escaped any new obligations. In the years after the first round of settlements and sub-settlements had been completed, the smaller under-proprietors lost more and more of their remaining rights to the taluqdars and, to some extent, to money-lenders and other men from outside. Many groups of once privileged tenants also suffered losses in the general process of enhancement of rents. The Government contributed fully to these developments. On the Government-managed estates of Mehdona, Kapradih and Sehipur in Faizabad district, for instance, several arrests were made for the non-payment of rents in full by underproprietors; and

> where tenants held reduced rates only by favour of the taluqdar, without any legal claim based on a former proprietory title, the Government exerted itself vigorously to bring rents up to the level of those paid by ordinary cultivators.[6]

Among the tenants, then, Brahmans and Thakurs suffered a progressive decline in terms of favoured rental rates as well as the areas of land leased out to them. Yet the pressure on them was light by comparison with that on the Kurmis and Muraos, cultivating castes with a reputation for efficiency who formed a considerable part of the tenantry, numbering in all about a million in Awadh in the 1880s. In Rae Bareli, in the decade following the first regular settlement of the district, during which prices rose only gradually,

[4]Ibid., pp. 131-3.

[5]P.J. Musgrave, 'Landlords and Lords of the Land: Estate Management and Social Control in U.P., 1860-1920', *Modern Asian Studies*, 6:3 (July 1972).

[6]Metcalf in Frykenberg (ed.), *Land Control*, pp. 133-4; see also *Collection of Papers Relating to the Condition of the Tenantry and the Working of the Present Rent Law in Oudh*, 2 vols. (Allahabad, 1883).

the increase in their rents varied between what was described as 'nominal' and 30-80 per cent, and actually reached a 100 per cent in one or two cases.[7]

With the taluqdari settlement, the bulk of the population of Awadh (just under 11½ million in 1881, rising to over 12 million by 1921) had in any case lost all their rights, which were unrecorded earlier and now excluded from the record. The vast majority of cultivators emerged as tenants-at-will on small holdings, or as landless labourers. In Lucknow district at the beginning of the 1880s, only a half per cent of the agricultural population held more that 50 *bighas* of land (a *bigha* = 5/8 acre). Six per cent held from 20 to 50 *bighas*, 11½ per cent 10 to 20 *bighas*, 15 per cent 5 to 10 *bighas*, and 39½ per cent less than 5 *bighas*. This was at a time when officials, who could scarcely be accused of liberality in these matters, felt that a cultivator needed at least 5 *bighas* to live 'reasonably'. The remaining 27½ per cent of Lucknow's agricultural population were classified as landless day-labourers.[8]

The resistance of Kurmi and other tenants on various occasions[9] could do no more than slow down these developments in particular areas. Nor did legislation that aimed at providing a modicum of security for the unprotected tenants and some control on the level of rent enhancements, significantly arrest the general deterioration. The landlords had too many cards up their sleeves, most of them the gift of the British Raj itself, to be seriously affected by such paper threats. They collected more than the recorded rents, instituted a system of unofficial taxation whereby the tenant paid a large premium or *nazrana* to be admitted or re-admitted to a holding, and often ignored the law altogether.[10] C.W. McMinn noted in the 1870s that taluqdar power was still great, in some ways indeed 'more absolute' than before, but now (constricted to narrower channels) it had 'meaner developments'.[11] The taluqdars now concentrated their efforts on screwing up their incomes from their estates, without any concern for protecting old tenants and dependants or improving their lands. The peasants of Pratapgarh

[7]Ibid., vol. I, p. 135.

[8]Ibid., vol. II, p. 400.

[9]F.W. Porter, *Final Settlement Report of the Allahabad District* (Allahabad, 1878), pp. 47-8; S. Gopal, *Jawaharlal Nehru: A Biography, vol. I* (London, 1975), p. 46.

[10]See G. Pandey, *The Ascendancy of the Congress in Uttar Pradesh, 1926-34; A Study in Imperfect Mobilization* (Delhi, 1978), p. 21.

[11]Quoted in Metcalf, *Land, Landlords and the Raj*, p. 175.

described this situation in their own idiom in conversation with the Deputy Commissioner of the district in 1920. Referring to the *murda faroshi kanun* (literally, the 'law for sale of the corpse'), i.e. the law permitting immediate enhancement of rent on, or sale of, the land of a dead tenant, they said that a new kind of Mahabrahman (the lowest among the Brahmans on account of the fact that he lives on funeral gifts) had come into being. The one object of this creature was to pray for an epidemic—just as the grain dealer prays for a famine—so that he might reap a rich harvest of *murda faroshi* fees. This Mahabrahman was the landlord. 'Before the ashes are cold on the pyre this Mahabrahman has to be satisfied.'[12]

To add to the misfortunes of the lower classes, population pressure on the land and the cost of living steadily increased from the later nineteenth century. In these conditions a very large section of the Awadh peasantry, both smaller landowners and tenants, sank into debt. As time went on they relied more and more heavily on their valuable crops, especially rice and wheat, to pay off interest and other dues, and the acreage under these crops increased. For their own consumption the bulk of the rural population depended on the inferior grains—maize, barley, *jowar* and *bajra*. One result of the growing demand for these inferior grains and the decline in the area over which they were cultivated, was that their prices rose even more sharply than the prices of wheat and rice in the first decades of the twentieth century.[13] It was a somewhat paradoxical index of the social dislocation that lay behind the revolt of the Awadh peasantry after the First World War.

January 1921 was the culminating point of a movement that had advanced very rapidly indeed from its inception towards the end of 1919. Kisan Sabhas, or peasants' associations, were being organized locally in Pratapgarh from the early months of 1920. By the middle of that year they had found a remarkable leader and coordinator in Baba Ramchandra, a Maharashtrian of uncertain antecedents who had been an indentured labourer in Fiji and then a *sadhu* (religious mendicant) propagating the Hindu scriptures in Jaunpur, Sultanpur and Pratapgarh, before he turned to the task of

[12]U.P.S.A, U.P. Rev. (A) Dept. File 753 of 1920; 'Report on Agrarian Disturbances in Pratapgarh', by V.N. Mehta, Deputy Commnr., Pratapgarh (hereafter, Mehta's Report), p. 4.

[13]M.H. Siddiqi, *Agrarian Unrest in North India: The United Provinces, 1918-22* (New Delhi, 1978), ch. II.

organizing Kisan Sabhas. Led by Ramchandra, members of the Pratapgarh Kisan Sabha sought the support of urban nationalists. It was then that Jawaharlal Nehru 'discovered' the Indian peasantry and found the countryside 'afire with enthusiasm and full of a strange excitment';[14] and then that the Kisan Sabha workers of the Congress who had endeavoured to extend their links in the villages of UP since 1918, began to work in association with the organizers of these independent local Sabhas, especially in Awadh.

Before the involvement of the nationalists from the cities, the Awadh Kisan Sabha movement had already gained considerable strength. There were reported to be 585 panchayats (village arbitration boards established by the peasants) working in Pratapgarh district alone. In the month or two during which Rure, the village in Pratapgarh where the first Kisan Sabha was established, was a centre of the movement, 100,000 peasants were said to have registered themselves with the association. These early efforts at organization had received indirect encouragement from the sympathetic attitude of the Pratapgarh Deputy Commissioner, V.N. Mehta, who asked Ramchandra and other peasant leaders to forward the peasants' complaints to him for examination and instituted inquiries regarding some of the more tangible allegations.[15] Now, with the growth of urban nationalist support, the movement advanced more swiftly still until it had engulfed large parts of Pratapgarh, Rae Bareli, Sultanpur and Faizabad districts, and established important footholds elsewhere. Its strength may be judged from the numbers of peasants who were said to have turned out for very different kinds of demonstrations: 40-50,000 to press for the release of Ramchandra from Pratapgarh jail in September 1920, 80-100,000 for the first Awadh Kisan Congress held in Ayodhya (Faizabad district) in December 1920.[16] Such estimates of the numbers involved in mass gatherings are of course notoriously unreliable. But even if we scale them down to one half or a third, as colonial officials did at the time, they indicate the rise of a movement of massive proportions.

[14] J. Nehru, *An Autobiography* (London, 1936; 1947 rpt), pp. 57, 51.

[15] Baba Ramchandra Colln. II (Nehru Memorial Museum & ' Library, New Delhi'; hereafter NMML), Acc. No. 610: RC XI, 'Autobiographical Notebook', p. 13; Ramchandra Colln. I (NMML) Acc. No. 163: 'Note' of 8 Aug. 194[?] and incomplete letter of 1939, pp. 5-6. For Mehta's role, see also Mehta's Report, p. 3.

[16] Siddiqi, op. cit., pp. 146-7.

Matters came to a head in January 1921, and soon after, the Awadh peasant movement, by now bereft of support from its erstwhile urban allies, was repressed by a determined attack on the part of the Government. It was not crushed, however, and a few months later it arose again in northern Awadh in the modified form of an Eka (unity) movement. We write of this as a continuation of the earlier, Kisan Sabha, phase of the struggle because the same kinds of forces were involved in its creation, and there was the same kind of ambiguous relationship between the Congress and the peasant rebels.[17] The Eka associations were aided in their initial stages by some Congressmen and Khilafatists of Malihabad, Lucknow district. But they quickly outstripped their beginnings, spread out widely and became very militant. The movement was strongest in certain districts of northern Awadh where the evils of grain rents and disguised rents abounded. The peasant associations now raised the cry for commutation to cash rents and resistance to demands for anything more than the recorded rent. They called at the same time for non-cooperation with the colonial regime. Before long, colonialist observers were complaining about the fact that the Indian Penal Code and the Criminal Procedure Code had 'no provision for a whole countryside arrayed against law and order'.[18] Yet the Congress leadership spared little time for the protagonists of Eka, and in due course this new phase of the movement was suppressed by a large force of armed police and military men.

There could have been no other outcome, given the positions adopted by the various contending forces in UP in early 1921. In the following pages we examine these positions at some length, for what they tell us about different assessments of the nature of political struggle in colonial India and the role of the peasantry in that struggle. The urban nationalist leaders and British officials have left behind more or less detailed discourses on the Awadh peasant movement of these years, alternative perspectives which reveal, we believe, their basic concerns and the extent of their

[17]As the officer specially deputed by the U.P. Govt. to inquire into the Eka movement, Lt Col J.C. Faunthorpe, put it, 'The Eka movement, which commenced towards the end of 1921, is a revival of the *Kisan Sabha* movement.' *United Provinces Gazette*, 13 May 1922, pt VIII (hereafter Faunthorpe's Report), p. 273.

[18]Clipping from *Englishman* (Calcutta), 28 Feb. 1922 in GOI, Home Dept., Pol. Branch, File 862 of 1922 (NAI, New Delhi).

understanding of the contradictions and possibilities existing in the situation. There are of course subtle, and sometimes not so subtle, variations between the language, say, of Gandhi and of Nehru, or the comments of the Liberals and those of the young non-cooperating Congressmen of 1920-22. Again there is a world of difference, on the Government side, between the response of someone like the Pratapgarh Deputy Commissioner, V. N. Mehta, and that of H. R. C. Hailey, his Commissioner and immediate boss in Faizabad Division, or Harcourt Butler, Lieutenant Governor and then (after 1920) Governor of UP: the first undertook an intensive tour of his district, interviewed 1700 witnesses and collected a mass of material on the basis of which he drew up a 111 page 'Report on Agrarian Disturbances in Pratapgarh' in 1920; the second described the report as 'partisan', 'one-sided', painting peasant grievances in 'lurid' colours; the third dismissed it simply as 'long and crude'.[19]

An appreciation of these variations is important for a proper reconstruction of the history of the period. Yet, in general terms, an official and a Congress stand on the Awadh peasant movement in these years, can be discerned. So can a general landlord position, though the landlords of Awadh were so much the puppets of their colonial masters by this time that they have left no significant deposition of their own. As for the peasants who set off this debate, no one took the trouble of recording their discourse. A small collection of papers, notes and diaries written by Baba Ramchandra mainly in the late 1930s and 1940s has been discovered, and this is in some ways very valuable. But we have no peasant testament outlining the impulses that moved them or defending the actions they took in 1919-22, not even an elaborate statement from Ramchandra. The peasants' view of the struggle will probably never be recovered; and whatever we say about it at this stage must be very tentative. Yet it seems important to try and piece together some part of it, from the isolated statements of peasants found in the documents and from the only other evidence we have—the message contained in their actions. Without this the historical record remains woefully incomplete. And the exercise is relevant for another reason too.

Historians of India have long debated the question of how mass

[19]U.P. Rev. (A) Dept. File 753 of 1920: Hailey to Keane, 26 Nov. 1920 and Butler's 'Note' of 17 Dec. 1920.

mobilization occurred in the course of the struggle for liberation from colonial rule. In the earlier writings, nationalist as well as colonialist commentators tended to treat the 'masses' (in this agrarian society, predominantly peasants) as essentially inert. When peasant insurrection occurred and swelled the tide of anti-imperialist agitation in the latter part of British rule in India, it was for the colonialists a sign of manipulation by 'outside agitators', for the nationalists evidence of mobilization by popular urban leaders. Colonialist (and neo-colonialist) historiography has not moved very far from this early position, although the theory of deliberate instigation of disturbance among ignorant and unconcerned people has been rendered somewhat superfluous by the discovery of 'factions', their members ever ready, in their hundreds if not thousands or indeed tens of thousands, to rise behind 'faction-leaders' in the latter's quest for the prestige and profits of office.[20] Liberal nationalist and Marxist historians, on the other hand, have gone on to make significant new statements regarding the politics of mass protest in India.

First, research indicated that many of the most important peasant insurrections in the country were largely autonomous, and that the intervention of 'outside' leaders was a marginal and, often, a late phenomenon. But while it was recognized that peasants had at times exercised an independence of initiative, their actions were seen as having been non-political or at best 'pre-political'. More recently some scholars have granted that these actions were in fact (at times) political, in the sense that they threw up a challenge to the established structure of authority and sought to create alternative centres of power. Yet the previous view persists: indeed, it remains dominant in the universities and among others interested in the recent history of the subcontinent, finding expression for instance, in the common equation of the Congress movement with the 'political' movement and of workers' and peasants' struggles with a 'social' one. And where some acknowledgement has been made of the political content of the latter, a new argument seems to have arisen. It is now suggested, in what might be called the last stand of traditional nationalist historiography, that these sectional struggles, of peasants and workers and other labouring and exploited classes, were out of step with the primary need of the 'nation' at that stage in its

[20]See D. Hardiman, 'The Indian 'Faction': A Political Theory Examined', in this volume.

history—the need to advance the anti-imperialist movement.[21]

The validity of some of these propositions cannot be fully tested until a good deal more research has been undertaken into modern Indian history, especially in the domain of mass movements and popular consciousness. Yet enough is known already about particular struggles, like that of the peasants in Awadh from 1919-22, to raise doubts about certain long-standing assumptions regarding what has come to be described as the relationship between popular struggles and the Indian national movement. It is the limited purpose of this essay to examine these assumptions in the light of what we know, from secondary as well as primary sources, about the Awadh peasant movement. I shall first analyse the very different contemporary responses to the political events of 1919-22 in Awadh, and then go on to consider whether historians commenting on peasant revolt and Indian nationalism have not too readily accepted the viewpoint of the better-educated and more vocal participants in the anti-colonial struggle in nineteenth-and twentieth-century India.

The Congress Response

In February 1921, when he visited UP, Gandhi issued the following *Instructions* to the peasants of the province:

> Attainment of swaraj or redress of grievances is imposible unless the following rules are strictly observed.
>
> 1. We may not hurt anybody. We may not use our sticks against anybody. We may not use abusive language or exercise any other undue pressure.
> 2. We may not loot shops.
> 3. We should influence our opponents by kindness, not by using physical force nor stopping their water supply nor the services of the barber and the washerman.

[21] See Bipan Chandra, *Nationalism and Colonialism in Modern India* (New Delhi, 1979) for the view that Gandhi and the post-World War I Congress 'aroused [the masses] to political activity', and for the above distinction between 'political' and 'social' struggle, pp. 127, 165, 183 and *passim*. There is a faint echo of this 'political'-'social' distinction also in Sumit Sarkar, *The Swadeshi Movement in Bengal, 1903-1908* (New Delhi, 1973), p. 515; and it is commonly voiced at academic seminars in India and elsewhere. The view that a peasant struggle was ill-timed, or diversionary, is expressed most clearly in Siddiqi, op. cit., pp. 217, 219. It is also reflected in Bipan Chandra, op. cit., p. 347.

4. We may not withhold taxes from Government or rent from the landlord.
5. Should there be any grievances against zemindars they should be reported to Pandit Motilal Nehru and his advice followed.
6. It should be borne in mind that we want to turn zemindars into friends.
7. We are not at the present moment offering civil disobedience; we should, therefore, carry out all Government orders.
8. We may not stop railway trains nor forcibly enter them without tickets.
9. In the event of any of our leaders being arrested, we may not prevent his arrest nor create any distrubance. We shall not lose our cause by the Government arresting our leaders; we shall certainly lose it if we become mad and do violence.
10. We must abolish intoxicating drinks, drugs and other evil habits.
11. We must treat all women as mothers and sisters and respect and protect them.
12. We must promote unity between Hindus and Muslims.
13. As amongst Hindus we may not regard anyone as inferior or untouchable. There should be the spirit of equality and brotherhood among all. We should regard all the inhabitants of India as brothers and sisters.
14. We may not indulge in gambling.
15. We may not steal.
16. We may not tell an untruth on any account whatsoever. We should be truthful in all our dealings.
17. We should introduce the spinning-wheel in every home and all—male and female—should devote their spare time to spinning. Boys and girls should also be taught and encouraged to spin for four hours daily.
18. We should avoid the use of all foreign cloth and wear cloth woven by the weavers from yarn spun by ourselves.
19. We should not resort to law courts but should have all disputes settled by private arbitration.

The most important thing to remember is to curb anger, never to do violence and even to suffer violence done to us.[22]

These *Instructions*, directed especially towards the peasants of Awadh who had so recently been responsible for acts of violence, may be taken as the final Congress comment on the peasant movement in Awadh. They were issued, we may be sure, after

[22] *Collected Works of Mahatma Gandhi*, vol. XIX (Ahmedabad, 1966), pp. 419-20

much soul-searching on the part of Gandhi, and a long period of trial-and-error on the part of the Congress leadership as a whole. In the ranks of the Congress and other organized nationalist parties, there were still some who favoured a continuation of the peasants' struggle. But in the thinking of the most important Congress leaders in the province and the country, January-February 1921 marked an important turning-point.

Numbers *1-3*, *9* and perhaps *8*, in addition to the concluding sentence of Gandhi's *Instructions*, reiterate the deep Gandhian concern for the maintenance of non-violence in all circumstances. It is notable, however, that the specific injunctions contained in them flow not simply from an abhorrence of physical violence in any form, but also from a precise knowledge of the actions taken by the Awadh peasants in the course of the development of the Kisan Sabha movement over the preceding months.

Instructions 1 and *2* were clearly intended to counter the kind of peasant activism that had broken out in Rae Bareli at the beginning of January 1921 and in Faizabad, Sultanpur and elsewhere a few days later. Peasants had attacked and looted bazars as well as stores of grain in the villages. They had destroyed and burnt property: straw belonging to the landlords, crops on the landlords' fields, large quantities of clothes, jewels and so on. *Instruction 2* related to this. So probably did *Instruction 15*, for destruction is no different from theft in the eyes of the propertied and their counsel.

Instruction 9 inveighed against the repeated attempts of peasants to liberate their leaders when they were arrested. Such attempts had led on more than one occasion in recent weeks to serious clashes with the police and to police firing. The most famous of these was the incident at Munshiganj bazar, a couple of miles from the centre of Rae Bareli town, on 7 January 1921. On that date thousands of peasants converged on the town from the early hours of the morning. The common object of those who turned out was to obtain the release of a popular leader. Most came because of rumours that Baba Ramchandra had been arrested and imprisoned in Rae Bareli jail. Some reported having heard that Gandhi had been detained there as well. The crowds probably also included some followers of Baba Janki Das, a local Kisan Sabha leader, who had been arrested in the district two days earlier and brought to the town but not, it was reported, before he could instruct his men to get people from Arkha (an early base of the

Kisan Sabha movement) to come and free him.[23] The numbers had soon swelled to an estimated 10,000, and the 'largest and most determined' section of the crowd was said to be at Munshiganj. The assembly was peaceful but refused to break up until their leaders had been released or rather, as it turned out, until a landlord and the police had fired several rounds at them, killing a number and wounding many more.

Just over three weeks later, on 29 January 1921, another man who called himself Ramchandra was arrested near Goshainganj railway station in Faizabad district. He had for some time before this been active in the area, urging peasants to refuse to pay their rents in protest against existing conditions, and advocating the justice of land being owned by its tiller. He had developed a large following—on account, it was said, of his radical preaching, *sadhu's* garb and, not least, his adopted name. When he was arrested crowds gathered at the station following a false report that the authorities intended to take him away by train They lay on the rails and prevented the train from moving, and were dispersed once again only after police firing and the arrest of eighteen of their number.[24] By this time, indeed, such confrontations between the police and the people had become fairly common. 'Even when minor agitators are tried for petty offences', the Deputy Commissioner of Bara Banki wrote in an affidavit submitted to the Court of the Judicial Commissioner of Awadh in the case instituted against Baba Ramchandra in February 1921, 'enormous gatherings assemble at the court house with the object of intimidating witnesses or to rescue the accused.'[25]

Gandhi no doubt wished to prevent the recurrence of the violent incidents that developed out of these situations. But in the process he attacked the very action that had first demonstrated the organized strength of the peasantry to the British administration and, more importantly, to the peasants themselves. Towards the end of August 1920, the Pratapgarh district authorities had arrested Baba Ramchandra on what appears to have been a fabricated charge of 'theft'. Arrested with him were Thakur Jhinguri Singh, who was

[23]U.P, G.A.D, 50/1921, Kws: J.A. St. John Farnon to Dy. Commnr., Rai Bareli, 19 Jan. 1921, and A.G. Shireff's 'Note' of 29 Jan. 1921.

[24]Siddiqi, op. cit., pp. 168-9.

[25]Motilal Nehru Papers, Group C (Legal) (NMML), File No. 44, 'King-Emperor v. Ram Chandra. Charge Under Sec. 124A 1PC, Court of the Judicial Commnr. of Oudh', affidavit submitted by C.W. Grant, Dy. Commnr., Bara Banki, 10 Feb. 1921.

one of the men responsible for the establishment of Kisan Sabhas in the district even before Ramchandra took a hand, and about thirty other peasants. Their plea for bail was refused. Three days later, when the arrested men were due to appear in court in Pratapgarh, 4-5,000 peasants marched to the town to see them—whereupon the hearing was either postponed or held secretly in jail. Upon this the crowd marched to the jail and held a peaceful demonstration outside: it dispersed only after officials had made a number of promises, the nature of which is not clear. Ten days later, a larger crowd (estimated variously at 10,000 to 40-50,000) congregated at Pratapgarh, drawn there by the rumour that Gandhi had come to get Ramchandra released. Gandhi was absent, but the peasants refused to budge until they had extracted a promise from the officials to release Ramchandra the next morning, then spent the night on the banks of the river Sai and re-assembled outside the jail at dawn As the crowd began to swell even more, the authorities lost their nerve; Ramchandra was released, spirited out of the jail under cover to prevent a stampede, and taken to a spot some distance away where from a tree-top he gave an audience to his followers. In their fear, officials had also assured the crowd that the grievances of the peasants would be investigated; and, if nothing came of this immediately, a few days later the case against Ramchandra, Jhinguri Singh and their co-accused was withdrawn.[26] It was a noble victory, but not one that Gandhi's injunctions would allow the Awadh peasants to repeat.

The origins of *Instruction 8* are equally hard to locate in the principle of non-violence alone. On the occasion of two mass rallies of the peasants, the Awadh Kisan Congress at Ayodhya on 20-21 December 1920 and a later conference at Unchahar in Rae Bareli on 15 January 1921, thousands of peasants practised 'non-cooperation' by travelling ticketless on the trains, and, when evicted, offered 'passive reistance' by lying on the rails until officials gave in and permitted them to travel free of charge. In January 1921, too, as we have noticed above, the peasants practised satyagraha by lying on the rails at Goshainganj (Faizabad) on the day of the arrest of the pretended Ramchandra. Years later,

[26]Siddiqi, op. cit., pp. 130-3. Ramchandra reports that the case against him and his comrades was got up by the Ramganj Estate. See his incomplete, undated letter in Ramchandra Colln., Acc. No. 163, Subject File No. 1—'Papers Relating to the Peasant Movement in Awadh, 1921'.

Jawaharlal Nehru recalled with pride these spontaneous acts of the Awadh peasants. The Non-co-operation Movement had begun, he wrote, and

> the *kisans* took to travelling in railway trains in large numbers without tickets, especially when they had to attend their periodical big mass meetings which sometimes consisted of sixty or seventy thousand persons. It was difficult to move them, and, unheard of thing, they openly defied the railway authorities, telling them that the old days were gone. At whose instigation they took to the free mass travelling I do not know. We had not suggested it to them. We suddenly heard that they were doing it.[27]

In February 1921, however, Gandhi advised, nay instructed, the *kisans* to refrain from such actions; and Nehru went along with him.

Numbers *8* and *9* of Gandhi's *Instructions* indicate that, in Gandhi's view as in that of the colonial regime, the peasants bore the responsibility for the preservation of non-violence—and for its break-down in any situation of clash with the authorities. *Instruction 3* shows that this was his view also of any confrontation between the peasant and the landlord. The instruction referred to physical force, but what was unique in it was the injunction against social boycott. It was precisely through this traditional practice that the Kisan Sabhas of Awadh had first signalled their arrival in the post-war political arena and through it too that they had considerably extended their influence. Towards the end of 1919, certain taluqdars of Pratapgarh who were guilty of severe exactions or other oppressive acts, found themselves up against such 'strikes' by the villagers. *Nau dhobi band kar diye gae,* i.e. the services of the barber, the washerman and other performers of menial but essential tasks, were withheld. More than a year later, in December 1920 and January 1921, this form of protest was still widespread in Pratapgarh and Sultanpur districts.[28] Now, after the outbreak of violence at various places, Gandhi sought to restore 'peace' by asking for the voluntary surrender of this time-honoured and effective weapon. No corresponding sacrifice was demanded of the landlords.

Indeed, the concern for the interests of the landlords went further. 'We may not withold taxes from the Government or rent

[27]Nehru, op. cit., p. 59.

[28]*Collected Works of Mahatma Gandhi*, vol. XX, p. 544; Siddiqi, op. cit., p. 111.

from the landlord' (*Instruction 4*). This was in line with *Instruction 7*: 'We are not at the present moment offering civil disobedience [this 'further step' was adopted by the Congress only in November 1921]; we should, therefore, carry out all Government orders.' But it was actuated by an altogether different argument as well: 'It should be borne in mind that we want to turn zemindars into friends' (*Instruction 6*). 'We should influence our opponents by kindness' (*Instruction 3*). 'Should there be any grievances against zemindars they should be reported to Pandit Motilal Nehru and his advice followed' (*Instruction 5*).

The use of the first person plural pronoun in Gandhi's *Instructions* was a delicate touch, typical of the man. But the delicacy of *Instruction 5*—'Should there be any grievances'—is of a different order. The long-suffering peasant masses of Awadh exploded in anger in 1920-21 in a situation of severe hardship. We have referred above to the well-nigh unchallengeable position guaranteed to the taluqdars by the British administration and—what was perhaps seen as part of that guarantee—the extremely insecure legal position given to the vast majority of tenants in Awadh. We have pointed also to the more or less general trend of immiserization of the peasantry under the weight of a stagnant economy coupled with population growth, rising prices and increasing demands for rent, interest and other dues. The First World War and its immediate aftermath brought new and crushing burdens: rocketing prices, uncertain harvests, War Loans, recruitment and sudden demobilization, and finally a quite disastrous season of epidemic disease. Added to these was renewed pressure from the landlords for enhanced rents, and much increased *nazrana* and other cesses, backed by the force of legal and illegal evictions of *bedakhli*. It was against *bedakhli* and *nazrana* that the peasants of Awadh protested most bitterly in 1920-21. And officials admitted the legitimacy of their protest, and therefore hastily moved to amend the Rent Act. 'There is no doubt', wrote the Commissioner of Lucknow Division having awakened to a new awareness of his surroundings in January 1921,

> that in the worst managed taluqdars' estates in this district [Rae Bareli] and others the tenants have been treated with such want of consideration and in some cases with such oppression by the landlords that one is compelled to sympathise with them.[29]

[29]U.P.,G.A.D. 50/1921, Kws: Commnr., Luknow to Chief Sec., U.P., 14 Jan. 1921.

It was not as if Gandhi knew less than this official about the extent of distress among the peasants. Among the more prominent leaders of the national movement, it was he who first vowed to identify himself with the poorest in the land (in language, in dress, in the food he ate) and to work for their uplift, precisely because of his awareness of their misery. But in Awadh at the beginning of the 1920s, he sought to play down the significance of the clash of interests between landlord and peasant, for tactical reasons as much, it appears, as out of any concern for non-violence. 'Should there be any grievances': in other words, if there were any examples of oppressive acts or punishment or cruelty which a peasant could not possibly tolerate any longer, he should—not protest, organize a social boycott of the oppressor, or perform satyagraha by sitting and fasting outside his house, but—refer the matter to Pandit Motilal Nehru, and follow his advice. Otherwise, outside the sphere of these extreme, absolutely intolerable grievances, 'You should bear a little if the zemindar torments you. We do not want to fight with the zemindars. Zemindars are also slaves and we do not want to trouble them.'[30]

Presiding at the Rae Bareli District Political Conference a few months later, Jawaharlal Nehru seconded Gandhi. The meeting appealed to tenants and zamindars to live in harmony, and 'although the recent Rent Act [the Awadh Rent Amendment Act which had in the meantime been rushed through the provincial legisature] had made their position worse, still they should patiently bear all their troubles, pay their rents and keep the welfare of the country in view'. Before then, the Congress message had gone out in still plainer terms: peasants in Faizabad Division were asked to give up organizing 'meetings', as well as 'disturbances', and to leave it to Gandhi to win Swaraj.[31]

It needs to be emphasized that Gandhi and other Congress leaders were concerned here not primarily with urging the peasants to foreswear violence and continue their struggle by non-violent means. They were urging that the struggle be abandoned altogether—in the interests of 'unity' in what they and later commentators have called the 'greater' struggle against the British.

[30]Gandhi to a peasant audience in Faizabad on 10 Feb. 1921, quoted in Siddiqi, op. cit., p. 180.

[31]Gopal, op. cit., pp. 61, 65. See also Siddiqi, op. cit., p. 179 for Jawaharlal's earlier expression of disapproval at the peasants' actions.

This idea of a united front with the landlords of Awadh in the anti-imperialist campaign bears pondering for a moment, for the landlords' dependence on the British (the 'slavery' that Gandhi spoke of) is obvious enough. Very few of the taluqdars performed any useful function in the rural economy, the man who was Settlement Commissioner of Rae Bareli in the 1890s recalled later: most of them were 'mere rent collectors'.[32] The British relied on these rent collectors. They were 'a very solid body', 'by no means a negligible quantity' and 'the only friends we have', the Lieutenant Governor of UP observed in 1920. Or again, as he noted in a memorandum justifying a demand for five reserved seats for the taluqdars in the new legislative council to be set up in the province under the reforms of 1919, 'they live on their estates. They are prominent in all good works. They take the lead in all movements for the improvement of the province and make generous subscriptions.'[33]

The mutuality of interests found here is noteworthy, for the taluqdars relied even more heavily on the British. Wherever the Kisan Sabha spread in 1920-21 their authority crumbled at a stroke: very few did 'anything else than shut themselves up in their houses or leave for the nearest town and complain of the supineness of the authorities'.[34] Then, like the village dog who sneaks out barking when danger has passed, the taluqdars returned to battle in February-March 1921, adamant in their refusal to agree to a liberal amendment of the Awadh Rent Act and insistent on the sanctity of the *sanads* (or patents) granted to them by the British after 1857. They were good landlords, one taluqdar asserted in a discussion regarding the proposed legislative amendments; therefore, 'the tenant . . . should only be the tiller of the soil, and he should not be given any rights'.[35]

[32]Butler Colln., vol. 75: S.H. Fremantle's comment on R. Burns's talk on 'Recent Rent & Revenue Policy in the United Provinces' in *Journal of the Royal Society of Arts* (20 May 1932), p. 674.

[33]Butler Colln., vol. 21: letters to H.E. Richards, 2 June 1920, and Vincent, 10 Nov. 1920; vol. 75: Memo prepared for the Southborough Committee, 1 Dec. 1918. Butler 'screwed' Rs 20 lakhs out of the Maharaja of Balrampur for the War Loan, and got him a knighthood in return. He had in fact intended to extract 50 lakhs, but because of a misunderstanding the subordinate official whom Butler sent to Balrampur asked only for 20 lakhs (Butler Colln., vol. 20: Butler to Hewett, 19 July 1918).

[34]U.P., G.A.D. 50/3/1921: Hailey to Lambert, 1 Feb. 1921; cf. also Butler Colln., vol. 80, Butler's notes on his meeting with taluqdars on 6 March 1921.

[35]Ibid; note on meeting with taluqdars, 12 Feb. 1921. For the emphasis on *sanads*, see esp. Raja Sir Rampal Singh's 'Taluqdars and the Amendment of the Oudh Rent Law' (Lucknow, n.d.), in ibid.

Nehru himself admirably summed up the position of the taluqdars in his *Autobiography*:

> The taluqdars and big zamindars . . . had been the spoilt children of the British Government, but that Government had succeeded, by the special education and training it provided or failed to provide for them, in reducing them, as a class, to a state of complete intellectual impotence. They did nothing at all for their tenantry, such as landlords in other countries have to some little extent often done, and became complete parasites on the land and people. Their chief activity lay in endeavouring to placate the local officials, without whose favour they could not exist for long, and demanding ceaselessly a protection of their special interests and privileges.[36]

But that was a later reflection. In 1921 Nehru and Gandhi looked aghast at the actions taken by the Awadh peasants against these creatures of imperialism. The symbolic significance of the Munshiganj events of 7 January 1921 when the landlord and the Deputy Commissioner lined up with the armed police against unarmed peasants and their local Congress allies, was missed. Or at least it was overlooked; for even at the time Nehru described the landlord as 'half an official' and wrote bitterly of 'the twins' (the British Deputy Commissioner and the Sikh landlord) who stood shoulder to shoulder at Munshiganj.[37] Yet, the Congress leaders looked to their landlord 'brothers' for support in the great struggle that was then raging against the British.

The Colonial View

A British intelligence official who travelled around a 'disturbed' area in December 1920 and January 1921 made what was in some ways a shrewder analysis of the political situation in the UP countryside, in spite of his need to justify the colonial power—which he did at every step. His assessment was based on a month's tour through the part of Allahabad district that bordered on Pratapgarh (Partabgarh in his report) and Jaunpur. Conditions differed here in significant respects from those that obtained in Awadh. Yet a strong Kisan Sabha movement arose in the same years, and there are so many features of similarity that this report on Allahabad, reproduced in full as an Appendix to this paper, may

[36]Nehru, op. cit., p. 58.

[37]*Selected Works of Jawaharlal Nehru*, vol. 1 (New Delhi, 1972), pp. 213, 224.

be taken as representative of the official discourse on the peasant movement in Awadh at this time.

Intended as a general report (and a secret one at that), this Intelligence Department document is far less selective than Gandhi's *Instructions*. Its ostensible purpose was to establish the identity of the opposing forces in the countryside and the reasons for peasant discontent. The report is therefore to the point about the causes of the Kisan Sabha movement.

> Everywhere . . . the great outcry is against bedakhli (ejectment), in spite of the large amount of marusi [*maurusi*, i.e. land held on a stable. occupancy tenure] land held by cultivators in these parts. (See p.193 below.)

The situation was far more serious in the neighbouring districts of Awadh where the great bulk of the tenants' land was *ghair-maurusi* (non-occupancy). But even in Allahabad,

> the idea prevails that the zamindars are avoiding the pinch of rising prices by taking it out of their tenants, both in the form of nazranas and by raising rents. When enhanced rents are not paid, the tenants are evicted, or in some cases the land is given for ploughing to others, without even the formality of an ejectment decree. (p. 193 below.)

The official's comments on the structure of colonial administration are equally frank. No one in the villages knew anything about the much-vaunted Montagu-Chelmsford reforms and the right of franchise conferred upon some people, he tells us, until Congress spread the word that votes should not be cast. But for the non-cooperators, the elections would have been 'even more of a farce' than they actually turned out to be. It would have meant, he adds in a significant observation, that 'the subordinate officials and well wishers of the government wishful to make the Reform Scheme a success would have brought voters to the polling stations as they did recruits to the colours and subscriptions to the War Loan.' (p. 195 below.) Elsewhere he pinpoints the contemporary social and political position of the landlords. 'The average zamindar is only concerned with collecting his rents and pays very little attention to improving the means of production, communication and irrigation on his estates.' 'The position taken by the zamindars is that they and their forefathers have been well wishers of the government, and it is up to that government now to help them out of their difficulties'. 'Their only wish is for things to go on the same as ever'. (p. 194 below.)

The major weakness in this report is the absence of any direct reference to the role of the colonial Government. The author plainly fails to make sufficient allowance for the fact that he is 'a European official', his assertion to the contrary notwithstanding. The point he wishes to stress most of all is that the Kisan Sabha agitation is 'not in any way anti-British nor even anti-Government'. The movement, he suggests, is basically directed against the landlords—and who can deny that the latter have in a large measure brought it upon themselves? He argues, further, in an interesting variation of the 'manipulation' theme, that the peasants are really quite ignorant of the larger issues at stake; they did not even know who Gandhi was, and actually said 'We are for Gandhiji and the Sarkar'. (p. 197 below.) We shall have more to say about this in a moment.

First, it may be noted that the intelligence official's clean chit to the Government and the Court of Wards, and his contention that the peasants were in no way anti-Government or anti-British, is contradicted by testimony that he himself inadvertently provides:

> The idea is a fixed one [in the minds of the villagers] that a poor man has no chance against a rich man in a contest in the courts, and who will say that there is not some truth in this under the system of civil and criminal justice as it has come to be practised in India. (p. 193 below.)

He admits, besides, that the peasants blame the Government for all their sufferings during the War and believe that they 'supplied the men and money' but got nothing in return. Finally, there is in the latter part of the report still more conclusive evidence against the intelligence man's claim that the Government was 'above it all'. Here it is stated that when it was announced to crowds of peasants that Gandhi had ordered that no votes be given, 'everyone' obeyed. 'For the present . . . Gandhi's word is supreme'. 'What he orders must be done'. (pp. 196-7 below.) That fact stood as an open challenge to the authority of the British. One should add that in a situation where the peasants were not even certain of who Gandhi was (as the intelligence report indicates), it is unlikely that they would always come to know what he had 'ordered'. Rather they must often have decided, by assumption, what his orders were. The point is of some importance for, as we shall see in the next section of this essay, in parts of Awadh Gandhi's name came to be used by peasant rebels, without any specific instructions from Gandhi, to deal out justice to the landlords and the police—the subordinate officials as well as the well-wishers of the regime.

The intelligence official's remarks regarding the supremacy of Gandhi, however, tell us a good deal more about the nature of the peasant movement in Awadh in 1919-22. They indicate the important role played by rumour in the rise of such movements. It is a common assertion that peasants, scattered and isolated by the conditions of their existence, are incapable of mobilizing themselves for political action. They need an 'outside leader', we are told—a Peasant King or a modern substitute, come to deliver the people from their thrall. Yet a Just, and usually distant Ruler has often been known to provide the necessary inspiration for peasant revolt. The belief in an 'outside leader' can also be seen as the obverse of a belief in the break-down of the locally recognized structure of authority; and rumour fulfils the function of spreading such a notion as efficiently as the leader from the town. Here lies the real significance of the myth of the Great Man: 'someone' has challenged the powers that be, 'someone' has come to deliver. Hence:

> The currency which Mr Gandhi's name has acquired even in the remotest villages is astonishing. No one seems to know quite who or what he is, but it is an accepted fact that what he orders must be done. He is a Mahatma or sadhu, a Pandit, a Brahman who lives at Allahabad, even a Deota. One man said he was a merchant who sells cloth at three annas a yard. Someone had probably told him about Gandhi's shop [the new Swadeshi store set up in the city of Allahabad]. The most intelligent say he is a man who is working for the good of the country, but the real power of his name is perhaps to be traced back to the idea that it was he who got *bedakhli* stopped in Partabgarh. It is a curious instance of the power of a name. (p. 196 below.)

A brisk trade in rumours arose in many parts of India during the First World War. Embellished, re-interpreted, modified and magnified as they were passed on from person to person, these rumours contributed significantly to the flood of mass risings in this period. There was a widespread belief that the British Empire was on the verge of collapse; the recruitment campaign grew ever more furious and fearful because its armies were decimated, there was a need to scrounge pennies from the people (the War Loans) because its coffers were empty. The advocacy of Home Rule took on a new meaning. The German King was sending troops to help the opponents of the Raj, it was said. The world was turning upside down. The day of the downtrodden had come. So stories concerning the coming of the Germans caused 'excitement' not only in the villages of Allahabad (p. 197 below.); they accompanied a whole variety of other mass uprisings in these years—agitation among the Oraons of Ranchi and Chota Nagpur (and in the distant tea-gardens of Assam) in 1915-16, violent revolt among the Santhals of Mayurbhanj (Orissa) in 1917 and the large-scale rioting in Shahabad (Bihar) on the occasion of the Baqr-Id in the latter year, for instance.[38]

The 'power of a name' was evident again in Awadh in the first years of the 1920s. Both 'Baba Ramchandra' and 'Gandhi' came to acquire an extraordinary appeal. This is highlighted by the huge demonstrations for the release of Ramchandra on different occasions, and the success of the 'pretender' Ramchandra at Goshainganj (Faizabad), noticed above. It is testified to also by the 'multiple personality' that Ramchandra appeared to develop during this period: he was reported to be 'in Bahraich on the 5th [January 1921] by Nelson, to be in Barabanki at the same time by Grant and in Fyzabad [Faizabad] by Peters'.[39]

Rumours about the presence of Gandhi added to the tumult on several occasions and, as we have already noted, brought thousands of peasants thronging to Pratapgarh jail in September 1920 and to Rae Bareli on 7 January 1921 when the firing at Munshiganj occurred. Less than a week later, the Commissioner of Faizabad reported that 'large numbers' of peasants were heading towards Rae Bareli (in which district a big meeting of peasant delegates was scheduled to be held, at Unchahar, on 15 January), having been told by their Kisan Sabhas that 'it was Gandhi's order that they are to go'.[40] But with these indications of the response to 'Gandhi' and 'Ramchandra', we have passed into the domain of the peasants' perspective on the political events of 1919-22.

[38]See IOL, London, L/P & J/6/1448 of 1916; L/P & J/6/1488 of 1917; L/P & J/6/1507 of 1918; GOI, Home Progs., Conf., 1919, vol. 52.

[39]U.P., GAD 50/1921, Kws: Hailey to Chief Sec., 15 Jan. 1921. Nelson, Grant and Peters were the Dy. Commnrs. of the three districts named.

[40]Ibid., Hailey to Chief Sec., 13 Jan. 1921.

The Peasants' Perspective

'We are for Gandhiji and the Sarkar'(p. 197 below) The peasants of UP, like peasant rebels elsewhere,[41] appear to have retained faith in the justice and benevolence of a distant ruler, the 'Sarkar', even as they revolted against his despotic agents. From this point of view, even the statement in the intelligence report on Allahabad district that the reverence for Gandhi was partly due to the belief that he had influence with the Government may be said to have had a grain of truth in it.

It is perhaps significant that in the Awadh of the early 1920s, those who spoke of Gandhi displacing the King at Delhi or in London tended to be men from the towns.[42] The peasants' own 'kings' were recruited locally. 'Gandhi Raj' would bring reduced rents, and

> *Babá Ram Chandra Ke rajwa*
> *Parja maja urawe na*
> (In the raj of Baba Ramchandra
> The people will make merry).[43]

The peasants' Gandhi was not a remote, western-educated lawyer-politician: he was a Mahatma, a Pandit, a Brahman, even a merchant 'who lives at Allahabad'. (p.196 below) Baba Ramchandra was more emphatically still a local man—a *sadhu* of renown in the districts of Jaunpur, Sultanpur and Pratapgarh, even before he gained a position of importance in the Kisan Sabha movement.

M.H. Siddiqi, citing the folk-rhyme regarding Ramchandra quoted above, rightly observes that the notion of *raja* (king) and *praja* (subjects) was 'so deeply ingrained in the psyche' of the peasant that he spoke even of popular peasant leaders in these terms.[44] The evidence from Awadh is indeed striking in this respect. Shah Muhammad Naim Ata, the descendant of a pious Muslim revered by Hindus and Muslims alike in the village of Salon (Rae Bareli district), became 'King of Salon' when he joined

[41]Cf. Gopal, op. cit., pp. 49-50n; I.J. Catanach, 'Agrarian Disturbances in Nineteenth Century India', *Indian Economic & Social History Review*, 3:1 (1966); Daniel Field, *Rebels in the Name of the Tsar* (Boston, 1976), *passim*.

[42]U.P., GAD 50/2/1921, D.O. No. 1620 from Office of Publicity Commnr., Naini Tal, 25 June 1921, quoting article in the *Leader* entitled 'Perversion of Peasants'; Siddiqi, op. cit., pp. 173n, & 178n.

[43]Ibid, pp. 200, & 112n.

[44]Ibid., pp. 122-3n.

the rebels in 1920. Jhinguri Singh, founder of what was probably the first Kisan Sabha of the movement in Rure (Pratapgarh district), was acclaimed 'Raja of Rure' and said to have 'swallowed all laws'. The pretender Ramchandra established his 'kingdom' in the region of Goshainganj (Faizabad district), held court and meted out justice before his arrest in January 1921. Thakurdin Singh, a servant of the Raja of Parhat, had done the same in some of the latter's villages in Pratapgrah district a couple of months earlier. In February 1922, again, it was reported that the leaders of the Eka movement had begun to assume the title of Raja and were moving about the countryside with 'large bodyguards of archers and spearmen'.[45]

The pithy rhyme from the Patti tahsil of Pratapgarh district thus captures a central feature of the traditional peasant view of the political world. There are rulers and ruled. And rulers are usually just: they must be, for their subjects to remain contented and for the normal functioning of the prescribed order of things. As we shall see, it was a view that at least some sections of the Awadh peasantry were to discard as their struggle matured between 1919 and 1922.

In the early stages of the Kisan Sabha movement, however, traditionalism was pronounced. One of the earliest forms of peasant protest to come to notice in Awadh during this period was the age-old practice of social boycott—*nau dhobi band*. The customary sanction of village caste panchayats was used to enforce the boycott among the peasants.[46] Caste solidarity and the authority of the caste panchayat appears also to have been of significance in the setting up of the Kisan Sabhas. The villages where the first Sabhas were established, such as Rure, Arkha and Rasulpur, had in their populations a large proportion of Kurmis and Muraos, 'superior' cultivating castes with a tradition of solidarity and independence, and it was among these castes that the Kisan Sabhas found their initial base.[47]

In southern and eastern Awadh as a whole the Kurmis were

[45]U.P., GAD 50/1921: telegram from Commnr., Lucknow to Chief Sec., U.P., 12 Jan. 1921; Mehta's Report, p. 3; S.K. Mitral and Kapil Kumar, 'Baba Ram Chandra and Peasant Upsurge in Oudh, 1920-21', *Social Scientist*, No. 71 (June 1978); extracts from the *Englishman* and the *Leader* as in *notes* 18 and 42 above. Cf. Pushkin's *The Captain's Daughter* for a picture of Pugachev, the Pretender.

[46] Siddiqi, op. cit., p. 111.

[47]Ibid., p. 117; W.F. Crawley, 'Kisan Sabhas & Agrarian Revolt in the United Provinces, 1920-21', *Modern Asian Studies*, 5:2 (1971), p. 101.

thought to be the 'mainstay' of the movement all the way from the last months of 1919 to the early part of 1921.[48] At more than one place in his notes and diaries, Baba Ramchandra reports how Thakur Jhinguri Singh and Thakur Sahdev Singh, the men who were responsible for drawing him into the Kisan Sabha movement, were aided in their earlier efforts to promote the movement by a number of 'honest, dedicated, self-sacrificing' Kurmis named Kashi, Bhagwandin, Prayag and Ayodhya. Jhinguri Singh, Sahdev Singh and their families initially had to bear the entire cost of looking after the thousands of peasants who in the early months of 1920 flocked to Rure to report their grievances. Then Bhagwandin, Kashi, Prayag and Ayodhya got together and proceeded to mobilize support from their caste-fellows. This they did so successfully that several thousand rupees were raised in a short while, and the movement gained a more secure footing.[49] Similarly, on the occasion of the great Awadh Kisan Congress held at Ayodhya in December 1920, the Rasulpur (Rae Bareli district) Kisan Sabha leader, Mata Badal Koeri, raised Rs 6000 from the Koeris who had come to attend the Congress.[50]

By the winter of 1920-21, the Kisan Sabha had gained considerable support among tenants and labourers of a wide range of castes, including Muslims. Caste consciousness may now have posed other problems for the organizers of the movement: hence, perhaps, the need for Ramchandra's directive that after meetings, local Ahirs should look after and feed Ahirs who had come from distant places, and Kurmis, Koeris, Muslims, Brahmans and others should do likewise.[51]

The peasant movement in Awadh was, in addition, marked by a pervasive religious symbolism. At the early peasant meetings Ramchandra and others commonly recited excerpts from Tulsidas's *Ramcharitmanas*,[52] the favourite religious epic of the Hindus in

[48]Ramchandra Colln. II, RC XIII; U.P. Rev. (A) Dept. File 753 of 1920: Hailey's 'Note' on Mehta's Report, dated 17 Dec. 1920; U.P., GAD 50/1921, Kws: Commnr., Faizabad to Chief Sec., U.P., 14 Jan. 1921.

[49]Ramchandra Colln. I, Subject File No. 1: 'Papers Relating to Peasant Movement in Avadh 1921', incomplete letter of 1939 and 'Avadh, U.P., ke kisanon par mere niji vichar' (14 July 1934). Translation from the Ramchandra papers is mine, except where otherwise stated.

[50]Ramchandra Colln. II, RC XI: 'Autobiographical Notebook', p. 35.

[51]Ibid., p. 12.

[52]Nehru, op cit., p. 53; D.N. Panigrahi, 'Peasant Leadership', in B.N. Pandey (ed.), *Leadership in South Asia* (New Delhi, 1977); p. 85. Old Congress workers of Sandila in Hardoi district recalled how Madari Pasi also 'recited *kathas* and held peasant meetings'.

northern India and especially beloved of people in this region: their own language, Awadhi, was after all the language of Tulsidas's composition, and places like Ayodhya (a few miles from Faizabad), the seat of Ram's kingdom, very much part of their world. The phrase 'Sita Ram' early became the chief rallying call of the movement—used by peasants of all communities, Muslims as well as Hindus, to bring out supporters for meetings and (at a later stage) for resistance to Government and landlord agents attempting to overawe members of the Kisan Sabhas, confiscate moveable property or take other action against the peasants.

Baba Ramchandra has a good deal to say about the words 'Sita Ram' in the course of his fairly sketchy writings on the movement. He recalls, in a note written in 1934, that when he first came to Awadh, the greeting *salaam* (usually addressed by one in an inferior station to one in a superior) was widely used. He promoted the use of the alternative, 'Sita Ram', which did away with such discrimination on grounds of status, and thus earned the displeasure of 'many of the praiseworthy [*sic.*] and respectable folk of the upper castes'. Gradually, however, he writes, 'Sita Ram', 'Jai Ram', 'Jai Shankar', caught on in place of *salaam*. And as the movement developed, and his own popularity increased, it was enough for Ramchandra to raise the slogan 'Sita Ram': the cry was promptly taken up in one village after another, and thus in a remarkably short space of time thousands would assemble to see him and hear his discourse.[53]

Elsewhere, Ramchandra writes with still greater pride of the phenomenal power of the peasants' new slogan. On one occasion, early in the history of the Kisan Sabha movement, a confrontation took place at village Bhanti (in Pratapgarh district) between the police and the agents of the Ramganj and Amargarh estates, on the one hand, and Thakur Jhinguri Singh and his co-workers on the other. 'On that side were the wielders of *lathis* and spears', Ramchandra records dramatically. 'On this side was the slogan "Sita Ram"... As soon as the cry of "Sita Ram" was raised, thousands of peasants poured out in waves from the surrounding villages.' It needed no more to make the police and other authorities change their tune: with the landlords' men, they left as quietly as possible.[54]

[53]Ramchandra Colln. I, Subject File 1: 'Avadh ke kisan par mere niji vichar' (14 July 1934); Nehru, op. cit., p. 52; interviews with the late Babu Mangla Prasad, one of the Allahabad Congressmen who had been drawn into the Pratapgarh peasant movement in 1920. [54]Ramchandra Colln. II: 'Autobiographical Notebook', p. 26.

In retrospect, indeed, Ramchandra attributes miraculous powers to the phrase 'Sita Ram'. He describes an incident in which a servant of the Amargarh estate forcibly cut a peasant's sugarcane crop for the purpose of feeding the Amargarh estate's elephants. As he returned with his loot loaded on an elephant, he was stopped by a Kisan Sabha worker named Prayag. 'The driver urged the elephant to advance upon him. But Prayag stood his ground, crying "Sita Ram". The elephant refused to advance.' Ramchandra goes on to report that in the part of Awadh where he was first based, the mango trees in the villages for several miles around bore fruit only once every three years. 'Because of the slogan "Sita Ram" they began to bear fruit every year.' He concludes: 'In the most difficult of situations, the peasants turned to the slogan "Sita Ram". And the slogan fulfilled their many different desires. As a result the organization [of the Kisan Sabhas] grew ever stronger.'[55] In other 'notes' written at around the same time, i.e. in 1939 or 1940, Ramchandra rues the fact that the peasants of Awadh were forgetting the two simple words that had brought them such great victories as the extraction, from the British, of the Awadh Rent (Amendment) Act of 1921 and the passing, by a Congress ministry, of the far more thorough U.P. Tenancy Bill of 1939.[56]

These reflections of a man who was by then inclining more and more to a left-wing position point to the religious type of consciousness[57] that the peasants brought to their struggle. That it was not just a 'half-crazy' *sadhu* who attached a special significance to the words 'Sita Ram' is attested to by other contemporary observations. The 'most serious feature' of the situation in January 1921, according to the Deputy Commissioner of Faizabad, was

> the immense danger which arises from an organization which at very short notice is able to collect enormous crowds. The existence of a definitely arranged rallying cry is another danger.

The last part of this statement was later elaborated thus:

[55]Ibid., p. 26-7.

[56]Ramchandra Colln. II, RC XIII; Ramchandra Colln. I, Subject File No. 1: 'Note' of 27 Dec. 1939. The 1939 Tenancy Bill received the Governor's approval and became law only in 1940 after the resignation of the Congress ministries.

[57]Ranajit Guha has drawn my attention to this concept which occurs in some of the early writings of Karl Marx.

One of the most powerful weapons at their [the peasants'] command is the war cry—Sita Ram Ki jai. They all say that when this is sounded, most turn out and to a very large extent this is done. It has become the cry of discontent.[58]

The hold of religious symbols on the mind of the peasant is perhaps also indicated by a story relating to the selection of Rure as the place where the first Kisan Sabha should be established. V. N. Mehta, after his enquiries into the movement, suggested that Rure was chosen partly because legend had it that Ram and Lakshman, the heroes of the *Ramayana*, had once rested there. Tulsidas wrote: '*raj samaj virajat Rure*' [the company of Princes honour Rure with their presence], and the people of Rure claimed that this was a reference to none other than their own village.[59] What better traditional sanction than this for the launching from here of a just and righteous political movement?

The idea of a just, or moral, struggle appears to have been fundamental to the peasants' acceptance of the necessity of revolt. Exploitation as such was not unjust. It was inevitable that some ruled and some conducted prayers and some owned the land and some laboured, and all lived off the fruits of that labour. But it was important that everyone in the society made a living out of the resources that were available. It was when the subsistence needs of the peasants of Burma and Indo-China were threatened in the colonial era that the fiercest peasant revolts broke out there.[60] It was similarly when the landlord decided to levy new and oppressive imposts in a period of considerable hardship for substantial sections of the peasantry that resistance was taken up in Awadh as morally right and necessary.

In Allahabad district, the intelligence officer noticed that there was a difference in the peasants' response on the estates of resident proprietors on the one hand and absentee owners on the other, and among the latter especially those of 'new men'—city *banias* and *mahajans* and the like.

There is nowhere any genuine objection to performing *hari* and *begari* [forced labour] according to immemorial custom for zamindars who

[58]U.P., GAD 50/3/1921: H.R.C. Hailey to Butler, 24 Jan. 1921; and 'Note' by Hailey, regarding views of himself, Peters and Scott O'Connor (enclosed with Hailey's letter to Lambert, 1 Feb. 1921). See also Nehru, op. cit., p. 53.

[59]Mehta's Report, cited in Siddiqi, op. cit., p. 115n.

[60]James C. Scott, *The Moral Economy of the Peasant* (California, 1976), *passim*.

> are seen and known, but there is a tendency to kick against working for and supplying nazrana, hathyana, motorana [all relatively new 'taxes'] etc. etc. for distant and unknown landowners at the bidding of foul mouthed karindas and sepoys.[61] (pp. 192-3 below.)

The feeling against 'new men' may have contributed to the peasant revolt in some of the Awadh districts too. The animosity displayed towards one or two Sikh taluqdars in Rae Bareli, it was suggested in January 1921, was because they were regarded as interlopers. On the estate of Sardar Amar Singh, the peasants were reported to have accepted the leadership of a Rajput occupancy tenant who had been dispossessed following the Mutiny.[62] In an attack on the estate of the small Kurmi taluqdar of Sehgaon-Pacchimgaon, also in Rae Bareli district, the peasants followed the Kurmi descendants of co-sharers likewise dispossessed after the Mutiny.[63] The adoption, as King of Salon, of Shah Naim Ata—descendant in a line of revered benefactors of the village—may also have been the result of a similar kind of sentiment.

There is evidence too of an acceptance of the long-established, 'fair' rights of the landlord—in Awadh as in Allahabad. A contemporary statement on the Awadh Kisan Sabha agitation made the point that the peasants' complaints regarding *begar, rasad* and so on were minor compared with their sense of outrage over *bedakhli* and *nazrana:* 'The former had been a custom for generations. The latter were of comparatively recent growth.'[64] In Pratapgarh, Mehta reported on the basis of his inquiries in October 1920, town-based politicians like Mata Badal Pandey had adopted the position that nothing more than the rent should be paid to the landlord; but 'the tenants have not yet fallen into line with them'.[65]

The 'Kisan pledge' to be taken on the formation of each new Kisan Sabha, which was drawn up in May or June 1920, still looked to the landlord (Thakur) for justice and protection from his oppressive agents (*ziladars,* peons and so on). It read as follows:

[61]*Nazrana* was the premium demanded from a tenant to allow him onto, or let him stay on the land. *Hathyana* and *motorana* were imposts levied on the peasants when a new elephant or a motor-car was bought by the landlord.

[62]U.P., GAD 50/1921, Kws: Commnr., Lucknow to Chief Sec., U.P., 14 Jan. 1921.

[63]H.R. Nevill, *Rae Bareli: District Gazetteers of the United Provinces of Agra and Oudh,* vol. 39, (Lucknow 1923), p.95; Siddiqi, op. cit., pp. 160-1.

[64]Faunthorpe's Report, p. 273.

[65]Mehta's Report, p. 57.

1. We Kisans shall speak the truth—not the untruth—and tell our story of woe correctly.
2. We shall not brook beating or abuses from anyone; we shall not lay our hands on anyone but if a ziladar or peon raises theirs on us we, five or ten of us, will stay his hand. If anyone abused us we shall jointly ask him to restrain himself. If he would not listen we would take him to our Thakur.
3. We shall pay our rent at the proper time—and insist upon a receipt. We shall jointly go to the house of the Thakur and pay the rent there.
4. We shall not pay illegal cesses like *gorawan* [*ghodawan*], *motorawan, hathiawan*. We shall not work as labourer without payment. If any peon catches hold of a Kisan (for forced labour) the rest of the villagers will not take their meals without setting him free. We shall sell *upli* (cow dung cakes), *patai* (sugarcane leaves for thatching) and *bhusa* (straw) at slightly cheaper than the bazaar rate but we shall not supply these articles without payment.
5. We shall not quarrel and if we do we shall settle it by a panchayat. Every village or two to three villages combined will form a panchayat and dispose of matters there.
6. If any Kisan is in trouble we shall help him. We shall consider other Kisans' joys and sorrows our own.
7. We shall not be afraid of constables. If they oppress [us] we shall stop him [them]. We shall submit to no one's oppression.
8. We shall trust in God and with patience and zeal we shall try to put an end to our grievance[s].[66]

Later a spokesman for the peasants explained, with reference to clause 4 above, that the amounts of *bhusa, upli,* etc. traditionally given, would still be provided free of charge; it was only anything demanded in addition that would have to be paid for as specified. And in October 1920, shortly after his liberation from Pratapgarh jail on account of the mass demonstrations of his followers, Ramchandra promulgated the rates of the customary dues, like *hari* and *bhusa, karbi* and *bhent,* that peasants were to pay.[67] It is in the light of the peasant's notion of a moral world, rather than in the simple terms of 'moderate' and 'radical' borrowed from elite discourse,

[66]This translation is found in ibid, pp. 109-10. The pledge appears over the name of Gauri Shankar Misra, vice-president, U.P. Kisan Sabha, but its language and Ramchandra's reconstruction of it in his writings (see undated, incomplete letter in Ramchandra Colln. I, File No. 1), suggest that Ramchandra and other local people had a major hand in drawing it up.

[67]Mehta's Report, p. 110.

that this position might best be understood. It is in this light too that we might comprehend the 'not altogether simple' demands[68] of the 3000 peasants led by Baba Janki Das and others, who besieged the house of Thakur Tribhuvan Bahadur Singh of Chandanian (Rae Bareli) on 5 January 1921 to obtain an end to ejectment and 'the turning out of a prostitute in the Taluqdar's keeping'.

The religious-ethical aspect of the peasants' demands was evident also in the oath taken by villagers in northern Awadh to signify the support of their villages for the Eka movement in the latter part of 1921 and the early months of 1922. An elaborate religious ritual accompanied the oath-taking. A hole dug in the ground and filled with water represented the sacred river Ganga. Over this, and in the presence of all the villagers—summoned, officials averred, by means of abuse, threats and social boycott—a pandit recited a prayer. A collection of four annas or more per head was made, and part of this was used to pay the pandit for his services. Finally, an oath was administered and a panchayat formed in order to settle disputes in the village. By the various injunctions of the oath, the peasants bound themselves to:

1. Refuse to leave their fields if illegally ejected.
2. Pay only the recorded rent.
3. Pay rent regularly at the agreed times.
4. Refuse to pay rents without being given receipts.
5. Refuse to perform *begar* for zamindars without payment.
6. Refuse to pay *hari* and *bhusa*.
7. Refuse to pay for the use of irrigation tanks.
8. Refuse to pay for grazing cattle on jungle and pasture lands.
9. Give no help to criminals in the village.
10. Oppose oppression by the zamindars.
11. Take all disputes to their own panchayat and abide by its decision.[69]

There are several points of similarity between the Eka oath and the earlier Kisan Sabha pledge. In both a traditional peasant morality finds expression. There was a proper share that the superior classes might claim: this was to be met promptly. Crime was to be opposed (Eka oath), truthfulness and trust in God maintained (Kisan Sabha pledge). Yet both emphasized, at the same time, the peasants' need for unity and self-help, especially reliance on their own panchayats for the purpose of settling all internal disputes.

[68] Siddiqi, op cit., p. 154. [69] Ibid., pp. 201-2.

It seems evident that there was already, in the earlier stages of the peasant movement, a growing tension between the traditional structure of agrarian society and the peasants' insistence on implementing traditional practice. Thus rents would be paid, but only if receipts were provided. Customary cesses would be met, but not any demand for larger quantities than usual, nor any new and illegal imposts. More generally, the peasants would resist oppression by the police and the landlord's agents, although they might still turn to the landlord for arbitration.[70] By the time of the Eka movement, this tension had been resolved to some extent by the adoption of a more militant stand against the traditional system as a whole. A commitment was still made to pay rents as agreed between landlord and tenant, but this was no longer the case even with customary cesses such as *hari* and *bhusa*. The peasants would no longer perform *begar* without remuneration, or pay for the use of irrigation tanks or pasture lands; for water, like air, was a gift of God, and the jungles and other uncultivated lands had for long (before the arrival of the British legal system and record of rights) been used in common. Finally, the peasants now declared their determination to resist any attempt to evict them illegally from their fields, and indeed to oppose all oppressive acts of the landlords. The surviving elements of deference, found in the expression of hope of justice from the landlord in the Kisan Sabha pledge, had disappeared.

This change of tone reflects another feature of the powerful peasant movement under discussion, its ability to overcome some of its own traditionalist limitations. Seeing how their landlords had acted, the Awadh peasants were learning to defend their interests. Many of the old links between the landlords and their tenants, labourers and other servants, had been eroded by the imposition of British order, the registration of rights, rigorous collection of rent, revenue and interest, the enforcement of all this in the courts of law, and most recently the exceptional pressure brought to bear on the peasantry during the First World War. Now, with the emergence of the Kisan Sabhas (working at times in association with Congress and Liberal volunteers) and the later Eka associations, the peasants' subservience broke down further.

[70]At another level the use of the traditional greeting 'Sita Ram' reflected the same tension—since it was promoted in part to do away with the peasant's consciousness of hierarchy and attitude of deference, and was opposed (as we have observed) by members of the more privileged classes.

Soon they launched into a more open attack on the old order. The movement had entered upon a significant new phase.

For the beginnings of this phase we have to look back to the events of December 1920 and January 1921. The great Kisan Congress at Ayodhya on 20 and 21 December 1920, attended by some 80-100,000 peasants, appears to have marked the turning point. After the Congress, the peasants first lay on the rails until they were permitted to travel home on the trains without purchasing tickets; then, back in their villages, took to protracted discussion of the events and decisions of the meeting 'in the local panchaits [panchayats] which have since been formed in almost every village'.[71] For the first time, an official commented, these villagers 'had begun to realise the power of an united peasantry—to realise that they themselves had the remedy of the most flagrant of their wrongs, the illegal exactions of the landlords, in their own hands'.[72]

By January 1921, another official reported after an investigation in Faizabad division, while most tenants professed 'a certain amount of attachment to the estates to which they belong', they appeared 'firmly determined to obey their [Kisan Sabha] leaders'. He went on to comment on the mass meeting scheduled to be held at Unchahar in Rae Bareli district on 15 January 1921, at which it was said Ramchandra would decide whether future rents were to be paid or not: 'The organization of the tenants' sabhas is now so far complete that it is probable that these orders will carry great weight, if [they are] not implicitly obeyed.'[73] As in Allahabad, a new authority had arisen. 'Gandhi's word is supreme.' Baba Ramchandra will be 'implicitly obeyed'.

As it happened, the peasants did not wait for the word of Gandhi, or of Ramchandra who was by this time working in close association with the leaders of the Non-cooperation Movement. It is evident that the presence of Gandhi and the Congress, and rumours regarding Gandhi's achievements in Champaran, were an important source of inspiration to the Awadh peasant in these years. The support of local Congressmen, Khilafatists and Liberals, and the intervention of men like Jawaharlal Nehru was also of consequence, helping to further inject the Kisan Sabhas with

[71]U.P. GAD 50/1921, Kws: St. John Farnon, Dy. Commnr., Rae Bareli, 19 Jan. 1921.

[72]Loc. cit.

[73]Ibid., Commnr., Faizabad to Chief Sec., U.P., 14 Jan. 1921.

nationalist symbols and slogans and of course giving them wider publicity. Yet, one must not exaggerate the role of the urban politician in the growth of the movement. Any suggestion that it was the Congress (or the Liberals) who politicized the peasantry and thus drew the Awadh peasant into the wider campaign against the British Raj, is belied by timing of the peasants' revolt and the violence of their actions.

It is clear that masses of peasants returned from the Ayodhya Congress with their own unexpected interpretation of the stated purpose of the gathering: 'to end landlord atrocities'. Ramchandra had appeared at the Congress bound in ropes, a dramatic gesture alluding to the bondage of the Awadh peasantry. Before the end of the conference he agreed to throw off his ropes since 'owing to the gathering, ejectment had already been done away with'.[74] The peasant audience took this act literally. Ejectment symbolized the oppressive authority of the landlords, and over the next three months this authority was attacked time and time again. The period saw widespread rioting in Rae Bareli, Faizabad and Sultanpur districts, and the extension of protest into other areas over matters that had not until then been brought into contention.

From the Faizabad division, officials reported a 'general refusal' to till the landlord's *sir* in Pratapgarh, Sultanpur and parts of Faizabad district.[75] The Raja of Pratapgarh, a leading taluqdar, received confirmation of the changed character of the struggle in January 1921 when he found tenants refusing his 'liberal' offer of fourteen-year leases which they had a short while earlier readily accepted. Around the same time, protests were beginning to be heard against demands for *rasad* and *begar* in Bara Banki, a district that had remained largely unaffected by the Kisan Sabha movement until then.[76]

In January 1921 there were also several instances of attacks on landlord property. These were concentrated in Rae Bareli district and the Akbarpur and Tanda tehsils of Faizabad district, but occurred elsewhere too. In Rae Bareli large bands appeared in several estates, destroying the taluqdars' crops and looting and destroying their storage places. 'From 5 January for some days the

[74]Siddiqi, op cit., pp. 148-9.

[75]*Sir:* land held by the landowner under title of personal cultivation.

[76]U.P. GAD 50/1921 Kws: letters of Commnrs., Faizabad and Lucknow Division to Chief Sec., U.P., 14 Jan. 1921.

district was practically in a state of anarchy.' In Pratapgarh there was an assault on the *ziladar* of Raja Bahadur Pratap Bahadur Singh. In Faizabad the terminal weeks of 1920 and the early days of 1921 brought isolated attacks on the servants of taluqdars, and the looting and burning of their straw. Then, following a meeting on 12 January 1921, which led to an attack on and the looting of the zamindars of Dankara, widespread rioting broke out in the district. Bands of 500-1000 men, women and children marched from place to place for the next two days, settling scores with their enemies.[77]

By this time, as we have already observed, many of the lower castes and landless labourers were involved in the agitation. At Fursatganj and Munshiganj bazars in Rae Bareli district, where police firing occurred on 6 and 7 January 1921 respectively, the multi-caste composition of the crowds was especially noted. Among these crowds were numbers of Pasis and members of other 'criminal' tribes who constituted a substantial section of the labouring population of the district. The prominence of the latter was attested to again by the official view that they were responsible for the 'indiscriminate' looting of village bazars and the concentration of rioting in the south-eastern tehsils of Rae Bareli.

In Faizabad, it was reported, Brahmans and Thakurs were not 'generally' in the movement, but 'all the lower castes are affected'. The rioters were said to consist chiefly of Ahirs, Bhars, Lunias and the untouchable Pasis and Chamars, i.e. the castes that provided the majority of the small tenants and agricultural labourers. Deo Narain, one of the two major Kisan Sabha leaders active in the district (the other was Kedar Nath), appears to have concentrated his propaganda efforts among the *halwas* (labourers) of the Brahman and Thakur zamindars and tenants, organizing them into numerous Kisan Sabhas. Consequently Pasis, Chamars, Lunias and other labouring castes were to the fore in the riots in Akbarpur and Tanda tehsils: they plundered the houses of high-caste villagers and their women too came out to attack the high-caste women.[78]

[77]Siddiqi, op cit., p. 165.

[78]U.P., GAD 50/1921 Kws: St. John Farnon to Dy. Commnr., Rae Bareli, 19 Jan. 1921; U.P. GAD 50/3/21: telegram from Commnr. of Faizabad to U.P.A.O., Lucknow, 16 Jan. 1921: and L. Porter to Governor, 19 Jan. 1921, report of interview with Raja Tawaqul Husain of Pirpur; also Siddiqi, op. cit., p. 166 and Panigrahi, op. cit., p. 95. C.A. Bayly has noticed the same sort of development in the neighbouring Allahabad district: by December 1920, he writes, the 'enraged lower peasantry had been joined by landless labourers,

The interests of the landless labourers and the smaller, unprotected tenants of Awadh converged to a large extent. And after December 1920, the actions of the peasants highlighted the concerns of these sections of the rural poor. Their attacks were extended to the bazars and other points where wealth was concentrated. The chief targets were the *banias* (merchants) who had exploited the difficult times to make large profits, but *sunars* (goldsmiths), weavers and others who were thought to have profited from the situation were also attacked in some places. Stores of grain belonging to the taluqdars were looted and destroyed. The houses of upper caste and prosperous villagers were attacked, and quantities of clothes, jewels and so on burnt and destroyed.[79]

At this more advanced stage of the struggle, the peasants also identified more clearly the forces that were ranged against them.[80] In Faizabad the targets of the peasants' violence spread out from the taluqdars and their direct agents to patwaris,[81] small zamindars, large cultivators and the high castes in general. They now covered all those who were on the side of the 'enemy'. This explains the attacks on upper-caste tenants, for as the Commissioner of Faizabad observed, many of these in Faizabad (and in Sultanpur) belonged to 'the same clans as the landlords' and 'opposed the formation of Sabhas in their villages'. Indeed, at this stage the higher castes in Faizabad turned more openly against the movement, welcomed the police, and on the latter's arrival 'plucked up spirit' to defend their property.[82]

suddenly caught by the rise in prices and the sharp turn of the labour market against them after the good months following the influenza epidemic of 1918. Offences against the liquor laws and attacks on the police by Pasis became frequent and in north Allahabad and Patti [Pratapgarh district] disorderly 'swarajya' crowds composed of unemployed Pasi and Chamar labourers became increasingly active during the next six months.' Bayly, 'The Development of Political Organization in the Allahabad Locality'. (Oxford D. Phil. thesis, 1970, pp. 369-71, 382.)

[79]U.P. GAD 50/3/1921; Siddiqi, op cit., pp. 151-3, 165.

[80]Siddiqi seems to accept the contemporary officials' view that the peasants were 'indiscriminate' in their attacks, and describes the local Sabhas as becoming 'totally anarchic' 'at the level of action' (ibid., p. 154). Yet the weight of the evidence points to a quite different conclusion, in spite of the instance Siddiqi singles out of an attack on weavers by 'some ten men'. (Ibid., pp. 150, 153.)

[81]In Awadh the patwari was looked upon as a servant of the landlord though he also performed several duties for the Government. Metcalf, *Land, Landlords and the Raj*, pp. 302-3.

[82]U.P., GAD 50/3/21: Commnr. of Faizabad to Chief Sec., U.P., 24 Jan. 1921; & U.P., GAD 50/1921 Kws: Commnr. of Faizabad's telegram and letter of 16 & 17 Jan. 1921; also Panigrahi, op. cit., p. 97.

It was in the very nature of these developments that the peasant rebels should soon come into direct confrontation with the law-enforcing authorities, who were unquestionably on the side of their enemies. An official diagnosis suggested in February 1921 that

> the kisans have come to appreciate the strength of numbers and having successfully defied the landlords are quite ready to defy Government authority. They have to a large extent lost all fear of the police.

It also reported a growing feeling of antagonism towards Europeans and the abuse of policemen for deserting their countrymen and serving an alien race. An important part of the local Kisan Sabha propaganda at this stage declared the taluqdars to be 'evil creations' of the Government; or, alternatively, described the Government as being 'in league with taluqdars, as guilty of murders and crimes, and above all as being condemned by Gandhi'.[83] All this had little to do with the Congress leaders. It was rather a product of the experience gained by the peasants in the course of their struggle. Given the structure of the colonial administration, the necessity of opposing European officials and the police arose from the very fact of opposing the landlords. This is evident from an examination of the circumstances surrounding even a few of the clashes between the peasants and the police in the Awadh countryside.

In the village of Sehgaon-Pacchimgaon, the peasants were aroused by news of the demonstrations and battles at Fursatganj and elsewhere in Rae Bareli district. In this situation they accepted the leadership of the dispossessed Kurmi co-sharers earlier mentioned and responded to their appeals to unite against the landlord. After the third week of January 1921 tension increased in the village. The villagers set loose the zamindar's cattle to graze on his sugarcane fields. Then, on a bazar day, they gathered and threatened to attack the landowner. The police intervened—to be attacked by the peasants. 'One constable was killed by a *lathi* blow, which smashed the back of his skull. The others retired two or three hundred yards using their guns.'[9] It was some time before the so-called 'ringleaders' could be arrested and the crowd dispersed.

Not long after this event another major clash occurred near the railway station of Goshainganj in Faizabad district. Here the

[83] U.P. GAD 50/3/21: Hailey's 'Note' enclosed with Hailey's letter to Lambert, 1 Feb. 1921.

pretender Ramchandra, who will by now be familiar to the reader, was active for several days in the last part of January 1921, advocating the non-payment of rent and apparently also the doctrine of 'land to the tiller'. Propagandists like him, officials observed, made 'the strongest appeal to the low castes and landless castes who are always little removed from starvation and are told that a millenium in the shape of swaraj is coming through the intervention of Mahatma Gandhi'. The Goshainganj Ramchandra actually did better. Such was his following for a short while that he was able to return land to peasants who had been ejected and order the explusion of others 'not true to the cause'. On 29 January 1921, then, it required a force of some seventy mounted policemen to arrest this one man. That afternoon crowds gathered thinking that he was to be taken away by a train at that time, and lay on the tracks to prevent the train from moving. When a large police force came forward to remove them, the peasants responded by attacking them with bricks lying near the station. The police had to fire thirty-three rounds before the crowds dispersed.

Later, in March 1921, the familiar sequence of mobilization against a landlord (in this case a widowed landlady) and then against the police when they intervened, occurred at Karhaiya Bazar in Rae Bareli district. In this area Brijpal Singh, a demobilized soldier from Pratapgarh, Jhanku Singh, another ex-soldier, Surajpal Singh and Gangadin Brahman, delivered numerous 'objectionable speeches' in the first three weeks of that month. A meeting, scheduled to be held at Karhaiya Bazar on 20 March, the weekly market day, was prohibited by the authorities, and orders issued for the arrest of the 'agitators'. But on that day, the peasants battled with the police, trading brickbat for buckshot, and rescued Brijpal Singh and Jhanku Singh when the police tried to arrest them. Indeed, the police were forced to retreat into the taluqdarin's house and here they were besieged by 'a yelling mob of several thousand people'. The arrival and direct orders of the white Sahib, the English Deputy Commissioner, failed to move the peasants. They continued their vigil all night and maintained a barricade the next morning to prevent 'motors' from entering or leaving the courtyard of the house. Another round of police firing was necessary before the peasants withdrew and their leaders were arrested. Jhanku Singh who was shot during the firing, later succumbed to his injuries, and at least two other peasants are known to have been killed.[84]

The transformation that had taken place in the Awadh peasants' struggle was recognized by the Magistrate at Pratapgarh who reported that what had started as a 'genuine tenants' agitation' soon assumed an 'openly political form' [*sic*].[85] In Faizabad, an official summary informs us, the result of the lectures delivered every three or four days all over the district by Deo Narain Pande, Kedar Nath Sunar and Tribhuvan Dutt was that

> meetings are held nightly *in every village* and a regular system of non-co-operation is being preached. Cultivators are told not to go to the courts, or to the tahsil or to the police, and to pay no rent. [emphasis added.]

At one of these nightly meetings, at which two police constables were beaten and slightly hurt, a number of papers were confiscated from the speaker: in the main, these were petitions to Gandhi describing various grievances regarding the peasants' fields, but they also consisted of two lists of men to be appointed to the posts of Deputy Commissioner, 'Kaptan Sahib' (i.e. Superintendent of Police), Daroga, etc.[86] In Karhaiya, as in Goshainganj (Faizabad), there is evidence of the rebels having established something in the nature of a parallel government. Brijpal Singh and Jhanku Singh in the former, and 'Ramchandra' in the latter, held frequent panchayats and tried criminal cases. Some villages in Rae Bareli even elected their own Deputy Commissioners, who then tried local cases.[87] In Tajuddinpur village in the district of Sultanpur, at about the same time, 'for a few weeks *swaraj* was proclaimed and a parallel government set up'.[88] It was a measure of the distance that the Kisan Sabha movement had traversed between the end of 1919 and the early months of 1921.

At this point the peasant movement in Awadh was more or less abandoned by the Congress leadership, and an emboldened admin-

[84] The last three paragraphs are based on Siddiqi, op. cit., pp. 160-1, 162-3, 168-70 and U.P., GAD 50/2/1921: Judgement of Khan Bahadur Md. Abdus Sami, Magistrate First Class, Rae Bareli, 25 April 1921, in Criminal Case 69, King-Emperor v. Brijpal Singh & others.

[85] *Report on the Administration of the United Provinces of Agra and Oudh, 1921-22* (Allahabad, 1922), pp. 31-2.

[86] U.P., GAD 50/3/21: L. Porter to Governor, 19 Jan. 1921: report of interview with Raja Tawaqul Husain of Pirpur, and Hailey to Butler, 24 Jan. 1921.

[87] Faunthorpe's Report, p. 273. [88] Gopal, op. cit., p. 55.

istation advanced to crush it—through the arrest of all of the most important peasant leaders, Ramchandra, Deo Narain and Kedar Nath among them, the widely publicized,[89] but ultimately trivial, amendment of the Awadh Rent Act, a sustained campaign of propaganda on behalf of the Government and a massive display of armed force.[90] Yet the movement was far from finished. Towards the end of November 1921 it burst forth again in the form of the Eka campaign.

The revival of the movement in this novel form may have owed something to an All-India Congress Committee resolution in November 1921 sanctioning 'full civil disobedience' including the non-payment of taxes. It was also encouraged initially by the efforts of certain Congressmen and Khilafatists based at Malihabad in Lucknow district, from whom it was suggested the movement got its new name—'Eka' or 'Aika' for unity. However, the Eka associations spread swiftly and it was not long before 'they got out of the control of the Congress people who were quite annoyed about it'.[91]

In Hardoi district, where the Eka movement first took root, tenants began to organize locally towards the end of 1921 to resist landlord attempts to collect more than the recorded rent. In Bahraich in early January 1922, there were two occasions on which tenants beat up *thekadars* (long-term lease-holders who collected rents on behalf of the taluqdars) and carried away the grain extracted from them as rent. Later that month bands of tenants were reported to be moving from village to village in the district demanding the immediate abolition of grain rents, through which the taluqdars and *thekadars* reaped virtually all the benefits of high prices. In Kheri district, the arrest of a Congress volunteer was the occasion for a demonstration by a considerable gathering,

[89]On 13 Jan. 1921, the U.P. Government telegraphed to various newspapers and to the Associated Press a press communique along the following lines: 'With reference to the suggestion that an enquiry must be held into the relations between the landlords and tenants in Oudh the Government is in possession of full information and has already decided to take up the question with a view to early legislation.' Further, 'Sir Harcourt Butler [the Governor] hopes as an old friend of both the landlords and the tenants of Oudh that they will avoid all action likely to cause a breach of the peace and will trust the Government to do justice.' (U.P., GAD 50/1921 Kws.) The Government also telegraphed all Dy. Commnrs. to 'have intention to legislate published in every Tahsil' (UP GAD 50/3/21).

[90]P.D. Reeves, 'The Politics of Order: "Anti-Non-Cooperation" in the United Provinces, 1921', *Journal of Asian Studies*, 25:2 (1966); Butler Colln., vol. 21, Butler to H.E. Richards, 4 Feb. 1921.

[91]Faunthorpe's Report, p. 274.

which besieged the police station and released the man. In the village of Kothi in Bara Banki district, again, the peasants' wrath was aroused; here a zamindar's peon was killed in March 1922 when he tried to collect rents.[92]

These and other such incidents reflect the force of the peasant movement as it swept through Hardoi, Bahraich, Kheri, Bara Banki, Sitapur and Lucknow districts. By the end of January 1922 the movement was very strong indeed in the Sandila tehsil of Hardoi district, and the landlords of the area more than a little perturbed. In February 1922 one police circle in Hardoi reported twenty-one Eka meetings in three days, with assemblies of 150 to 2000 people. In the same month Kishan Lal Nehru visited Atrauli (Hardoi district) in order to try and reassert a Congress hold on the movement. But he found that Madari, an untouchable Pasi by birth who had become the acknowledged leader of the Eka movement, was 'in full command'. Indeed at this stage, as the movement spread to thirty more villages, Madari completely severed his connections with Malihabad and shifted the Eka headquarters to Sandila in Hardoi district.[93]

Yet this symbolic and significant break from the Congress did not make the Eka movement any less 'political', even if we take the narrow view of equating the political with the avowedly nationalist. On the contrary. The official report on the Eka movement, produced by Lieutenant-Colonel J.C. Faunthorpe, I.C.S., in April 1922, sought to draw a distinction on this ground between the Kisan Sabha and the Eka phase of the agitation. In the former, Faunthorpe wrote, 'the animosity of the peasants was directed entirely against the taluqdars and not against Government officials. In the Eka movement this is not so much the case.' The official biographer of Jawaharlal Nehru writes that 'though the Congress had little to do with the Eka Movement . . . the Eka associations soon began to pass political resolutions'. According to the police at the time, too, there was little to distinguish Non-cooperation from Eka in the preachings of men like Baba Garib Das, a Pasi turned *sadhu* who was active in Bara Banki in March 1922.[94] Perhaps the most striking evidence of all is Madari's attempt to extend the appeal of the movement at the very time

[92]Loc. cit; Siddiqi, op. cit., pp. 196–204.

[93]Ibid., p. 200 & n.; Faunthorpe's Report, p. 274.

[94]Ibid., 273; Gopal, op. cit. p. 57; Siddiqi, op. cit., p. 204n

when he shifted its headquarters from Malihabad to Sandila. In order to do this, it was reported, he 'adjusted local differences' and urged zamindars to join the Ekas. In the weeks that followed, large numbers of petty zamindars did so.[95]

The provincial authorities in UP were in no doubt about the political implications of the Eka movement. From the end of 1921 they used their 'most autocratic powers' to break the Eka and the Congress organizations.[96] In Awadh this intervention again led to open clashes between the police and the peasants. When the police tried to arrest Madari in February 1922—having made 'arrangements on a somewhat elaborate scale' [97] for the purpose—several thousand peasants gathered to frustrate their effort. Indeed Madari was not to be apprehended until June that year, in spite of the handsome Rs 1000 reward that the authorities offered for his arrest. In March 1922 the peasants of Hardoi provided further evidence of their political feelings, when a large crowd of Pasis attacked a police party that was making inquiries about Eka meetings in village Udaipur in the Shahabad police circle. In the police firing that followed, two of the attackers were killed.[98] Ultimately the forces at the disposal of the Government proved to be too great for the proponents of Eka to match on their own. Confronted by large bodies of armed and mounted police and a squadron of Indian cavalry, the Eka movement went under.

Conclusion

When peasant violence erupted in January 1921 to set off the debate on the social and political condition of Awadh, the British were quick to sum up its causes. 'It has for long been obvious that the Oudh Rent Act requires amendment.' 'In the worst managed taluqdars' estate . . . the tenants have been treated with such want of consideration and in some cases with such oppression by the

[95]Faunthorpe's Report, p. 281. Siddiqi argues that the participation of the small zamindars was 'not entirely political'. He quotes the instance of one landowner whose involvement was attributed by officials to a desire to advance his personal interests, but then goes on to tell us that most of the zamindars who supported the movement did so either because they were Khilafatists or because of 'the crushing weight of the revenue demand which made them join the ranks of the tenants' (op. cit., pp. 206-7). It is not easy to conceive of many choices more political than that.

[96]Reeves, op cit., p. 273.

[97]Faunthorpe's Report, p. 274.

[98]Loc. cit. See also Siddiqi, op. cit., p. 204 & n.

landlords that one is compelled to sympathize with them.' The administrators themselves, fair-minded officials, representatives of a great empire, were above it all. Venerable justices of the peace, their influence would count, their neutrality could scarcely be called into question. The assessment turned out to be inaccurate. The days were gone when the Raj could pose as an impartial referee, standing on high and whistling 'foul play'. Local struggles tended more and more to get caught up in the general wave of anti-imperialism sweeping through India Even as the officials in Awadh were making their pious pronouncements on the reasons for the 'disturbances', the peasants had begun to attack the symbols and servants of the British Raj.

The colonialists could never comprehend this development. Then and later their explanation of it was to be in terms of the ignorance of the Indian masses and the manipulation of them by self-interested politicians. Yet they needed no prodding to realize its potential consequences. They wavered for a brief moment in mid-January 1921, even asking the bigger and more 'responsible' nationalist and peasant leaders to mediate and bring their moderating influence to bear on the peasants.[99] Then they moved with determination—and 'sympathy' was less in evidence than armed and mounted police and contingents of Indian troops.

Other participants in the debate could not match such clarity of vision or firmness in action. It was a period of learning, of trial-and-error, and uncertainty all round—among the peasants as among their urban well-wishers. Gandhi and Nehru recognized and indeed stressed that the Awadh peasant movement was anterior to and independent of the Non-cooperation Movement, though there is evidence too of the interaction between the two and the strength one lent to the other. Hesitantly, yet surely, the Congress leaders were drawn into the conflict between the peasants and their oppressors. In the end, however, they came around to the view that if the peasants' struggle was allowed to continue, it might hinder the development of the national movement against the British. The interests of that 'larger' struggle, the need for 'national unity', necessitated the shelving of such sectional struggles for the time being. The argument appears to have a good deal of force in it and some recent historians have been tempted to

[99]U.P., GAD 50/1921, Kws: telegram from Commnr., Lucknow to Collector, Rae Bareli, 14 Jan. 1921.

accept it *in toto*. The grounds on which they do so, however, require closer examination.

A united front of the whole Indian people—landlords and peasants, millowners and manual labourers, feudal princes and the tribal poor—in the anti-colonial campaign was scarcely feasible: no major struggle for change anywhere has ever achieved such unity. If, then, the statement is diluted to one urging the 'widest possible unity' on the basis of the only demand held in common by most Indians, the demand for Swaraj, we are still in the position of begging the question. What did the demand for Swaraj in fact signify? Is the idea of liberation from colonial rule to be equated with the narrow vision of the eviction of the white man from India? It is doubtful if a single one of the more important Congress leaders had a notion of Swaraj that was restricted to the simple physical eviction of the British from Indian soil. Had this been the sum total of the nationalist demand, the British would in all probability have been willing to submit to it long before they did. The concept of Swaraj had inherent in it the idea of greater individual freedom, equality and justice, and the hope of accelerated national and consequently individual development. Whether articulated by a Gandhi, as in his *Hind Swaraj,* or a Nehru, as in Jawaharlal's 'socialist' phase, or by the humblest nationalist sympathizer, the idea of Swaraj had built into it the dream of 'a new heaven, a new earth'—increased participation by all in the making of the decisions that affected them, reduced burdens (of rents and other taxes and imposts), an end to oppression.[100] The question then was how best to organize to bring this about.

The appeal to the need for *national unity* in the pursuance of this goal is plainly rhetorical. It needs to be re-phrased in terms of an appeal for *a particular kind of alliance,* seen as being necessary for the furtherance of the anti-imperialist struggle. It should be evident that the nature of the Swaraj that eventuated from this struggle would depend very much on the nature of the alliance (the 'unity') that was forged. From this point of view, the Congress' insistence in 1921-2 on a united front of landlords as well as peasants and others, was a statement in favour of the *status quo* and against any radical change in the social set-up when the British finally handed over the reins of power. The advice to peasants to give up organizing

[100]See Saadat Hasan Manto's story 'Naya Qanoon' for an interesting portrayal of such expectations.

'meetings' and 'disturbances' and to leave politics to the professionals, was a statement against mass participatory democracy and in favour of the idea of 'trusteeship'—the landlords and princes acting as trustees in the economic sphere, Gandhi and company in the political. In the two and a half decades following 1922, sections of the Congress did abandon this stance, under the impetus particularly of the workers' and peasants' struggles that arose in various parts of the country during the years of the Depression and after. But the main body of Congressmen stood by the position worked out by Gandhi and other leaders in 1921-2.

The sort of alliance that the Congress leadership settled on at that juncture was of crucial significance in determining the future course of the anti-imperialist struggle in India. Yet it is too easy to present a scenario of a dynamic urban-based party conducting the struggle, and at certain points making a choice between a variety of passive onlookers who might be expected to sympathize with their objectives. Referring to the debate between pro-slavery (conservative) and abolitionist (liberal) writers on American slavery, Genovese has pointed out that both viewpoints treat the Blacks 'almost wholly as objects, never as creative participants in a social process, never as half of a two-part subject'.[101] So, in the case of colonial India, the peasants have generally been treated as beneficiaries (economically) of an increasingly benevolent system or victims of an oppressive one, 'manipulated' (politically) by self-seeking politicians or 'mobilized' by large-hearted, selfless ones. Both viewpoints miss out an essential feature—the whole area of independent thought and conjecture and speculation (as well as action) on the part of the peasant.

From the stand-point of many an Awadh peasant in the 1920s, we would suggest, there was a Gandhi different from the one we know and a promise of Swaraj also different from the one that we do not so much *know* as *assume*; just as from his predecessor's point of view there had been, in the nineteenth century, a 'benevolent' but inaccessible white queen, quite different from the 'benevolent' Queen addressed and perhaps seen by the western-educated Moderate members of the Indian National Congress. This man, with his own peculiar expectations of Gandhi and Swaraj, jumped into the fray in Awadh in the years 1919-22. Beginning with petititions,

[101] Eugene D. Genovese, 'American Slaves and their History' in A. Weinstein and F.O. Gatell (eds.), *American Negro Slavery* (New York, 1973), p. 186.

and demonstrations against the landlords's agents, he went on to show his faith in locally-organized panchayats in preference to the British courts, to non-cooperation with the railway authorities and further, in places, to a campaign for the non-payment of taxes and attacks on the landlords and the police. At the very moment of Gandhi's imaginative Non-cooperation Movement, he and thousands of his comrades arose to present a parallel and powerful challenge to the entire structure of colonial authority in UP. They threw up thereby the real and immediate possibility of an anti-imperialist movement very different from any until then contemplated by the urban nationalist leadership. And to press their point they marched scores of miles first, in June 1920, from Pratapgarh to Allahabad, and then, in the succeeding months, to several Kisan Conferences to meet their Congress leaders and learn from them how they should proceed.

It was not, thus, an abstract question of whom the Congress might choose as ally, and then educate and train for political action. The peasants of Awadh had already taken the lead in reaching out for an alliance. As Ramchandra put it:

> It was felt that if we could link our Kisan movement with some established organization, or gain the support of well-to-do [privileged?] groups and lawyers, then this movement would become the future of India.[102]

As it happened, the Congress leadership declined this offer—on account of its concern for the maintenance of non-violence, its uncertainty as to the possible repercussions of encouraging a broad-based peasant movement, or a dim but growing awareness of its own class interests.

Recent statements on the peasant movement in Awadh have asserted that 'the Congress and the Liberals had helped the Kisans to stand on their feet'[103] and to 'defy not just the landlords but even the Government'.[104] How far and in what way this was true has already been indicated. For the sake of the completeness of the historical record, it needs also to be said that the same people helped, by their refusal of continued support, to bring the peasant movement to its knees. It has been argued, in addition, that while the Liberals appreciated the class interests of the peasants better

[102]Ramchandra Colln. I, Subject File No. 1: incomplete letter of 1939.
[103]Siddiqi, op. cit., p. 217. [104]Gopal, op. cit., p. 55.

than the Congress—witness their support for the amendment of the Awadh Rent Act—'the Congress, as a more advanced political force that wanted to end British rule in India, devoted its energies and attention towards preserving unity between different classes'.[105]

Here the historian faithfully reproduces the Congress leaders' assessment of the peasant movement in Awadh as fundamentally misguided. On the basis of the evidence so far available, this is not a position that is easy to uphold. Indeed it may more reasonably be argued that, as their struggle matured, the peasants of Awadh sensed more accurately than the urban leaders did, the structure of the alliance that held up the colonial power in UP and the range of forces that might combine to fight it. The very 'moderation' of Madari Pasis' effort to enrol the support of the smaller zamindars stands testimony to that. In this situation, a pronouncement of the error, or ill-timing, of the peasant movement can come only out of an uncritical acceptance of the Congress leaders' point of view. It does not flow from an analysis of the actual conditions of anti-colonial struggle in the 1920s.

Madari, Sohrab, Isharbadi: three names, and the caste affiliation of the first-named (a Pasi), is all we know about these Eka leaders who, with others as yet unnamed, for several months in 1921 and 1922, guided a powerful peasant movement against the colonial rĕgime and its local collaborators.[106] It is a telling comment on the importance that historians and others have so far attached to the history of the subaltern.[107] Some scholars have indeed expressed their prejudice quite plainly. 'To organize was difficult enough, to

[105]Siddiqi, op. cit., p. 217.

[106]The long lists of 'freedom-fighters', *Svatantrata Sangram ke Sainik,* drawn up district by district, by the U.P. Government in connection with the celebration of the Silver Jubilee of Indian independence, does not contain entries for any of these leaders. Madari Pasi and the village he is supposed to have come from are mentioned in the introductory note to the volume on Hardoi district. In a brief visit to the district I sought to use this lead in order to try and find out more about Madari, only to discover that Madari never came from a village of that name, that a village with that name does not exist in the concerned tahsil, and that old Congressmen (mentioned in the list of 'freedom fighters') spoke of Madari as they would of a 'bad character' or at best an inconsequential one: so heavily does the ĕlitist heritage sit upon us. I did not have the time to pursue my inquiries after Madari and other Eka leaders on that occasion, but feel sure that further effort will yield useful information.

[107]We use this term (as we use 'elite') as a convenient short-hand to distinguish the lower, labouring and exploited classes from the upper, relatively privileged groups in different parts of the society.

organize in the face of repression was not possible for Madari.' Thus Majid Siddiqi, in the only published monograph on the peasant movement in Awadh.[108] This comment on the configuration of forces then existing in the country betrays the élitist viewpoint of its author, for the picture appears very different from the peasants' perspective.

By the winter of 1921-2, the peasant movement in Awadh had overcome many, though by no means all, of its own traditionalist limitations. Yet, its localism and its isolation remained. To get over these it needed an ally among other anti-imperialist forces in the country. But the chief candidate for this role, the party of the growing urban and rural petty bourgeoisie, had turned its back on the peasant movement long before that time. What a commentator wrote on another popular struggle, in another time and another land, is perhaps more appropriate in the context:

> The petty bourgeoisie encouraged insurrection by big words, and great boasting as to what it was going to do. [But] wherever an armed conflict had brought matters to serious crisis, there the shopkeepers stood aghast at the dangerous situation created for them; aghast at the people who had taken their boasting appeals to arms in earnest; aghast at the power thus thrust into their own hands; aghast, above all, at the consequences for themselves, for their social positions, for their fortunes, of [at?] the policy in which they were forced to engage themselves . . . Thus placed between opposing dangers which surrounded them on every side, the petty bourgeoisie knew not to turn its power to any other account than to let everything take its chance, whereby, of course, there was lost what little chance of success there might have been, and thus to ruin the insurrection altogether.[109]

[108]Siddiqi, op. cit., p. 202n. Kapil Kumar has recently completed a doctoral dissertation on the peasant movement in Avadh, for the University of Meerut. When published, this should tell us a good deal more about the Eka movement.

[109]F. Engels, *Germany: Revolution and Counter-Revolution* (London, 1969), p. 105.

[9]
Cultural Transformations

Pierre Brocheux

Economic development, the formation of new social classes with diverse lifestyles and philosophies, and foreign influences all combined to produce new cultures and mentalities in Indochina. The experiences, ideas, and moral and religious values introduced by colonization found expression in literature, music, and the fine arts. They informed certain new behaviors, though never fully eliminating the preexisting ways of thinking or living, if only because they had an unequal effect on different peoples and social classes, and in different ways in the cities than in the countryside.

The Vietnamese, the Cambodians, the Lao, and the ethnic groups of the highlands all reacted to the new situation at different rates and to different degrees. Some reacted to modernization with stubborn resistance and rejection. At other times, however, they adopted it unknowingly, through ephemeral infatuations. The search for multiple syntheses between past and present, native and outsider, East and the West, was probably never successful. The form of interaction that took shape was, inevitably, syncretic. Full cultural comprehension and assimilation would take much longer to achieve than the eighty years of French colonization.

FRENCH CULTURAL INITIATIVES

Economic, social, and technical changes are agents of cultural evolution, but in a colonial regime in particular, the policies of the imperialist state are likewise influential. The state defined the direction of education policy, publishing, even the orientations of the press and cinema. Through subsidization or outright censorship, the state facilitated or hindered the circulation of people and ideas. The state also policed local customs and thus could accelerate or hinder changes in mentalities.

From Assimilation to Relativism

Did the colonial state in Indochina have a clearly defined cultural project that it carried out in concrete ways? Or was the state content simply to identify the direction that should be followed, one that could be inflected and even changed? Certainly, the spread of French civilization was the acknowledged goal. But did that really mean that French civilization would replace existing cultures? Even today, we ridicule the phrase "Nos ancêtres, les Gaulois" (Our forefathers, the Gauls), which Indochinese and African children were obliged to recite. However, in practice, teachers were not gullible enough to believe that they could inculcate into their students the belief that they were descendents of the Celts. The very traditions and the daily lives of the pupils themselves served to belie the recitation. Over the years, the phrase became more a symbol of educational routine than the accurate reflection of a political goal. What was scandalous was less the recitation of this phrase than the application of a teaching curriculum identical to the one being used in the metropole and the use of textbooks that were poorly adapted to the colonized milieu. Untangling these three interlinked elements of colonial cultural policy—the cultural assimilation of the colonized, the colonial desire to realize some sort of social genesis, and the political centralism of the Third Republic—would never be easy.

Over time, a better knowledge of Far Eastern civilizations forced the French rulers to change their cultural and educational approaches as they realized the absurdity of trying to turn the Indochinese into Frenchmen. Many French policymakers long established in the colony understood the irreducible originality of local civilizations. They conceded that there would be persistent resistance to the imposition of new psychologies and attitudes. And they worried that the spread of humanist, republican, liberal, and democratic components of French culture could have unforeseen repercussions on the colonized societies. In 1930, Governor-General Pierre Pasquier expressed his doubts to the journalist René Vanlande:

> For thousands of years, Asia has possessed its personal ethics, its art, its metaphysics, its dreams. Will it ever assimilate our Greco-Roman thought? Is this possible? Is it desirable? Until today, to our knowledge, it [Asia] has only proceeded by imitation. It has endeavored to take a path parallel to ours. There is juxtaposition. Can it be an intimate penetration? Where can one find the cement and the ties between Asia and ourselves? We, the Gauls, we were the Barbarians. And, in the absence of our own light, we illuminated ourselves, after some resistance, with the light that came from Rome. The glue of Christianity completed this fusion. But in Asia, without speaking of the distance between races, we find souls and minds molded by the oldest civilization of the globe.[1]

These remarks testify to a change within the French attitudes towards foreign cultures. Gwendolyn Wright has correctly pointed out that the cultural innovations that had appeared in France since the beginning of the twentieth century (the rebirth of French regionalism, the artistic movements of fauvism, cubism, etc.), had some influence on the governing powers in Indochina. For example, the famous Governor-General Albert Sarraut was an art critic and connoisseur. The new relativistic approach and questioning of the ideal of universal beauty—of which Europe was supposedly the depository—weakened French pretensions to cultural hegemony.[2] Pasquier's reflections on education were more concrete: "It must be admitted: we turn out batches of teachers and professors based on the educational philosophy that gave the Third Republic such an admirable pedagogical nursery. . . . But is this really what the old, conservative people of Annam want?"[3]

That said, it is important not to rely solely on the intentions proclaimed in official speeches. An examination of the cultural evolution of the Indochinese peoples under French rule—the initiatives of the colonizers and the responses from the colonized—is indispensable.

Colonizing Education

According to an anticolonialist slogan, France built more prisons than schools in Indochina. In reality, the French government made significant, sustained efforts to further education there. The statistics testify to a marked growth in the number of public schools, an increase in the size of the teaching corps, and a substantial rise in the number of students. To this, one can add the large number of private educational establishments in urban areas (see app. 10).

We can distinguish three major periods in the creation of the Indochinese educational system: 1860–1917, 1917–1930, and 1930–1945. The first phase was marked by the quest for an appropriate system. Between 1860 and 1917, the French were chiefly concerned with conquering the eastern part of the Indochinese peninsula and establishing their rule there. They were still too imbued with a sense of the superiority of their own culture to esteem the cultures—themselves different from one another—of those they were colonizing. At the same time, Republican France itself saw profound changes in the definition of both the means and ends of education.

The reforms of Jules Ferry not only changed France; as we shall see, they also had an impact on the colonies. Around 1890, when the question "What education for our colonies?" was being debated in the metropole, French colonial administrators on the spot simultaneously began to take into account Indochina's idiosyncrasies. The Public Instruction Code promulgated by Governor-General Albert Sarraut (1917–19) established "higher education and defined the programs and teaching cycles for each level" of the Indochinese schooling system, although it in fact did no more than create the legal context for it. The educational system that came into being under Governor-General Martial Merlin (1922–25), however, experimented with the single-school *(école unique)* approach before its metropolitan counterpart. "Pedagogical innovations had just started: the creation of a communal educational system in Annam, the renovation of the pagoda schools in Cambodia, then in Cochinchina, and finally in Laos, and education for the ethnic minorities. . . . Classes were no longer to be taught in French, but in the local languages. . . . Textbooks were written expressly for them. All aspects of primary education were experimented with to allow a widespread development of mass schooling."

The crisis of the 1930s, which assumed not only an economic dimension, but also a political one, was the start of a period of budgetary restrictions that slowed creativity and innovation. Only the educational sector dubbed "penetration" continued to develop, because the populations themselves took charge. Several upper schools were restructured, and the equivalency of French and Indochinese diplomas was established.[4]

For this, Cochinchina served as an educational laboratory, marked by the implementation in 1879 of Franco-indigenous education based on the French public school model.[5] The first modern schools spread from the south into the northern protectorates of Vietnam, such as the College of Interpreters in Hanoi (1886). These schools produced the first generation of intellectual cultural intermediaries, such as Truong Vinh Ky and Paulus Cua in Cochinchina, Nguyen Van Vinh (who founded the influential publication *Dong Duong Tap Chi* [The Indochinese Review] in May 1913), Pham Huy Ton, Pham Quynh, and Tran Trong Kim, among others. In the quest for a coherent educational policy, the colonial regime seems to have long tried to restructure the traditional education that had remained intact in Annam and Tonkin. In 1908, there were more than 15,000 schools in these two protectorates where Chinese characters were taught, with perhaps 200,000 pupils,[6] not counting the official schools in district and provincial seats. The French hoped to transform the traditional schools "into an immediate means of instruction and intellectual penetration."[7] This was certainly the aim of the May 31, 1906, reform elaborated by Governor-General Paul Beau and his director of education, Henri Gourdon. It opened the way for the creation of the first Conseil de perfectionnement de l'enseignement indigène (Council for the Improvement of Indigenous Education), created on November 14, 1905, under the direction of metropolitan and local Masonic lodges. The reform reorganized Franco-indigenous education—officially created in Tonkin in 1904, in Cambodia in 1905, and in Annam and Laos in 1906. It established the principle of one school for every village, and made Quoc ngu the mandatory written language of instruction in the ethnically Viet regions of Tonkin, Annam, and Cochinchina. Chinese ideograms became from that point no more than an object of study. To a larger extent, elementary aspects of French were introduced in upper-level primary schools *(primaires supérieures)* and teacher training colleges *(écoles normales)*, and language skills were tested through a variety of literary contests.

TABLE 5.1 Number of public school students in Vietnam and Cambodia, 1920–1945

Vietnam			
Years	Primary cycle	*Primaire supérieur*	Secondary
1920	1,126,000	2,430	—
1923	—	—	83
1929	—	—	121
1938–1939	287,500	4,552	465
1940–1941	518,737	—	5,637
1943–1944	707,285	—	6,550

Cambodia		
Years	Public primary	Renovated "pagoda schools"
1930	15,700	—
1939	—	38,000
1945	32,000	53,000

SOURCES: For Vietnam through 1939: G. P. Kelly, *Franco-Vietnamese Schools 1918–1938* (Madison, Wis.: Southeast Asia Publications, 1982); for Vietnam, 1940–1941: J. Gauthier, *L'Indochine au travail dans la paix française* (Paris: Eyrolles, 1949), p. 35; for Vietnam, 1943–1944: *Annuaire statistique de l'Indochine, 1939–1946*. For Cambodia: J. Delvert, "L'oeuvre française d'enseignement au Cambodge," *France-Asie* 125–126–127 (October–November 1956).

In 1907, in an attempt to combat nationalism, Paul Beau created the Indochinese University in Hanoi with three divisions for instruction in literature, law, and science. In its first year, however, the university counted only ninety-four students and seventy-four auditors. In January 1908, colonial circles, concerned by events in Annam (the anti-tax revolts in Quang Nam), closed the university, which was not reopened until 1917, when departments of Medicine and Pharmacy, Veterinary Science, Education, Watercourses and Forestry, Commerce, Finance, Law and Administration, and Fine Arts were added. In 1928, the School of Medicine became a fully operational faculty. The Indochinese University had as one of its distinctly affirmed goals the training of administrators. During World War II, when communications with France were interrupted, the university expanded and diversified its teaching, as well as its recruitment. In 1941, for example, it had a Science Department and also a Department of Architecture. In 1943–44, its final year (the university was closed when the Japanese ended French rule in 1945), the Departments of Law, Science, Medicine, and Pharmacy registered a total of 1,222 students: 837 Vietnamese, 346 French, 18 Cambodian, 12 Lao, 8 Chinese, and 1 unspecified. There were also 353 registered in other disciplines, for example, 130 in the Department of Fine Arts, 99 in Watercourses and Forestry, 46 in Veterinary Science, and 78 in other fields (Public Works, Architecture, etc.).[8]

TABLE 5.2 Students at the University of Hanoi, 1922–1944

Years	1922	1929	1938–1939	1941–1942	1942–1943	1943–1944
No. of Students	500	511	457	834	1,050	1,575

In the capitals and the towns, modern education was not without its successes. The Quoc Hoc College in Hue, founded in 1896 and reformed in 1905, is a case in point. It welcomed 787 students between 1899 and 1905. However, in the rural areas, modern education often failed: "In the course of my tours," Ha Dong's resident wrote in 1909, "I realized that the local schools for the most part existed only on paper."[9] Nevertheless, these modern schools, in tandem with the penetration of Western culture, led to the rapid retreat in the use of Chinese-based ideograms, as noted above. The traditional literary contests suffered from the competition represented by the new educational methods. Little by little, traditional exams lost their value, since, in the new context, they could no longer open the way to social promotion and professional advancement. In 1912, there were only 1,330 candidates taking part in the triennial contest in Nam Dinh, in Tonkin, as opposed to over 6,000 in 1906. The form of the examinations was modified in 1913, and the last triennial competitions occurred in Nam Dinh in 1915 and in Hue in 1919. The adoption of Quoc ngu and French as languages of instruction, combined with the demise of traditional examinations in the schools, shattered the essential mechanisms by which the ruling elite had been affiliated to the Confucian Sino-Vietnamese universe. It also dealt a blow to schools for the study of Chinese characters and the official government schools in Hue, which were in any case dismantled in 1919 and replaced by Franco-indigenous schools under the control of the Protectorate.

The Goals and Results of Colonial Education

The Règlement général de l'instruction publique of December 21, 1917, envisaged as the true "charter for Indochinese education," rationalized the entire educational apparatus. This set of regulations did not seek to exclude the colonized from modern knowledge and education, since these were among the colonial system's most powerful weapons. Rather, it aimed to channel the use of education into the service of three clearly conceived goals—to inspire and control the content and the transmission of written knowledge within the villages; to transmit to some extent a minimal modern mass education, on which the colonial system depended for its basic functioning; and, at the same time, to adapt the colonized elite to the functions assigned to them by the colonial system. Thus, while attempting to economize as much as possible (education represented 6% of the local and general budget expenses in 1930, and 7.8% in 1942), the regime adopted a strategy fairly close in its fundamental logic to that underwriting a similar school system in the metropole, one that excluded the masses from intellectual professions. In Indochina, the central concern was not the French school, which was only very marginally accessible to colonized youth, but a parallel network of Franco-indigenous schools (see table 5.1). This system prioritized primary teaching. In 1924, it was divided into an Elementary Primary Cycle (of three years) and a Primary Cycle (of two years, then three in 1927), extended by two highly selective examinations into upper primary and secondary "local" education. At the end of this, the latter provided a "local" *baccalauréat* (the French equivalent of the high school diploma), and, for a very small minority, admission to the Indochinese University. The system certainly produced a modern elite, but it was numerically a very restricted one, and most of its members had only a primary education. In 1930, 34,371 candidates earned an Indigenous Elementary Primary Studies certificate (as compared to 47,214 in 1942). Of this number, 16,933 received certificates indicating that they had learned French, and 4,379 received Franco-indigenous Primary Studies certificates (12,696 in 1942). However, of this total, only 648 received Franco-indigenous diplomas (1,124 in 1942), and only 75 earned the "local" *baccalauréat*.

From a social and political point of view, upper primary education was very significant. In the 1930s, it was the part of the educational system that generated the lower middle class of civil servants, employees, and professional revolutionaries. Secondary teaching played an analogous role, but tended to produce writers, journalists, or civil servants of a middle or superior rank. The high-school level was a seedbed for the Indochinese University in Hanoi and French universities and hence the antechamber through which those who entered into the liberal professions passed.

In 1932, there were 541 students, of whom 20 were French or foreigners, at the Indochinese University. In 1942, three law degrees and nine doctorates in medicine, pharmacy, and dentistry were conferred; there were 69 admissions to the first year of medical studies; and 42 certificates for advanced studies in the sciences were awarded. This was, however, a culturally truncated elite. Its largest groups, mainly Vietnamese, were civil servants (26,941 in 1941–42). Nearly all of them served as lower-level clerks and teachers (16,000 in 1941–42). Of the teachers, the overwhelming majority taught at the primary school level, and most of them were mere auxiliaries. This elite was long excluded not only from positions of command and organization, but also, in spite of the belated creation of the Hanoi School of Sciences, from theoretical work, especially scientific theory, which could only be studied in metropolitan France and was therefore only marginally accessible to the colonized. It was not until 1930 that the first scientific doctorate (in physics) was granted in Paris to one of the colonized, the Vietnamese Hoang Thi Nga, whereas Cambridge admitted its first Indian student as early as 1865. The Tata family had created the Indian Institute of Sciences in Bangalore in 1911—though in a country, it is true, that had been conquered since the eighteenth century. This elite was

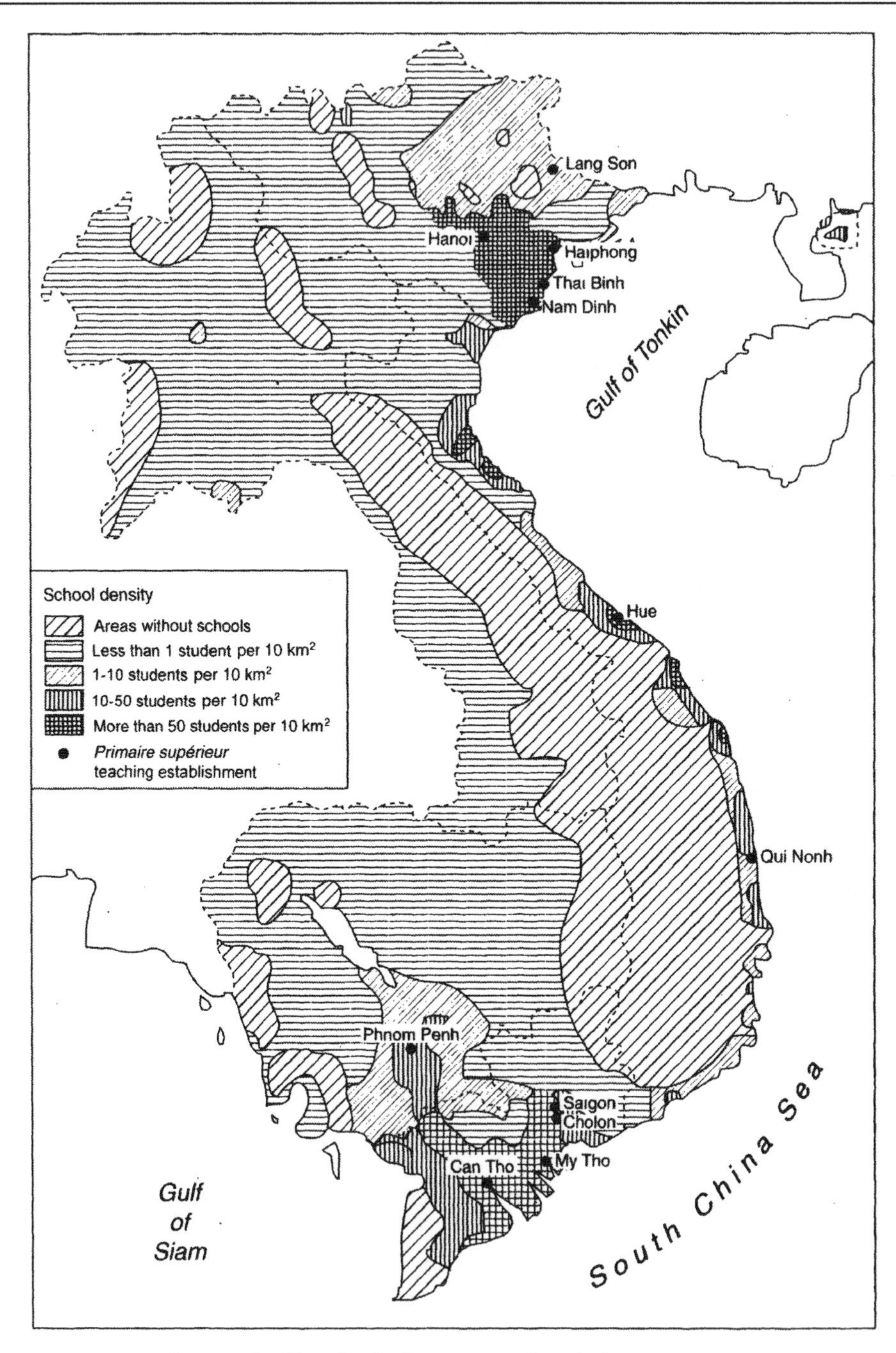

MAP 5.1. Distribution of public schools. (Exposition coloniale de 1931, Gouvernement général, *Le service de l'instruction publique en Indochine en 1930* [Hanoi, 1930].)

also under ideological surveillance, and indeed, viewed with suspicion by the colonial state. The minister for the colonies cautioned in 1919:

> It is advisable that we only go down the reformist road with extreme prudence. . . . It is precisely the natives educated in our methods and in our ideas who are the most dangerous enemies of our authority and the most resolute partisans of a *home rule* [said in English] in which we would have no place. There is no doubt, in fact, that the education provided in France does not correspond to any real need of the indigenous populations, or to their mentality. There, more than anywhere else, it is advisable not to open up the speculative domain of ideas too extensively, but, on the contrary, to encourage the acquisition of only the most essential knowledge.[10]

Although the number of Vietnamese children without schooling for lack of means (poverty, but also lack of schools and of teachers) can be estimated at around 100,000 in 1944, the schooling of youngsters increased constantly after 1930. Moreover, the important deficiencies that affected rural areas and the lower social categories in the cities cannot be attributed entirely to a deliberate Malthusian logic on the part of the French. In 1944, a critical assessment of the Association for the Diffusion of Quoc ngu (Hoi truyen ba quoc ngu)—a private Vietnamese and even crypto-communist initiative—underlined the geographical limitation of the group's actions to villages in the Hanoi vicinity, and blamed its failures on the psychological obstacles thrown up by the rural people themselves.

The Question of Language

A major educational problem was the selection of the language of instruction. While French would, of course, be preeminent, it was inconceivable that all Indochinese could be schooled in that language. It was thus necessary to maintain the vernacular languages as instruments of communication among the indigenous peoples. The organization of two categories of teaching, one reserved for French and the other called "Franco-indigenous," respected the linguistic duality of every territory of the Indochinese Union (Cochinchina, Annam, Tonkin, Laos, and Cambodia).

An example of this is the diffusion of Quoc ngu, the transcription of Vietnamese into Latin characters, which under the French became the national writing system of the Vietnamese. However, the ultimate success of this writing system was neither desired nor foreseen by either the colonizers or the colonized. Established in the seventeenth century by European Catholic missionaries, Quoc ngu was originally a means of transcription designed to facilitate evangelization. Although Alexandre de Rhodes undoubtedly played an active role in the perfection of Quoc ngu, Portuguese Jesuits played a central role in this endeavor by forging the new transcription on the basis of Portuguese.[11] During the colonial period, the French believed that the Chinese characters and the *nom* system (the demotic Vietnamese script based on Chinese characters) could not be instruments of modernization.

Besides, a rejection of the Chinese or *nom* characters allowed the French to end the cultural monopoly of the existing literate elites who used Chinese characters, thereby undermining their prestige and their authority. By replacing Chinese with French, the colonizers thus counted on creating a new cultural playing field tilted to their own advantage. This project was clearly stated at the time: "The Annamese within our Protectorate and under our direction are in fact influenced by China. More than ever, the literate class is intellectually under its dependence; it knows and thinks only through China, according to her and far behind her . . . its characters being the only vehicle of instruction for this class. This will be the case as long as the present situation endures, as long as it is not replaced by the national language in everyday usage and by French as the vehicle of higher education."[12]

In the 1880s, the French were still not conscious of the inherent difficulties of generalizing the use of French, although they quickly realized the importance of Quoc ngu as an intermediary language that would allow the Vietnamese to familiarize themselves with French. What was lost sight of was the vision of Gabriel Aubaret, a French Navy officer fluent in Chinese and Vietnamese, who negotiated the 1864 treaty ceding the three provinces of Cochinchina to France. Aubaret assigned a revolutionary role to the new roman transcription system: "This common language, solidified through our use of Latin characters, opens a clear path for our civilizing ideas to penetrate; and who knows whether it will be in this way that European science, so absolutely unknown in the Far East because of the insurmountable difficulty of terms, will be understood one day? We can hope that some of the Annamese people, whose future is in our hands, will acquire an incontestable moral superiority over the remainder of Cochinchina; to solidify a language through writing is, after all, a revolution almost comparable to the discovery of printing."[13]

Meanwhile, French was taught in all Indochinese schools. The certificate of Franco-indigenous primary studies (CEPFI), the end of the first level of colonial education in Vietnamese countries, included a dictation in French (five spelling mistakes resulted in elimination). As a result, until the 1930s, the failure rate sometimes reached as high as 70%. But opinions and practical arrangements surrounding this francophone principle varied. Gustave Dumoutier (1850–1904), who directed education in Annam-Tonkin at the turn of the century, reestablished the teaching of Chinese characters and introduced Quoc ngu in the schools of Annam and Tonkin. In 1930, an essay in Quoc ngu appeared in tests for the CEPFI, as well as an optional examination in Chinese calligraphy. Starting in 1930, it was decided that ethics, history, and geography did not have to be taught in French. Echoing Governor-General Pierre Pasquier, Alexandre Varennes, himself a former governor (1925–27), warned against teaching the natives that France "is their homeland," and cautioned: "Make sure they have an Asian education that is useful to them in their country."[14] In the same vein, a teacher named Émile Tavernier published a booklet in Saigon in 1933 entitled *De la nécessité d'écrire l'histoire de l'ancien empire d'Annam* (On the Necessity of Writing the History of the Ancient Empire of Annam). Reverence for Vietnamese culture was accentuated during World War II, so that the radical Vietnamization of teaching in 1945—which was clearly a voluntary break with the colonial past—can be considered as a logical, inevitable outcome of this earlier process, something which the most farsighted French had already conceded.

It was only in the aftermath of World War I that the Vietnamese, seeing that French domination was well established, decided they had to deal with the linguistic question. Several figures defended the idea of making Quoc ngu the national form of writing. This was notably the opinion upheld by the nationalist Phan Van Truong in 1912, when he created a Hoi than ai dong bao (Countrymen's Club) in Paris. It was at this time that he wrote a pamphlet that was a true "defense and illustration of Quoc ngu." According to him, this new form of writing was a tool for literary creation and scientific teaching, not just a simple means of communication between the French and the native population. Later, when he returned to his homeland, Truong continued to promote the diffusion and teaching of Quoc ngu, for example, to the Société cochinchinoise pour la promotion des études (Cochinchinese Society for the Promotion of Education) in 1925. The importance of the role that Truong played in the intellectual, and therefore political, history of his nation can hardly be overemphasized.[15]

Then, in the 1930s, Quoc ngu became a tool of political proceedings and modern Vietnamese literature. The initiatives of the colonizers also affirmed the rise of Quoc ngu. There was no precise cultural program in this domain, but Indochina's Gouvernement général did take note of two or three facts that incited it to take an interest in cultural questions. For one thing, the 1907 Dong Kinh Nghia Thuc (Dong Kinh [Hanoi] School of the Just Cause) had demonstrated that in the absence of governmental measures, the Vietnamese had the will and the capacity to establish a politically uncontrolled organization of modern popular education (see below). Second, Chinese reformist literature (Kang You-wei and especially Liang Qichao) had penetrated Vietnam and introduced the Vietnamese to the ideas of Montesquieu, J.-J. Rousseau, Darwin, Spencer, and so on. The Chinese Republican movement and the revolution of 1911 worried colonial authorities. And, lastly, German activity in the Far East in the early twentieth century alarmed the French.[16]

To take on these threats, the Gouvernement général relied on literary modernists and the supporters of a Franco-Vietnamese colonial contract, as embodied in the official policy of "collaboration and Franco-Vietnamese harmony." The first initiative was the creation of the magazine *Dong Duong Tap Chi,* which appeared between 1913 and 1920. Its moving spirit was Nguyen Van Vinh (1882–1926), an enthusiastic partisan of French culture, who was joined by Phan Ke Binh, Tran Trong Kim, Nguyen Van To, Pham Duy Ton, and the poet Tan Da. The magazine violently attacked the traditionalist literati, and the French therefore came up with a new magazine, *Nam Phong Tap Chi* (Wind of the South), which was officially launched on July 1, 1917. This was followed, two years later, by the creation of the Association pour la formation intellectuelle et morale des Annamites (Association for the Moral and Intellectual Education of the Annamese). The idea originated with Louis Marty, who was the interim director of the Indochinese Sûreté and a man with remarkable political skills. He became the mentor of numerous young Vietnamese radical intellectuals. Marty laid out the objectives of *Nam Phong Tap Chi* as follows:

> The subjects to be treated will be very freely chosen, so as to preserve sufficient independence and impartiality in this collection, without which this work of propaganda will suffer the fate of earlier similar attempts, which failed because of the naïve and clumsy administrative bias that inspired them.... The head of the Political Office of the Gouvernement général is its unofficial promoter.... The two main editors, Pham Quynh and Nguyen Ba Trac, took this magazine under their wing, so that it would preserve an exclusively indigenous character in the eyes of the public.[17]

Nam Phong received a monthly subsidy of four hundred piastres from the Gouvernement général, which decided to entrust the direction of the new enterprise to a remarkable man who, like Nguyen Van Vinh, had been trained at the School of Interpreters. Writer, translator, and essayist, versed in Chinese, Quoc ngu, and French, Pham Quynh and his mentor, Marty, touched a sensitive chord in linguistic nationalism. The magazine also played a fundamental role in the intellectual life of Tonkin and Annam until around 1924. It was an invaluable tool in the diffusion of Quoc ngu and cleared the way for the take-off of Vietnamese literature and language. As Pham Quynh wrote at the time: "To be Vietnamese, we must respect and cherish the language of our country. We must place Vietnamese above French and Chinese. I am someone who, because I truly love Vietnamese, has voluntarily dedicated his whole life to giving this language an independent literature, so that my people do not have to endure the eternal fate of studying and writing in a language borrowed from a foreigner."[18]

The initiators of *Nam Phong* wanted to channel the intellectual aspirations of the Vietnamese middle class their way and screen foreign intellectual contributions themselves. In this sense, Pham Quynh played the role of a Confucian scholar, monarchist, and elitist. His linguistic purism only allowed for borrowings from Chinese in the building of a Quoc ngu vocabulary. His monopolistic control over the selection of French authors published (though he excluded contemporary writers) greatly limited the influence of *Nam Phong* to the advantage of the radical publications that appeared after 1923, notably, *La cloche fêlée* (The Cracked Bell), edited by Nguyen An Ninh. These, paradoxically, were published in French.

With the same cultural preoccupations in mind, Pierre Pasquier founded the Buddhist Institute of Phnom Penh, destined to receive three thousand monks and to divert the Buddhist clergy from going to Siam. The Buddhist Institute, associated with the Orientalist Suzanne Karpelès, was not only destined to shield the Khmer monks from the influence of the Thai monasteries, it was also the crowning achievement of a cultural project that solidified a renaissance movement within Khmer culture. This began in 1914 with the creation of the School of Pali (the religious writing of southern India in which the Buddhist canonical texts had been written) in Cambodia, located in Phnom Penh. This was reorganized in 1922 and renamed the Pali School of Higher Learning. In 1924, these French initiatives were followed by the founding of the Royal National Library of Cambodia, whose director was Karpelès. The Buddhist Institute was opened shortly thereafter. These creations in the capital depended on a network of pagoda schools, some of which were progressively brought up to date. This was the case in the provinces, as well as in areas in Cochinchina inhabited by the Khmer Krom, the Cambodian inhabitants of the Mekong Delta, conquered by the Vietnamese in the nineteenth century. The first pagoda schools to be reformed dated from 1908–11, but they really took off only in 1930. The introduction of new subjects (arithmetic and geography, for example) into the curriculum pointed up the modernization of the traditional Cambodian education system. According to Pascale Bezançon, Louis Manipoud was the driving force behind this educational policy. He devoted himself to this reform with particular conviction and tenacity in the province of Kampot, where he was inspector of primary schools between 1924 and 1936.[19]

These educational institutions doubled the size of the network of schools without undermining it. Pupils sat for the Certificate of Elementary Indigenous Studies with a 48% success rate in 1935. In 1930, 3,332 students were enrolled in 101 renovated schools. In 1939, 908 reformed schools counted 38,834 students; and finally, in 1944, 47,555 students studied in 992 reformed schools. In Cochinchina, in 1941, 5,837 Khmer children attended this type of school. Such schools demonstrate the flexibility and adaptability of a French policy usually considered to have been assimilationist and unpragmatic.

The Revival of Arts and Crafts

Colonial authorities and individuals attempted to rebuild or to renovate other cultural domains in Indochina. These initiatives principally concerned traditional arts and monuments. In Cambodia, Annam, and Tonkin, the French tried to halt the decline of the arts and to stimulate their development. The situation had become particularly alarming in Cambodia. The artisan of the Cambodian arts renaissance, Georges Groslier, explained the reasons for this deterioration in a long report:

> For about the past sixty years, Khmer traditions have been subjected to the direct influence of the West. . . . By comparison to the European arriver, the highest mandarin

> is no longer a great character in the eyes of the masses. He tries to acquire our superiority, which he only understands in its vain and superficial aspects, in order to reestablish his lost prestige in new garb. The Khmer aristocracy (and I mean by this term the entire ruling class), the only one that associates with the Europeans, quickly moved ahead of the people: it abandoned them . . . out of one and a half million inhabitants, ten thousand, if you will, have come over to our side. Therefore, on one side, there is an invariable popular mass, on the other, the rich, directing element, the motor, in the midst of a full Europeanization. . . . All these purchasers of puerile imported consumer goods—notables, well-to-do farmers, princes of all kinds of blood—stopped looking to the local craftsmen. Previously . . . all mandarin Khmer of some quality had their share of cabinetmakers and goldsmiths, troupes of musicians and dancers, sculptors and artists. . . . In 1909, I met . . . the last high mandarin who still had some actresses. And in 1917, only the king maintained workshops, which were in a distressing state of anarchy and disintegration. . . . The misfortune spread among the pagodas, for every monastery also had its artists. But monasteries started building with reinforced concrete, which only Chinese workers know how to do, buying paper flowers from the glass showcases of Western shopkeepers, importing glass chandeliers from the Bazar of the Hôtel de Ville in Paris in honor of the statue of the Buddha, and the popular artists, without any work, became rarer, receded into the background, and practiced their crafts less and less.[20]

Here, Groslier was alluding to a census of craftsmen. In 1917, there were a hundred and thirty of them located throughout the country. The majority, to subsist, had to rely on farming. In Phnom Penh, a town of thirty-five thousand Cambodians in 1925, there were only thirty-two artisans, of whom twenty were attached to the court.[21]

Although they did not decline so dramatically, Vietnamese arts and handicrafts showed similar signs of decline. The causes were comparable, the weakening of imperial patronage being one of the most important. In 1897, according to an anonymous colonial official, in Vietnam, "Working in jade and ivory was almost completely abandoned. As for the enamel work once practiced in palace workshops . . . its technique is lost, and there are no longer any enamel workers in Hue."[22] This decline, he added, was "especially caused by European influences of dubious taste," which had "brought about an incontestable degeneration of styles," leading to an "extreme scarcity of clientele." In 1937, the official French milieu finally agreed on the need to revitalize the Indochinese arts. This shift was founded on the recognition of their aesthetic value, but it can also be explained by the realization that they were expressions of cultural identity: "It seems that we must assume the role of conserving the artistic domain of the people whose education we have undertaken, the unique character and originality of their national art, to help them rediscover elements that they have misjudged or forgotten, and to emphasize their identity rather than impose our own. This is especially true with regards to the Far Easterners who have created unparalleled works of art and who have achieved very admirable results in all branches of art."[23]

Finally, in 1924, the Gouvernement général founded the École des beaux-arts de l'Indochine (School of Fine Arts of Indochina) under the direction of Victor Tardieu. Renamed the Higher School of Fine Arts of the Indochinese University in 1937, the establishment recruited new masters capable of training handicraft artists. It also taught Western techniques of sculpture and oil painting to student artists and included a Department of Applied Arts. There was a debate about the mission of the School of Fine Arts, which pitted those who wanted to train only craftsmen against those who strove, in line with the demands of a part of Vietnamese opinion, to make the school a training ground for artists devoted to what were known as the major arts.[24] From 1937, the choice leaned toward the second orientation, in the same way that "Indochinese Physicians" became "Indochinese Doctors." It can therefore not be said that colonial education was just an institution destined to shape performers and underlings, a kind of "discount education."

The colonial administration and the promoters of the renaissance and development of indigenous arts took care to associate the schools with museums, which brought together many ancient artifacts from French Indochina and elsewhere in the area. This provided sources of inspiration for artisans and artists and played a role in shaping public tastes. The Albert Sarraut Museum formally opened in Phnom Penh on April 13, 1920, and by 1924, it was already exhibiting 2,202 original objects, some dating to the classical period. In 1923, the Khai Dinh museum opened in Hue, whereas Hanoi was home to the Louis Finot Museum and Saigon boasted the Blanchard de la Brosse Museum.

The organizers of the art schools did their best to support the students they had trained and ensure them outlets for the sale of their artistic work. For example, the Office des corporations cambodgiennes (Office of Cambodian Corporations), founded in 1920, was an outlet for Khmer artisans. The corporate associations of Gia Dinh and Thu Dau Mot, founded in 1933, and the Société annamite d'encouragement à l'art et à l'industrie (Annamese Society for the Support of Art and Industry), created in 1934, did the same in eastern Indochina. These associations encouraged local artists to participate in exhibitions in Indochina, as well as internationally, in France (in Paris in 1925, 1931, and 1937) and in San Francisco (1939). They also organized contests offering prizes or diplomas.

The Modernization of Artistic Education

Restoration work had started earlier through the implementation of artistic education throughout the colony. The first school in Indochina was founded in 1917, in Phnom Penh. Its mission was to restore an original Cambodian artistic patrimony that was in danger of disappearing completely. The teachers were all Cambodian artists and were entirely free of French tutelage. A rigorous selection process admitted seventy students in 1937. Cochinchina possessed three provincial schools where so-called minor arts were taught. A school was founded in Bien Hoa in 1903 for artisans working in bronze and ceramics, which had fifty students in 1937. A school was founded in Gia Dinh in 1913 for the teaching of the decorative arts, design, engraving, and lithography, which had from seventy to ninety students in 1937. In Thu Dau Mot, a school was founded in 1901 for woodworking, cabinetwork, sculpture, and inlays of mother of pearl and wood.

The efforts accomplished in favor of artistic instruction and the promotion of the fine arts bore fruit. Traditional techniques such as lacquering and silk painting in the classic style were vigorously maintained. The principal innovations were oil painting and the introduction of European perspective in the composition of paintings. Although the realism of the traditional arts remained predominant, romanticism and even Western realism made themselves felt. One of the realist painters most appreciated by the Vietnamese and European public was Nguyen Phan Chanh. He received honors from *L'Illustration,* which reproduced several of his works in its special 1932 Christmas edition. Among the more eccentric artists was Ta Ty, the first Vietnamese cubist painter. Lastly, owing to French influence, caricature and humorous drawing found support from an expanding Vietnamese press. In the pages of the magazine *Phong Hoa,* the genre immortalized Ly Toet and Xa Xe, two fictional Vietnamese rustics invented by the poet Tu Mo, who are victims of their own naïveté.

The Introduction of Broadcasting and Cinema

Other forms and tools of modern cultural expression appeared relatively early in Indochina. Broadcasting was introduced at the end of the 1920s. In 1938, in Cochinchina, Vietnamese owned 59% of all radios, while the Chinese accounted for 17%. Two private radio stations in Saigon were particularly successful: Radio Boy Landry and Radio Michel Robert. They broadcast music programs and Asian theater, which took up more airtime than their French programs. As for cinema, there were, from 1932, twenty-seven public cinemas in Tonkin. The two French companies that owned twenty-two of these theaters projected 80 to 100 talking films and 150 silent films per year. In Annam, eleven cinemas showed films regularly; however, it was in Cochinchina that the cinema truly thrived and was most diverse, not only in the origins and genres of the films it showed but also in the audiences they attracted. Cochinchina had thirteen movie theaters, in addition to traveling entrepreneurs who showed films in the provinces. In all, Cochinchina ran a total of 100 talking films in 1932. As for Cambodia, it had seven cinemas, where 324 silent films were shown. Laos had only three. The clientele of the grand cinemas of Hanoi and Saigon was primarily French; elsewhere, however, it was mostly Indochinese or Chinese.[25]

Lenin was not the first to understand the ideological and political role that cinema could play. The French authorities were also concerned about the impact of the "Seventh Art" on the populations of the colonies. They paid attention to the content of each film, whether French or foreign. In 1932, the huge success of the American director Lewis Milestone's *All Quiet on the Western Front* (1930) in Hue worried the authorities, who considered the film to be dangerously pacifist. Although the Soviet filmmaker Vsevolod Pudovkin's *Storm over Asia* (1928) presented "French characters in a favorable light," a ban was recommended in 1938 because its subject matter dealt with violent revolt.[26] Chinese films that had the capacity to provoke anti-Japanese demonstrations were equally censored. Except in particular cases, a fairly liberal policy governed the importation of films on social topics, even if they were "bitter," as long as they were "not subversive." However, the authorities paid more attention to the effects produced by movies displaying naked women and prolonged kissing. One French official observed at the time: "The indigenous audience members react to certain somewhat daring scenes with loud hilarity that embarrasses the European viewers."[27]

Governor-General Pasquier was supportive of using movies in schools, and the local chief of education in Annam reported that, from 1926, films were used as teaching tools in the major educational establishments of Hue, Vinh, and Qui Nhon.[28]

THE INITIATIVES OF THE COLONIZED

In developing education, in restoring the monumental and artistic past with a success attested by the magnificent work accomplished at Angkor by the École française d'Extrême-Orient (French School of the Far East), and in encouraging intellectual publications, the French made it clear that they intended to influence the cultural evolution of the Indochinese. But France was but one side of the coin. The Indochinese were able to draw on different or contrary references within this same French culture and opposed countervailing values to those the colonizers officially attempted to instill into them.

Education, the Press, and Publishing

The Vietnamese attempted to attain the sources of modernity by themselves, while refusing or evading those that the colonizers filtered and then offered them. The first step toward seizing the opponent's secrets was the Dong Du (Voyage East) movement. From the outset, it combined a political project with a cultural program. Through the work of Phan Boi Chau, and inspired by the Japanese model (which was reinforced by the Japanese defeat of the Russians in 1905), this movement sought to maintain traditional moral values and politics. Chinese characters remained its language of expression. The principal effect of the Dong Du's cultural program was its contribution to the intellectual and political evolution of involved individuals rather than the elaboration of a new culture. By rubbing shoulders with Japanese and then Chinese reformers, the Dong Du confirmed to the Vietnamese that they were right to search for inspiration and suggestions from the West. This experience paralleled the rallying of intellectuals to Quoc ngu.

The earliest attempt at real, autonomous cultural development was the Dong Kinh Nghia Thuc (DKNT) movement mentioned above, which coincided not only with the French crackdown on the Dong Du and the expulsion of Vietnamese by the Japanese government but with numerous initiatives by Hanoi in support of popular education and periods of study in France, such as those by the Association d'aide aux Annamites pour des études supérieures et techniques en France (Association of Aid to Annamese for Advanced and Technical Studies in France) and the Association de soutien aux étudiants en France (Association of Support for Students in France). Thus began the phase that followed the Dong Du: that of the Tay Du (Voyage West).

On March 3, 1907, a group of "patriotic and progressive" literati founded the Dong Kinh Nghia Thuc in a room on Silk Street (Hang Dao) in Hanoi. Members paid a monthly contribution of five piastres. The school provided the paper, pens, and ink. Every evening, four to five hundred listeners hurried to conferences where one could learn characters, Quoc ngu, and French, as well as the main disciplines of the French educational curriculum. The latter request represented a Vietnamese desire to attain educational parity with the colonizer. Traditional customs were debated, as well as more purely intellectual questions. The Vietnamese thus familiarized themselves with Montesquieu's *L'esprit des lois*, Rousseau's *Le contrat social*, and the evolutionist writings of Darwin via Chinese and Japanese translations and commentaries. Numerous translations in Quoc ngu were completed, and the romanized language even served as the main vehicle of instruction. Women were admitted to DKNT classrooms both as students and as teachers. Several works published by the DKNT have recently been discovered, notably, the *Tan dinh luan ly giao khoa* (New Manual of Morals), *Quoc dan doc bao* (Reading Book for the People), and *Quoc van tap doc* (Book of Readings and National Literature). These books, which extol moral and civic virtues, patriotism, and national solidarity, reveal the extent to which ethics was at the heart of the DKNT educational program. Its leaders believed that morality was "the quintessence of national honor and the origin of education."

The DKNT thus assigned an important place to modern knowledge. However, this school associated it with the culture of so-called ancestral values and virtues in order to affirm the originality and cohesion of a Vietnamese nation linked by blood ties and consecrated through its 4,000 years of existence. This implied a cardinal and imperative duty: piety and loyalty to the sovereign and the homeland.[29] Unsurprisingly, in December 1907, the colonial authorities closed the school.[30]

The Dong Kinh Nghia Thuc nonetheless marked a cultural turning point in two ways. First, the classically trained literati (Luong Van Can, Tang Bat Ho, and Nguyen Quyen, for example) gave their stamp of approval to the use of the romanized Quoc ngu writing system, transforming an instrument of foreign penetration into a tool of internal communication and national cultural unification. Moreover, Quoc ngu was much more effective for facilitating mass education than Chinese-based characters had ever been. By teaching a syllabus very close to the one being proposed by the French and by studying Western philosophers, the organizers and their pupils broke away from cultural xenophobia. They distinctly separated Western culture from the enterprise of colonial conquest, thus abolishing traditional reticence about participating in Western or Western-derived schools.

The French government understood that it had an interest in not suppressing, and even in exploiting this local desire for modern knowledge. In 1909, the colonial state created the School of the Protectorate, a secondary establishment reserved for young Vietnamese. In 1913, it encouraged the launching of *Dong Duong Tap Chi* by Nguyen Van Vinh, who had likewise participated in the Dong Kinh Nghia Thuc. And ten years after it had closed, the government reopened the Indochinese University in Hanoi. Moreover, the Dong Kinh Nghia Thuc cleared the way for an intellectual collaboration that supplemented political or "supporting" collaboration with the colonizer. Later on, some of the translators for the magazine *Nam Phong* were men who had been active in the Dong Kinh Nghia Thuc, such as Nguyen Huu Tien, Nguyen Don Phuc, and Nguyen Van To, among others.

Thanks to the rise of Quoc ngu in particular and the spread of education in general, the publication of periodicals and books became a notable part of Indochinese intellectual life, above all in Vietnam. From 1924 on, despite obstacles stemming from government censorship, financial constraints, and lack of professional experience, the press witnessed a remarkable boom. Many modern writers started their careers in journalism before becoming well enough known to make their livings as novelists, poets, or essayists. The first newspapers were official organs, mainly destined to broadcast the colonial administration's decisions and authorized texts. The official and private media, even those printed in Quoc ngu, were originally French-owned. One of the most famous French newspaper owners and editors was François-Henri Schneider. Paradoxically, it was in this kind of publication that the first Vietnamese challenges to colonial domination appeared. For example, the famous patriot Gilbert Chieu wrote his major political harangues against colonial domination in the pages of the informational paper *Luc Tinh Tan Van* (The New Gazette of Six Provinces [i.e., Cochinchina]), which belonged to Schneider.

The most remarkable periodicals in terms of the talent of their authors and the ideas and debates they presented were, in Saigon, *La cloche fêlée,* edited by Nguyen An Ninh and Phan Van Truong (1923–28), *Dong Phap Thoi Bao* (1923–27), *Trung Lap Bao* (1924–33), *Duoc Nha Nam* (1928–37), and *Phu Nu Tan Van* (1929–34). In Hanoi, one could read *Trung Bac Tan Van* (1919–45), also owned by Schneider, *Thuc Nghiep Dan Bao* (1920–33), and *Khai Hoa Nhat Bao* (1921–27), among other periodicals. Huynh Thuc Khang succeeded in publishing *Tieng Dan* in Hue from 1927 to 1943 by himself, with scant resources.

During a short period of time corresponding largely to the duration of the Popular Front government in France, the legal communist and left-wing press experienced a brief but intensive expansion, which is addressed elsewhere in this work. In 1937, the Gouvernement général tallied a total of 110 dailies and 159 magazines and bulletins. In 1938, there were 128 daily publications and 160 magazines and bulletins. In 1939, 128 dailies and 176 magazines and bulletins were in operation.

The activity of the Indochinese publishers was, without doubt, the most sustained of all those in the French colonial empire. Thanks to laws requiring copies of all books to be sent to the Bibliothèque nationale in Paris, that library now holds a collection of some sixteen thousand works in Quoc ngu, mostly relating to religious matters. Vietnamese authors and editors, however, wrote on a great range of topics. Among these editors, Dao Duy Anh, a lexicographer whose French-Vietnamese dictionary is still a classic, had an extremely important role in popularizing philosophical ideas, notably Marxism. He edited a series of brochures to introduce the ideas of Jean-Baptiste Lamarck, Charles Darwin, Auguste Comte, Karl Marx, and H. G. Wells to Vietnamese readers. He also provided clarifying introductions with titles like "What Is Religion?" or "What Is Society?" or "What Is the Nation?" In addition, Dao Duy Anh attempted to collect documents relating to ancient Vietnamese history and to analyze these texts following the methods of the French historian Charles Seignobos.[31]

Many of these works contained a glossary of new words in Quoc ngu. In other areas, there was a medical encyclopedia published in Haiphong in 1930, followed fourteen years later by two medical dictionaries. Several books on applied sciences—electricity, physics, chemistry, agronomy—appeared between 1929 and 1934. Booksellers also offered practical guides on car mechanics, accounting, shorthand and typing, photography, and so on.[32]

The popularization of science is also evident in periodicals such as *Nam Phong* (1917–21) and *Phu Nu Tan Van*, to name only two major titles. After 1921, however, two magazines were published that were specifically devoted to the popular dissemination of scientific and technical knowledge. In Saigon, *Khoa Hoc Pho Thong* (Science) appeared from 1934 to 1942. In Hanoi, *Khoa Hoc Tap Chi* (Scientific Journal), edited by the agronomist and engineer Nguyen Cong Tieu, sold an average of two thousand copies between 1931 and 1940. Tieu was especially well known for his research on azolla, or duckweed fern, used as a green agricultural fertilizer. He was admitted to the Scientific Council of Indochina, which depended on the governor-general. There, he sought to reconcile the scientific spirit (i.e., rationalism) with Confucianism.[33] The success of the popularization of sciences, notably applied sciences, testified to the open mind of the urban Vietnamese and perhaps pointed up a certain scientific naïveté.

Meanwhile, the illiteracy rate remained very high. The rise in the number of publications in Quoc ngu should not prevent us from seeing that they were essentially destined for the urban middle class. Nevertheless, lectures, public commentaries, and oral transmission of information and opinions should be taken into account when trying to gauge the actual spread of new intellectual knowledge during the colonial period.

Changes in Customs and Ideas

An anecdote related by the French journalist Andrée Viollis illustrates the gap between two Vietnamese generations:

> In one of those towns I found out that an Annamese dignitary wanted to make my acquaintance. His son, a fellow student of my daughters' at the Sorbonne, had visited me in Paris. He is a tall, handsome boy, of studied elegance, with slicked-back hair, who seemed to attend dances no less assiduously than he did classes. Then there is the father, a classic mandarin, dressed in his refined robes, his hands in his sleeves, bowing with dignity; he does not even know French and his customary compliments are translated by an interpreter, as he repeatedly bows. It is impossible to associate this character straight out of a Chinese screen with the very Parisian image of the young regular of the Boul' Mich' [Boulevard Saint-Michel, in the heart of the student quarter in Paris]. Separated by years, but also by the insurmountable barrier of ideas, customs, and habits, how will this father and son be able to understand and listen to each other? I am told that this excellent civil servant, who has made significant sacrifices for the education of the young man, patiently awaits his return. Is the young man also eager to return to his country? Will he rebel against the tyranny of his indigenous environment or against the French yoke and its constraints? It is a moving problem that evokes serious reflection.[34]

This narration ends with a question. But Governor-General Pasquier recounted to the journalist René Vanlande how the son of a mandarin had ridiculed his father by accusing him of having conceived him in a moment of drunkenness. One can imagine how monstrous such a statement must have seemed in a society where filial piety was a capital virtue. Without a doubt, the reported case is extreme. Nevertheless, a cultural malaise existed, and not only among those "returning from France." At one point, it even became fashionable to speak only in French. The writer Nam Xuong wrote a satirical piece that was an adaptation of Molière's *Le bourgeois gentilhomme.* The principal character, a "French Annamese" rejects his parents because they have an "indigenous odor" and resorts to an interpreter because he is ashamed to speak in his native tongue. There were also some ephemeral infatuations like the creation of a Tino Rossi club in Hanoi by about twenty young Vietnamese "fans." Beyond this, and more profoundly, a new way of living was emerging, one that increasingly collided with the values that had been cultivated for centuries in Vietnam.

The French conquest first of all disrupted the notion of political duty by raising the important question of to whom obedience and loyalty should be directed—to the sovereign who had surrendered to the invader, to the monarchy, independent of the sovereign, or to moral beliefs in themselves? One either had to accept the new rulers or fight them to the end. This predicament eventually forced the Vietnamese to begin to separate politics from ethics. This was new.

Parallel to the political questions created by the colonial process were cultural issues that threatened the very soul of the nation *(quoc hon)* and its national essence *(quoc tuy)*. Confronted by superior foreign power, traditional ideology could be perceived as the cause of weakness and, consequently, of defeat and servitude. It could also be held responsible for delaying modernization, since Confucianism was sometimes seen as impermeable or even hostile to the scientific and technical spirit. It could even be written off as "feudal," a hindrance to the renaissance of the nation. But did this mean it was necessary to accept the values that the colonizers sought to impose on the colonized, or accept those unleashed by the colonizers' very presence? Whatever the topic of a debate—linguistics, philosophy, literature, history, education, or ethics—and whatever the theme of a literary work, one always encountered the question of the nation's destiny, whether it be decadence, disappearance, or rebirth. All movements, all organizations, all intellectual schools or currents inevitably had to deal with this matter.

During the 1920s and 1930s, as seen by the malaise among the youth and the debates on the status of women, Vietnamese society was shaken in its key institution—the family. What seemed most menacing to the cohesion of the familial and national collectivities—which were inseparable in the Vietnamese context—was the emancipation of the individual. This constant conflict imposed limits on all movements whose objective was the transformations of relations between the generations and the sexes.

The main Vietnamese women's organization was created in 1926 in Hue. Placed under the patronage of a man, Phan Boi Chau, and directed by Mme Dam Phuong, the Association des femmes pour l'étude et le travail (Association of Women for Work and Study) adopted as its primary goal equal rights in education and preeminence in familial responsibilities. The latter point was portrayed as the foundation of patriotic sentiment. The ideal of the liberated woman was best symbolized by the Trung sisters, heroines who had taken part in a tenth-century insurrection against the invading Chinese armies.

Other militants went farther by pronouncing their rejection of "feudal customs," meaning arranged marriages, one-sided chastity, and especially the "Three Submissions" and the "Five Virtues." These questions were debated within the narrow circles of the urban middle class. Furthermore, it was in Hue, the imperial city and capital of conservatism, that women were the most active. The weekly *Phu Nu Tan Van* (Feminine Gazette, or Modern Women's News) reached a peak circulation of 8,500 copies, progressively expanding the themes it treated in its pages. The importance of these themes was reflected in the fact that the paper's audience consisted of as many men as it did women. The control of the magazine by the Marxist Phan

Van Hum, starting in 1933, put an end to its eclecticism. From that point on, it emphasized less the obligations owed to the national community than the social duties owed to hard-working, underprivileged women. In this sense, the liberation of women was only conceived of to the degree that it was in line with collective obligations. The point of view expressed by the Indochinese Communist Party situated itself within an analogous perspective. The emancipation of women was inseparable from the liberation of the proletariat. This was an important departure from conservative positions and official wishes as they were expressed by the author of a work on *La femme dans la société annamite* (Woman in Annamese Society): "The Annamese woman has in all times been a model of great purity. She is the guardian of a high moral culture; in the setting of the family, she has fulfilled herself for millennia, independent of our social and national adventures."[35]

At the end of 1930, the colonial administration reduced the Association of Women for Work and Study to a simple patronage association, and *Phu Nu Tan Van* ceased to appear in 1934. In the meantime, other groups of women from Cochinchina and Annam were forbidden to meet or had their associations dispersed.

If the ideological battles revealed what moved hearts and minds, we know very little about what actually happened in the families themselves. It is reasonable to imagine that few radical changes occurred, since even "French naturalized" families continued to observe local customs in the family domain and in the relations it generated. Through the legal and economic changes, and even under the appearance of French manners, cultural identity persisted.

Nevertheless, the young men and women of the urban middle class began to move down the path of physical and intellectual transformation. Physical education, sports (and notably European football), swimming, tennis, and traditional martial arts, but also English boxing, progressively developed. This occurred first in scholarly establishments, then spread with the expansion of sporting associations. In 1937, the first summer camps allowed a still modest number of schoolchildren (four to five hundred in each *ky*) to go to the beach or the mountains.[36] The first municipal swimming pool reserved for Indochinese opened in Saigon in 1937.[37] The first Boy Scout groups were started in 1930, and the first Girl Scouts emerged in 1936. Beginning in 1935, the Scouting movement, which numbered eight thousand members, as opposed to only a hundred in 1930, possessed its own magazine. La Fédération des scouts d'Indochine (The Federation of Scouts of Indochina) was formed in 1937 and opened a school for leaders in Bach Ma (close to Hue). The Scouts provide us with an interesting case: conceived as an organization fit to instill discipline, fidelity, and respect for hierarchy, it simultaneously gave young Indochinese an opportunity to acquaint themselves with modern techniques of organization and action. It taught them to take the initiative and to help others. It allowed them to become familiar with the rural population when they came to the aid of the poor or victims of disasters.

In 1932, a group of young girls from Hanoi organized a march to Haiphong. While few reached their destination and many were the objects of ridicule, the event garnered a great deal of attention, because it was understood that girls from good families did not travel by foot. In 1936, some girls from Saigon decided to start cycling, and one of them attempted to ride the 1,800 kilometers from Saigon to Hanoi.

Indeed, in traditional society, physical exercise was considered scandalous, let alone exposing parts of the body to the sun and to the eyes of others. This cultural reticence was only overcome very slowly and with great difficulty. In 1936, Mme Françoise Brachet, principal of the Hanoi Teacher's Training School for young girls, recounted that

> in fifteen years, ideas have changed. When I arrived to Hanoi in 1921, all of my students wore a black *cai ao.* It was so sad that I tried to allow them, at least, to wear a violet *cai ao.* The families there were violently opposed to this. However, today violet is the color of the uniform of the Annamese women. Today, my students wear colored dresses. Another thing: in attempting to give them gymnastics lessons and let them sing to the harmonium, I almost unleashed a revolution. In this office, I saw mothers kneeling . . . in protest. Only the *Kham Tien,* prostitutes, sing and make gestures with their arms. Now, all my pupils sing. Every morning, they have half an hour of physical education. Their professor is a young French noncommissioned officer and the families approve.
>
> But there is something more important. Shaped by our ideas, the young Annamese no longer accept what was the rule for their mothers. No one is willing to become a "second-rank spouse." On this point, they do not give in, whatever the insistence or the threats of their parents.
>
> They have acquired a sense of their personal dignity. They require an independent budget, and one now sees an astounding thing, in Annam: young couples get settled in their own houses, and the young woman frees herself from the authority of her mother-in-law.[38]

Although her remarks are limited to the modest proportions of a particular social stratum (teachers), the observations of Mme Brachet provide us with a window into social changes in colonial Vietnam. Incontestably, some transformations had occurred within the span of a decade. To Tam, the heroine of a melodramatic novel by Hoang Ngoc Phach published in 1925 (said to have been inspired by the 1848 novel *La Dame aux camélias* by Alexandre Dumas *fils*), who is forced by her parents to marry a man she does not love, and who dies as a result, was perhaps not quite representative of that generation. To Tam chooses submission; other young people chose suicide, whether because of love or because they could no longer tolerate domestic discipline. The son of a provincial judge explained his suicide in a letter published in *Phu Nu Tan Van* of May 25, 1931, as follows: "Can one imagine that a man of twenty-four years, married and the father of a family, still living at the expense of his parents, would be obliged to ask for their permission every time he wanted to spend a coin or take a step out of the house, never daring to do anything according to his own will? Such a life is not worth living."

The essayist Truong Tuu (born Nguyen Bach Khoa) provided his own insightful commentary on the evolution of the young: "Individualism and Western romantic literature surge into our country like a hurricane carrying away all the souls. In the long-cleared soil of Vietnamese sensitivity, these two spiritual factors have found sufficient conditions to take root and develop themselves. Waves of youngsters who grew up amid the collapse of Confucianism move away from the rationalistic spirit to go straight to art and love. They forget reason. They know only nature and the heart."[39]

After a period of withdrawal from traditional values, the philosophical and religious men and doctrines redeployed and redefined themselves around the challenges caused by the intrusion of French culture, as well as by social and political tensions.

The "Return" to Traditional Values

Working in the neotraditionalist Chinese style of the 1920s and 1930s, Tran Trong Kim, Freemason, scholar, and primary school inspector, attempted to adapt Confucianism to the modern world by associating intuition with reason, while allowing them their respective and separate domains. But the metamorphosis of Confucianism into metaphysics considerably weakened its impact on social reality. Pham Quynh, on the other hand, cultivated a Confucianism of an "ethical order," using Charles Maurras to counter the critical approach of Jean-Jacques Rousseau and the ideas of French liberal thought in general. A deep connivance developed between this conservative current and the colonial authorities as they faced the intellectual and political evolution of the youth and the social and political movements of the peasantry and the workers in the early 1930s in particular. Using a lexical approach to the elementary school textbooks published by the chancellor's office of the Hanoi Education Department between 1925 and 1930, the sociologist Trinh Van Thao has arrived at the following conclusion:

> The crushing hegemony of the cultural and moral values derived from the conservative milieu and the Confucian ideology (focused on the master-king and the father), the ramifications of a familial and patriarchal system, which insisted heavily upon the omnipresence of paternal authority (notably through the three feminine submissions), underscored by an essentially agricultural economy and a rural and communal civilization, leaves no doubt as to the cultural impregnation exercised by the *Nam Phong* group on our authors, with whom they maintained privileged relations (creating a literary and philosophical, if not political, community).... [T]he undeniable success of the manuals (*Quoc van giao tu*), and their resonance in the collective Vietnamese memory during the years of humiliation and contrition (1925–45), suggest a people nostalgic for the traditional values of conservative Confucianism, which were taken, rightly or wrongly, to be the authentically national values.[40]

The stakes were equally high for Vietnamese Buddhism, which found itself confronted with similar challenges. Given the historical role that Buddhism had played in the history of the Vietnamese state, it could not remain indifferent to the cultural and societal transformations taking place during the colonial period. The rapid rise of the Cao Daist religion in the mid 1920s, for example, coincided with the uproar caused by the trial of Phan Boi Chau and the death of Phan Chu Trinh, the economic crisis of 1929, and the loss or muddling of moral landmarks. Similar factors gave rise to the revival of Buddhism in Asian countries such as Burma and Siam, where religion was associated with national movements or the monarchy. A spiritual reform movement developed in Vietnam in response to modernity, material progress, and advances in science and technology. Quoc ngu literacy and publication took on new importance as means of spreading religious doctrine and training a clergy capable of assuming these new tasks. Above all, religion became integral to philosophical-political debates, such as Nguyen An Ninh's 1937 *Critique du bouddhisme* (Critique of Buddhism), which posed the question "God or the poor?" (underlining the permanent tension in Buddhism between the quest for enlightenment, or personal salvation, and collective salvation). In the 1930s, Cochinchina, Annam, and Tonkin all had Buddhist associations, and sometimes even provincial sections. In 1937, the Association bouddhiste du Tonkin (Buddhist Association of Tonkin) announced that it had two thousand monks and nuns and ten thousand adherents. Annam was said to have three thousand monks and nuns. Attempts to federate the associations into a national body did not, however, succeed. The Buddhists had varying attitudes to French domination. They were mostly apolitical, but certain provincial associations in Cochinchina sheltered young patriotic monks, such as those of the Phat giao tan thanh nien (New Buddhist Youth) association of Saigon. In contrast, the Société des études bouddhistes de Cochinchine (Society of Buddhist Studies of Cochinchina) was regarded as pro-government, according to the historian Tran Van Giau.[41]

The Vietnamese Catholic community comprised 1,300,000 adherents (not including 74,000 in Cambodia) out of a total Vietnamese population of 15 million in 1931. Evangelization rarely reached into Laos. Of its 1,500,000 inhabitants only 18,964 were Catholic (and the overwhelming majority of these were ethnic Vietnamese). In Vietnam, the Catholic community stood out not only for its large number of believers but also for the growing importance of the indigenous clergy, who, with 1,062 priests and 3,129 nuns in 1931, outnumbered their European counterparts. From 1933 to 1938, three Vietnamese acceded to the rank of bishop: Monsignors Nguyen Ba Tong, Ho Ngoc Can, and Ngo Dinh Thuc.[42] Catholic educational works saw a particular expansion after 1934, along with the Jeunesse étudiante chrétienne (Christian Student Youth) and the Jeunesse ouvrière chrétienne (Christian Youth Workers), not to mention the Scouts. And Vietnamese national literature proudly includes the Catholic Han Mac Tu (1912–40) among its greatest romantic poets.

The Vietnamese were drawn to religious novelty. This was especially the case in Cochinchina, a "frontier" region and fertile ground for acculturation, where the Cao Dai and Hoa Hao religions developed quickly.

Millenarianism and Messianic Movements

Cao Dai, the Great Religion of the Third Period of Salvation, was born in 1926 within a narrow circle of spiritualists founded by the prefect Ngo Van Chieu. When Le Van Trung, a French-naturalized civil servant, former member of the Cochinchina Conseil de gouvernement, and colonial counselor, and the "pope" *(pape)* Pham Cong Tac took over the leadership, Cao Dai changed. From an esoteric circle, it was transformed into a religion, attracting thousands of members. Its structure was comprised of a clerical hierarchy, which built its Holy See *(Toa thanh)* near the town of Tay Ninh. Caodaism incorporated Buddhist, Confucian, and Taoist elements, unified by the catalyst of prophetic spiritualism. This, more than syncretism and the invocations of the exotic spirits of Victor Hugo, Joan of Arc, and Jesus Christ, was undoubtedly the reason for its popular success. One could interpret this doctrine as a means for the new Vietnamese upper class to affirm their equality with the French. Spiritualism was a transcultural common denominator, symbolically represented in the narthex of the Holy See in Tay Ninh by a fresco of three historic figures: the Tang-era Chinese poet Li Tai Po, the sixteenth-century Vietnamese scholar Nguyen Binh Khiem, and the nineteenth-century French poet and novelist Victor Hugo.

But although it was a religion of landowners and middle-class civil servants, Caodaism penetrated the peasant world, where it presented itself as the bearer of new social relations founded on mutual trust, notably between landowners and farmers. Cao Trieu Phat, on his return from France, where he was a sergeant-interpreter from 1914 to 1918, founded an ephemeral labor party, followed by the Caodaist sect of Bac Lieu in 1926. Phat asked his farmers to address him as "Brother," rather than "Sir." When the nationalist revolution of 1945 came, he joined the Viet Minh.

French incomprehension and suspicion of this new outpouring of local elite aspirations put the two on a collision course. In the 1930s, the Tay Ninh Cao Dai sect established relations with Prince Cuong De through the intermediary of the Japanese businessman cum spy Mituhiro Matushita. Police repression, the closing and the occupation of the Holy See in 1940, and the exile of Pham Cong Tac to the island of Nosy Lava (near Madagascar), conferred great prestige on Caodaism, as well as political power under favorable circumstances.[43]

The historical conjuncture was equally important in the growth of the Buddhist religious sect called Hoa Hao, named after the birthplace of its prophet, Huynh Phu So. Historians identify it, like Caodaism, as a political-religious sect, due to the role it played in the first Indochinese war. In fact, its political-military apparatus was only a superstructure, which did not survive historic vicissitudes. If the religious current of Hoa Hao was momentarily orientated toward temporal objectives, it did not exist any less as a cluster of beliefs and rituals destined, like all religions, to put people in harmony with nature and one another, and to organize these relationships.

Huynh Phu So was the guide of what might have remained a local sect, like so many others that emerged in Cochinchina. However, his charisma, his alleged healing powers, and his gift of prophecy attracted scores of peasants to his movement, and not just the poor. Moreover, his murder by the Viet Minh in April 1947 conferred on him that all-important martyr's halo. During his lifetime, he presented himself as the reincarnation of the Master Buddha of Peace in the West (Phat Thay Tay An). Doan Minh Huyen, the first known incarnation, appeared in 1849 in the hills around Chau Doc, located along the frontier between present day Cambodia and Vietnam. Distributing amulets bearing the four ideograms *buu son ky huong* (mysterious fragrance from the precious mountain), he preached the religion of Dao Lanh (The Good). At once a mystical current and a communal organization that devoted itself to the clearing of virgin land, Dao Lanh was inevitably drawn into the resistance to the return of the French to the Mekong Delta. The millenarianism and the messianism of this religion also found an additional objective in a war against the French. It allowed the Hoa Hao prophets to identify the apocalypse and the advent of the "Era of Justice and Light" with Vietnam's national liberation. What was exhibited was therefore a form of the dominant Buddhism purified of cultural pomp and without a clergy. The Hoa Hao religion became implanted in a very specific terrain located at the confluence of Khmer, Viet, and Chinese pioneer zones, where the "orthodox" framework of the Confucian literati was weakest, if not nonexistent. The local population expected a great deal from the Hoa Hao's claim to be "those who take care of people" *(cuu dan do the).* Every reincarnated Buddha was both a minister to the soul and a healer of the body. Indeed, both the vigor and the weakness of this religion resulted from the charisma of one figure. This explains its ups and downs, and also the fact that it remained circumscribed within narrow geographical boundaries.[44]

Cambodia and Laos probably offered a deceiving appearance of tranquility because of the absence of dramatic events and an apparent continuity in social and mental structures. Popular Buddhism, inseparable from the local setting, assured religious homogeneity. The Buddhist monarchies in western Indochina, even though dependent, had not, as in Vietnam, undergone the double dissociation of the institution from the ruler, on the one hand, and the monarchy from the nation, on the other. Lao and Khmer monarchs do not seem to have suffered a similar erosion of their prestige in the eyes of the people. Modern education was neither the locus nor the instrument of upheaval, since it only touched a handful of the aristocracy's sons and daughters. Was it not symptomatic that, until World War II, the sons of Khmer or Lao nobility prepared for the *baccalauréat* by attending high schools in eastern Indochina—Albert-Sarraut (in Hanoi), Chasseloup-Laubat (in Saigon), or Yersin (in Dalat)?

The Rise of Modern Literature in Vietnam

The advent of modern literature in Vietnam was preceded by a long tradition of writing by the literati that was strongly influenced by the Chinese model and written in Chinese characters.[45] The Vietnamese masterpiece *Kim Van Kieu* written in the first years of the nineteenth century, affirmed the existence of original Vietnamese literature through its verse and its title. This literature was always lively in the nineteenth century, producing the notable works of Nguyen Dinh Chieu and the nonconformist poet Ho Xuan Huong.

In the period 1913–30, the flourishing of journalism established Quoc ngu in print, and in so doing forged and sharpened the instrument necessary for the creation of modern literature. Newspapers and magazines were the original vectors of this blossoming literature, thanks to their publication of poems, novellas, and serial novels. The magazine *Dong Duong Tap Chi* published the works of Tan Da (alias Nguyen Khac Hieu, 1889–1939), considered a pivotal writer, who ensured the transition from classical poetry to what was called "new poetry" *(tho moi)*. In 1939, the writer Phan Khoi recalled:

> I have known M. Nguyen Khac Hieu (Tan Da) since 1918, when I came to live in Hanoi and wrote for the *Nam Phong* magazine. On a cold spring evening, I was lying down, reading, upstairs from the office of the magazine, on Cotton Street—the floor reserved, at the time, as lodging for Nguyen Ba Trac. A visitor arrived. M. Trac made the introduction: "This is M. Nguyen Khac Hieu." At that moment, it was as if an electric current passed through me. I felt dread and fright. I got up quickly! This is true. The name of Nguyen Khac Hieu, at that time, was no small thing, and this name had even more solemnity for me than for others. When I heard it, I shivered. This is true. Consider that literary writings in Quoc ngu in this period were still very rare, and literary creation was even rarer. Yet I had already read texts in the *Dong duong tap chi* such as "The Internal Content of Every Being." I had just arrived in Hanoi when "The Small Dream" *[Giac mong con]* was published, and I could not have had a greater admiration for the author, who was truly talented. I said to myself of him: "Pham Quynh and Nguyen Van Vinh only write following the books and thoughts of the French; as for this guy, he writes his own thoughts; it is he who is truly a creator."[46]

It is generally agreed that Tan Da was the greatest Vietnamese poet of the first half of the twentieth century. French literature influenced Vietnamese writers through translations or the reading of texts in French. The choice of French authors was varied, ranging from Abbé Prévost to Victor Hugo. But the poetry Tan Da wrote was primarily romantic. It portrayed the self and its passions as a source of scandal, and therefore something that created a rupture with the conformist heritage and environment. The southern writer Ho Bieu Chanh used the novel to moralize about social reality. Playwrights were familiar with Corneille's *Le Cid* and *Horace*, and with the plays of Molière, translated and published in *Nam Phong*. The success of the performance of Molière's *Le Malade imaginaire* in Vietnamese on April 25, 1920, was an important event.

After 1930, literature became both a mirror of and a catalyst for social change. That year saw the start of a second period in the development of Vietnamese literature. Its rise was marked by the supremacy of the "Autonomous Literary Group" (Tu Luc Van Doan; TLVD) and the "New Poetry" movement. Described as romantic, the two literary trends affirmed themselves through breaks with the past and its literary traditions. The starting point of New Poetry was the publication of the poem "The Old Lovers" by the reformist scholar Phan Khoi in March 1932: "We are not spouses but lovers. Why therefore speak of fidelity and eternity!"

Taking up the perspective of the "returnee from France," Hoang Tich Chu extolled the adoption of French syntax in the writing of Quoc ngu. TLVD writers used a concise, clear style, taken from classic French literature. They tried as far as possible to avoid Chinese terms, turns of phrase, and literary allusions, such as the unchanging images of wind, snow, flowers, and the moon.

Gathering together the novelists Khai Hung, Nhat Linh, Hoang Dao, and the poet Tu Mo around the publishing house Doi Nay (Our Times) and the magazine *Phong Hoa* (Mores and Customs),[47] the TLVD was a powerful agent of cultural renewal. *Phong Hoa* not only published literary works but also took the initiative in publicizing ideological debates, such as the polemics on the emancipation of women, the implications of Confucian ethics, and controversies (during 1935–39) between advocates of "art for art's sake" (such as the romantics Luu Trong Luu, Thieu Son, and Hoai Thanh) and those of "art for life" (the Marxist critic Hai Trieu is a good example). The artist-designer of the group, Nguyen Cat Tuong, reformed the traditional costume of Vietnamese women, making it essentially what it is today.

Not only did the TLVD poets—The Lu, Xuan Dieu, Luu Trong Luu, Che Lan Vien, and Huy Can—adopt a French style of verse that was freer than that of Chinese, but their poetry was also lyrical. They sang of love and nature and exalted the role of the poet. "We, the poets of today, we do not want to, indeed we cannot, feel and be moved in his way [that of Tan Da]. Our deep feelings are much more complex, we suffer, we feel much more, and when we burst with joy, the joy also takes on strange colors and nuances."

Already in 1930, a clear and vigorous realist trend had begun. During the period marked by the economic crisis of 1929 and the social and political uprisings rocking Indochina in 1930, the writers Vu Bang, Vu Dinh Chi, and Vu Trong Phung published numerous suspenseful novels about the urban proletariat, prostitution, and usury, among other things. Meanwhile, Vietnamese readers increasingly gained access to the works of Balzac, Flaubert, Tolstoy, Dickens, Barbusse, Gide,

Dostoevski, and Goethe. Between 1936 and 1939, the prestige of the TLVD declined, because it not only had to compete with social realist writers who benefited from greater press and publishing liberty, but also to take into account the social and political questions that were now on the agenda. The novelists Ngo Tat To, Nguyen Cong Hoan, Nguyen Hong, and Nam Cao chose to write about the people, notably those in rural areas, and the class oppression that was overwhelming them. They expressed a social critique, like novelists of the TLVD, but in a populist and Marxist vein.

Nhat Linh and his friends also attacked the "feudal," mandarin, and bourgeois society, which oppressed the individual. The literature of the TLVD was an affirmation of the "I" in the face of the collective. The literary controversies, like the one around *Kim Van Kieu,* were underpinned by different beliefs about the nature of Vietnamese society and the role of intellectuals in society. The cultural debate was deepened by political rifts. In 1939, *Ngay Nay* (Today), the other magazine of the TLVD, reproduced the French press's approval of André Gide's *Retour de l'URSS (Return from the U.S.S.R.).* It was not only a confrontation between literary movements, but also an ideological war between communists and their sympathizers, on the one hand, and intellectual "bourgeois individualists," on the other. Not all the novels, poems, or essays, however, fell into the previously cited movements. There were original and unclassifiable writers such as Nguyen Tuan (born in 1913), who excelled at nostalgic chronicles of an introspective and intimate character. And there was also a militant literature that flourished in prisons. In the late 1930s, the young poet To Huu became famous for his revolutionary lyricism. Popular literature also thrived in the shape of *ca dao* (anonymous couplets) and *cheo* theater, in its renovated urban forms. The classical theater of the *tuong* and the modern *cai luong* (reformed theater) always drew large audiences.

In contrast, modern literary creations were largely absent in Cambodia. One can only cite one modern novel. In 1938, Rim Kin (1911–59) published *Suphat.* The reasons the author provided to explain his decision to write shed light on why Khmer literature developed slowly. Rim Kin was a student at the Sisowath High School, where Vietnamese were as numerous as Cambodians, if not more so. The markets in Phnom Penh teemed with Vietnamese books, and Rim Kin decided to take up his pen in order not to be "disgraced before foreigners."[48]

An Unfinished or Impossible Fusion?

An overview of Vietnamese intellectual and artistic creation during the "eighty years of French colonization" would be incomplete if nothing were said of the existence of works written in French by Indochinese, as well as those written by French authors in, or about, Indochina.

Among the first group, the names of three men stand out, to whom modern Vietnamese culture is indebted even if, until 1933, nationalist opinion viewed them unfavorably and minimized their role. Two Catholics, Truong Vinh Ky, better known by the name of Petrus Ky (1837–1898), and Huynh Tinh Cua, also known as Paulus Cua (1834–1907), were intermediary figures between traditional culture and that imposed from the outside. As scholars trained in Sino-Vietnamese studies and interpreters for the French government, they made scholarly contributions in the domains of philology and lexicography. Paulus Cua produced an important dictionary, *Dai Nam Quoc am tu vi* (1895). They did not, however, confine themselves to this area. Both transcribed and translated Chinese and Vietnamese works into Quoc ngu. Furthermore, Paulus Cua founded the first newspaper printed in Quoc ngu, *Gia Dinh Bao* (1865). What the third man, Pham Quynh, did to assure the vitality of national writing has been described earlier in this chapter.

These three figures, along with others, laid the foundation of modern Vietnamese culture. Other writers, however, wrote their works in French rather than their mother tongue. Given this, should we count them as Vietnamese (or Cambodian, in the case of the poet Princess Yukhanthor) creators, or should they be included under the heading of francophone literature? The novels and poetry of Nguyen Tien Lang and Pham Van Ky are part of a context of cultural mingling that some have claimed they desired themselves.[49] In contrast to what happened to those who adopted European techniques in the plastic arts,[50] in literature, the tool of expression they used propelled them to the margins of their national culture. Consequently, with the exception of militant nationalists who wrote polemics in French (Nguyen Ai Quoc, alias Ho Chi Minh, and Nguyen An Ninh), Indochinese writers of the French language have been placed with the cohort of French writers of colonial literature.

The domain of Indochinese French literature is extremely rich. As early as 1930, René Crayssac inventoried the archival and fictional production. The authors "are legion," he wrote, and the list of works that he presents is indeed impressive—and will certainly grow longer in the future.[51] Through a great quantity and variety of genres, and a range of quality and talent, these works include examples of descriptive and often superficial travel literature; of exotic literature, at its best, a quest for initiation into the world of the Other; as well as colonial literature, which was predominant. The latter was the mirror of the colony, as well as the bearer of the colonial ideology that saw the Indochinese as the "property" of the colonizers. Certain authors, however, tried to penetrate the indigenous world and explored the problems posed by European intrusion. Sympathy and even empathy were not absent. Some authors were highly perceptive, among them Albert de Pouvourville and especially Jean Marquet, Herbert Wild, and Mme Chivas-Baron. All demonstrated a true consciousness of the colonial situation, of its contradictions and injustices.

In the end, literature and the fine arts found literary themes and sources of inspiration in Indochina: the exotic scenery, certainly, but also an affirmation of universal ethical values. However, this colonial literature created by French writers was tied up with the destiny of the empire. "It is remarkable, for example," one author has noted, "that the literature of the quests and protests of the 1930s for the first time took into account misery, injustice, repression, protests, and revolts, without ever arriving at an acknowledgment of the contradictions of a colonial system, whose legitimacy was never questioned. . . . From this point of view, [Louis] Malleret's dream of a fusion of the East and West, manifested in art and literature, remained an illusion."[52] The same author, with good reason, identifies the novelist Jean Hougron (1923–), who was writing during France's final war in Indochina, as a privileged witness of the fall of "white power." Was their audience mainly French or Indochinese? Did they influence the Indochinese, in particular, the artists? In terms of artistic influence, Victor Hugo, Molière, André Gide, and suspense novels had the greatest impact on Indochinese and especially on Vietnamese readers.

The questions raised about the French writers of Indochina resurface with regard to those working in the plastic arts. Were they only colonial artists, for whom Indochina was nothing more than an inspiration? Did they, at best, simply popularize European art (methods and aesthetic), or at worst, merely propagate the politics of foreign domination? Or were they influenced to the point where their stay did not leave them untouched and they became "orientalized"? One analysis of their work concludes:

> One does not find in their paintings any strained sentiment: there is only harmony. The effects of sickness, death, and old age are absent. The paintings also leave aside the tensions born of colonization. André Maire, for example, overlooks the war, although he remained in Vietnam until 1958; his paintings represent Indochina in such a way as to invoke the image of a country imprinted with the serenity of the "Asian philosophies." Seduced by Indochina, these artists wished to provide an enticing image of it. Their role was not to attain objectivity but rather to paint with all their sensibility. . . . They were fascinated by Indochina, and their paintings translate what they felt naturally, without the pressures of propaganda, which, in official commissions, demanded of painters that they idealize the image of Indochina.[53]

On the other hand, Indochina did not bring France a renewal of plastic arts comparable to that which Japanese and African art inspired among European impressionist and cubist painters. The meeting and blending of two cultures, their interactions, have yet to studied; it is a wide-open field for historians.

APPENDIX 10

Franco-indigenous School System in Indochina, 1930 and 1942

Levels of schooling (in 1930)	Teaching staff (in 1930)	Number of students		Language of instruction (in 1930)	Diplomas (in 1930)
		1930	*1942*		
Franco-indigenous elementary schooling: • elementary cycle at 397 full-course schools • classes at 2,835 elementary schools • classes at 4,531 establishments of academic initiation: renovated pagoda schools, etc.	Official schools: • 4,727 assistant schoolteachers and instructors (often educated at Franco-indigenous *primaire supérieur* schools) Establishments of academic initiation: • 5,452 teachers (former ideogram teachers, graduates of elementary and sometimes primary cycles, pagoda school teachers)	338,379	546,504	Native language, with an initiation to French in most elementary schools (85,000 students in all)	Certificate of indigenous elementary primary studies. Created in 1924, it included optional exams in French or Chinese.
Franco-indigenous primary schooling: 397 full-course schools	1,572 schoolteachers: graduates from teacher training colleges, holding either a diploma of *primaire supérieur* school studies or a *primaire supérieur* school teaching certificate and a certificate of pedagogical aptitude	40,367	63,611	French, with study of the native language and Chinese (Pali in Cambodia and Laos)	Certificate of Franco-indigenous primary studies, including native language, Chinese, or Pali exams.

(continued)

APPENDIX 10 *(continued)*

Levels of schooling (in 1930)	Teaching staff (in 1930)	Number of students		Language of instruction (in 1930)	Diplomas (in 1930)
		1930	*1942*		
Franco-indigenous *primaire supérieur* schooling: 21 establishments (*primaire supérieur* school classes, schoolteacher training colleges, first cycles of Franco-indigenous middle and high schools)	126 French and native *primaire supérieur* teachers	4,615	6,163	French, with study of the native language and Chinese or Pali	Diploma of Franco-indigenous *primaire supérieur* studies (approximately equivalent to the French elementary school certificate)
Franco-indigenous secondary schooling (3 years): Franco-indigenous high school of the Protectorate (Hanoi), Petrus-Ky Franco-indigenous high school (Saigon), Quoc Hoc middle school (Hue)	314 French and native graduate teachers	157	697	French, with study of the native language and Chinese or Pali	Certificate of qualification in Franco-indigenous secondary instruction, or the local baccalaureate in two parts, made equivalent to the French baccalaureate (except in medicine) in January 1930
Professional schooling	137 instructors and foremen	1,680	3,461		Professional diplomas
TOTAL	12,328, of which 12,014 are native (8,891 in the three Ky)	385,198	620,436		

Notes

1. R. Vanlande, *L'Indochine sous la menace communiste* (Paris, 1930).

2. Wright, *Politics of Design*, pp. 199–200.

3. Pierre Pasquier, memorandum to Governor-General Merlin, "L'enseignement primaire en Annam," December 31, 1922.

4. Bezançon, *Colonisation éducatrice?*

5. See G. P. Kelly, *Franco-Vietnamese Schools, 1918–1938: Regional Development and Implications for National Integration* (Madison, Wis., 1982), and "Colonial Schools in Vietnam, 1918 to 1938," in *Proceedings of the 2nd Annual Meeting of the French Colonial Historical Society* (Milwaukee, 1976); Gouvernement général de l'Indochine, *Le Service de l'Instruction publique en Indochine en 1930* (Hanoi, 1930).

6. "Situation de l'enseignement indigène," report of P. Beau to the minister of the colonies, 2 July 1907, Centre des archives d'outre-mer, Aix-en-Provence [henceforth cited as CAOM], Fonds du Gouvernement général, 2579.

7. P. Beau, *Situation de l'Indochine de 1902 à 1907* (Paris, 1908), p. 315.

8. *Annuaire statistique de l'Indochine, 1939–1946*. According to the "Tableau statistique de l'enseignement en Indochine," CAOM, NF Indo. 1323, there were a total of 1,528 students in 1944 (1,210 of them in the sciences, medicine, pharmacy, and law.)

9. Quoted in V. Floquet, "Étude de la vie rurale au Tonkin d'après les rapports des résidents supérieurs (1908–1930)" (MA thesis, Aix-en-Provence, 1992), p. 70.

10. Note from the Ministry of the Colonies, Service de l'Indochine, to the Inspection générale de l'instruction publique, November 11, 1919, quoted by P. Bezançon, "La rénovation des écoles de pagodes au Cambodge" (MA thesis, Paris, 1992).

11. R. Jacques, "Le Portugal et la romanisation de la langue vietnamienne: Faut-il réécrire l'histoire?" *Revue française d'histoire d'outre-mer* 85, 318 (1998): 21–54.

12. M. Pietri of the École française d'Extrême-Orient to the governor-general regarding the doctoral examination of 1910, Hanoi, February 3, 1911.

13. *Code annamite: Lois et règlements du royaume d'Annam* (Paris, 1865), 1: vi.

14. Parliamentary debate on the budget for the colonies, January 1930.

15. Quoted by Marr, *Vietnamese Anticolonialism*, p. 149.

16. Governor-general, letter to the minister of the colonies, September 15, 1917, CAOM, NF Indochine 56.

17. L. Marty, "Au sujet de la revue *Nam Phong*," CAOM, NF Indochine 56.

18. Pham Quynh, *Nam Phong*, no. 20 (February 1919).

19. Bezançon, "Rénovation des écoles de pagodes."

20. G. Groslier, "Rapport sur les arts indigènes du Cambodge," CAOM, Agence FOM 911, 1925.

21. Ibid.

22. Resident superior of Annam to governor-general, "Rapport sur les industries d'art indigènes," CAOM, Agence FOM 911, April 1925.

23. *Les écoles d'art de l'Indochine* (report produced for the Exposition internationale des arts et technique de Paris, Section coloniale), CAOM, Agence FOM 911, 1937, p. 8.

24. *Truong dai hoc my thuat Hanoi, 1925–1990* (The École supérieure des beaux-arts of Hanoi, 1925–1990) (Hanoi, 1990).

25. Governor-general, report to the minister of the colonies, CAOM, Affaires politiques 1733, 27.9.1932.

26. CAOM, Affaires politiques 1734.

27. CAOM, Affaires politiques 1733.

28. "Note sur le cinéma scolaire en Annam," CAOM, Affaires politiques 1733, 2.6.1932.

29. *Van Tho Dong kinh Nghia thuc: Prose et poésies du DKNT* (Hanoi, 1997), pp. 180–81.

30. Tran Huy Lieu et al., *Lich Su thu do Ha-noi* (History of the Capital of Hanoi) (Hanoi, 1960).

31. Dao Duy Anh, *Nho nghi chieu hom* (Memoirs and Reflections of the Evening) (Ho Chi Minh City, 1989). A lively press was the main means by which Cochinchinese urbanites participated in public life, as P. Peycam highlights in "Intellectuals and Political Commitments in Vietnam: The Emergence of a Public Sphere in Colonial Saigon, 1916–1928" (PhD diss., London, 1999).

32. See C. Rageau's catalogue of the collection of documents in Quoc ngu in the Bibliothèque nationale, or D. G. Marr, *Vietnamese Tradition on Trial, 1920–1945* (Berkeley, 1981).

33. Nguyen Van Ky, *La société vietnamienne face à la modernité: Le Tonkin de la fin du XIXe siècle à la Seconde Guerre mondiale* (Paris, 1995).

34. Viollis, *Indochine S.O.S.*, p. 78.

35. Dang Phuc Thong, *La femme dans la société annamite* (Hanoi, 1931), p. 3. The responses of Vietnamese women to the challenges they had to face are soundly analyzed by

Bui Tran Phuong, "Viêt Nam, 1918–1945: Genre et modernité. Émergences de nouvelles perceptions et expérimentations" (PhD diss., Lyon, 2008).

36. CAOM, Agence Fom 238.

37. Ibid.

38. H. Célarié, *Promenades en Indochine* (Paris, 1937), pp. 176–77.

39. Truong Tuu, in *Tao Dan*, no. 1 (March 1939): 25.

40. Trinh Van Thao, *L'école française en Indochine* (Paris, 1995), pp. 179–80.

41. *Su Phat trien cua tu tuong o Vietnam tu the ky XIX den cach mang Thang Tam*, vol. 2: *He Y thuc Tu san va su bat luc cua no truoc cac nhiem vu lich su* (The Ideological Evolution of Vietnam from the Nineteenth Century to the August Revolution, vol. 2: Bourgeois Thought and Its Powerlessness in the Face of the Historical Tasks) (Ho Chi Minh City, 1993). See also *History of Buddhism in Vietnam*, ed. Nguyen Thai Thu (Hanoi, 1992), part 5.

42. C. Lange, "L'Église au Vietnam," in *Les prodromes de la décolonisation de l'Empire français 1936–1956* (Paris, 1986).

43. Nguyen Tran Huan, "Histoire d'une secte religieuse au Vietnam: Le caodaisme," in *Tradition et révolution au Vietnam* (Paris, 1971); J. S. Werner, *Peasant Politics and Religious Sectarianism: Peasant and Priest in the Cao Dai in Vietnam* (New Haven, Conn., 1981).

44. Hue Tam Ho Tai, *Millenarianism and Peasant Politics in Vietnam* (Cambridge, Mass., 1983).

45. This section is based on M. M. Durand and Nguyen Tran Huan, *Introduction à la littérature vietnamienne* (Paris, 1969); *Littératures contemporaines de l'Asie du Sud-Est*, ed. P.-B. Lafont and D. Lombard (Paris, 1974), particularly the contribution of Nguyen Tien Lan; Bui Xuan Bao, *Le roman vietnamien contemporain: Tendences et évolution du roman vietnamien contemporain, 1925–1945* (Saigon, 1968); and Vu Ngoc Phan, *Nha van hien dai* (1942; reprint, Glendale, Calif., 1980).

46. Phan Khoi, "Le poète Tan Da et moi," *Tao Dan Tap Chi*, nos. 9–10 (July 16, 1939).

47. Ten thousand copies of the magazine *Phong Hoa* (Mores and Customs) were printed in 1933.

48. Rim Kin quoted by Khin Hoc Dy, "Le développement économique et la transformation littéraire dans le Cambodge moderne," *Mondes en développement*, no. 28 (1979): 798. Rim Kin's novel *Suphat*, translated by Gérard Groussin, has been published in French under the title *Sophat: Ou les surprises du destin* (Paris, 1994).

49. E. Pujarniscle, "Philoxène ou de la littérature coloniale," in *Le Roman colonial* (Paris, 1987).

50. On November 15, 1929, an exhibition of painting and sculpture was inaugurated in Hanoi. New aesthetic tendencies inspired by the West were remarked upon. One French journalist wrote of the "birth of the Annamese school of beaux arts"; see *Nam Phong*, December 1929.

51. René Crayssac, *Extrême-Asie: Revue indochinoise*, July 1930; for the period after 1930, see R. Cornevin, "La vie culturelle: la littérature d'expression française," in Académie des sciences d'outremer, Commission Indochine, *Indochine, alerte à l'histoire: Ni opprobre, ni oubli* (Paris, 1985), pp. 197–208.

52. See H. Copin, *L'Indochine dans la littérature française, des années vingt à 1954: Exotisme et altérité* (Paris, 1996), and B. Hue et al., *Littératures de la péninsule indochinoise* (Paris,

1999), a book published within the framework of the history of francophone literature that testifies to the richness of colonial literature, yet at the same time restricts its social and cultural impact. Indeed, is this literature a minor key of twentieth-century French literature? Can its authors aspire to a universal dimension or are their works of only documentary value?

53. N. André-Pallois, *L'Indochine: Un lieu d'échange culturel? Les peintres français et indochinois (fin XIXè-XXè siècle)* (Paris, 1997), p. 193.

[10]

'OUR STRIKE': EQUALITY, ANTICOLONIAL POLITICS AND THE 1947–48 RAILWAY STRIKE IN FRENCH WEST AFRICA

BY FREDERICK COOPER

University of Michigan

THE strike of African railway workers which began in October 1947 was an event of epic dimensions: it involved 20,000 workers and their families, shut down most rail traffic throughout all of French West Africa, and lasted, in most regions, for five and a half months. As if the historical event were not large enough, it has been engraved in the consciousness of West Africans and others by the novel of Ousmanne Sembene, *God's Bits of Wood*. Sembene dramatizes a powerful strike effort weakened by the impersonal approach of trade unionists, by the seductions of French education, and by the greed of local élites. The strike is redeemed by its transformation into a truly popular movement dynamized by women, climaxing in a women's march on Dakar led by someone from the margins of society and leading to a coming together of African community against the forces of colonialism.

Sembene's novel both complicates the task of the historian and lends it importance: the written epic may influence oral testimony, yet the fictional account enhances the sense of participants that their actions shaped history. When a group of Senegalese graduate students and I went to the railway junction of Thiès to begin a project of collecting testimonies, some informants expressed resentment of Sembene for turning 'our strike' into his novel.[1] What needs most to be unpacked is the connection of the labor movement to the independence struggle: the two were both complementary

[1] The quoted phrase comes from an interview with Amadou Bouta Gueye, 9 Aug. 1994, Thiès. Oumar NDiaye, interviewed the same day, made much the same point. These interviews were part of a workshop and field studies program conducted in August 1994, by Dr Babacar Fall of the Ecole Normale Supérieure, Université Cheikh Anta Diop, Dakar, and the present author. A series of training sessions for graduate students was led by Dr Robert Korstad of the Center for Documentary Studies of Duke University, and I accompanied groups of students who interviewed eyewitnesses in Dakar and Thiès. The students participating in these interviews included Aminata Diena, Makhali NDaiye, Oumar Gueye, Alioune Ba, Biram NDour, and Ouseynou NDaiye. I am particularly grateful to Ms Diena for setting up the Thiès interviews and to Mr M. NDaiye, Mr Ba, and Mr Gueye for organizing the Dakar interviews. This workshop in turn was inspired by a visit that Dr Fall and I made to Thiès in July 1990, in which a graduate student working with Dr Fall, Mor Sene, took us to interview two important witnesses to the 1947–8 events. Mr Sene has himself contributed to the historiography of the strike in his master's thesis, 'La grève des cheminots du Dakar-Niger, 1947–1948' (Mémoire de maîtrise, Ecole Normale Supérieure, Université Cheikh Anta Diop, 1986–7). Following the 1994 workshop, students in Dakar will conduct interviews as part of their research on their own theses and dissertations, and will contribute tapes to an archive of contemporary oral history under the supervision of Dr Fall. Tapes of interviews cited here are preserved at the Ecole Normale Supérieure. My collaboration with Dr Fall in the study of African labor history over the last nine years has been a deeply

and in tension with one another. My goal in this article is both to re-examine the question of how to locate the railway strike in the history of post-World War II West Africa and to point to questions that need further research, for the very extensive nature of this social movement – embracing the colonies of Senegal, the Soudan, Guinea, the Ivory Coast and Dahomey and intersecting a wide range of local contexts, communities, and political struggles – means that it contains many histories and requires the attention of many historians. The research begun in Senegal gets at only some of these histories, and time is running out on the lives and memories of the people involved.

The all-too-neat assimilation of social and political struggles is a matter of hindsight: once independence was achieved, all forms of contestation against French rulers and bosses appear to be part of a seamless pattern of ever-broadening, ever-growing struggle. Some sort of connection is not in doubt; the problem is to pry apart its complexities and ambiguities. The strikers were able to hold out for over five months because they were so well integrated into the African communities in which they lived, but their demands, if realized, would have had the effect of pulling them out of close communities into a professionally defined, non-racial body of railwaymen. The union's goal from 1946 onward was the creation of the *cadre unique*, a single scale of wages and benefits for Africans and white Frenchmen alike. Such a system would widen the gap between the life experiences of railwaymen and those of the peasants, pastoralists and merchants among whom they lived. In political terms one can argue the opposite: to the extent that the strike movement drew from anticolonial sentiments that went beyond the workplace and to the extent that the strike gave Africans a sense of empowerment in their confrontations with the French government, anti-colonial politics risked diluting the work-centered goals of the strike movement. The idea of independence would sever the French connection which was the ideological basis for the railwaymen's claims to equality of wages and benefits with French workers, while opening the union's considerable organizational achievements to co-optation by political parties whose primary concerns lay elsewhere.

In fact, the union and the major political movements of the day remained in uneasy relationship. The men who were the ultimate beneficiaries of decolonization – the Senghors and the Houphouët-Boignys – did not make the cause of the strikers their own. Senghor, more so than other party leaders, maintained contact with the union and when the strike was over moved decisively to bring its leaders into his political fold and under his eyes – a process which increased the union's influence and decreased its autonomy. For many strikers, the behavior of politicians was disillusioning, and for the union structure, the very success of the strike left potentially conflicting alternatives between becoming, as one veteran put it, the 'auxiliaries' of a political party or else focusing as a union on the kinds of claims they could make that stood a good chance of success within the framework of industrial relations emerging out of the strike. If the strike, as a popular movement,

gratifying one, and I would like to thank him for all the help he has given me along the way, for his comments on an earlier draft of this article and for his leadership in setting up the 1994 workshop.

gave thousands of people a sense of collective strength, the strike – as a process carried out through certain kinds of institutions – defined the terrain of contestation in a narrower way.

This article points to the kind of questions that further oral research across the strike zone will illuminate. Among documentary sources it gives particular emphasis to reports by police spies present at numerous strike meetings. They must of course be used with care, since spies have a tendency to see what their superiors want them to see. But it is clear that the strikers earned the grudging admiration of their opponents, who had clear reasons to try to learn something of what was going on among them. Taken together, available sources offer multiple points of access to an extraordinarily complex social movement.[2]

THE CONTEXT: STRIKE MOVEMENTS AND THE MODERNIZATION OF IMPERIALISM

The strike must be understood in the context of a French government anxious to find a new basis of legitimacy and control in an era when social and political movements in the colonies were asserting themselves with new vigor. These two processes shaped one another: as African movements sought to turn the government's need for order and economic growth into claims to entitlements and representation, officials had to rethink their policies in the face of new African challenges. The truly agenda-setting movement of the immediate post-war years was the Senegalese general strike of 1946. Up to that point, the French sociology of Africa admitted to only two categories, *paysans* and *évolués*. Officials hoped to achieve economic growth by eliminating forced labor, reducing the tax burden on peasants, and improving infrastructure devoted to agriculture, and to attain political stability by granting *évolués* a modest degree of participation in the governing institutions of France itself. The strike movement – beginning in the port in December 1945, extending to commercial establishments in January, and turning at mid-month into a general strike – involved everyone from African civil servants to dockworkers to market sellers (with the conspicuous exception of railwaymen). Confessing his inability to control events, the Governor General welcomed a labor expert from Paris who proceeded to make workers a focus of policy. The general strike ended as officials negotiated with individual categories of workers, granting collective bargaining agreements to each one in turn. By February the strike movement was over, and ordinary laborers had won significant wage increases; government workers were getting family allowances based on a percentage of the indemnities granted to the top ranks; unions were recognized; and wage hierarchies were expanded and bonuses granted for seniority.

[2] The spies' reports appear in the archives as 'Renseignements', often with a notation such as 'African source – good'. Most came from the Sûreté at Thiès, where the almost daily mass meetings were held, but reports from other regions are also used. Archival sources from the Archives Nationales du Sénégal include (from the Government General of Afrique Occidentale Française) series K (labor), 17 G (politics), 2 G (annual reports), and (from the government of Senegal) series D (political and administrative files). The series IGT (Inspection Générale du Travail) and AP (Affaires Politiques) are from France, Archives Nationales, Section Outre-Mer, Aix-en-Provence. The abbreviation 'AOF,' for Afrique Occidentale Française, occurs frequently in the notes.

Out of the strike came a newly empowered Inspection du Travail that sought to use French models of industrial relations to gain a measure of control over an increasingly differentiated labor force and to promote 'stabilization' as an antidote to the kind of mass, boundary-crossing movement they had just faced. There emerged as well a labor movement able to turn officials' hopes for stability and the assimilationist rhetoric of post-war French imperialism into African workers' claims to French wage and benefit scales. Over the next several years, the labor question focused on the details of what stabilization and 'equal pay for equal work' would mean and on efforts of both workers and labor inspectors to devise an empire-wide *Code du Travail* that would guarantee basic rights and bound conflict within a set of legally defined procedures. Family allowances, minimum wages, wage hierarchies, and trade union rights were all the objects of negotiations, mobilization, and strikes.[3]

Politics was meanwhile being changed from above and from below. Seeking to demonstrate that what were once called colonies were now an integral part of Greater France, citizenship was extended from the few acculturated urban centers to all French territory and – with a limited but gradually expanding franchise – elections were held throughout French Africa from late 1945 onward for positions in the French legislature. As old-line politicians like Senegal's Lamine Gueye tried to maintain control of their parties, 'youth' organizations challenged them in cities and rural constituencies were organized, most strikingly by the Société Agricole Africaine in the Ivory Coast, leading to the formation of a cross-territorial political party, the Rassemblement Démocratique Africain (RDA).

In the middle of the ferment within Senegal over both trade unions and politics was François Gning, Secretary General of the Syndicat des Travailleurs Indigènes du Dakar-Niger, headquartered in Thiès. He had led this union of skilled and long-term African railwaymen since the mid-1930s, and he was an active member of Lamine Gueye's socialist party, the Section Française de l'Internationale Ouvrière (SFIO). His union was the most important group of workers to refuse to participate in the 1946 general strike. His socialist affiliations – the socialists were then in the government in France – were a major factor inhibiting his room to maneuver. It was not a popular stance.[4] As early as December 1945, railwaymen at a meeting in Thiès were talking about a strike, in opposition to Gning.[5] This did not come off, but after the Dakar general strike, Gning and his Comité Directeur decided to start a strike fund, part as sensible preparation, part as delaying tactic. He hoped that 'the example furnished by the groups that recently

[3] Frederick Cooper, 'The Senegalese General Strike of 1946 and the labor question in post-war French Africa', *Can. J. Afr. Studies*, XXIV (1990), 165–215 and 'Le mouvement ouvrier et le nationalisme: la grève générale du 1946 et la grève des cheminots de 1947–48', *Historiens et Géographes du Sénégal*, VI (1991), 32–42.

[4] There was considerable discontent on the railway in the period before the Dakar strike. Renseignements, 9, 27 Apr. 1943, 7 Sept. 1944, 27 Feb. 1945, 11 D 1/1392.

[5] Governor General to Minister, 19 Jan. 1946, 17 G 132. The other side of Gning's connections was that, from 1944 until his dethronement in 1946, he had access to the Governor General and negotiated a number of concessions for the railwaymen. Renseignements, Thiès, 30 Aug., 1, 4 Sept. 1944, K 329 (26); Renseignements, 10 Jan. 1946, and Directeur du Réseau, transcript of meeting of Conseil du Réseau, 24 Jan. 1946, K 328 (26).

went on strike will allow railwaymen to reflect on the gravity of an act which constitutes a two-edged sword'.[6]

Politics and trade unionism came together in the opposition to Gning's maneuverings in the principal railway junction and repair center at Thiès. In April 1946, officials reported agitation among the railway workers, who felt they had not received what they deserved from their restraint during the general strike. In May, security officials learned that a movement to oust Gning was being organized by a group from the Union des Jeunes de Thiès, who were also active members of the railway union. Here developed an extraordinary conjuncture of the political ideals of a group of young, educated men and a workforce that was largely non-literate. From mid-1945, the Union des Jeunes was led by a clerk (Abdoul Karim Sow) and a school teacher (Mory Tall), and included several people with clerical jobs on the railway. Its goals were simultaneously political, cultural and intellectual – to promote our 'general development', one leader recalled.[7] Its meetings brought out a youthful vigor against the perceived lethargy of older Senegalese politicians and a new combativeness toward the French, even though neither it – nor any other significant political group – was at this time calling for independence.[8] Its attacks were highly personal – the Commandant de Cercle at Thiès was a target – and the administration replied in kind by transferring Tall to a remote northern town, where he promptly organized another Union des Jeunes. The organization published a newsletter, *Jeunesse et Démocratie*, and entered a complicated dialogue with the local section of the SFIO, also led by Gning. It alternated between criticism of the doyen of Senegalese socialist politicians, Lamine Gueye, and attempts to make up with him.[9] The aggressive moves of the 'Jeunes' to remake politics within the SFIO at Thiès led Gning to resign in frustration as its Secretary General.[10]

Gning was a Catholic and his mentor, Lamine Gueye, while Muslim like

[6] Syndicat des Travailleurs Indigènes du Dakar-Niger, Circulaire no. 10, 1 Feb. 1946, signed by Gning, in K 325 (26).

[7] Mory Tall, interview, Thiès, 9 Aug. 1994, by Aminata Diena, Biram NDour, Alioune Ba and Frederick Cooper.

[8] Tall told an early meeting of the 'Jeunes' of the need to 'bring about in a short time a complete assimilation in all domains with Europeans and a larger participation of the indigenous element in the administration of the country'. The union apparently began as an offshoot led by the militant Tall against the conservative Gning within yet another of the discussion-cum-political groups of the immediate post-war years, the Comité d'Etudes Franco-Africaines. Renseignements, 26 June 1945, 11 D 1/1396. The Comité faded while the union took off. Chef du 2e Secteur de la Sûreté to Commandant de Cercle, 13 Oct. 1945, 11 D 1/1396.

[9] Commissaire de Police, Thiès, to Commandant de Cercle, Thiès, 22 Aug., 27, 28 Sept. 1945; Renseignements, Thiès, 3 Dec. 1945, 11 Sept. 1946; Commissaire de Police to Chef de la Sûreté du Sénégal, 22 Nov. 1945; Commandant de Cercle, note for Governor of Senegal, 26 Apr. 1946; Chef du 2e Secteur de la Sûreté to Chef de la Sûreté du Sénégal, 20 July, 13 Nov. 1945; Note by Chef de la Police Spéciale du Réseau Dakar-Niger, 7 Aug. 1945, in 11 D 1/1396. The Union des Jeunes established contacts with Léopold Senghor and felt they had his sympathy despite his unwillingness at the time to follow them in criticizing his mentor, Lamine Gueye. Renseignements, 17 May 1946, 11 D 1/1396.

[10] Commissaire de Police to Commandant de Cercle, 28 Sept. 1945, 11 D 1/1396; Renseignements, 22 Sept. 1945, 11 D 1/1392.

most peasants and workers, was from the old élite of the Quatre Communes, which had long enjoyed French citizenship and were seen to be distant by most rural Senegalese. The leaders of the Union des Jeunes were Muslim, and one of them, Ibrahima Sarr, came from a family with connections to marabouts, the leaders of the Muslim brotherhoods which held great influence in rural Senegal. Sarr was also well educated: a graduate of a leading trade school, *écrivain* in the *cadre local supérieure* since 1938.[11]

Gning, an *évolué* conscious of having earned his privileges, was unable to assimilate one of the basic lessons of the January 1946 strike: that workers of all levels were laying claim to basic entitlements. He would not attack the privilege of the top cadres, thinking it inconceivable that an ordinary worker 'receive the same indemnities as a Governor'.[12]

Following their attacks on Gning in the Thiès section of the SFIO, the militants of the Union des Jeunes spearheaded a 'revolution' within the railway union, attacking Gning's non-combative approach, his failure to join the successful 1946 strike, and his alienation of non-élite workers.[13] After meetings of the Comité Directeur, demonstrations calling for Gning's resignation, and a public meeting of 1,000 railwaymen at Thiès on 23 May 1946 at which he was repeatedly denounced, Gning resigned. Ibrahima Sarr took over, installing a Comité Directeur largely led by other clerks but including representation of all divisions.[14]

[11] On Sarr's background, see Sene, 'Grève des cheminots'. His pre-strike activism in the Union des Jeunes was noted by police informants. See Chef du 2e Secteur de la Sûreté de Thiès to Commandant de Cercle, 9 July 1945, Note by Chef de la Police Spéciale du Réseau Dakar-Niger, 7 Aug. 1945, 11 D 1/1396. Sarr was listed in the latter document as one of the editors of *Jeunesse et Démocratie*. His connection to a leading Mouride marabout and its importance to the strikers was described by a well-informed strike veteran. Mansour Niang, interview, Dakar, 4 Aug. 1994, by Makhali NDiaye, Aminata Diena, Alioune Ba and Frederick Cooper.

[12] Renseignements, 6 Apr. 1946, K 328 (26); Renseignements, 14 May 1946, enclosing transcript of meeting of 4 May 1946 of Comité Directeur, K 352 (26). The director of the railway system, like Gning, thought that a progressive policy aimed at the élite of railway workers had 'produced fruit'. In particular, he argued that reforms of December 1945 which had opened up the *cadre secondaire* to Africans, who could compete for posts 'with equality of credentials or of merit', had contributed to the willingness of this élite to co-operate with the union leadership in keeping the rest of the personnel on the job during the January strike. These reforms had permitted 1,100 Africans (out of 20,000) to be examined for possible promotion into the *cadre secondaire*. Directeur du Réseau, Compte Rendu on the Conseil du Réseau, 24 Jan. 1946, K 328 (26).

[13] 'Revolution' was the word used by a strike veteran Adoulaye Souleye Sarr, interview, Thiès, 22 July 1990, by Mor Sene, Babacar Fall and Frederick Cooper. He pointed to the milieu of Thiès as the incubus of the revolution.

[14] Renseignements, 22, 23, 24, 25 May 1946, 11 D 1/1392. Gning bitterly attacked the 'conspiracies' of certain *écrivains* associated with the Union des Jeunes but accepted the will of the assembly, wishing the union well in trying to find a Secretary General 'more sincere' than he. Sarr had been transferred by the railway administration from Thiès to Dakar because of his activities in the Union des Jeunes, but the railway transferred him back so he could be near the union headquarters at Thiès, and he was promoted to the *cadre secondaire* on 1 Jan. 1947. Commissaire de Police to Chef de la Sûreté du Sénégal, 25 May 1946, 11 D 1/1392. For a list of members of the Comité Directeur, see Renseignements, 19 July 1946, 11 D 1/1392. This narrative and explanation is quite close to that given by informants, notably Oumar NDiaye, Amadou Bouta Gueye (interview, Thiès, 9 Aug. 1994), Mansour Niang (interview, 4 Aug. 1994), and Abdoulaye Souleye Sarr (interview, 22 July 1990).

Sarr's inaugural speech to the committee, in May 1946, printed and circulated to the men, was at the same time an attack on colonialism and a perceptive use and extension of the new French colonial rhetoric against the old. He called for

> the liberation of the worker, giving him sufficient means so that he can live honorably and relieving him, above all, of the singular and painful nightmare of uncertainty about the next day, in other words, the abolition of antiquated colonial methods condemned even by THE NEW AND TRUE FRANCE which wishes that all its children, at whatever latitude they may live, be equal in duties and rights and *that the recompense of labor be a function solely of merit and capacity.*[15]

The new union regime had a base to start: Gning's union was the oldest in French West Africa, and his connections to the Socialist Party and the Government General in 1936–8 and 1944–6 had brought some concessions without strikes. But Sarr was promising to remedy the union's greatest limitation since the 1930s. In fact, the most important railway strike in recent memory, at Thiès in 1938, had been conducted over the opposition of the union, and Gning's élitism had put the largest category of railway workers – the auxiliaries – outside of the union's embrace. Auxiliaries often worked for years if not a lifetime and many were highly skilled; but the railway limited the number of its permanent employees, the *cadres*, to increase its control and decrease its costs. In 1938, a dissident union of auxiliaries had challenged Gning as much as the railway. Their aggressive attempts to shut down the railway had ended in military violence and the fatal shooting of six strikers. The tragic incident was quickly exploited by rightists in Dakar and Paris to eliminate officials who had encouraged bargaining with African trade unions, and the labor movement remained all but dormant until the end of World War II.[16] Reviving his old union after the war, Gning soon learned that the world of labor had changed for good.

Sarr promised to bring auxiliaries and cadres into a single organization and a single struggle. The union's demands consistently had two dimensions: to equalize benefits for all railwaymen in the cadres with no distinctions of origin or race, and secondly to integrate all auxiliaries into the cadres. The demands were both about equity in compensation and about dignity, especially the dignity of lower-ranking workers. The ultimate demand was for a *cadre unique*, a single hierarchy defined by skill and seniority that would set aside the old distinctions of colonial/metropolitan and cadres/auxiliary.[17]

Sarr's other major achievement was to forge a French West Africa-wide

[15] Renseignements, 28 May 1946, K 352 (26); Sene, 'Grève des cheminots', 46. In July, Sarr and his colleagues, still fearing a comeback by Gning, played out an unpleasant little game: they threatened a strike unless the Direction of the railway transferred Gning away from Thiès. The demand was refused, but Sarr was put off by a promise to arrange a meeting with the Governor General and the moment passed. Renseignements, 27 July 1946, 17 G 527.

[16] Iba der Thiam, 'La grève des cheminots du Sénégal de Septembre 1938' (Mémoire de maîtrise, Université de Dakar, 1972).

[17] A month into his tenure, Sarr was criticized at a meeting of auxiliaries for not doing enough for them, and he responded with a meeting to assure them that he was and made the integration of all railwaymen into the *cadre unique* the main theme of his tour of the lines. Renseignements, 27 June, 2 July 1946, 11 D 1/1392. Abdoulaye Souleye Sarr recalled that in the early days lower ranking workers were called *travailleurs indigènes* rather than *cheminots* (interview, 22 July 1990).

movement. The *coup de main* that overthrew Gning had been very much a Thiès-centered event; a mass meeting was its climax. Thiès was a very special kind of place: residence and workplace were thoroughly integrated, and railwaymen from diverse parts of Senegal and the Soudan shared common conditions in this double sense; the bonds formed at Thiès in turn travelled up and down the rail line that ran from Dakar to Bamako. It was not clear at first that the new leaders had support along the line, let alone in the other systems of French West Africa. But within a month of his takeover, Sarr embarked on a series of visits, beginning with the Soudan in June 1946 and culminating in a tour of the other railway lines on the eve of the 1947 strike. He told everyone of his desire to end the distinction between cadres and auxiliaries, pleaded the common cause of the workers against the Federation-wide railway administration, and encouraged the payment of dues and contributions to the strike fund. The union organizations on the different lines brought themselves together as the Fédération des Syndicats des Cheminots Africains, and ceded central direction to the Comité Directeur of the Dakar-Niger branch, headquartered in Thiès. In February 1947, the Dakar-Niger branch claimed to have added over 700,000 francs to the fund of 92,000 left by the old leadership – it was ready for a test.[18]

All this took place against the background of what police reports often called 'effervescence' at various points in the West African railway system and in other professions as well. Dakar now seemed a center of calm, and the Governor General attributed this to the success workers had already achieved in that city. Short, localized strikes and strike threats were reported in Dahomey, Guinea and the Ivory Coast.[19] In 1947, in French West Africa as a whole, 164 collective conflicts were reported to the Inspection du Travail, although the vast majority was settled without incident and strikes focused on wage disputes. By then, 133 unions in the public sector and 51 in the private had been officially organized. In Dakar, 40 per cent of workers belonged to unions; by the next year, officials believed that 20 per cent of all wage workers in French West Africa had joined a union. The large majority of the unions affiliated to the Conféderation Générale du Travail

[18] Syndicat des Travailleurs Africains de la Région Dakar-Niger, Transcript of Assemblée Générale of 9 Feb. 1947, K 459 (179); Sene, 'Grève des cheminots', 47–50; Renseignements, 20 June, 2 July 1946, 11 D 1/1392. The politics of the unions in each line remain to be elucidated, as does the obvious question of why they were willing to cede so much control to Thiès. Some powerful personalities, notably Gaston Fiankan in the Ivory Coast, existed in the different lines. The Federation-wide organization paralleled efforts in the same years of individual trade unions to organize confederations first within each territory, then on the level of French West Africa. The Conféderation Générale du Travail was the most successful at forging this kind of centralized organization. AOF, Inspection Générale du Travail, Annual Reports, 1947, 1948.

[19] Governor General to Minister 20 Apr. and 19 June 1946, 17 G 132; Renseignements, Dahomey, June, July, Aug. 1946, and Report of the Gendarmerie Nationale, Porto Novo, 13 Aug. and 18 Sept. 1946, K 352 (26); Renseignements, Guinea, 1 July 1947, Aug. 1947, and Gendarmarie Nationale, Conakry, report, 1, 5 Aug. 1947, K 352(26); Renseignements, Soudan, 8 June 1946, 7 July, 3 Aug. 1947, K 352(26); Chef de la Région Abidjan-Niger to Directeur, Chemins de Fer de l'AOF, 20 Sept. 1946, 17 G 591; Ivory Coast, Police et Sûreté, Rapport Politique Mensuel, 3 Oct. 1946, and Renseignements, 6 May 1947, 17 G 139; Report of Commandant du Peloton de Marché d'Abidjan on strike movement at Tafiré (Korhogo), 16–17 Aug. 1946, 17 G 138.

(CGT), with the African confederation retaining considerable autonomy despite its affiliation with the communist-led, metropolitan organization. But the Fédération Syndicale des Cheminots remained autonomous of any of the central union organizations.[20]

The other side in the rail dispute was also changing, opening up uncertainty about the status of railwaymen as government employees just as civil servants achieved success in the strike of 1946. The railways had been under the Direction des Travaux Publics. Effective 17 July 1946, they were reorganized as the Régie des Chemins de Fer de l'Afrique Occidentale Française (AOF), which would today be called a parastatal organization and which was described at the time as an 'organization of public utility attached to the private sector and constrained to rules of industrial and commercial operations'. It was administered by a director, M. Cunéo, who reported to a Conseil d'Administration chaired by the Secretary General of the Government General and consisting of 16 members appointed by the administration, eight representatives of the Grand Conseil (the elected legislative body of French West Africa), five representatives of the workers (of whom three were named by the unions), and three representatives of the users of railway services. The board was autonomous in its position, but not in its majority membership, while the status of the Régie implied that its own financial condition – and not the resources of the Government General, or by extension, France – constrained its expenditures. The reorganization meant that railway workers would no longer benefit from a *statut*, as did civil servants, but would come under a *convention collective*, like the metal workers, the bakery workers or commercial workers. Railway workers could not automatically claim the gains acquired by the civil service, and railway officials had an excuse for not responding to political pressure. The Régie became a distinct battleground, consistent with the government's overall strategy of regaining initiative after the unified mobilization it had faced in the general strike of 1946.[21]

The Régie's personnel was organized hierarchically, in a manner parallel to the bureaucracy: the *cadre supérieur* was entirely European, the *cadre commun supérieur* mostly so. The *cadre secondaire* was mixed and the *cadre local* was, essentially, African. All the cadres were either housed or received equivalent indemnities; the indemnities of zone and for family charges were highly skewed toward the superior, largely European, cadres. But most important, the auxiliaries did not receive housing or indemnities; they could be fired for minor offences; they were in many respects treated like temporary workers even though most served for years. And they were the large majority of railway personnel. In 1946, the railway employed 478

[20] AOF, Inspection Générale du Travail (IGT), Annual Report, 1947, 56–9; *ibid.*, 1948, 83. One reason the railwaymen shied away from the CGT or other *centrales* was that white railwaymen were mostly in the CGT, and their overt racism and unwillingness to make common cause with Africans was not a strong advertisement for solidarity. Jean Suret-Canale, 'The French West African railway workers' strike, 1947–48', in Robin Cohen, Jean Copans and Peter C. W. Gutkind (eds.), *African Labor History* (Beverly Hills, CA, 1978), 152, n. 8.

[21] AOF, IGT, Annual Report, 1947, 60–1; Sene, 'Grève des cheminots', 16. The importance to strikers of the *statut* issue was emphasized by Mansour Niang (interview 4 Aug. 1994).

Europeans and 1,729 Africans in the various cadres, plus 15,726 auxiliaries.[22] This structure was very difficult to defend in principle – but useful in practice, especially given the precedent set by government cadres in 1946. Government officials, however, did see that a more coherent structure might offer possibilities of reducing the staffing level of the railway. The direction of the railway agreed: they wanted a smaller and more efficient staff – realizing that the days of the derisorily paid multitude were ending – and they wanted the unions to co-operate.[23] There was room for bargaining.

In August 1946 the Fédération des Travailleurs Africains submitted its demands for a *cadre unique* and for the integration, over time, of the permanently employed auxiliaries into the cadre. The Governor General, under current labor law, appointed a Commission Paritaire, in which representatives of the two sides discussed the issues dividing them. Between December and April, twenty rounds of bargaining were held, most of them 'confused, tedious, broken up by stormy discussions'. Unions representing European workers made the procedures more divisive by their overt defense of racial privilege and rejection of the *cadre unique*. In April 1947, the African union, its demands unmet, staged a theatrical coup: it withdrew from the Commission Paritaire and staged a strike at the moment when the President of France and the Colonial Minister – Marius Moutet – were visiting Senegal.[24]

The three-day strike – throughout French West Africa – was a brilliant maneuver, and it appeared to have worked.[25] Under the pressure of Moutet's presence – as well as that of Governor General Barthes, Lamine Gueye, Léopold Senghor, and other luminaries – the parties agreed on the necessity to create a *cadre unique*, but also to reduce the staffing level of the railway, with the layoffs to be worked out by another Commission Paritaire which would consider seniority and skill. The creation of the *cadre unique* would require working out a table of equivalencies, so that people would be slotted into the correct positions.[26]

[22] AOF, Direction Générale des Travaux Publics, Direction des Chemins de Fer et Transports, Annual Report, 1946, quoted in Suret-Canale, 'Railway workers' strike', 152, n. 5.

[23] This was precisely the kind of thinking that emerged from the 1946 general strike. Cooper, "The Senegalese General Strike'.

[24] Inspecteur Général du Travail, 'La Grève des Cheminots de l'AOF (1/10/47–16/3/48)', IGT 13/2; AOF, IGT, Annual Report, 1947, 60; Renseignements, 19 Aug. 1946, 11 D 1/1392; Suret-Canale, 'Railway workers' strike', 134–5. Sarr, in explaining the withdrawal from the Commission, told an assembly of workers on 9 February, 'The "toubabs", in perfect unity, lined up against us in the Commission Paritaire'. He and others complained of the racist comments continuously made by representatives of European workers in the commission, and warned of 'a battle with the Europeans'. The latter phrase was used by Mody Camara. Renseignements, 1, 10 Feb. 1947, K 377 (26).

[25] Police spies reported on a series of meetings at Thiès in early April at which the strike was planned: leaders calculated that high officials would accept union claims to avoid the embarrassment of having their President witness an ongoing strike. There were also rumors that 3,000 Africans were about to lose their jobs, and the strike thus had a defensive element to it. Renseignements, 11, 13 Apr. 1947, and Gendarmerie Nationale, Thiès, Rapport, 14 Apr. 1947, K 377 (26). For reports on the strike, see telegrams from the Governors of Dahomey, the Ivory Coast, Guinea and the Soudan, 20–23 Apr. 1947, *ibid.*

[26] Protocole de fin de grève, 19 Apr. 1947, K 377 (26).

The acceptance of this protocol suggests that the highest levels of the government were unwilling to contest the principle of the *cadre unique* and the integration of auxiliaries. They did not want to defend overtly the discriminatory structure of a colonial labor force against the universalistic claim to equality among all workers. In April, the most far-reaching issue seemed theoretically solved. The issues over which the October strike was to be fought were less than earthshaking; the Director of the Régie later referred to them as 'points of detail'.[27] The real issue was power: who was to control the process by which new modalities of labor organization would be worked out?

In the months after April, two developments took place. The worsening economic situation in metropolitan and overseas France led to a renewed attempt by officials to hold down prices and wages throughout the French domains, the first attempt in Africa having failed during the 1946 strike. In late April and May, Governors General were told to avoid a 'general readjustment of wages of a profession'. Despite fears of renewed general strikes, officials on the scene had to push for restraint.[28] The wages of railwaymen were a major factor in the cost of goods exported and imported. In August, the railway claimed that its 1947 budget was in the red and that the integration of around 2,000 auxiliaries into the cadre would more than triple the deficit and require a 130 per cent increase in railway rates in order to bring it back to equilibrium, in lieu of which a subsidy from the government would have to be forthcoming.[29]

Secondly, in May 1947, the coalition governing France changed. The Communist Party was formally expelled, and a Center-Left coalition took power, although Moutet remained Colonial Minister until November. This meant that certain kinds of debates and certain kinds of compromises did not have to take place within the French government. The new Cabinet did not overtly reverse past labor or imperial policy – it remained committed to rationalizing the workplace and working for a Code du Travail – but it was more open to other sorts of imperatives. In metropolitan France, a bitter railway strike promptly ensued.[30]

Although the Conseil d'Administration of the Régie des Chemins de Fer overlapped in membership and personnel with the Commission Paritaire that had negotiated the agreement of April, it voted in August to reject the accord. This kind of contradiction was in fact part of what the creation of the Régie was all about: government-appointed members put on their parastatal hats, pleaded autonomy and fiscal accountability, and sent the agreement into limbo.[31]

For the union, this was nothing less than a betrayal. By summer's end, Sarr was mobilizing forces for a strike, and angry workers were even

[27] Note sur la proposition de loi présentée par M Mamadou Konaté tendant à la création d'un cadre unique des chemins de fer de l'AOF, incl. Cunéo to Governor General 30 Mar. 1950, K 43(1).

[28] Circular signed by Secretary General Marat (for Minister) to Hauts Commissaires, 29 Apr. 1947. For warnings of a general strike, see Inspecteur du Travail Combier (Senegal), Note d'étude, 17 Apr. 1947, and letter to Secretary General, 13 May 1947, IGT 13/4. [29] Note sur l'équilibre financier de la Régie, 12 Aug. 1947, K 459 (179).

[30] Marie-Renée Valentin, 'Les grèves des cheminots français au cours de l'année 1947', *Le Mouvement Social*, CXXX (1985), 55–80. [31] Sene, 'Grève des cheminots', 55–7.

criticizing him for not doing so forcefully enough.[32] They had to cross muddied waters to define issues: the call for a *cadre unique* was a dramatic demand for equal conditions of work – linking the feelings of workers who experienced racial discrimination on a daily basis with the assimilationist rhetoric of the French state – but the other side responded by both accepting and rejecting the *cadre unique*. The union's demand that railwaymen of all ranks be paid the indemnity of zone (the supplement to wages intended to offset geographical differences in cost of living) at the same rate rather than at rates favoring the top ranks was met not with denial but with claims that perhaps the indemnity of zone was a bad idea and should be eliminated for all workers.[33] The issue of integrating auxiliaries into the cadres was not contested either, but issues of effective dates and the standards for integration (general versus selective) were pressed by the Régie.[34] Officially, the disputed issues boiled down to: the effective date for integrating auxiliaries into the cadres; how workers were to be reclassified in forming the *cadre unique*; where examination barriers were to be set for promotions; conditions for leaves; which employees would receive housing; and whether the indemnity of zone would be uniform or would depend on rank.

At the beginning of September, Sarr told an assembly at Thiès that 'The colonialist spirit of the Europeans has once again revealed to us its force'. He explained the detailed issues in dispute. With unanimous agreement, a strike date was set for 10 October. He persuaded proponents of an immediate strike that it was first necessary to make the rounds of the railway depots – including the Ivory Coast, Guinea and Dahomey – and he soon set off on his journey. The Ivoirien union leader, Gaston Fiankan, declared that the Abidjan-Niger region would join the Dakar-Niger in the strike, and he was soon holding meetings in various locations in the Ivory Coast to consolidate support. As Sarr went off to prosyletize the Soudan, French security reported 'Up to now, he is getting confidence and unanimity for the strike along the entire line'. Returning from the Soudan, Sarr appeared before another assembly at Thiès attended by, according to police, 7,000 people. Awaiting him, the crowd beat drums, engaged in 'wild dances' and waved three big French flags. He was escorted to the meeting by cyclists and arrived amidst cries of 'Vive Sarr'.[35]

Just before the strike deadline – on October 7 by one account – Léopold Senghor came to Thiès to meet in private with the Comité Directeur. He told them he was with them in their struggle. Lamine Gueye, meanwhile, already had a strained relationship with the current union leadership and had had an ugly confrontation in Thiès with the 'Jeunes' when he tried to reconcile

[32] Renseignements, 25 Aug. 1947, K 377 (26).

[33] Governor General to Minister, 28 June, 16 Sept. 1947, K 459 (179). This indemnity could rise as high as 7/10 of the base wage; it was a *de facto* mechanism for equalizing base wages while maintaining substantial inequalities. The Governor General claimed to be thinking about suppressing this for civil servants – which would set a precedent, although technically no more than that, for railway workers – and replacing it with an indemnity of residence which would apply only to high-cost areas and apply without distinction of rank or origin. The Governor General, however, feared that opening up this issue raised the possibility of a general strike throughout the civil service and railways.

[34] Mémoire of Régie for the Comité Arbitral, 27 Oct. 1947, K 459 (179).

[35] Renseignements, Thiès, 1, 11 Sept. 1947, and Renseignements, Ivory Coast, 16, 18 Sept., 1947, K 377 (26); Sûreté, Synthèse mensuelle, Oct. 1947, 17 G 527.

them with Gning after Sarr's coup in the railway union. Gueye, according to informants, was willing to talk to the union leaders, but he warned them of the dangers of a strike rather than giving his support. The strikers would remember the difference, even though Senghor failed to back the strikers publicly as he had in private.[36]

The Governor General talked to the union leaders on the eve of the strike and tried to intimidate them. The Inspection du Travail made a last ditch attempt at conciliation. The union felt it had fulfilled all the preconditions for a legal strike by virtue of the fact that it had been jumping through hoops for over a year; officials claimed that these were not the hoops prescribed by law and that the dispute should go to arbitration over the listed items in dispute. An arbitrator and the arbitration appeal panel eventually did hear the case and made their rulings later in the month. This action was too little, too late, and without waiting for the hearing, the union began its strike as planned on 10 October throughout all branches of the railway in French West Africa and on the wharfs in Dahomey and the Ivory Coast under the Régie's jurisdiction. The walkout was virtually complete among the 17,000 railwaymen and 2,000 workers at the wharfs, and it remained that way: on 1 November, 38 Africans were on the job.[37]

SOLIDARITY AND SURVIVAL

Reading police reports – several per day during the five and a half months of the strike – reveals some of its remarkable features: the union's largely successful attempt to preserve unity until January, when the Abidjan-Niger region defected, but the other regions held solid; the fear of the administration that the hiring of strikebreakers or other repressive measures would provoke reactions which it could not control, and its delay for a month before it tried – with only marginal success – to reconstitute a work force and increase traffic; the slowness of African politicians and political parties – and the new institutions of the Union Française – to take cognizance of this act of enormous political and economic importance until the strike was three months old; and the way in which the struggle, as it wore on, became more and more about the strike itself, and its ending reflected the fact that each side had proved its toughness and was ready for the next round – and the next form – of contestation.[38]

The most fascinating question about the conduct of the strike – how such a large and diverse body of workers maintained themselves physically and as a coherent force – requires further investigation. Asked this question, informants stress solidarity within the railway community, connections to farmers, merchants and others in a position to help, and good preparation by

[36] I have not seen any mention of the meeting with Senghor in the archives – apparently the police spies missed this one. It was reported independently by two knowledgeable informants in Thiès, Amadou Bouta Gueye and Oumar NDiaye (interviews, 9 Aug. 1994). It is conceivable that the railway union's later support for Senghor is being pushed backwards, but these informants (both *délégués du personnel* at the time) are quite specific about this meeting. On Gueye's clash with the Union des Jeunes, see Renseignements, 27 May 1946, 11 D 1/1392.

[37] Governor General to Minister, 11 Oct. 1947, IGT 13/2; AOF, IGT, Annual Report, 1947, 62.

[38] For a narrative approach to the strike, see Sene, 'Grève des cheminots'.

the union itself (see below). The question obviously puzzled officials – who were predicting the strike's imminent collapse from its first days to its final months – and the most perspicacious official accounts reached a surprising and frightening conclusion.

The security services gradually learned that railwaymen had a complex web of affiliation within the communities in which they lived. A police spy overheard reports to a meeting at Thiès of a strike official's tour of Senegalese depot towns: at Kaolack a 'humble cultivator gives us 400F'; at Tambacounda, the merchant El Hadj Abou Sy gave sheep to the railwaymen, and local notables, marabouts and merchants offered 20,000 francs and ten tons of millet; at Guinguinéo investigation of a rumor that the marabouts were hostile to the strike proved false, and the strikers' emissary found that the entire population 'is with us with no reserve'.[39] In fact, the leading marabouts of the Islamic confraternities of Senegal – who were close to the administration – used their influence against the strike but closer to ground level the religious organization seems to have been more supportive.[40] Informants claim that marabouts would not support the strike in public but that many were either supportive or neutral in private.[41]

Other reports suggested that merchants in Senegal played a particularly important role in providing assistance, in the form of money, food and trucks to transport food. This was particularly so in Thiès where the health of almost the entire business community depended on the custom of railwaymen.[42] The newspaper *L'AOF*, read by many *évolués*, publicized a collection drive to benefit railwaymen: it reached 134,615 francs in late November and 454,555 by mid-December.[43] The union, according to an informant, channelled its strike funds to men with families, figuring that single men could improvise more easily.[44]

In Abidjan, the Ivory Coast railway union issued an 'Appeal to Africans' in late October and asked 'all black associations' to provide material aid. In November, the union was providing 300 francs to any needy striker who asked for it. 200,000 francs had been paid out in Abidjan, 100,000 each at

[39] Renseignements, 19 Nov. 1947, K 378 (26).

[40] The Grand Marabout of Tivaouane, Ababacar Sy, told a religious meeting in January 1948, 'France is good and generous', and workers would get satisfaction only if they politely asked their employers after having accomplished their tasks. 'God the all-powerful has said he will never help his "slave" who, in demanding things impolitely and with hatred, puts forward his desire to possess'. Renseignements, 26 Jan. 1948, K 379 (26). The powerful marabout Seydou Nourou Tall also worked against the strike. Renseignements, 29 Oct. 1947, K 457 (179).

[41] Of the leading marabouts, Cheikh Mbacke is mentioned as having been supportive, but the tolerance of lower level marabouts is what was stressed most in interviews. Informants stressed their personal acquaintance with marabouts at the time. Oumar NDiaye and Amadou Bouta Gueye (interviews, 9 Aug. 1994) and Mansour Niang (interview, 4 Aug. 1994).

[42] Renseignements, 14 Nov. 1947, K 457 (179). A list of donors published in *Réveil*, 20 Nov. 1947, also listed a number of local politicians, merchants and union groups in railway towns such as Diourbel and Kaolack, as well as Dakar and Thiès. Informants noted the importance of merchants' help: Oumar NDiaye and Amadou Bouta Gueye (interviews, 9 Aug. 1994), Mansour Niang (interview, 4 Aug. 1994).

[43] *L'AOF*, 25 Nov., 12 Dec. 1947. The newspaper gave considerable coverage to the strike, although its patron, Lamine Gueye, took a hands-off position throughout its course.

[44] Oumar NDiaye (interview, 9 Aug. 1994).

Port-Bouet, Grand-Bassam, Agboville and Dimbokro.[45] Such support was not unanimous – some citizens of Abidjan refused to donate because the strike had deprived them of meat – but it was substantial.[46] At Conakry, in Guinea, the union appealed to Lebanese shop-owners and African civil servants. According to the police, 'The majority of merchants and civil servants (Customs, post and telephone, auxiliary doctors) have contributed sums between 300 and 500 francs'.[47] In Dahomey, the Inspection du Travail thought that the mass did not look favorably on the strikers but they nonetheless were receiving 'loans of considerable magnitude for their strike fund, coming not only from notables or autochthonous groups, but also from certain Europeans'. The Governor thought that the *évolués* were supportive because the claims for equal indemnities with Europeans struck a chord with them.[48]

Railwaymen did a great deal themselves to organize food provisions. Most workers had not cut themselves off from their rural roots. They had family members who farmed and could either provide a place for strikers to return to or directly supply them with grain or fish. Interviews in 1990 and 1994 underscored the importance of the family mechanism in sustaining the strikers.[49] Union leaders told many workers to return to their villages to reduce the burden for feeding those who remained in the depot towns. Near the smaller stations along the lines, railwaymen sometimes had their own fields and could devote their energies to growing their food as the strike wore on.[50]

Women clearly played a major role in the strike, although one female informant distinguished between their participation in the violent strike of 1938 – where she and other women passed stones to male strikers who threw them at police and strikebreakers – and their role in the non-violent, carefully controlled strike of 1947. Testimonies so far collected stress the role of women within family units – their efforts to find food, their work in market-selling or other non-wage activites to sustain family income.[51] They composed songs supporting the strike and its leaders and taunted strike breakers: their position in railway communities created an atmosphere where *défaillants* (strike breakers) would not want to live. This is a subject which requires further investigation, but it appears less likely that women acted as

[45] Renseignements, 31 Oct., 7 Nov. 1947, K 379 (26).

[46] Renseignements, 10 Nov. 1947, K 379 (26).

[47] Renseignements, Coyah, 20 Dec. 1947, K 379 (26).

[48] Inspection du Travail, Dahomey, to IGT, 4 Nov. 1947, K 457 (179).

[49] Adboulaye Souleye Sarr (interview, 22 July 1990), Amadou Bouta Gueye and Oumar Ndiaye (interview, 9 Aug. 1994), Mansour Niang (interview, 4 Aug. 1994).

[50] Renseignements, Thiès, 4 Dec. 1947, and Ivory Coast, 9 Nov. 1947, K379 (26); IGT, AOF (Pierre Pélisson), Report on Strike, 24 Jan. 1948, IGT, 13/2; Abdoulaye Soulaye Sarr, (interview, 22 July 1990).

[51] Khady Dia, who sold peanuts by the Thiès train station, compared the role of women in the two strikes. Interview, Thiès, 9 Aug. 1994, by Aminata Diena, Alioune Ba, Oumar Gueye and Frederick Cooper. Abdoulaye Souleye Sarr (interview, 22 July 1990), Oumar NDiaye and Amadou Bouta Gueye (interviews, 9 Aug. 1994) also suggested that Sembene may have elided the role of women in the two strikes. Informants call the 1938 strike 'la grève de Diack', after its leader Cheik Diack, while the 1947–8 strike is known as 'la grève de Sarr'. All informants stress the importance of women's efforts to sustain families during the long strike.

a distinct entity – let alone that such an entity was led by someone from the margins of Muslim society like Sembene's character Penda – than that they acted as parts of families and communities. Sembene's women's march is absent from oral testimonies and the police record. It remains to be seen how much their actions in turn affected the way these structures operated and altered the meanings of gender within laboring communities, as well as the extent to which the increasing value and security of male wage packets changed power relations within households.[52]

The union itself had realized in its preparations for the strike that the supply question would be crucial. There already existed a *co-operative indigène* headquartered at Thiès and Bamako, which constituted a kind of bulk-buying organization for railway workers. On the eve of the strike, the co-operative leaders, close to the union leadership, had stocked their stores. The strike – not by coincidence – occurred at the end of the harvest season when supplies were at their best. During the strike, the co-operative supplied food and other necessaries to strikers on credit – afterward officials reported the co-operative 1,560,000 francs in debt for food delivered before or during the strike. 'During the entire strike the co-operative sustained you', appealed Sarr to union members as he tried to raise money to pay off the debt.[53] A strike committee official boasted to a meeting at Thiès, with a dig at the marabouts of the Mouride brotherhood, about the work of the co-operative: 'Now ... that we have assured our supplies and have for certain a little money, we are like the 'Cheikh Mourides' [Mouride marabouts]; we do not work but we have our provisions; we thus have people who work for us, it is Allah who is with us'.[54]

In January, three months into the strike, Pierre Pélisson, the head of the Inspection du Travail in French West Africa, reached a startling conclusion about the ability of Africans to conduct a long strike: 'Here the means of defense are very different – and singularly more effective – than in the case of metropolitan strikes because the roots of the labor force are deeper and its

[52] It is hardly likely that the extensive network of police spies would have missed a public event like a march of women from Thiès to Dakar. Sembene's account was specifically denied by Abdoulaye Souleye Sarr (interview, 22 July 1990) and Amadou Bouta Gueye (interview, 9 Aug. 1994), and contradicted by Khady Dia (interview, 9 Aug. 1994). There is a report from December 1947 that when eight workers decided to return to work at Thiès 'a band of women and children gathered in front of their (the returnees') homes and began to insult and threaten them', so that the ex-strikers had to wait for the police to disperse the crowd before reporting to work. Gendarmarie Nationale, Thiès, Report, 23 Dec. 1947, K 379 (26). See also Sene, 'Grève des cheminots', 91, who cites an interview with Mame Fatou Diop, on the importance of songs and the taunting of strike breakers. For a literary analysis of women in Sembene's novel, see F. Case, 'Workers' movements: revolution and women's consciousness in *God's Bits of Wood*', *Can. J. of Afr. Studies*, xv (1981), 277–92.

[53] Renseignements, Thiès, 26 Oct. 1947, K 43 (1); Renseignements, Thiès, 17 Sept. 1948, 5 Aug. 1949, 11 D 1/1392; Abdoulaye Souleye Sarr (interview, 22 July 1990); Jacques Ibrahima Gaye, article in *L'AOF*, 17 Oct. 1947, clipping in K 457 (179).

[54] N'Diaye Sidya, quoted in Renseignements, 29 Oct. 1947, K 457 (179). Food supply became part of the struggle between the two sides. The co-operative supplied food only to strikers, not to railwaymen who went back to work, and officials thought this a major reason why few workers went back to work on the Dakar-Niger. The Régie tried itself to organize the delivery of rice from the Soudan to railwaymen at Thiès and Dakar who went back to work. IGT, AOF, to Deputy Dumas, 6 Jan. 1948, K457 (179).

needs less imperious in Africa than in Europe'.[55] Pélisson had been taught an important lesson: the degree of proletarianization was not an accurate measure of the power of strikers, and the success of the strike lay in the integration of the strikers into the strikers' own communities.

PROLETARIANS, POLITICIANS AND MOBILIZATION BEYOND THE RAILWAY

It was in regard to other proletarians that the solidarity of the strike movement was the most ambiguous. Pélisson noticed this too, writing that most wage workers outside the railway distanced themselves from railwaymen, and the latter 'have not benefited from their effective support but only from habitual demonstrations of sympathy'. In Dakar, wage workers were in the midst of peaceful negotiations over another round of wage revisions; no general strike movement emerged in support of the railwaymen.[56]

At times, it looked as if the solidarity of the railwaymen would take on an even wider dimension. In early November the Commission Administrative of the Union des Syndicats de Dakar discussed what to do to support the strikers. The leading veterans of the 1946 strike, Abbas Gueye and Lamine Diallo, tried to convince a 'reticent assembly' of the need for a general strike. They pointed out to civil servants in particular that they shared a fundamental interest in a unified indemnity of zone. But other speakers pushed for 'more moderate' approaches, such as protest meetings, collections of funds and delegations to the Governor General, and it was the latter position which prevailed.[57] In Guinea, the Union Régionale Syndicale de Guinée passed a motion of support for the railwaymen, 'whose demands were theirs as well'. But there was no common action for the common demands.[58] In the Ivory Coast in November, the Union Locale des Syndicats, affiliated to the CGT, decided 'that it could not support the action of the railway union because [it was] not affiliated to the CGT'.[59] Around that time, some civil service unions were thinking about a general strike, but they would not act until they heard from the Rassemblement Démocratique Africaine and its leader Houphouët-Boigny. They were to get no encouragement from him.[60]

The trade union movement, in West Africa and in France, did better by the railwaymen in a financial sense. CGT unions in the region contributed, according to a French CGT source, about two million francs. The National Solidarity Committee of the CGT in France gave 500,000, while other contributions came from French railway unions and another CGT bureau. The RDA in the Ivory Coast gave 350,000 – although its support became increasingly suspect.[61]

What other unions and political parties did not do was organize sympathy strikes, stage large demonstrations or otherwise try to turn the strike into a wider social and political movement. The lack of common action is all the more notable because there was considerable trade union anger at the time

[55] IGT, Report, 24 Jan. 1948, IGT 13/2. [56] *Ibid.*
[57] Report of meeting, 4 Nov. 1947, K 379 (26); Renseignements, 7 Nov. 1947, K 457 (179). [58] Resolution of Union Régionale de Guinée, 18 Nov. 1947, K 379 (26).
[59] Governor, Ivory Coast, to Governor General, 21 Nov. 1947, K 237 (26).
[60] Renseignements, Ivory Coast, 9 Nov. 1947, K 379 (26).
[61] Suret-Canale, 'Railway workers' strike', 147.

of the strike over the withdrawal by a new Minister of Overseas France of a Code du Travail which Moutet had tried to implement by decree just before he left office in November 1947.[62] But the causes never were linked, the Code protests fizzled, and the Code debate disappeared into French political institutions for another five years.

Some trade unionists in Senegal were reluctant to lend their support to railway workers in 1947 because railwaymen had not helped them during the general strike of 1946. Moreover, the civil service, metal trades, commerce and industry unions were now engaged in regular negotiations through institutions set up as a result of that strike. As the annual reports of the Inspection du Travail make clear, the 1947–8 railway strike stands out in both years, during which disputes were narrowly focused and easily contained within existing negotiating frameworks. The fact that most of the concessions made to civil servants in Dakar were extended to other parts of French West Africa, and the spread of Dakar-type agreements to other key businesses in West Africa changed the politics of labor on a wide scale. Focusing the labor question on union-management relations within each branch of industry, commerce or government and making workers less inclined toward another venture in solidarity had been the Inspection's strategy since January 1946, and Pélisson recognized even in the midst of the railway strike that the strategy was working.[63]

The relationship of the railwaymen to organized politics was equally ambiguous. The RDA, which like the railway crossed territorial borders, maintained its distance. In the run up to the strike, Sûreté thought that the RDA was fighting against the strike call, hoping that its failure would lead to Sarr's ouster and open up the autonomous union to takeover by pro-RDA leaders.[64] In February 1948, the *Voix de la RDA*, published in Dakar, saw fit to rebut a charge that the strike had been called by the RDA by writing, 'Sarr, the federal secretary of the railway union, whose courage and combativity we admire, is not RDA'. The newspaper insisted that it respected 'trade union independence', and that while it agreed with the demands of the union, 'We had the courage to declare to the railwaymen: on the local level we could do nothing. It was the business of the railwaymen and only the railwaymen to take up their responsibilities'. It claimed that the RDA had tried in the metropole to bring pressure on the government to settle the strike and blamed its opponents for the failure of that initiative.[65]

This article probably represented the view of the RDA leadership in

[62] At the Grand Conseil, Senghor noted the 'emotion the suspension of the application of the Code du Travail raised among workers' and urged legislative action. *Bulletin du Grand Conseil*, 29 Jan. 1948, 277–8. See also Renseignements, 19, 28 Jan. 1948, K 439 (179); Directeur des Affaires Politiques, Note pour M. le Ministre, 20 Dec. 1947, AP 2255/1. For more on the Code, see Frederick Cooper, *Decolonization and African Society: The Labor Question in French and British Africa*, forthcoming ch. 7.

[63] IGT, Report, 24 Jan. 1948, IGT 13/2. The 1948 Annual Report of the Inspection du Travail for French West Africa (90) termed the railway strike 'the only important collective conflict' of the year. It claimed credit for the 'favorable evolution' of the situation. There were many more disputes registered with the Inspection in 1947, but they had not led to many serious strikes, a fact for which the Inspection also took credit. *Ibid.* 1947, 59.

[64] Renseignements, 1 Sept. 1947, K 377 (26).

[65] *La Voix de la RDA* was published regularly as a special section of the *communisant* Dakar newspaper, *Réveil*. This article appeared in no. 283, 5 Feb. 1948.

Dakar. The leading light of the party, Houphouët-Boigny was playing a more complicated game. Security officials kept hearing reports of Houphouët-Boigny's covert opposition to the strike. In early November, they reported he had told the strike committee 'that the deputies from French West Africa had not been consulted before the breaking out of this strike, inopportune at this time of year, and that as a result he was not going to be mixed up in their affair'. Two weeks later, security reported, 'In his house, last Sunday, the deputy Houphouët had said to his friends that the strikers have not acted skillfully, that they should have accepted the advantages conceded in the course of this strike, gone back to work in order to renew their demands later and obtain the "full rate" (the full indemnity of zone) by successive steps'. At that point, he said he would go to Dakar to see what he could do.[66]

In Dakar he sang a different tune. Houphouët-Boigny told a meeting called by the Union des Syndicats Confédérés de l'AOF on 7 December that he and his RDA colleague Gabriel d'Arboussier pledged support to the railwaymen 'in their struggle against colonialism' and assured them of the 'presence of the RDA beside you to defend their demands which are legitimate'. The pro-RDA newspaper *Réveil* noted the absence at this meeting of the parliamentarians from Senegal (who were not RDA).[67]

But by this time most of the West African parliamentarians, Houphouët-Boigny included, were pursuing a goal which, however worthy, was not quite the same as the anti-colonialist rhetoric implied. At the time of the union meeting, Houphouët-Boigny and other deputies were in Dakar for the December–January meeting of the Grand Conseil de l'AOF, French West Africa's major deliberative body. They took advantage of their collective presence in Dakar to talk to leading officials and to try to persuade the Governor General to intervene. Houphouët-Boigny and his rival counselor, Lamine Gueye, both told Pélisson of 'their concern not to mix politics with an affair that must remain strictly professional and simply to bring their purely obliging support to settling a conflict whose importance to the country is considerable'.[68] The parliamentarians told both the Inspecteur Général du Travail and the Governor General that their concern was to end the strike 'so prejudical to the economy of the country as well as to the interests of the Régie and of the railwaymen themselves'. They were rebuffed by Governor General Barthes, who refused to call into question the October ruling of the arbitrators.[69] But in any case, these interventions show the tone of the politicians two months into the strike: a sentiment of regret over the hardships caused by the strike and hope for a quick settlement, but an evasiveness about the substantive issues and an unwillingness to support the strikers unambiguously and publicly.

Houphouët-Boigny reported the meetings to the Grand Conseil, but the effort of some members to debate the strike failed, as its president, Lamine Gueye, claimed the Conseil had no say on such a matter. Gueye went on to distance himself from the strikers, noting that while the interests of the railwaymen were affected by the strike, 'those of the entire country are as

[66] Renseignements, Ivory Coast, 5, 18 Nov. 1947, K 379 (26).
[67] *Réveil*, no. 268 (15 Dec. 1947) and no. 269 (18 Dec. 1947).
[68] IGT to Governor General, 12 Dec. 1947, K 457 (179). [69] *Ibid.* IGT 13/2.

well'. At a subsequent session in January, a counselor from Dahomey, Apithy, introduced a resolution asking for a delegation of the Conseil to try to get the government to intervene and attacked Lamine Gueye for failing to act. But this merely led to a brief and bitter exchange of accusations between RDA and Socialist deputies. Several delegates opposed intervention on the grounds that the Conseil did not have jurisdiction. Senghor said contacts had been made with the incoming Governor General, whose presence would raise the possibility of compromise in this 'painful conflict'. He added, 'The role of Grand Counselors is not to have a partisan debate here or to tear each other up and thus to tear up Africa, but to study the technical means to bring a solution to the conflict'. Apithy withdrew his resolution. French West Africa's most powerful political actors had failed even to express a collective opinion on the most salient issue of the day.[70]

Meanwhile, Houphouët-Boigny was doing his bit to end the strike in his home territory. The railwaymen of the Ivory Coast broke ranks in early January and gave up the strike. Pélisson wrote, 'According to our information, this result is due to M. the Deputy Houphouët who succeeded in persuading the African railwaymen to return to work despite the counter-propaganda of M. Sarr'.[71] The police reports from the Ivory Coast (see below) reveal a pattern of intrigue in January which resulted in the union's defection; Houphouët-Boigny's influence on some members of the union leadership – although not its leader, Gaston Fiankan – may well have been crucial. None of this should be surprising: the Ivoirien branch of the RDA had emerged from a group of cocoa planters and was rapidly expanding its power in agriculture as much as in politics. The harvest-time strike obviously affected their prospects with particular acuity.

Senghor was among the deputies who joined the settlement initiative in December and January. He was the only major political figure at the time to have given some indication of support – if only in private – to the strikers and he remained in contact. Senghor sent a letter to the minister, enclosing a list of demands of the union as well as a 'History of the Situation' written by Sarr. His own interpretation was truly Senghorian: 'In any case, the claims relative to the suppression of racial discrimination seem to me to be well founded, even if one can dispute the wage rates. In effect, one cannot speak of a *cadre unique* if there is discrimination within the interior of the cadre, discrimination which is moreover condemned by the Constitution of the IVth Republic'. He appealed for a settlement not on the basis of the April accords, but on the 'spirit of the Constitution of the IVth Republic which proclaims that the Union Française is a union founded on the equality of rights and duties, without discrimination based on race or religion'. Avoiding

[70] AOF, Bulletin du Grand Conseil, Procès-Verbal, 23 Dec. 1947, 80–1, 31 Jan. 1948, 320–1. The assembly of the Union Française – the deliberative (but nearly powerless) body intended to allow full discussion of issues facing Overseas France among colonial and metropolitan deputies – had a longer debate on the strike, ending in a resolution calling on the administration to 'resolve' the conflict and not to sanction the strikers. The debate is nonetheless notable for the invocation by supporters of the strikers of images of France's unity, on its progressive role in the world, and on the importance of equality within it to justify favorable treatment for African railwaymen. Débats, Sessions of 6, 12 Feb. 1948, 69–74, 78–89.

[71] Pélisson to M le Deputé Dumas, 6 Jan. 1948, IGT 13/2.

the mundane complexities of a labor dispute, Senghor defined the issue as one of constitutional principles and racial equality.[72]

By then, the Comité Directeur of the union had already criticized both Senghor and Lamine Gueye 'for having placed themselves on the side of the Administration and for their support of Cunéo'.[73] When the December discussions among parliamentarians assembled for the Grand Conseil meeting and the meetings with the Governor General got nowhere, Fily Dabo Sissoko, deputy from the Soudan, began to intervene as well.[74] Since the Soudanais railwaymen were crucial to the Dakar-Niger branch, officials hoped that he would have sufficient influence to get one group of workers to give up the strike in exchange only for promises that Sissoko would use his good offices on the union's behalf after railwaymen returned to work. Sissoko and his allies told officials that the Soudanais railwaymen had 'total confidence' in the Deputy of the Soudan, and that his intervention would insure that 'the Soundanais will detach themselves from the Senegalese and it is certain that overall movements similar to the strike of 11 October will not recur'.[75] Sissoko suggested token concessions, such as changing the date on which auxiliaries would acquire permanent status, but the real message was 'about the influence that the Deputy Fily Dabo Sissoko could have on the end of the strike'.[76] The Régie agreed to the date change, insisting that this promise 'is made to you and you alone to help you in your good offices to bring about an effective return to work and would only apply if the return occurred on the date indicated'.[77]

Sissoko talked directly with Sarr, who was frightened of the potential split in the strike movement within the Dakar-Niger. But the Comité Directeur would have none of this: they interpreted the offer as a 'word game' and as 'sabotage'. Sarr was instructed on 29 January 1948 to reject Sissoko's initiatives: 'A scalded cat fears cold water... and we cannot base our return to work on a promise, above all when that promise is stripped of any guarantee'. Sarr showed the telegram to Sissoko, who was angered and gave indications that he would actively intervene to get the Soudanais railwaymen to go back to work.[78]

[72] Senghor to Minister, 26 Nov. 1947, K 457 (179).

[73] Renseignements, 17 Dec. 1947, K 457 (179).

[74] Sissoko had earlier telegraphed the Ministry to remind them of the 'lamentable situation of several thousand families' affected by the strike, of the 'economic perturbation' leading to a 'fiasco' in the 1948 harvest, and of the unfortunate effects of turning the strike into a 'test of force'. Sissoko to Ministry, telegram, 3 Dec. 1947, IGT 13/2. This language was fully consistent with the tack being taken by most of the West African deputies.

[75] Note signed by Pillot, for the Dakar-Niger Réseau, for M le Directeur Fédéral de la Régie des Chemins de Fer de l'AOF, and sent by Cunéo to the President of the Conseil d'Administration, 19 Jan. 1948, K 457 (179). The administration was thinking that they could split off the Soudanais as early as the end of December. Renseignements, Thiès, 27 Dec. 1947, K 457 (179).

[76] Note by Pillot, K 457 (179).

[77] Secretary General of Government General, to Sissoko, 29 Jan. 1948, copy enclosed Inspection du Travail, Bamako, to IGT, 7 Feb. 1948, K 457 (179).

[78] Inspection du Travail, Bamako, to IGT, 7 Feb. 1948, Moussa Diarra, on behalf of Comité Directeur, telegram to Sarr, 29 Jan. 1948, and Renseignements, 4 Feb. 1948, K 457 (179). Another telegram sent by the Comité Directeur at Thiès to the Soudan attacked the entire initiative of Sissoko: 'Regret to put you on guard against the bad propaganda of the Sage of the Soudan who despite promises of devotion to cause attempts

The Inspection du Travail in Bamako reported that Sissoko indeed asked workers to go back, effective 2 February. The union appealed to them to hold fast. And this they did: at Bamako only seven workers returned to work on the day indicated.[79] Sissoko's intervention did little more than discredit him, although it may have made the union leadership nervous enough to look more favorably on the next settlement initiative in early March.

It had taken the leading elected politicians of French West Africa two months to intervene, and their efforts over the next two months accomplished little more than splitting the railwaymen of the Ivory Coast from their comrades elsewhere. Although Senghor, in a private letter to the minister, had assimilated the cause of the strikers to his anti-racist cause, he had done nothing to tap the popular mobilization that was part of the strike. Houphouët-Boigny had invoked the spectre of colonialism in a Dakar speech, but at virtually the same time he was working behind the scenes to end the strike in the Ivory Coast.

In Senegal, Senghor is said to have helped to settle the strike. This perception is more a consequence of what happened after the strike than what he did during it. Senghor realized that the union was one of the most important organized blocks of voters in the territory, and he set about straightening things out.[80] He made Sarr a candidate on his ticket for the Assembly of the Union Française, and he was duly elected in 1953. He is remembered in Thiès for having incorporated the railway workers union into his political movement, but with more than a hint that the workers did more for him than he for them.[81]

The story does not end here. As part of the leadership of Senghor's Bloc Démocratique Sénégalais, Sarr – who did not forget his origins – allied himself with the left wing of the party, and in particular with Mamadou Dia, who became Senghor's Prime Minister after independence. But when Dia and Senghor broke, and Dia and his allies were accused of crimes against the state, Sarr, along with Dia, was imprisoned, a fate he had not suffered at the hands of the French government.[82]

None of this negates the argument – which is the main point of Sembene's fictionalized account – that the struggle itself galvanized a *popular* sentiment

---

negative propaganda of destruction through numerous telegrams and letters addressed to Soudan. Consider intervention of this man as destruction orchestrated with directors of Régie at their visit to Bamako'. Diarra to Moriba Cissoko, 4 Feb. 1948, in Renseignements, Soudan, 5 February 1948, K 379 (26).

[79] Inspection du Travail, Bamako, to IGT, 7 Feb. 1948, K 457 (179).

[80] A month after the strike, as Suret-Canale notes, Senghor finally wrote an article on the subject, in which he in fact mentioned that he 'did not write a single article on the question and ... if I dealt with it at times in my speeches, I did so voluntarily, in measured terms'. He claimed support for the principle of nondiscrimination and, in practical terms, for compromise. The quotation is from *La Condition Humaine*, 26 Apr. 1948, as translated in Suret-Canale, 'Railway workers' strike,' 145.

[81] Mory Tall, Oumar NDiaye and Amadou Bouta Gueye (interviews, 9 Aug. 1994), Mansour Niang (interview, 4 Aug. 1994).

[82] The same thing happened to another leading labor leader of the 1950s, Alioune Cissé. His militant trade unionism never landed him in jail under the French, but Senghor put him there for his role in organizing a general strike in 1968 – an irony he remains well aware of, as he does in the case of Sarr (interview, Dakar, 4 Aug. 1994, by Oumar Gueye, Alioune Ba and Frederick Cooper).

hostile to the hypocrisies of the colonial regime and led to a sense of empowerment among the strikers whose implications undoubtedly went beyond the sphere of labor. But organizationally, things were not so clear. Neither the major parties nor the major trade union confederations made the railwaymen's cause their own. Neither gave the railwaymen much reason to have confidence in their ability to represent the cause of labor. The strike of 1947–8 was a railway strike of extraordinary proportions, but it began and ended as a railway strike.

THE AMBIVALENCES OF COLONIAL REPRESSION

The government side of the issue leaves its puzzles too: why officials allowed a disruptive strike to drag on so long without being either more repressive or more conciliatory. The government at first had no idea that it would face a long strike: 'The strike will no doubt last a few weeks. It is unpopular in all milieux – merchants, politicians, and workers'. This expectation may be why virtually nothing was done until November to try to maintain railway traffic.[83] And the arrogance of the assumption that the Régie would soon prevail no doubt communicated itself to the well-placed network of spies, who kept telling their bosses that the strike was about to collapse.[84] Self-deception was thus an important element in prolonging the strike.

Although the Régie had conceded the *cadre unique* and the integration of auxiliaries in April, it was struggling for the power to give content to those ideas. Increasingly, the strike itself became the principal issue. On the very eve of the strike, Governor General Barthes, in his last-ditch meeting with union leaders, lectured them on 'the terms of the law and my intention of insuring that it is respected'.[85] He immediately (and in accordance with those terms) sent the dispute to an arbitrator and then to an arbitrational committee – which on 31 October in effect affirmed the agreement of April 1947 and on the whole agreed with the Régie's interpretation of it. From the first, the Governor General and the Régie insisted that the arbitration proceedings alone had legal standing and that negotiation over them was out of the question. The stance led to a virtual loss of contact between Régie and union, and the Inspection du Travail, whose interventions had been critical to settling previous strikes, was largely frozen out of the action.[86] Only in

[83] Directeur Fédéral de la Régie to Directeur de l'Office Central des Chemins de Fer de la France Outre-Mer, 10 Oct. 1947, IGT 13/2.

[84] For example, Renseignements, 25 Oct. 1947, K 457 (179): 'One detects considerable discontent among the strikers who without any doubt did not expect a strike of this length. If it weren't for religious superstition, many would already have returned to work'. A week later, the report was, ''The enthusiasm of the beginning has completely fallen ... the women in particular are starting to get agitated and can expect that 50 per cent at least of the strikers demand to return to work'. Renseignements, 3 Nov. 1947, K 43 (1). Still later, it was the 'profound weariness' of the strikers which gave rise to expectations for a quick end to the strike. IGT to Governor General, 15 Dec. 1947, K 457 (179). The strike still had three months to go.

[85] Governor General to Minister, 11 Oct. 1947, IGT 13/2.

[86] AOF, IGT, Annual Report, 1947, 62. See for example the transcript of the meeting of the Conseil d'Administration of the Régie, 15 Nov. 1947 (K 459 [179]), at which Cunéo remarked: 'Whatever may be the consequences of the strike of African personnel, it seems that respect for the decisions of the judiciary, respect for legality, forbids the opening of new negotiations'.

December were some minor concessions being talked about: making the integration of auxiliaries retroactive to 1 July instead of 15 July, allowing 'individual' reclassifications of some railwaymen in categories where the union had demanded systematic reclassification, and allowing fifteen instead of ten days leave in case of marriages, births and deaths.[87] But it was still on the grounds of the sacrosanct nature of the arbitration decision that the Governor General refused the December initiative of the West African parliamentarians.[88] As late as 3 February, the administration in Dakar claimed that even sending an Inspecteur du Travail to talk to the union would be interpreted as a sign of loss of will, and that it was still necessary that the affair 'end by the total execution of the arbitration ruling'.[89]

Yet at the same time, the administration pulled its punches. At first it did nothing to enforce the arbitrator's judgment: it did not arrest the strike leaders, replace the illegally striking workers with new recruits, or requisition the workers, which would have put them under military discipline. All these options were discussed within the Government General and in Paris, but all were at first considered provocative. Only in the first week of November did the Régie make known its intention to hire replacements for the strikers, and even then the Governor General saw it necessary to explain that 'now, traffic must be assured as far as possible, despite the prolonged absence of African railwaymen'. The minister agreed, but wanted such hiring kept to a 'strict minimum'.[90] Such drastic measures as conscripting strikers into military service were viewed with considerable skepticism at the highest levels of the Ministry. Officials were no doubt reluctant to escalate for fear of going against their own initiatives of the post-war era: to constitute a new approach to labor based on ending forced labor, developing a system of industrial relations, and incorporating trade unions into that system. Measures intended to crush the union and coerce unwilling workers into the workplace would not help the cause. As Robert Delavignette, then head of Political Affairs in the Ministry in Paris, put it 'the strong style directed at the strikers will not itself resolve the problem (one has seen this in the recent past, even in AOF), if the government gives the impression of going back, after a detour, on trade union freedom and on the abolition of forced labor'.[91]

[87] The latter concessions were made apropos of an attempt by a deputy and a leader of the Confédération Française des Travailleurs Chrétiens, Joseph Dumas, to mediate the dispute, with the proviso that if the mission failed the Régie would undertake massive publicity of the terms offered in order to induce railwaymen to break with their union and go back to work. IGT to Governor General, 15 Dec. 1947, K 457 (179). The Inspecteur Général du Travail, Pélisson, wanted to let railway workers know that their wages might be revised in parallel with revisions being planned for the civil service, and that he favored giving 'at least partial satisfaction' to the railwaymen, while trying 'to save the face of the Régie'. But the Régie was not interested in saving face, and Dumas was left with narrow possibilities for maneuver, and predictably failed. IGT Note for Dumas, 18 Dec. 1947, K 457 (179).

[88] *Paris-Dakar*, 26 Dec. 1947, and Minutes of Grand Conseil, 24 Dec. 1947, cited in Suret-Canale, 'Railway workers' strike,' 145, 153, n. 25.

[89] Affaires Courantes, Dakar, telegram to the new Governor General, Béchard, 3 Feb. 1948, IGT 13/2.

[90] Governor General to Minister, telegram, 5 Nov. 1947, and Minister to Governor General, telegram, 7 Nov. 1947, IGT 13/2.

[91] Delavignette, 'Grève des chemins de fer et des wharfs en AOF', 13 Dec. 1947, IGT, 13/2. For the context of post-war labor policy – notably the assertion of legitimacy through the abolition of forced labor and the attempt to build a more differentiated,

It was only in mid-November that Sarr was brought to court 'for having ordered the strike in violation of the decree of 20 March 1937 on compulsory arbitration'. Fiankan, the Ivory Coast leader, had been prosecuted earlier and sentenced to three months in prison for interference with the liberty to work, although he was not in fact jailed and his conviction was overturned on appeal. Sarr was sentenced on 11 December 1947 to twenty days in jail and a fine of 1,200 francs for leading an illegal strike, but he never served his sentence: in April, after the strike, the appeals court commuted his sentence to a fine of 100 francs, suspended. Significantly, the prosecutors went after Fiankan again immediately after the Ivory Coast strike was broken and they were anxious to remove him from the scene lest he start it up again. He was convicted of threatening people who returned to work and sentenced to six months in prison on 22 January, but his sentence was later reduced on appeal to two months and a fine, and in the end he was pardoned. There were also some prosecutions in Dahomey and Guinea, most of which ended in acquittals.[92]

Nor did the Régie play another card it had: many of the strikers lived in railway housing, concentrated in various *cités* in key depots. One of the demands of the union was to open such housing to auxiliaries: lodging was quite valuable given the poor infrastructure of colonial towns, and the linkage of housing to job was part of the stabilization strategy of post-war governments. The Régie kept threatening to expel strikers from their homes unless they returned to work, but it did not do so.[93] Perhaps its caution came from the notion – repeated often in reports in the immediate post-war years – that African labor was inherently unstable, all too likely to jump from job to job or return to village life. It was the most experienced and skilled workers who were housed, and it would have been consistent with thinking on the 'stabilization' issue for the Régie to fear that once such workers left the *cités*, they might never be heard from again.

The weapons that the Régie was left with, then, were to manipulate the divisions within the work force and try to get enough manpower in place to run the railway system well enough to avoid economic paralysis. By November, the Régie had started to hire new workers and it kept issuing appeals to strikers – with a mixture of promises and threats – to go back individually. The appeal stressed that the Régie had already agreed (and the arbitration award made this explicit) to the reorganization of the cadres, in some form at least, and to the integration of at least a significicant number of auxiliaries. The poster distributed to the Ivory Coast, for example, pointed out that these measures would mean a 'large raise' for the cadres and

stable, manageable labor force see Cooper, *Decolonization and African Society*. Both policies came to the fore in 1946, as did the new development program, and French officials were eager to demonstrate to a world increasingly skeptical of denials of self-determination that social, economic and political development were at the heart of colonial policy.

[92] Governor General to Minister, 20 Nov. 1947, IGT 13/2; Directeur, Sûreté, to IGT, 15 Sept. 1948, K 458 (179).

[93] Cunéo (Director of Régie) draft letter to all regional directors, 9 Jan. 1948, reminding them that strikers, as of 28 November 1947, had been 'detached' from the Régie and warning them that if they did not return by 15 January they would be dislodged: K 457 (179). For earlier threats, see Renseignements, 19 Nov. 1947, K 378 (26), and Inspection du Travail, Guinea, to IGT, 19 Nov. 1947, K 457 (179).

'a very large raise for qualified auxiliaries'. The threat was that, as of November, strikers had been officially 'detached' from their posts, but that the regime would take them back with seniority intact if they returned immediately and not at all if they held out.[94]

None of this was very effective until the Ivory Coast gave way in early January. As of 1 November, three weeks into the strike, 487 Europeans and 38 Africans were trying to run a railway. By 2 January, 836 strikers had gone back to work and 2,416 new workers had been hired. Even if one accepts the Régie's claim that it really needed only 13,500 men, not the 17,000 it had had before the strike (and after the strike the Régie came up with a new figure of 15,000), the Régie had only recovered little over a quarter of its African workforce. In the crucial 'material and traction' section of the Dakar-Niger line, which included locomotive drivers and other running personnel, less than a sixth of the posts were filled on 2 January. Indeed, the entire Dakar-Niger branch remained solid: 1,125 workers of both races were all there was to do the job of 6,765. The Conakry-Niger line – 1,196 at work out of 2,014 – and the Abidjan-Niger line – 1,424 out of 3,111 – were shakier.[95]

After the return to work in the Ivory Coast, the administration hoped that the other lines would give way, but their most serious attempt, via Fily Dabo Sissoko, to hive off a large section of workers from the union failed. As of 1 February 1948, the active workers as a percentage of theoretical staffing stood at 32 per cent on the Dakar-Niger, 54 per cent on the Conakry-Niger, and 16 per cent on the Benin-Niger. Overall, this meant that 34 per cent of staffing needs were being met.[96]

Officials thought that the union was able to prevent hiring through its influence in the railway centers.[97] Even where new workers were signed on, they did not necessarily work well. This was particularly the case at the wharfs in the Ivory Coast where a mixture of European and African strikebreakers, plus a detachment from the Marine Nationale flown from Dakar to the Ivory Coast, had been put to work. 'The results have not lived up to our hopes, because the detachment which was sent was composed of unskilled workers who had never driven the equipment that was confided to them and which was relieved at the end of a month on the scene just when the Marines began to get used to the material they were using'.[98]

[94] Annex to Renseignements, Ivory Coast, 30 Dec. 1947, K 379 (26). Boldface and underlining in original.

[95] IGT, AOF, to IGT, Paris, 8 Jan. 1948, IGT 13/2; AOF, Inspection du Travail, Annual Report, 1947, 62. In February, Africans *en service* for the Régie founded a new Professional Association, headed by none other than François Gning. The call to its first meeting stated, 'We speak to you here with a French heart for the true France'. Its goal was to 'constitute in the heart of the Régie a true family of railwaymen where love of work will be the uniting trait between management and staff'. Even at this meeting, objections were made to Gning's leadership. The Association would give rise to a union, which would contest Sarr's union after the strike, but without a great deal of success. Renseignements, 8 Feb. 1948, K 457 (179).

[96] On these three lines, 839 workers had returned to their posts (including a few who had never left them) and 2,155 had been hired. Situation de la Régie au 1er Fevrier 1948, K 457 (179). [97] Governor General to Minister, 21 Nov. 1947, IGT 13/2.

[98] Directeur Général de l'Office Central des Chemins de Fer de la France Outre-Mer, Note, 15 Dec. 1947, IGT 13/2. Similar disappointment was felt with strike-breaking labor on the wharf in Dahomey. Dahomey, Inspection du Travail, Annual Report, 1947, 33.

Traffic had plunged after the strike and had only partially been restored. In mid-February, passenger traffic on the Dakar-Niger was at 12 per cent of its recent average, goods traffic at 43 per cent. On the Conakry-Niger, passenger traffic was at 20 per cent, goods at 48 per cent. On the Benin-Niger, passenger traffic stood at 10 per cent, goods traffic at 30 per cent.[99] Its effects were felt not only in the damage it was doing to the French campaign to resupply the metropole, but also in the scarcities of goods that were occurring throughout French West Africa and which threatened the painful effort that was being made to provide incentives to peasants to grow marketable crops and workers to work.[100] In fact, the timing of the strike was crucial in this sense: France had with fanfare launched a 'development' initiative in 1946, and the railway strike served both to undermine its economic goals and take the luster off its ideological intervention.

At the end of January, about 300 men from the French railways were sent to Dakar to provide skilled labor, particularly in the troublesome Traction division. Some white CGT leaders and the anti-colonial press urged them not to act as strike breakers, and apparently some asked to be taken back to France or else subtly undermined their own presence by pretending that their equipment was not properly functioning. The fact that the French locomotive drivers were not familiar with the steam locomotives still in use in Africa – and which African drivers knew intimately – may have contributed to the subsequent decision to accelerate dieselization of the system.[101]

However much the administration's actions fell short of all-out combat, the union's achievement in holding together for so long stands out. There is no question that leadership played a big part in it: the strike had been extensively discussed within railway communities in advance and scrupulously planned. Sarr had made the rounds of the depots and cemented a personal identification of the cause with himself and with the strike committee. He ordered his followers to 'stay home and not to indulge themselves in any outside demonstration or any sabotage' – an order which was by all indications followed.[102] In Thiès, the strikers held daily open meetings, where doubts and concerns were aired, but peer pressure was maintained. Whenever there were signs of wavering along the Dakar-Niger line, Sarr went on tour and reaffirmed the personal ties and the group loyalties. Security officials were convinced that this direct approach was effective: 'Before the passage of Sarr, many of them were getting ready to return to work; afterwards, they have again decided, more so than ever, to continue the strike'.[103] Fily Dabo Sissoko – in the midst of his effort to get

[99] Affaires Courantes, Dakar, to Minister, 14 Feb. 1948, IGT 13/2.

[100] Inspection du Travail, Guinea, to IGT, 19 Nov. 1947, K 457 (179); Delavignette, Grève des chemins de fer...', 13 Dec. 1947, IGT 13/2.

[101] Gendarmerie Mobile, Rapport, 15 Nov. 1947, K 43 (1); Suret-Canale, 'Railway workers' strike', 140; Abdoulaye Soulaye Sarr (interview, 22 July 1990); Sene, 'Grève des cheminots', 117.

[102] Renseignements, 25 Oct. 1947, K 43 (1). His warning was later published in *Réveil*, 20 Nov. 1947. The orders against demonstrations were passed out in the Soudan as well. Renseignements, Bamako, 11 Oct. 1947, K 43 (1).

[103] Renseignements, 13 Nov. 1947, K 457 (179), in regard to Sarr's trip to the Soudan. There are extensive reports from police spies of meetings at Thiès and elsewhere. See, for example, Renseignements, 29 Oct., 25 Dec. 1947, *ibid.* and Renseignements, 16 Oct. 1947, K 43 (1).

the Soudanais back to work – told French officials that 'The Soudanais considered themselves bound to the union Leader by a pact which it would be dishonorable to break'.[104]

However impressive the leadership, collective and personal, it was clearly rooted in railway communities – in towns like Thiès and Kayes, where railway workers and their families lived together as well as worked together, and where they were part of broad networks linking them to merchants and farmers in the area. In any case, Pélisson, the Inspecteur Général du Travail noted a crucial aspect of solidarity on the railway: it crossed all ranks.

It is important to observe that the [strike] order was followed not only by the agents of the permanent cadre and the auxiliaries eligible to be integrated into it, the only people with an interest in the agreement under discussion, but also by the mass of ordinary auxiliaries – manual laborers for the most part – and by the personnel of the wharfs whose situation was not at all in question. Led into this behavior by a limitless confidence in their leaders and their directions, undoubtedly as well by fear and at times by concern to keep their word, the African railwaymen have until now kept up, calmly and with respect for public order which is much to their credit, a strike whose prolongation seemed, however, more and more like a dead end.[105]

DEFECTION, DEFIANCE AND AN AMBIGUOUS RESOLUTION

The strike broke first in the Ivory Coast. Pélisson attributed this to the behind-the-scenes machinations of Houphouët-Boigny, but it is also clear that a second tier of union officials staged a kind of coup while Fiankan, the Secretary General of the Abidjan-Niger railway union, was out of the country. The Ivory Coast union was clearly divided, and the officers whom Fiankan had replaced when he became Secretary General had, as early as November, intrigued against him. Fiankan for a time wavered in his support of the strike. Houphouët-Boigny had reportedly told the union leaders of his disapproval of the timing of the strike and their failure to consult him. When the news of the failure of the intervention of the deputies in December reached Abidjan in a telegram from Sarr on 30 December, it led to a tense meeting of a hundred railwaymen, presided over by Djoman, the Adjunct Secretary. Sarr's telegram was pessimistic, but argued that the only way for railwaymen to keep their jobs was to carry the strike to a successful conclusion. Maitre Diop, a lawyer and member of the Grand Conseil just returned from Dakar, confirmed the failure of the Dakar initiative. The Regional Director had shrewdly timed an offer (quoted above) to rehire all workers on the Abidjan-Niger who returned to work at that time, promising wage increases that would flow from the reclassifications approved in the arbitration ruling. The meeting divided between those who favored a return to work and those who wanted to await the return of Fiankan.[106]

The next day, Fiankan was being blamed for his absence (he was in

[104] Sissoko therefore saw convincing Sarr as the key. He miscalculated the nature of the union leadership, however, since the strike committee ordered a wavering Sarr not to give in. Governor, Soudan, to Governor General, 12 Jan. 1948, K 378 (26).

[105] IGT, Report, 24 Jan. 1948, IGT 13/2.

[106] Renseignements, Ivory Coast, 14, 15 Nov., 30 Dec. 1947, K 379 (26). On Houphouët-Boigny's role, see Renseignements, 5 Nov. 1947, *ibid.* and IGT to Deputy Dumas, 6 Jan. 1948, IGT 13/2.

Dakar), and the supporters of the strike were rapidly becoming discouraged. Over the next few days, the failure of the parliamentarians to settle the strike weighed heavily on a divided and depressed group of trade unionists. Sarr was blamed for starting the strike, 'traitors' for trying to end it. Diop and Djoman came out for a return to work. This was decided on 4 January, effective the next day. When Fiankan returned on 5 January, the men had gone back.[107] Meeting with a group of railwaymen at Treichville, Fiankan called them 'traitors to your comrades in Dahomey, Guinea and the Soudan' and demanded why they had gone back. 'It was the Committee in accord with Maitre Diop who gave the order to go back', he was told. Fiankan urged them to strike again. They replied, 'We have suffered enough'.[108]

Leadership was clearly of the utmost importance in maintaining such a strike.[109] The Ivory Coast workers went back essentially under the terms of the arbitration decision, which provided that auxiliaries would be integrated into the cadres in accordance with their qualifications. The members of the cadres were, as promised, taken back to their old posts, but auxiliaries found that the conditions of their return were indeed problematic. The Régie had promised that the strikebreakers hired in the interim – and there were 755 of them out of a theoretical staffing of 3,111 – would keep their jobs, and it was the less senior auxiliaries who would bear the brunt. The Government General in Dakar – despite fear of trouble from the Governor in Abidjan – was content for the laid off auxiliaries to learn that a 'strike always carries risks above all when it takes place outside legal procedures'.[110]

All this served notice that the government was going to play as tough when workers went back as they had when they were out on strike. Perhaps this experience contributed to the determination of the other regions to hold out and to the union's toughness in the post-strike period.

It was only when a new High Commissioner came to French West Africa that further movement took place. Paul Béchard, taking advantage of his arrival, undertook to talk to the principals beginning 26 February. Béchard, as he himself later told it, decided that taking the legalistic line to its logical conclusion – by firing the railwaymen for violation of the arbitration ruling – was 'a brutal solution of rupture with unpredictable political consequences'. He sought a 'last try at conciliation', and he issued a series of proposals based on, but slightly modifying, the arbitration ruling:

(1) In regard to the union's claim to make the integration of auxiliaries retroactive to 1 January 1947, he proposed 1 May 1947 in regard to pay and 1 January 1947 in regard to seniority. The Régie had wanted 1 October and the arbitrator 15 July.

[107] Renseignements, Ivory Coast, 31 Dec. 1947, 3, 4, 7, 8 Jan. 1948, K 379 (26).

[108] Renseignements, 7 Jan. 1948, K 379 (26). At Port-Bouet the next day, Fiankan was greeted with such hostility that he had to leave. *Ibid.*, 8 Jan. 1948.

[109] The strike had not been as solid on the Abidjan-Niger line as on the other lines. On the former, 519 workers had returned to work by 1 January 1948, out of a theoretical labor force of 3,111. On the Dakar-Niger, only 236 out of 6,765 had given up by that date, while only 71 workers on the other two lines combined went back before the new year. IGT, AOF, to IGT, Paris, 8 Jan. 1948, IGT 13/2.

[110] Governor, Ivory Coast, to High Commissioner, telegram, 12 Jan. 1948, and Affaires Politiques, Administratives et Sociales to Governor, Ivory Coast, telegram, 20 Jan. 1948, K 378 (26).

(2) In regard to the reclassification of certain agents in the *cadres secondaires*, Béchard maintained the Régie's equivalence tables, but granted extra seniority to the agents in question.
(3) In regard to where examinations would be required to pass between scales, he placed examination barriers where the Régie wanted them, and also where the union wanted them.
(4) In regard to the union's demand for 15 days annual leave, in addition to a month's vacation, which the Régie had rejected and the arbitrator reduced to ten days, the High Commissioner agreed to 15, but only for family events and only if necessities of service permitted.
(5) In regard to the union's demand for the provision of lodging or a compensatory indemnity to all agents, he agreed with the Régie's position, supported by the arbitrator, that this could not be guaranteed for all.
(6) In regard to the union's demand for a uniform indemnity of zone, at the rate then accorded the highest rank – as opposed to the Régie's and the arbitrator's proposal for incorporating the old, hierarchical indemnities into a hierarchical wage scale and adding an indemnity of residence for places with a high cost of living – Béchard held firm to the Régie's position.

The High Commissioner decided in addition that there would be no punishment for striking, that the Régie would take back all its personnel in the cadres, that all auxiliaries currently at work would be kept on, and that striking auxiliaries would be taken back in order of seniority until the staffing levels had been filled.[111]

The High Commissioner was going along with the Régie on the issues where concessions would be the most costly. In both cases – housing and the hierarchical indemnities – he was not denying an agreed-upon benefit to railwaymen, but preserving the Régie's power to determine the modalities of implementation. In particular, the Régie retained wide discretion to maintain differentiation in emoluments: the incorporation of the highly unequal indemnity of zone into wages would preserve hierarchy, while the smaller and egalitarian indemnity of residence – applied by place and not by rank – would give lip service to equalizing adjustments for variations in the cost of living. Housing would be an emolument that could be used flexibly by the Régie to attract those categories of workers it wanted most. None of these differentials was explicitly racial, nor had any of them been that way in the Régie's offer or the arbitrator's ruling. On the other questions, Béchard's decisions appeared positively Solomonic: each side could claim it got something out of the battle. These proposals, of course, could have been made months earlier.

Union leaders, after discussing the proposal among themselves came back the next day, 15 March, expressing overall acceptance of the proposals but with a single objection: they wanted a guarantee that all auxiliaries would get their jobs back. Béchard later congratulated himself for having 'the intuition that this exigency constituted the stumbling block to the return', for the union had to protect its rank and file. By 4 a.m. he had a compromise: he would still protect those who had returned to work before the negotiated

[111] High Commissioner's narrative of strike, 1 Apr. 1948, K 458 (179).

settlement but agreed to take back in principle all striking auxiliaries. But within a month, and after negotiations between the Régie and the union, a new staffing table – providing for a reduction of the workforce – would come into effect and auxiliaries' rights to keep their jobs would depend on seniority and competence. Striking auxiliaries who had filled, before the strike, the conditions for integration into the cadres would keep the benefits of the transition program. He also made a slight concession on one of the strike issues, easing the examination barriers for passing between certain ranks. Strike days would not be paid. As compensation for the increased cost of living, the Régie was to raise (retroactive to 1 January 1948) wages, expatriation and displacement benefits, and management benefits by 20 per cent, and increase an indemnity of residence for Dakar, Abidjan and other cities. The 20 per cent in this context hardly seemed to be the technical adjustment it was alleged to be but a response to a disciplined strike. Any disagreements over the implementation of the agreement would go to a commission including one representative of the High Commissioner, and two each from the Régie and the union.

The Régie and the union accepted these proposals, and the return to work was fixed for that Friday, 19 March. Béchard concluded his report on the strike, 'It left no victors, no vanquished. Reasons for excessive bitterness for one side or the other have been avoided. Work could be resumed on solid bases, ignoring former divisions, in good order and with confidence'.[112]

Sarr, returning to Thiès after signing the agreement, claimed that the High Commissioner had 'given us concessions which the Régie did not want to give us ... Thus, comrades, our honor is safe and we will return to work having shown that we were men who know what we want'. He did not want strikers to get into disputes with nonstrikers: 'We will resume work calmly, and with discipline'. The end of the strike was celebrated with a long march at Thiès, followed by meetings and dancing. It was an occasion of joy, an expression of confidence in organization and unity. In the years that followed, many children of railwaymen were named after Ibrahima Sarr.[113] The end of the strike is remembered today as a 'magnificent' victory bringing equality and the end of racial discrimination within the labor force, as a 'clear improvement' in the lives of workers, as an achievement won on behalf of the auxiliaries integrated into the cadres.[114]

AFTERMATH

Almost immediately, the two sides plunged into a struggle over the staffing table, over deciding which auxiliaries would be kept and over how integration would take place. The intensity of the disputes must have reminded everyone

[112] High Commissioner's narrative, 1 Apr. 1948, K 458 (179); Protocole de Reprise du Travail, 15 Mar. 1948, IGT 13/2.

[113] Renseignements, 16 Mar. 1948, K 458 (179); Sene, 'Grève des cheminots', 104, 112. The administration feared that auxiliaries, who were still at risk, might try to block the return to work, but Sarr vowed to defend them, and officials noted that 'we must assume that he will not give way on this point'. Renseignements, 16 Mar. 1948, K 458 (179).

[114] Abdoulaye Souleye Sarr (interview, 22 July 1990), Oumar NDiaye and Amadou Bouta Gueye (interview, 9 Aug. 1994) and Mansour Niang (interview, 4 Aug. 1994).

concerned of why the strike had been fought so determinatedly.[115] Management asserted its prerogative to fire people for incompetence or other reasons; the union had the implicit threat of another strike behind its demands.

The discussions over the labor force reduction lasted over two years. The Régie had intended to reduce its 17,000-man force even before the strike began; such a reduction was its quid pro quo during the April negotiations for agreeing to restructuring the cadres and integrating auxiliaries. In the midst of the strike, and probably for political purposes, it claimed it only needed 13,500. But when it came to listing necessary workers, the Régie found it needed to ponder the question – amidst challenges from the union – and then came up with a figure of 14,748 in June 1948. Given the fact that over 2,000 strike-breakers had been hired (not counting the Abidjan-Niger branch) and had to be kept on under the terms of the Protocol, this meant that as many as 5,000 workers could have lost their jobs. But as further delays ensued – including protracted and heated negotiations throughout the summer – many workers left voluntarily, while new works projects and the need to take care of neglected maintenance increased needs, so that by September the number of workers in jeopardy was around 2,500.[116]

Some of the voluntary resignations apparently resulted from union members making life difficult for the *défaillants* or *jaunes*, as strike-breakers were called.[117] From the very start, the union challenged management on so many points that the director complained that his regional directors

> find themselves in an annoying situation *vis-à-vis* the unions because of the fact that they are constantly accused of violating the end of strike protocol with threats of informing the Governor General or the Inspecteur Général du Travail. The authority necessary for the execution of a public service is dangerously disturbed.[118]

What was happening was good, hard negotiating, carried out within the new Commission at the federal level (as well as the Conseil d'Administration of

[115] The Inspection du Travail realized immediately that the question of rehiring auxiliaries would be the crucial one in the upcoming weeks. Pélisson thought that the less senior auxiliaries, who were vulnerable to lose their jobs, should be clearly informed of this, so that any who had taken other jobs during their strike could decide if it were advisable to keep them. He thought that Inspecteurs du Travail, not the Régie, should be the ones to break the bad news. IGT, circular to Inspecteurs Territoriaux du Travail, 17 Mar. 1948, IGT 13/2.

[116] These ups and downs are traced in IGT to Inspecteur Général des Colonies, 6 Sept. 1948, K 458 (179), and can be followed in Renseignements, June–September 1948, 11 D 1/1392. The 14,748 figure was agreed to, by a vote of 11–2, at the meeting of the Conseil d'Administration of the Régie, 25 June 1948, transcript in IGT 13/2. At this time, the plan was to fire 2,500 unskilled workers on 31 July, followed by three batches of 850 each of skilled workers. The actual firings turned out to be considerably less drastic.

[117] Inspecteur Territorial du Travail, Dahomey, to IGT, 1 Apr. 1948, IGT 13/2; IGT, Réglement de la grève des chemins de fer africain de l AOF, 24 Sept. 1948, *ibid.* The tension at Thiès was heightened by the presence of the union of nonstrikers organized on the Dakar-Niger by Gning. But for all of Gning's obsequiousness *vis-à-vis* the administration, the latter wanted no part of his union, for it knew where the power lay, and it systematically denied it a place on the bodies which negotiated terms of layoffs and rehirings. High Commissioner to Gning, 15 June 1948, K 458 (179).

[118] Directeur Fédéral de la Régie des Chemins de Fer to Inspecteur Général du Travail, 9 Apr. 1948, K 458 (179).

the Régie) and within each of the branch lines. The Régie recognized the need to balance its desire to minimize costs with a desire for an 'appeasement policy', and in bargaining sessions the union insisted on 'the social side of the problem'. This meant avoiding brutal layoffs while using the labor force to assure neglected maintenance and the 'modernization of its equipment and its installations', which the Régie had proclaimed its goal. One top official admitted that in the course of 115 hours of meetings, the two sides had come closer together and concessions had been 'pulled out of the Régie', which admitted that its first tables were too theoretical and that more staffing was needed.[119] Then, from June through September, the details of where the axe would fall were negotiated. By this time, attrition had eased the problem somewhat, some of the workers hired during the strike were fired for incompetence and others for faults committed before the strike, and the union negotiated that layoffs take place in three batches, in August, September and October. Lists were generated by trade and seniority, and they were given to the union. Regional commissions heard disputes. Most, according to the Inspection, were settled unanimously. The axe did fall: the August firings consisted of 671 on the Dakar-Niger, 92 on the Conakry-Niger, 112 on the Abidjan-Niger, and 258 on the Benin-Niger, a total of 1,133. In September, 380 workers were fired. At Thiès, where the problem was regarded as 'the thorniest', the Inspecteurs got 348 rehired as temporaries, and encouraged others to seek work as dockers in Dakar or laborers on a development scheme on the Senegal River.[120] In Dahomey and in the Ivory Coast, the union succeeded in getting significant numbers of workers slated for lay off to be reinstated.[121]

The Inspecteur Général du Travail admitted that 'the social malaise remains considerable', particularly the tension between white and black railwaymen. He hoped that the departure of some European railwaymen

[119] Statements of Pillot and Mahé for the Régie and Ousmane N'Gom for the union, Transcript of Meeting of Conseil d'Administration des Chemins de Fer de l'AOF, 25 June 1948, IGT 13/2.

[120] IGT, 'Réglement de la grève des chemins...' 24 Sept. 1948, IGT 13/2. The union's role in establishing lists of workers to be fired was not defined in the Protocol of 15 March, but was apparently offered 'spontaneously' by the Régie when it came up with its staffing table, undoubtedly to insure that the union was complicit in hard decisions that had to be made. This lengthened the proceedings, and let attrition take care of part of the problem. IGT to Sarr, 28 Oct. 1948, K 458 (179). In October, the Régie, with the consent of the union, decided to pension off auxiliaries over 55 years of age, claiming that the life-pensions or layoff indemnities were expensive, but that this would leave a more effective workforce (and would presumably ease the anxieties of younger workers). The rival union, led by Gning, complained about this, but got little more than an explanation of why the main union, Sarr's, and the Régie, had agreed to it. IGT to Gning, 18 Oct. 1948, K 458 (179).

[121] In the Ivory Coast, 342 scheduled layoffs were reduced to 187. Inspection du Travail, Ivory Coast, Rapport sur l'evolution de réglement de la grève de la Régie des Chemins de fer de l'AOF (Région Abidjan-Niger), 28 Aug. 1948; Inspection du Travail, Dahomey, Rapport sur l'évolution de réglement de la grève des cheminots Africains de la Région Bénin-Niger, 25 Aug. 1948, K 458 (179). In the Soudan, most of the laborers laid off were quickly rehired, as were 73 of the 202 skilled workers. The biggest problem was auxiliaries whose skills were specific to railway work. Governor, Soudan, to High Commissioner, 9 Oct. 1948, K 458 (179).

would ease the way both to hiring more Africans and improving the atmosphere. In any case, Pélisson acknowledged, a bit grudgingly, that the union 'had done its duty in defense of the railwaymen'.[122]

The union had to accept its share of responsibility for the process, but also credit for protecting its own men and inducing strike-breakers to quit. It concluded,

having rid ourselves of the nightmare of staff compression, the situation of all the comrades who remain will be correspondingly improved. All qualified auxiliaries will soon be integrated into the cadre. The agents of the cadre will in several days receive their recalls, fruits of a struggle that will be forever remembered. Thus all will be paid their true value and the frightening number of auxiliaries will diminish considerably by their integration into the *cadre unique* which does not distinguish white or yellow or black, but only workers, period.[123]

But people did get hurt in this process, and in November a group of auxiliaries massed in front of Sarr's home to protest that the union was not looking after their interests and had not accomplished the promised integration of auxiliaries. They accused him of fostering his own political ambitions.[124] Indeed, the process of integrating auxiliaries was slow and partial, and some railwaymen continued to press (unsuccessfully) to regain the status of civil servants while civil servants pressed (successfully) for their own version of the *cadre unique*, with equal benefits regardless of origin.[125]

The concrete gains were significant. The post-strike plan was for 2,500 auxiliaries to be integrated into the cadres. By 1950, the cadres had gone from around 12 per cent of the work force before the strike to over 31 per cent.[126] A financial evaluation of the Régie in 1952 concluded that the cost of integrating auxiliaries was one of the major factors leading to the high freight charges and precarious financial situation of the Régie, as were the substantial raises – estimated at 77 per cent – given auxiliaries since 1948. Officials pointed out in reply that the costs of the 1947 strike were still being paid and that social relations in French West Africa's largest enterprise were important not only in themselves but were 'necessary, as the strike of 1947 proved, for the sound functioning of the Régie itself. I believe that technical progress

[122] IGT, 'Réglement de la grève des chemins...', 24 Sept. 1948, IGT 13/2.

[123] Circular signed Abdoulaye Ba from the union to union subdivisions, apparently intercepted by Sûreté and filed as Renseignements, 8 Sept. 1948, K 458 (179).

[124] 'La vie syndicale en AOF', 31 January 1949, AP 3406/1. There were more protests later in 1949. Renseignements, n.d. [*c.* Nov. 1949] 11 D 1/1392.

[125] Labor reports noted 'malaise' in the civil service and railways. The former received legal assurance of equal pay and benefits from the 'Lamine Gueye Law' of 1950, although its implementation remained a subject of contestation. IGT, 'Rapport: cessation d'application du Protocole de reprise du Travail sur les Chemins de Fer de l'Afrique occidentale française', 2 July 1949, IGT 13/2; Ibrahima Sarr, for Fédération des Syndicats des Cheminots Africains de l'AOF to Inspecteur Général du Travail, 18 Aug. 1952, 18G 163; High Commissioner to Minister, 20 Nov. 1948, Union des Syndicats Confédérés de Dakar, Revendications, 1 May 1949, Secretary General, Services des Etudes, Note pour l'Inspecteur Général du Travail, 18 May 1949, High Commissioner to Minister, 12 Jan., 25 Feb. 1950, all in K 424 (165).

[126] IGT to Inspecteur Général des Colonies, 6 Sept. 1948, K 458 (179); Directeur Fédéral de la Régie to IGT, 30 June 1950, K 43 (1).

and social progress cannot be separated'.[127] This was a lesson that officials could not forget, and unions would remind them if they did, while rank and file might remind their union leaders if they neglected the human interests that were at stake.

In the aftermath of the strike, its political implications remained to be worked out. The administration had fought the strike as a labor dispute, not as a contest over colonial authority, restraining its authoritarian hand but stubbornly insisting on following its industrial relations procedures. The union had also fought the strike as a labor dispute, restraining itself from public demonstrations more extensive than the regular mass meetings of railwaymen at Thiès. If the rhetoric of Sarr from his first speech in May 1946 onward was filled with attacks on colonialists, it also contained numerous references to the role Africans had played as in the French military, defending French freedom, and this – along with working side by side with French railwaymen – was seen as legitimating the claim to equality of pay and benefits.[128] Similar strategies were used by others to turn the rhetoric of unity and assimilation in the Union Française into claims to entitlements: the veterans' slogan, for example, was 'equal sacrifices, equal rights'.[129] The French reference point was in fact vital to the union's entire argument: the plea for an end to racial discrimination in regard to indemnities, housing and other issues assumed the existence of a unit within which equality could be pursued.

Forty-seven years later, a former railwayman denied that the 'spirit of independence' was behind the strike; the central issue was 'respect of professional value'.[130] Yet the political meanings of the strike are more complicated than that. Equality with French railway workers was a formal demand, yet the spirit of defiance and the anger against French colonial practices could not be so neatly bounded. Nor could the self-confidence gained by the disciplined conduct of a social movement over five and a half months and a vast space be limited to the issues formally at stake. In regard to questions of popular consciousness, the vision of Sembene's novel remains germane to histories of the post-1948 era.

But popular consciousness does not make movements in a vacuum. Organization is a key concern, and here one finds a double ambiguity, in relation to trade union organization and to political parties. The community mobilization on which the strike depended was channelled – in the strike and its aftermath – through the railway union and its Comité Directeur. The very success of its negotiations drew it into a framework of industrial

[127] Mission Monguillot, 'Situation Financière de la Régie Générale des Chemins de Fer de l'AOF', Rapport 93/D, 10 Apr. 1952; Directeur Général des Finances to Monguillot, 5 May 1952, and High Commissioner to Monguillot, 17 July 1952, AP 2306/7.

[128] For example, Sarr told an audience at Kayes in November: 'We have suffered famine and thirst and we have marched naked to defend purely French interests; nothing prevents us to suffer as much today when it is a question of our own interests.' Renseignements, 31 Nov. 1947, K 457 (179). The Comité Directeur included *anciens combattants*, who remained proud of their service to both causes. Abdoulaye Souleye Sarr (interview, 22 July 1990), Amadou Bouta Gueye (interview, 9 Aug. 1994).

[129] Myron Echenberg, *Colonial Conscripts: The Tirailleurs Sénégalais in French West Africa, 1857–1960* (Portsmouth, NH: Heinemann, 1991), 152.

[130] Mansour Niang (interview, 4 Aug. 1994).

relations, modelled on French labor law and French practices. The union, over time, became more of a union.

And whatever the potential implications of the strike to anti-colonial politics, they were in fact channelled through the structures of political parties. The networks created by the union and by the strike as well as the memories and sentiments to which it gave rise were both enlisted in a wider cause and tamed. Senghor was the West African politician who accomplished this with particular acuity. Spending much time as a deputy in Paris and more tending to organizational work in Dakar, Senghor needed a mechanism to get beyond the limitations of the Dakar-centered politics of his mentor, Lamine Gueye. Senghor had not stood publicly by the side of the railway workers. His breakthrough occurred in reaching out to them – as he did to other constituencies via leaders, networks and pre-existing institutions. The Mouride brotherhoods were key constituents in rural areas, labor in the towns. Two of the candidates he kept on his slate after his break with Lamine Gueye in 1949 and his founding of the Bloc Démocratique Sénégalais were Sarr (for the Assemblée de l'Union Française) and Abbas Gueye, one of the heroes of the 1946 Dakar general strike (Assemblée Nationale).[131]

In the memories of participants, there is both pride and bitterness at this process: assertions that the railwaymen's actions set the stage for wider population mobilization, identification with Senghor as a political 'phenomenon'. But one hears from workers as well a disappointment that their own union leaders had become estranged in putting on the *boubou politique* (the robes of politics) and that their interests were being set aside in the scramble for office and the enjoyment of its perquisites. They feared that they would lose the power that derived from their professional focus and become only the 'auxiliaries' of the political parties.[132] By the mid-1950s, the political activities of union leaders would become a source of controversy within the railway union and indeed within the labor movement of French West Africa in general.[133]

CONCLUSION

There remained, in 1948, a great deal for African union leaders to accomplish, on the railroad as well as outside. But in following up the strike, as much as in the strike itself, they had shown that the representatives of African workers would be present where their interests were being discussed. The 1947–8 railway strike was above all a contest over power within a system of industrial relations that had only just been brought to French Africa. No longer willing to defend explicitly and overtly a system of job classifications

[131] 'La vie syndicale en AOF au cours de l'année 1948', 31 Jan. 1949, including High Commissioner to Minister, 2 Feb. 1949, AP 3406/1. This report makes it clear that the union remained clear of political involvement during the strike, but that afterward politicians, and Senghor in particular, realized that 'the African railwaymen constitute in effect a very important electoral trump card in Senegal'.

[132] The phrase *boubou politique* was used in an interview by a former government worker and low-level official in a civil service union, while the notion of becoming 'auxiliaries' to political parties comes from Mory Tall. Moussa Konaté, interview Dakar, 8 Aug. 1994, by Frederick Cooper and Alioune Ba. Tall interview, by the *équipe de Thiès*, 9 Aug. 1994.

[133] This theme is discussed at length in Cooper, *Decolonization and African Society*, ch. 11.

by race or origins, colonial officials were nonetheless willing to fight for power within the structure of bureaucratized industrial relations machinery they had created, over the details of what the wage hierarchy would be and the precise terms of access to different points within it. Hierarchy and differential access to resources were to remain fundamental to the modernized colonialism of the post-war era, and the strike of 1947–8 revealed the impossibility of separating neatly the impersonal structure of a modern institution from the racialized history of colonial rule. In so far as the struggle forced colonial officials to assert ever more vehemently that they did not mean for the new hierarchy merely to reproduce the old, in so far as control of that hierarchy had to be shared with a militant union, officials were made to confront the fact that colonial authority was no longer as colonial as it once was. Such a realization was an important part of the reconsideration by French political leaders and civil servants in the mid-1950s of the strategies and institutions on which French rule depended.[134]

The determination and unity of the African railway workers made clear, for then and thereafter, that their voices would be heard. But the government of French West Africa made its point too: African unions could fight and they could win, but within certain legal and institutional structures. The very battle brought both sides ever deeper into those structures, and neither tried to take the battle outside. The railway workers drew on the strength of their communities – ties of family, commerce and religion within Thiès most notably – whereas proletarian solidarity across occupational lines or a wider African mobilization against colonialism could not be organized. At the end of 1948, a government report, reflecting on a year which had witnessed one titanic labor conflict – and a host of routine disputes and negotiations easily contained within the recently created structures of the Inspection du Travail – applauded the form in which the two sides had joined their conflict: 'Social peace can only profit from such a crystalization of forces around two poles, certainly opposed but knowing each other better and accepting to keep contact to discuss collective bargaining agreements and conditions of work'.[135]

Perhaps. The clearest sign that the terrain of struggle became more closely framed, defined and narrowed was that nothing quite like the general strike of 1946 or the railway strike of 1947–8 occurred again under French rule.[136] For the railway and the government, the strike had a high cost in wages and benefits and a higher one in the lesson learned that the new social engineering strategies of the post-war era would give rise to new forms of struggle and new claims to entitlements. The question this would eventually leave in official minds had profound implications: was it politically wise to use France as a model for Africa and assert that the French empire represented a single entity when that legitimated African claims for a French standard of

[134] This is a major theme of the concluding part of my *Decolonization and African Society*. [135] 'La vie syndicale en AOF', 31 Jan. 1949, AP 3406/1.

[136] The largest subsequent event was a one-day general strike in November 1952 throughout French West Africa, spearheaded by the CGT and intended to bring pressure on the French legislature to pass the Code du Travail. There were co-ordinated strikes in 1953 over the terms of implementation of that code, but while those strikes revealed impressive co-ordination they did not entail the kind of community dynamic of the earlier ones.

living? For African railway workers integrated into the cadres, the material gains of the strike were considerable, but this achievement left open the question of whether African communities would be strengthened or segmented by the higher incomes of a distinctly defined body of men. The strike of 1947 had drawn its strength simultaneously from the communities of the railwaymen and the union's seizure of the institutions and rhetoric of post-war French imperialism as the bases for its demands. The railwaymen now faced the question of whether their strength could serve a broader population or whether in attaching themselves to the cause of national politics the strength would be drawn out of the labor movement and into political institutions where their interests, their sense of community and their visions would be lost.

SUMMARY

This essay is both a reinterpretation of the place of the French West African railway strike in labor history and part of an exploration of its effects on politics and political memory. This vast strike needs to be studied in railway depots from Senegal to the Ivory Coast. Historians need both to engage the fictional version of the strike in Ousmanne Sembene's *God's Bits of Wood* and avoid being caught up in it. Interviews in the key railway and union town of Thiès, Senegal, suggest that strike veterans want to distinguish an experience they regard as their own from the novelist's portrayal. They accept the heroic vision of the strike, but offer different interpretations of its relationship to family and community and suggest that its political implications include co-optation and betrayal as much as anticolonial solidarity. Interviews complement the reports of police spies as sources for the historian. The central irony of the strike is that it was sustained on the basis of railwaymen's integration into local communities but that its central demand took railwaymen into a professionally defined, nonracial category of railwayman. The strike thus needs to be situated in relation to French efforts to define a new imperialism for the post-war era and the government's inability to control the implications of its own actions and rhetoric. Negotiating with a new, young, politically aware railway union leadership in 1946 and 1947, officials were unwilling to defend the old racial wage scales, accepted in principle the *cadre unique* demanded by the union, but fought over the question of power – who was to decide the details that would give such a cadre meaning? The article analyzes the tension between the principles of nonracial equality and African community among the railwaymen and that between colonial power and notions of assimilation and development within the government. It examines the extent to which the strike remained a railway strike or spilled over into a wider and longer term question of proletarian solidarity and anticolonial mobilization.

[11]

Authority, Gender & Violence

The War Within Mau Mau's Fight for Land & Freedom

JOHN LONSDALE

Introduction: Memory is not History

History moves us forward, into the unknown. Whether in hope or in fear we face futures we imagine, either going our way or coming to get us. We cannot foretell the outcome of any encounter, or what else is round the corner. Try as we may to pray or plan, neither petition nor prudence can make life other than a gamble – on the will of God or the wiles of men.[1] Luo say, with truth, 'You know where you came from, not where you are going.'[2] Only with the future behind us can we read history with a storied sense of direction. We can remember it backwards, and no longer have to guess. We know what happened next – or what is comforting to believe, or plausible to claim, we caused to happen next. We can all recall self-regarding narratives of the past. They keep us going.[3] And if we cannot pocket one in triumph then we can either keep failure quiet or blame it on some enemy's foul play.

Historians are tossed about on this tidal flow of anxious guesswork and therapeutic memory. Our profession teaches us to explain people's actions in their own time, in the face of uncertain futures, when all decisions were a venture, when anything might happen. As human beings, however, we are also partisan, and we know better than the actors we study. Their unknowable futures have since become known; their unforeseen outcomes have shaped our own heroic myths. Some of their causes have prospered, others failed or were crushed. We want to know why. Who benefited and at whose expense? But hindsight is a notoriously unfair tribunal and the 'judgment of history' often pre-judged.

The tension between history, as people once faced its 'confused alarms of struggle and flight',[4] and narrative memories of what might have been is particularly acute in the case of Kenya. The Mau Mau Emergency that overshadowed the last years of colonial rule exacted a grievous price in blood and treasure. The ordeal divided Kenyans against each other, whether in forest ambush or at the conference table, even as they fought or argued against the British. Since independence different Kenyans have likewise tasted freedom's variegated fruits, some sweet, others rotten, still others poisoned. They have searched the past for the roots of inequality.

Partisan questions about the Mau Mau war have therefore echoed round Kenya's political arena during 40 years of independence. How historically necessary was Mau Mau? Did its secretive sectarian violence alone have the power to destroy white supremacy? Or did it merely sow discord within a mass nationalism that – for all the failings of the Kenya African Union (KAU) – was bound to win power in the end? Did Mau Mau aim at freedom for all Kenyans? Or did moderate, constitutional, politicians rescue that pluralist prize from the jaws of its ethnic chauvinism? Has the self-sacrificial victory of the poor been unjustly forgotten, and appropriated by the rich? Or are Mau Mau's defeats and divisions best buried in oblivion?

Contradictory answers to such questions have since supported one political cause after another. Their afterlife is a proper subject for study.[5] But we should not deceive ourselves. To dissect Kenya's memories is to explain, not Mau Mau, but its mythic presence in later struggles for mastery. Two problems in oral tradition are relevant here, self-censorship and the false connectedness that memory lends to the discontinuities of actual historical contexts. Kenya's historians have barely begun to address the issue of therapeutic forgetting. We can detect partisan recall, or recognize politically expedient half-truths – such as Kenyatta's 'We all fought for freedom', that denied an exclusive patriotic virtue to Mau Mau. But, unlike historians of Zimbabwe's liberation war, students of Kenya have yet to examine the healing rituals that underlie the politics of a once wartorn locality, the psychodynamics of personal loss and recovery, or a peasant culture that doggedly silences past setbacks in order to face the future without flinching.[6] Memories of Mau Mau, too, must have been cleansed, to promote healing, but we have not considered the implications for historical method. We must also be aware, secondly, that the past is always another country where people did things differently. The men and women of Mau Mau had hopes and fears that may seem to resemble ours. The similarity of human motive through time is one of historiography's major snares. A seeming familiarity of recorded thought can blind us to the often silent heart of a past context, by which thought was shaped and to which it was addressed. Yet contextual fidelity, as Bethwell Ogot long ago insisted, is, after textual rigour, the historian's chief defence against the partisanship of memory.[7]

However self-disciplined most of us have been, historians have nonetheless written with different known futures for Mau Mau in mind – the changing Kenyan presents to which we have wished to speak. The first scholars, at the time of independence, wrote cleansing histories for self-government. They proved that Mau Mau's militants were neither savages nor madmen, as British propaganda had portrayed them, but ordinary people, driven to extraordinary lengths of political commitment, clearly fit for self-rule. Thereafter historians addressed what they saw as the failings of the new 'Kenyatta state'. Following intellectual fashion and Kenya's own debates, they first saw it as a neo-colonial dependency and then as a corrupt ethnocracy. Each type of successor state was held to have betrayed its parentage, an appropriately contradictory Mau Mau. In the first of these retrospective narratives the movement acted as the cutting edge of a national working class. The Kenyatta state had clearly suppressed, or ideologically cleansed, that radical story in the interest of the new ruling alliance, between the national petty-bourgeoisie and international capital. In the second, ethnically charged but still class-conscious, view Mau Mau became a Kikuyu peasants' army. These, as is the common fate of peasant rebels, had been dumped by their patrons when the latter no longer needed, indeed, had come to fear, their plebeian battering ram. In 1969 – that fateful year which saw Tom Mboya murdered, Kikuyu oath-taking revived to retain power in the house of Muumbi, and a massacre among Kenyatta's Luo audience at Kisumu – this last view seemed to be confirmed. Many Kenyans now imagined Mau Mau as an elite bid for Kikuyu dominion, as the British had also once warned. In the 1990s, however, the regime overturned Kikuyu privilege, sometimes with a force that recalled early-colonial punitive expeditions. Within the 'peoples' republics of the *matatus*' (Kenya's minibuses) many reacted by remembering Mau Mau, once again, as radical democracy in action. Its healing image was different now; it stood for the poor in general, who in turn had become the suffering people of God.[8] Mau Mau, in short, is an indelible symbol round which Kenya's antagonistic afterthoughts will continue to swarm. Historians have analysed Mau Mau accordingly, as symptom or cause of Kenya's divisions, or both. This is another attempt at explanation. But it is based on a premise about the human condition. It approaches Mau Mau not as the focus of divided memories but as a prime case in a common history of quarrelsome genders and argued authority. An effort to be contextually faithful is the only healing to which an historian can legitimately aspire.

Food, Freedom, and Kenya's Peasantries

What has always concerned Kenyans is what preoccupies humanity as a whole: the question of what to make of our lives. A context none can escape, the domestic future demands decision with each unforgiving day. It cannot be deferred – unlike, say, a declaration of war. How can we win honour, build a household and feed posterity, and exercise the responsibility we owe our seniors and juniors? These are questions about how to make respectably productive genders, according to our cultural lights and economic status. They amount to an audit of personal freedom, since, unless we are free to choose otherwise, we can neither shoulder responsibility nor win a reputation. To focus on gender, generation and honour is to prove oneself to be a child of one's time, like any other historian. But private life is a common concern. It is not of itself politically charged, as the issue of Mau Mau's ethnicity is politically charged. Moreover, to ask how far the Kenyans of half a century ago thought they were free to decide their destiny is to share in their uncertainty, presuming nothing about their future beyond its unknowability. To marry, to procreate, to cultivate, to herd livestock, were (and are) all fearful gambles. Freedom alone can transmute such throws of the dice into responsible choices. That is why people try to protect it. But they also take out insurances against its risks, at some acceptable cost to their autonomy in terms of duty to coalitions of kin, neighbours and political patrons. It is this universal need for freely contracted responsibility and its reciprocal obligations that makes Mau Mau's call for land and freedom part of Kenya's common history rather than its divided memory.

How then did twentieth-century Kenyans construe freedom within their many economies of reputation?[9] We cannot answer precisely, but they have left us clues. When in 1992 Oginga Odinga, who paid as dearly as any in its cause, was asked what freedom meant he replied by picturing 'a good and considerate father with many children'. Such a man would check any bullying tendency in one child that denied freedom to its siblings. He would correct the lazy child, who could not be free if he or she let others down. He must protect the timid child from losing his (or her) rights to more assertive offspring. In short, freedom needed hierarchical protection, self-discipline and leadership. But who, Odinga was asked, would protect the protector? He took this to mean protection from power's temptations: 'That is a matter for the culture, morality and good sense of the nation', he replied. 'In political practice, the people themselves are the protectors of the protector.'[10] So Odinga thought freedom must respect the storied past that shaped a people's culture. He could have said the same in 1952.

Kenyatta, who owed much to Odinga, had come to the selfsame view of freedom long before that, in the 1930s, in his British exile. It was his inherited culture, he believed, that taught a man the 'mental and moral values' that encouraged him 'to work and fight for liberty'. He also agreed that what fitted a man for public duty was his private management of a large, productive and potentially fractious household.[11] A Luo *ker*, Paul Mbuya Akoko, agreed that freedom was wealth, well earned. To work for, and depend on, another was to be unfree. Conversely, the wealthy had duties toward juniors, clients, and servants. His fellow Luo sage, Oruka Rang'inya, thought likewise. A free man was one who had many warrior sons, and well-stocked granaries (Rang'inya had ten wives to fill his) that enabled him to feed more than his own household in time of famine. Social inequality – he did not quite say – created obligations as well as rewards. Three attributes, he thought, helped one to attain such plutocratic freedom: hard work, self-discipline and respect for others.[12] Kikuyu, proverbially, said the same: self-mastery, self-restraint (*wiathi*), was the beginning of wisdom, a quality earned by senior elders. A productive life proved one's capacity to make the peace that protected the industrious freedom of others.[13]

The Kuria of Western Kenya endorsed an equally censorious ethic. Their elders had to show self-discipline in household careers of ordered growth, straightness, or *oboronge*, before they were trusted to protect the potential for moral growth in others.[14] Expert accumulation of the resources needed for survival was the similarly stern criterion of elderhood and ethnicity among Kenya's pastoral Maasai. Alternative identities, like womanhood and warriorhood, had little pull against this patriarchal hegemony.[15] This same harsh necessity lies behind President Moi's ruling ideology, derived from his Kalenjin upbringing. Leadership, he has said, is what 'liberates and galvanises the people's ability into a dynamic force', by freeing 'the constructive talents of the individual citizens'. As 'the art of prosperity' it is also 'a force for change'. Its fruits depend as much on the 'moral rectitude' of obedient followers as on their leaders' training.[16] Moi has here generalized the linkage that Kenyans hope to see, locally, between straightness in their protective elders and the freedom of juniors to achieve their own responsible ends. This household philosophy would be endorsed by even the least typical of Kenya's citizens, the Swahili townsmen of the coast. Their sense of honour, *heshima*, is shaped by patrician manners and an Islamic, bookish, code of enlightenment peculiar to their own commercial, urban, history. But *heshima* also grows with the considerate 'relations of communication and exchange' that are implicit in all the 'upcountry' notions of elderhood quoted above.[17] All these aspirations to honour presumed household property in land, or livestock, or credit, all means of subsistence. Mortal and moral life together needed both land and freedom.

The questions that put Mau Mau at the heart of Kenya's history, then, are these. How far, by the mid-twentieth century, did households differ, regionally, in their hopes or fears for their future freedom to produce on their own land? Where did foreboding about such prospects most aggravate relations between genders and generations? Did it become harder for some (but not other) young people to marry, become adult and feed a future at all? Kenya's societies were never equal but, in some regions, did freedom's protectors, wealthy elders, find it impossible to soothe local disputes that could no longer be resolved by the old remedy of clan fission and migration? Were elders then galvanized to regain peace-making authority by leading anti-colonial protest? Or were they compromised by their propertied self-interest, and outflanked by hungrier spirits among juniors who contrived to break their local dependence by access to outside support?

The relative propensity of different peasantries to revolt has been the subject of much theoretical strife. Yet it has proved difficult to apply any theory derived from Eurasia to sub-Saharan Africa. Some have questioned how far African cultivators can be called peasants at all.[18] But the end of sociological theory is the beginning of social history. The problem is that Africanist historians have employed class labels too precise to be usable, like poor, middle and rich peasants or – among their oppressors – landlords, merchants and planters. We have paid less attention to the household conflicts suggested above, partly because it is harder to find the evidence, partly also because, when found, it relates, rather distressingly for theory, to any and every class or political economy. It confuses generalization further if rich and poor face a similar intimate unease, especially if their attempts to relieve it are then rooted in specific cultural histories and memories.

Intimate unease, nonetheless, must surely be our quarry. It makes normal behaviour perilous and abnormal action a possible deliverance. Householders normally try to get by on their own, helped by reciprocities conventional to their local coalitions. Ordinarily, most people appear to accept their unequal status, no matter how guilty or rebellious their inner thoughts. But a pervasive sense of unease makes collective protest, even violence, thinkable, led either by natural leaders anxious for their legitimacy, or, if only they can break their ties of obligation, by their juniors. Open resistance from below requires that people see a continued deference, however hollow, to be more hazardous than joint action, in alliance with unreliable outsiders, against powers better armed than they. 'Exploitation without rebellion', it has been said, seems 'a far more ordinary state of affairs than revolutionary war'.[19] To explain Mau Mau, therefore, we need a better sense of how a domestic desperation that could detonate public violence varied across Kenya's social geography. Without it we are merely – to quote Eric Stokes on the historiography of the Indian mutiny/rebellion a century earlier – 'striking matches in the dark'.[20]

Here is another match struck in the dark. No matter how little we know of Kenya's household histories, it is nonetheless clear that colonial rule disturbed the bedrock issues of straightness and growth. Kenyatta charged that alien rule destroyed the spirit of manhood by denying to Africans the power of decision. Postwar pamphleteers agreed.[21] Dr Carothers, who investigated the mind of Mau Mau, would also have understood. He was haunted by the memory of how, on his official safari of inquiry, Kikuyu inmates greeted him at each detention camp with the chorused reproach of 'Boy! Boy! Boy!'[22] Many women also found marriage more stifling than before; some shocked men by using market freedoms to escape household ties; a few became the first African owners of urban property. Genders were clearly on edge, but not everywhere to the same extent.[23] So too were generations. Some mothers deplored their daughters' looseness, freed from cultural discipline. Migrant labour gave young men the economic liberty to marry without their fathers' aid.[24] By the mid-1940s, however, land shortage and the rise of rural capitalism had in some parts turned the tables on the young; many were finding it harder to marry at all.[25] But some elders felt that their duty to defend ancestral land from white ambition was now so far beyond them that they were prepared, reluctantly, to share it with their juniors. These were the dilemmas that 'straddling' peasantries, all who marketed their labour as well as their produce, had to argue about.[26]

In due course, domestic debate created new public spheres, in which equalities of discourse challenged hierarchies of opinion.[27] Literacy,

Qur'anic or biblical exposition, a secular press, official *barazas*, and local native councils (LNCs) structured their 'horizontal comradeships'.[28] Kenyatta's 'inherited cultures', Kenya's tutors in liberty, inspired new local historiographies, narratives of ethnic virtue that deserved political reward.[29] Standardized print-vernaculars began to edge out local dialects in 'lexicographic revolutions'.[30] New patriotisms, moral ethnicities, appeared, within which to renegotiate, in changing times, the freedoms, duties and protections that promoted civic virtue, in hope of restoring an equitable, not equal, social order that would allow all who worked to eat.[31]

A Political Geography of Intimate Unease

The urgency of these debates was very uneven, if such crude indices as British anxiety or African anger are any guide.[32] Kenya's many economies of reputation faced varied futures by the mid-twentieth century. In most localities, a confidence in their continued tactical mobility, within coalitions of collective insurance, allowed individual households to pursue a canny survival. By contrast, tactical immobility, helplessness in face of an inexorable social extinction that one's natural leaders either abetted or appeased, could prompt people to search for allies outside the little coalitions that now spelt danger rather than protection. This seems to be the only safe generalization to make about rural rebellion.[33] But extinction can take two forms, physical or social. Survival in subsistence crises, such as severe famine, seems as often as not to demand a selfish isolation. Threats to household autonomy in production and exchange, on the other hand, have more potential to arouse co-operation. This hypothesis suggests two riders to any explanation of rural resistance. Some social force must be felt to threaten a peasantry; and external allies must be available to help peasants resist. It is futile to try to understand rural rebellion by looking at cultivators and pastoralists alone. In colonial Kenya one must also assess the changing strategies of the regime, of white settlers and of African big men, the peasants' patrons; and ask to whom else rural householders could turn.[34]

To examine, so far as one can, tension within and between households can thus be no more than a first step in understanding. Such fissures may have fired people to challenge their leaders' accommodations with the British, but colonial policy itself coloured the future that householders imagined. Colonial rule also rested on African supports. The politics of collaboration was narrow. It offered much, but to few. It exacerbated existing social difference and created new political power. But only in some regions, in pursuit of particular policies, did the African props of British rule become socially insupportable, by undermining rather than promoting the industrious freedoms of other men's households. Only after recognizing this knotted relationship between state and society can we attempt to compare Kenya's regions according to the relative likelihood that their domestic fractures would, if allies were found, endanger the regime. This contour map of susceptibility to rebellion has nothing intrinsically to do with ethnicity. It charts, rather, the uneven impact of colonial rule and rural capitalism, upon both the spirit of manhood and household entitlement to produce and eat. It is a regional, not a 'tribal', map. But political effects cannot be deduced from socio-economic causes alone. Kenya's ecologically based ethnicities, as already argued, were developing spheres of public debate. What follows, then, has to be more than a mere social geography. Ethnic patriotisms gave to regional difference an increasingly discordant set of political narratives.

In brief, the political potential of intimate social unease increased with proximity to Kenya's centre. Agrarian politics was a distorted mirror of physical geography. The colony's hot, semi-desert, plains were, in political terms, a cool periphery. Full of intrigue and banditry, they rarely alarmed official Nairobi. But as Kenya's highlands climbed to cooler altitudes, from ranchland to cultivated fields, and populations thickened, so politics heated up. On the pastoral periphery, African social structure disciplined domestic discord. Plains people were also regaining some tactical mobility with respect to the state. Cleavages of age and gender were sharper among those cultivators who were least tactically mobile. Their autonomy was threatened most by unequal access to land, education and markets. Friction was more likely, but not inevitable, the closer one lived to the line of rail, Nairobi and the White Highlands. This was also the area most critical to British control, most sensitive to white settler alarm and where the state's few forces could most easily be deployed.[35] Yet British rule suffered no crisis such as might have unified any forces of discontent. There was no mutiny, as in the India of 1857, to create a vacuum in power. By contrast with the years after the first world war, African taxation supplied a declining share of the state's income. A more distant contrast with the great war is also apposite. Unlike Russia in 1917, there were no shivering bread queues in Nairobi, nor did the Abyssinia and Burma campaigns turn the King's African Rifles (KAR) into a revolutionary mob. The KAR had returned victorious, marching to a song that predicted, with a productive, manly, optimism that was not always betrayed: 'When we have beaten the enemy we shall return home. The children will be waiting to clap their hands. We shall start to dig our fields, And herd our cattle for ever.'[36] In the 1940s, then, Kenyans faced their futures neither forced nor drawn together, but regionally apart. Efforts to resolve issues of local community withstood any attempt by the KAU to appropriate a wider unity. Only within their ethnically distinct public spheres were strangers likely to volunteer alliance.[37]

To begin, then, in the northern plains, the two-thirds of Kenya that are almost desert. Some of their hardy peoples had fought exhausting wars against British conquest, while losing many livestock to drought and disease. Their markets were then shut for decades by quarantines that protected white ranchers from competition and cattle plague. In the 1930s depression herders compared tax-hungry DCs to hyenas. In the early

1940s the number of cattle requisitioned to feed the army again threatened breeding stocks. This dismal sequence meant that northerners were repeatedly preoccupied with rebuilding their herds, an aspiration to which colonial policy belatedly adjusted in the late 1940s. Kenya never became a large beef producer, as officials hoped, but at least its pastoralists could now pursue the politics of accumulation without intolerable state meddling. They continued to define large stock owners as honourably straight and the poor as feckless others. The latter were no longer 'us', on whose behalf patrons should act, but of no account, obliged to seek asylum elsewhere as fisherfolk or cultivators. A British official termed the outcome 'unregulated autocracy'. Pastoral chiefs were critical of colonial rule, of course, but remained self-confident allies, neither troubled by dissent from below nor with much reason to rebel themselves. In the sputnik era, a northern DC might still mount his police on ponies, the better to combat stock theft and grazing feuds.[38]

Other pastoralists were centrally placed and, through service in army or police, more able to upset the applecart of colonial rule. These were the several peoples who in the 1940s began to call themselves Kalenjin, 'I say to you', proof of a new public sphere, uttering a common vernacular. But Kalenjin had three good reasons not to carry anti-colonial feeling to the point of sustained opposition, even if they did cause the British periodic alarm. First, their peoples retained room to expand their mixed economies. Tugen herds surreptitiously grazed the Lembus forest reserve and white border ranchlands, from which they were only from time to time expelled. Some Kipsigis stockmen emigrated to Maasailand. Nandi squatters in the Uasin Gishu district suffered few restrictions on their customary rights to cultivate and graze portions of white farms. Second, thanks to this continued ability to eat well in freedom, internal Kalenjin politics upheld a vigorous rural capitalism among men who might otherwise have caused trouble. These were young elders, often armed with Christian literacy, who fenced in lineage commons, upgraded cattle and grew more maize – in the Kipsigis case, for sale as rations to the tea planters of Kericho. Their livestock market also expanded, as more densely populated groups, like Luo and Kikuyu, began to de-stock, selling off cattle and buying in meat. Such alternative leadership, finally, as the prophetic *orkoiik* might have provided for younger sparks, had long been suspect to many Kalenjin. There was, then, little intimate cause to co-operate in rebellion. When others took to arms in Mau Mau, Kalenjin could also exploit the enlarged security forces' payroll and the anxious flattery the British lavished on them.[39]

Mixed farmers carried more political weight than herders. While pastoralists controlled three-quarters of Kenya's land, they numbered less than 14 per cent of the population.[40] Stockowning black farmers were the main taxpayers, school-parents and migrant workers. Nearly half of them lived west of the Rift Valley, in the old Nyanza province. For the sake of brevity, these must do representative duty for all Kenya's African mixed farmers – save only Kikuyu. The most numerous Nyanza groups were

Luo, Luyia and Gusii. All enjoyed superior access to modern education. Their council expenditure on schools and other public services soared after the second world war. Luyia and Gusii agriculture boomed. Luo and Luyia men, up to half their adult male population at any time, migrated throughout East Africa, from Kampala to the Indian Ocean, often in skilled jobs on the railway, the region's best employer.

Luo had good reason to resist postwar British attempts to reform their husbandry and land law, with the aim of making more intensive cultivation ecologically sustainable. But Luo were scarcely up against a wall. They had little fear of white settlers, to Odinga a 'distant horror'; the threat they now faced came from the state, not from their own coalitions. Luo lineages retained a resilient talent for spreading farming's risks. An uncertain subsistence on poor, and erratically watered, land fostered reinsurance with kin and interlocked land holdings, resistant to individualizing reform. Luo capitalists ploughed wide acres only when colonists, over the Tanganyikan border, and not at home. Any new inequality between Kenya Luo was caused more by education and clerical employment elsewhere. Distinctions between 'owners' of land and 'tenants', *weg lowo* and *jodak*, were strained, but scarcely to breaking point; new competitions in production had not yet subverted old reciprocities of patronage. When, therefore, the British tried to reform land usage they faced an almost solid opposition, led by wealthy elders, *jodong gweng'*, whose reputation still rested on their ability to protect the subsistence of the poor. At the intimate levels of household and lineage, Luo agreed that private freedoms were still publicly compatible with each other. Unity made an entirely passive resistance entirely effective.[41]

Some Luyia peoples, in the southeast of their region, one of the most populous corners of Kenya, faced a deeper foreboding. Young men had adopted a radical politics, accordingly. They failed to make any wide impression. Their local base was riven with clan faction;[42] further afield, Luyia were never a 'tribe'. Their collective name, (Ba)Luyia, first mooted in the 1930s, was derived from the grove where clan elders took counsel, *oluyia*. There were hundreds of these, all independent, all over Buluyia. Another vernacular recognition of a newly enlarged public sphere, the name was long seen as subversive of all local hierarchy. Elders thought it 'an assertive appellation', usurped by juniors.[43] These elders, *maguru*, were able to thwart British tenurial reform, like Luo *jodong' gweng*, thanks to the same authority to mediate between litigious neighbours. There was little intimate discord on which to build a wider, rival, sway. The wealthiest Luyia group, Bukusu, were too divided between plough-owning maize barons and poor farm-squatters, whose religious enthusiasm in the charismatic *Dini ya Msambwa* movement had little staying power. Elsewhere, any broader Luyia patriotism was balked by unhappy memories of the sub-imperialism once exercised by the Wanga 'royal' line, through whom the British had first tried to rule the area.[44] There was plenty of individual conflict, but little corporate unease, among the prosperously litigious Gusii.[45]

JOHN LONSDALE

The Well-fed, the Ravenous and the Greedy[46]

This sketch of a relative absence of unease in Nyanza must do duty for the rest of postwar, highland, cultivating, Kenya; for the rest, that is, save for the peoples who called themselves Kikuyu, whose anxiety was distinctive in four ways. They feared more for land and freedom than other groups, with a dismay felt by the wealthy scarcely less than the poor. Their unusually large diaspora, next, faced social extinction. Their townspeople, further, seemed to have repudiated reputation. Their public sphere, finally, was sharply divided between desire for local autonomy and need for political solidarity, between dynastic and generational authority, and by mutual fear of sorcery. Of no other region of Kenya, not even of those that had lost more land to white settlement, could all this be said.

First, no Kenya peasantry knew sharper contrasts between profit and ruin. This was due in part to the loss of some – 6 per cent – of their land to white settlement. Kikuyu saw that as the source of their hatreds. Central location divided them more. By the 1940s they had caught up with Nyanza's education; their farmers had intensified production, more than others more distant, to supply Nairobi with food and fuel; their traders were busier. Not all could exploit these advantages. Postwar educational reform that stiffened entry criteria for primary education closed for many the door of opportunity; some trades offered no more than survival for the poor, women especially. Many feared that their coalitions, the sub-clan *mbari* that once welcomed industrious dependants, had, by contrast with Luo *gweng'*, become dynastic engines of exclusion against juniors, women and clients. Closure of entitlement to assiduous growth became punitive when the postwar labour of state-enforced soil conservation fell mainly upon poor men's wives. Many land-poor households were desperate, with no defence in sight. Few wealthy elders were any more confident. Their children would surely lack land in the next generation. A growing mistrust in *mbari* was not the only sense in which Kikuyu felt up against a wall.

Inequality, second, gave Kikuyu the largest emigrant African population outside their 'reserves': by 1950, 30 per cent of their total number. Most were farm-labour tenants, squatters, on the White Highland plateaus – formerly Maasailand – that abutted the Rift Valley. This diaspora was unique in Kenya. The next largest outflow came from Buluyia, but that was only 18 per cent of all Luyia. Moreover, while for every 100 Kikuyu emigrant females there were 136 emigrant males, in the Luyia case there were 186 males and, for Luo, no less than 272.[47] Many whole Kikuyu households had emigrated; others sent out more single men. If not landless before they went, the former found their reserve land rights harder to reclaim with every passing year. Squatters had to struggle if they were to be counted as 'us', enfolded within the sphere of Kikuyu patronage – and not cast-offs, like failed pastoralists. After 1945, their settler employers, formerly patrons of peasant colonization, turned against them – as whites hesitated to turn on Kalenjin – and curtailed their rights to hoe and graze, reducing them to wage labourers. Squatters, *athikwota*, urgently needed to reclaim their imagined Kikuyu citizenship, to appeal for redress or refuge. They knew, intimately, long before Ngugi wa Thiong'o, how Mau Mau fed on the anxieties of exile.[48]

In 1946 the diaspora's leaders petitioned the British colonial secretary, Arthur Creech-Jones. Farm squatters told him that they were suffering social extinction at the hand of their white patrons. They were being 'gradually exterminated', reduced 'to the status of slaves' and on 'a sinking ship'. The ex-squatters whom the government had settled at Olenguruone felt, still more painfully, that they were being unmanned. The British thought them state tenants. The Kikuyu thought themselves owners of land granted in lieu of alienated ancestral acres. They protested that the settlement's rules, which prescribed impartible inheritance, forced men 'to divorce our wives and denounce fatherly rights to our sons'. Livestock and cultivation were also restricted. Since parental authority was thus subverted, household solidarity had to be engineered. Juniors were keen to share in responsibility; without productive entitlements in the highlands, how else could they support their parents in old age? Needing a common front to resist state dictate, the ex-squatters administered one of the oaths of commitment their culture offered. Normally only male elders, trustees for juniors, took such oaths; but times were not normal. Elders had been shorn of fatherhood. They had no option but to share it with wives and children. A great vulgarization of authority occurred. Elders shuddered, but the British, not their juniors, were to blame. Looking back, many saw the Olenguruone oath, with its unnatural collusion of genders and generations, and its outcome, the eviction of its participants, as the start of Mau Mau.[49]

Cultural innovation in Nairobi, *gecombaini*, the place of strangers, was more shocking still. Respectable men like Kenyatta commuted to the city from their homes in Kiambu or, if from more distant Murang'a and Nyeri, from rented rooms a bus ride out of town. Kikuyu townswomen were notoriously independent. Swahili, who had failed to make the capital as urbane as Mombasa, thought Kikuyu men savages, *acenji*, for exerting so little control. Nairobi Kikuyu thought differently, but their attempts to rewrite the norms of reputation made matters worse. Young men banded together as the *Anake a Forti*, the Forty Group. But not all had been initiated in 1940. They recruited regardless of their members' circumcision year, rejecting the authority of the wealthy elders who sponsored initiation annually. More impudently still, they claimed that their parents had been born, initiated and married in 1940 too, an insult to all concepts of ordered growth in seniors. They were almost certainly from land-poor families. There were shreds of respectability about the *Anake a Forti*, nonetheless. Many being unmarried, they had the decency not to assume elder status and took no oath of solidarity. They also repatriated prostitutes and women in short dresses, while acting, it was said, as pimps themselves. Kikuyu politics, from 1948, centred on rival efforts to control such hooligans. Elders were anxious to discipline them, militant trade unionists happy to use them.[50]

This observation introduces the fourth, decisive, distinction in Kikuyu unease: its highly disputatious public sphere. No other vernacular region had such competitive institutions within which one might attempt to recreate a social order in which all could eat the unequal fruits of their toil. All such attempts faced insoluble problems, however, rooted in moral and political thought. Not even the proclamation of the Emergency – to many, a British declaration of war – made it easy for Kikuyu to decide which of their many fences they could no longer sit upon.

Kikuyu moral-political thought was twice divided. Vertical, kin-based, loyalty to *mbari*, opposed horizontal solidarity in age-sets or *riika*. Dynastic charters of separately sweated *mbari* progress also clashed with the collective cleansing promised in the costly ritual of generational renewal called *ituika*.[51] History taught the perils of this divided counsel, not least the failure to persuade the (Carter) Land Commission of the early 1930s to return alienated Kikuyu land. The toughest interest groups, the hundreds of sub-clan *mbari*, were also the most divisive. Their elders had sole responsibility for their land, as in Luoland and Buluyia. They could not share it without surrender – although, as at Olenguruone, land elders began to accept that the impatience of juniors was a forgivable response to closure of opportunity. Age-sets, next, ladders of straightness, were increasingly splintered. Some youths were still initiated collectively, by tradition; some in a missionary hospital without due ritual; yet others, children of the poor, by the roadside. Some young women, daughters of keen Christians, escaped the discipline of genital surgery entirely. Ideas of generational authority, finally, had become blurred over time, but no less powerful for that. The last *ituika* had been celebrated at the turn of the century. Its cleansing ideas had supported young Christian readers, *athomi*, in their sometimes scandalous innovations in the 1920s.[52] Thoughts of renewal were in the air once again.

Successive leaders tried to control Kikuyu responses to the intimate perils of the postwar world by redefining one institution after another: *mbari*, age-set and generation. Koinange wa Mbiyu, a senior official chief, had redeemed some dynastic authority, shattered by Judge Carter's deafness to *mbari* pleas, by founding the Githunguri Teacher Training College in 1939. He was also responding to the prophecy of Chege (Mugo) Kibiru, associated with symbols of *ituika*, that the 'red strangers' would depart once Kikuyu had learned their wisdom. Koinange's federation of lineage heads, *Mbari*, could, however, only encourage each *mbari* to act for itself. *Mbari* thus printed claim forms for land elders to use at need. These specified that 'Many centuries past' A, son of B, had 'purchased a large portion of land from' C, for X goats, Y rams and Z 'pots of honey'. Any more unified 'tribal' front, would, in Kikuyu political theology, have been illegal, offensive to the spiritual forces that protected each *mbari*'s land.[53] But *Mbari* could take up less specifically land-linked causes, such as the plight of the squatters. In a plea to Creech Jones, supported by the thumb-prints of two other senior chiefs, Nderi and Wambugu, Koinange used language very similar to the squatter petitioners. 'Man is compelled to sell his goats and sheep to divorce his wives, and is forced in Olenguruone and Rift Valley areas to denounce his fatherly right to his children in order to limit their family to the area of allotment given to these slave squatters.'[54] The Kikuyu public sphere was clearly thick with private lines of communication. It was well informed by the public prints. It was also, however, haunted by fears of sorcery, fostered by rural capitalism's mutual suspicions. Koinange's *Mbari* would have had no authority were it not backed by a new oath of commitment, *uiguano*, or 'unity', that foreswore sorcery between its elders.

Kenyatta, who returned from Britain in 1946, earned still less power to co-ordinate opinion than his father-in-law Koinange. Based at Githunguri, he tried to energize the horizontal political principle latent in the *riika* age-sets. The vernacular press encouraged their competition to fund the college, but with short-lived success. Rural elders suspected *riika* treasurers of selling accelerated eldership in their oaths of commitment; and *riika* allegiance was to their own members, not to some wider project.[55] The strategy with which Kenyatta intended to employ the projected unity can only be inferred, from scanty evidence. Like other elders, he exhorted Kikuyu to work, since prosperity was its own argument for political reward. He also had a historical precedent in mind, to which he often referred. This was the sequence in which the killing of 25 Africans, who in March 1922 had demanded the release of the jailed Harry Thuku, had been followed by the Colonial Office's Devonshire Declaration that Kenya was an African, not a settler, territory. Kenyatta seems to have believed that punitive excess had shamed London into political concession. And until 1951 he had friends in the British Labour government, whose instincts he thought he understood. In an account of the Thuku incident for the British press, Kenyatta had stressed the African protesters' discipline, under their chiefs' authority. To African audiences he now warned that their tree of freedom would be watered by blood, not European blood but their own, that of 'twenty Kenyattas'.[56]

This strategic analogy would explain Kenyatta's hostility to youthful criminality. The British must be given no pretext for whatever bloody act of panic they would surely commit, unnerved by whatever peaceful protest a disciplined unity might sometime deliver. Kikuyu elders often reminded themselves, too, that armed resistance had brought nothing but loss in the past.[57] Violence would also outrun the elders' control. Kenyatta's conservative convictions were plain to see in front of a rowdy crowd, over 20,000 strong, at the KAU's mass meeting outside Nyeri in July 1952. 'KAU is not a fighting union that uses fists and weapons. If any of you here think that force is good, I do not agree with you... I pray to you that we join hands for freedom and freedom means abolishing criminality...' He then invited the crowd to welcome senior chief Nderi. To 'tremendous jeers' Nderi promised that 'Our Government knows that you are hungry and it will feed you.'[58] Three months later he was dead, murdered by Mau Mau.

Nderi used a household metaphor that his young audience shouted down. Their nickname, coined by opponents, was 'Mau Mau'. The most plausible of its many attempted explications is 'the greedy eaters'. In the Great Hunger of the 1890s this name had characterized warriors who raided their own neighbourhoods. A term of disapproval, it nonetheless suggested that the greedy were not solely to blame. Their parents should have fed them then, as the government was again failing to do in 1952. Kikuyu had an apt proverb for the moral ambiguities of rapaciousness: 'The well-fed calls the ravenous greedy.' Elders were reluctant to condemn the commitment oaths that landless young men were taking in Nairobi. It was greedy to demand large fees for oaths, and wrong for the young to assume authority. It was also understandable, for they were hungry.[59]

Mau Mau was the outcome of a competition for the authority to take action. Elders in *Mbari*, with Kenyatta, had authority but lacked cohesion. They failed to find the unity of peaceful pressure enjoyed by Luo *jodong' gweng*. Kikuyu elders had invested in well-fed power, but it now offered no growth to juniors. The young were famished at the elders' table. Their militants had little of their own to invest in politics, and greedily demanded it of others. This competition makes a strict definition of Mau Mau impossible, until after British countermeasures had separated the hesitant from the desperate. Until then Mau Mau was less a movement than a partisan sector of a crowded arena. The political songs, or *nyimbo*, are the best evidence.[60] They scarcely mentioned violence but extolled the peasant virtues of labour and responsibility; they sneered at the well-dressed ones who would bear no fruit; and told the elders to keep silent, as if it was time for another *ituika*. Sung by urban youths who could no longer look to rural patrons for land, who had to act for themselves, they nonetheless voiced the hopes of people worthy to be peasant allies. The slum-dwellers of Nairobi enjoyed the tactical mobility that squatters and the land-poor in the reserves lacked, and shared the peasants' sweaty ideology. All the same, Kikuyu seem to have been reluctant to resort to arms. It took Kenyatta's arrest to persuade many that violence was respectable. It took the settlers' repatriation of squatters and rough handling by the police to recruit most forest fighters, in their own defence. 'War is not porridge', Kikuyu say. Porridge is cooked in households, by creatively fulfilled genders. These are what the forest war failed to provide.

Gender and Generalship

In the forest war the internal struggle for reputation was as fierce as the outward fight for freedom. Men and women wrestled with questions of self-discipline, gender and literacy that were, at bottom, about power and its claims on self-mastery. In trying to win authority over each other the Mau Mau forest fighters experienced all the crises of intimate unease that other Kenyans, in less desperate circumstances, have had to face in the 40 years since independence.

To look, first, at the general issue of self-discipline: a forest song recalled what Kenyatta had said at the Nyeri mass meeting of the KAU: 'Vagrancy and laziness do not produce benefits for our country.'[61] Those whom Kenyatta had then condemned as hooligans now proved to have their own rigorous standards of straightness in fighting to benefit their country. Forest leaders condemned all ill-disciplined fighters as *komerera*, a name that connotes both cowardice and the idleness that Kenyatta had condemned. *Komerera* were bandits, as distinct from warriors under discipline. As vagrants they perpetrated anti-social violence, refused to cook for their leaders, and failed to fight the British. They personified the nightmare 'other', for Mau Mau military discipline as much as for the Kikuyu civic virtue for which Kenyatta had called. Forest leaders thus disowned much of the evil barbarism that whites attributed to Mau Mau. *Komerera* thuggery was politically disastrous, and unworthy of their cause.[62] The split between politically principled fighters and *komerera*, many of whom may have been politically ignorant refugees from police reprisals or victims of Mau Mau press-gangs,[63] was, however, not as serious as the forest war's conflicts over gender and education. *Komerera* were 'not us', and were marginalized; quarrels of gender and education were at the heart of Mau Mau's agonized spirit of manhood.

The forest's struggle for honour was toughest in matters of gender.[64] Men and women fighters found they could not relate as adults. Liberation wars may well demand the sacrifice of the self-mastery to which their militants so hungrily aspire – along with the well-fed Odinga, Rang'inya, and Kenyatta. Warriors discussed their predicament in the light of the remembered past. Kikuyu had conventionally recognized two stages of gender relations after circumcision of both sexes at puberty had initiated them as sexual beings. Religious and social change, however, meant that the behaviour proper to both stages was now uncertain. Before marriage – soon after initiation for women, but for men often not until they were senior warriors, in their early twenties – there had once been relatively free relations between age-mates, including non-penetrative intercourse, *nguiko*. By the 1940s older Kikuyu were blaming Christianity for the allegedly new scandal of premarital pregnancy. White missionaries, they said, had condemned disciplined premarital sex as promiscuity and young Christians, in response, had abandoned not *nguiko* but its prudential rules against conception.[65] In the past, marriage had then conferred on men sole reproductive – but not exclusive sexual – rights in their wives.[66] Christianity had apparently brought guilty subterfuge to this area of sexual hospitality too. Economic relations between the genders had also changed. They had been relatively equal in pre-colonial times. By the 1950s poor men, a growing majority, had become ever more dependent on their wives for farm management and commercial skill. Many men found this hard to stomach.[67] Neither stage of gender relations, not even in their current state of disarray, was available to the forest fighters. Nor did fighters make good husbands and fathers. Mau Mau's attempts to regulate its own behaviour, under unprecedented moral and physical pressure, divided its fighters bitterly, fatally so in the case of the senior forest commander, Dedan Kimathi, who fell victim to his subordinates' anger.

Mau Mau guerrillas accepted that proper marital relations could exist only outside the forest, in what one of their senior officers, Karari Njama, called the 'normal world'.[68] Njama's memoirs are so much more reflective and apparently more reliable than those of other forest fighters that one must be careful not to assume his views were typical. His is a partisan account, largely but not blindly favourable to the literate Kimathi, and critical of the unlettered Stanley Mathenge, whose leadership the former usurped in 1953.[69] Nevertheless, while Njama may have taken a more than usually censorious view of wartime sexual liaisons, his attitude to marriage seems to have been shared by all in the forest, male or female. Kahinga Wachanga, Njama's rival in other respects, made the same distinction between 'wives' in the reserve and 'women' in the forest. Moreover, the relative anonymity of female lovers, fighters and auxiliaries that is found in all male memoirs and deplored by feminist scholars, may well be explained by the men's concern to protect unmarried female honour after the war was over, back in the normal world.[70]

If wartime marriage was difficult, parenting was a burden; in the end its labours broke the will to fight. Individually, Njama gave what little he could to support his family, lamenting that in the forest he made a poor husband and father.[71] Collectively, male and female activists shared parental roles in the absence of mothers in detention or fathers in the forest. A British official thought this was what most impressed people about Mau Mau.[72] Those who supplied food, arms, shelter and information were, in effect, Mau Mau's mothers and daughters.[73] Eventually, however, the hunger and oppression of nurturing insurgent sons or husbands while also performing punitive labour for the British caused the rural population to share the white opinion that Mau Mau was evil. This parental change of heart was the strongest pressure on many forest fighters to end the war.[74]

Surrender also promised a return to the 'normal world' and true responsibility. The most stirring event in some memoirs is not a forest battle but marriage at the end of the war, or a return to the marital household. J. M. Kariuki recounted his postwar wedding at greater length than his first oath.[75] Kikuyu associated marriage with adult proprietorship; no man should marry without land on which a wife could support her children. The heavy moral cost of the insurgents' war, then, is shown by the opposing fighters' nicknames, which denoted their respective marital status. A loyalist Kikuyu guard was *kamatimu*, a spearman, but also a junior elder, qualified as such by marriage and fatherhood. By contrast, forest fighters were *itungati*, in past usage warriors sufficiently experienced to form a rearguard and entitled to marry, but who had rarely done so. Most Mau Mau *itungati* were thus the 'boys' that colonial usage now made so insulting, and who were fighting against their seniors in gendered straightness.[76]

All this is to say that war and married adulthood did not mix. Male insurgents resented that. We know less of how women felt at the time; there is only one woman's memoir. Historians did not consult female memories until a quarter of a century later. Most women served Mau Mau as mothers and sisters, the supply line without which the forest war would not have lasted a week. They rarely became fighters themselves. Some of those who have since reminisced to scholars have relished the unusual degree of power and autonomy that the war allowed them to enjoy, as is often true of gender relations in wartime; but there was also female pain and submission. Wangui, the *kabutini* or 'little platoon' allocated to look after Njama's needs, accepted with resignation the household and sexual tasks that Mau Mau required of her: 'Wherever I might go under the sun, I think these same duties would follow me.'[77]

Most male fighters, most of them young, will have been unmarried. But premarital sexual relations, whether historically open or promiscuously modern, were also impossible. There were too few women, constituting 5–20 per cent of the forest armies.[78] Kikuyu moreover, like many peoples, thought sexual intercourse out in the bush to be taboo. It was thought especially dangerous to warriors on active service. In pre-colonial times this would have been a raid, of only of a few days' duration. Men feared that sex weakened them or brought 'calamity'. The forest leaders, accordingly, at first tried to ban sexual intimacy and to segregate men from women. These rules, alien to normal Kikuyu sexuality, sought to avert male jealousy as much as to keep them 'clean'; although if married men slept with their wives while on home leave in the reserve some thought that they should be ritually purged before returning to the forest.[79] But the martial celibacy appropriate to cattle raids soon wavered in face of constant war; leaders were said to be the worst offenders.[80] Cohabitation became inevitable.

But sex was dangerous. Forest leaders tried in vain to contain its explosive potential by reinterpreting older disciplines. With Mathenge in the chair, the Nyandarwa area's commanders decided in July 1953 that they must replace unenforceable celibacy with regulated cohabitation. Meeting on the upper reaches of the Mumwe river, they recognized women as fellow soldiers – an outrage to their grandfathers – but then tried to restrict their status and sexuality. Men resolved that women's only role was to be camp caterers; they must also all 'marry' by public notice. 'Adultery' by either party would bring corporal punishment. These rules adjusted former relations between warriors and women to the unprecedented length of the war and an unequal sex ratio. The Nyandarwa leaders met again in August, now under Kimathi, high on the Mwathe moorlands. No source tells us why or how, but women had gained much in the intervening month. They could now be promoted up to the rank of colonel. They could choose with whom to live, as they had normally been free to choose premarital partners or husbands in the past. They could also keep insurgent officers out of their affairs until a couple wished to register 'as man and wife'. These were all gains in responsible freedom. But the Mwathe meeting also agreed to prohibit 'divorce'. The ban was ostensibly designed to prevent men's homicidal sexual intrigue. All present must, however, have known that the chief cause of divorce in the 'normal world' was women's desire to escape from mistreatment by men.[81]

It is important not to misunderstand these debates. They were not about what they seem to be: monogamy, or indeed marriage itself. No bridewealth was, or could be, exchanged; there was no obligation to tell a couple's parents, nor any customary celebration. There was no discussion of these deficiencies, however, nor yet a principled decision to ignore them. Njama, present at both meetings and their only reporter, was just the sort of man to have recorded their arguments, if any, at anguished length. This lack of debate is highly significant and, on reflection, not surprising. Mau Mau leaders were looking only to discipline premarital sexuality to an extent not previously necessary, not to revolutionize marriage, with all its implications for social reproduction. The Mwathe rules of August 1953 followed the traditional practices of unmarried love so far as possible, and tried to minimize the dangers to which the unheard-of length of the war exposed their inevitable violators. That forest liaisons were not marriage is best seen in the contrast that Mau Mau made between loyalist, enemy, women and female insurgents. It was parallel to the distinction already noted between loyalist *kamatimu* fathers and guerrilla *itungati* 'boys'. It was resolved that Mau Mau should not deliberately kill loyalist women, since they would be mothers. By contrast, it was 'bad discipline' for women forest fighters to fall pregnant. An offender 'lost her honour' and her gun; her partner was subject to 'punitive chores'.[82] Insurgents were clearly expected to practise premarital *nguiko*, not coition, in obedience to older conventions of unmarried love.

These rules were traditional in spirit but revolutionary in practice. They caused division between officers and men, formally on Mount Kenya, disputatiously so in the Nyandarwa theatre of war. In the Mount Kenya forest, General China seems to have formalized a military command structure in the sphere of gender relations. He not only tried to enforce the rules of faithful cohabitation on all, he forbade his officers to enter into amatory competition with other ranks. This was scarcely a hardship, since he also arranged for women leaders in the reserve to introduce officers to local girls, presumably *airitu*, initiated but unmarried young women. China thus provided senior men with a militarily secure waiver of the formal, if widely ignored, ban on abducting females into the forest. Had he so chosen (we do not know), he could have justified this unequal male sexuality by appeal to precedent. Senior warriors had always had the power – or so they reminisced to Louis Leakey in the 1930s – to impose on juniors a high price of admission to the pleasures of female company.[83]

On Nyandarwa, Field Marshal Kimathi seems also to have enjoined sexual discretion on his commanders, in return for employing the women's escort agency.[84] But he abused his own rules. His best fighting general, Kago, protested at Kimathi's abduction of women food suppliers. Kago narrowly escaped execution for his effrontery, fled from the shelter of the forest, and based himself in the Murang'a reserve, soon to be killed in battle.[85] Colonel Wamugunda likewise criticized Kimathi's dangerous fondness for women's chatter while there was a war on. General 'Knife-in-the-buttocks', Kahiu-Itina, even accused him of turning 'the majority of guerrilla women into prostitutes' by loving them 'too much'.[86] The policeman Ian Henderson may not have been far from the mark in referring to Kimathi's 'harem'. Njama, who knew Kimathi's habits from closer quarters, wrote, rather, of the serial polygyny, equally against the rules, by which he changed his partners every few months.[87]

Kimathi's private failings had fatal public consequences. In the end, he was betrayed to Henderson by a turncoat forest fighter whom Kimathi had condemned to be flogged for presuming, although a common soldier, to sleep with a woman.[88] Long before that, Kimathi's refusal to punish his brother Wambararia for trying to murder two sexual rivals had finally convinced his critics that he was a tyrant, placing himself and his kin above the law.[89] The gender conflict was, indeed, located within a wider forest struggle. This ranged literates and unlettered against each other over the fundamental question of authority. It was not a new problem. Kenyatta had thought colonialism undermined African manhood in general. The British thought Mau Mau, lacking authority, had recruited by magic and intimidation. Forest fighters themselves were just as troubled by the relations between authority and freedom.

There are good grounds for suggesting that the experience of their own tyranny destroyed Mau Mau morale in the forests, just as British tyranny destroyed imperial authority at Hola camp.[90] The commonest forest criticism of Kimathi and his main supporters, in what became the Kenya Parliament, was that they suffered from the faults of literacy. This label covered many failings in the liberating authority conventionally expected of leadership.[91] The opposition to Kimathi took Mathenge as their leader, the only commander to refuse commissioned rank. His followers were mostly unlettered, but one, Kahinga Wachanga, was among the best educated in the forest. The crux of their resistance to Kimathi may be seen in the name they gave themselves, Kenya *Riigi*, after the door that protects a household. Their memoirs nowhere explain this self-description. That it was deliberate becomes clear if one measures their complaints against Kimathi against what we know of Kikuyu – or other Kenyan – political thought. Arising within stateless peoples, preoccupied with reputations, not institutions, it is better termed moral thought. The aspects most relevant to the *Riigi*–Parliament conflict were summed up by Kenyatta in the axioms, 'A man is judged by his household'; 'A good leader begins in his own homestead'; and, what a man achieved as manager of a polygynous family, a man was 'expected to do on a larger scale in the interests of the community as a whole.'[92] But Kenyatta did not go as far as he might; he did not explore the contradiction at the heart of Kikuyu thought that made the power of this civic virtue so parochial. He omitted to quote the proverb that set the limits on authority: 'nobody else can close the door of another man's hut.' Each householder must be his own master.[93] Mathenge remembered this proviso; Kimathi, it seems, forgot.

By their choice of name, *Riigi's* unlettered men declared that their distrust of mission-schooled Mau Mau leaders was rooted in the issue of authority. Forest-fighters needed it. They were obsessed with what appear to be inappropriately luxuriant ranks – field-marshal, general, and so on. Essential for large formations, one might think them an encumbrance to mobile bands with poor communications, private sources of supply, and needing the discretion to resolve the parochial politics of their rural bases. But this was a political war. Mau Mau fought, locality by locality, but to establish a wider power. Independent bands had a tactical advantage over brigaded British battalions, but no hope of concerted influence. It was to bridge this gap between fragmented guerrilla tactics and united political strategy that Mau Mau leaders multiplied their ranks. But these were menacing symbols of state-like intention, not insurgent solutions, just as Koinange's *Mbari* and Kenyatta's *riika* had threatened local autonomy rather than delivered unity in the bygone days of peace.[94] The *Rügi* critique of Parliament is the best illustration of why Mau Mau could neither be a tribally united movement nor would ever have been managed by its hero, Kenyatta.

Both Kimathi's men in Parliament and Mathenge's in the *Rügi* accepted that authority must rest on straightness of achievement. In that they agreed with Kenyatta, and countless elders of other Kenyan peoples before him. But they disagreed on what constituted achievement and the scope of its authority. *Rügi* leaders agreed with Kimathi's chief secretary, Njama, that 'activities proved abilities'. But they objected when he construed that proverbial axiom to mean that 'it would be as difficult for the illiterate people to lead the educated persons as it is for the blind to lead one with eyes'.[95] The *Rügi* developed five lines of attack on literate pretensions. In their view the educated were cowards, were ashamed of their identity, flouted the rules of reputation, and despised both labour and a morality grounded in religion. It was a formidable list of complaints. It showed that social change (and war) had generated open argument in a public sphere, not the psychic trauma of a secretive people that many whites thought had caused Mau Mau. But even reasoned debate was enough to wreck the fragile cohesion of the guerrilla war.

The first *Rügi* complaint has often been echoed by Kenya's radical historians: that the educated had deserted the insurgent cause at the first sign of danger. It was closely linked to the second – on which radical scholars are silent – that literates did not love the ethnic traditions that *Rügi* held dear.[96] Mathenge and his lieutenant, Kahiu-Itina, had a third, still graver, criticism. Even the few literates who fought in the forest flouted the test of proper authority. This was set by the small community that alone could swear to one's reputation: one's clan, neighbours, or insurgent band. Mathenge, from the same locality as Njama, accused the latter of coming home only 'as a visitor', both ignorant outsider and of unknowable integrity. His secretarial responsibilities distanced him from those who knew him, making it difficult for people to trust him, as Njama himself admitted. Where Njama praised Kimathi for unselfish management of his subordinates' affairs, Mathenge refused to infringe other men's rights to close their own *rügi*. 'I should know', he said, reminding Njama of a core principle of stateless politics, 'that home is the starting point'; you could not 'find [the] feathers [of success] along other men's paths'. Kahiu-Itina similarly rejected Njama's argument that he owed it to his electors to attend Parliament. His constituency, his *itungati* band, 'were still living with him and ... they knew very well whether he led them well or not'.[97] The localities to which *Riigi* leaders answered had a sharp eye for manly virtue; Parliament's assent to Kimathi's dictatorship, by contrast, suggested that literate power was blind to vice. *Riigi* were proud not to be packed with Kimathi's 'yes yes men',[98] just as the domestic *riigi* defended moral autonomy. Insistence on the authenticity of face-to-face, land-bound, civic virtue had earlier inspired 'loyalist' resistance to Mau Mau claims to collective power: there was no known test by which to gauge the militants' reputation and thus their authority.[99] Suspicion of distant state power remains one of the pillars of Kenya's political culture today.

As recorded by their chief secretary, Njama, the educated Parliament men rebutted these first three points of the *Riigi* case against them, line by line. First, not all literates were cowards, and that jibe in any case misread the nature of modern power: the pen was now mightier than the sword. Even unlettered fighters agreed that Western schooling could satisfy African hunger. They sang that, had Kikuyu not been educated, 'Then neither the European Nor the Asian [would] lose sleep Worrying about how to satisfy their needs ... The need for a spear is gone, Replaced by the need for a pen. For our enemies of today Fight with words.' Njama also denied one had to be conservative to preserve one's identity. Mau Mau must be free to choose the best and discard the worst of both ancestral and European cultures. 'Every generation makes its own customs, invents its songs and dances, makes its rules and regulations, which all die a natural death with that generation,' he observed, in a typically Christian view of the radical nature of past transfers of generational power at *ituika*.[100] He could have said, just as truly, that modern Kikuyu probably had a more coherent view of tradition than their ancestors, since the first generation of Christian 'readers' had been so anxious to record rather than betray the past: Kenyatta chief among them with his patriotic ethnography, *Facing Mount Kenya*.

The heart of the dispute lay in the literates' reply to the *Riigi* thesis that authority rested on reputation within the small moral community. Kimathi and Njama countered that the unlettered were selfish intriguers who fanned clannish jealousy for lack of personal merit. Literate statesmanship was, by contrast, an arduously acquired skill, not conferred by favour. A real leader was 'a man of good ideas'. Personality was not enough; it died with the man. Ideas outlived a leader's death.[101] Njama thought the dangers of reputation were all too well illustrated by Kahiu-Itina's wretched career. He had initially been a martinet; strict discipline had earned him his fearsome nickname. He had separated officers from other ranks, and men from women. There had been a woman to tend every camp fire. By late 1954, however, Kahiu-Itina had become a leader of the *Riigi* opposition. He now hated literates, and had abandoned his privileges to live with his men, 'so as to preach equality in order to gain popularity by criticising the other leaders'. Rank thus had a twofold virtue in Njama's eyes. By preserving the leaders' unity it ensured obedience among their subordinates. Competition for popularity courted anarchy. Njama was particularly contemptuous of Mathenge's dangerous leadership style: 'very popular, inactive and incapable'.[102]

Njama's views allowed Parliament men to call for nomination rather than elections to fill vacancies, on the one-party thesis that electoral success 'depended on either popularity or deceitful propaganda and not on merit'. It took a *Riigi* general, Kimbo, to put the case for multi-party democracy. Njama's argument that it was best to criticize Parliament from within was, Kimbo thought, politically naive. Criticism inevitably created enmity, and a critic within a single party would have none to defend him – and no chance, therefore, of pressing his criticism; 'but an enemy from another party would be defended by his party'.[103] Mau Mau was therefore divided by an issue central to all multicultural politics, not in Africa alone. Is equal citizenship best preserved by neutral, culture-blind, institutions or by laws that recognize the cultural particularity within which people are formed as social beings? In the parochial mosaic of Kikuyu culture, that was the nub of the argument between Parliament and *Riigi*.[104]

The next issue between educated and unlettered focused on the range of power rather than sources of authority. Who would allocate the Rift Valley land held by white settlers and never, before British rule, worked by Kikuyu? To great applause, Kimathi declared in August 1953 that his officers would get white farmland in lieu of pensions, after Mau Mau had won the day for African rule. But within the year General Kimbo was insisting that the first claim on Rift Valley land lay with fighters who, like him, had worked it as squatters. Sweat conferred property right. They did not want anyone from the Kikuyu reserve – who would have included Kenyatta – to become 'their master who would divide unto them their lands'.[105] Squatter suspicion of their educated cousins in the reserve was a large element in the *Riigi* opposition. Later history showed they had good reason. At independence, they were forced to share their White Highlands inheritance with competitors, Kikuyu and others, who had never before put a hoe to its soil.

The final issue between Parliament and *Riigi* was more complex. It was bound up with religion, the deepest source of moral authority and, to close the circle, in all probability linked to gender. Kahiu-Itina, second only to Mathenge among *Riigi* leaders, accused educated men of intellectual subservience to white missionaries who hated everything Kikuyu. They also used their uneducated followers as 'merely stone walls' on which to build their personal futures. In late 1954 Njama was alarmed by the spread of an insubordinate doctrine that he attributed to the *komerera*, but could as well have come from the *Riigi*. The idea was getting about that domestic service for leaders, the household chores that every soldier knows, were 'slavery'. Leaders 'never collected firewood or made their own fires, yet they were the most famous fighters ... The true liberty was equality of all persons in which one was free from anyone's rule.' This complaint legitimized idle, cowardly, *komerera* practice. Too dangerous to ignore, Njama had to confute it if leaders were not to be 'abandoned by the *itungati*'.

Njama chose to attack subversion at its root, by theological argument. He 'tried to prove' to a leading egalitarian – who had nonetheless taken the title Lord Gicambira – 'that there was no equality of persons on this earth'. The dissidents replied that 'man was the master of this earth and he could make changes to suit his desires'. Within days of this religious controversy Njama was fortified in his beliefs by surviving a British bombing raid through the power of prayer, holding his ground while the dissident social levellers faithlessly ran away.[106] While their egalitarianism could be found in both the ancestral religion that the *Riigi* defended and in the colonial Christianity they attacked as the source of literate arrogance, in practice both cosmologies supported differentiation in wealth and power. What was new was the dissidents' humanism: 'man was the master of this earth'. Neither elders nor Christians could allow that. No Mau Mau source makes the connection but it seems reasonable to suppose that the *Riigi* rejection of the literates' Christianity, seen at its most radical here, stemmed in part from outrage that, as Kahiu-Itina had put it, the educated Kimathi had prostituted Kikuyu women. It was a common accusation that Christianity had destroyed the discipline of *nguiko*; parents had long seen girls' education as the road to prostitution. The fault of literacy, it appears, was not simply that it enabled leaders to escape the scrutiny of the small community. Its alien theology violated the very basis of community, that shared calculus of gendered straightness, arrived at by the consensus of generations of householders who had each won reputation in defending household reputation behind their own *riigi*.

Conclusion

Even in the forest, to outsiders a thicket of evil, Mau Mau insurgents faced the same issues of authority as other Kenyans and, from different perspectives, debated the future of self-mastery under a civilized order that protected land and freedom. These hooligans, as Kenyatta thought them, had been initiated, through the oath that Mau Mau called 'circumcision', into the spirit of manhood. They became – or so many of them imagined – Kenyatta's rearguard, his *itungati*. Even with their mothers' aid they did not, however, win the fight for Kenya's freedom. They made it impossible for the British to continue to rule as they had done before. The 'second prong', the civil side of counter-insurgency, necessarily entailed giving Africans more representative power in central government, at the expense of Kenya's immigrant whites and Asians. This alone was a great achievement for Mau Mau. It was, however, a Pyrrhic victory; the movement was destroyed, and destroyed itself, in the winning. Its militants earned none of the collective, executive, control that General Kimbo knew was secured by party. That was won later, by other, better educated, men. Their political parties competed for the power that the United Kingdom devolved, in response to parliamentary boycotts and at round-table conferences, when a wider, pan-African, process of decolonization made it impossible for the British to continue to rule Kenya at all. If, as Mathenge said, 'home is the starting point', then it was marriage, not the status of forest veteran, that was decisive to the fighters' future reputations. Their memoirs, as already noted, support him in the joyful domesticity of their endings. But the *riigi*, or door, of household responsibility inevitably divided warrior *itungati* who had now become junior elders, *kamatimu*. As Kikuyu say, 'Birds that land together [to feed] fly up separately [when satisfied]' or, more plainly, 'Young men agree to seek their fortune together; when it comes they part company.'[107] That, in a word, is the tragic history not only of Mau Mau but of all human experience of conflict between solidarity and freedom, as all Kenya's peoples well know.

Notes

1. With apologies to Michael Whisson, 'The Will of God and the Wiles of Men – an Examination of the Beliefs Concerning the Supernatural Held by the Luo', EAISR conference paper, Makerere (1962).
2. A.B.C. Ocholla-Ayayo, *Traditional Ideology and Ethics among the Southern Luo* (1976), 237. I try not to use the definite article in referring to ethnic groups; it gives a false impression of socio-political unity.
3. John Lonsdale, 'Agency in Tight Corners: Narrative and Initiative in African History', *Journal of African Cultural Studies* 13 (2000a): 5–16.
4. Matthew Arnold, 'Dover Beach' (c. 1850).
5. As the chapters by Marshall Clough, E.S. Atieno Odhiambo, Bethwell Ogot and James Ogude make clear.
6. For Zimbabwe, Richard Werbner, *Tears of the Dead: The Social Biography of an African Family* (1991); Heike Schmidt, 'The Social and Economic Impact of Political Violence in Zimbabwe 1890–1990: a Case Study of the Honde Valley', (1996); Jocelyn Alexander, JoAnn McGregor & Terence Ranger, *Violence and Memory: One Hundred Years in the 'Dark Forests of Matabeleland* (2000), Chap. 11. For a start for Kenya, Greet Kershaw, *Mau Mau from Below* (1997), pp. 15–18, 259, 265, 323–5; followed in John Lonsdale, 'Contests of Time: Kikuyu Historiography, Old and New', in Axel Harneit-Sievers (ed.), *A Place in the World: New Local Historiographies from Africa and South Asia* (2002), pp. 201–54.
7. Bethwell A. Ogot, 'History, Ideology and Contemporary Kenya', presidential address to the Historical Association of Kenya annual conference, 27 Aug. 1981.
8. In thematic sequence as follows: (i) Carl G. Rosberg & John Nottingham, *The Myth of 'Mau Mau': Nationalism in Kenya* (1966); and John Spencer, *KAU: the Kenya African Union* (1985). (ii) Maina wa Kinyatti, *Mau Mau: A Revolution Betrayed* (2000); Frank Furedi, *The Mau Mau War in Perspective* (1989); Sharon B. Stichter, 'Workers, Trade Unions, and the Mau Mau Rebellion', *Canadian Journal of African Studies* 9, 2 (1975): 259–75. (iii) Tabitha Kanogo, *Squatters and the Roots of Mau Mau* (1987); David W. Throup, *Economic and Social Origins of Mau Mau, 1945–1953* (1987); Bethwell A. Ogot, 'Politics, Culture and Music in Central Kenya: A Study of Mau Mau Hymns, 1951–1956'; and Benjamin E. Kipkorir, 'Mau Mau and the Politics of the Transfer of Power in Kenya, 1957–1960', both in *Kenya Historical Review* 5, 2 (1977): 275–86 and 313–28. (iv) E. S. Atieno-Odhiambo, 'Democracy and the Ideology of Order in Kenya', in Michael G.

Schatzberg (ed.), *The Political Economy of Kenya* (1987), pp. 177–201; Galia Sabar-Friedman, 'The Mau Mau Myth: Kenyan Political Discourse in Search of Democracy', *Cahiers d'études africaines* 35, 1 (1995), 101–31; François Grignon, 'La démocratisation au risque du débat? Territoires de la critique et imaginaires politiques au Kenya 1990–1995', in Denis-Constant Martin (ed.), *Nouveaux langages du politique en Afrique orientale* (1998), pp. 29–112; Grace Nyatugah Wamue, 'Revisiting Our Indigenous Shrines through Mungiki', *African Affairs* 100 (2001): 453-67.

9. A term I owe to my colleague Craig Muldrew, it is preferable to Goran Hyden's 'economy of affection' in his *Beyond Ujamaa in Tanzania: Underdevelopment and an Uncaptured Peasantry* (1980), pp. 18–19.
10. Henry Odera Oruka, *Oginga Odinga: His Philosophy and Beliefs* (1992), pp. 107–8.
11. Jomo Kenyatta, *Facing Mount Kenya: The Tribal Life of the Gikuyu* (1938), p. 317 for the quote; pp. 9, 11, 76, 175, 194, 265, 310, 315–16 for household skills. See further, John Lonsdale, 'Kenyatta, God and the Modern World', in Jan-Georg Deutsch, Peter Probst & Heike Schmidt (eds), *African Modernities* (2002b). Women were not convinced of men's managerial restraint: Inge Brinkman, *Kikuyu Gender Norms and Narratives* (1996).
12. Mbuya (formerly [Chief] Paulo Mboya) and Rang'inya, quoted in Henry Odera Oruka, *Sage Philosophy: Indigenous Thinkers and Modern Debate on African Philosophy* (1991), pp. 144, 122. Gerald J. Wanjohi, *The Wisdom and Philosophy of the Gikuyu Proverbs: The Kihooto World-View* (1997), p. 90, objects that Mbuya's Christianity made him a dubious interpreter of Luo thought, but his perspective parallels that of the non-Christian Rang'inya.
13. Wanjohi, *Wisdom, passim.*
14. Malcolm Ruel, *Belief, Ritual and the Securing of Life: Reflexive Essays on a Bantu Religion* (1997), Chap. 1.
15. Thomas Spear & Richard Waller (eds) *Being Maasai: Ethnicity and Identity in East Africa* (1993), especially Waller's 'Conclusions', pp. 290–302.
16. Daniel T. arap Moi, *Kenya African Nationalism: Nyayo Philosophy and Principles* (1986), pp. 78–9. The president does not reflect on possible differences between principle and practice.
17. John Middleton, *The World of the Swahili: An African Mercantile Civilisation* (1992), pp. 191–200.
18. Allen Isaacman, 'Peasants and Rural Social Protest in Africa', *African Studies Review* 33 (1990): 1–120; Robert Buijtenhuijs, 'The Revolutionary Potential of African Peasantries: Some Tentative Remarks' (1991); Wunyabari Maloba, *Mau Mau and Kenya: An Analysis of a Peasant Revolt* (1993), pp. 1–19; John Young, *Peasant Revolution in Ethiopia: The Tigray People's Liberation Front 1975-1991* (1997), Chap. 1.
19. James C. Scott, *The Moral Economy of the Peasant: Rebellion and Subsistence in Southeast Asia* (1976), p. 4.
20. Eric Stokes (ed. C.A. Bayly), *The Peasant Armed: The Indian Rebellion of 1857* (1986), p. 225. For everyday resistance, Isaacman, 'Peasants'; James C. Scott, *Weapons of the Weak: Everyday Forms of Peasant Resistance* (1985).
21. Kenyatta, *Facing Mount Kenya*, p. 211; and Cristiana Pugliese's chapter in this volume.
22. The late Dr Carothers, interviewed at Havant, Hampshire, 26 July 1989.
23. Cynthia Hoehler-Fatton, *Women of Fire and Spirit: History, Faith, and Gender in Roho Religion in Western Kenya* (1996); Luise White, *The Comforts of Home: Prostitution in Colonial Nairobi* (1990); Claire C. Robertson, *Trouble Showed the Way: Women, Men, and Trade in the Nairobi Area, 1890–1990* (1997); Tabitha Kanogo, 'The Medicalization of Maternity in Colonial Kenya', in E. S. Atieno Odhiambo (ed.), *African Historians and African Voices: Essays Presented to Professor Bethwell Allan Ogot* (2001), pp. 75–111.
24. Jean Davison, *Voices from Mutira: Lives of Rural Gikuyu Women* (1996); Luise White, 'Work, Clothes, and Talk in Eastern Africa: An Essay about Masculinity and Migrancy', in E.S. Atieno Odhiambo, *African Historians*: 69–74.
25. John M. Lonsdale, 'KAU's Cultures: Imaginations of Community and Constructions of Leadership in Kenya after the Second World War', *Journal of African Cultural Studies* 13 (2000b): 113–14.
26. Greet Kershaw, *Mau Mau from Below* (1997), Chap. 6. For an economic history based

upon Michael Cowen's concept of straddling, see, G. Kitching, *Class and Economic Change in Kenya: The Making of an African Petite-Bourgeoisie* (1980).

27. Jürgen Habermas, *The Structural Transformation of the Public Sphere* (English translation, 1989).
28. Benedict Anderson, *Imagined Communities: Reflections on the Origin and Spread of Nationalism* (1983), p. 16.
29. David W. Cohen & E.S. Atieno Odhiambo, *Siaya: The Historical Anthropology of an African Landscape* (1989), pp. 35–50; Lonsdale, 'Contests of Time'. Kanogo's 'Medicalization of Maternity' reveals lively LNC debates on gender and moral economy.
30. Anderson, *Imagined Communities*, p. 80.
31. John M. Lonsdale, 'The Moral Economy of Mau Mau: Wealth, Poverty and Civic Political Kikuyu Thought', in Bruce Berman & John M. Lonsdale, *Unhappy Valley: Conflict in Kenya and Africa* (1992), Book 2, especially pp. 461–8; John M. Lonsdale, 'Moral Ethnicity, Ethnic Nationalism and Political Tribalism: The Case of the Kikuyu', in Peter Meyns (ed.), *Staat und Gesellschaft in Afrika: Erosions- und Reformprozesse* (1996a), pp. 93–106; and Bethwell A. Ogot's chapter in this volume.
32. For official anxiety, Bruce Berman, *Control and Crisis in Colonial Kenya: The Dialectic of Domination* (1990), Chaps 3, 5, 7; Joanna Lewis, *Empire State-Building: War and Welfare in Kenya 1925–52* (2000).
33. Scott, *Moral Economy*, Chaps 1 and 2; Hyden, *Beyond Ujamaa*, p. 18; and Buijtenhuijs, 'Revolutionary Potential', pp. 19–24, all in disagreement with Eric R. Wolf, *Peasant Wars of the Twentieth Century* (1973), pp. 291–3.
34. Barrington Moore, *Social Origins of Dictatorship and Democracy: Lord and Peasant in the Making of the Modern World* (1967), pp. 453–83.
35. For this last point, see David Percox's chapter in this volume.
36. Orlando Figes, *A People's Tragedy: The Russian Revolution 1891–1924* (1996), pp. 263, 300–8; 'Tufunge Safari', adapted from Anthony Clayton, *Communication for New Loyalties: African Soldiers' Songs* (Ohio University Papers, Africa Series 34, 1978), p. 37.
37. Lonsdale, 'KAU's Cultures'.
38. For resistance, John Lamphear, *The Scattering Time: Turkana Responses to Colonial Rule* (1992); for an official hyena, Paul Tablino, *The Gabra: Camel Nomads of Northern Kenya* (1999), p. 232; for market history, R. M. A. van Zwanenberg, with Anne King, *An Economic History of Kenya and Uganda, 1800–1970* (1975), Chap. 5; Philip Raikes, *Livestock Development and Policy in East Africa* (1981), pp. 191–203; and advice from Richard Waller. For age and property, Paul Spencer, *The Samburu: A Study of Gerontocracy in a Nomadic Tribe* (1965); Neal Sobania, 'The Historical Tradition of the Peoples of the Eastern Lake Turkana Basin, c. 1840–1925' (1980); David M. Anderson & Vigdis Broch-Due (eds), *The Poor Are not Us: Poverty and Pastoralism in Eastern Africa* (1999). For the DCs' view, Charles Chenevix Trench, *The Desert's Dusty Face* (1964); Terence Gavaghan, *Of Lions and Dung Beetles: A 'Man in the Middle' of Colonial Administration* (Ilfracombe, 1999), Chap. 16, quote from p. 166.
39. J. W. Pilgrim, 'Land Ownership in the Kipsigis Reserve', EAISR conference paper, July 1969; Robert A. Manners, 'The Kipsigis of Kenya: Culture Change in a "Model" East African Tribe', in Julian H. Steward (ed.), *Contemporary Change in Traditional Societies: I, Introduction and African Tribes* (1967), pp. 205–359; Diana Ellis, 'The Nandi Protest of 1923 in the Context of African Resistance to Colonial Rule', *Journal of African History* 17 (1976): 555–75; Christopher Youe, 'Settler Capital and the Assault on the Squatter Peasantry in Kenya's Uasin Gishu District, 1942–1963', *African Affairs* 87 (1988): 393–418; Sally Kosgei, 'Land, Resistance, and Women among the Kipsigis', African Studies seminar, University of Cambridge, March 1988; David M. Anderson, 'Black Mischief: Crime, Protest and Resistance in Kenya's Western Highlands', *Historical Journal* 36 (1993): 851–77; David M. Anderson, *Eroding the Commons: Politics in Baringo, Kenya, c. 1890–1963* (2002).
40. Calculated from 'African Population of Kenya Colony and Protectorate: Geographical and Tribal Studies' (East African Statistical Department, Nairobi, mimeo, 1950), pp. 5–6.
41. Susan C. Watkins, 'Local and Foreign Models of Reproduction in Nyanza Province,

Kenya', *Population and Development Review* 26 (2000): 725–59; John M. Lonsdale, 'Rural Resistance and Mass Political Mobilisation amongst the Luo', in François Bédarida et al. (eds), *Mouvements Nationaux d'Indépendance et Classes Populaires aux XIXe et XXe Siècles en Occident et en Orient*, Vol 2 (Paris, 1971), pp. 459–78; Parker Shipton, 'The Kenyan Land Tenure Reform: Misunderstandings in the Public Creation of Private Property', in R.E. Downs & S.P. Reyna (eds), *Land and society in Contemporary Africa* (1988), pp. 91–135; John Iliffe, *A Modern History of Tanganyika* (1979), p. 316; Oginga Odinga, *Not Yet Uhuru* (1967), p. 61.

42. Author's interviews with former officials of the North Kavirondo Central Association: Luka Lumadede Kisala, at Vihiga, 12 April 1965; Andrea Jumba, in Tiriki, 13 April 1965; and John Adala, at the Lumumba Institute, Nairobi, 27 April 1965.
43. KNA, SF/Adm. 4/1. III: S.H. Fazan to Chief Secretary, 5 Sept 1940.
44. Gideon Were, *A History of the Abaluyia of Western Kenya, c. 1500–1930* (1967); Günter Wagner, *The Changing Family among the Bantu Kavirondo* (1939); Norman Humphrey, *The Liguru and the Land* (1947); Audrey Wipper, *Rural Rebels: A Study of Two Protest Movements in Kenya* (1977), Part III; Jan J. de Wolf, *Differentiation and Integration in Western Kenya: A Study of Religious Innovation and Social Change among the Bukusu* (1977), pp. 180–91.
45. Robert Maxon, *Conflict and Accommodation in Western Kenya: The Gusii and the British, 1907–1963* (1989); Stephen Orvis, *The Agrarian Question in Kenya* (1997).
46. This section is based on Rosberg & Nottingham, *Myth*, Chap. 7; Spencer, *KAU*, Chaps. 5–7; Kershaw, *Mau Mau from Below*, Chap. 7; Michael Cowen, 'Capital and Household Production: the Case of Wattle in Kenya's Central Province' (1979); Apollo Njonjo, 'The Africanization of the "White Highlands": A Study in Agrarian Class Struggles in Kenya, 1950-1974' (1978); Throup, *Economic and Social Origins*; Furedi, *Mau Mau War*; Kanogo, *Squatters*; Lonsdale, 'Moral Economy'; Fiona Mackenzie, *Land, Ecology and Resistance in Kenya, 1880-1952* (1998). References will be given only to support quotations and points of detail.
47. Calculated from 'African Population of Kenya Colony' (1950).
48. P. Wyn Harris, 'The Problem of the Squatter', draft memo, 21 Feb. 1946: KNA, LAB 9/1040. For Ngugi's exile Mau Mau, see James Ogude's chapter in this volume, p. 283.
49. Samuel Koina, Mara Karanja, Njoroge Kagunda et al. to Arthur Creech-Jones, 22 July 1946: PRO, CO 533/544/2/3. For concern for parents, Muga Gicaru, *Land of Sunshine: Scenes of Life in Kenya before Mau Mau* (1958), p. 161.
50. Jomo Kenyatta to John Dugdale, 14 Aug. 1950: PRO, CO 533/566/7/15.
51. A proposition elaborated in my 'Moral Economy', 'Contests of Time', and 'The Prayers of Waiyaki: Political Uses of the Kikuyu Past', in David Anderson & D. Johnson (eds), *Revealing Prophets: Prophecy in Eastern African History* (1995), pp. 240–91.
52. For *ituika* in the 1920s, D. Peterson, 'Writing Gikuyu: Christian Literacy and Ethnic Debate in North Central Kenya 1908–1952' (2000), Chaps. 3 and 4.
53. Wakahihia Clan Claim, 19 Aug. 1946: PRO, CO 533/544/2/66.
54. Memorandum on African Land Tenure, Social, Economic and Politics in Kenya [sic] (n. d., 1946): CO 533/544/2/16.
55. Josiah M. Kariuki, *'Mau Mau' Detainee* (London, 1963), p. 11, for Kenyatta's mastery of age-set courtesies. Kershaw, *Mau Mau from Below*, pp. 201, 219, for his problems with Kikuyu political culture.
56. Johnstone Kenyatta, 'An African People Rise in Revolt: The Story of the Kenya Massacre: How Harry Thuku Led the Great Struggle against Imperialism', *Daily Worker* (London, 20, 21 Jan. 1930); Director of Intelligence to Chief Native Commissioner, 1, 3 June 1947: KNA, MAA 8/8.
57. Lonsdale, 'Prayers of Waiyaki'.
58. [Ian Henderson], 'Kenya African Union Meeting at Nyeri', Appendix F to Colonial Office, *Historical Survey of the Origins and Growth of Mau Mau* (Cmnd. 1030, 1960), pp. 301–8.
59. For 'Mau Mau', Kershaw, *Mau Mau from Below*, Chap. 7, and Joanna Lewis's chapter in this volume. For the proverb, Ngumbu Njururi, *Gikuyu Proverbs* (Nairobi, 1938), p. 38: thanks to Rebecca Affolder for a reminder.
60. As in Louis S.B. Leakey, *Defeating Mau Mau*, (1954), Chap. 5; Maina wa Kinyatti (ed.),

Thunder from the Mountains: Mau Mau Patriotic Songs (1980). Both collections must be read with due awareness of their editors' biases.

61. Donald Barnett & Karari Njama, *Mau Mau from within: Autobiography and Analysis of Kenya's Peasant Revolt* (1966), p. 180.
62. *Ibid.*, pp. 213, 221, 293–5, 376, 390, 397, 479, 498; Waruhiu Itote (General China), *'Mau Mau' General* (1967), pp. 139-41. For measures to 'cool the heat of war' and disperse its evil: L.S.B. Leakey, *The Southern Kikuyu before 1903* (1977), Chap. 24.
63. Barnett & Njama, *Mau Mau from Within*, p. 151; Renison Githige, 'The Religious Factor in Mau Mau', (1978), p. 59; Maloba, *Mau Mau and Kenya*, p. 115.
64. My views on forest gender relations are now different from those summarized in my 'Mau Mau's of the Mind: Making Mau Mau and Remaking Kenya', *Journal of African History* 31 (1990): 420. What follows is an expansion of my 'Moral Economy', pp. 455–9.
65. Kenyatta, *Facing Mount Kenya*, pp. 155–60; Leakey, *Southern Kikuyu*, pp. 810–13.
66. Kenyatta, *Facing Mount Kenya*, p. 181; Leakey, *Southern Kikuyu*, Chap. 19.
67. Lonsdale, 'Moral Economy', pp. 340–1, 355–9. White, *The Comforts of Home*, and Robertson, *Trouble Showed the Way*, give insight into relations between (amongst others) Kikuyu men and women.
68. Barnett & Njama, *Mau Mau from Within*, p. 435.
69. Henry Kahinga Wachanga (ed. Robert Whittier), *The Swords of Kirinyaga: The Fight for Land and Freedom* (1975), p. x.
70. For female anonymity, Jean O'Barr, 'Introductory Essay', in Muthoni Likimani, *Passbook No, F. 47927* (1985). For male dispraise of female activism: K. Santilli, 'Kikuyu Women in the Mau Mau Revolt', *Ufahamu* 8 (1977/8): 143–59; Cora A. Presley, *Kikuyu Women, the Mau Mau Rebellion, and Social Change in Kenya* (1992), Chaps 7–8. Greet Kershaw suggests anonymity may show male respect.
71. Wachanga, *Swords*, 37; Barnett & Njama, *Mau Mau from Within*, 435.
72. For Mau Mau support for widows and orphans: Barnett and Njama, *Mau Mau from Within*, pp. 223, 361; Mohammed Mathu, *The Urban Guerrilla* (1974), pp. 42, 76; Maina wa Kinyatti (ed.), *Kenya's Freedom Struggle: The Dedan Kimathi Papers* (1987) p. 85. For collective parenting, Ngugi Kabiro, *Man in the Middle* (1973), pp. 53, 67; Kanogo, *Squatters*, p. 146. For popular approval, Peter Marris to DC Nyeri, 25 May 1954 (courtesy of Greet Kershaw).
73. Kiboi Muriithi, with Peter Ndoria, *War in the Forest* (1971), p. 24; Gucu Gikoyo, *We Fought for Freedom* (1979), pp. 50–1, 124, 192–3; Karigo Muchai, *The Hard Core: The Story of Karigo Muchai* (1973), p. 21; Wambui Waiyaki Otieno (ed. Cora A. Presley), *Mau Mau's Daughter: A Life History* (1998), Chap. 3.
74. Wachanga, *Swords*, p. 94; Barnett & Njama, *Mau Mau from Within*, pp. 434–6; and Caroline Elkins's chapter in this volume.
75. Waruhiu Itote, *'Mau Mau' General*, pp. 223–7; Mathu, *Urban Guerrilla*, pp. 86–7; Muchai, *Hard Core*, pp. 84–5; Wachanga, *Swords*, pp. 151–2; Joram Wamweya, *Freedom Fighter* (Nairobi, 1971), p. 199; J.M. Kariuki, *'Mau Mau' Detainee* (1963), pp. 148, 172–7.
76. Kenyatta, *Facing Mount Kenya*, p. 108; Leakey, *Southern Kikuyu*, pp. 748, 1051.
77. Contrast Kanogo, *Squatters*, pp. 143–9 or Presley, *Kikuyu Women*, Chap. 7, with Barnett & Njama, *Mau Mau from Within*, pp. 242–3. The single female memoir, Otieno's *Mau Mau's Daughter*, must be read with care.
78. The lower estimate is given in Barnett & Njama, *Mau Mau from Within*, p. 226, the higher in Ian Henderson, with Philip Goodhart, *The Hunt for Kimathi*, (1958), p. 18.
79. Barnett and Njama, *Mau Mau from Within*, pp. 165, 187, 194–5, 242, 244, 291–2; Gikoyo, *We Fought*, pp. 60–1, 63-5, 113–14; Itote, *Mau Mau General*, 78; Mathu, *Urban Guerrilla*, pp. 55–6; Wachanga, *Swords*, p. 37.
80. Barnett & Njama, *Mau Mau from Within*, pp. 215, 219.
81. *Ibid.*, pp. 221–2, 247–9. Mau Mau regulations resembled the KAR's, for which see Timothy Parsons, *The African Rank-and-File: Social Implications of Colonial Military Service in the King's African Rifles, 1902–1964* (Portsmouth NH and Oxford, 1999), ch. 5.
82. Itote, *'Mau Mau' General*, pp. 127–38 for women and the rules of war; Kanogo, *Squatters*, p. 147, for sanctions against pregnancy. For relations between warriors and initiated

girls: Leakey, *Southern Kikuyu*, Chap. 18 (p. 721 for a precedent for Mwathe's compulsory pairing). For a contrary view, that fighters reconstituted Kikuyu marriage as monogamy: White, 'Separating the Men', pp. 10–15.

83. Itote, *'Mau Mau' General*, pp. 78, 281–2, 285–90; cf. Leakey, *Southern Kikuyu*, pp. 716–22; Barnett & Njama, *Mau Mau from Within*, p. 248.
84. Itote, *'Mau Mau' General*, pp. 285, 289–90.
85. Gikoyo, *We Fought*, p. 110.
86. Kinyatti, *Kenya's Freedom Struggle*, pp. 93, 73.
87. Henderson, *Hunt*, p. 33; Barnett & Njama, *Mau Mau from Within*, p. 443.
88. Henderson, *Hunt*, p. 67.
89. Barnett & Njama, *Mau Mau from Within*, pp. 379-80, 397, 400–1.
90. For which see the chapters in this volume by Elkins and Lewis. Did the chastened British reaction to the 'Hola massacre' bring some satisfaction to Kenyatta, with its echoes of their response to the Thuku incident of 1922?
91. For more on Mau Mau literacy see D. Peterson's chapter in this volume.
92. Kenyatta, *Facing Mount Kenya*, pp. 76, 175, 315.
93. G. Barra, *1000 Kikuyu Proverbs* (1939), no. 782. Atieno Odhiambo tells me Luo say the same. For a parallel Luo debate see, David Parkin, *The Cultural Definition of Political Response: Lineal Destiny among the Luo* (1978), Chap. 7
94. Maloba, *Mau Mau and Kenya*, Chap. 6, is illuminating on this issue.
95. Barnett & Njama, *Mau Mau from Within*, pp. 395, 398. Njama, Kimathi's secretary, is unfortunately the only extensive source for the forest debate, but he saw both sides, in deserting Kimathi for Mathenge while criticising both.
96. Complaints by Mathenge and two *Riigi* generals, Kimbo and Kahiu-Itina, in *ibid.*, pp. 336, 397, 471.
97. *Ibid.*, pp. 394–6, 399, 453, 481.
98. *Ibid.*, pp. 401, 471.
99. Lonsdale, 'Moral Economy of Mau Mau', pp. 436–7.
100. Barnett & Njama, *Mau Mau from Within*, pp. 239, 337. For Christian views of *ituika*, Peterson, 'Writing Gikuyu', and Lonsdale, 'Contests of Time'.
101. Barnett and Njama, *Mau Mau from Within*, pp. 396, 451, 445.
102. *Ibid.*, pp. 165, 299–300, 397–9, 443.
103. *Ibid.*, pp. 415, 401.
104. For example, Charles Taylor, *Multiculturalism and 'The Politics of Recognition'* (1992).
105. Barnett and Njama, *Mau Mau from Within*, pp. 374, 402.
106. *Ibid.*, pp. 397–8, 406–9.
107. Barra, *1000 Kikuyu Proverbs*, no. 23; Njururi, *Gikuyu Proverbs*, no. 28; Justin Itotia with James Dougall, 'The Voice of Africa: Kikuyu Proverbs', *Africa* 1 (1928): 486.

[12]

People's War, State Formation and Revolution in Africa: A Comparative Analysis of Mozambique, Guinea-Bissau, and Angola[1]

by

Patrick Chabal

University of East Anglia

What can revolution imply for Africa? In the following discussion I take my cue from the compassionate Guinean who relieved me of the growing anxiety which I had developed at being labelled a 'redfoot' when, in 1979, I was doing research in Guinea-Bissau. I had worried a great deal about this, echoes of red terror in mind, until the tale of 'redfeet' was unravelled for me by this kind soul who had given me a lift. 'You see', he said like a schoolteacher, 'since we had to gain independence through armed struggle and since we are committed to socialism, we have attracted the attention of all of you, Europeans and Americans. Can't manage a revolution at home so you're looking for one in the Third World. First, it was China, then Vietnam, then Cuba, then Algeria. Today it is us. In a few years you will tell us that our revolution has failed and you'll move on to some other place: Western Sahara perhaps?' I protested, but to no avail, that I was no 'redfoot' but an academic. 'Yes, of course', he said, grinning.

To what extent and in which ways do wars of national liberation usher in new post-colonial states substantially unlike those born of constitutional decolonisation? Political independence in Angola, Guinea-Bissau, and Mozambique (hereafter referred to as lusophone) came by way of armed conflict. Zimbabwe followed. Namibia is also at war. The success of the lusophone nationalists was seen by many to redraw the political map of independent Black Africa. The supporters of the lusophone nationalists as well as their opponents recognised the historical significance of what came to be labelled the second wave of African independence. The governments of the three lusophone countries, and later that of Zimbabwe, claimed and were perceived to be committed to socialist development. The socialism of which they spoke did not echo earlier claims of African socialism, a socialism which the new regimes disowned, and from which they derived little inspiration.

More significantly, the political organisation of these three countries, based on the structures of the parties as they evolved during the long decade of armed struggle, was in many respects more akin to revolutionary parties outside of Africa than to the first wave of African nationalist parties.[2] It was scarcely credible that this was so only because the lusophone parties had received the bulk of their financial aid and equipment from Eastern countries. War, then, had mattered. Or had it? Could it be that we were just being dazzled, all political 'redfeet', by the glitter of the firmly held Kalyishnikov as the new flag unfurled – socialist brotherhood and revolutionary fervour?

The argument implicit in the claims of many Africanists sympathetic to the new regimes is that the process of a people's war causes fundamental changes in the political, social, and economic structures of the colony, changes which did not obtain in countries which decolonised constitutionally and which now open the door to further revolutionary changes.[3] For them, a successful people's war leads, first, to the emergence of a 'revolutionary class alliance' of radical *petits bourgeois*, workers, and peasants which had hitherto not existed in Africa. The war requires total commitment and thus weeds out those *petits bourgeois* unprepared to move towards socialism. Political mobilisation demands the ability to forge an alliance between *petit bourgeois* leadership and peasants. The gap between elite and mass is closed. The post-colonial state is, therefore, in the hands of true revolutionaries.

Secondly, it is argued, a successful people's war is predicated on the creation of a well organised, united, and ideologically homogeneous political party. In practice such parties are more radical in their socialist orientation and more committed to socialist changes than any of their constitutional predecessors in Africa. Thus, it is claimed that the lusophone nationalist parties evolved structures, policies, and an ideology which can be used as effective instruments of revolutionary change after independence.

The third argument put forward by those who view the revolutionary potential of the three lusophone countries with optimism is that the nationalist parties had already achieved significant political, social, and economic changes in the liberated areas before independence. New forms of political institutions had been created from below, new forms of collective production and distribution had been introduced, new social and economic priorities had been defined. New bonds of national identity and solidarity were now at hand. People's war would succeed, where constitutional decolonisation had failed, in bringing revolution to Africa and thus in laying the foundations for a non neo-colonial path to development: a transition to socialism. What is claimed, then, if only implicitly, is that, like the Chinese Communist Party or the Vietminh, the three lusophone parties possess the apparatus, the men, the skills, the ideology, and the experience to see the revolution through.[4]

Many historians of Africa, however, are dubious about these claims.[5] They reject the contention that a successful nationalist struggle is a sounder basis for revolution (which, in any case, they doubt is about to occur in Africa) than the previous less violent and less spectacular forms of decolonisation characteristic of the 1950s and 1960s. They put forward three broad counter-arguments. First, revolution is the cant of modern nationalism. Nationalists fighting a war utter the slogans which will get them the material and political support they require. The aim of nationalists is independence, not revolution: heed not their rhetoric. Secondly, even assuming that this new generation of nationalists somehow *is* dedicated to revolution, it is naive to suggest that the political and military campaign designed to force a colonial power to negotiate independence heralds a new revolutionary dawn. The one has historically little to do with the other. Finally, and perhaps most crucially, the experience of other so-called African socialist states dedicated to revolution has shown that the social and economic under-development of African societies, and the constraints imposed by the world market economy from which they cannot expect to detach themselves, foreclose any hope of emulating the Russian or Chinese examples. There is, therefore, no reason to believe that, simply because they were successful in the prosecution of nationalist wars, the leaders of the lusophone countries can be more successful in achieving a revolutionary transformation of society than their equally ambitious predecessors in Africa.

These claims and counter-claims can only be sorted out by means of a sharper and more explicit conceptual apparatus than has hitherto been available. I propose to initiate the process of conceptual clarification by addressing the two questions which are implicit in the debate on the political significance of the nationalist struggles in the three lusophone countries. In what ways did it matter, firstly, that the post-colonial state in Angola, Guinea Bissau, and Mozambique was born of an armed struggle (or what I shall call a people's war)? Does the process of people's war usher in the establishment of radically distinct post-colonial states in Africa? More generally, is there a correlation between the nature of the post-colonial state and the success of the people's war which preceded independence? Secondly, is it either legitimate or even meaningful to infer that the emergence of a distinct post-colonial state is causally related to the development of a revolutionary process in the three lusophone countries? Does the creation of a 'people's state' lead to the transition to socialism? Or to put it more bluntly, when, if ever, is a nationalist waving a gun a revolutionary?

Usefully to discuss these two questions requires conceptual clarification in respect of the assumptions made in the usage of notions such as revolution, state, and, crucially, people's war.[6] Although there is no firm consensus on the subject, most political scientists and historians would agree that a revolution requires not only the overthrow of the existing political state – whether indigenous or foreign – by a counter-elite but more importantly the ability by the new political masters, the new elite, to establish a radically distinct social and economic order. A successful revolution can be seen to have occurred when the initial phase of 'political' revolution is followed by a 'social' revolution. Historically, most modern revolutions have undergone a period of civil or people's war and have been, in most instances, carried out by Marxist professional revolutionaries who, through the agency of a well organised and politically efficacious party, have aimed at establishing a socialist state. What sort of society they have envisaged and whether they can be said to have succeeded need not impinge on the conceptualisation of the process of revolution.

Since the Vietnamese revolution, however, the issue of nationalism has been paramount in the political process of what are generally recognised as the more recent revolutions. That this has been so is historically linked with the end of colonial rule and the struggle in much of the non-Western world to move away from ever sharper neo-colonial relations. Nationalism has been broadened to imply economic independence, that is some degree of autonomy from the constraints of the world-market economy. It is clear, therefore, that the meaning as well as the concept of revolution has changed in the second half of the twentieth-century – Vietnam and Cuba emerging as the two poles of the most relevant 'model', much as China and Russia had been earlier.[7] It may well be that the failure of most revolutionary attempts in Latin America and the apparent consolidation of the Ethiopian revolution point to the next historical step in the development of new forms of political and social revolutions. Whether the Ethiopian revolution, however, is a 'model' for what African revolutions would look like is not altogether very convincing given the peculiar and in many ways unique features of the country's social and economic structures.[8] It is simply not clear what revolution in lusophone Africa (or anywhere else in Africa) would mean. What follows, therefore, is no more than a cockshy.

The political component of an African revolution would imply, minimally, the acquisition and establishment of political power in a post-colonial state whose structure, personnel, and policies would derive not from its colonial predecessor but from the legitimacy of a vanguard mass party rooted in the countryside. Social revolution in Africa would mean the development of policies leading to a form of autonomous economic development in which agriculture would be modernised through the establishment of new structures of production and distribution and in which industrial advance would be tailored to the economic needs of the country and to its potential for self-sustained growth. In short, revolution in Africa (and here the lusophone revolutionaries rejoin their earlier counterparts on the continent) must mean the establishment of a state capable of breaking with the all too familiar pattern of neo-colonial development common, in its successful or failed version, to most African countries. Historically, therefore, although not causally, the formation of such a state must come before revolution.[9]

What of the state, then, that all too elusive monster which so fascinates social scientists and, of late, historians as well? Like all monsters it is more useful unseen but present. About the state one can ask a number of questions and any conceptualisation must ultimately depend on the questions asked. Here, I follow Lonsdale who, in his extraordinarily catholic paper, has given us some hope as well as some means of understanding, *historically*, the notion of state in Africa. As he pithily writes:

> Otherwise than in myth, states do not have origins; they are formed. Origins are magical events; formation is slow, often very slow, social and political process .... Only states without a past look like the simple instrument of their dominant class; and even revolutionary states have pasts .... There are periods when states do appear to have origins, to take on new forms, autonomously to exert or instrumentally to transmit power more inclusively in a burst of law making. Historical eras do come to an end, new ones do begin; even people living at the time can be aware of that.[10]

Decolonisation appeared to be one such period, so that the formation of the post-colonial state matters.

How it matters is a question for analysis and analysis requires some conceptualisation. Lonsdale's gallant efforts at unpacking the layers of meaning attached to the notion of the state are not in vain. The state can be conceptualised through its four inter-connected structures: its apparatus, its representative estates, its ideology, and its material base.[11] At any one time in history, the state is the resultant of the conflict extant in the process of relationships between these structures. By definition, therefore, the state is not an a-historical hydra nor is it simply the political instrument of a given class but, like other concepts, a code-word for the analysis of the connection between historically specific processes and structures. The merit of this approach, beyond its obvious coherence, is to make it possible to conceptualise the state, that is to ask the right questions about it, in its relation to social processes and over time. State formation becomes amenable to analysis in the complexity of the transition between two historical eras. Questions can be asked which make possible comparisons between the process of state formation in different areas of the world, under different historical circumstances. It also becomes possible to ask whether state formation in eighteenth or nineteenth-century Europe is conceptually relevant to state formation in Africa in the second half of the twentieth century.[12]

Here I am essentially concerned with state formation in Africa, the key question of the epoch of decolonisation. The issue is whether historically different forms of decolonisation lead to the formation of significantly distinct post-colonial states. By now the liberal and radical post-mortems of the death of the dream of socialist states on the morrow of the first wave of independence rejoin, though for opposite reasons, in their conclusions: 'revolutionary nationalists' become bulwarks of conservatism once in power. Because the post-colonial state was essentially unchanged after independence, the argument is made, radical leaders were able to use revolutionary rhetoric to conceal, in most cases not very effectively, private plundering and the social reproduction of their privileges. Fanon was right![13] Or to put it another way, these radical nationalists inherit a post-colonial state which it is in their interest to make prosper as a neo-colonial state.[14] To liberal and radical critiques alike, then, the independence of these countries was nothing but the Africanisation of the colonial state. Independence did not imply a radical re-definition of the state, much less therefore a revolution.

The argument implicit in much of the writing on Angola, Mozambique, and Guinea-Bissau is that, to follow Lonsdale's conceptualisation, the post-colonial state of these countries is significantly different in its apparatus, representative estates, ideology, and material base *because* of the nationalist wars.[15] What this means is that the structures of the post-colonial states in these countries (though like most other African countries they are one-party states) are new. They do not derive from the colonial apparatus as it was inherited at independence but from the political and administrative organisation which sustained the party's effort in the liberated areas. The nature and legitimacy of these new political structures are determined by the experience of political mobilisation not by colonial white papers. The representative estates of the new state have joined in what is referred to as a 'revolutionary class alliance' of *petits bourgeois*, workers, and peasants. Such a political coalition, it is argued, was not to be found in countries which underwent constitutional decolonisation. The process of war has enabled the most radical section of the *petite bourgeoisie* to assume the leadership of the party. The requirements of massive peasant participation in the political process of mobilisation gives them a powerful political voice in the party. The balance of political forces in the state is thus subtantially different from what it was in the earlier wave of independent African countries.

Similarly, the ideology of the new states has, through the political process of war, evolved squarely towards the more radical end of socialism. More importantly, it is contended, this ideology was born of political mobilisation and, because it is congruent with the structure of the party, it can be used for revolutionary purposes. In other words, it is no longer rhetoric but the ideal fashioned out the blood, sweat, and tears of a truly popular political movement. It is also an indigenous ideology because the harsh reality of the war has eliminated the political clichés picked up in London, Paris, Lisbon, or Moscow.

Finally, it is argued, even the material base of the new states has changed in ways which were not possible for those other African nations which inherited the economy, as well as the administration, of the colonial state. The point here is not that the material resources of the lusophone states were somehow altered by the war (in fact they were; agriculture, in particular, was badly damaged) nor that the dependent economic position of lusophone Africa differs from other African states, but rather than the wars have led to changes in the aims as well as in the organisation of economic production and distribution. The economic priorities of the new states have been redefined and means are now at hand to implement them. The experience of political mobilisation, the necessity to become economically self-sufficient in the liberated areas and the existence of a popular party to affect economic change at the local level, all re-define the potential action of the new state on its material base. The Chinese and Vietnamese cases are implicit 'models' here. The claim, in effect, is that the material base of the liberated areas (the image of the society to be) has already been re-shaped during the armed struggle.[16]

These are impressive claims – particularly when earlier assertions about the radical nature and revolutionary promise of the post-colonial state in Africa have disappeared without echo.[17] Meaningfully to assess these claims in the case of lusophone Africa demands that we understand the process of nationalist (or people's) war. Simply to *assume* that a people's war leads *ipso facto* to the formation of a radical post-colonial state which holds the key to a successful transition to socialism is not good enough.

The argument, as I see it, involves two steps. First, how successful was the nationalist war in each case? How do we gauge the success or failure of people's wars? Secondly, is there a correlation (and if there is what is its nature) between the success of a nationalist war, the distinctiveness of the post-colonial state, and the potential for revolution in Angola, Mozambique, and Guinea-Bissau?

I proceed, then, with what I take to be the process of people's war in Africa in the third quarter of the twentieth century, using the three lusophone countries as my source material.[18] Historically, people's wars have assumed the form of a guerilla war in which the indigenous nationalist movement has sought to mobilise the largest possible section of the predominantly rural population to challenge and eventually eliminate foreign political and military control. Although very much a military conflict, the nature of a people's war is, to my mind, essentially political and cannot, therefore, be reduced to military parameters.[19] There are three broad areas of enquiry relevant to my first concern, the assessment of the success of a people's war, and to its potential for revolutionary change. First, to what extent has the nationalist party achieved effective political control over the territory it claims and what degree of political legitimacy has it acquired in the country as a whole? Secondly, to what extent does the party represent the political articulations of social forces during the anti-colonial struggle – that is, what is its political complexion and its potential as an agency for societal transformation? Thirdly, with what success has the party managed to promote meaningful political, social, and economic changes in the liberated areas *before independence*?

The key to the success of a people's war lies in the party's ability to achieve effective political mobilisation, that is, the ability to generate sufficient *active* political support for its aims and actions. In concrete terms, success here means not only to be able to operate freely in the countryside, receiving food, shelter, and protection, but also, and crucially, to be able to recruit members locally. This requires the mobilisation of the rural population, an extremely difficult task under any circumstances, however ill-disposed it may be towards the established colonial state.[20] Villagers are suspicious of outsiders, justifiably 'parochial' in their concerns, and, if anything, millenarian rather than socialist. Thus, the gains of political mobilisation are always likely to be fragile and reversible. Mobilisation depends ultimately on the ability of party cadres to convince individuals and communities that their interests will best be served by the nationalists.[21] Although such mobilisation can be achieved by various means (and it has been achieved by various means in different settings), the methods used are not politically neutral. The use of ethnic hostility (as in Angola) or of terror (as in Algeria) has obvious consequences and may become self-defeating. Finally, however successful political mobilisation has been, the coalition of interests between villagers and party is relatively unstable. Once independence is achieved, the party's political ambitions may clash with the demands of the villagers.

Successful political mobilisation is predicated on the party's capacity to overcome three internal contradictions. The first concerns one of the most essential components of successful political mobilisation in Africa, that is the creation of over-arching ties of supra-ethnic loyalties and a sense of national identity. The paradox is that successful mobilisation demands, not the abolition of ethnic sentiments (if that were possible), but rather the politicisation of ethnicity for nationalist purposes.[22] Here the role of the party is crucial: it is both the agency through which ethnic mobilisation is channelled and the organisation through which ethnic particularisms are transcended into a new state. The party must reconcile its conflicting interests between the need to achieve national unity and the use of local and parochial issues for purposes of mobilisation. In Africa, all nations had to be created out of colonies through some form of political mobilisation, but a successful people's war requires far more unambiguous commitment to national unity if the armed struggle is not to be jeopardised. Ethnic nationalism, of course, has no such dilemma.[23]

The second contradiction inherent in the process of a people's war is that the party needs to maintain *political control* of the war in a period when military efficiency is at a premium, when the dynamics of war favour the military men and when the requirements of a successful political campaign do not always coincide with those of military effectiveness. Here I am assuming, on the basis of most people's wars (the most significant exception being Cuba) that military success is dependent on the success of political mobilisation. There seems, in fact, little doubt that in Africa at least (and probably elsewhere as well) the development of successful people's war is determined by the extent to which the party has secured *active* political support. The failure of the UPC in Cameroon illustrates the point.[24]

The third contradiction is that the party must maintain a balance, and avoid a split, between the internal and external wings of the party in a situation where the lack of effective communication channels tends to isolate the fighting men from the external leadership. Here two observations can be made. First, a people's war is unlikely to be successful so long as it is conducted from outside the country: a strong and autonomous internal party organisation is essential. Second, exile politics are likely to be detrimental to the party's overall effectiveness.[25] The aim of any nationalist party engaged in a people's war must be to reduce its dependence on external bases and to become politically self-sufficient in the interior.

People's wars, by their very nature as anti-colonial struggles, are international in character. Both the rulers of the colonial state and the nationalists seek to legitimise their action internationally and to acquire allies, if not active support. Successful diplomacy of national liberation movements, therefore, is essential.[26] Broadly, such diplomacy must manage, first, to gain the support of neighbouring countries and to procure the necessary bases. Secondly, it needs to create, and preferably to maintain, nationalist unity in order to win international recognition as the sole legitimate nationalist organisation. Thirdly, the party must secure financial aid and military equipment. Finally, the nationalists must generate the largest and most vocal metropolitan and international opposition to the colonial war in order to obtain, ultimately, the widest and most prompt recognition of the independent government of the country. Hence, the importance of remaining non-aligned.

The ultimate significance of people's wars, however, does not lie in the nationalists' ability to mobilise villagers into bands of guerillas. The lusophone parties claimed, like their predecessors elsewhere in the world, that their aim was to construct a new society, not merely to expel the colonial forces. The measure of their success in doing so must initially be gauged by an examination of their achievements in the liberated areas.[27] Here, three inter-related issues are of particular significance: (i) the extent of effective party control in the liberated areas and the rate of progress in extending these areas; (ii) the effectiveness of the party in creating a genuinely popular leadership; and (iii) the nature and extent of socio-economic reconstruction in the liberated areas. The legitimacy of each nationalist party and the validity of its claims to form the first independent government depend largely upon success in the liberated areas.

* * *

The different outcomes of the three people's wars in lusophone Africa are best understood through an analysis of the degree to which each party managed successfully to mobilise the countryside and the extent to which it overcame the contradictory demands made on it by the process of war.[28] The conclusion which emerges is that there are broad similarities between the PAIGC and FRELIMO but that the MPLA is a party with substantially different political experience and achievements.[29] The PAIGC was the most adept in its prosecution of a people's war. It was most successful in achieving nationalist unity, in carrying out political mobilisation and in establishing new political structures in the liberated areas. At independence it had achieved the largest degree of control over its territory and its overall political legitimacy was high. The PAIGC certainly was a popular party as it integrated the historic nationalist leadership and the next generation of cadres who had emerged during the war. The party had also managed to advance the reorganisation of the liberated areas and was active in their reconstruction. Not surprisingly, it posed the most serious political and military threat to the Portuguese.

FRELIMO, despite serious difficulties throughout the 1960s, eventually managed to follow the same route as the PAIGC. Once it had overcome the weaknesses which threatened to split the Mozambican nationalists further and once it had assimilated the lessons of the failure of the early military campaigns, it developed a successful strategy of political mobilisation which, by 1974, had borne fruit.[30] Because of the size of the country (and other contextual factors) and because of the political costs of the early mistakes, FRELIMO had not achieved control over as high a proportion of the country as the PAIGC.[31] Where it had, however, it had done so by a similar process and its achievements in the liberated areas compared favourably with those of the Guinean party. FRELIMO was certainly a military force to reckon with and posed a serious military threat to the colonial armed forces. Colonial rule was not in immediate danger, however, as there was *de facto* military stalemate.

The MPLA, on the other hand, never overcame the ethnic, political, and military obstacles which stood in the way of its nationalist and socialist ambitions. Without Cuban support from 1975, the MPLA might have been eliminated whereas there was little doubt that both the PAIGC and FRELIMO would take power at independence. Briefly, the MPLA had little success in the development of a people's war because it could not progress either effectively or substantially with political mobilisation in the countryside.[32] It was the least successful of the three lusophone parties in overcoming the three central contradictions which are the most damaging to the success of a people's war.[33] The outcome of the Angolan nationalist conflict was therefore more the result of strictly military factors and outside intervention than the product of the political process of mobilisation which is so essential to the strength of the post-colonial state and to its distinctiveness as a new, more independent, and radical instrument of political change. To my mind, then, the Angolan state at independence was not only weaker but also less structurally distinct from the colonial state than either Mozambique or, even more, Guinea-Bissau.[34]

Furthermore, my analysis clearly indicates why and how the political process of people's wars differs in kind from that of constitutional and legal decolonisation. Although it is often argued that nationalist wars are nothing more than the pursuit of nationalist goals by military means, the process of political mobilisation ensures that this is not really the case. People's wars differ from constitutional decolonisation in three fundamental respects: (i) successful political mobilisation requires a form of political collaboration between a modern party and the rural population which was not necessary, and thus did not obtain, during constitutional decolonisation; (ii) the demands of a guerilla war lead to the development of political parties whose organisation, leadership, ideology, and political effectiveness are in fact more akin to parties committed to revolution than to those political organisations which negotiated independence in the rest of Africa; (iii) successful people's wars usher in the establishment of states the legitimacy and structure of which owe little to their colonial predecessors.

The PAIGC, FRELIMO, and to a much more limited extent the MPLA, were thus the first African nationalist parties in a position to replace, rather than simply inherit, the colonial state. Thus, it would appear that the potential role of the new states as instruments for revolution is greater in those three countries (although less in Angola) than it ever was in any other African colony – much as it was greater in Vietnam than in India.

Whether revolution is thereby more likely in any or all of the three lusophone countries is an entirely different and essentially empirical question. The issue is clear, if not easily resolved. Even if we assume that the leadership of the three states is genuinely committed to revolutionary change, are they in a better position than their equally ambitious nationalist predecessors elsewhere in Africa to carry out such a revolution? I return to an assessment of the claims of those who view the revolutionary potential of the three countries with optimism, and examine in turn the three arguments which they put forward. However, the generalisations I make on the basis of a comparison of the three nationalist movements must always be seen in the context of the significance of the differences between the three cases. It is difficult, in some instances, to argue that the MPLA can be usefully compared to the other two parties.[35]

The Nature of the 'Revolutionary Class Alliance'

The 'optimists' (as I shall call them) put forward two arguments. First, they contend that the process of war itself has enabled the most radical section of this class alliance to assume the leadership of the party. Secondly, they believe that the requirements of massive peasant participation in the political process of mobilisation gives them a 'passive veto' over the party and thus ensures that their voice will be heard. This, it is argued, fundamentally distinguishes the process of a people's war from any other form of decolonisation.[36]

Leaving aside the problem raised by the definition of these various classes (peasants, workers, and *petits bourgeois*) and by the meaning of 'passive veto', a few observations can be made.[37] In Guinea-Bissau and Mozambique, the process of political mobilisation did indeed lead to the development of parties which differed greatly from earlier African nationalist parties. Although the original leadership of the PAIGC and FRELIMO did not differ in either class origin or social status from their counterparts elsewhere in Africa (assimilated, educated, professional, middle class), the process of war saw the emergence of a 'second generation' of cadres who rose to the top because of their political skills and, in both instances, this new leadership ultimately displaced the first generation.[38]

It is equally true that this new leadership owes its political status to the party and not to 'traditional ethnic' affiliation or to the urbanised middle classes which took power in most of Africa. These 'party men' see themselves as, and in many instances indeed are, the representatives of those who did not have a voice under colonial rule and who still have no say in most African countries. Their 'natural' constituency is in the countryside where the party is most popular. Their commitment lies with the construction of a new social order which is not to be found in Africa today, rather than in the maintenance of the neo-colonial *status quo*. To that extent the leadership of the PAIGC and FRELIMO is radical, albeit in different ways. By contrast, the leadership of the MPLA, although socialist in ideology, is more akin to previous nationalist parties precisely because the process of war did not lead to the same degree of political mobilisation in the countryside. The party's 'natural' constituency remains in the cities (primarily Luanda).[39]

But, however distinct the leadership of the three lusophone parties is seen to be, there is no structural reason why this radical *petit bourgeois* leadership, as Cabral himself pointed out, should 'commit suicide as a class' in order to pursue a revolutionary path after independence.[40] Whether they do so cannot meaningfully be determined by the nature of the class alliance which the party is supposed to embody. Nowhere in Africa have the workers, as a class, shown great proclivity towards revolution. Nor, and that is more damaging to the case, is there any evidence that the peasants are revolutionary or even that their voice, if it is to be heard after independence, will necessarily radicalise the leadership.[41]

There are two fallacies in presuming an active political role by the peasants.[42] In the first instance, although it is true that the requirements of political mobilisation gave the rural population a *de facto* political veto during the war, there is no reason to believe that such veto can be maintained after independence when the party leadership assumes control as the new government. During the war the power of the villagers lay in the party's dependence on their cooperation. But, unless specific political structures have been created which ensure villagers a voice commensurate with their numbers, their participation in the war does not automatically guarantee them power after independence.[43] A crucial factor in lusophone Africa is likely to be the economic potential of the country.[44] Where there are virtually no other resources but agriculture, as in Guinea-Bissau, the countryside will have to be placated if production is to increase. On the other hand, Angola's immense oil and mineral wealth may well persuade the government to initiate a 'forced march' forward towards industrialisation – of which the countryside will inevitably be the main victim.

Secondly, and again to quote Cabral, the 'peasantry is not

revolutionary'.[45] Thus, even if the countryside should retain a passive veto after independence, there is no reason to believe that this would favour a revolutionary transformation of society. The history of revolutions seems to indicate that peasants (villagers) do not, and perhaps cannot, share the political aims of a modern socialist party. There are many historical precedents for thinking that a socialist leadership tends to favour forms of economic development which may not be to the benefit of the countryside. In such cases it is more likely than not that conflict will arise between party and villagers.[46]

In sum, then, it is not certain that the nature of the class alliance embodied in any or all of the lusophone parties is necessarily favourable to revolution. Independently from the question of whether it is possible to define a 'revolutionary class alliance' in the context of Africa, it seems causally simplistic to suggest that the process of class coalition which obtained during the nationalist wars is structurally more revolutionary than in other forms of decolonisation. What weakens the argument of the 'optimists'' here is their assumption that the radical ideological commitment of the leadership reflects the revolutionary nature of the existing nationalist class alliance rather than the greater need to utilise ideological mobilisation to move such a class alliance towards a more revolutionary project.[47]

The Nature of the Party

In the twentieth century the party has visibly been the driving force of most revolutions. The 'optimists' argue here that it is politically of the greatest significance that the wars in lusophone Africa have led to the emergence of political parties which are structurally different from their earlier nationalist counterparts in Africa. Three arguments are most commonly put forward to show why the PAIGC, FRELIMO, and the MPLA are now in a position to pursue a revolutionary course. First, their ideology, leadership, and policies are 'revolutionary'. Secondly, their organisation of and their integration into local political life provides them with the tools to affect change. Thirdly, the parties have acquired legitimacy not only as nationalist organisations but, crucially, as instruments of socio-economic change.

There is a *prima facie* case in favour of these arguments, with the proviso (rarely made) that the MPLA differs greatly from the other two parties. The political requirements of a successful people's war – the development of effective political mobilisation and the need to administer the reconstruction of the liberated areas – have created parties which have acquired a vastly different political experience from that of Congresses lobbying for constitutional reform. The obstacles which the PAIGC and FRELIMO had to overcome, the relative failure of the MPLA, the difficulties of ZANU and ZAPU in Rhodesia, all point to the uniqueness of political organisations capable of succeeding in war.[48]

In structure, leadership, and ideology, the three lusophone parties do differ from earlier African nationalist parties. All three are firmly committed to modern (as opposed to Africa) socialism. The party leadership has had to evolve a form of socialist ideology adapted to the country.[49] Consequently, a form of socialist ideology, understood and accepted by the party cadre and available for further mobilisation, emerged early. This experience differs significantly from those African countries, such as Guinea (Conakry), Tanzania, Uganda, or the Congo, which turned to the Left in the mid-sixties, a few years after independence.

The ideology of the lusophone parties is more pragmatic and their socialist objectives more suitably modest than those adopted, for example, in Ghana or Guinea (Conakry). More importantly, the process of war created a party apparatus based on the experience of implementing policies which, at the outset, did not look promising. The party organisation was severely tested and the war itself carried out a ruthless selection of the most competent political cadres. In short, the PAIGC and FRELIMO (unlike the MPLA) emerged at independence as toughened, effective, and self-confident political organisations with a clear sense of political identity, realistic ambitions, and considerable political experience.

It is equally true that the PAIGC and FRELIMO (more than the MPLA) had acquired political legitimacy as instruments of change at the local level in the liberated areas unlike other African parties.[50] War forced the three parties to create local political structures integrated in some way to indigenous village administration. This required not only collaboration in village and regional committees but also the creation of local party structures capable of reconciling local demands with party directives. Councils of elders or other so-called traditional forms of local government combined or fused with local party committees and some villagers themselves assumed important positions in the party hierarchy. Finally, the party's legitimacy depended on what it did rather than, as in much of Africa, on what it promised to do.

There were, however, vast differences between the three lusophone territories, differences which will undoubtedly affect their political evolution and which considerably reduce the value of generalisations about the three cases. The PAIGC could reasonably claim at independence to have acquired full legitimacy and to be in control of a national party organisation extending all the way down to the local level. The 1972 and 1976 elections have clearly indicated that the PAIGC's constituency was in the countryside and that, although not universally popular, it had support in all areas of the country.[51] FRELIMO was at independence less advanced in that it did not control the southern half of the country where, in any case, political mobilisation had not been as extensively carried out as FRELIMO would have wished.[52] However, the party's national legitimacy was not seriously in dispute and its political experience enabled it rapidly to extend the new party structures to the whole country. In Angola the situation was different. At independence the MPLA controlled little of the country beyond a small Mbundu base and some liberated areas along the Eastern border. The tripartite nationalist division along ethnic lines and the lingering war against UNITA robbed the MPLA of much of its national legitimacy. Finally, the MPLA had far less political experience in the countryside, much of which was without party organisation at independence.

There is thus little to dispute the argument that the PAIGC, FRELIMO, and (to a much lesser extent) the MPLA differed from their earlier African nationalist counterparts. There is, however, equally little to suggest that such significant political differences as exist either amount to or are a prelude to revolution in lusophone Africa.[53] Scepticism must remain, not because these parties could not be used as instruments of revolution – clearly they could insofar as they do not differ in structure, leadership, personnel, or ideology from parties which did carry through the hoped-for revolution – but because revolutions are rare and their occurrence cannot be anticipated either on the basis of the pronouncements of party leaders or from an examination of the nature of the party as such. Self-proclaimed revolutionary leadership and effective party machines are essential to the process of revolution. They are, however, far from sufficient, unless, that is, one believes in the ability of any revolutionary party to carry out a revolution from above, under any circumstances. Most political scientists (whether Marxist or not) would argue that revolutions rarely occur unless there are *social and economic*, as well as political, factors which are favourable to revolutionary change. Whether in the case of the three lusophone countries, as in the case of other nationalist revolutions, there are sufficient structural (as distinct from political) forces helping the revolutionaries is not altogether clear.

The three lusophone parties were initially set up as nationalist, not revolutionary, parties and their success as such cannot form a reliable guide to their potential as agencies of socio-economi change. The course of development followed in the three countries since independence would suggest, if anything, that there is no obvious correlation between the two. The PAIGC, ostensibly the most successful of the three parties, has pursued the most moderate and pragmatic path since independence. The MPLA and FRELIMO, although vastly different, have both opted for 'scientific socialism' and a 'Marxist-Leninist path to development'.[54] The political orientation of each party is not, therefore, necessarily a result either of the process of war or of the party's achievements in the liberated areas.

Reconstruction in the Liberated Areas: A New Society?

It is here that the claims of the 'optimists' are most ambitious and far reaching. To them, the achievements of the three lusophone parties in the liberated areas provide the foundations of the future revolution. In order to assess these claims it is best to discuss separately the three main areas of party policies: political, economic, and social. In the political sphere two questions require examination: the degree and significance of political mobilisation in the country and the nature of the political institutions established *before independence*. As concerns the parties' economic policies, it is necessary to assess the degree to which structural changes have actually occurred in agriculture and whether such changes can form the basis of a socialist economy. Finally, a consideration of the social implications of people's wars must include a brief (and probably impossible) evaluation of the claim that a 'new man' has emerged in the liberated areas.[55]

Briefly, the development strategy pursued with varying success by the three parties aimed at creating a popular leadership and a party organisation capable of integrating local socio-political structures (like councils of elders) into a new political system. The key to their efforts was the village committees designed to work in collaboration with the local party. On the whole, the three parties found it more convenient to utilise rather than replace pre-existing political structures. People's stores, health clinics, schools, security forces, and 'agricultural brigades' were set up locally. Every effort was made to improve agricultural methods and to increase production by developing new cooperative forms of production. Finally, the three parties sought to impart a new political ethos to the population of the liberated areas. These were their aims.[56] What have they in fact achieved?

a. *Political Change:* Political mobilisation was most complete and thorough in Guinea and northern Mozambique. In Angola, the MPLA was not really in a position to 'develop' the liberated areas. In Angola, as in Mozambique, the Portuguese had set up 'strategic hamlets', thereby restricting the impact of the party's attempts at reconstruction.[57] Where political mobilisation succeeded, however, the three parties relied heavily on existing local political structures (traditional authorities). In most instances, anti-colonial sentiments in the village amounted to a desire for a return to 'traditional' socio-political institutions rather than for integration into a modern socialist party organisation. The extent to which the three parties actually managed to change the structure of local political institutions must have been limited.[58]

Although village committees did form the linchpin of local administration in the liberated areas and although they enjoyed a certain degree of autonomy in their dealings with the party, it is unlikely that they acted as instruments of socio-political change.[59] There is thus little ground to suggest that the experience of political mobilisation and of war-time collaboration between villagers and party turned village committees into 'revolutionary cells'.

However, in Guinea-Bissau and Mozambique, such experience does represent a political resource which was never available to other African nationalist parties at independence. Undoubtedly, the most original and significant political innovation occurred in Guinea-Bissau, where the PAIGC held elections before independence to establish independent representative political institutions.[60] Whether this attempt to institutionalise popular participation in the emergent party-state is revolutionary cannot be determined at this point. What is clearer is that the political changes which were achieved in the liberated areas of Guinea-Bissau and Mozambique did not (perhaps could not) fundamentally alter local socio-political structures. In most twentieth-century revolutions, revolutionary parties were able to set up new forms of political organisations largely *because* the socio-political order was in the process of disintegration and a new one was wanting.[61] This does not seem to have been the case in lusophone Africa.

b. *Economic Change:* Similarly, the economic context within which the lusophone nationalists launched their armed struggles differed substantially from that of most other countries where revolutions have taken place. The existing structure of land ownership, the degree of economic exploitation and misery, and the social organisation of village life were not similar to those of, for example, Russia, China, or Vietnam. With few exceptions, there was no private African ownership of land and, in the lusophone countries, food was readily available. The villagers' grievances did not question 'traditional' patterns of agricultural production but only attacked the most obvious abuses of the colonial economy, most notably plantation labour and taxation.[62]

Thus successful political mobilisation in the countryside did not require an 'economic programme' nor did it require significant reforms, much less revolutionary change. As a result, the lusophone parties merely sought to sever the liberated areas from the colonial economy and to increase production; they did not innovate much. This was largely achieved by a return to traditional methods of cultivation and an increase in labour input rather than by the implementation of structural change. Despite the efforts of a leader like Cabral, who was more aware than most of the necessity to transform agriculture, little was achieved.[63] For example, there is no evidence to suggest that much progress was made in Guinea-Bissau towards some form of collective agriculture during the war. The structure of agricultural production remained essentially unchanged in the liberated areas.

Although the people's stores fulfilled their role during the war, state control of marketing which has derived from it since independence has not proved effective.[64] In fact, the disastrous effects of the wars compounded with the very serious economic difficulties faced by the three governments have led to a collapse of agricultural production and consequent food shortages. There is precious little here to cheer those who envisage a form of socialist development based on the Chinese, rather than the Soviet, model. Although the primary resources of Angola might make the Soviet option more feasible there, Guinea-Bissau and Mozambique cannot expect to follow that route.

c. *Social Change:* Has the war led to new forms of socio-political consciousness? In the absence of reliable data, speculation would be otiose. All that can be said is that the more successful political mobilisation was, the greater the social consensus it achieved. In Guinea-Bissau and Mozambique, political unity has been attained; ethnic, regional, and racial divisions have, for the time being, been neutralised and non-particularistic institutions are operating effectively.[65] The same cannot be said of Angola. There is some ground for hoping, although no more than that, that the nature of the political institutions which have been established in Guinea-Bissau and Mozambique will make it possible to avoid the politicisation of ethnic, religious, racial, or other potentially divisive forms of social identity.[66] In these two countries there is support for the 'socialist ideals' put forward by the government and a commitment to social goals which is rarely found in Africa. But clearly, such socialist commitment is an eminently evanescent commodity which may facilitate the party's attempt to transform society in the short run but which cannot replace new forms of political mobilisation in the long term. Revolutions do succeed in part because they have fired the imagination of many and because they are perceived as pursuing legitimate goals. But only structural change can consolidate the political gains of the war.

* * *

I think it clear that the drama of armed struggle did matter in Guinea-Bissau, Angola, and Mozambique. It was more than a mere trick of the light. The requirements of a successful people's war helped in the formation of a post-colonial state which differed substantially from those born of constitutional decolonisation. But what of revolution, then?

The wars in the three lusophone countries were launched because the nationalists could not achieve their aims through peaceful negotiations. The political, economic, and social context within which these were launched was not in any sense 'revolutionary', as it is plausible to argue that it was in Russia, China, or Vietnam.[67] The existing political order, the colonial state, was not crumbling. Colonial rule had not led to massive economic exploitation and wide-spread social disruption, as it had in Vietnam for example. Nor was there, as there was in Russia and China, a collapse of the agricultural system and famine. There were not, in short, many of the 'revolutionary pre-conditions' which students of revolution have identified in other instances.[68] In a real sense, therefore, the nationalists were not in any position to mobilise the population on the basis of the economic and social grievances which have been paramount in most twentieth-century revolutions.

Moreover, and perhaps more discouragingly for the 'optimists', the international economic context within which most African countries must develop is not favourable to socialist revolution. Short of the barbaric extremes which total 'socialist autarky' (on the Cambodian model) imposes on third world countries, there is little scope for an African country to control the nature of its economic links with the world market. Paradoxically, from the viewpoint of underdevelopment theory, Guinea-

Bissau, the most successful politically, is in the weakest economic position because it is entirely dependent on the export of agricultural products, whereas Angola may be one of the few countries in Africa with the resources to exercise a large degree of control over its economic development. In Guinea-Bissau it is very unlikely and in Mozambique improbable that industrialisation can serve as the engine of socialist development. The range of choices open to these two countries, especially Guinea, is not auspicious for development outside the world market and without outside financial aid.[69]

But the sceptics' mirth at these apparently gloomy conclusions could well be premature. There may not be a causal relationship between people's war and revolution in lusophone Africa but there is no sound reason for thinking that revolutions *cannot occur*. Revolutions are only defined as such in hindsight. The creation out of armed struggle of novel post-colonial states in lusophone Africa can be seen as a *political* revolution. It may be, although the odds are not very favourable, that hard ideological labour, dedicated revolutionary leadership, and an efficient party machine will move one (or more) of these countries through a *social* revolution.

NOTES

1. A preliminary version of this article was presented at the panel on 'The Nature of the State in Africa', Twenty-fifth Annual Meeting of the African Studies Association, Washington, DC, 4-7 November 1982. I am grateful to the members of the panel, especially Nelson Kasfir, Frank Holmquist, and Richard Joseph, for their useful comments. The material used for this article largely derives from the research done for the last chapter of my book: *Amilcar Cabral: Revolutionary Leadership and People's War* (Cambridge, 1983), henceforth referred to as *Cabral*.
2. For a discussion of the first and second waves of African socialism, see, for example, Carl Rosberg and Thomas Callaghy (eds), *Socialism in Sub-Saharan Africa* (Berkeley, 1979).
3. In what follows I have drawn on the arguments of many. See more particularly, Bonnie Campbell, *Libération nationale et construction du socialisme en Afrique* (Montreal, 1977); John Saul, *The State and Revolution in Eastern Africa* (London, 1979); Basil Davidson *et al., Southern Africa: The New Politics of Revolution* (Harmondsworth, 1977); Thomas Henriksen, 'Marxism and Mozambique', *African Affairs*, 77 (1978), 441-62; Basil Davidson, 'African Peasants and Revolution', *Journal of Peasant Studies*, 1 (1974) and 'Questions about Nationalism', *African Affairs*, 76 (1977); James Mittelman, *Underdevelopment and the Transition to Socialism: Mozambique and Tanzania* (New York, 1981).
4. Bonnie Campbell writes, for example: 'La poursuite et les impératifs de la lutte armée ont transformé de manière fondamentale le contenu idéologique de l'indépendance nationale en substituant au nationalisme "traditionnel" un nationalisme révolutionnaire – phénomène qui se concrétise par la transformation radicale de la pratique et donc des structures en place'. Campbell, *op. cit.*, 15.
5. They have not, however, cared to put their arguments in writing. I am grateful to John Lonsdale for talking me through these arguments.
6. For a cogent review of theories of revolution, see Theda Skocpol, *States and Social Revolutions* (Cambridge, 1979); on people's wars, see Eric Wolf, *Peasant Wars of the Twentieth Century* (New York, 1969).

7. For a useful discussion of the concept of modern revolutions, see John Dunn, *Modern Revolutions* (Cambridge, 1972) and 'Understanding Revolutions', *Ethics*, 92 (1982).
8. For a controversial account of the Ethiopian case, see Fred Halliday and Maxine Molyneux, *The Ethiopian Revolution* (London, 1981).
9. For an argument in favour of such causality, see Mittelman, *op. cit.*, 7.
10. John Lonsdale, 'States and Social Processes in Africa: a Historiographical Survey', *African Studies Review*, 24 (1981), 154.
11. *Ibid.*, 156.
12. See Thomas M. Callaghy, 'External Actors and the Relative Autonomy of the Political Aristocracy in Zaire' in this collection.
13. Frantz Fanon, *The Wretched of the Earth* (New York, 1968).
14. See, among many, Colin Leys, *Underdevelopment in Kenya: the Political Economy of Neo-Colonialism* (London, 1975), 207-12.
15. This is what I take to be the most coherent of these arguments, although they have not been expounded in this form.
16. See, for example, Campbell, *op. cit.*, 33-8.
17. See Thomas Callaghy, 'The Difficulties of Implementing Socialist Strategies of Development in Africa: The "First Wave" ', in Rosberg and Callaghy, *op. cit.*, 112-30.
18. On Guinea-Bissau, see *Cabral* and Lars Rudebeck, *Guinea Bissau: A Study of Political Mobilisation* (Uppsala, 1974). On Mozambique, see Thomas Henriksen, *Mozambique: A History* (London, 1978) and Luis Serapiao and Mohamed El-Khawas, *Mozambique in the Twentieth Century: From Colonialism to Independence* (Washington, 1979). On Angola, see John Marcum, *The Angolan Revolution*, I and II (Cambridge, 1969, 1978) and Douglas Wheeler and René Pélissier, *Angola* (London, 1971).
19. A point which Henriksen, for example, seems to have overlooked in 'People's War in Angola, Mozambique and Guinea Bissau', *Journal of Modern African Studies*, 14 (1976).
20. For a comparative perspective, see Wolf, *op. cit.*
21. For a comparison with China and Vietnam, see Mark Selden, 'People's War and the Transformation of Peasant Society: China and Vietnam' in Edward Friedman and Mark Selden (eds), *America's Asia: Dissenting Essays of Asian-American Relations* (New York, 1971).
22. For the most comprehensive discussion of ethnicity and politics in the context of Africa, see Nelson Kasfir, *The Shrinking Political Arena* (Berkeley, 1976), chapters 2 and 3.
23. For a discussion of ethnic nationalism in Angola, see Réne Pélissier, *Le Naufrage des Caravelles* (Orgeval, 1979), 99-140.
24. For a revealing account of the UPC rebellion, see Richard Joseph, *Radical Nationalism in Cameroun: Social Origins of the UPC Rebellion* (Oxford, 1977).
25. On this point, see Marcum, *The Angolan Revolution,* II, 3.
26. For a discussion of what I mean by diplomacy of national liberation in the context of Guinea-Bissau, see *Cabral*, chapter 3, section E.
27. Which in the case of Guinea-Bissau is assessed in *Cabral*, chapter 4, and Rudebeck, *op. cit.*, chapters 4-6.
28. *Cabral, op. cit.*, chapter 7.
29. The comparative analysis of the people's wars in the three countries is to be found in *Cabral, op. cit.*, chapter 7. Contrast with Henriksen, 'People's War in Angola, Mozambique and Guinea Bissau'.
30. See Walter Opello, 'Pluralism and Elite Conflict in an Independence Movement: FRELIMO in the 1960s', *Journal of Southern African Studies*, 2 (1975).
31. Henriksen, *Mozambique*, 226-7.
32. For a sympathetic account of their success, see Basil Davidson, *In the Eye of the Storm: Angola's People* (Garden City, 1972).
33. See my discussion of the MPLA's difficulties in *Cabral*, chapter 7.
34. See Marcum, *The Angolan Revolution,* II, conclusion.
35. It is, however, necessary to examine the three parties comparatively not only because, on paper, they are very similar but also because in most of the literature it is often assumed that they in fact were.

36. See, among many, Saul, 'Free Mozambique' in *The State and Revolution in Eastern Africa*, 79-92.
37. There is little agreement on the definition of these classes in the context of Africa. For a review of the arguments, see, *inter alia*, Stephen Katz, 'Marxism, Africa and Social Class: A Critique of Relevant Theories', Occasional Monograph Series, 14, Centre for Developing Area Studies, McGill University, 1980.
38. For a discussion of this process in Guinea-Bissau, see Patrick Chabal, 'Party, State and Socialism in Guinea Bissau', *Canadian Journal of African Studies*, forthcoming; in Mozambique, Barry Munslow, 'Leadership in the Front for the Liberation of Mozambique' in *Collected Papers*, Centre for Southern African Studies, University of York, Part I, pp. 139-66, Part II, pp. 114-27.
39. David Birmingham, 'The Abortive Coup in Angola, 1977', *African Affairs*, 77 (1978).
40. Amilcar Cabral, *Revolution in Guinea* (London, 1969), 89.
41. A somewhat naive view which Cabral did not hold, *ibid.*, 50.
42. There is a vast literature on the political role of the peasants. See, among others, John Lonsdale, 'State and Peasantry in Colonial Africa', in R. Samuel (ed), *People's History and Socialist Theory* (London, 1981); Ken Post, ' "Peasantization" and Rural Political Movements in West Africa', *Archives Européennes de Sociologie*, 13 (1972); John Saul and Roger Woods, 'African Peasantries' in Teodor Shanin (ed), *Peasant Societies* (Harmondsworth, 1971).
43. Even in Guinea-Bissau, where such political structures were set up (through elections) before independence, there occurred in the five years after independence a gradual but significant loss of power on the part of the countryside. This was one of the factors which precipitated the November 1980 coup in Bissau. On the coup, see my articles in *West Africa* (15 December 1980), 2554-6; (22/29 December 1980), 2593-4; and (12 January 1981), 62-3.
44. A point generally valid for most African countries. See, for example, John Dunn, *West African States: Failure and Promise* (Cambridge, 1978), 11.
45. Amilcar Cabral, *Revolution in Guinea*, 50.
46. Wolf writes about the role of peasants in modern revolutions: '... the peasant is an agent of forces larger than himself .... The peasant's role is thus essentially tragic: his efforts to undo a grievous present only usher in a vaster, more uncertain future'. Wolf, *op. cit.*, 301.
47. See Campbell's reasoning here: 'Ces nouvelles relations sociales rendues nécessaires par la dynamique de la lutte impliquent une transformation radicale des structures et souvent le création de structures tout à fait nouvelles .... Le lutte de libération est donc un processus cumulatif, et génère sa propre dynamique. Les conditions nécessaires pour son avancement deviennent en fait les moyens de l'approfondissement du contenu idéologique de la lutte et la meilleure garantie de sa consolidation et de son succès'. Campbell, *op. cit.*, 37-8.
48. For a relevant comparison with Vietnam and China, see Selden, *op. cit.*
49. For a useful comparison see the analysis of the last three party congresses in Luis Moita, *Os Congressos de FRELIMO, do PAIGC e do MPLA: una analise comparativa* (Lisbon, 1979).
50. In the case of Guinea-Bissau, see Rudebeck, *op. cit.*, 146.
51. See my discussion of the 1972 elections in *Cabral*, chapter 4, section E.
52. Henriksen, *Mozambique*, 226-7.
53. As John Saul seemed to imply in 1975: A revolutionary nationalism which has broken through the barrier of Portuguese "ultra-colonialism" now stands poised to confront the more subtle dangers of a threatened neocolonialism'. *The State and Revolution in Eastern Africa*, 55.
54. See Molita, *op. cit.*
55. Generally, there has been too little research done here to provide enough comparative material. For a beginning on Guinea-Bissau, see James Cunningham, 'Guinea Bissau 1956–74: A Re-Assessment', *African Affairs*, forthcoming.
56. For a discussion of the Guinean case, see *Cabral*, chapter 4.

57. See Gerald Bender, 'The Limits of Counter-Insurgency: An African Case', *Comparative Politices*, 4 (1972).
58. This, however, is almost never discussed in the literature even though the experience of other 'rural revolutions' shows that it is a crucial point.
59. See Rudebeck's cautious conclusions about Guinea Bissau. Rudebeck, *op. cit.*, 248-52.
60. *Cabral*, chapter 4, section E.
61. See Skocpol, *op. cit.*
62. For two different views on the relevance of the plantations of northern Angola, see René Pélissier, *La Colonie du Minotaure* (Orgeval, 1978) and Mario de Andrade and Marc Ollivier, *La guerre en Angola: étude socio-économique* (Paris, 1971).
63. Cabral was an agronomist and, earlier, had conducted the first agricultural survey of Guinea. See his comments in 'Le rôle social de la paysannerie', in *Unité et Lutte*, 1 (Paris, 1975).
64. In both Guinea-Bissau and Mozambique there have been moves to return to some form of private trading and commerce.
65. By neutralised I mean that they are not, at the moment, politically salient. I am not implying, however, that they may not become politically salient in the future. I do not subscribe to the view that such forms of social identity 'disappear' with modernity. I am simply concerned here to analyse under what historical circumstances they become more or less salient.
66. These forms of social identity need not necessarily be divisive but, historically, they have often been so during the end of colonial rule and the first few years of independence in Africa. Revolution itself is no guarantee that such forms of social identity will not become politically salient again as quite clearly they have become in some countries which underwent a revolution.
67. See here Dunn, *Modern Revolutions*, and Skocpol, *op. cit.*
68. Wolf's comparative analysis is most relevant here.
69. All three countries have established, or seek to establish, close economic links with the West and with such economic agencies as that set up by the Lomé Convention.

Part IV
Modes of Solidarity

[13]

Between a Moment and an Era: The Origins and Afterlives of Bandung

Christopher J. Lee

At the Rendezvous of Decolonization

> No race possesses the monopoly of beauty, intelligence, force and there is room for all of us at the rendezvous of victory.
>
> —Aimé Césaire, *Cahier d'un retour au pays natal* (1939)

IN NOVEMBER 2006, China hosted a summit of forty-eight political leaders from countries across Africa, the third in a series sponsored by the Forum on China–Africa Cooperation (FOCAC) since 2000. Widely covered in the international media, this three-day event in Beijing aimed to crystallize a common agenda between China, with its burgeoning global role in the post-cold war world, and Africa, a continent described on posters in Beijing as "the land of myth and miracles."[1] Publicized as a benevolent occasion with promises of aid and trade agreements reflective of a novel global partnership outside the West, this meeting equally marked a new and ambivalent turn for many observers in Europe and North America concerned with China's increasing influence on a continent that has been perceived by Chinese leaders as "up for grabs." That China's intentions are unsurprising and historically familiar—many have cited its aggressiveness as reminiscent of European colonialism—has not mitigated these anxieties. Consumer markets and resources such as oil have been key incentives for recent Chinese attention. In particular, international criticism following the 1989 Tiananmen Square Massacre, the rise of US hegemony after the cold war, and the 1997 Asian financial crisis have forced China to reconsider its foreign policy, with Sino-African relations forming a central component of this shift toward restoring its global presence and power. Unrestricted foreign aid from China has in turn been attractive for a number of African nation-states, especially governments such as Zimbabwe's and Sudan's that have fallen into disfavor with the IMF, the World Bank, and Western governments generally. China's respect for sovereignty and noninterference has characterized this approach. Since 2005, China has consequently become Africa's third most important trading partner following the US and France, thus superseding Great Britain. The Forum's slogan of "Peace, Friendship, Cooperation, Development" therefore sums up the working sensibility found between both sides, though it also conceals a complex set of unsteady power relations that currently undergird this alignment.[2]

The rhetoric of newness surrounding the Forum also obscures an equally complicated past, not only between China and Africa but between Asia and Africa generally. The present collection seeks to amend this empirical and conceptual gap, to restore a chronology and trajectory of historical experience that have been marginalized by conventional area-studies analysis. Like many projects preceding it, this volume is concerned with the complex foundations, experiences, and aftereffects of the modern history of colonization and decolonization during the 20th century. As such, it builds upon work published over the past thirty years that has sought to respond to and redress the frameworks of political economy and social knowledge produced by global imperialism. Unlike many of its predecessors, however, this volume departs from a metropole-colony focus, asserting the impact and consequent importance of connections within the global South in the making of this history. It specifically uses the 1955 Afro-Asian Conference in Bandung, Indonesia, as a central point of orientation, being an occasion—diplomatic and symbolic—

when twenty-nine African and Asian countries met to discuss the possible futures of the postcolonial world. Indeed, a recent resurgence of interest in Afro-Asian relations and the fiftieth anniversary of the conference—which established the New Asian-African Strategic Partnership (NAASP), whose official declaration reinstated the Ten Principles of the Bandung Communiqué—have revived focus on the meeting.[3] This restoration, however, has also risked simplifying the complexities of 1955. From one point of view, the conference constituted a foundational moment of the early postcolonial era, manifesting the rendezvous of victory presaged metaphorically by Aimé Césaire. But from another vantage point, it equally contained the existential predicaments of newfound sovereignty and the internal and external political claims and responsibilities that would soon challenge it, particularly those generated by the cold war. In sum, Bandung comprised a complex intersection of "imagined communities"—in the influential nation-making sense as defined by Benedict Anderson—but also a set of politically constrained "represented communities" as described more recently by John Kelly and Martha Kaplan, being constituted and limited by institutionalized acts of law, diplomacy, and the structural legacies of colonial rule. Bandung contained both the residual romance of revolution, as well as the *realpolitik* of a new world order in the making.[4]

This volume is therefore poised between several interrelated but often disparate fields: cold war history and postcolonial studies, global history and area studies, diplomatic history and sociocultural history. The attraction of Bandung as an event is its capacity to bring these subjects into conversation with one another, presenting a historical moment and site generative of intersecting vantage points and their storied outcomes. Indeed, the contributions to this volume speak from and to these different academic audiences through a variety of social themes—gender, law, technology, labor, ideologies of development, foreign aid, and religion among them. Yet they are unified by a concern for community formation—or, more specifically, a geopolitical *communitas*, as discussed later—beyond the reaches of political, geographic, and historical convention. The case studies on offer here do not seek to reconstitute a triumphal narrative of postcolonial autonomy and assertion—a tact that has animated many recent discussions of Afro-Asian relations thus far—but instead recuperate a more usable past by identifying the varied locations and complex, situated meanings of "Afro-Asianism," an ill-defined term that has signaled both a cold war-era ideology of diplomatic solidarity as well as a more general phenomenon of intercontinental exchange and interracial connection. This volume does not pretend to cover every aspect of this history, nor does it emphasize one meaning of this expression over another. Given the still-early stage of this research field at present, we are more focused on identifying the occasions, archives, thematic realms, and analytic techniques for addressing this history. If Bandung in retrospect offered a "diplomatic revolution" for the postcolonial world, a subsequent question emerges as to how a sociocultural turn can be applied to this diplomatic history, to connect this event to preexisting area-studies agendas that have privileged the agency of local people and communities.

The essays that follow, in sum, explore these scales of power and geography not only to examine the ramifications of Bandung itself, but to add greater empirical depth to meanings of the postcolonial, a stronger area-studies perspective to cold war scholarship, and, at the broadest level, a more concerted emphasis on how political projects based in the "majority world" shaped global history during the latter half of the 20th century. But why this specific historical moment, and, furthermore, how might Bandung be situated and understood from the point of view of the present? In what ways does the Bandung conference complicate conventional exit-and-entry narratives of decolonization and generalized assertions about "the postcolony" by highlighting new forms of "political community" beyond the nation-state? In short, how does this history speak to concerns expressed with growing frequency regarding the disjunctures between 20th-century decolonization, postcolonial criticism, and the political problems of sovereignty in the global present by charting the possibilities and predicaments of the early postcolonial period? To answer these crucial questions, it is appropriate to start with a discussion of the precursors and afterlives of the Bandung moment.[5]

A Brief History of the Future, circa 1955

> For many generations our peoples have been the voiceless ones in the world. We have been the unregarded, the peoples for whom decisions were made by others whose interests were paramount, the peoples who lived in poverty and humiliation. Then our nations demanded, nay fought for independence, and achieved independence, and with that independence came responsibility. We have heavy responsibilities to ourselves, and to the world, and to the yet-unborn generations. But we do not regret them.
>
> —President Ahmed Sukarno of Indonesia, Opening Address of the Asian-African Conference, April 18, 1955

Decolonization poses fundamental challenges for the historian. From an empirical standpoint, it is both a contingent moment of political independence *and* a long-standing process with deep roots, at times originating with the act of initial colonization itself. It is an experience that is at once uniquely individual in scope—to people, communities, and nation-states alike—and in retrospect seemingly universal: the world witnessed a momentous wave of newly independent nation-states during the second half of the 20th century, more than doubling the number of members in the United Nations. Yet despite its relative ubiquity as a political process for many parts of the world, it is not easily contained within uniform frames of analysis, or time. The early episodes of decolonization in the Western hemisphere preceded that of Africa and Asia by almost two centuries, with the American Revolution (1776–83) and the Haitian Revolution (1791–1804) subverting the imperial presence of Great Britain and France respectively in the New World. Indeed, the early modern political independence of nation-states in North and South America antedated the formal colonization of Africa and in ways influenced this new shift in political direction for Europe during the late 19th century. Asia similarly experienced European imperialism within a time frame of its own, with initial Western intrusion concurrent to parallel endeavors in the Americas during the early modern era and the final vestiges of this process relinquished as late as Great Britain's handover of Hong Kong

Introd.1. Prime Minister Jawaharlal Nehru of India and President Gamal Abdel Nasser of Egypt arrive in Bandung

to China in 1997. Thus, the precolonial period in Africa does not overlap chronologically with Asia's precolonial period, in the same sense that Latin America's postcolonial period has existed for some time whereas it is still just starting for parts of Asia and Africa. Our schematic frames of chronological reference—the precolonial, colonial, and postcolonial eras—accordingly face the challenge of synchronicity. The timing of decolonization can be out of joint when transnational and transregional comparisons are made. Further complicating such matters have been trends of subimperialism, the rise of former colonies such as the United States, South Africa, and China, for example, into roles of regional and global dominance, a development that decenters Europe as a point of reference but introduces new complications in the chronological placement and meaning of decolonization in world history. Imperialism has reproduced itself in various changing forms over time and continues to do so to the present.[6]

Decolonization consequently presents a problem of narrative and analysis. It is not an expression that is easily transferred between contexts with a common definition intact. Like the nation-state with which it is intrinsically connected, decolonization on the surface lends itself wide use, as a process and baseline for narratives of autonomous economic development and political modernization. However, as with these issues, the outcomes are more often assumed than achieved, with a persistent risk being recourse to historical teleology to provide an explanatory structure.[7] Mindful of this problem, social historians for the most part have focused on explorations of nationalism, interrogating its claims of representation, but venturing little beyond the boundaries of the nation-state at hand or chronologically further into the postcolonial period to follow its changing meanings.[8] Recent work has attempted to address the internal, qualitative differences between settler and non-settler colonies, but, as underscored by the insights of diplomatic historians, other geopolitical contexts—the cold war in particular—must also be pointed to as crucial external factors in shaping and at times prolonging decolonization, as in Southeast Asia and southern Africa.[9] From the vantage point of another involved field, postcolonial studies, the term "postcolonial" itself—to which decolonization is also intrinsically tied—has often been essentialized through interpretive assertions that have sought to read and inscribe a common set of experiences across much of the former colonial world.[10] The universality of condition imparted by such terminology therefore deserves critical vigilance as well. Decolonization and its correlative expressions, in sum, present an ongoing predicament, enabling comparison while equally posing the concession of oversimplification. Furthermore, they underscore the disjunctive manner by which these issues are currently addressed among political scientists, economists, anthropologists, historians, and literature scholars. It is best approached as a situated process that requires attention to local case studies as well as broader patterns of event and meaning across space and time. Rather than simply signaling a linear, diplomatic transfer of power from colonial to postcolonial status, decolonization equally constitutes a complex dialectical intersection of competing views and claims over colonial pasts, transitional presents, and inchoate futures.

Opportunities are provided in this set of tensions as well. If empirical generalization is to be avoided, processes of decolonization offer an entry point for rethinking the specific conditions and local causes for political change, in addition to more broadly experienced continuities that have attended such shifts. As observed with the political dilemmas of many postcolonial leaders, the transition from colonial to postcolonial status was often thin on autonomy and thick with ongoing entanglements. Political sovereignty did not automatically translate into economic self-sufficiency or cultural independence, as seen in the writing of such figures as Kwame Nkrumah, Julius Nyerere, and Jawaharlal Nehru.[11] Revisiting moments of decolonization consequently presents an opportunity for recapturing the senses of optimism, frustration, and uncertainty that characterized such occasions. Such emotive qualities found in the speeches and writings of figures who attended Bandung in 1955 reflect a lack of comfort through the absence of any stable trajectory, and they explain in part why contemporary narratives of anticolonialism and decolonization have often resorted to forms of romance, as David Scott has recently argued. In Scott's view, anticolonial histories

> have tended to be narratives of overcoming, often narratives of vindication; they have tended to enact a distinctive rhythm and pacing, a distinctive direction, and to tell stories of salvation and redemption. They have largely depended upon a certain (utopian) horizon toward which the emancipationist history is imagined to be moving.[12]

This interpretive situation has in turn created a sense of disconnection between the failures of the postcolonial present and the complex visions of postcolonial futures expressed during moments of decolonization. Frederick Cooper, for example, has pointed to empirical

Introd.2. Local popular reception of the arrival of international delegations in Bandung

gaps in recent critical work that has assigned postcolonial blame on past colonial projects, a common approach that can often obscure the importance of the late colonial and early postcolonial period in shaping the era that followed.[13] In this way, it is important to reexamine the events and features of decolonization in order to restore the competing strategies and complex visions that not only sought to achieve future outcomes, but at the time sought to inventively reshape the legacies of the past to serve such present endeavors.

Bandung was such an occasion. In retrospect, it can be seen as a pivotal moment placed in mid-century between colonial and postcolonial periods, between the era of modern European imperialism and the era of the cold war. It summarized an alternative chronology of world events organized by intellectuals and activists of color who had been subjected to forms of colonialism, racism, and class oppression. This historical sequence includes such precursors as the series of Pan-African Congresses that took place beginning in 1900, the 1911

Universal Races Congress in London, the League Against Imperialism meeting held in Brussels in 1927, and the two Pan-Asian People's Conferences held in Nagasaki (1926) and Shanghai (1927).[14] At a deeper level, Bandung also served as a culmination of connections and relationships that had crossed the Indian Ocean world for centuries.[15] The common ground shared and frequently cited at the conference was the history of Western imperialism in Asia, Africa, and the Middle East since the sixteenth century. These claims similarly extended to a broader set of thematic experiences including racism and cultural discrimination, which further attracted such noted observers as Richard Wright, the African American novelist.[16] The meeting therefore captured and represented a complex global present, one that signaled political achievement but also future uncertainty. Of the twenty-nine countries that sent official delegations, many had attained independence, though there were others, particularly from Sub-Saharan Africa, which still remained under the last remnants of colonial rule. Not all were former colonies either. Constituting a diverse spectrum, participants included leading lights of the postcolonial world, such as India and Egypt, as well as countries that had recent imperial legacies of their own, namely Japan.[17] From cultural, religious, and linguistic standpoints, the differences between attendees were equally pronounced. And yet, it is essential to recognize that the organizers themselves acknowledged such factors of division, resting their contingent solidarity and sense of purpose on a shared history of Western aggression.[18]

The immediate backdrop to the conference were two meetings in 1954 between Indonesia, Burma (Myanmar), Ceylon (Sri Lanka), India, and Pakistan—often referred to collectively as the Colombo Powers. Concerned with cold war tensions in Vietnam and Southeast Asia generally, one meeting was held in Colombo, Sri Lanka, in April with a second held in Bogor, Indonesia, in December. Prime Minister Ali Sastroamidjojo of Indonesia, a vocal critic of Western intervention in Asia, originally proposed the idea of an Asian-African conference as a response to the 1954 founding of the Southeast Asia Treaty Organization (SEATO) sponsored by the United States. Delegations were to be drawn from the existing Afro-Asian group within the United Nations. However,

Introd.3. Premier Zhou Enlai of China with Prime Minister Ali Sastroamidjojo of Indonesia at the Bandung Airport

the invitation list soon expanded, reflecting a diplomatic, rather than strictly continental, logic. Jawaharlal Nehru of India, for example, insisted that China be included as part of his foreign policy agenda to foster productive regional relations despite the forced acquisition of neighboring Tibet by China in 1950. This move eliminated Taiwan as a possible participant, given the tense Strait Crisis which then remained unresolved. Apartheid South Africa was also eventually excluded, as were North and South Korea which still maintained a cease-fire following the Korean War (1950–53). Israel was also voted down for fear that Arab and Muslim countries would not attend. Invitations ultimately were sent to Egypt, Turkey, Japan, Libya, Lebanon, Jordan, Syria, Iran, Iraq, Saudi Arabia, Yemen, Afghanistan, Nepal, Laos, Cambodia, Thailand, North and South Vietnam, the Philippines, Ethiopia, the Gold Coast (Ghana), Sudan, Liberia, and the Central African Federation.[19] With China and the Colombo Powers included, twenty-nine countries in total attended, comprising a group nearly half the size of the U.N. and ostensibly representing an estimated 1.5 billion people, thus underscoring the numeric significance of the meeting. But of these countries, only six were from Africa, which tilted much of the agenda toward concerns found in Asia, including the Middle East.

The conference took place between April 18 and 24, 1955. The location of Bandung was significant, as it was one of the most important cities in Indonesia. Indonesian President Ahmed Sukarno had received his university education and started his career as a political activist there, publishing the journal *Indonesia Muda* and helping found the Partai Nasional Indonesia.[20] More importantly, the choice of a metropole outside the West marked a symbolic departure from its Pan-African and League Against Imperialism antecedents, underscoring the new geographic sphere of autonomy found in the nascent postcolonial world. Although a certain diplomatic complexity undergirded the meeting, the public atmosphere achieved at the conference evinced this sensibility of a new era in world history. Social activities, panels, and receptions scheduled throughout the week contributed to this mood of excitement, with the centerpiece of the conference being the opening addresses given by various heads of state, a who's who of postcolonial leaders.[21] It was also this platform through which political tensions and opportunism emerged, posing immediate questions about the viability and longevity of Afro-Asianism as a political ideology and front. As with Sukarno, Bandung offered an unparalleled occasion for Nehru to consolidate his position as a recognized world leader, providing a diplomatic stage for his vision of nonalignment from the U.S. and Soviet Union, an idea that would gain traction in the years that followed. For Gamal Abdel Nasser of Egypt, it enabled him to ascend to a status equivalent to that of Nehru—a position soon consolidated by the 1956 Suez Crisis—in spite of the ambiguities of the coup that placed him in power in 1952. Given its exclusion from the U.N., Zhou Enlai, China's foreign minister, similarly perceived Bandung as a moment of legitimating China in the purview of its regional neighbors. Despite tensions with the US over Taiwan and North Korea and its concurrent alliance with the USSR, the Bandung meeting presented a forum through which China could state its peaceful intentions and overcome a sense of isolation within the international community.

*Introd.*4. Premier Zhou Enlai, who was also China's foreign minister, delivering his address at the Bandung Conference

However, beyond this "great men" perspective on the conference were issues and situations that underscored not only competing visions of the future, but how such visions were informed and supported by the new global order being established by the United States and Soviet Union. In a recent acclaimed survey of the cold war, Odd Arne Westad has contended that this period's greatest impact was on the Third World—not the theater of Europe as so often assumed—since American and Soviet policies ultimately formed a continued pattern of colonialism, if by revised means, with aspirations of political, economic, and ideological control.[22] In many cases, the imperial "man on the spot" had been replaced by a member of the new postcolonial elite, as famously warned by Frantz Fanon. Among the participants, Communist China, with its then-close relations with the Soviet Union, was perhaps the most widely viewed proxy for superpower interests, although other countries maintained similar sets of connections. Iran, Iraq, Pakistan, and Turkey, a member of NATO, had recently signed the Baghdad Pact with Great Britain on February 24, 1955 to form the Central Treaty Organization (CENTO) with the direct intention of limiting Soviet interests in the Middle East. In parallel, SEATO—with its members Thailand, the Philippines, and again Pakistan in attendance—had been formed in 1954 with the same intent. Japan and Saudi Arabia similarly had strong unilateral ties with the US. Yet, the most visible cold war fault line existed between North and South Vietnam, both of which took their opening addresses as an opportunity to accuse the other of escalating tensions within Indochina.[23] Following the French defeat at Dien Bien Phu, the 1954 Geneva Accords had granted independence to Vietnam, albeit dividing it into a pro-communist North and anti-communist South, eventually leading to the Vietnam War involving the US. Other speeches identified similar ongoing and future conflicts, perhaps most conspicuously the Palestinian and anti-apartheid struggles.

The conference thus captured a complex set of individual and group aims. The immediate outcome of the conference was a final communiqué that reinstated the desire for greater economic cooperation and cultural exchange, recognition for human rights and self-determination, the condemnation of new and future forms of imperialism, and the

Introd.5. The Liberian delegation in attendance

need to pursue policies that would promote world peace. It is important to recognize that nonalignment as a stated principle shared by all in attendance was not an outcome of the Bandung meeting, yet again a reflection of the formal and informal security agreements that many participants had already arranged and, moreover, the priority placed on individual sovereignty. Indeed, only India, Burma, and Indonesia supported the idea explicitly. However, the more momentous result was the *feeling* of political possibility presented through this first occasion of "Third World" solidarity, what was soon referred to as the Bandung Spirit. In defining this sentiment of a new future that transcended the bounds of member states, Vijay Prashad writes

> What they meant was simple: that the colonized world had now emerged to claim its space in world affairs, not just as an adjunct of the First or Second Worlds, but as a player in its own right. Furthermore, the Bandung Spirit was a refusal of both economic subordination and cultural suppression—two of the major policies of imperialism. The audacity of Bandung produced its own image.[24]

The Bandung Conference of 1955 consequently generated what has often been taken as self-evident: the idea of a Third World. Furthermore, in contrast to many contemporary understandings of this expression, the Third World was embraced as a positive term and virtue, an alternative to past imperialism and the political economies and power of the US and the Soviet Union. It represented a coalition of new nations that possessed the autonomy to enact a novel world order committed to human rights, self-determination, and world peace. It set the stage for a new historical agency, to envision and make the world anew. The recent history of imperialism and colonialism across Africa and Asia had informed these ideals. Although the 1952 origins of this expression preceded the conference by three years, Bandung captured in palpable form the potential of what this global coalition and its political imagination might mean.[25]

Still, the elusiveness of solidarity suggested by the word "spirit" equally characterized the aftermath of the conference. Indeed, although the sense of unity caught the Eisenhower administration off guard, the tense balance of cooperation and respect for individual

Introd.6. Members of the Gold Coast (Ghana) and Indian delegations during a recess

sovereignty among the delegates became more pronounced in the years that followed.[26] Unilateral and regional security arrangements such as SEATO and CENTO remained unchanged with few exceptions, as with the departure of Iraq from CENTO in 1958. The United States and Soviet Union continued to make regional inroads during the 1950s, escalating tensions particularly in the Middle East and Southeast Asia. The Vietnam War alone demonstrated an inability of Afro-Asian nations to dispel foreign geopolitical influence and guaranteed that peace, as aspired to in the Bandung communiqué, would not be the prevailing norm in Asia during the cold war. The Arab-Israeli conflict and the late decline of white minority rule in southern Africa—in Southern Rhodesia, Angola, Mozambique, and apartheid South Africa—would pose equally persistent challenges. Perhaps more politically damaging to the Bandung Spirit than these externally influenced cases were episodes of delegate nations themselves coming into conflict, at times violently. The Sino-Indian Border Conflict of 1962 as well as similar disputes between India and Pakistan undermined the possibility of solidarity within the subcontinent. The Sino-Soviet split also presented a diplomatic complexity for former Bandung participants, despite the surface suggestion of a new nonalignment. A final setback to the principles of the communiqué was the gradual testing and acquisition of nuclear arsenals by China (1964), India (1974), and eventually Pakistan (1998).

Such factors accumulated over time, however, and the vision of future opportunities articulated at Bandung was not foreclosed in the short term. Nasser became an early beneficiary by quickly moving to position himself as a leader of the Third World, a status enhanced by the global support Egypt garnered during the 1956 Suez Crisis, when Great Britain and France failed, under international pressure, to regain control over the Suez Canal. In December 1957, the Afro-Asian Peoples' Solidarity Organization (AAPSO) was established in Cairo, marking a new endeavor in the wake of Bandung. The Soviet Union and China both became involved in its activities. AAPSO proved to have even wider reach than the Bandung meeting itself, by including a range of political and cultural organizations as opposed to official delegates from African and Asian states. The conferences it organized between 1958 and 1965 continued the Bandung Spirit by emphasizing professional exchange, cultural connections, women's coalitions, and youth participation (see the chapters by Bier and Brennan in this volume for the prominent role of Egypt). Furthermore, meetings were held within an expanding range of locales including Guinea, Ghana, and Tanzania. The most important post-Bandung development, however, was the institutionalization of nonalignment through the founding of the Non-Aligned Movement (NAM). The Belgrade Conference of Non-Aligned Nations convened in September 1961 by Yugoslavia's Josip Tito, who sought greater autonomy from the USSR, initiated this formal alliance, revising once again the meaning of Afro-Asianism. The second conference held in Cairo in October 1964 had delegations from forty-seven states in attendance, a growth attributable to the wave of decolonization in Sub-Saharan Africa. Combined, these two mutual, if at times competitive, efforts at sustaining a Third World bloc manifested a high point for Afro-Asian solidarity by 1964. However, this trend was dramatically cut short a year later with the failure to coalesce the proposed second Afro-Asian meeting to be held in Algiers in 1965, the result of unresolved differences between China, Indonesia, India, and the Soviet Union, whose involvement in the intervening years had become ineluctable.[27]

With the period of colonial rule receding and the individual options and abilities of postcolonial political autonomy better understood, the original fervor of Afro-Asianism as an ideology shifted and declined thereafter, though it did not entirely disappear. The Vietnam War, the late decolonization of southern Africa, the antiapartheid struggle in South Africa, and the Arab-Israeli conflict continued to offer reasons for protest against continuing forms of imperialism and Western intervention. In parallel, the "development" and "modernization" aspects of solidarity discourse gained ground aside the political, taking root in local contexts and leading to debates, struggles, and continued speculation over the viability of transposing certain ideas, like Maoism, beyond their place of origin (see chapters by Burgess, Monson, and Lee). Translation, in its pragmatic and ideological forms, was a constant issue. Still, new connections were also fostered, particularly in Latin America with the 1966 founding of the Organization of Solidarity with the People of Asia, Africa and Latin America in Havana, Cuba, and the emergence of a broader tricontinentalism. If the reach of such projects embody in organizational form the kind of problematic essentialism of "the postcolonial" as addressed earlier, it is nevertheless important to recognize their institutional legacies that still continue today. In addition to the NAM, the Group of 77—established within the UN in 1964 to aggregate the interests of developing countries—has since enlarged to include 130 countries. The NAM itself continues, if in a weakened and less certain form after the cold war, to provide a forum for leaders and nation-states in Africa, Asia, and Latin America.[28]

A more decisive failure on the part of the original "Bandung regimes"—as Samir Amin has called them—and their successors has been within the political realm internal to their borders, rather than the version of late internationalism they sought to define and mobilize.[29] One-party states, authoritarian regimes, abuse of human rights, and economic discrepancies between elites, workers, and peasants have all too often characterized the social and political conditions of nation-states within the Third World, contributing to its pejorative valence in expression. Although such conditions can be traced in many cases to the political influence and financial backing of the United States and the Soviet Union, they nevertheless point to failures of leadership and inherited structural legacies of rule—what Frederick Cooper has referred to as the "gatekeeper" state, wherein power is highly centralized and vertically structured, such that political participation is strictly regulated.[30] Combined, such elements have undermined the core ideals of the Bandung communiqué. What Frantz Fanon warned in *The Wretched of the Earth* (1961) regarding the rise of a new comprador bourgeoisie in postcolonial countries has been consummated too often in too many places.[31] Working from this horizon, David Scott has asked if our postcolonial present of "less developed countries" (LDCs)—whether located in Africa, Asia, or Latin America—is characterized by forms of failure, how might this condition be traced to the moment of decolonization? What alternative futures were present at the time, and why have so many been rendered moribund? He argues that such questions return us to a set of fundamental political foundations and serve to re-engage academic scholarship with the conditions and problems of the present.[32] In a stimulating critique of Benedict Anderson, John Kelly and Martha Kaplan similarly have suggested that answers to the present may rest in the difference between "imagined communities" and "represented communities," that decolonization was not so much an exit but instead an entry into a global political scenario that shared structures and protocols with the preceding colonial era.[33] These concluding observations therefore highlight the analytic and political need for ongoing empirical investigation and critical vigilance; to develop more fully integrated conversations between diplomatic history, social history, and postcolonial criticism; and, in sum, to acknowledge the possibilities and contradictions of Bandung—its placement between constituting a moment and representing an era. The next section outlines how this volume intersects with this broad endeavor.

Imagined Communitas—*Rethinking "Political Community" along the Afro-Asian Divide*

Prasenjit Duara has written that there are "remarkably few historical studies of decolonization as a whole, despite the importance of the subject."[34] In a similar vein, Stephen Ellis has admonished historians of Africa for continuing to focus on the precolonial and colonial periods even though the postcolonial period and its history are continuing apace fifty years hence.[35] Speaking to a Latin American audience, Gilbert Joseph has similarly cited the need for bringing Latin American studies—and, by extension, area studies—into better conversation with scholarship on the cold war, to achieve an intellectual rapprochement that recognizes their shared history and disciplinary origins.[36] At the most fundamental level, the following essays aim to amend this research situation by contributing a set of case studies that help to outline the possible parameters of these related fields. In short, the scope of this volume is panoramic, extending beyond the event of the Bandung meeting to consider the locations, practices, and politics that created senses of community across the Afro-Asian divide. The history of connections between both continents, if not exactly hidden, has often been occluded by what have become the conventional concerns of area-studies scholars since the 1960s. Beyond occasional comparative studies, Afro-Asian relations have been marginalized until quite recently by conceptual frameworks that have either centered historical change as emanating from Europe—world-systems theory being a key example—or emphasized the local and regional dynamics of African and Asian communities making their own history, if not always under conditions of their choosing.[37] Yet, as the Bandung meeting itself emphasized, the backdrop to these contrasting approaches has been the history of modern imperialism on both continents. Not only did acts of Western intervention serve as defining experiences in many locales, but they also left durable intellectual legacies that have shaped how such acts would be interpreted after their denouement. Area-studies scholars, who have been poised between such legacies and the possibility of their critique, have undertaken a range of efforts, both theoretical and empirical, to challenge the uncritical reproduction of imperial knowledge. This endeavor has not only interrogated the internal contradictions of the colonial archive, but has variously sought to articulate countermodernities, alternative modernities, decolonial thought, and the "provincialization" of Europe—a sequence of related projects that have shared a common purpose designed to recover a space of agency, history, and social knowledge beyond Western influence.[38]

Attempting a shift away from such West-Rest dialectics, research on Afro-Asian relations has blossomed recently among a number of scholars drawn from cultural, literary, and American studies. In part, this research turn has been an outgrowth of multiculturalism in the American academy since the 1980s, further intersecting with contemporary concerns over US imperial ambitions during the 20th century. Within a brief space of time, this effort has underscored the historical importance of transracial coalitions in the making of modern social movements.[39] However, a striking absence in this developing subfield is the presence of area-studies scholars and their views on intercontinental, rather than solely interethnic, Afro-Asian connections. Africa and Asia are symbolically invoked, but often empirically absent. In parallel, recent scholarship on the Indian Ocean world has made substantial headway in defining a new framework analogous to the Black Atlantic, thus creating a geographic and thematic space for reconsidering the histories of Africa and Asia in mutually constitutive ways. But these studies so far have centered on the precolonial and colonial periods, leaving open questions as to the shifting contours and meaning of this setting for the postcolonial period.[40] Finally, a third agenda of interest—related to the critical projects mentioned previously, albeit with a stronger empirical focus—has been the writing of new imperial histories. Building upon the prescient insights of such thinkers as Hannah Arendt, Aimé Césaire, and Edward Said, this turn has helped account for interregional dynamics by examining the circuits of knowledge and experience that transformed European and colonial worlds alike.[41] Similar to Indian Ocean studies, this field by its very nature has remained entrenched in the colonial era, exploring the tensions of empire but leaving the tensions of postcoloniality aside. Overall, these loosely related agendas have shared a common purpose to work against conventional analytic binaries and to push geographic boundaries through critical explorations of how political space is defined. Even the contours and dynamics of continental thinking having come under scrutiny, with questions as to how the geographies that define our expertise have intellectual structures that furtively limit our spatial frames of reference and interpretation.[42]

This collection is situated amid these multilayered conversations. Its key distinctions from these existing projects are, first, its active attempt to move chronologically into the postcolonial and cold war periods—thus departing from the new imperial agenda and current work on the Indian Ocean—and second, to locate more firmly an intercontinental geography of historical agency and meaning, in order to avoid certain risks of parochialism found in area studies as well as the existing US-centered Afro-Asian literature. Indeed, to interrogate the area-studies paradigm is to readdress an enduring intellectual legacy of the cold war era that is still with us, a critical task of which we are quite conscious. But beyond these concerns over time, place, and disciplinary knowledge rests, at the center of our agenda, the question of "political community"—specifically, what its contours, content, and viability have been in the context of the postcolonial world beyond the archetype of the nation-state. This basic question dwelled at the heart of the Bandung meeting as the preceding section suggests, yet it is an idea that has animated a number of events and political formations of the modern era, from ideologies of Pan-Africanism and Pan-Arabism to more recent intergovernmental organizations at regional and global levels such as the Southern African Development Community (SADC), the Organization of the Petroleum Exporting Countries (OPEC), and the Nonaligned Movement itself. For sure, these ideas and bodies are diverse in their outlooks—serving varying degrees of cultural, economic, and political intent—and, although transnational in principle, they have typically been instruments at the service of individual state agendas. However, despite these limitations, which evince the risks of overdetermining their import, these bodies do outline a realm of community politics situated between the nation-state as such and outsized global political entities, namely the United Nations. Indeed, the continued use and dependence on political units—in particular, the nation-state and empire—which matured during the 19th and 20th centuries marks a distinct analytic constraint in contemporary scholarship, given the proliferation of these alternative political models. These new structures are not entirely defined by these existing categories, nor do they approximate alternative community forms, such as diaspora, that have been anchored by descent-based identities. In this view, political conditions have outpaced the evolution of our mainstream analytic vocabulary. The recent imperial turn to explain contemporary US foreign policy appears to be an all-too-clear reflection of this state of categorical impasse, making presumptive conclusions of behavior instead of raising new questions of definition and practice.[43]

Rethinking political community requires, then, a removal from this safety of terminology. A better strategy is needed beyond labeling multipolar phenomena as transnational. This proposal does not necessarily mean inventing new language per se. Rather, recourse to empiricism and social process—how such terminology is understood and redefined on the ground—is needed. Attention to the relationships between decolonization, the rise of interregional bodies, and the interpersonal, sociopolitical practices that constituted such efforts is required. The term "community," of course, is generic enough for wide application. But it does possess a deep genealogy and an existing set of distinct uses. In his classic study *Gemeinschaft und Gesellschaft* (1887), Ferdinand Tönnies drew a distinction between "community" (*Gemeinschaft*) and "society" (*Gesellschaft*), the former organized around a shared set of values and the latter characterized by self-interest.[44] These elements for thinking through the dynamics of community have carried over in contemporary employment of the expression. The most influential recent use of the term "community" has arguably been in relation to nationalism and the nation-state, as outlined by Benedict Anderson in *Imagined Communities* (1983). Anderson's argument contains a compelling focus on the role of popular imagination as a political practice, enabled through the rise of print media. This approach has sparked debate, though, with critics such as Partha Chatterjee and Manu Goswami drawing attention to the structural role of colonialism and global capital in the making of national territorial spaces and, more generally, a functional nation-state system in the wake of mid-20th century decolonization.[45]

Other scholars have embraced Anderson's intervention, but have also cited a need to expand the parameters of his expression. Extending Chatterjee's question of *whose* imagined community, Dipesh Chakrabarty, for example, has suggested that scholars should "breathe heterogeneity into the word 'imagination'" in order to open its wide-ranging sites and expressive possibilities.[46] Taking a different angle, Frederick Cooper has similarly decried two prevailing misuses of "community": first, its synonymous relationship with the nation-state, which reduces the diverse meanings of the term and the complex scale of relations they have inhabited; and second, how "community" is often employed to capture a sociohistorical alternative or counterpoint to Western modernity and its claims to universalism, rather than being mobilized to create a link between the two. Simplification in both cases has reproduced categorical norms that fail to highlight examples of innovation and entanglement that have animated connections between individuals, organizations, and states.[47] Returning to the question of representation, Martha Kaplan and John Kelly have cited the related insufficiency of "imagination" as a means for explaining community formation during the colonial and postcolonial periods. A better grasp of the institutional limitations and the ritual practices of community legitimation is needed to understand the political and material obstacles that postcolonial countries have faced.

These comments that derive primarily from research on the colonial and early postcolonial periods equally pertain to the present. Contemporary globalization has generated wide-ranging discussion about the function and meanings of community in a context increasingly defined and managed by nonstate actors. Arjun Appadurai has pointed to how states have sought "to monopolize the moral resources of community" through heritage projects and equating "state" with "nation," in order to counter competing trends of transnational separatist movements.[48] Michael Hardt and Antonio Negri, echoing Cooper, have criticized how "the nation becomes the only way to imagine community," that too often the "imagination of a community becomes overcoded as a nation, and hence our conception of community is severely impoverished."[49]

Meanwhile, David Held has contended that national governments are not the arbiters of power they once were, since the contemporary rise of "political communities of fate"—which he defines as "a self-determining collectivity which forms its own agenda and life conditions"—increasingly transcend their boundaries of control.[50] Recent changes in the global scale of political interaction therefore do not herald the deterioration or end of "community" as such but have only escalated its role and stature. This "return to community"—through incipient nationalisms, indigenous-people movements, and the mobilization of religious identities—has refreshed questions of individual-versus-group interests in determining the viability of political ideals of equitable justice and democratic practice.[51]

This volume takes such contemporary developments seriously, as highlighted at the start. But it seeks to flesh out the history between late colonialism and these observations of the global present.[52] Indeed, this book does not seek to overdetermine Bandung as a direct precursor to current political trends or suggest that contemporary China-Africa relations have assumed without revision the mantle of mid-20th-century Afro-Asianism. Instead, it aims to articulate a complex history composed of a constellation of political communities that have cut across the Asia–Africa divide during the 20th and early 21st centuries. These communities have been inspired by ideas that transcend conventional political geographies. But they have also been made by individuals who have been both empowered and limited by political resources, language, and other day-to-day realities (see Bier, Brennan, Burgess, Monson, Lee, and Prestholdt in this volume).

As proposed here, uniting these diverse and challenging conditions and the way people managed them is not only the question of "community" but the practices and habits of *communitas*. This expression is most closely associated with the ethnographic work of Victor Turner on social custom and ritual. But taken as a political process, it offers several compelling features that apply to the concerns of this volume. First, *communitas* is related to, but also distinct from, community, which Turner describes as grounded in a particular geography. Instead, *communitas* is defined by "social relatedness" that comprises a "community of feeling." Turner references Tönnies's use of

Gemeinschaft as a point of orientation, with this expression's argument for community based on sentiment, not locality or blood. The second important feature of *communitas* is its transitory, liminal status and subsequently antistructural character. Unlike the more generic and static expression "community," which conveys a ready-made quality, *communitas* is in movement, an interval moment of creative possibility and innovation, and therefore an active rite of passage thought to be necessary, yet equally perceived as destabilizing. It embraces what Andrew Apter has called "critical agency," a capacity to mobilize social discourse and challenge existing norms.[53]

Applied here, *communitas*—and its existential, normative, and ideological forms—provides a term for capturing the complex dimensions and meaning of decolonization and the diverse political communities inaugurated by it.[54] It cites the demands and rituals of what it takes to be a community—nation-state or otherwise—on the world stage, as well as the potential for challenging those rules. Of particular use is its emphasis on political feeling rather than a structured community per se, which relates to the spirit of Bandung, but also its inventive, transitional qualities that reflect the cold war fluidity of political alignments and nonalignments. Employing Turner's taxonomy to its full extent, one can argue that an existential *communitas*—based on a shared experience of Western imperialism—informed an ideological *communitas* that intended to provide a distinct, even utopian alternative to the preceding era through a discourse of Afro-Asian solidarity. Indeed, as the previous section noted, the US and Soviet Union were quick to intervene to mitigate the possibility of a permanent and influential Afro-Asian bloc from taking hold—what Turner would call a normative *communitas*. The idea of an imagined *communitas* proposed here, therefore, conjoins Turner and Anderson with the intent of advancing a more active notion of "community," one emphasizing elements of movement and innovation in the face of existing structures of a global nation-state system. It aims to step beyond the subjective and often rhetorical qualities of "imagination" to represent both the strong sense of political purpose postcolonial communities had as well as the practical limitations they faced, diplomatic and otherwise. Embracing *communitas* as a political phenomenon at this level therefore asks what it takes to be a viable community international in scope, the diplomatic rituals of recognition as well as the more local practices of self-constitution involved. It demands examination of the strengths and weaknesses of such communities, with their potential for alternative views that provide forms of critical authority, but also the challenges they face based on political feelings that could shift and subside.

These observations intimate the constraints of the translocal communities that followed Bandung and, at a broader level, the improbability of long-term Afro-Asian solidarity. Yet their histories, if at times ephemeral in nature, offer another angle as well: that significant patterns of interaction can be pointed to, addressed, and explored in depth. The chapters that follow present case studies that examine the grounded ways this interaction took place and held influence, charting a history intended to flesh out empirically the period between Bandung and the global present. They are at once social and intellectual, diplomatic and cultural, and are defined as much by strategic intention as they are by geographic obstacle. They reveal not tensions of empire, but tensions of postcoloniality—the complex and at-times contradictory set of aims and conditions situated between the rhetoric of revolution and the pragmatism of governance, defiance of the West and continued forms of economic and political need. Tensions of postcoloniality, in sum, refer to inherited colonial legacies and possible postcolonial futures that African and Asian countries had to negotiate. Whether in "strong" or "weak" form, the political communities described here serve to reposition how the term "community" itself might be understood against the paradigms of empire and the nation-state, by working through variable modes of *communitas* as a means of understanding the opportunities and impediments for alternative communities of fate and the realm of political futures they have had to offer.

Tensions of Postcoloniality—Locations, Practices, Politics

This edited volume works at three levels. First, it aims to enhance developing discussions on this neglected aspect of world history through focused case studies—from South Africa, to Tanzania, to Egypt, to Southeast Asia, to Central Asia—that demonstrate the variety, complexity, and wide-ranging geography of Afro-Asian relations during the last century. It should be emphasized that, with several key exceptions (see Chakrabarty, Go, Adas, and Burton), this topic is approached from the vantage point of scholars working within Africa. In this regard, the essays here intend to speak to contemporary Afro-Asian relations, particularly those with China, as suggested at the start of this introduction. Yet this volume also seeks to de-center a narrow emphasis on China, pointing to multiple histories of connection between both continents. This relates to a second level. Through a case-study approach, the essays of this book equally demonstrate the research and methodological possibilities of this field: from empirically based examples that locate the state and nonstate archives of such history, to more conceptually driven pieces that provide ways of interpreting and thinking about the Afro-Asian world. As stated before, the precursors and afterlives of the Bandung moment present an opportunity to rethink the interactions between social history, cultural history, intellectual history, and diplomatic history—the latter in particular a genre that remains underdeveloped within area studies, especially for Africa.

At the broadest level, this collection aspires to address and contribute to contemporary debates over transnationalism, globalization, and the crossing of area-studies boundaries—to articulate the meaning of these expressions and agendas through grounded illustrations. We do not propose an autonomous realm of knowledge or experience beyond the West—a turn that continues to reemerge, whether under the rubric of "alternative modernities" or "decolonial" thought—but rather we seek to interrogate the historical relations of power at micro- and macro-levels that make such agendas at best limited. Such positions not only risk simplifying the spatial dimensions of political and cultural power to generic locations of "inside" and "outside," but in the same manner they reinstate rather than dissolve the very perception of such boundaries that were first established through histories of imperialism, and later redeployed by cold war politics. This third dimension of the book therefore encapsulates the thrust of the project as a whole: to identify the contours of a new research agenda that speak to, and build upon, existing discussions in area studies, global history, and postcolonial studies that are critical of such preexisting conventions of geography and power and their genealogical origins. This volume does not pretend to offer complete coverage or conclusively answer the questions it raises. It does not chart a sequence of diplomatic events typical of many cold war histories. Rather, it positions the Bandung meeting as a means of bringing the aforementioned issues and disciplines together. Straddling the colonial and postcolonial worlds, Bandung provides a new chronology and an event-centered focus for examining the postcolonial period.

The volume is divided into three parts. The first section—entitled "Framings: Concepts, Politics, History"—is devoted to a conceptual and empirical stage setting for the essays that follow. Dipesh Chakrabarty leads off with a study of three key concepts—anticolonialism, postcolonialism, and globalization—by examining their genealogical origins and interrelations in various decolonization projects, including Bandung. This chapter is an effort at outlining and unifying these interrelated, though often separate, ideas that have defined a broad agenda shared by many area-studies scholars working today. It furthermore offers a useful historical and theoretical structure for the essays that follow. Michael Adas, for example, examines the effects that World War I had on the genesis of anticolonialism during the interwar years. As his wide-ranging chapter underscores, these effects were not isolated but formed a broader pattern of experience and meaning across Africa and Asia against the effects of European imperialism. In sum, his essay outlines the political terrain and intellectual origins of rationales that would lead to Bandung in 1955. Julian Go follows with a similar set of political questions posed after World War II, examining how postcolonial independence in Africa and Asia can be fruitfully understood through a lens informed by constitutional law, thus serving to separate the rhetoric of autonomy from the demands of legal *realpolitik*. Go's essay therefore refrains from uncritically valorizing the spirit of Bandung by instead situating the development and reconfiguration of the post–World War II global order from the perspective of constitutional practices that typically underscored continuity, rather than departure, from Western practices. In sum, these essays examine the early challenges of community formation faced in the Afro-Asian world.

With this foundation, the second section—entitled "Alignments and Nonalignments: Movements, Projects, Outcomes"—transitions to the multiple afterlives of the Bandung moment, with particular attention to the role of local contexts, practices, and meanings in the articulation of this broader geography. Laura Bier's essay explores how Afro-Asianism intersected with a nascent Third World feminist movement based in Cairo through AAPSO during the late 1950s and 1960s. Despite the open embrace of these two ideologies as a common front, Bier underscores how cultural challenges remained, with prevailing views that were often informed by Western cultural discourse inherited from the colonial period. James Brennan similarly examines the importance of Cairo, offering a detailed discussion of how the Egyptian government under Nasser mediated discourses of anticolonialism and pan-Islamism in East Africa during the 1950s and 1960s through the Swahili broadcasting of Radio Cairo. His essay underlines the technological means of diplomatic engagement that states and anticolonial movements had at their disposal for communicating ideas of Third World solidarity, yet also the local dynamics of race and nationalism that complicated any easy acceptance of Afro-Asian solidarity. Venturing further in this geographic direction, the next two chapters explore Chinese-sponsored "development" projects in East Africa. Gary Burgess investigates the exchange of students, official visitors, and "modernization" experts between Zanzibar and China during the 1960s, along with the corresponding complexity of the ideological connections between Mao, Nyerere, and Abdulrahman Mohamed Babu, each of whom aspired to a "usable future." In parallel, Jamie Monson discusses the history of Chinese development experts and African workers on the TAZARA railway in postcolonial Tanzania and Zambia during the 1960s and 1970s. Complementing Burgess's chapter, this essay points to the more practical demands and day-to-day aspects of Afro-Asian interaction beyond rhetorical gestures toward "modernization," as well as the deep history of cooperation with China that has reemerged today. Moving to a different context, Christopher Lee's biographical essay on father–son activists James and Alex La Guma examines the role travel had in fostering diplomatic relationships between South African activists and the Soviet government over the course of the 20th century. Central Asia proved to be a particularly important site of these travels, illustrating the development possibilities that a socialist South Africa might experience as described by Alex in his memoir *A Soviet Journey* (1978).

The final section of the volume—"The Present: Predicaments, Practices, Speculation"—builds upon the empiricism of the previous section and returns to the conceptual questions in the first. Moving beyond state-and-social-history narratives, the chapters of this section address present challenges developing between Africa and Asia, exploring issues of continuity and change in relations between both continents since the end of the cold war. Denis Tull's essay provides a useful overview of China's growing involvement in Africa and how it suggests more problems than benefits for African nation-states, thus marking a decisive shift in Afro-Asianism as an ideology of solidarity since Bandung. Focusing on a separate set of politics that are equally important, Jeremy Prestholdt offers a parallel analysis of the rise of Osama bin Laden as an icon of anti-Western revolution among communities in the Indian Ocean region, especially coastal Kenya, today. Building upon recent work by Mahmood Mamdani and others, he questions whether bin Laden has joined the symbolic ranks of Mao and Che Guevara and what the implications this discourse has for understanding Afro-Asian political ideologies of the present.[55] Combined, both essays suggest the continued growth of regional interaction with patterns that recall the past as well as signal different visions of the future.

In sum, this volume considers the past, present, and future of political communities in this contingent world. It intimates an alternative history and geography of the 20th century that challenges not only Eurocentric accounts, but also contributes to ongoing discussions of transnationalism and globalization in a committed empirical fashion. It presses for a reconfiguration of viewpoint and consequently a reassessment of conventional accounts of the 20th century. Indeed, as Antoinette Burton suggests in her insightful epilogue, the occasion of Bandung forces a reorientation not only with how the fields of postcolonial and cold war studies might be readdressed chronologically and empirically, but also how the mobility and redefinition of race, class, and gender in the wake of Bandung subsequently demand a thorough reappraisal of how these categories were transformed in variable ways between the receding experience of modern imperialism and our global present.

To those who were present and those who observed from afar, the 1955 Bandung Conference was a watershed moment, a historical juncture that served as a summary point for previous anticolonial activism and a new baseline by which the accomplishments of the postcolonial world were to be measured. Although essays found here address pertinent theoretical issues connected to this moment, the majority provide historical case studies that lend substantive empirical weight to the premises of the volume. The net effect of these strengths is that we can start to move beyond the theory-driven conventions of postcolonial studies and, armed with evidence, begin to think more concretely and extensively about how to sharpen our reconception of postcolonial history and that of the 20th century. Bandung must not be understood as an isolated moment, but instead be situated within a rich and varied history of intercontinental exchange that it shaped and still continues today.

Notes

1. Joseph Kahn, "China Opens Summit for African Leaders," *New York Times*, November 2, 2006.

2. It should be noted that as this volume went to press, a Fourth Forum meeting was to be held in November 2009 in Egypt. For an overview of the past and present of this relationship, see, for example, Jan S. Prybyla, "Communist China's Economic Relations with Africa, 1960–64," *Asian Survey* 4, no. 11 (1964): 1135–43; George T. Yu, "Sino-African Relations: A Survey," *Asian Survey* 5, no. 7 (1965): 321–32; George T. Yu, "China's Failure in Africa," *Asian Survey* 6, no. 8 (1966): 461–68; Harish Kapur, *China and the Afro-Asian World* (New Delhi: Prabhakar Padhye, 1966); George T. Yu, "Dragon in the Bush: Peking's Presence in Africa," *Asian Survey* 8, no. 12 (1968): 1018–26; John K. Cooley, *East Wind Over Africa: Red China's African Offensive* (New York: Walker, 1965); Bruce D.

Larkin, *China and Africa, 1949–70: The Foreign Policy of the People's Republic of China* (Berkeley: University of California Press, 1971); Tareq Y. Ismael, "The People's Republic of China and Africa," *Journal of Modern African Studies* 9, no. 4 (1971): 507–29; Alaba Ogunsanwo, *China's Policy in Africa, 1958–71* (London: Cambridge University Press, 1974); George T. Yu, *China's African Policy: A Study of Tanzania* (New York: Praeger, 1975); Alan Hutchison, *China's African Revolution* (Boulder: Westview Press, 1976); Warren Weinstein, ed., *Chinese and Soviet Aid to Africa* (New York: Praeger, 1975); Alvin Z. Rubenstein, ed., *Soviet and Chinese Influence in the Third World* (New York: Praeger, 1975); Martin Bailey, "Tanzania and China," *African Affairs* 74, no. 294 (1975): 39–50; Martin Bailey, *Freedom Railway: China and the Tanzania-Zambia Link* (London: Collings, 1976); Richard Hall and Hugh Peyman, *The Great Uhuru Railway: China's Showpiece in Africa* (London: Victor Gollancz, 1976); Gao Jinyuan, "China and Africa: The Development of Relations Over Many Centuries," *African Affairs* 83, no. 331 (1984): 241–50; Philip Snow, *The Star Raft: China's Encounter with Africa* (London: Weidenfeld and Nicolson, 1988); George T. Yu, "Africa in Chinese Foreign Policy," *Asian Survey* 28, no. 8 (1988): 849–62; Ian Taylor, "China's Foreign Policy towards Africa in the 1990s," *Journal of Modern African Studies* 36, no. 3 (1998): 443–60; Deborah Bräutigam, "Close Encounters: Chinese Business Networks as Industrial Catalysts in Sub-Saharan Africa," *African Affairs* 102, no. 408 (2003): 447–67; Chris Alden, "Red Star, Black Gold," *Review of African Political Economy*, nos. 104/5 (2005): 415–19; Lindsey Hilsum, "Re-enter the Dragon: China's New Mission in Africa," *Review of African Political Economy*, nos. 104/5 (2005): 419–25; Michael Klare and Daniel Volman, "America, China and the Scramble for Africa's Oil," *Review of African Political Economy*, no. 108 (2006): 297–309; Denis M. Tull, "China's Engagement in Africa: Scope, Significance and Consequences," *Journal of Modern African Studies* 44, 3 (2006): 459–79; Ian Taylor, *China and Africa: Engagement and Compromise* (London: Routledge, 2006); Chris Alden, *China in Africa* (London: Zed, 2007); Daniel Large, "Beyond 'Dragon in the Bush': The Study of China-Africa Relations," *African Affairs* 107, no. 426 (2008): 45–61.

3. For recent work on Afro-Asianism, which has been unusually, if not entirely, American-focused, see, for example, Vijay Prashad, *Everybody Was Kung-Fu Fighting: Afro-Asian Connections and the Myth of Cultural Purity* (Boston: Beacon Press, 2001); Robin D. G. Kelley, *Freedom Dreams: The Black Radical Imagination* (Boston: Beacon Press, 2002), chapter 3; Andrew F. Jones and Nikhil Pal Singh, eds., *The Afro-Asian Century*, special issue of *Positions* 11, no. 1 (2003); Bill V. Mullen, *Afro-Orientalism* (Minneapolis: University of Minnesota Press, 2004); Heike Raphael-Hernandez and Shannon Steen, eds., *Afro-Asian Encounters: Culture, History, Politics* (New York: New York University

Press, 2006); Vijay Prashad, *The Darker Nations: A People's History of the Third World* (New York: New Press, 2007); Fred Ho and Bill V. Mullen, eds., *Afro Asia: Revolutionary Political and Cultural Connections between African Americans and Asian Americans* (Durham: Duke University Press, 2008). On the fiftieth anniversary of the Bandung meeting, see R. M. Marty M. Natalegawa, ed., *Asia, Africa, Africa, Asia: Bandung, towards the First Century* (Jakarta: Department of Foreign Affairs, Republic of Indonesia, 2005); John Mackie, *Bandung 1955: Non-alignment and Afro-Asian Solidarity* (Singapore: Editions Didier Millet, 2005). For the NAASP, which South Africa, a country that did not officially participate in the original Bandung meeting, has taken a lead in overseeing, consult: <http://www.naasp.gov.za/index.html>.

4. Benedict Anderson, *Imagined Communities: Reflections on the Origin and Spread of Nationalism* (London: Verso, 1983); John D. Kelly and Martha Kaplan, *Represented Communities: Fiji and World Decolonization* (Chicago: University of Chicago Press, 2001), 22, 23.

5. On these disjunctures, see Arif Dirlik, *The Postcolonial Aura: Third World Criticism in the Age of Global Capitalism* (Boulder: Westview Press, 1997); David Scott, *Refashioning Futures: Criticism after Postcoloniality* (Princeton: Princeton University Press, 1999); Ania Loomba, et. al., eds., *Postcolonial Studies and Beyond* (Durham: Duke University Press, 2005). On generalized assertions about the postcolony, see Achille Mbembe, *On the Postcolony* (Berkeley: University of California Press, 2001).

6. On modern decolonization and its variability, see, for example, Prosser Gifford and William Roger Louis, eds., *The Transfer of Power in Africa: Decolonization, 1940–1960* (New Haven: Yale University Press, 1982); Prosser Gifford and William Roger Louis, eds., *Decolonization and African Independence: The Transfers of Power, 1960–1980* (New Haven: Yale University Press, 1988); John Darwin, *Britain and Decolonisation: The Retreat from Empire in the Post-war World* (Basingstoke: Macmillan, 1988); Frederick Cooper, *Decolonization and African Society: The Labor Question in French and British Africa* (Cambridge: Cambridge University Press, 1996); M. E. Chamberlain, *Decolonization: The Fall of the European Empires* (Oxford: Blackwell, 1999); John Springhall, *Decolonization Since 1945: The Collapse of European Overseas Empires* (New York: Palgrave, 2001); James D. Le Sueur, ed., *The Decolonization Reader* (New York: Routledge, 2003); Prasenjit Duara, ed., *Decolonization: Perspectives from Now and Then* (New York: Routledge, 2004); Raymond F. Betts, *Decolonization* (New York: Routledge, 2004); Hendrik Spruyt, *Ending Empire: Contested Sovereignty and Territorial Partition* (Ithaca: Cornell University Press, 2005); David Luis-Brown, *Waves of Decolonization: Discourses on Race and Hemispheric Citizenship in Cuba, Mexico and the United States*

(Durham: Duke University Press, 2008); Frederick Cooper, "Possibility and Constraint: African Independence in Historical Perspective," *Journal of African History* 49, no. 2 (2008): 167–96. For various popular and academic studies of "empire" and its reproduction, see, in addition to works previously cited, Michael W. Doyle, *Empires* (Ithaca: Cornell University Press, 1986); Michael Hardt and Antonio Negri, *Empire* (Cambridge: Harvard University Press, 2000); Niall Ferguson, *Empire: The Rise and Demise of the British World Order and the Lessons for Global Power* (New York: Basic Books, 2003); Noam Chomsky, *Hegemony or Survival: America's Quest for Global Dominance* (Boston: Metropolitan Books, 2003); Chalmers Johnson, *The Sorrows of Empire: Militarism, Secrecy, and the End of the Republic* (Boston: Metropolitan Books, 2004); Rashid Khalidi, *Resurrecting Empire: Western Footprints and America's Perilous Path in the Middle East* (Boston: Beacon Press, 2004); Frederick Cooper, "Empire Multiplied," *Comparative Studies in Society and History* 46, no. 2 (2004): 247–72; Frederick Cooper, *Colonialism in Question: Theory, Knowledge, History* (Berkeley: University of California Press, 2005), especially chapter 6.

7. For recent critiques of development teleologies, see, for example, James Ferguson, *The Anti-Politics Machine: "Development," Depoliticization, and Bureaucratic Power in Lesotho* (Cambridge: Cambridge University Press, 1990); James Ferguson, *Expectations of Modernity: Myths and Meanings of Urban Life on the Zambian Copperbelt* (Berkeley: University of California Press, 1999); Arturo Escobar, *Encountering Development: The Making and Unmaking of the Third World* (Princeton: Princeton University Press, 1995); Akhil Gupta, *Postcolonial Developments: Agriculture in the Making of Modern India* (Durham: Duke University Press, 1998).

8. On the challenges of nationalism, see, variously, Partha Chatterjee, *Nationalist Thought and the Colonial World: A Derivative Discourse?* (London: Zed, 1986); Partha Chatterjee, *The Nation and Its Fragments: Colonial and Postcolonial Histories* (Princeton: Princeton University Press, 1993); Jean Marie Allman, *The Quills of the Porcupine: Asante Nationalism in an Emergent Ghana* (Madison: University of Wisconsin Press, 1993); Prasenjit Duara, *Rescuing History from the Nation: Questioning Narratives of Modern China* (Chicago: University of Chicago Press, 1995); B. A. Ogot and W. R. Ochieng, eds., *Decolonization and Independence in Kenya, 1940-93* (Athens: Ohio University Press, 1995); Geoff Eley, ed., *Becoming National: A Reader* (New York: Oxford University Press, 1996); Susan Geiger, *TANU Women: Gender and Culture in the Making of Tanganyikan Nationalism, 1955–1965* (Portsmouth, NH: Heinemann, 1997); E. S. Atieno Odhiambo and John Lonsdale, eds., *Mau Mau and Nationhood: Arms, Authority, and Narration* (Athens: Ohio University Press, 2003); Gregory H. Maddox and James L. Giblin, eds., *In Search of a Nation: Histories of Authority*

and Dissidence in Tanzania (Athens: Ohio University Press, 2005); Elizabeth Schmidt, *Mobilizing the Masses: Gender, Ethnicity, and Class in the Nationalist Movement in Guinea, 1939–1958* (Portsmouth, NH: Heinemann, 2005); Elizabeth Schmidt, *Cold War and Decolonization in Guinea, 1946–1958* (Athens: Ohio University Press, 2007). On the postcolonial challenges of nationalism and historiography, see Terence Ranger, "Nationalist Historiography, Patriotic History and the History of the Nation: The Struggle over the Past in Zimbabwe," *Journal of Southern African Studies*, 30, 2 (2004): 215–34.

9. On settler colonialism and its legacies, see Caroline Elkins and Susan Pedersen, eds., *Settler Colonialism in the Twentieth Century: Projects, Practices, Legacies* (New York: Routledge, 2005). On the intersection between decolonization and the cold war, see Robert J. McMahon, *Colonialism and the Cold War: The United States and the Struggle for Indonesian Independence, 1945–1949* (Ithaca: Cornell University Press, 1981); Matthew Connelly, *A Diplomatic Revolution: Algeria's Fight for Independence and the Origins of the Post–Cold War Era* (Oxford: Oxford University Press, 2002); Todd Shepard, *The Invention of Decolonization: The Algerian War and the Remaking of France* (Ithaca: Cornell University Press, 2006); Odd Arne Westad, *The Global Cold War: Third World Interventions and the Making of Our Times* (Cambridge: Cambridge University Press, 2005); Gary Baines and Peter Vale, eds., *Beyond the Border War: New Perspectives on Southern Africa's Late-Cold War Conflicts* (Pretoria: UNISA Press, 2008).

10. On critiques of the expression "postcolonial" and its use, see Ella Shohat, "Notes on the Postcolonial," *Social Text*, nos. 31/32 (1992): 99–113; Anne McClintock, "The Angel of Progress: Pitfalls of the Term 'Postcolonialism,'" *Social Text*, nos. 31/32 (1992): 84–98; Arif Dirlik, "The Postcolonial Aura: Third World Criticism in the Age of Global Capitalism," *Critical Inquiry* 20, no. 2 (1994): 328–56; Stuart Hall, "When was 'the Postcolonial'? Thinking at the Limit," in *The Post-Colonial Question: Common Skies, Divided Horizons*, ed. Iain Chambers and Lidia Curti (New York: Routledge, 1996): 242–60; Scott, *Refashioning Futures*. For an attempt at bridging an existing divide between imperial history and postcolonial studies, see Dane Kennedy, "Imperial History and Post-Colonial Theory," *Journal of Imperial and Commonwealth History* 24, no. 3 (1996): 345–63.

11. Kwame Nkrumah, *Neo-colonialism: The Last Stage of Imperialism* (New York: International Publishers, 1965); Kwame Nkrumah, *Consciencism: Philosophy and the Ideology for Decolonization* (New York: Monthly Review Press, 1970); Julius K. Nyerere, *Ujamaa: Essays on Socialism* (Oxford: Oxford University Press, 1968); Jawaharlal Nehru, *The Discovery of India* (New York: Penguin, 2004).

12. David Scott, *Conscripts of Modernity: The Tragedy of Colonial Enlightenment* (Durham: Duke University Press, 2004), 8.

13. Cooper's critique is directed primarily toward Mahmood Mamdani, *Citizen and Subject: Contemporary Africa and the Legacy of Late Colonialism* (Princeton: Princeton University Press, 1996). See Cooper, *Colonialism in Question*, ch. 1.

14. It should be noted that the First Congress as such was held in 1919, with the 1900 conference serving as a key precursor. See P. Olisanwuche Esedebe, *Pan-Africanism: The Idea and Movement, 1776–1991* (Washington, DC: Howard University Press, 1994). On the Universal Races Congress, see, for example, Universal Races Congress, *Record of the Proceedings of the First Universal Races Congress, Held at the University of London, July 26–29, 1911* (London: P. S. King and Son, 1911); Paul Rich, "'The Baptism of a New Era': The 1911 Universal Races Congress and the Liberal Ideology of Race," *Ethnic and Racial Studies*, 7, no. 4 (1984): 534–50; Susan D. Pennybacker, "The Universal Races Congress, London Political Culture, and Imperial Dissent, 1900–1939," *Radical History Review*, 92 (Spring 2005): 103–17; Mansour Bonakdarian, "Negotiating Universal Values and Cultural and National Parameters at the First Universal Races Congress," *Radical History Review*, 92 (2005): 118–32. On the League Against Imperialism, see, for example, Robert J. C. Young, *Postcolonialism: An Historical Introduction* (Oxford: Blackwell, 2001), 176–77; Vijay Prashad, *The Darker Nations* (New York: New Press, 2007), ch. 2. On Pan-Asianism—which, it must be noted, also contributed to Japan's imperial ambitions—see Prasenjit Duara, "The Discourse of Civilization and Pan-Asianism," *Journal of World History*, 12, no. 1 (2001): 99–130; Sven Saaler and J. Victor Koschmann, eds., *Pan-Asianism in Modern Japanese History: Colonialism, Regionalism and Borders* (London: Routledge, 2007); Cemil Aydin, *The Politics of Anti-Westernism in Asia: Visions of World Order in Pan-Islamic and Pan-Asian Thought* (New York: Columbia University Press, 2007). For a recent study of the "global color line," see Marilyn Lake and Henry Reynolds, *Drawing the Global Colour Line: White Men's Countries and the International Challenge of Racial Equality* (Cambridge: Cambridge University Press, 2008).

15. For past and present examples of this growing historiography, see Joseph E. Harris, *The African Presence in Asia: Consequences of the East African Slave Trade* (Evanston: Northwestern University Press, 1971); K. N. Chaudhuri, *Trade and Civilization in the Indian Ocean: An Economic History from the Rise of Islam to 1750* (Cambridge: Cambridge University Press, 1985); Sugata Bose, *A Hundred Horizons: The Indian Ocean in the Age of Global Empire* (Cambridge: Harvard University Press, 2006); Thomas R. Metcalf, *Imperial Connections: India in the Indian Ocean Arena, 1860-1920* (Berkeley: University of California Press, 2007).

16. Richard Wright, *The Color Curtain: A Report on the Bandung Conference* (New York: World Publishing Company, 1956).

17. Turkey and China also had imperial legacies, if not as recent as Japan's.

18. A number of studies on the conference exist in the fields of international relations, Southeast Asian studies, and diplomatic history. For a selection, see George McTurnan Kahin, *The African-Asian Conference: Bandung, Indonesia, April 1955* (Ithaca: Cornell University Press, 1956); A. Appadorai, *The Bandung Conference* (New Delhi: Indian Council of World Affairs, 1955); Carlos P. Romulo, *The Meaning of Bandung* (Chapel Hill: University of North Carolina Press, 1956); David Kimche, *The Afro-Asian Movement: Ideology and Foreign Policy of the Third World* (New York: Halstead Press, 1973); A. W. Singham and Tran Van Dinh, eds., *From Bandung to Colombo* (New York: Third Press Review, 1976); Robert A. Mortimer, *The Third World Coalition in International Politics* (New York: Praeger, 1980); Roeslan Abdulgani, *The Bandung Connection: The Asia-Africa Conference in Bandung in 1955*, trans. Molly Bondar (Singapore: Gunung Agung, 1981); Prashad, *The Darker Nations*, ch. 3.

19. The British Central African Federation—consisting of Northern Rhodesia (Zambia), Southern Rhodesia (Zimbabwe), and Nyasaland (Malawi)—did not send a delegation.

20. Prashad, *The Darker Nations*, 34, 35.

21. For speeches, see Asian-African Conference, *Asia-Africa Speaks from Bandung* (Jakarta: Ministry of Foreign Affairs, Republic of Indonesia, 1955).

22. Westad, *The Global Cold War*.

23. Asian-African Conference, *Asia-Africa Speaks from Bandung*, 146, 147, 150, 151.

24. Prashad, *The Darker Nations*, 45, 46.

25. On the 1952 origins of the expression "Third World," see ibid., 10, 11.

26. On the perspective of the Eisenhower administration, see Matthew Jones, "A 'Segregated' Asia? Race, the Bandung Conference, and Pan-Asianist Fears in American Thought and Policy, 1954–1955," *Diplomatic History*, 29, 5 (2005): 841–68; Jason Parker, "Cold War II: The Eisenhower Administration, the Bandung Conference, and the Reperiodization of the Postwar Era," *Diplomatic History*, 30, 5 (2006): 867–92. For another view of the Bandung moment from the viewpoint of African American activists, see Penny M. Von Eschen, *Race against Empire: Black Americans and Anticolonialism, 1937–1957* (Ithaca: Cornell University Press, 1997), ch. 8.

27. Prashad, *The Darker Nations*, 46, 47.

28. On the history of nonalignment, see, for example, Lawrence W. Martin, ed., *Neutralism and Nonalignment: The New States in World Affairs* (New York: Praeger, 1962); Cecil V. Crabb Jr., *The Elephants and the Grass: A Study of*

Nonalignment (New York: Praeger, 1965); G. H. Jansen, *Nonalignment and the Afro-Asian States* (New York: Praeger, 1966); J. W. Burton, ed., *Nonalignment* (London: Andre Deutsch, 1966); K. P. Misra, ed., *Non-Alignment Frontiers and Dynamics* (New Delhi: Vikas Publishing, 1982); A. W. Singham and Shirley Hune, *Non-Alignment in an Age of Alignments* (London: Zed, 1986); M. S. Rajan, V. S. Mani, and C. S. R. Murthy, eds., *The Nonaligned and the United Nations* (New Delhi: South Asian Publishers, 1987); Roy Allison, *The Soviet Union and the Strategy of Non-Alignment in the Third World* (Cambridge: Cambridge University Press, 1988).

29. Amin as cited in Scott, *Refashioning Futures*, 144. See also Samir Amin, *Re-reading the Postwar Period: An Intellectual Itinerary* (New York: Monthly Review Press, 1994).

30. Frederick Cooper, *Africa Since 1940: The Past of the Present* (Cambridge: Cambridge University Press, 2002).

31. Frantz Fanon, *The Wretched of the Earth*, trans. Constance Farrington (New York: Grove Press, 1963).

32. Scott, *Refashioning Futures*.

33. Kelly and Kaplan, *Represented Communities*, 5.

34. Duara, ed., *Decolonization*, 1.

35. Stephen Ellis, "Writing Histories of Contemporary Africa," *Journal of African History*, 43, no. 1 (2002): 1–26.

36. Gilbert Joseph, "What We Know and Should Know: Bringing Latin America More Meaningfully into Cold War Studies," in *In from the Cold: Latin America's New Encounter with the Cold War*, ed. Gilbert M. Joseph and Daniela Spenser (Durham: Duke University Press, 2008), 7.

37. For world-systems theory and its variants, see, for example, Andre Gunder Frank, *Crisis in the World Economy* (London: Heinemann, 1980); Giovanni Arrighi, *Chaos and Governance in the Modern World System* (Minneapolis: University of Minnesota Press, 1999); Immanuel Wallerstein, *World-Systems Analysis: An Introduction* (Durham: Duke University Press, 2004). An important critique is Frederick Cooper, et. al., *Confronting Historical Paradigms: Peasants, Labor, and the Capitalist World System in Africa and Latin America* (Madison: University of Wisconsin Press, 1993).

38. On countermodernities, see Paul Gilroy, *The Black Atlantic: Modernity and Double Consciousness* (Cambridge: Harvard University Press, 1993). On alternative modernities, see Dilip Parameshwar Gaonkar, ed., *Alternative Modernities* (Durham: Duke University Press, 2001); On decoloniality, see Walter D. Mignolo, *Local Histories/Global Designs: Essays on the Coloniality of Power, Subaltern Knowledges, and Border Thinking* (Princeton: Princeton University Press, 2000); Walter D. Mignolo, ed., *Coloniality of Power and*

De-colonial Thinking, special issue of *Cultural Studies*, 21, nos. 2–3 (2007). On "provincializing" Europe, see Dipesh Chakrabarty, *Provincializing Europe: Postcolonial Thought and Historical Difference* (Princeton: Princeton University Press, 2000).

39. In addition to the work of Bill Mullen and Robin Kelley cited in fn 3, see Cynthia A. Young, *Soul Power: Culture, Radicalism, and the Making of a U.S. Third World Left* (Durham: Duke University Press, 2006); Besenia Rodriguez, "'Long Live Third World Unity! Long Live Internationalism!': Huey P. Newton's Revolutionary Intercommunalism," *Souls: A Critical Journal of Black Politics, Culture and Society*, 8, no. 3 (2006): 119–41; Judy Tzu-Chun Wu, "Journeys for Peace and Liberation: Third World Internationalism and Radical Orientalism during the U.S. War in Vietnam," *Pacific Historical Review*, 76, no. 4 (2007): 575–84.

40. For more recent studies in addition to those mentioned above, see Patricia Risso, *Merchants and Faith: Muslim Commerce and Culture in the Indian Ocean* (Boulder: Westview Press, 1995); Shihan De S. Jayasuriya and Richard Pankhurst, eds., *The African Diaspora in the Indian Ocean* (Trenton: Africa World Press, 2003); Edward Alpers, Gwyn Campbell, and Michael Salman, eds, *Slavery and Resistance in Africa and Asia* (New York: Routledge, 2005); Engseng Ho, *The Graves of Tarim: Genealogy and Mobility across the Indian Ocean* (Berkeley: University of California Press, 2006); Edward Alpers, Gwyn Campbell, and Michael Salman, eds., *Resisting Bondage in Indian Ocean Africa and Asia* (New York: Routledge, 2007); Jeremy Prestholdt, *Domesticating the World: African Consumerism and the Genealogies of Globalization* (Berkeley: University of California Press, 2008). On the Black Atlantic, see, inter alia, John K. Thornton, *Africa and Africans in the Making of the Atlantic World, 1400–1680* (Cambridge: Cambridge University Press, 1992); Gilroy, *The Black Atlantic*; Brent Hayes Edwards, *The Practice of Diaspora: Literature, Translation, and the Rise of Black Internationalism* (Cambridge: Harvard University Press, 2003); Christopher L. Miller, *The French Atlantic Triangle: Literature and Culture of the Slave Trade* (Durham: Duke University Press, 2008).

41. See, for example, Hannah Arendt, *The Origins of Totalitarianism* (New York: Harcourt Brace, 1951); Aimé Césaire, *Discourse on Colonialism* (New York: Monthly Review Press, 2000 [1953]); Edward W. Said, *Culture and Imperialism* (New York: Vintage, 1993); Nicholas B. Dirks, ed., *Colonialism and Culture* (Ann Arbor: University of Michigan Press, 1992); Frederick Cooper and Ann Laura Stoler, eds., *Tensions of Empire: Colonial Cultures in a Bourgeois World* (Berkeley: University of California Press, 1997); Catherine Hall, ed., *Cultures of Empire: Colonizers in Britain and the Empire in the Nineteenth and Twentieth Centuries* (New York: Routledge, 2000); Antoinette Burton, ed., *After the*

Imperial Turn: Thinking with and through the Nation (Durham: Duke University Press, 2003); Kathleen Wilson, ed., *A New Imperial History: Culture, Identity and Modernity in Britain and the Empire, 1660–1840* (New York: Cambridge University Press, 2004).

42. For critiques of continental thinking, see V. Y. Mudimbe, *The Invention of Africa: Gnosis, Philosophy and the Order of Knowledge* (Bloomington: Indiana University Press, 1988); Walter D. Mignolo, *The Idea of Latin America* (London: Blackwell, 2005); Martin W. Lewis and Kären E. Wigen, *The Myth of Continents: A Critique of Metageography* (Berkeley: University of California Press, 1997). For texts that have engaged with the specific limitations of area studies, see Dirlik, *The Postcolonial Aura;* Arif Dirlik, Vinay Bahl, and Peter Gran, eds., *History after the Three Worlds: Post-Eurocentric Historiographies* (New York: Rowman and Littlefield, 2000); Masao Miyoshi, ed., *Learning Places: The Afterlives of Area Studies* (Durham: Duke University Press, 2002).

43. The trend of labeling the US as an imperial power is not entirely new, an earlier, influential view being William Appleman Williams, *Empire as a Way of Life* (Oxford: Oxford University Press, 1980); William Appleman Williams, *The Tragedy of American Diplomacy* (New York: Norton, 1988 [1959]). Recent studies that explore the deep history of this trajectory in the American case include Greg Grandin, *Empire's Workshop: Latin America, the United States, and the Rise of the New Imperialism* (New York: Metropolitan Books, 2006); Michael Adas, *Dominance by Design: Technological Imperatives and America's Civilizing Mission* (Cambridge: Harvard University Press, 2006); George C. Herring, *From Colony to Superpower: US Foreign Relations Since 1776* (Oxford: Oxford University Press, 2008). For another critical view of the category of "empire," see Cooper, "Empire Multiplied."

44. Ferdinand Tönnies, *Community and Civil Society,* ed. Jose Harris, trans. Jose Harris and Margaret Hollis (Cambridge: Cambridge University Press, 2001).

45. On the former, see Manu Goswami, "From *Swadeshi* to *Swaraj*: Nation, Economy, Territory in Colonial South Asia, 1870 to 1907," *Comparative Studies in Society and History,* 40, no. 4 (1998): 609–36; Manu Goswami, "Rethinking the Modular Nation Form: Toward a Sociohistorical Conception of Nationalism," *Comparative Studies in Society and History,* 44, no. 4 (2002): 770–99; Manu Goswami, *Producing India: From Colonial Economy to National Space* (Chicago: University of Chicago Press, 2004). On the nation-state system and decolonization, see Kelly and Kaplan, *Represented Communities.* For studies that followed Anderson, at times critiquing him, see Chatterjee, *Nationalist Thought and the Colonial World;* Chatterjee, *The Nation and Its Fragments,* especially chapter 1; E. J. Hobsbawm, *Nations and Nationalism since 1780: Programme, Myth, Reality*

(Cambridge: Cambridge University Press, 1992); Sara Castro-Klarén and John Charles Chasteen, eds., *Beyond Imagined Communities: Reading and Writing the Nation in Nineteenth-Century Latin America* (Baltimore: Johns Hopkins University Press, 2003).

46. Chakrabarty, *Provincializing Europe*, 149.

47. Cooper, *Colonialism in Question*, 20, 31, 140. See also Frederick Cooper, "Conflict and Connection: Rethinking Colonial African History," *American Historical Review*, 99, no. 5 (1994): 1516–45.

48. Arjun Appadurai, *Modernity at Large: Cultural Dimensions of Globalization* (Minneapolis: University of Minnesota Press, 1996), 39.

49. Hardt and Negri, *Empire*, 107. It should be emphasized although a common ground is cited here, Cooper has been sharply critical of Chakrabarty and of Hardt and Negri. See Cooper "Empire Multiplied"; Cooper, *Colonialism in Question*, ch. 1.

50. David Held, "Democracy and Globalization," in *Re-imagining Political Community: Studies in Cosmopolitan Democracy*, eds. Daniele Archibugi, David Held, and Martin Köhler (Stanford: Stanford University Press, 1998), 21, 24.

51. For discussion, see Janna Thompson, "Community Identity and World Citizenship," in *Re-imagining Political Community*, 179–97.

52. Cooper, *Colonialism in Question*, 17, 18.

53. Victor Turner, *Dramas, Fields, and Metaphors: Symbolic Action in Human Society* (Ithaca: Cornell University Press, 1974), 201–03; Andrew Apter, *Beyond Words: Discourse and Critical Agency in Africa* (Chicago: University of Chicago Press, 2007). For a separate exploration of *communitas*, see Roberto Esposito, *Bíos: Biopolitics and Philosophy*, trans. Timothy Campbell (Minneapolis: University of Minnesota Press, 2008), especially the translator's introduction.

54. On these different forms, see Victor Turner, *The Ritual Process: Structure and Anti-structure* (Chicago: Aldine, 1969), 132.

55. Mahmood Mamdani, *Good Muslim, Bad Muslim: America, the Cold War, and the Roots of Terror* (New York: Pantheon, 2004).

[14]

RETHINKING THE COLD WAR AND DECOLONIZATION: THE GRAND STRATEGY OF THE ALGERIAN WAR FOR INDEPENDENCE

Matthew Connelly

October and November 1960 were two of the coldest months of the Cold War. Continuing tensions over Berlin and the nuclear balance were exacerbated by crises in Laos, Congo, and—for the first time—France's rebellious *départements* in Algeria. During Nikita Khrushchev's table-pounding visit to the United Nations, he embraced Belkacem Krim, the foreign minister of the Gouvernement Provisoire de la République Algérienne (GPRA). After mugging for the cameras at the Soviet estate in Glen Cove, New York, Khrushchev confirmed that this constituted de facto recognition of the provisional government and pledged all possible aid. Meanwhile, in Beijing, President Ferhat Abbas delivered the GPRA's first formal request for Chinese "volunteers." U.S. President Dwight D. Eisenhower asked his National Security Council "whether such intervention would not mean war." The council agreed that if communist regulars infiltrated Algeria, the United States would be bound by the North Atlantic Treaty to come to the aid of French President Charles de Gaulle and his beleaguered government. After six years of insurgency, Algeria appeared to be on the brink of becoming a Cold War battleground.[1]

What are scholars to make of such episodes? Even without knowing its particular origins or outcome, numerous studies would suggest that little good could result from bringing the Cold War into a colonial conflict. Historians have long been critical of how the United States imposed its global priorities regardless of local contexts, confused nationalists with communists, and supported colonial powers rather than risk instability.[2] With the opening of Soviet archives, scholars have also begun to document how Moscow subordinated revolutions in Asia to its own security interests and exploited conflicts in China and Korea for material advantage.[3] But comparatively little attention has been paid to how anti-colonial nationalists, for their part, approached the superpower rivalry. Some scholars assume that they were inevitably losers—even pawns—in that larger game; that it was at best a distraction.[4] But even without access to their archives, others have surmised that leaders such as Mohammed Mosaddeq and Gamal Abdel Nasser found opportunities as well as risks in the Cold War compe-

Matthew Connelly is Assistant Professor of History and Public Policy, University of Michigan, Ann Arbor, Mich., 48109, USA. E-mail: mattconn@umich.edu

tition.[5] The question, then, is not whether the Cold War was a "good" or a "bad" thing for anti-colonial nationalists. Rather, it is how they dealt with the challenges it posed in the formulation of their foreign policies.

With the opening of the Algerian archives—along with those of France, the United States, and the United Kingdom—it is now possible to document elite decision-making during the Arab world's most bitter anti-colonial conflict. How, it is asked, did Algerians relate their independence struggle to superpower rivalries, and how did the strategies they pursued influence international politics and contribute to their eventual victory? Although much work remains to be done, it is already clear that the Algerian perspective places episodes such as the one described earlier in an entirely new light. Thus, even while Abbas was warning Western journalists that a communist intervention would be a "disaster for the whole world," Krim worked with his North African allies to exaggerate the danger and drive France to the negotiating table.[6] Indeed, years before the Algerians launched their fight for independence, they had planned to harness the Cold War to their cause. Exploiting international tensions was part of a grand strategy that backed diplomatic lobbying with demonstrations of mass support, attracted foreign media with urban terror, and used U.N. debates to inspire peasant revolutionaries. But the boldest stroke came in 1958, when the Algerians established a provisional government and demanded diplomatic recognition despite the fact that they could not control any of the territory they claimed. The precedents they set would show the way and smooth the path for other national liberation movements. This article will show how, rather than being mere pawns of the great powers, the Algerians rewrote the rules of the game.

The origins of the grand strategy of the Algerian War can be traced to the last day of World War II in Europe. Nationalists had associated themselves with American anti-colonialism and organized celebratory marches. These quickly turned into bloody clashes in which French forces massacred from 6,000 to 45,000 Algerians—mass graves and an official cover-up made an exact accounting impossible.[7] Algeria's leading opposition figure, Messali Hadj, then turned to electoral politics. His new party, the Mouvement pour la Triomphe des Libertés Démocratiques (MTLD), won municipal offices across Algeria. But in the 1948 elections, Interior Minister Jules Moch had the MTLD's candidates arrested while local authorities stuffed ballots for "*Beni oui-ouis*"—Muslim yes-men.[8]

Later that year, the MTLD asked the head of its paramilitary wing, Hocine Aït Ahmed, to advise on how the party might win Algeria's independence through force of arms. Aït Ahmed was only 27 years old at the time and had never been formally educated in matters of strategy. Even so, he displayed considerable erudition in his report. He analyzed both earlier rebellions against the French and examples from abroad—the 1916 Easter uprising in Ireland, the Yugoslavian resistance, Mao's Long March, and Indochina—while incorporating insights from Carl von Clausewitz, Ernst Jünger, and B. H. Liddell Hart. All this led him to a sobering conclusion: "[i]f one considers dispassionately contemporary military history . . . one would search in vain even among the fights of colonized peoples against the European powers as great a disproportion in the forces facing each other." Algeria was only 400 miles from France, and, unlike any other colony, it was constitutionally an integral part of the republic. Moreover, unlike Indochina, most of Algeria was arid, exposed terrain ideal for the employment of air power. Above all, virtually no other anti-colonial movement had had to deal with such a sizable and politically powerful settler population—the 1 million *pieds noirs,* who exercised a virtual right of veto over French Algerian policy through their lobby in the National Assembly. For all of these reasons, Aït Ahmed ruled out a popular uprising, a liberated zone, or mass demonstrations. He prescribed nothing less than *une grande stratégie* for a truly revolutionary war, relating finances, logistics, morale, propaganda, and foreign policy. This article focuses on this last aspect: the foreign policy of national liberation.[9]

If Algerians had to "integrate the people's war in the international context," it was only because Aït Ahmed did not think they could hope to prevail otherwise. Thus, their "vital force" was "the historic movement which leads the peoples of Asia and Africa to fight for their liberation. . . . They will follow our example as we follow the example of other peoples who liberated themselves by force of arms or who are fighting still." But Aït Ahmed stressed that this was a "dogmatic and sentimental" principle, practical only to the extent that it would cause France to disperse its forces. Instead, their foreign policy would be independent and eminently flexible: "placing the good on one side and the bad on the other would be to ignore the complexity and ambiguity of elements that determine the interest of each country or group of countries." He knew that the United States, in particular, would never allow North Africa to pass under Soviet influence.[10]

Yet the Americans' interest created potential leverage, as Aït Ahmed pointed out. Even if the Americans would never be allies, he would exploit their rivalry with the Soviets to undermine their alliance with France. "Our strategy will follow this guideline in diplomatic matters: When we intend to put on our side of the scale an act of support from a Socialist country we will think at the same time of removing from the colonial side of the scale the weight of Western support." In December, the MTLD Central Committee approved the report in near-unanimity.[11]

In the following years, the MTLD would more often be divided, as younger militants such as Aït Ahmed chafed under Messali's autocratic rule. After six years, they finally broke away to form the Front de Libération Nationale (National Liberation Front; FLN) and launch the war for independence. It was soon apparent that Aït Ahmed's report had either inspired the FLN's strategy or reflected the views of its other leaders. The FLN's 1 November 1954 proclamation declared among the front's aims the "internationalization of the Algerian problem" and accorded it the same emphasis as the struggle's internal, military dimension.[12]

Aït Ahmed joined with his brother-in-law Mohammed Khider, a former National Assembly deputy, and Ahmed Ben Bella, a twice-decorated veteran of the Italian campaign, to form the FLN's first external delegation. Aït Ahmed and Khider's orders were to defeat French efforts to define Algeria as an internal affair and to take the FLN's case to the United Nations. Aït Ahmed would represent the FLN in New York and at international conferences, while in Cairo Khider was responsible for the overall direction of FLN diplomacy. Meanwhile, Ben Bella traveled throughout the Middle East and North Africa arranging arms shipments to the forces fighting in the interior.[13]

At the time, anti-colonialism was only beginning to emerge as a coordinated, international movement, and recently emancipated states were still a small minority at the United Nations. Consequently, the Algerians found it difficult to make headway. In

December 1954, neutral Asian countries meeting in Colombo, Sri Lanka, refused even to mention them in their final communiqué, explaining that it was up to the Arab states to take the lead.[14] On Khider's urging, Saudi Arabia did petition the U.N. Security Council. But most Arab League members were unwilling to challenge French claims that Algeria was juridically an internal affair. The Iranian representative who held the council's rotating presidency declared the whole business to be "perfectly absurd."[15]

Nevertheless, the Quai d'Orsay noted that the Saudi petition had "revealed the supposed existence of an Algerian question to American public opinion, which had been totally unaware of it before." The Interior Ministry was therefore asked to provide information on the number of rebels and the scale of their operations to help "reduce the present events to their exact proportion."[16] In fact, initially the FLN consisted of fewer than 2,500 mujahedin possessing no more than 400 rifles.[17] But the French were already concerned that diplomatic and military actions, however ineffectual in isolation, could together amplify Algerian demands through international organizations and the media, redounding to their disadvantage in world, and especially American, opinion.

The tensions the Algerian war would create in Franco-American relations were already apparent in a National Security Council meeting held three weeks after it began. Admiral Arthur Radford, chairman of the Joint Chiefs of Staff, pointed to the central dilemma facing American policy: "the possibility of either losing our whole position in the Middle East by offending the Arabs, or else risking the rupture of our NATO position by offending the French." While Radford advocated "outright support of the Arabs," Secretary of State John Foster Dulles prevailed on President Eisenhower to allow him quietly to urge his French counterparts to implement reforms leading to greater autonomy.[18]

The Bandung conference of Asian and African states in April 1955 exacerbated the Americans' apprehensions. Learning the lessons of the earlier conference, the Algerians prepared the ground by sending propaganda missions to the Colombo countries and joined representatives of the French protectorates of Morocco and Tunisia in a united North African delegation. They obtained a resolution recognizing that all had a right to independence.[19] Almost immediately there was a sharp increase in the number of FLN attacks in Algeria, from 158 in April to 432 in May.[20]

Philippe Tripier has attributed the escalation to the conference, marking the start of a pattern: "every important international event affecting the allies or sympathizers of the Algerian uprising would immediately have an effect on Algerian opinion and on the morale of the rebels themselves." Conversely, every reported exploit of the rebels within Algeria aided the FLN's allies and irritated the friends of France. "One noticed a phenomenon of resonance and reciprocity," Tripier concluded, "a natural interaction between the Algerian event and its global context." Indeed, in September 1958 the French delegation to the United Nations ordered a chart showing the correspondence between General Assembly debates on Algeria and the incidence of FLN attacks in Kabylia.[21]

Although many different factors determined the level of rebel activity, Tripier's account does reflect the perception of French security forces that the FLN's campaign abroad kept the rebellion alive—not surprisingly, because he served as an intelligence officer during the war. There is also ample contemporary evidence. In September 1955, for instance, the director-general of security in Algiers complained that "it would be difficult to restore calm as long as the nationalists felt they were going to get help from outside."[22] The French therefore concluded that they could not avoid doing battle with the FLN in the international arena, waging the Algerian war as a kind of world war—a war for world opinion.

The most fiercely contested terrain would be the United States and the United Nations. The French counted on U.S. military and especially diplomatic support, assuming it could easily command a majority in the General Assembly.[23] But in 1955, seventeen states—most of them Eastern bloc or Afro-Asian—were to gain membership. Even so, Aït Ahmed doubted that he had the votes to place the Algerian question on the agenda. Hoping to influence the outcome, shopkeepers in Algiers staged their first general strike on the opening day of the debate while the French deployed troops at strategic points around the city. Once again, an FLN diplomatic campaign coincided with a sharp increase in armed attacks.[24]

On 30 September 1955, the delegates voted in "an electrified atmosphere," as Aït Ahmed later recalled, with his deputies "counting on their toes." They won by a single vote, provoking thunderous applause and an abrupt walkout by the French foreign minister, Antoine Pinay.[25] At a dinner party in New York that evening, Pinay launched what a startled British ambassador described as "a ferocious attack" on his Soviet counterpart's support for the FLN.[26] Absent primary evidence, one can only surmise that this vote was part of Khrushchev's new Third World strategy. He had scored his first major success earlier that month by supplying arms to Egypt, breaking a Western monopoly in the Middle East. After it was announced that Krushchev would visit India, Burma, and Afghanistan—where he promised additional aid—Dulles concluded that "[t]he scene of the battle between the free world and the communist world was shifting."[27]

In November, the United States helped the French U.N. delegation adjourn discussion of the Algerian question. But at the same time, American diplomats began a series of meetings with the FLN. They were particularly impressed with Aït Ahmed, whom they described as "silken in tone and marble-hard in content." Aït Ahmed warned that "the attitudes of an independent North Africa toward the West would depend on the circumstances in which she won her independence."[28] Ben Bella, for his part, claimed that the FLN had "closed the door" to the communists. Still, he subtly played on American anxieties, criticizing U.S. support for France not only because it hurt its image in North Africa, but also because it "weakened the defenses of Western Europe against the Soviet Union." Indeed, the Americans were increasingly concerned about the shift of French forces from NATO to Algeria. Ben Bella was equally astute in suggesting what they might do about it:

> There was no thought, he said, that the United States should exert public pressure on France. Such a move would be bound to fail. He hoped however that the United States, behind the scenes, would continually urge the French in the direction of finding a peaceful solution through negotiations with the Algerian Nationalists.[29]

In fact, behind the scenes the United States did urge the French to make concessions and seek a negotiated settlement.[30] In Paris, everyone from communists to conservatives accused Washington of playing a "double game"—pretending to back France while secretly favoring the rebels.[31]

In February 1956, a new French government under Prime Minister Guy Mollet resolved to grant Tunisia and Morocco "independence within interdependence," calculating that with aid and advisers France could retain these countries as allies, or at least prevent their aiding the FLN. But Mollet complained to U.S. Ambassador Douglas Dillon that the Moroccans "are constantly telling [the] French that they can obtain [aid] more easily and in greater quantities from [the] U.S. than they can from France." The prime minister insisted that the United States not allow North Africans to play the allies off against each other.[32]

In March, a series of reports arrived in Washington indicating a "dangerously sharp rise in anti-American sentiment." Without a strong, public statement of U.S. support for France in North Africa, Dillon predicted "an explosion."[33] Conversely, the new foreign minister, Christian Pineau, pledged that his government "was really determined to reach [an] agreement with [the] Algerian nationalists," though they could succeed only with U.S. support.[34] Washington finally extended only token aid to the former protectorates, prompting the Tunisians to joke that they would use the money to build an embassy in Moscow.[35] At the same time, Eisenhower approved a qualified but well-publicized endorsement of French policy in Algeria.[36]

Undeterred, Aït Ahmed simply redoubled his efforts, pressing the Afro-Asian caucus to convene a special session of the General Assembly and petition the Security Council. "[T]he more we push the U.S. to implicate itself with colonialism," he predicted, "the closer will be the day when they will see themselves obliged to bail out." He urged his allies to make *démarches* to all the NATO capitals, especially to Washington and London. At the same time, he called on Khider to obtain "the most extreme positions possible" from the Arab League. These efforts were interconnected and mutually reinforcing: "extreme" positions by the league would lend urgency to the *démarches* of even "moderate" states such as India, while the collective weight of the Afro-Asian world would compel France's allies to press for a compromise peace.[37]

The one weak link was Nasser, heretofore the Algerians' most valued supporter. Worried about French arms shipments to Israel, he was now exploring a possible rapprochement. The bargaining began in March 1956, when Pineau paid a surprise visit to Egypt. Nasser promised not to oppose any settlement in Algeria that had the support of its Muslim population and agreed to arrange a meeting between a French representative and the FLN.[38] In the next three weeks, there was a significant decline in the size of Egyptian arms shipments, which the FLN attributed to the Pineau–Nasser meeting.[39] Both Aït Ahmed and Khider also noted a weakening of Egypt's diplomatic support at the United Nations and the Arab League.[40]

Nasser's point man on North Africa, Mohamad Fathi al-Dib, suggested that he make a deal with France. Noting France's ability to destabilize the region, he would require that country to limit both military aid and Jewish emigration to Israel; to assist in the settlement of the Palestinian problem; and to continue opposing British efforts to form a regional defense organization, the Baghdad Pact. Thus, at the same time a political solution in North Africa was beginning to seem possible, Egypt would make it contingent on these and other French concessions that had nothing whatever to do with Algerian independence—but everything to do with Egypt's problem with Israel.[41]

Yet even if Pineau had wanted to make this deal, he probably would not have been able to pull it off. Both Mollet and Defense Minister Maurice Bourgès-Maunoury had a deep, sentimental attachment to the Israelis and might have been repulsed rather than tempted by the offer. Moreover, the French government had been powerless to stop the Defense Ministry from sending the Israelis tanks and planes.[42] The Israelis, for their part, were pushing hard from the other direction. As early as June 1955, Shimon Peres, then director-general of the Israeli Defense Ministry, had observed that "[e]very Frenchman killed in North Africa, like every Egyptian killed in the Gaza Strip, takes us one step further towards strengthening the ties between France and Israel."[43] Israel's Mossad assisted France's Service de Documentation Extérieure et de Contre-Espionnage (SDECE) with intelligence on Nasser's aid to the FLN, which made a French–Egyptian rapprochement even more unlikely.[44] So, too, did a statement by Israeli Prime Minister David Ben-Gurion praising France as the only country to supply Israel with weaponry. On 15 May, the Paris daily *Le Monde* reported that the Israelis had contracted for another dozen Mystère IVs, the latest generation of French jet fighters.[45] That same day, Nasser asked Dib to re-evaluate Egypt's policy. Quickly reversing course, he decided to step up support for the FLN.[46]

Egypt's increasing aid encouraged the French tendency to view the FLN as a mere instrument of Nasser's ultimate ambition "to re-create the empire of Islam around Egypt," as Mollet explained it to Anthony Eden. When Egypt nationalized the Suez Canal in July 1956, Pineau vowed to respond with force, even without allied support.[47] The French finally brokered the agreement that would bring Britain and Israel into the war together. But, ironically, France was preparing to strike at Nasser at precisely the moment the FLN was repudiating Egyptian influence.[48]

On 20 August, the FLN's leadership within Algeria met secretly in the Soummam valley to compose a common platform.[49] None of the external delegation attended, so Ben Bella could not counter criticism that he was too close to Nasser and had not provided enough arms. The congress's platform openly criticized "the Arab states in general, and Egypt in particular":

> Their support for the Algerian people's struggle was limited and was subjected to the fluctuation of their general diplomacy. France exerted a special form of pressure on the Middle East by means of her economic and military aid and her opposition to the Baghdad pact.

The platform denied any role to Algerian communists and condemned the equivocal position of the French Communist Party. Conversely, it downplayed "the rather embarrassed declarations forced out of the representatives of the United States, Great Britain, and NATO" in support of France.[50]

Most significantly, the Soummam congress did not envisage a military victory. Instead, it looked for "the total weakening of the French army to make victory by arms impossible." Equally important, the FLN would work for "the political isolation of France—in Algeria and in the world."[51] Toward that end, the platform foresaw a permanent office at the United Nations and in the United States, as well as a delegation in Asia. In fact, by October 1956 there would be eight FLN bureaus: in Cairo, Damascus, Tunis, Beirut, Baghdad, Karachi, Djakarta, and New York. The Soummam congress also called for "mobile delegations" that would visit various capitals and international cultural, student, and trade-union meetings. The FLN had already formed a labor affiliate, the Union Générale des Travailleurs Algériens, and would create a commercial association the following month, the Union Générale des Commerçants Algériens. While forming links with their counterparts abroad, these organizations would coordinate labor and commercial strikes during the next U.N. debate. They also facilitated indirect contributions to the FLN, including important sums from the CIA, which thereby hedged the public U.S. position behind France.[52]

Thus, the FLN's international strategy—particularly the campaign to undermine U.S. support for France—was a sustained effort that withstood temporary setbacks and had the support of the party's top leaders. The Soummam platform did establish the principle that the interior leaders would have primacy over the exterior, but only because FLN foreign policy was deemed too important to be delegated. The most influential among these leaders, Ramdane Abbane, had already dispatched a personal envoy—Dr. Lamine Debaghine—with nominal authority over the rest of the external delegation. Although Debaghine soon quarreled with his new colleagues—Ben Bella "almost strangled him on several occasions," according to Khider—the clash was of personalities rather than policies.[53]

The proof came in October 1956, when the French intercepted a plane carrying Khider, Aït Ahmed, Ben Bella, and Mohammed Boudiaf (who had served as liaison to Algeria's Western front). The French introduced their captives as "Ben Bella and his associates," reflecting both his close ties to Cairo and the French view that they all worked for Nasser. But once officials read their papers, they admitted that the internal leadership was in charge, not the FLN diplomats, and certainly not Ben Bella (though he benefited enormously from the publicity).[54] The internal leaders simply dispatched new representatives abroad to continue their policies under Debaghine's direction.

The arrest of the external delegation and the Suez fiasco only heightened American doubts about Paris's ability to contain the conflict and conclude a compromise peace. Indeed, by this point the best-known Algerian moderate, Ferhat Abbas, had gone over to the FLN. In his first State Department meeting in November 1956, he warned that the war increased the danger of communist infiltration. If the French succeeded in actually decapitating the FLN, "red Maquis" would take over.[55]

Abbas was exaggerating, as there were now close to 20,000 armed regulars in the Armée de Libération Nationale (ALN). In January 1957, the ALN executed almost 4,000 attacks around the country, including more than one hundred within the capital itself—a nearly tenfold increase since May 1955.[56] But the FLN leaders continued to direct their efforts at defeating the French abroad. As Abbane put it:

> Is it preferable for our cause to kill ten enemies in some riverbed in Telergma, which no one will talk about, or rather a single one in Algiers, which the American press will report the next day? Though we are taking some risks, we must make our struggle known.[57]

On 2 January, the FLN's new representative in New York, M'Hammed Yazid, called for U.N. sponsorship of renewed negotiations based on a recognition of Algeria's right to independence.[58] That same day, the head of ALN forces in Algiers, Larbi Ben M'Hidi, began to prepare for a general strike. "As the UN session approaches," he explained, "it is necessary to demonstrate that all the people are behind us and obey our orders to the letter." This would negate the French government's argument against negotiating—that is, that the FLN represented no one if it did not actually represent Nasser. The rest of the leadership agreed unanimously, and leaflets announced and explained the action as directed at the U.N. debate.[59]

In what became known as the Battle of Algiers, French paratroopers marched into the Algerian capital, broke the strike, and systematically dismantled Ben M'Hidi's organization. In the following months, the French would send 24,000 Muslims from the city to internment centers, where torture was systematically practiced. This was more than four times as many as the entire FLN organization there, and almost 10 percent of the city's total Muslim population. By the end of the year, nearly 4,000 people had disappeared without a trace.[60]

Meanwhile, Abbas and Yazid struggled to win support for a forceful U.N. resolution, but they were outgunned and outspent. Mollet met with no fewer than thirty-six ambassadors in Paris, while in New York Pineau personally lobbied most heads of delegations.[61] When diplomacy did not suffice, SDECE agents distributed outright bribes.[62] The French Information Center, for its part, delivered propaganda films to American television stations that were shown more than 1,500 times to an estimated 60 million viewers. The $450,000 that the French Information Center was estimated to have spent on a full-page advertisement in the thirty-one largest U.S. newspapers was more than ten times the FLN office's entire budget.[63]

The Algerians were finally forced to settle for a compromise resolution that merely called for "a peaceful, democratic, and just solution . . . conforming to the principles of the United Nations charter."[64] With the sacrifices being made in Algiers, this could only disappoint the FLN leadership. That same day, they decided to abandon the city and direct the rebellion from Tunis. Even before they arrived, Ben Bella's representative was attacking their record. "We have risked the dismantling of the revolutionary organization to make a noise at the United Nations," he exclaimed. "It's stupid and ridiculous!"[65]

Yet as Abbane had anticipated, the risks the FLN ran were repaid with media attention in France and around the world. Indeed, as French methods came to light, the Battle of Algiers began to appear as a Pyrrhic victory. Authorities banned articles and books about torture, but this merely lent these works cachet and did not stop FLN publicists from citing them to argue that France had violated the U.N. resolution. Translations of Henri Alleg's *La Question* became best-sellers elsewhere in Europe and in the United States.[66] Censorship also made "the worst impression abroad," as the French Director of Information and Press Pierre Baraduc pointed out in March 1958.[67] Even writers who condemned the FLN, Ambassador Hervé Alphand reported, "observed that the persistence of terrorism implicitly attests to the fact that France cannot take the situation in hand. . . . [L]ittle by little, [this] prepares American public opinion for the idea that the Algerian question is on the way to becoming an international problem."[68]

French propagandists therefore began to ignore the war and emphasize their efforts to "develop" Algeria. As Baraduc argued, "Each time that one can speak of something other than blood in Algeria . . . this is progress for pacification because it represents a return to normal."[69] Yet a "return to normal" did not interest newsmen attracted to a story with strong visuals and plenty of violence. Although the FLN could not equal France in its propaganda output, the FLN gained a decisive advantage in "free media."

The radio and television formats rewarded the FLN for creating controversy and providing combat footage, whereas the French would not even dignify their adversary with a debate. The host of a CBS radio program, Blair Clark, resorted to letting an FLN spokesman sitting in the studio debate the network's correspondent in Algiers.[70] Similarly, Chet Huntley of NBC TV's *Outlook* program showed clips taken by mujahedin using a portable camera. Perhaps the scenes of children crying beside their parents' corpses and French soldiers falling to the ALN were staged, as the French maintained, but they obviously made a greater impact than propaganda films such as *Water, Crops, and Men.*[71] And what did it matter if, as Paris complained, Italian and German correspondents who thought they were accompanying FLN raids never really left Tunisia? By making the rebels appear to control parts of Algeria, these reports buttressed the FLN's claims to international recognition. As one French diplomat later remarked about FLN visits to the State Department, "It's not the reality of what they say or do, but the way it is represented in the radios of Tunis and Cairo and the myth that it gives life to in [Algeria]." Indeed, this "myth" of a conquering army and diplomats with entrée to every chancellery would gradually help to transform reality within Algeria itself, inspiring nationalists to persist in their struggle and making the once unassailable notion of *Algérie française* itself seem illusory.[72]

In the near-term, the FLN focused on inciting international opposition to the Algerian war and using Tunisia as a safe haven in which to regroup its forces. The French, for their part, began to fortify the border with electrified fences, minefields, and radar-directed artillery. This led to a series of clashes that drew in Tunisia's own small army, leading President Habib Bourguiba to threaten to turn to Egypt or the Eastern bloc for arms that France now refused to supply.[73] The Tunisian arms crisis, as it came to be known, culminated in November 1957 with an Anglo-American decision to provide a small but symbolic shipment, despite the vociferous objections by the new French government led by Prime Minister Félix Gaillard. As Eisenhower described it, Gaillard had threatened "a complete breakup of the Western alliance."[74]

Yet the worst crisis came in February 1958, when the French bombed a Tunisian border village that they alleged to be an ALN base, inflicting scores of civilian casualties. Within hours, Bourguiba had brought foreign correspondents and cameramen to the scene, and the resulting articles and images created a public-relations fiasco for Paris. After barricading French troops in their bases, Bourguiba threatened to petition the U.N. Security Council before accepting American and British mediation. All through the talks, Bourguiba sought to expand their mandate to include a settlement of the Algerian war while rejecting any measures that might have hindered the ALN.[75] Meanwhile, the rebel command sent whole battalions against the French border fortifications, leading to some of the most intense fighting of the war.[76]

By word and deed, passivity and aggressivity, the Tunisians and Algerians together were forcing each of the foreign powers to weigh in on the future of North Africa. Virtually all had struggled to avoid an unqualified commitment to either French Algeria or independence—America playing a "double game," Germany conducting a "double strategy," Italy pursuing a "two-track" policy, Britain publicly supportive but privately skeptical[77]—because none, not even the USSR, wanted to see French influence eradicated in the region. Thus, the Soviet deputy foreign minister urged Paris to undertake "an 'audacious' initiative" or risk being replaced by the United States.[78] Indeed, Dulles had already told Alphand that it was "indispensable that you look for a political solution while there is still time." He warned, "[W]hatever may be the French determination to continue the fight, . . . financial conditions could, at some point, stand in their way." Only two months before, France had narrowly averted a balance-of-payments crisis thanks to loans from the United States, the International Monetary Fund, and the European Payments Union. Dulles noted that certain, U.S. senators had asked him to go back on the decision. With a new financial crisis looming, and France ever more isolated, his words carried considerable weight.[79]

A week later, the American member of the "good offices" mission, Robert Murphy, sought British support in demanding that France accept a cease-fire and an international conference on Algeria. If Paris did not agree, the United States would be forced to provide political, economic, and military support to Tunisia and Morocco—thus placing America behind France's adversaries in a public and definitive fashion.[80] The perception that the United States was unfairly pressuring Paris caused the downfall of the Gaillard government. But leading candidates to succeed him were prepared to work with the Americans. On 1 May, René Pleven told U.S. Ambassador Amory Houghton that he "would hope that we would be willing to use our contacts with [the] FLN, if good enough, to try to get it to discuss a cease-fire." Mollet, for his part, favored sending a negotiating team to meet with the Algerians.[81] Their long and patient efforts to secure U.S. support for a negotiated settlement appeared to be on the brink of success.

But rather than submit to a "diplomatic Dien Bien Phu," the *pieds noirs* rose up on 13 May, and, under the leadership of the local army commanders, demanded the return of de Gaulle. Assuming full powers on 1 June, de Gaulle quickly settled the border conflict with Tunisia and restored confidence in France's ability to end the war. Yet it soon became clear the general would make peace only on his own terms, which did not include political negotiations with the FLN or full independence for Algeria.[82]

De Gaulle's return was a massive setback for the FLN's international strategy. "We've settled into the war, the world has also gotten used to it," the FLN's chief of armaments and logistics, Omar Ouamrane, bitterly observed two months later. The world would "continue to turn to the Algerian war as long as it lasts, if necessary until the last Algerian." The ALN had suffered demoralizing losses in assaults on the French border fortifications. Soon they would become all but impenetrable as French forces set to work stamping out the insurgents of the interior. Diplomatically, de Gaulle could "permanently bar the way to the West and neutralize the Eastern bloc," Ouamrane wrote. "He has already succeeded in partially cutting us off from our own brothers." After making a separate deal with de Gaulle, the Tunisians joined the Moroccans in urging the FLN to accept less than full independence.[83]

Instead, Ouamrane called for a "truly revolutionary political and diplomatic action"—though it was an action that Aït Ahmed had already suggested nearly two years before. In fact, Ouamrane was inspired by a study he had written in his prison cell in the Santé.[84] Here is how Ouamrane summarized Aït Ahmed's critical insight:

> Our whole policy consists of requesting, of demanding our independence. We demand it from the enemy. We want that our brothers, our friends, the U.N. recognize it. We ask it of everyone except ourselves, forgetting that independence proclaims itself and is not given.[85]

Aït Ahmed argued instead that by unilaterally declaring independence and establishing a provisional government, the FLN could drive France to the negotiating table. First, re-establishing the *dawla*—or state—was the dream of generations of Algerian

Muslims; it would now inspire them to persist in their struggle. The Arab and Asian states would be "forced, by their public opinion and by mutual competition for interests and prestige, to conform their actual policy to their profession of faith." By obtaining their recognition, Algeria would be perceived as an integral part—rather than merely as an outward sign—of the Afro-Asian movement, which was the object of increasing superpower competition. And if the provisional government won recognition from the communist states, the Americans might be led to end their "complacency and capitulations" to French blackmail. Finally, a campaign for recognition could be conducted continuously, unlike the once-a-year test of strength in the U.N. General Assembly. Each success would galvanize the energy of the Algerian people and help convince Paris that the process was irreversible.[86]

So on 19 September 1958, Ferhat Abbas called a press conference in Cairo to announce the formation of the GPRA, with himself as president. Despite having discouraged this initiative, Morocco and Tunisia immediately extended diplomatic recognition, explaining to Paris that they would otherwise be subject to attack from more militant states such as Egypt and Iraq—just as Aït Ahmed had anticipated. Indeed, every Arab state except Lebanon immediately joined them.[87] China's recognition came within the week, followed shortly by North Vietnam, North Korea, and Indonesia. All together, thirteen of some eighty-three states recognized the GPRA within ten days of its creation.[88]

While the GPRA sent delegations to the communist states, its forty-five representatives abroad—accredited and not—were initially concentrated in Middle Eastern and Western European countries, twenty in total.[89] In theory, they reported to Debaghine, now designated foreign minister. But given the circumstances in which they worked, all of the GPRA's ministries had to deal with other governments—or evade them—in order to carry out their functions. By June 1960, French intelligence counted 177 GPRA officials in thirty-eight countries, not counting Tunisia and Morocco. But this figure included—and doubtless excluded—dozens working clandestinely as recruiters or money collectors in emigrant communities.[90] Although all of this was inimical to rational organization, it would have been impossible for the Foreign Ministry's small staff to oversee the entirety of Algerian activities abroad.[91] Rather than implying the insignificance of foreign affairs for the GPRA this attested to its all-encompassing importance. With a Ministry of Armaments dealing with everyone from German arms dealers to communist China, and a Ministry of General Liaisons running bagmen and agents across Europe and the Middle East, nothing was "foreign" to the new government. Indeed, in 1960 even the "minister of the interior," Lakhdar Bentobbal, concluded that "each one of our agencies, military, political, diplomatic, social, associational or otherwise should act in its area according to the same objective: *INTERNATIONALIZATION*."[92] In that year, the French estimated, the GPRA's expenditures abroad—for arms purchases, maintenance, support for refugees, and so on—had nearly equaled expenditures in the five Algerian *Wilayat*. The GPRA was like a state turned inside out.[93]

De Gaulle's strategy was to reverse this process of internationalization and isolate the GPRA. Like his predecessors, he believed that the provisional government would not otherwise acknowledge defeat.[94] His main concern was that the Algerians and their allies would exploit the competition between the United States and the USSR, observing that "the Arabs were past masters in playing off one white power against another."[95] He therefore called for a tripartite organization that would divide the world into French, British, and American spheres of influence. In September 1958, he warned that such an organization was "indispensable," and that France "subordinates to it as of now all development of its present participation in NATO." Thus, both sides escalated their international campaigns without fundamentally altering their strategies.[96]

During the U.N. debate on Algeria in December 1958, three GPRA ministers toured China, North Vietnam, and North Korea. Soon the press was reporting that they had requested economic and military aid—even volunteers. Yet this visit did not provoke a violent reaction from the West, as a GPRA official noted. Indeed, the United States refused to vote with France's supporters at the United Nations. More than half of the U.N. General Assembly explicitly recognized the GPRA, though a resolution calling for "negotiations between the two parties" failed by a single vote to obtain the requisite two-thirds majority. The U.S. abstention was "incontestably a success" from Abbas's standpoint, encouraging the Algerians' efforts to exploit the escalating "war of nerves" between the putative allies.[97] The French U.N. representative, for his part, observed that "[i]f the FLN has lost ground in Algeria, there is little doubt that it has gained a good deal on the international level and in all the countries of the world where it has sent missions, especially the United States and the United Nations."[98]

There were a number of reasons for the American abstention, but the main one remained Dulles's and Eisenhower's determination not to alienate Third World opinion. It is indicative of this attitude that what worried the secretary about de Gaulle's tripartite proposal "was not so much its impact on NATO countries but the disastrous effects it would have on countries in Africa and the Middle East."[99] De Gaulle retaliated by withdrawing the French Mediterranean fleet from NATO command.[100] His new prime minister, Michel Debré, instructed French ambassadors that Algeria was now the "first priority" of the government and its foreign policy. "[I]t is imperative that the rebellion lose the support and complacence that it currently benefits from," he asserted, "and that it feel abandoned and asphyxiated."[101]

Denying the GPRA diplomatic recognition was therefore critical to French strategy. Since September 1958, Lebanon and Mongolia had joined the group of states that recognized the provisional government. French spokesmen privately suggested that a Muslim or Arab country could not do otherwise. But if de Gaulle was not unduly exercised by anything Ulan Bator said or did, he warned in April 1959 that Paris would sever ties with any "responsible" state that followed suit. Nevertheless, nothing was done to Ghana after it accorded de facto recognition that summer, thus extending the zone of French tolerance to all of Africa. Otherwise, in trying to isolate the GPRA, France risked isolating itself.[102]

Algeria's evident importance to Paris encouraged unfriendly states to turn the war to their advantage. In August 1959, Soviet Foreign Minister Andrei Gromyko warned his French counterpart, Maurice Couve de Murville, that Moscow would drop the restraint it had displayed on Algeria if Paris continued to back West Germany on Berlin.[103] Conversely, German Chancellor Konrad Adenauer's support for French Algeria—including tolerance for SDECE operations against arms traders and GPRA officials in West Germany—mitigated the credit de Gaulle hoped to obtain for his uncompromising stance, even if Adenauer was too skilled a statesman to link these issues explicitly.[104] Francisco Franco, on the other hand, called on de Gaulle to end tolerance toward dissident Spanish emigrés, as Madrid had already done vis-à-vis the Algerians. De Gaulle flatly refused, denying any equivalence between the Spanish republicans and the Algerian provisional government, but the whole conversation must have been distasteful to him.[105] It was from such episodes that de Gaulle concluded that Algeria "undermines the position of France in the world," as he said at the time. "As long as we are not relieved of it, we can do nothing in the world. This is a terrible burden. It is necessary to relinquish it."[106]

So on 16 September 1959, de Gaulle declared: "[t]aking into account all the givens—Algerian, national, and international—I consider it necessary that the principle of self-determination be proclaimed from today." After peace was restored, Muslims would decide their own future in a referendum to which de Gaulle would invite "informants from the whole world." At first some actually dismissed the speech as intended only for foreign consumption. De Gaulle himself privately explained that he hoped "to defuse the debate at the U.N. at the end of September."[107]

Yet despite de Gaulle's acceptance of self-determination, the Americans still refused to associate themselves with his Algerian policy. "How could we say that we support the French and still not damage our interests?" Eisenhower asked in an August 1959 National Security Council meeting. Interpreting a proposed policy statement, he stated that "a solution 'in consonance with U.S. interests' meant that we should avoid the charge that we were one of the colonial powers." He would not openly side with de Gaulle, no matter what he proposed, as long as it was not immediately accepted by the Algerians.[108]

Eisenhower's reasoning shows why, as the French representative Armand Bérard wrote in July 1959, "the evolution of the situation in North Africa and that of our position at the U.N. are going in exactly opposite directions."[109] Indeed, by that point the number of ALN regulars within Algeria had declined by a third from its peak, while a quarter of their weapons lacked parts or ammunition. Moreover, morale was suffering: the proportion of prisoners to killed rose from 27 percent to 42 percent over the same period, and there was a doubling in the monthly rate of rebels voluntarily rallying to the French.[110] The impossibility of breaching the border fortifications without staggering losses prevented reinforcement while creating disciplinary problems in the armies left idle on the frontier, problems that contributed to a deterioration in relations with Tunisia and Morocco.[111]

The evolution Bérard traced was not inexorable. In fact, the U.N. General Assembly resolution calling for negotiations barely missed the required two-thirds majority. But after having achieved virtually the same result as in 1958 despite making a maximum effort to win over world opinion, it was now clear that de Gaulle could not domesticate the Algerian question. The cause of Algerian independence had taken on a life of its own at the United Nations and around the world. And this, in turn, had begun to help sustain loyalty to the provisional government within Algeria despite the reversals suffered by the ALN. French officials touring Algeria in January 1960 discovered that "the successes, even relative, of the FLN in the international arena seem to have deeply affected Muslim opinion."[112]

Yet de Gaulle would have to overcome the opposition of the *pieds noirs* and his own military, who did not see why they had to concede to the GPRA what it could not win in the field. That same month, another settler uprising once again forced de Gaulle to rule out political negotiations. Debaghine's successor as foreign minister, Belkacem Krim, therefore embarked on the risky strategy that culminated in the episode described at the outset of this article. Debaghine had already provided the rationale in an October 1959 memorandum. Noting that U.S. support for France weakened the moment it was rumored that China might back the Algerians, he proposed that they continue to escalate. De Gaulle's difficulties increasingly affected the West, Debaghine noted, and "[t]he process is going to intensify":

> The Arab states will commit themselves further, and so too will the Afro-Asian countries. On the French side it will be necessary to involve the West even more. The radicalization of the war, with the co-belligerence of the Arab countries and the participation of Chinese volunteers, will lead in the end to a confrontation between the West and the East. . . . The final stage is the intervention of China. This will lead the West to put a stop to the war in Algeria. If not this would be world war.[113]

Krim confirmed this shift in Algerian strategy in "Our Foreign Policy and the Cold War," one of the first memoranda he wrote as foreign minister. The Algerians would no longer present themselves as potential allies of the United States or limit themselves to threats to turn to "the East." Although the goal remained the same—to exacerbate divisions in the West and thereby exert indirect pressure on Paris—they would pursue it through a policy of brinkmanship, confronting France's allies with actual and increasing communist support.[114] This aid might also help militarily, but for Krim that was secondary. Thus, when he formally called for foreign volunteers—initially limited to the Arab and African states—there was no discussion of how they might actually be used. "The modalities of putting this into practice will be discussed and debated later," he explained in an internal note. "Right now what matters is to conduct a vigorous propaganda [campaign] around the principle of volunteering and above all to demonstrate, if the war continues, de Gaulle alone will be responsible and world peace will be directly threatened." For Krim, both African and Arab support were alike a "means of pressuring the East and the West."[115]

Thus, even while the Algerians' international strategy came to encompass East and West, North and South, it remained interdependent and essentially political in nature. Support by African and Arab states sought after by the superpowers would compel the communists to provide more active assistance, while the threat of increasing communist influence or even direct intervention would cause France's allies to compel a settlement. Yet, as in the earlier phase, a weak link could cause the whole plan to unravel. That weak link was now located in Moscow.

The Soviets had always been reluctant to give the Algerians more than their General Assembly votes. In addition to their solicitude for French communists and fear that the United States would fill any vacuum in North Africa, more forthright support would cost them a valuable bargaining chip in relations with de Gaulle—especially while the Berlin question was unsettled and a summit in Paris was imminent. Indeed, Krim was nervous about a rapprochement between the great powers, as he made clear during a conversation in Beijing on 1 May 1960. He told the Chinese vice premier that he "would have loved to see . . . the Soviet Union adopt very firm positions like those of the government of the People's Republic of China" and asked him to make certain that Khrushchev acted as an advocate for colonized peoples.[116] Considering their divide-and-conquer strategy, the Algerians had reason to fear that a relaxation in superpower tensions "would materialize on our backs," as they had told Indian Prime Minister Jawaharlal Nehru two years before.[117] But that same day, the Soviets shot down Gary Powers's U-2 spy plane. De Gaulle backed Eisenhower in the midst of the collapsing summit, and, in retaliation, Khrushchev condemned his "war against the Algerian people that has lasted five years and for which France needs American support." This ended the danger that détente posed to Algerian diplomacy.[118]

When the Soviets extended de facto recognition to the GPRA in October, Yazid demanded a meeting with a high-level U.S. State Department official to warn that the pro-Western faction was losing power.[119] Later that month, Abbas formally appealed for Chinese "volunteers." At the same time, Morocco's Crown Prince Hassan told the British ambassador that the Algerians had delivered a written request to admit them. He warned British Prime Minister Harold Macmillan that he could not delay their entry more than two months, urging progress toward peace talks before the U.N. General Assembly debated the question. Macmillan called it "a very dangerous" proposal and urged Hassan not to force the Western powers to choose between Paris and the GPRA. Bourguiba tipped off the Lebanese ambassador—who quickly passed the tip on to his French colleague—that soon "Chinese hordes" would sweep across North Africa.[120]

In fact, Hassan and Krim concocted this request for the express purpose of "putting pressure on Macmillan," as Krim noted at the time. "Result: Macmillan felt the pressure." The GPRA's foreign minister was equally pleased with Hassan's self-imposed deadline, "[w]hich leaves the Anglo-Americans two months to make their move and avoid letting Algeria become a theater of the Cold War." Little did they know that Krim and Hassan were talking about only forty technicians, hardly the makings of a horde. Even so, the Moroccans were genuinely reluctant to admit the Chinese, with the minister of the interior suggesting instead that they might join the GPRA as co-belligerents. But Krim insisted, explaining that "Chinese and Russian intervention has a much greater political effect because it constitutes a more immediate danger for the West."[121]

The British and the Americans quickly rose to the bait. On 26 October, London pressed de Gaulle to declare his peaceful intentions or risk defeat in the U.N. General Assembly. A week later, the U.S. State Department stepped up the pressure, warning that it would not otherwise defend the French position. The very next day, de Gaulle declared that he was prepared to negotiate with the GPRA over a referendum in Algeria that he admitted would inevitably result in an independent republic.[122]

Nevertheless, the GPRA continued to press for a resolution that called for a U.N.-supervised referendum. There was no chance that the French would allow it, but they continued to fear that diplomatic victories strengthened the Algerian bargaining position.[123] Ironically, by this point the Algerians themselves would have opposed a U.N. intervention, mindful of the chaos then occurring in the Congo. But, as they explained to Yugoslavia's Marshal Tito, "we also knew, on the one hand, that General de Gaulle was frightened by the idea of an internationalization of the Algerian problem and that, on the other hand, our proposition would deepen the divisions that reign among France's allies."[124]

Yet while neither Paris nor the GPRA considered the United Nations capable of halting hostilities, the U.N. General Assembly debate had taken on a life of its own in Algeria. In August 1960, a meeting of top French officials in Algiers found that most Muslims increasingly thought that only the United Nations could end the conflict. The French Delegate General's monthly report for September agreed. Similarly, in October de Gaulle's adviser on Algeria found that Muslims were showing increasing interest in the provisional government's activities abroad and the upcoming U.N. General Assembly debate. Indeed, Bentobbal urged them "not to place too much hope in the decisions of the U.N. so as not to be disappointed." But they appeared not to listen, even placing hopes in the outcome of the American presidential election because of its potential impact in Algeria. Thus, a correspondent who visited an ALN camp high in the Atlas mountains at the time was astonished to find grizzled mujahedin asking what John F. Kennedy's chances were against Richard M. Nixon, doubtless recalling a 1957 speech in which Kennedy had called for Algerian independence. On the night of the election, ALN fighters listened to transistor radios as the returns came in, cheering whenever Kennedy pulled ahead, cursing when Nixon threatened to overtake him.[125]

In December 1960, as the debate was about to begin in New York, de Gaulle decided to go to Algeria. In five days he faced four separate assassination plots and innumerable mobs of angry *pieds noirs*. But while this was fully expected, no one was prepared for the Muslims of Algiers and Oran to mount a massive counter-protest. Marching in the thousands from the Casbah, they waved homemade Algerian flags and chanted "long live the GPRA!"—much to the surprise of the provisional government itself. It was all the more shocking for rioting *Algérie française* activists, forcing them to wheel around and close ranks with the police.[126]

Meanwhile, the demonstrations in Algiers led France's supporters in New York to waver. Once moderate delegations, such as India's, violently attacked the repression. Even normally friendly representatives from Francophone African states such as Mali and Togo defected.[127] The paragraph calling for an internationally supervised referendum failed by a single vote. But a majority of sixty-three to eight demanded guarantees for self-determination for the whole of Algeria—de Gaulle had floated rumors of a possible partition—and insisted on a U.N. role. As a French army report noted, "Nearly all the nations of the world have thus proved their will to end the Algerian conflict, if need be by foreign intervention."[128]

Once again, Algerians had paid a heavy price for a diplomatic victory. Yet perhaps the most significant casualties were three political myths, as the *New Yorker* magazine's Paris correspondent, Janet Flanner, wrote at the time: the myth that Algeria was French, that only a handful of rebels wanted independence, and that de Gaulle alone could impose peace.[129] It also marked the moment at which another "myth" became reality: the once mythical notion that a national liberation movement could triumph without having liberated any of the national territory. It was the culmination of the strategy Aït Ahmed had first articulated more than a decade before, a strategy that all along aimed at establishing a mutually reinforcing relationship between the Algerians' diplomatic campaigns abroad and manifestations of popular support at home. Although more than a year of negotiations remained—during which the Algerians would continually threaten to invite direct intervention by their Soviet and Chinese supporters—independence was at hand.[130]

This article can only begin to suggest the kinds of research made possible by the opening of the GPRA archives, which will doubtless enrich our understanding of the social, cultural, and military aspects of the Algerian war. But one can offer some tentative conclusions about its international history, especially because we can compare the Algerian archives with those of France and its two main allies, the United States and the United Kingdom. For instance, the inverse relationship between France's military strength and the progressive weakening of its hold on Algeria has been called the "supreme paradox" of this long struggle.[131] This paradox now appears to be a matter of perspective. Even before the war began, the FLN leaders did not consider winning a conventional victory to be possible. At the peak of their military strength, they continued to conduct operations for the purpose of achieving diplomatic and propaganda victories. And even when they invited outside intervention, it was intended to compel France's allies to force de Gaulle to negotiate.

From the point of view of French governments, on the other hand, the problems this strategy presented were indeed paradoxical and ultimately insuperable. Concentrating on the war within Algeria—the initial response of both the Fourth and Fifth Republics—allowed the nationalists to develop diplomatic, military, and economic resources abroad with which to harry the French on every front. But engaging them in the external arena made the war even more of an international struggle, one in which France had to deliver and receive blows and risk becoming vulnerable to its adversaries and dependent on its allies. French attempts to isolate the Algerians led to crises in which the French themselves were isolated, and their own efforts to win over international opinion led them to move steadily toward conceding independence. Where once holding on to Algeria appeared like "the last chance for French power," the GPRA's international campaigns finally convinced French leaders that they had no chance of restoring their stature without relinquishing Algeria.[132] We cannot know when and how the Algerians might have won without pursuing this strategy. But it is altogether clear that their adversaries always considered their support abroad to be their main strength and ultimate refuge.

Just as Algeria's independence is impossible to explain without placing it in an international context, the war had an equal if not opposite impact on the outside world—what Elie Kedourie called "prodigious peripeties."[133] It accelerated decolonization in Morocco, Tunisia, and Sub-Saharan Africa; it contributed to France's decision to back Israel and confront Nasser; it triggered the fall of the Fourth Republic and the return of de Gaulle; and it provoked de Gaulle into beginning the withdrawal of French forces from NATO commands. And although the Algerians never sent foreign volunteers into combat, their example attracted and influenced key figures in the next generation of national liberation movements. Thus, when the ALN marched in a victory parade through its main base in Morocco, Nelson Mandela was there to see it, having come to learn revolutionary strategy and tactics. The mujahedin appeared to Mandela like an apparition of the future ANC forces. And when the FLN finally entered Algiers in triumph, Yasir Arafat was in the crowd cheering. He would consciously model Fatah after the FLN. Soon Algiers became known as the "Mecca of the revolutionaries."[134]

In fact, other revolutionary movements would have to develop their own strategies, though the Algerians had shown that it was not enough simply to play off the superpowers. Instead, they exploited every international rivalry that offered potential leverage—revisionist against conservative Arab states, the Arab League against Asian neutrals, China against the USSR, the communist powers against the Western allies, and, above all, the United States against France itself. To that end, the Algerians projected a more or less "moderate" or "pro-Western" image according to the tactical needs of the moment, encouraging outsiders to view personal rivalries among Algerian leaders through their own geo-political and ideological preconceptions. Consequently, a lessening of international tensions was potentially disastrous, as in the case of France and Egypt and, still more, the United States and the USSR. Yet the Algerians did not need to win support from both sides in all these different struggles. As Aït Ahmed had predicted, it was no less effective to use aid from the communist powers to undermine France's position among its allies.

No amount of diplomatic virtuosity would have sufficed if the GPRA's activities abroad had not visibly resonated with the people it represented. The genius of the provisional government's grand strategy was to ensure that political, diplomatic, and military campaigns were mutually reinforcing, so that Algiers and New York, Beijing, and Paris, became theaters in the same struggle. By thinking and acting globally to attain their goals at home and abroad, the Algerians revealed how even a stateless and embattled people could be authors of their own history, a history in which the Cold War was a small but essential part.

NOTES

Author's note: I am grateful to all those who commented on earlier versions of this article, especially Daniel Byrne, Charles Cogan, Juan Cole, Jeffrey Herbst, Martin Thomas, and the anonymous reviewers of *IJMES*. I am also indebted to Hocine Aït Ahmed, Mabrouk Belhocine, and Rédha Malek for granting interviews, and to Daho Djerbal, Samer Emalhayene, William Quandt, and Fadila Takour for advice and assistance in organizing a research trip to Algiers. This work was made possible through the financial support of the Center for Middle Eastern and North African Studies and the Office of the Vice President for Research at the University of Michigan.

[1]"Note," 5 October 1960, Ministère des Affaires Etrangères (hereafter, MAE), Paris, Europe 1944–60, URSS, dossier 271; La Grandville to Couve de Murville, 7 October 1960, MAE, Mission de liaison algérien (hereafter, MLA), Action Extérieure, URSS, dossier 88; Abbas to Zhou Enlai, 24 October 1960, Mohammed Harbi, ed., *Les Archives de la révolution algérienne* (Paris: Editions Jeune Afrique, 1981), 527–28; 466th meeting of the National Security Council, 7 November 1960, *Foreign Relations of the United States* (hereafter, *FRUS*, with year and volume) 1958–60, vol. 13 (Washington, D.C.: Government Printing Office, 1992), 706.

[2]William Appleman Williams, *The Tragedy of American Diplomacy: United States Foreign Policy 1945–1980* (New York: W. W. Norton, 1959, 1988); Robert J. McMahon, "Eisenhower and Third World Nationalism: A Critique of the Revisionists," *Political Science Quarterly* 101 (1986): 453–73; Gabriel Kolko, *Confronting the Third World* (New York: Pantheon, 1988). More recently, scholars have credited the Eisenhower administration with an appreciation for the force of anti-colonial nationalism, particularly in the Middle East and North Africa, while emphasizing the dilemmas it presented for U.S. policy. See H. W. Brands, *The Specter of Neutralism: The United States and the Emergence of the Third World, 1947–1960* (New York: Columbia University Press, 1989); Peter Hahn, The *United States, Great Britain, and*

Egypt, 1945–1956: Strategy and Diplomacy in the Early Cold War (Chapel Hill: University of North Carolina Press, 1991); Egya N. Sangmuah, "Eisenhower and Containment in North Africa, 1956–1960," *Middle East Journal* 44 (1990): 76–91; Irwin M. Wall, "The United States, Algeria, and the Fall of the Fourth French Republic," *Diplomatic History* 18 (1994): 489–511.

[3]See, for instance, Vladislav Zubok and Constantine Pleshakov, *Inside the Kremlin's Cold War: From Stalin to Khrushchev* (Cambridge, Mass.: Harvard University Press, 1996), 54–62; Chen Jian, "The Sino-Soviet Alliance and China's Entry into the Korean War," Cold War International History Project (hereafter, CWIHP) Working Paper No. 1 (1993), 8–9; Kathryn Weathersby, "Korea 1949–50: To Attack, or Not to Attack? Stalin, Kim Il Sung, and the Prelude to War," CWIHP *Bulletin*, no. 5 (1995), 3.

[4]Paul Gordon Lauren, *Power and Prejudice: The Politics and Diplomacy of Racial Discrimination*, 2nd ed. (Boulder, Colo.: Westview Press, 1996), 220–21; Thomas Borstelmann, *Apartheid's Reluctant Uncle: The United States and Southern Africa During the Early Cold War* (New York: Oxford University Press, 1993), 195.

[5]Zachary Karabell, *Architects of Intervention: The United States, the Third World, and the Cold War, 1946–1962* (Baton Rouge: Louisiana State University Press, 1999), 65–67; Fawaz Gerges, *The Superpowers and the Middle East: Regional and International Politics, 1955–1967* (Boulder, Colo.: Westview Press, 1994), 38–39, 245–46.

[6]Waverly Root, "Offer of Massive Chinese Aid Hangs over Algerian Talks," *Washington Post*, 20 July 1960, A8, and see later for an analysis of the episode. The GPRA archives are quite accessible—especially when compared with some of those in France—*pace* Charles-Robert Ageron, "A Propos des Archives militaires de la Guerre d'Algérie," *Vingtième Siècle* 63 (1999): 128–29.

[7]Charles-Robert Ageron, *Modern Algeria: A History from 1830 to the Present*, trans. Michael Brett (London: Hurst, 1991), 98–102; John Ruedy, *Modern Algeria: The Origins and Development of a Nation* (Bloomington: Indiana University Press, 1992), 147–50. For evidence of the cover-up, see Bergé to Bringard, 17 June 1945, Archives d'Outre-Mer (hereafter, AOM), Aix-en-Provence, Ministère des Affaires Algériennes (MAA), dossier 586, and Barrat, "Additif à mon Rapport sur les événements de Guelma," 27 June 1945, ibid.

[8]Moch to Schuman, 31 January 1948, AOM, MAA, dossier 18; Charles-André Julien, *L'Afrique du Nord en Marche. Nationalismes Musulmans et Souveraineté Française* (Paris: Julliard, 1952), 284–88.

[9]"Rapport d'Aït Ahmed," December 1948, in Harbi, *Les Archives*, 15–49. Harbi's collection has long been virtually the only source of internal documents from the nationalist movement. It still serves as a valuable supplement to the state archives.

[10]Ibid., 43–44.

[11]Ibid., 44; Hocine Aït Ahmed, *Mémoires d'un combattant: L'esprit de l'indépendance, 1942–1952* (Paris: Sylvie Messinger, 1983), 156–58. The Moroccans and Tunisians also emphasized the international aspect of their independence struggle, and they, too, sought to exert pressure on France's allies by pointing to the danger of communist expansion in North Africa. See Allal al-Fassi, *The Independence Movements in Arab North Africa, 1948* (New York: Octagon Books, 1970), 381–94, and Habib Bourguiba's July 1946 letter to Ferhat Abbas, reprinted in Samya El Méchat, *Tunisie, Les Chemins vers l'Indépendance, 1945–1956* (Paris: L'Harmattan, 1992), 259–63.

[12]The proclamation is reprinted in Harbi, *Les Archives*, 101–103.

[13]M'Hammed Yazid, "Rapport," July 1957, in Harbi, *Les Archives*, 172–73.

[14]Ibid. See also Hocine Aït Ahmed, "Bandoeng Trente Ans Après," *Jeune Afrique*, no. 1272 (1985), 18.

[15]Khider to Djouad Zakari, 14 December 1954, Centre National des Archives Algériennes (hereafter, CNAA), Algiers, Le Fond du GPRA, MAE, dossier 1; Hoppenot to Mendès France, 5 January 1955, MAE, Série ONU, dossier 546; Mendès France to Mitterrand, Service de l'Algérie, 13 January 1955, no. 189, ibid.

[16]Mendès France to Mitterrand, 13 January 1955, no. 327, MAE, Série ONU, dossier 546; Gillet to Mendès France, 11 December 1954, ibid.

[17]Mohamad Fathi al-Dib, *Abdel Nasser et la Révolution Algérienne* (Paris: L'Harmattan, 1985), 23.

[18]225th Meeting of the NSC, 24 November 1954, *FRUS* 1952–54, vol. 2, 792.

[19]Yazid, "Rapport," 173; El Méchat, *Tunisie, Les Chemins vers l'Indépendance*, 231–33; Aït Ahmed, "Bandoeng," 18–19.

[20]Philippe Tripier, *Autopsie de la guerre d'Algérie* (Paris: Editions France-Empire, 1972), 211; John Talbott, *The War Without a Name: France in Algeria, 1954–1962* (New York: Knopf, 1980), 53.

[21]Tripier, *Autopsie,* 210–12; Langlais to Algiers, 4 September 1958, MAE, Série ONU, dossier 557.

[22]Clark to Dulles, 19 September 1955, U.S. National Archives (hereafter, USNA), College Park, Md., RG59, Central Decimal Files, 751S.00. For other examples, see Dillon to Dulles, 25 July and 16 November 1956, ibid.

[23]Lodge to Dulles, 1 November 1955, *FRUS* 1955–57, vol. 18, 230. U.S. military aid was rapidly winding down in the aftermath of the Indochina war, though Paris sought approval for the transfer of previously supplied equipment.

[24]Clark to Dulles, 23 September 1955, USNA, RG59, Central Decimal Files, 751S.00; Slimane Chikh, *L'Algérie en Armes, ou, Le Temps des Certitudes* (Algiers: Office des Publications Universitaires, 1981), 421.

[25]Aït Ahmed to Margaret Pope, 15 October 1955, Aït Ahmed personal papers; Guiringaud to Pinay, 4 October 1955, MAE, Série ONU, dossier 546; Aït Ahmed, interview, Lausanne, August 1998.

[26]Dixon to Macmillan, 1 October 1955, Public Record Office (hereafter, PRO), Kew, U.K., PREM 11/902.

[27]267th Meeting of the NSC, 21 November 1955, Dwight D. Eisenhower Library (hereafter, DDEL), Abilene, Kans., Ann Whitman File (hereafter, AWF), NSC Series.

[28]Memorandum of Conversation (Memcon) Root, Bovey, Looram, and Aït Ahmed, 5 December 1955, USNA, RG59, Central Decimal Files, 751S.00; Memcon Aït Ahmed, Bovey, 16 May 1956, ibid.

[29]Memcon Nes, Allen, Ben Bella, Ali Hawazi, 6 December 1955, USNA, RG59, Central Decimal Files, 751S.00; Chase to Dulles, 25 February 1956, USNA, RG59, Central Decimal Files, 751S.00.

[30]See, for instance, Dulles to Dillon, 27 May 1955, *FRUS* 1955–57, vol. 18, 219–20.

[31]Dillon to Dulles, 4 October 1955, *FRUS* 1955–57, vol. 18, 222–24. On the double game, see Pierre Mélandri, "La France et le 'Jeu Double' des États Unis," in *La Guerre d'Algérie et les Français,* ed. Jean-Pierre Rioux (Paris: Fayard, 1990), 429–50.

[32]Dillon to State, 21 February 1956, USNA, RG59, Central Decimal Files, 751S.00. On Morocco's and Tunisia's use of U.S. aid to win greater autonomy from France, see I. William Zartman, *Morocco: Problems of a New Power* (New York: Atherton Press, 1964), 27, and Carol Mae Barker, "The Politics of Decolonization in Tunisia: The Foreign Policy of a New State," (PhD. diss., Columbia University, 1971), 240–41, 349.

[33]Dillon to Dulles, 2 March 1956, *FRUS* 1955–57, vol. 18, 115–16.

[34]Dillon to Dulles, 4 February 1956, USNA, RG59, Central Decimal Files, 751S.00.

[35]Thomas Brady, "Tunisian Rebukes U.S. on Aid Policy," *New York Times,* 11 May 1957, 1, 6.

[36]"Text of Address by Ambassador Dillon on North Africa," *New York Times,* 21 March 1956, 4.

[37]Aït Ahmed to Khider, 7 April 1956, CNAA, GPRA, dossier 1.

[38]Pineau to Mollet, 14 March 1956, MAE, Secrétariat Général, dossier 56; Keith Kyle, *Suez* (London: Weidenfeld and Nicolson, 1991), 116; *L'Année Politique, 1956* (Paris: Presses Universitaires de France, 1957), 279–80.

[39]Al-Dib, *Abdel Nasser,* 120–21; Harbi, *Le FLN: Mirage et Réalité* (Paris: Editions Jeune Afrique, 1980), 174.

[40]Khider to Aït Ahmed and Yazid, 9 May 1956, CNAA, GPRA, dossier 2.

[41]Al-Dib, *Abdel Nasser,* 123–32. It is not clear whether the Egyptians actually offered this deal. But Mollet did publicly reaffirm his opposition to the Baghdad Pact, betraying a commitment to Anthony Eden: Kyle, *Suez,* 116; see also Chauvel to Massigli, 15 March 1956, MAE, René Massigli Papers, vol. 95.

[42]Charles G. Cogan, "The Suez Crisis: Part I, The View from Paris," paper presented at a conference on the Suez Crisis and Its Teachings, American Academy of Arts and Sciences, Cambridge, Mass., 15–16 February 1997, 18.

[43]Matti Golan, *Shimon Peres,* trans. Ina Friedman (London: Wiedenfeld and Nicolson, 1982), 36.

[44]Zachary Karabell, "The Suez Crisis: Part I, The View from Israel," paper presented at a conference on the Suez Crisis and Its Teachings, 14–15; Cogan, "The View from Paris," 18–19. For French intelligence reports that would suggest new—and well-informed—sources, see the unsigned "Note" by Sous-Direction de Tunisie, 5 March 1956, MAE, Cabinet du Ministre, dossier 157, Tunisie; "Note sur les ingérences egyptiennes en Afrique du Nord," 20 October 1956, MAE, Cabinet du Ministre, dossier 155, Algérie, Loi Cadre.

[45]Cogan, "The View from Paris," 17–18; Kyle, *Suez,* 117–18.

[46]Al-Dib, *Abdel Nasser,* 145–49.

[47]Memcon Mollet, Eden, 11 March 1956, *Documents Diplomatiques Français,* 1956, vol. 1, no. 161 (Paris: Imprimerie Nationale, 1988) (hereafter, *DDF,* with year and volume); Cogan, "The View from Paris," 3. See Matthew Connelly, "Taking off the Cold War Lens: Visions of North-South Conflict During the Algerian War for Independence," *American Historical Review* 105 (2000): 739–69, for how images and ideas about Africa and Islam helped to shape French policy.

[48]Bernard Droz and Evelyne Lever, *Histoire de la guerre d'Algérie (1954–1962)* (Paris: Editions du Seuil, 1982), 103.

[49]The platform was released in November 1956 and is reprinted in Tripier, *Autopsie,* 571–601.

[50]Ibid., 578–79, 598–600.

[51]Ibid., 583.

[52]Guy Pervillé, "L'insertion internationale du F.L.N. algérien," *Relations Internationales* 31 (1982): 374, 377; Richard J. Barnet, *Intervention and Revolution: The United States in the Third World,* rev. ed. (New York: Mentor, New American Library, 1972), 316–17.

[53]Tripier, *Autopsie,* 600; Khider to Aït Ahmed; 1 August 1956, CNAA, GPRA, dossier 1; Mabrouk Belhocine, interview, Algiers, December 1999.

[54]Dillon to Dulles, 31 October 1956, USNA, RG59, Central Decimal Files, 651.71.

[55]Memcon Bovey, Abbas et al., 29 November 1956, *FRUS* 1955–57, vol. 18, 255–58; Wall, "The United States, Algeria," 493–94.

[56]Tripier, *Autopsie,* 78–79.

[57]"Directive number 9" (fall 1956), as quoted in Jacques Duchemin, *Histoire du FLN* (Paris: La Table Ronde, 1962), 263–64.

[58]Georges-Picot to Pineau, 4 January 1957, *DDF* 1957, vol. 1, no. 17.

[59]Yves Courrière, *Le Temps des Léopards, La Guerre d'Algérie* (Paris: Fayard, 1970), 2:448–50, 473. See also Tripier, *Autopsie,* 130.

[60]Courrière, *Le Temps des Léopards,* 2:516–17; Henri Alleg, *La guerre d'Algérie* (Paris: Temps actuels, 1981), 2:466–69; Gilles Manceron and Hassan Remaoun, *D'une rive à l'autre: La Guerre d'Algérie de la mémoire à l'histoire* (Paris: Syros, 1993), 177–78.

[61]"Minute" from the Secrétariat des conférences to Georges-Picot, 23 January 1957, MAE, Série ONU, dossier 549.

[62]Douglas Porch, *The French Secret Services: From the Dreyfus Affair to the Gulf War* (New York: Farrar, Straus and Giroux, 1995), 366.

[63]Bureau de New York, "Rapport d'Activité," 18 February 1957, CNAA, GPRA, dossier 4.5; Vaurs to Langlais, 15 March 1958, MAE, MLA, propagande, dossier 1; "Le Cabinet du Ministre Résident et les titres d'ouvrages et de brochures qu'il a diffusé depuis 15 mois" (n.d., but c. early 1957), Archives Nationales, Paris, Bidault Papers, 457AP, box 110.

[64]"Note: La Question Algérienne à la XIeme Session de l'Assemblée Générale," 9 March 1957, MAE, Série ONU, dossier 551.

[65]Alistair Horne, *A Savage War of Peace: Algeria, 1954–1962,* rev. ed. (New York: Penguin, 1987), 224.

[66]De Guiringaud to Pineau, 3 April 1957, *DDF* vol. 1, no. 290; Pineau circular, 13 April 1957, ibid., no. 312.

[67]Baraduc to Gorlin, 22 March 1958, AOM, 12/CAB/234.

[68]Alphand to Pineau, 14 June 1957, MAE, MLA, vol. 23 bis. (provisoire), Action extérieure, Etats-Unis, December 1956–December 1957, Cote EU.

[69]Baraduc to Gorlin, 22 March 1958.

[70]Vaurs to Pineau, 6 October 1958, MAE, Série ONU, dossier 559.

[71]Alphand to Baraduc, 14 June 1957, MAE, Direction Amérique 1952–63, Etats-Unis–Afrique du Nord, dossier 32.

[72]"Note sur le rôle réservé par le F.L.N. à la Presse, au profit de sa propaganda," 11 May 1957, MAE, Série ONU, dossier 544; "Exploitation de la Presse par la Propagande du FLN," n.d., MAE, MLA, propagande, dossier 2; Lebel to Langlais, 16 June 1959, MAE, MLA, vol. 24 (provisoire), Action extérieure, Etats-Unis, January 1958–June 1959, Cote ML 4.

[73]Jones to Dulles, 4 September 1957, *FRUS* 1955–57, vol. 18, 679–80.

[74]Diary entry, 14 November 1957, *FRUS* 1955–57, vol. 18, 758–61. Both the French and the Americans were influenced by their experience with Egypt, which first turned to the Soviets after Washington refused

to deliver new weaponry. For a more extended analysis, see Matthew Connelly, "The Algerian War for Independence: An International History" (Ph.D. diss., Yale University, 1997), 289–311.

[75]Accounts of the Sakiet crisis can be found in Wall, "The United States, Algeria," 503–11, and Matthew Connelly, "The French–American Conflict over North Africa and the Fall of the Fourth Republic," *Revue française d'histoire d'outre-mer* 84 (1997): 20–27.

[76]Tripier, *Autopsie,* 163–66; *L'Année Politique, 1958* (Paris: Presses Universitaires de France, 1959), 249–50.

[77]Mélandri, "La France et le 'Jeu Double'," 429–33; Müller, "Le réalisme de la République fédérale," 418–21; Rainero, "L'Italie entre amitié française et solidarité algérienne," 394–95, all in Rioux, *La Guerre.* Regarding Britain, see Martin Thomas, *The French North African Crisis: Colonial Breakdown and Anglo-French Relations, 1945–62* (New York: St. Martin's Press, 2000).

[78]Dejean to Pineau, 17 March 1958, MAE, Europe 1944–60, URSS, dossier 271.

[79]Alphand to MAE, 5 March 1958, Direction Amérique 1952–63, Etats-Unis–Algérie, dossier 33 (provisoire). On U.S. economic leverage, see Connelly, "French–American Conflict," 9–27.

[80]Beeley to Lloyd, 12 March 1958, PRO, PREM 11/2561.

[81]Houghton to State, 1 May 1958, USNA, RG59, Central Decimal Files, 751.00.

[82]For a discussion of de Gaulle's Algeria policy, see Connelly, "Algerian War," chap. 7.

[83]Ouamrane to the Comité de Coordination et d'Exécution (or CCE, the FLN's highest decision-making body), 8 July 1958, in Harbi, *Les Archives,* 189–93. Regarding Tunisia and Morocco, see the *procès-verbaux* of the June 1958 Tunis conference, reprinted in Harbi, *Les Archives,* 414–26.

[84]The study is reprinted in Hocine Aït Ahmed, *La Guerre et l'Après-guerre* (Paris: Editions de Minuit, 1964), 9–57. In his Introduction, Aït Ahmed doubts that his study ever reached the CCE, but Ouamrane attached it to his report, and its influence is evident in the "Rapport de la Commission gouvernementale sur la Formation d'un Gouvernement provisoire de l'Algérie libre," 6 September 1958, reprinted in Harbi, *Les Archives,* 210–14. Aït Ahmed first suggested forming a provisional government in August 1956: see Khider to Aït Ahmed, 17 August 1956, CNAA, GPRA, dossier 1.

[85]Ouamrane to CCE, 8 July 1958, 191–92; Aït Ahmed, *La Guerre,* 25.

[86]Aït Ahmed, *La Guerre,* 25–29, 33–36, 55.

[87]Parodi to MAE, 18 September 1958, MAE, MLA, Action Extérieure, Maroc, dossier 48.

[88]"Liste des Etats Ayant Reconnu le G.P.R.A.," 22 November 1961, MAE, Secrétariat d'Etat aux Affaires algériennes (hereafter, SEAA), dossier 6.

[89]"Les Animateurs de la Rebellion Algérienne," 16 October 1958, MAE, Série ONU, dossier 560.

[90]See SDECE note number 23754/A in MAE, SEAA, dossier 6, and the "Condense des Renseignements" for Debré, Division Renseignement, Etat-Major général de la défense nationale, 10 November 1959, MAE, MLA, Action Extérieure, R.F.A., dossier 4.

[91]Pervillé, "L'insertion internationale," 375–77. See also Chikh, *L'Algérie en Armes,* 418–19.

[92]The emphasis is in the original: Lakhdar Bentobbal, "Plan d'organisation pour l'Organisation politique," 12 November 1960, CNAA, GPRA, dossier 8.2.

[93]"Les Dépenses du FLN a l'Extérieur de l'Algérie," Delegation Générale du Gouvernement en Algérie, Bureau d'Etudes, 2 May 1960, AOM, 14/CAB/193; "Les Dépenses du FLN a l'Intérieur de l'Algérie," 16 April 1960, AOM, 14/CAB/48.

[94]Jebb, "Record of conversation with General De Gaulle," 20 March 1958, PRO, PREM 11/2339.

[95]"Mr. Dillon's Interview with General de Gaulle on January 10th," attached to Jebb to Lloyd, 18 January 1957, PRO, PREM 11/2338.

[96]De Gaulle to Eisenhower, 17 September 1958, *FRUS* 1958–60, vol. 7, 81–83. Regarding the Algerian motive behind de Gaulle's tripartite proposal, see Connelly, "Algerian War," 380–86, and Irwin M. Wall, "Les Relations Franco-Américaines et la Guerre d'Algérie 1956–1960," *Revue d'Histoire diplomatique* 110 (1996): 79–80.

[97]Mostefai, "Quelques idées sur les tâches actuelles," 22 December 1958, CNAA, GPRA, dossier 5.3; Abbas, "Rapport de Politique Générale," 20 June 1959, idem; "L'Algérie et l'Actualité internationale," c. January 1959, ibid., dossier 8.2.

[98]"Question Algérienne," n.d. (c. January 1959), MAE, Série ONU, dossier 557; Georges-Picot to Couve, 16 December 1958, ibid.

[99]Caccia to Lloyd, 25 October 1958, PRO, PREM 11/3002. For other reasons that the United States would not support de Gaulle on Algeria, see Mélandri, "La France et le 'Jeu Double'," 440–42.

[100]Memcon Herter, Alphand, 3 March 1959, USNA, RG59, Records of the Policy Planning Staff 1957–61, lot 67D548, box 136, France; Lyon to Herter, 6 March 1959, *FRUS* 1958–60, vol. 7, 185–86.

[101]Memcon Debré, Couve et al., 14 March 1959, MAE, Cabinet du Ministre, Cabinet de Couve de Murville, dossier 212bis, Algérie confidentiel. See also "Instruction: Lutte contre les activités du F.L.N. à l'étranger," 2 April 1959, AOM, 14/CAB/177.

[102]Mohamed Bedjaoui, *La Révolution algérienne et le droit* (Brussels: International Association of Democratic Lawyers, 1961), 124–27.

[103]"Note," 8 August 1959, MAE, Secrétariat Général, dossier 60.

[104]Memcon Verdier, Ritter von Lex et al., 18 November 1958, MAE, MLA, Action Extérieure, R.F.A., dossier 2; Seydoux to Couve, 16 April and 22 April 1959, ibid., dossier 3; Porch, *French Secret Services,* 371–72; Müller, "Le réalisme de la République fédérale," 424–28.

[105]Memcon de Gaulle, Castiella, 5 September 1959, MAE, Secrétariat Général, dossier 60.

[106]Alain Peyrefitte, *C'était de Gaulle* (Paris: Fayard, 1994), 59.

[107]Charles de Gaulle, *Discours et Messages: Avec le Renouveau, Mai 1958–Juillet 1962* (Paris: Plon, 1970), 117–23; Jean Lacouture, *De Gaulle: 3. Le Souverain, 1959–1970* (Paris: Editions du Seuil, 1986), 69–71.

[108]417th Meeting of the NSC, 18 August 1959, DDEL, AWF, NSC Series.

[109]"Note: la question à la XIVème session . . . ," 23 July 1959, MAE, Série ONU, dossier 561. See also "Schéma d'un plan d'action," 5 June 1959, ibid.

[110]Tripier, *Autopsie,* 331–38; Harbi, *Le FLN: Mirage,* 244–50; Commandement en Chef des Forces en Algérie, "Evolution de la situation militaire en Algérie," July 1959, Service Historique de l'Armée de Terre (hereafter, SHAT), Paris, 1H, 1751, dossier 2.

[111]Abbas, "Rapport de Politique," 20 June 1959 CNAA, GPRA, dossier 5.8; Yazid to Krim, Bentobal, and Boussouf, "La Politique Nord-Africaine," 6 September 1959, CNAA, GPRA, dossier 17.2.

[112]Essig to Delouvrier, 13 January 1960, AOM, 14/CAB/142.

[113]Debaghine to GPRA, 27 October 1959, CNAA, GPRA, dossier 5.3; Debaghine to GPRA, 17 November 1959, in Harbi, *Les Archives,* 272–74.

[114]Krim, "Notre Politique extérieure et la Guerre froide," 13 March 1960, CNAA, GPRA, dossier 5.3.

[115]Krim, "Note sur Notre Politique Actuelle," "Notre Politique à Moyen Orient," "Note sur Notre Politique dans le bloc Afro-Asiatique," all dated 13 March 1960, CNAA, GPRA, dossier 5.10.

[116]Memcon Krim, Boussouf, Francis, and Ho Long, 1 May 1960, CNAA, GPRA, dossier 5.12.

[117]Ibid. Adda Benguettat and Cherif Guellal, "Rapport," c. March 1958, CNAA, GPRA, dossier 3.3.

[118]Dejean to Couve, 28 May 1960, MAE, MLA, Action Extérieure, URSS, dossier 87.

[119]Dillon to Houghton, 11 October 1960, USNA, RG59, Central Decimal Files, 651.51s.

[120]Abbas to Zhou Enlai, 24 October 1960, in Harbi, *Les Archives,* 527–28; Chauvel to Couve, 27 October 1960, *DDF* 1960, vol. 2, no. 186; Macmillan to Lloyd, 28 October 1960, PRO, FO 371, 147351; Memcon Macmillan, Home, Hassan, 28 October 1960, PRO, PREM 11/3200; Raoul Duval to Couve, 17 November 1960, MAE, Asie-Oceanie 1956–67, Chine, dossier 523.

[121]"Entrevue avec Moulay El Hassan," 21 October 1960, CNAA, GPRA, dossier 8.4; "Rapport du Ministre des Affaires Extérieures sur son Séjour au Maroc," c. October 1960, ibid.

[122]"Note pour le Ministre," 26 October 1960, MAE, Cabinet du Ministre, Cabinet de Couve de Murville, dossier 212bis, Algérie 1959–62; Bérard to Couve, 1 November 1960, ibid.; Alphand to Couve, 3 November 1960, ibid.; De Gaulle, *Discours,* 257–62. It is, of course, difficult to prove that international pressure accounts for this particular decision, and Couve de Murville was at pains to correct the impression that the timing had created—even while admitting to his American counterpart that the policy shift was "in line with your concern": Couve to Herter, 7 November 1960, MAE, Cabinet du Ministre, Cabinet de Couve de Murville, dossier 212bis, Algérie 1959–62. For a more detailed discussion of the importance of international, and especially American, pressure on de Gaulle's policy, see Connelly, "Algerian War," chap. 7 and 8.

[123]Lacouture, *Le Souverain,* 136; Carbonnel to Bérard, 6 October 1960, MAE, Cabinet du Ministre, Cabinet de Couve de Murville, dossier 212bis, Algérie 1959–62.

[124]Memcon Tito, Abbas et al., 12 April 1961, in Harbi, *Les Archives,* 509; Bentobbal, "Directives Générales."

[125]Comité Central de l'Information, "Procès-Verbal," 19 August 1960, AOM, 14/CAB/177; Delegation Générale du Gouvernement en Algérie, Affaires Politiques, "Rapport Mensuel sur l'évolution de la situation générale," 13 September 1960, AOM, 15/CAB/74; Bernard Tricot, *Les Sentiers de la Paix: Algérie 1958/*

1962 (Paris: Plon, 1972), 194; Bentobbal, "Directives Générales"; Richard Mahoney, *JFK: Ordeal in Africa* (New York: Oxford University Press, 1983), 22.

[126]Lacouture, *Le Souverain,* 137–41.

[127]"Note: a/s l'Inde et la question algérienne," 10 March 1961, MAE, Asie 1944 . . . , Inde 1956–67, dossier 248; Bérard to Couve, 21 December 1960, AOM, 15/CAB/149.

[128]Lieutenant-Colonel Thozet, "La Politique du GPRA de la 15o session de l'Assemblée Générale des Nations Unies a l'ouverture des pourparlers d'Evian," 14 June 1961, SHAT, 1H, 1111/3.

[129]Janet Flanner, *Paris Journal,* ed. William Shawn, vol. 2: 1956–65 (New York: Harcourt Brace Jovanovich, 1988), 162.

[130]See, for instance, Joxe to de Gaulle, 3 June 1961, MAE, Cabinet du Ministre, Cabinet de Couve de Murville, dossier 212bis.

[131]Jean Lacouture, *Algérie, La Guerre est finie* (Brussels: Editions Complexe, 1985), 11.

[132]Charles-Robert Ageron, "'L'Algérie dernière chance de la puissance française,' Etude d'un mythe politique (1954–1962)," *Relations internationales* 57 (1989): 113–39.

[133]*Islam in the Modern World and Other Studies* (London: Holt, Rinehart and Winston, 1980), 213–14.

[134]Nelson Mandela, *Long Walk to Freedom* (New York: Little Brown, 1995), 259–60, and testimony at the Rivonia Trial, 1963–64, track 11.1 *Apartheid and the History of the Struggle for Freedom in South Africa,* CD-ROM (Bellville, South Africa: Mayibuye Center, University of the Western Cape, 1993). On Arafat, see Alan Hart, *Arafat: A Political Biography* (London: Sidgwick & Jackson, 1994), 102–104, 112–13, 129–30; Barry Rubin, *Revolution Until Victory? The Politics and History of the PLO* (Cambridge: Harvard University Press, 1994), 7, 10. On Algiers as a Mecca, see John P. Entelis, *Algeria: The Revolution Institutionalized* (Boulder, Colo.: Westview Press, 1986), 189.

[15]

Decolonising 'French Universalism': Reconsidering the Impact of the Algerian War on French Intellectuals

JAMES D. LE SUEUR

Introduction

More than any other colonial confrontation, the French-Algerian War (1954–62) forcibly demonstrated North Africa's impact on a major European power. The war in Algeria triggered a series of events that toppled the Fourth Republic, affected intellectual life and destroyed long-standing myths about the universality of French culture. On a grand scale, therefore, the decolonisation of Algeria forced a fundamental reconsideration of politics, the status of intellectuals and the role of French culture in the world. This reconsideration had, in fact, become so extreme that by the conclusion of the war in March 1962, the French nation was suffering from an unprecedented identity crisis. In short, the French-Algerian War and the process of decolonisation disrupted France and French perceptions of France on a level not seen since the German Occupation and, one can argue, even since the French Revolution. Unquestionably, France and Algeria continue to feel the repercussions of this 'uncivil war', and historians have only just begun to delve seriously into this troubled past. Recent brazen admissions of torture by French generals such as Paul Aussaresses and Jacques Massu have renewed national and international debates over how historians of modern France and the French government ought to proceed.[1]

Due to the severity and the importance of the Algerian crisis, there is a sense of urgency to research on the French-Algerian War because it continues to affect France and Algeria, and by extension Europe and North Africa. Furthermore, because the legacy of decolonisation is seldom effortlessly forgotten, memory of the war will continue to pass from national history into national mythology. This is most certainly the case with regard to Algeria because the legacy of the war and decolonisation reverberate in contemporary debates over historiography, language, ethnicity, immigration, gender relations, political ideology, morality, torture, violence and religion. The

Moroccan-born novelist and writer Tahar Ben Jelloun best characterises the extent of this legacy in his recent book *French Hospitality: Racism and North African Immigration*:

> Between France and Algeria, a memory still survives. But it is not a healthy one. It is a wounded part of a shared history that has not managed to accept reality. Neither the war of liberation nor the independence that followed have really been recorded in the great book of French history. A kind of amnesia affects that part of the story of decolonisation, which has been stated but not assimilated into France's social and political awareness.[2]

For intellectual and cultural historians of France, the Algerian War is thus one of the most important moments of the twentieth century. French intellectuals' responses to the war and to the changes it brought became such a strident feature of everyday life in the *métropole* that it would be impossible to present an accurate portrait of the post-World War II era without weaving the colours of the Algerian debates into France's social fabric. Yet, despite the seminal place the war and decolonisation occupy in the tapestry of modern France, a proper assessment of its impact on the life-world of intellectuals has suffered much neglect. In part, this is attributable to a noticeable tendency among many historians of twentieth-century France (until recently) to marginalise colonial history, or to write the history of French decolonisation following a core-periphery model. This core-periphery model tends to view decolonisation through the lens of convenient notions of colonial hegemony – Eurocentric by nature and superficial by deed. This lens projects France's image onto the passive colonies, as receptacles of French ideas, politics and problems. Some efforts have been made to correct this imbalance, such as Robert Malley's *The Call from Algeria* (1996). This chapter is meant to complement and extend this and other praiseworthy efforts to reverse the optics in the writing of history about Algeria and France.

In many ways, however, my chapter is unconventional. In it I will illustrate how the French-Algerian War transcended military and political concerns but its goal is not to illuminate France's impact on Algeria and the Maghreb but rather the war's impact on French intellectuals. Ultimately, this means that we must be prepared to see colonialism and decolonisation as a dialogical process, where historians chart the pathways of communication between two or more interlocutors (or communities), rather than as a monologue where subservient and mute colonies listen to the humdrum voice of European colonial powers. Having said that, I must issue a caveat here: this article does not focus on the relationship between Algerian intellectuals and French intellectuals. Rather, it investigates the relationship between the war in

Algeria and French intellectuals. Specifically, it will demonstrate how the war determined, undermined and, in many cases, set the parameters of debates in France over identity and intellectual legitimacy for French intellectuals.

In short, I believe that an understanding of the period of decolonisation – especially the decolonisation of French Algeria, which after all was the only French overseas possession actually administrated (from 1848) as if it were three regular French provinces – should provide historians with a useful vantage point from which to view one of the most important questions – if not the most important question of the modern period – the question of identity. It is no accident that the decolonisation of French Algeria triggered a fundamental re-evaluation of French (especially French intellectual) identity.

By 1954, when the war of liberation began, after 124 years of colonisation, the French population in Algeria numbered almost 1 million, the Muslim population about 8 million. The transition away from European colonial hegemony was especially poignant for France. More than other European states, decolonisation threw metropolitan France into severe political and economic crises. The reasons for this are clear: its colonial 'superpower' status had become part and parcel with French national identity; France had a large settler population in Algeria; the military was still reeling from its recent, stinging defeat in Indo-China; and many French politicians and intellectuals continued to insist on France's civilising mission and the universalism of French culture. For over a hundred years French colonial theorists had applied enormous pressure on the national community to affirm that civilising mission and to ensure that colonialism and universalism would be the measure of French national eminence. This, of course, would have grave consequences during the era of decolonisation.

The importance of decolonisation is no doubt attributed to the fact that the process of decolonisation overlapped with (and perhaps even triggered) the issues posed by postmodernism. Decolonisation – as a cultural and intellectual phenomenon – highlighted the ambiguities and strains in the traditional boundaries between the observer and the observed. In other words, decolonisation upset the colonial imbalance and threw the European world-view into chaos. As Martin Evans explains:

> Decolonisation revealed the world as fluid, decomposing, recomposing and changing and destroyed the historical certainties that underpinned the imperialist preconceptions of the world. The emergence of liberation movements in Indochina and North Africa turned the colonial world upside down, and revealed its myths as historical and cultural, rather than natural and eternal. Suddenly, colonised peoples, whom imperialism had confined to the margins of history as inert objects,

> showed themselves to be dynamic subjects capable of overthrowing French colonialism.[3]

In other words, the effects of decolonisation on the French intellectuals' conceptions of selfhood very closely resembled the transformative effects that modernity once had on pre-modern conceptions of the identity.

In order to underscore why decolonisation was so important for France, I would like to consider a claim Charles Taylor (1992) has made in his recent book, *Multiculturalism and the 'Politics of Recognition'*.[4] According to Taylor, modern conceptions of personal identity emerged following the collapse of the Old Regime's rigid and fixed social categories. In other words, Taylor locates the emergence of the modern self at the crisis point when the static categories of social ranking gave way to the pressures of modernity. It is possible to apply the mechanics of this same theory to the decomposition of the colonial world. Because colonialism implied relatively static categories of identity (with some important exceptions), there was a stable sense of the French national identity *vis-à-vis* Algeria during the colonial era.[5] There were also pragmatic aspects of this identity. For example, in Algeria, all but a handful of elite Muslims were literally considered second-class citizens. Europeans, in the same French 'provinces', were legally and socially 'superior'. It follows, using Taylor's remarks about identity, that decolonisation – like modernity in Europe – would force a fundamental reconsideration of the idea of self, both in France and in Algeria.

It also follows that French intellectuals reflecting on this changing identity ushered in by decolonisation would pay a heavy price for theorising about French and Algerian identity during the war. For example, in an interview I conducted with the French philosopher, Paul Ricoeur, he stated that the French-Algerian War was enormously important for French intellectuals because it unleashed a crisis of French identity. But why did it do so? Because the war and the whole process of decolonisation challenged the seminal assumption about French culture. In Ricoeur's words, the war forced an 'honest coming to terms' with the fact that French culture was not 'universal'.[6] In a very profound sense, decolonisation in North Africa set the terms by which the entire French nation (and especially intellectuals) could adjust to a scaled-down post-colonial world devoid of France's civilising mission.

It must also be noted that, on the political level, the French – especially the intellectuals – seldom agreed with one another anyway, and the French Fourth Republic was exceptionally fragile when the war broke out on 1 November 1954. Struggles among communists, non-communists, Marxists, non-Marxists, liberals and non-liberals were common-place within the patchwork of French national politics. The Vichy purges of the Nazi collaborators and the beginnings of the Cold War only served to accentuate these debates. However, struggle or no struggle, one idea in which many French intellectuals continued to believe explicitly or implicitly was *French* universalism. The notion of French universalism also formed the bedrock of French colonial policy, especially in Algeria. It was this universalism (a product of the French Revolution and the Enlightenment), ironically, that, according to historians, allowed many intellectuals to waiver uncomfortably on the Algerian question because French colonialism in Algeria simultaneously contradicted and affirmed universalist intentions and ideals.

While French and Algerian intellectuals rethought the question of national and personal identity, tried to comprehend the loss of *French* universalism, and attempted to understand the national significance of the demise of French power overseas, the French-Algerian War also presented them with a unique opportunity to re-assert intellectual legitimacy. At the very least the war opened doors to new paradigms of identity politics. After all, crisis can be a time of enormous productivity, and this was certainly the case for French intellectuals. The desire to reassert intellectual legitimacy was no doubt due to the fact that the war erupted at the precise moment when French intellectuals, especially the French left, realised that it was entering a period of crisis.[7] Violence, identity and the question of intellectual legitimacy, therefore, forced intellectuals during the war to make a choice: either situate their privileged status as intellectuals within the new France, the post-colonial France, or attach their status as intellectuals to an empire in peril. Very few intellectuals (Jacques Soustelle is among the important exceptions) opted for the latter.[8]

To best demonstrate how the war in Algerian impacted French intellectuals, I have chosen to focus on two episodes of heightened intellectual activity during the war: the formation of the anti-colonial movement in 1955 called the Comité d'Action des Intellectuels contre la Poursuite de la Guerre en Afrique du Nord (hereafter referred to as the Comité) and the actions of a group of avant-garde intellectuals, the so-called 'Jeanson Network', accused of treason in 1960 for aiding the Front de Libération Nationale (FLN).[9] I am aware that the Comité and the Jeanson Network do not speak for the totality and complexity of the war, and that Algerian voices are generally not present here, but I have selected these issues as important examples of how the decolonisation of French Algeria conditioned debates among intellectuals over legitimacy and identity in France. I have addressed the issue of the war's impact on Algerian intellectuals elsewhere.[10]

Anti-colonialism and Intellectual Identity

On 5 November 1955, in the Salle Wagram (an important auditorium and meeting hall in Paris), the Comité was founded by Dionys Mascolo and Louis-René Des Forêts, Robert Antelme and Edgar Morin with this telling statement: 'In addressing ourselves against this war [in Algeria], we defend our own proper principles and liberties. The war in North Africa puts, in fact, the Republic in danger'.[11] Understanding that events in Algeria directly impacted political life in France, the Comité's four initiators wanted to assemble something similar to a federation of intellectuals which would fight against the colonial regime and underscore the group's independence from political parties.[12] Their success was astonishing. In a very short time, they succeeded in collecting the signatures of hundreds of writers, artists,[13] professors and journalists on their first manifesto.[14] The signers of the manifesto called for all other like-minded intellectuals and writers to join them in their 'just cause' and their struggle against repression, racism, blocked negotiations, and for the liberation of the continent of Africa.[15]

It was a force to be reckoned with, but soon after it was formed, the Comité's anticolonial agenda provoked a heated and thoughtful debate with Jacques Soustelle, the last governor general of Algeria (from 1955–56) about intellectual legitimacy. It was certainly no accident that Soustelle, the man who led the charge against this anti-colonial Comité, was also one of France's pre-eminent anthropologists. Yet, as an anthropologist, Soustelle was incredibly Eurocentric and believed himself to incarnate the virtues of modern France. As an intellectual, Soustelle unquestionably privileged the French nation as a bearer of progress and civilisation and made no apologies for it. Additionally, he believed that French technology, progress, science and rationality was superior to the Algerians' indigenous culture and religion, Islam, which he distrusted. Hence, in his press release issued on 7 November 1955, Soustelle challenged the anti-colonial Comité's right to speak for the Algerian nationalists' cause and to address the public as intellectuals. He followed this bold claim with a piece published in *Combat* on 26 November, which he poignantly called 'A Letter of an Intellectual to a Few Others'. This was not a response to the Comité per se but rather to a few intellectuals, whom Soustelle considered his intellectual peers.[16] Soustelle stated that as an academic he maintained his firm belief in the value of thought, research and intellectual engagement. On the other hand, he argued, the Comité had substituted 'vague passionate images' (of anticolonialism) for the rigors worthy of the intellectual's profession.[17] In addition, Soustelle continued, this (or any) anticolonial movement was bound to be careless and dishonest. Intellectuals, he wrote, were 'only justified if they behave in this instance and more than ever as intellectuals, that is to say with concern for honesty and clarity which are in some respects our mark'.[18]

The following week on 3 December 1955, the Comité published its 'Response to the Governor General of Algeria'. In self-defence, the Comité characterised intellectuals as those who can use 'scientific rigor' in order to analyse a situation as complicated as that of Algeria.[19] The Comité confronted Soustelle with his failure as a professional intellectual to see the French role in the conflict, for misrepresenting the historical dimensions of colonialism and for escalating violence through his policy of repression. Furthermore, it claimed that Soustelle had forfeited his intellectual legitimacy by insisting that the conflict's violence originated with the Algerians.[20] Soustelle's silence on the reasons for Algerian nationalists' violence deformed the French intellectuals' identity. This was especially true since French intellectuals needed to be honest about colonialism: 'Who rapes, pillages, kills, massacres and tortures, in effect, in Algeria? The French authorities, isn't it?'[21]

The Comité therefore defended Algerians by distancing itself from the practices of French colonialism (especially those of Soustelle), and in an effort to drive the legitimacy wedge between colonialists and anticolonialists intellectuals, it opened the topic of torture. Evoking the wounds of the Nazi era, the Comité asserted that France had become a '*régime concentrationnaire*' in Algeria and this pervaded all levels of the French bureaucracy, police and administration.[22] France needed to stop this fascist, colonial behaviour immediately. The Comité called on Soustelle (as a politician, but not as an intellectual) to commission an inquiry into the reported human rights' violations in Algeria. If this were not done, and since violence was systematic, the French military and civilians would be guilty of collective assassinations.[23] Only if Soustelle had the courage to face the horrors of colonialism, could the truth come out and could France and Algeria remain on good terms. The Comité stated, '[t]he path that we want to see our country take is neither abandonment nor war: it is that of co-operation in friendship and confidence between two peoples equal in responsibilities and dignity'.[24]

Naturally enough, Soustelle continued with business as usual. As governor general, Soustelle tried to implement his key policy, that of integration. Without question there was a deep-seated paternalism in Soustelle's policy and a very stable sense of French authority. Consider for a moment a 'declaration' he delivered on Radio-Algérie in January 1956, which illuminates his Panglossian view of French colonialism:

> For Algeria's own good, she must stay French. Algeria without France would mean poverty in countless ways. Who else in the world would replace what France gives to Algeria? Who else would replace the

> millions of francs that Algerian workers send from metropolitan France? Foreigners who encourage the rebellion or who give advice to France are interested in Algeria only because they want to drill oil wells and dig mines there, but they are not interested in building roads or constructing schools. I say that the separation of Algeria and France would be for Algeria, and especially for its Muslim people, the worst of all catastrophes. Secession is ruin. ...

And he continued:

> Neither directly nor indirectly, through whatever form it may be, will I allow secession. As long as I am responsible here, as long as I am in charge of Algeria, everyone, friends and adversaries alike, should know that I will not consent to anything which will distance Algeria from France. ...[25]

In other words, to Soustelle's understanding, France and Algeria could never be separated; colonialism was the best of all possible worlds; there was no solution for Algeria outside of France; the Algerian Muslims were, in a sense, capable of being true citizens because they were slowly being Westernised by French civilisation.

As Soustelle asserted his role as a political leader to the Muslim and European population in Algeria, the epistolary polemic continued between him and the Comité. On 10 January 1956, the Comité re-issued its call for authentic intellectual activity by stating that when it came to colonialism, intellectuals and governmental authority were incompatible. It was therefore 'sadly comical' to engage in a polemic with a governor general masked in an intellectual's uniform.[26] And it was 'comical' because Soustelle had tried to preserve the respect due to him as an intellectual while simultaneously upholding the intellectually and morally dubious policies of the French government in North Africa – especially the practice of so-called concentration camps in Algeria; furthermore, it was 'sad' because this cost lives and paralleled attempts by the German Gestapo to cover its systematic tortures with propaganda. Soustelle and men like him simply corrupted France from within, which was as dangerous to the French nation as collaboration had been. Soustelle had become a propagandist. That was all. Hence, by becoming a vehicle of an oppressive state, Soustelle forfeited his privileged status as a French intellectual. '[Soustelle had] not known how to remain an intellectual, according to the intellectuals', the Comité argued, because he had transgressed the border separating intellectuals from the state. In other words, Governor General Soustelle's role as a propagator of colonial warfare and a de facto defender of torture removed him categorically from the

Decolonising 'French Universalism'

FIGURE 1
PARALYSED ON THE LEFT SIDE

Note: One of several cartoon postcards created between 1958 and 1961 by Siné (Maurice Sinet).
Source: Courtesy of Maurice Sinet.

roster of legitimate French intellectuals even before he was replaced as governor general by the new resident minister Robert Lacoste in 1956.[27]

In effect, the Comité had won the battle with Soustelle for the right of anti-colonialists to call themselves intellectuals. The Comité-Soustelle debate was one of the first important signs of how the war would affect the composition of intellectuals within the *métropole*. However, a simple question still remained. Could the Comité sustain its cohesion and its monopoly of intellectual legitimacy given its diversity of intellectual and political commitments? In other words, could the Comité sustain its cohesion and its monopoly of intellectual legitimacy given the diversity of its constituency?

The limits of a unified anti-colonialist movement were soon tested as the Comité's intellectuals dealt with divisions within Algerian nationalism itself. Choosing which Algerian nationalist group to support – the FLN or Messali Hadj's MNA (the Movement National Algérien) – undermined unity by raising the issue of whether the Comité as a group could determine orthodox anti-colonialism.[28] Put differently, could the Comité legitimately endorse one form of Algerian nationalism over another? Inevitably, the question of Algerian nationalism directly impacted the unity of the anti-colonialist movement in France.

Discord Within the Comité: Is There an Orthodox Anti-colonialism?

Aside from the general agreement that France was inevitably intertwined with the events in Algeria, the question of choosing sides created deep fissures which ran the length of the French intellectual community. Yes, the Comité had proved itself to be firmly on the ground of intellectual legitimacy because it had so far shown that it would stand up for universal justice and equality, but where would this newly created federation of intellectuals go from here? How could it move from theory to practice? In this next phase, this struggle to create a praxis of anticolonialism, the Comité was not coherent and proved incapable of finding a comprehensive position. This paralysis was not entirely its fault; there were several important phenomena simply beyond its control: the problem of violence in Algeria, Cold War politics and other domestic affairs. However, the issue of choosing sides in the conflict between rival Algerian nationlist groups nearly destroyed the Comité.

Importantly, the Comité tended to side with the FLN for various reasons, and the preference of the Comité's leaders for FLN over the MNA created the first crack in the wall of a united anticolonial front.[29] There are many examples of this, but one striking one occurred when two Comité members, Francis and Colette Jeanson, published their *L'Algérie hors la loi,* a book favouring the FLN. Immediately, another prominent Comité member, the *pied noir* journalist, Jean Daniel, attacked their endorsement in an article called 'Between Sorrow and Shrugged Shoulders'. Daniel criticised the Jeansons for making it appear that the FLN was the only Algerian nationalist movement French intellectuals could support. And, Daniel correctly predicted that choosing sides in the Algerian nationalist question would destabilise the anticolonial movement. But this was demonstrative of another, more dangerous concern. Daniel insisted that in choosing sides, Francis Jeanson was guilty of the same sin as Soustelle because 'Jeanson believed himself to incarnate Algeria'.[30] In other words, the Jeansons' self-arrogation of the position of a legitimate anti-colonialist intellectual illustrated a larger problem that would henceforth colour all leftist intellectuals' discussions of Algeria. As Daniel put it: 'There is now an orthodox anti-colonialism just as there is an orthodox communism. The dogma of this orthodoxy is not the well-being of the colonised but the mortification of the colonisers'.[31] In this sense, Daniel claimed, Jeanson's solidarity with the FLN evidenced bad faith because the Jeansons were acting as if they were uniquely 'qualified to give out certificates of Algerian patriotism to the Algerians of [their] choice'.[32]

On 26 January, the well-known anarchist writer, Daniel Guérin, published a similar critique of the Jeansons' work in the interest of 'public opinion'.[33] Beginning with praise for what he considered a courageous and over-due book on Algeria, Guérin attacked its treatment, 'without any attempt at impartiality', of the diverse tendencies of the Algerian revolutionaries.[34] According to Guérin, the Jeansons' wilful omission of Messali Hadj, claimed by many to be the father of Algerian nationalism, was unjustified and unfounded.

Francis Jeanson responded to Jean Daniel, but not to Guérin, in an unpublished but semi-open letter. Knowing that *L'Express* would not publish it, he had copies printed and sent to approximately 100 'well chosen' Parisian intellectuals.[35] Jeanson argued that membership in the Comité should produce reciprocal respect for individual intellectual differences.[36] However, Jeanson chastised Daniel for pretending that a real political force existed inside Algeria other than the FLN. As a result, Jeanson defended himself against Daniel's charge that he was dividing the French left with radical, orthodox, anti-colonial politics. The time had come, Jeanson contended, to choose between Algerian resistance organisations because there were only two forces left in Algeria: the army and the resistance (*maquisards*). Fence-sitting at this point only played into the hands of neo-colonialism disguised as current anti-colonialism.

Ironically, however, the death blow to the Comité came not with disagreements within the Comité over which nationalist position to take *vis-à-vis* war in Algeria, or even over which nationalist group to endorse, but with the Soviet army's suppression of the Hungarian nationalists in November 1956. On 23 October 1956, students at Budapest University set off a national uprising by demonstrating for national independence. Within five days, the country was almost completely liberated from the Soviets. But, by 4 November, the Soviet tanks had entered the capital, and Igmar Nagy, the leader of the independence movement, first sought refuge in the Yugoslav Embassy but was soon captured and deported to Romania. The Soviet suppression of Nagy's movement created a problem for French intellectuals: as they sought to adjust to the shifting sands of universalism, the anti-colonialist intellectuals, during their debates with Soustelle, had made a convincing argument about the need to condemn colonialism around the globe based on universal principles. In fact, the Comité had made the universalism of the French republican 'Rights of Man' ideology the hallmark of its crusade against colonialism in North Africa and the foundation stone of intellectual legitimacy. However, Nagy's arrest and deportation – and the arrest of hundreds of opposition intellectuals by the Soviet regime – forced the Comité once again to rethink its own legitimacy because the universalism of its message would again be called into question if its members did not unilaterally condemn this new Soviet imperialism. To understand the full import of this catch-22 position, it is helpful to recall the intent of the founders of the Comité. Embittered by the ineffectual partisan politics of the post-WWII era, the initiators wanted to keep the Comité apolitical. However, after the Soviets smashed Hungary's democratic uprising as the world looked on, it was clear that politics could not be kept out of the Comité. Communist or non-communist sympathising intellectuals faced an incredible dilemma: would they criticise or break away from the Communist Party in order to save the Comité from disgrace?

The first move by important members of the Comité came on 8 November 1956, when the directors of the left-oriented *France observateur* published its text 'Against Soviet Intervention'.[37] Those who signed the text agreed that 'socialism' could not be 'introduced with bayonets'.[38] On 9 November 1956, in an article for *L'Express,* Sartre denounced the crimes of Budapest: 'I entirely and without any reservations condemn the Soviet aggression. Without making the Soviet people responsible, I repeat that its current government has committed a crime ... which today goes beyond the Stalinism that has already been denounced'.[39]

If the effects of taking sides with different Algerian nationalist movements already put the intellectual unity of members of the Comité on shaky ground, Budapest was the ultimate and most destructive test of whether the universal foundations of anti-colonialism, as embodied in the Comité, could withstand both internal and external scrutiny. The executive head of the Comité discussed its position *vis-à-vis* Hungary, and on 21 November the Comité asked its members to choose from among three possible responses to Budapest: 1) to concentrate on fighting against the war in Algeria, despite the similarities between the Soviet suppression of Hungary and French pacification of Algeria; 2) to condemn, with equal force, the war in Algeria and the repression of Budapest; 3) not only to condemn, without reserve, the force used in Hungary, but to demand that all members of the Comité announce publicly their condemnation of the Soviet Union.[40]

Reactions were diverse but resulted in the dissolution of the Comité. For example, Jean-Marie Domenach, the editor of the moderate left Christian journal *Esprit,* admitted that the events of Budapest posed questions 'of logic, of coherence, and of morality'.[41] Knowing that the success of his journal depended on public opinion, Domenach continued, it was not possible for him to continue collaborating with a committee, which did not publicly condemn the Soviet intervention in Hungary. Then, in a general meeting of the Comité on 26 November, Daniel Guérin spoke out against denouncing the Soviet suppression because, unlike Domenach, he argued that it was a 'bad idea' to risk destroying a committee whose 'unique mission was to continue to struggle against the war in Algeria'.[42] Sartre also started his own petition to voice opposition to the Soviet suppression of Budapest.[43]

Decolonising 'French Universalism'

Ironically, Budapest helped destroy the Comité by separating the Comité from its original objective, which was to fight against the war in Algeria.[44] Understandably, the Comité's founders were dismayed at its sudden downfall. Edgar Morin recounted its paralysing effect: 'It was not possible to denounce French imperialism in Algeria, without denouncing something analogous to what the Soviet Union was doing in Hungary'.[45] In his private notes just after Budapest and in reference to the attempt to call for a meeting of the Comité to denounce Budapest, Dionys Mascolo asked himself ironically: would a vocal communist member of the Comité participate today in a 'meeting for the right of people to dispose of themselves' against a communist regime with the same level of commitment as he displayed in attacking French policy in Algeria? 'Sinister joke ... Now the Comité is paralysed by the smallest possibility of talking tomorrow of the people's right to dispose of themselves'.[46] Mascolo then asked the communists to leave the Comité in order for it to continue its war against colonialism.[47] Seeing the damage that the communists' refusal to leave had caused to the Comité, he resigned on 11 November 1956, and he wrote the following:

> It is not only odious, it is ridiculous to protest against the arrest of a few militant anticolonists in the company of men who elect to treat the workers, soldiers, and intellectuals in the Hungarian insurrection as fascists just as Soustelle and the traitors of the socialist government of the official France call the Algerian militants terrorists and bandits. I am not sectarian, but anticolonialism should be total: It is a principle.[48]

Budapest, however, was not an isolated incident of discord among the members. It merely pushed the left-oriented Comité over the precipice. The Comité's assumed universalism and unity ensured by the open battles with Soustelle suddenly dissipated as it confronted a new species of imperialists: the Soviets. By late 1956, the French-Algerian War and other world events momentarily rendered it impossible to unify intellectual identity and orient public opinion through such a large organ as the Comité, and many French intellectuals asked themselves if they would have a chance to restore universalism.

The Jeanson Network, or the Treason of the French 'Self'?

For some of the important members of the Comité the answer was, yes, there would be another chance, but this chance would come with the aid of the FLN, and it would radicalise the idea of intellectual engagement and challenge the very idea of universalism. Francis Jeanson, for example, took the initiative to mobilise the French left, or 'avant-garde' intellectuals, as he called them. After the Comité dissolved, Jeanson went underground and created a sophisticated network which provided weapons, money and supplies to the FLN. Eventually, he attracted a large group of committed intellectuals who followed him into clandestineness. It was his affiliation with the FLN that eventually drove him underground in 1957.[49]

Jeanson's decision to enter into an alliance with the FLN was therefore taken with two primary objectives in mind: 1) ending the war in Algeria by supporting the only effective Algerian revolutionary movement, and 2) unifying the French left in order to save French democracy. This unity was particularly important because the principal issue for the French left was no longer merely cultural and political reconciliation with the Algerians. Rather, many leftist intellectuals wanted to use the idea of universal revolutionary activity – embodied in the Algerian FLN – as a means to re-unite the fragmented left in order to secure individual and collective freedoms.

In making this co-operation between the revolutionary French and Algerian public, Jeanson believed that he could foster intellectual engagement based not only on 'theoretical' concerns but also on those 'inscribed within an everyday context'. In other words, French intellectuals' calls to end the Algerian war would make it possible to bridge the gap between 'action' and 'practical reflection' by illustrating to the French public that there really was 'something to do' for the Algerians.[50] Aware that the consequence of taking the FLN's side would lead to the charge of treason, Jeanson claimed that the charge was false because, according to France's official rhetoric, the rebellion was merely a civil war in which the Algerians were considered 'French citizens'.[51] But the crime of collaborating with these 'French citizens' (the FLN) was worth the penalty, he claimed, if the alternative was to admit that he belonged to the same community of men as General Massu and Prime Minister Debré.[52] Moreover, since it was indisputable in 1960 that the Algerians would achieve political independence and that France was heading toward fascism by prolonging the war, he argued that it was in France's political interest to guarantee future relations with the Algerian government.[53] The dual purpose, saving France and ensuring that the French would not be condemned '*en bloc*' as fascists by the Algerians after independence, would forge a future Franco-Algerian solidarity.[54]

In the May 1960 issue of *Esprit*, Jean Daniel disagreed with the French avant-garde's position on the FLN, which endorsed violence. 'Violence', he claimed, 'had posed the problem; it did not suffice to solve it.'[55] As for the commitment of the French left, Daniel wrote that it wanted to profit from the revolutionary spirit of Algerian nationalism and this 'intellectual slippage was very perceivable'.[56] As a result, Daniel continued, the French avant-garde left had overlooked fundamental and disturbing facts about Algerian nationalists in order to blindly 'sacralise' the FLN as a revolutionary movement.[57] This activity of the French left was no better than 'Stalinist intellectuals [who] sacralised the Communist Party'.[58]

Les Temps modernes replied to Daniel.[59] Admitting that it desired the unification of the left with the FLN, Sartre's journal stated that it was important not to accept de Gaulle's version of peace with Algeria because: 'if de Gaulle makes peace, it will be good for the Algerians, but bad for the left'.[60] The real problem was simple: 'Peace ... did not justify the Gaullist order'.[61]

The so-called 'Jeanson Network' was discovered in early 1960.[62] In total, 23 members of the network, 17 French and six Muslims were arrested, while five – including Jeanson – managed to avoid arrest.[63] The network's trial, which began on 5 September 1960 and lasted for months, provoked an unprecedented national debate on the limits of intellectual engagement and the impact of the war on France and the intellectual community.[64] It forced avant-garde leftist intellectuals to face the legal charge of treason, which the anti-colonial Comité never confronted. Eventually, nine members of the Jeanson network were acquitted; 15 (including Jeanson and four others still at large) were sentenced to the maximum sentence which was ten years and 70,000 NF in fines, and three others received less severe penalties. Perhaps, it was just this charge of treason that created the greatest fissures within the French intellectual community. Yet, for Jeanson's supporters there was a common cause: motivating French public opinion against the war in Algeria and using the possibility of a civil war in France to rejuvenate the French left.

Out of this changing relationship among the members of the French left and between the French and Algerians, a central question emerged: whose war was the French-Algerian War? Jeanson himself tried to answer this question with his *Notre guerre*, published at the end of 1960 because he realised that the war had called French identity into question. It was, Jeanson wrote, in order 'to really be French' that intellectuals like him were 'now working to reconstitute a national community' by fighting alongside the FLN.[65] Hence, the question was not whether or not the war was a French or Algerian one, but rather how the French could engage in the war which was not their own on the side of the Algerians in order to reconstruct their own national community without becoming any less French? Jeanson did not deny the implicit risk of losing one's French identity during the struggle. In Jeanson's words, those working with the Algerians 'faced two inverse risks: that of being so accepted that we become submerged, absorbed, lost, Algerianised; and that of being rejected for having kept our distance'.[66] The network members tried to account for this, he said, by attempting 'to be totally *with*, and in consequence, totally *ourselves* ... For three years, we have worked *for* the FLN ... *without being "under its orders", or without being "for sale"*'.[67] Hence, the problem for the French was to show solidarity with the Algerians and yet maintain their autonomy from the Algerians.

As for the charge that the French involved in the Jeanson network were betraying their national community, Jeanson claimed that '*the real TREASON* was the renunciation – active or passive – of the profound resources of the country, the only chance to realise an effective community, of everything that can, in the end, constitute a real showing of France at work'.[68] It was only by working for the conclusion of a warranted peace, a real peace, which could assure a continued co-operation and friendship between the French and Algerians, that the 'Gaullist magic' could be dispelled. That was the true meaning of the war for France. It was, in fact, according to Jeanson, the only way to restore France's real significance in the world. In other words, if France did not live up to its intellectual and moral heritage, which was founded on the universal principles of equality and fraternity, it would never be in a position to recover its status as a world leader, nor would its intellectuals be able to hold their heads high. And, for the avant-garde French left, trapped by de Gaulle's illegitimate rise to power in 1958, trapped by the illegalities of the French army and the unstoppable use of torture and mass killing, trapped also by their own desire to take an active role in a revolution that was not their own, the paradox was obvious: how could the French avant-garde left not be, as Jeanson said, 'Algerianised' through its involvement in the Algerian Revolution?

In this sense, following Charles Taylor's argument cited above, the French-Algerian War was the ultimate litmus test for French intellectuals who were placed in the awkward position of defending the universal values of their personal, collective and national identities on the one hand, and, on the other hand, siding with a people who largely denied this universalism. It was unquestionably a cruel paradox: to affirm and subvert at the same time. This is certainly what Paul Ricoeur had in mind when he stated that the decolonisation of French Algeria provoked a national crisis the likes of which had not been seen since the Enlightenment and the demise of the Old Regime. To affirm by subversion, this was for intellectuals such as Jeanson, the only truly orthodox anti-colonial position. Finally, what is particularly significant about this period and these series of transformations is that they unleashed intellectual and ideological processes and positions that eventually heralded the advent and the crisis of the post-modern intellectual.

Decolonising 'French Universalism'

ACKNOWLEDGEMENTS

Sections of this article will appear in James D. Le Sueur, *Uncivil War: Intellectuals and Identity Politics During the Decolonisation of Algeria* (Philadelphia: University of Pennsylvania Press 2001). I wish to thank Julia Clancy-Smith and John Ruedy for inviting me to participate in 'The Maghrib in World History' conference in Tunis in 1998 during which this article was first presented. I would also like to thank Jean Daniel and the late Dionys Mascolo for allowing me to consult their private papers.

NOTES

1. See 'Je me suis resolu à la torture ... J'ai moi-même procédé à des executions sommaires', *Le Monde*, 24 Nov. 2000; 'Si la France reconnaissait et condamnait ces pratiques, je prendrais cela pour une avancée'. Entretien avec le général Jacques Massu, vainqueur de la bataille d'Alger, *Le Monde*, 22 Nov. 2000; and General Aussaresses, *Service Spéciaux Algérie*, 1955, 1957 (Saint-Amand-Montrond: Perrin, 2001).
2. Tahar Ben Jellloun, *French Hospitality: Racism and North African Immigrants*, trans. Barbara Bray (New York: Columbia University Press 1999) p.11.
3. Martin Evans, 'The French Army and the Algerian War: Crisis of Identity' in Michael Scriven and Peter Wagstaff (eds.), *War and Society in Twentieth Century France* (New York: Berg 1991) pp.152–3.
4. See Charles Taylor, *Multiculturalism and the 'Politics of Recognition'* (Princeton: Princeton University Press 1992).
5. Those who come most readily to mind are intellectuals who one could call colonial/cultural hybrids such as Albert Camus, Jean Amrouche and Mouloud Feraoun.
6. Interview with Paul Riceour, Paris, 20 Oct. 1993.
7. Many important intellectuals including Raymond Aron, Maurice Merleau-Ponty and Georges Gurvitch acknowledged during the epoch of the French-Algerian War that the social sciences and philosophy were in crisis.
8. For an extended discussion of the war's impact on Camus and Soustelle, see Le Sueur, *Uncivil War* (note 1). See also James D. Le Sueur, 'Before the Jackal: The International Uproar over *Assassination!*', an historical essay accompanying *Assassination! July 14*, by Ben Abro (Lincoln: University of Nebraska Press 2001).
9. The sources used in this article dealing with both the Comité and the 'Jeanson Network' are from private archives, which have not been consulted before, unpublished materials in public archives, published texts and interviews I have conducted.
10. See Mouloud Feraoun, *Journal, 1955–1962: Reflections on the French-Algerian War*, ed. and intro. James D. Le Sueur, trans. Mary Ellen Wolf and Claude Fouillade (Lincoln: Nebraska, University of Nebraska Press 2000) and Le Sueur, *Uncivil War* (note 1).
11. Comité d'Action des Intellectuels contre la Poursuite de la Guerre en Afrique du Nord (S.l.n.d) p.2.
12. Edgar Morin, *Autocritique* (Paris: Seuil 1970) pp.191–3.
13. André Breton and other surrealists signed the manifesto, thus signalling the re-introduction of the surrealists into politics.
14. Among the names on the original manifesto in November 1955 were: Claude Lévi-Strauss, Paul Ricoeur, François Mauriac, Georges Gurvitch, Roger Martin du Gard, Louis Massignon, Gaston Wiet, André Breton, Jean Wahl, Jean-Paul Sartre, Régis Blachère, Jean Daniel, Marguerite Duras, Henri Lefebvre, Jean Cocteau, Jean-Jacques Mayoux, Jean-Marie Domenach, Jean Genet and Charles-André Julien. There were several hundred names in total. It is important to point out that Soustelle had also been active in antifascist committees on the eve of World War II.
15. Comité d'Action des Intellectuels contre la Poursuite de la Guerre en Afrique du Nord (S.l.n.d) p.2.

16. About the Comité, Soustelle says that 'a certain number of honourable signatures mixed with unknown ones, who, without doubt, were desirous to leave their obscurity, and with a few *demoiselles* quite unqualified to treat the problems of which they knew nothing. As much as I worried little about the specialists, the unknowns and the *demoiselles,* I attached greater importance to the opinions of writers and professors [*universitaires*] that I respected and among whom I counted friends. That is why I decided to respond'. Jacques Soustelle, *Aimée et souffrante Algérie* (Paris: Plon 1956) p.170. Among the '*demoiselles*' to whom he was referring were Marguerite Duras, Simone de Beauvoir and Françoise Sagan.
17. At the outbreak of the Algerian War, Soustelle was directeur des études at the École Pratique des Hautes Études, but was formally detached on 1 February 1955 for the duration of his functions as governor general of Algeria. He was later reinstated to his post at the École on 20 March 1956.
18. Jacques Soustelle, 'Lettre d'un intellectuel', *Combat* (26 Nov. 1955), p.1.
19. 'Réponse au Gouverneur Général de l'Algérie', Comité d'Action des Intellectuels contre la Poursuite de la Guerre en Afrique du Nord (Paris, 3 déc. 1955) p.2.
20. Ibid. p.3.
21. Ibid. p.2.
22. For an expanded version of this argument see Claude Bourdet, 'Votre Gestapo d'Algérie', *France observateur* (13 Jan. 1955) pp.6–7. For analysis of the issue of torture during the war, see James D. Le Sueur, 'Torture and the Decolonisation of French Algeria: Nationalism, "Race", and Violence in Colonial Incarceration' in Graeme Harper (ed.), *Colonial and Post-Colonial Incarceration* (London: Continuum 2001).
23. Comité d'action des Intellectuels contre la Poursuite de la Guerre en Afrique du Nord, 'Réponse au Goverheur Général de l'Algérie' (Paris, s.d.) p.2.
24. Ibid. p.4.
25. Déclaration de Monsieur Jacques Souste Soustelle Gouverneur Général de l' Algérie Radio-Algørie le 12 janvier 1956.
26. 'Réponse du Comité, 10 January 1956, in 'Réponse au Gouverneur Général de l'Algérie', p.6.
27. It could not have come as a great surprise to many of the Comité members that Soustelle, who had been instrumental in placing de Gaulle in power in May 1958, was eventually forced into exile for his extreme right-wing activities. Soustelle was finally granted amnesty in 1968, along with the rest of de Gaulle's opponents and members of the OAS and the CNR. See Le Sueur, 'Before the Jackal' (note 9).
28. Messali Hadj (1898–1974) was one of Algeria's most important nationalist leaders. In 1926 he became the leader of the Étoile Nord-Africaine which was based in France. In 1933, Messali recreated the ENA, changing its name to La Glorieuse Étoile Nord-Africaine. The French Popular Front disbanded the ENA in 1937, after which Messali founded the Parti du Peuple Algérien (PPA). After the PPA had been disbanded by the French, Messali formed another group, Mouvement pour le Triomphe des Libertés Démocratiques (MTLD), which succeeded the PPA. After World War II, he took over the leadership of Amis du Manifeste et de Liberté (AML) which had been created by Ferhat Abbas. During the French-Algerian War, he directed the Movement National Algerien (MNA), which was the rival of the FLN.
29. Many French intellectuals later admitted that they chose the FLN because its leaders tended to be more western: they dressed like Frenchmen, they spoke French well, they were Marxists or extreme leftists, as opposed to Messali Hadj, the leader of the MNA, who wore traditional North African clothing, had a long beard and remained a devout Muslim and a religious leader.
30. Jean Daniel, 'Entre le chagrin et le haussement d'épaules', *L'Express* (13 Jan. 1956) p.11.
31. Ibid.
32. Ibid.
33. Daniel Guérin, 'L'Algérie hors la loi', *France observateur* (26 Jan. 1956) p.12.
34. Ibid.
35. Jeanson wanted to offer a response to Daniel, one which would be private enough to keep

the already sceptical public opinion from turning against intellectuals and the higher causes of Algerian nationalism and anticolonialism. Interview with Francis Jeanson, 11 Dec. 1993.

36. Francis Jeanson to Jean Daniel (16 Jan. 1956) p.1. Archives Guérin, 721/91/4, Bibliothèque de Documentation Internationale Contemporaine (BDIC).
37. According to Martinet, after the *France observateur* criticised Soviet intervention, the number of subscribers to the newspaper increased substantially. Interview with Gilles Martinet, Paris, 2 March 1994.
38. 'Contre l'intervention', *France observateur*, 8 Nov. 1956. Also reprinted in full in: Jean-François Sirinelli, *Intellectuels et Passions Françaises: Manifestes et pétitions au XXe siècle* (Paris: Fayard 1990) pp.177–78. It should also be noted that on 29 Nov. 1956 an open letter written by Soviet writers was published in *France observateur* along with a rebuttal written by Colette Audry, Simone de Beauvoir, Janine Bouissounouse, Jean Cau, Claude Lanzman, Michel Leiris, Claude Morgan, Marcel Péju, Henri Pichette, Gérard Philipe, Promidès, J.-F. Rolland, Claude Roy, Jean-Paul Sartre, Tristan Tzara and Louis de Villefosse. The Soviets defended the Hungarian suppression on the grounds that the 'uprising' was motivated by fascists and anti-revolutionaries. Additionally, the Soviets argued that the same French intellectuals who had condemned the Soviet actions in Budapest had not shown equal force in condemning the recent French aggression against Suez.
39. Jean-Paul Sartre, 'Après Budapest', *L'Express* (9 Nov. 1956) p.15.
40. Comité d'Action des Intellectuels to its members, Paris (21 Nov. 1956) Fonds *Esprit*, ESP2. E1-02.02, Institut Mémoire de l'Edition Contemporaine (IMEC), Paris.
41. Jean-Marie Domenach to the Comité d'Action des Intellectuals, Fonds *Esprit*, ESP2, E1-02.02, IMEC.
42. Daniel Guérin, *Ci-gît le colonialisme: Algérie, Inde, Indochine, Madagascar, Maroc, Palestine, Polynésie, Tunisie – Témoignage militant* (Paris: Mouton 1973) p.95.
43. When he met Francis Jeanson on his way to Éditions du Seuil, Sartre offered the petition to Jeanson for his signature condemning the invasion. Reading the names, which Sartre had just begun to collect, Jeanson saw that they were all names of ex-communists, i.e., anti-communists, and to Sartre's surprise, Jeanson said: 'We'll talk about it tomorrow'. It was never discussed further. Although Jeanson was not a member of the Communist Party, he did not want to align himself with others on Sartre's list known to be extreme anti-communists. Interview with Francis Jeanson, 11 Dec. 1993.
44. Interview with Edgar Morin, 4 Dec. 1993.
45. Morin, *Autocritique* (note 13) p.197.
46. Notes of Dionys Mascolo. Private papers of Dionys Mascolo.
47. Interview with Dionys Mascolo, 16 February 1994.
48. Dionys Mascolo to the Comité, 19 Nov. 1956. Mascolo papers. André Mandouze was a prominent French intellectual living in Algeria whose vocal support for the FLN led to his arrest by the French authorities.
49. Having lived in Algeria for several years, Jeanson had also been one of the first French intellectuals to write about the impending revolution. In his articles which appeared in *Esprit* in 1950, Jeanson attempted to bring the French out of their 'sleepwalking' with respect to Algerian nationalism. Jeanson claimed that it was important for him to go into hiding and was actually asked to do so by the leader of the FLN in France because he had 'in his hands' all the information concerning the FLN's activities in France. Interview with Francis Jeanson, 11 December 1993.
50. 'Francis Jeanson, Lettre à Jean-Paul Sartre', *Les Temps modernes*, 169–70 (April–May 1960) p.1541.
51. Ibid. p.1544.
52. Ibid. This comment is well on the mark, given Massu's and Ausseresses's recent admissions concerning the use of torture against Algerians.
53. Ibid.
54. Ibid. pp.1546–7. *Les Temps modernes* followed the same logic and continued with the theme of intellectual commitment espoused by Jeanson in its editorial, 'The French left and the

FLN'. See *Les Temps modernes* 167–8 (Feb.–March 1960) pp.1169–73. The journal also attacked de Gaulle's policy in Algeria and depicted him as a potential fascist threat to French democracy.

55. Jean Daniel, 'Socialisme et anti-colonialisme,' *Esprit* 284 (May 1960) p.810.
56. Ibid. p.811.
57. Ibid.
58. Ibid. pp.813–14.
59. 'Réponse à Jean Daniel', *Les Temps modernes*, 169–70 (April–May 1960) pp.1530–4.
60. Ibid.
61. Ibid. p.1534.
62. For the most complete history of the development of the Jeanson network, see Hervé Hamon and Patrick Rotman, *Les porteurs de valises: La résistance française à la guerre d'Algérie* (Paris: A. Michel 1979).
63. Jeanson was in Switzerland throughout the trial.
64. 4 September 1960 when *Le Monde* announced that 121 intellectuals (writers and artists) had signed the Manifesto for the 'right of insubordination' against the French-Algerian war. The Manifesto of the 121 was made public on the day before the trial of the 'Jeanson network' began in Paris. Dionys Mascolo, one of the original founders of the Comité was again one of the principal motivators for the Manifesto of the 121. Others included France's most prominent leftist intellectuals including Robert Barrat, Simone de Beauvoir, André Breton, Marguerite Duras, Michel Leiris, Jérôme Lindon, Dionys Mascolo, Jean-Jacques Mayoux, Jean-Paul Sartre and Pierre Vidal-Naquet. However, a group of moderate French intellectuals quickly countered the Manifesto of the 121. This group, led by Maurice Merleau-Ponty, signed a less provocative manifesto which underscored the moral choices the government was forcing upon the youth, but did not advocate the right of desertion. The signatures on the manifesto totalled over a thousand. Among the names were Raymond Aron, Jean-Marie Domenach, Roland Barthes, Georges Canguilhem, Jean Cassou, Jean Dresch, Claude Lefort, Jacques Le Goff, Edgar Morin, Paul Ricoeur and Daniel Meyer.
65. Francis Jeanson, *Notre guerre* (Paris: Minuit 1960) pp.14–15.
66. Ibid.
67. Ibid. p.48. The reference to being for sale came from the French presses at the time of the Jeanson Network trial. Many in the French media claimed that the members of the network had been seduced by attractive Algerian men and by money into working with the FLN.
68. Ibid. p.117.

[16]

'Daddy Wouldn't Buy Me a Mau Mau'

The British Popular Press & the Demoralization of Empire

JOANNA LEWIS

By the time news reached Blighty that Kenya's government had declared an Emergency on 20 October 1952, Mau Mau already meant something to many in the United Kingdom – whether young or old, white-collared or working class, rampant English bulldog or critical Celt sulking on the fringe. That something was scarcely nice. For many it was disturbing.[1] Parents disciplined delinquent offspring by threatening that Mau Mau would come and get them if they did not eat their greens. MPs compared each other's rowdy behaviour in the Commons with Mau Mau terror.[2] Mau Mau even had its own pop song, the first line of which appears in this chapter's title.[3] Clearly, Mau Mau had become a British household word. It brought empire into everyday language and popular culture in a way not seen since the phrase 'the black hole of Calcutta' had entered colloquial speech over a century before.

This chapter studies how Kenya's Emergency was reported in key sections of the popular press, the medium through which politicians and public squared up to each other via journalists, editors, and proprietors, and where news jostled with entertainment and often lost out. It asks three thus far neglected questions. What were British working women and men told about Mau Mau when they opened their penny papers? What can we then infer about the popular politics of decolonization? And what light does this case study throw on the popularity of empire in twentieth-century Britain? For the threatening nature of Kenya's Emergency for the British public was not simply the *racial* terror of black men wielding carving knives to mutilate domestic pets and close family members, the staple of earlier studies.[4] Mau Mau drew on another popular discourse too, that of a class-driven distrust for the bearers of imperial power in colonial Africa.

The British Popular Press in the 1950s

That Mau Mau reached so many readers was a consequence of a cheap and cheerful mass media. With a buoyant commercial press, a public broadcasting service – mainly audio, but becoming televisual – and with newsreels continuing to be part of the cinema's entertainment, the postwar British public enjoyed unprecedented exposure to the world beyond the privet hedge. Official propaganda and censorship during the second world war had highlighted the role of mass communication in modern life. For many – George Orwell most famously – it was a deadly force, much to be feared. For not only did the communicative power of print hold sway over a population with unparalleled rates of literacy that, for the first time, spanned all generations. In addition, photographic and film techniques were improving; more and more publications were using photos, with ever sharper images, to reinforce that print.

As for the times themselves, there was much to ponder. The cold war had frozen international relations in an atomic age. At home, the legacy of the 'people's war' still soured daily life. Household essentials were short, economic recovery slow. Sugar was rationed until 1953, 'the year the war really ended'.[5] Conflict continued overseas. There were new institutions of public power, the United Nations, the welfare state and the first landslide Labour government, with many trades union MPs – even if it was dumped by the electorate in 1951. Meanwhile the public could gaze on the two young princesses. The press splashed Elizabeth's tour of Kenya even before her father's death made her queen, at Treetops Safari Lodge. And there was much to distract, thanks to the dazzling new glamour of Hollywood and the latest ready-to-wear 1950s fashion chic. The death of Queen Mary reinforced a nostalgic continuity with Victorian times; the coronation in April 1953 further titillated patriotic sentiment.

By the 1950s, London's popular press reached out to a nation of millions of readers. While the age of the interfering press baron was gone and editors controlled their paper's content, newspapers remained loyal to particular partisan traditions and political parties. Social and class allegiance continued to be a peculiar feature of the British press.[6] The two biggest national dailies, each with other associated titles, were the *Daily Mirror* and *Daily Mail.* Both had been founded by Lord Northcliffe (Alfred Harmsworth). The *Daily Mail* began the era of mass circulation dailies in 1896. The *Daily Mirror* started in 1903 'as a boudoir paper for – and produced by – women' although this approach soon foundered, to be replaced by a male agenda.[7]

Both papers shared similar features whilst appealing to different sections of the reading public. Both relied on sales to create revenue, unlike broadsheets that relied on advertising income. Both were tabloid, in that they used photographs to illustrate, even to tell, the news. Yet both took the reporting of foreign news seriously – much more so than any tabloid or, indeed, many broadsheets, today. Both were morning dailies, printed in London. The *Mail* had a circulation of around 2.3 million and the *Mirror* 4.5 million. The latter claimed the largest daily sale in the world (later, the universe). With an average of two more adults reading a newspaper in addition to the purchaser, actual readership was much higher, at over 15 million. These newspapers were therefore read by a significant proportion of the electorate. In the 1960s, up to 90 per cent of British adults read a national daily, many more than today.[8]

Both newspapers claimed to be independent. In practice they were loyal to a particular political party, and readers remained loyal to their chosen paper. Until the mid-1950s, popular dailies remained steadfastly partisan. The *Daily Herald* and *Daily Mirror* backed the Labour Party; the *Daily Mail* supported the Conservatives. After 1955, the press began to realize that close political links could damage commercial sales. The popular press increasingly fell out with its natural allies, at least on specific issues. In the 1950s celebrity columnists like William Conner, or 'Cassandra', the *Mirror*'s pungent political commentator, moulded mass opinion by the force of their personality. Both papers also used the royal family to reinforce their worldview. The *Mirror* was the more popular of the two, a 'super-popular' tabloid with more of its readers drawn from the blue-collar working class. It had fewer pages to cover hard news than the *Mail* and gave more space to sport and photographs. It favoured direct and startling headlines, short news summaries and generous dollops of royalty.

The *Mail* reached out to the white-collar, lower-middle class and to aspirant blue-collar workers. It was a longer read, reported hard news and politics in greater depth, and offered advice on personal finance. It was bought by a broader and more affluent section of working people, as evidenced by its regular television reviews. However, it echoed the super-tabloids in its human-interest angles, and stories of the bizarre, some of them home improvement tips. Who could forget the 'Rise and fall of the aspidistra' in September 1952?[9] Yet it took itself seriously as a newspaper first and foremost, sometimes even giving alternative opinions on current affairs, if in a biased format. What distinguished the *Mail* was its use of figures in authority to convey the news, reflecting its belief in law and order. Above all, it offered readers a conservative vision of the world that reinforced and reflected support for the Tory government of the day.

These papers cannot be dismissed as irresponsible intermediaries between the news as it broke and political opinion as it had already formed. The relationship between the press, public opinion (low politics) and politicians (high politics) is never straightforward, nor easily elucidated by historians. It would be snobbish and foolhardy to ignore the role of low politics in such major political processes as the United Kingdom's comparatively peaceful disengagement from empire. To their enormous combined readership the *Mail* and *Mirror* expressed strong views on colonial rule.[10] Yet studies of the domestic opposition to empire focus on political parties and disregard press and public.[11] Popular dailies have been discounted for their self-interested and shallow approach to colonial affairs, and derided for their sensationalism. However, as this chapter will show, the coverage of colonial news was a serious business in the 1950s, especially when a crisis erupted, involving British troops and provoking international criticism.[12] A seemingly ghoulish outbreak of violence and supernatural activity in a colony long romanticized as a playground for the

British ruling class – over there, overpaid and over-sexed, with aristocrats yielding to altitude, alcohol and adultery – offered Britain's mass media a compelling and money-making saga. There was enormous visual potential in the wild men of the forest, British soldiers in khaki combats and the English rose at target practice. But Kenya's popular fascination had roots deeper than such sexy aesthetics. Another clash was also unfolding, in which popular culture and populist politics began to look increasingly at odds with each other. Racist images of 'darkest Africa' engulfed in savage barbarism now competed with a class politics that relied on a rhetoric of 'us and them', in which white settlers and the government were, for a working-class readership, more 'them' than 'us'.

For the *Mirror*, Kenya's crisis exposed defects in colonial policy in general and the Conservative government's backward approach to African nationalism in particular. That it used sensationalism and gimmicks to engage the audience is no cause to dismiss its content on grounds of distortion but, rather, to analyse it as a means to dramatize remote news through the medium of low political discourse. Big headings, bold writing and everyday language, supported with photographs, were needed to 'hit hard and hit often' working people shattered by their working lives.[13] Tabloid headings offer rich insights into the cultural mores of the time. They had to convey instant meanings to conventional opinions. Mau Mau was an important source of images in the twentieth-century West's representation of Africa.[14] It is time for the historiography of decolonization to get into step with the *Mirror's* masthead slogan of the time, and move 'forward with the people'.

'The Greedy Eaters'

To assess the coverage of Mau Mau, we must know what the public already knew, or were told, about colonial Africa. An important difference between the *Daily Mirror* and the *Daily Mail* was their coverage of Kenya before October 1952. *Mail* readers had a long-standing sympathy with white settlers in Africa; they knew the colonists' views on black incapacity, and believed settlers would best ensure that colonies paid. The ideological framework into which Kenya's news was placed was already well established in the right-wing press. Plans to create a federation of the Rhodesias and Nyasaland had recently reunited readers with settler hopes and fears. Typically, the *Mail* had gone straight to the top and interviewed Sir Godfrey Huggins, prime minister of Southern Rhodesia.[15]

Huggins's interview presented the core themes in the British popular news out of Africa. They would recur in Kenya's imminent news bonanza. First, settlers knew what was best for Africa, much better than the 'ideologists of Whitehall', whom Huggins derided for interfering on behalf of native interests. The danger for Africa came from meddling by 'ill-informed Socialist functionaries', and from any future 'Socialist Government' that desired a 'native controlled state like the Gold Coast'. Settlers knew best, secondly, because Africans were stuck in primitive stupor. 'The local black people ... like to be told what to do', not consulted, since 'only 60 or 70 years back these people were so primitive that they had never invented nor even seen a wheel ... all loads being carried by women'. Catering to the *Mail*'s female readership also helped the settler cause. A piece headed 'The Women May Decide in New Dominion' gave female settler views. They were opposed to giving Africans more political freedom. That might make white women more vulnerable to African men. They resented the way African men treated their women. Political progress might also create a servant problem.[16] While the last point might not have pulled the heart-strings of hard-pressed and still-rationed Brits, the other two were money in the bank. The anti-Mau Mau cause would soon draw on these reserves.

Nonetheless, the *Mail* also billed the Central African Federation as 'Africa's great experiment in black and white'. According to its correspondent Ward Price, British settlers should be left to run the colonies as self-governing dominions because they were a progressive force. They would improve African townships. They were protecting good race relations in a manner far wiser than the Afrikaners. The *Mail* derided the apartheid policies of the latter for 'clinging to the past and trying to arrest the march of time'.[17] Even the right preferred its imperial white knights to show an aptitude for modernization and to behave in ways that marked them as superior to anti-imperial South Africa.

By September 1952 Kenya had snatched the headlines from these dominion daydreams. From now on the *Daily Mail's* attention to Kenya was unflinching. This is in part explained by the emotional capital already invested in the lives of whites in the tropics, but Mau Mau was in any case a journalist's dream and a press proprietor's early retirement package. Kenya's crisis fed racial prejudice and lined city pockets. There were at least three dominant patterns in the presentation of Mau Mau: its sensational character; its threat to honest citizens and to law and order; and the vivid photographic endorsement of both views.

The *Mail* naturally emphasized Mau Mau's lurid violence. On Saturday 13 September, the front page opened with 'Kenya unrest to be probed. New attacks by Mau Mau. Swordsmen surround mission'. The report itself told how the secretary of state for the colonies, Oliver Lyttelton, now took a serious view of an anti-European movement, but a violent knife attack had failed. The opinion of the former governor, Sir Philip Mitchell,[18] was quoted to discredit Mau Mau: 'the last despairing kicks and struggles of superstition'. On the following Monday, the paper went for the oathing option. 'How Recruits Join Mau Mau – Secret Terrorist Movement Enrols 200,000 in Kenya' was accompanied by a small photograph of an alleged oathing arch, described as a 'sign of terror'. It was the same height as a wicker basket placed next to it and was decorated with what were said to be sheep's eyes but looked more like soft marshmallows.[19] The revelation that Kikuyu feared the number seven added a frisson of black magic.

One of the most effective articles to exploit Mau Mau's potential as a diabolical terrorism came from a regular *Daily Mail* Africa reporter, Ralph Izzard. Entitled 'Educated Men Organising the Pagan Terrorists', with the subheading 'Threat of Death Keeps the Mau Mau Secrets', it was accompanied by a small photo of the governor, Sir Evelyn Baring, whose life had allegedly been threatened by the 'Mau Mau Court of Justice'. Beginning with the dawn discovery of a corpse buried upside down, Izzard elaborated on the meanings of the term 'Mau Mau', before detailing the bloody and magical rituals of an oathing ceremony. With only speculation about the name to go on, there was much to exercise the imagination, from 'all devouring', to 'Mombi African Union', to 'man-eater ... who devours human flesh ... having a head "as big as granary basket", long hair and two mouths filled with sharp teeth, the second being concealed at the back of the neck'.[20] Izzard could at least confirm that it was the undercover wing of the Kenya African Union (KAU). Their tactics differed, but their aims were the same. The KAU had done little more than 'boycott European customs such as drinking European beer and knocking western-style hats off African heads'. Mau Mau was a Kikuyu movement because that tribe was overpopulated and land-starved. But Izzard showed little sympathy. It might well be a revolt of the envious have-nots, against the haves, but the fault was their own; as 'wasteful' cultivators, they had resisted new farming methods.[21]

A second framework for the *Mail*'s reports on Kenya was the threat to law and order. If Mau Mau was diabolical, loyalist forces were naturally on the side of the angels. Headlines and articles pushed this line. The front-page report of chief Waruhiu's murder on 8 October 1952 is a good example. Its headline, 'Mau Mau Shoot Africa's Churchill', was a nice allusion to Britain's own wartime spirit. Other splashes followed: 'Terrorism not yet at peak', and 'Mau Mau threaten to kill Baring'. Photographs reinforced the *Mail's* reading of a situation that was black-and-white in more ways than one. There were two in-house styles. First, photos were often reproduced next to, or incorporated in, an article. They normally represented a senior white official like Baring, or a military officer. On 13 October the main headline was backed by a photo of 'RAF moustached, ex-fighter pilot, Police Inspector Kenneth Price'. On inside pages the story reappeared as 'Ex-RAF Fighter Pilot Joins Battle with the Mau Mau Terrorists', and was illustrated by three action shots: 'Interrogation', 'Hunting', and 'Watching'.[22] But if a story had a pagan slant, like the Mau Mau initiation arch, then a photo could reinforce the sense of threat: Kenyatta was shown with his hands raised, as if to cast a spell.[23] Kenya photographs also appeared, secondly, in the paper's special montage section. Here action shots vied with snaps of royalty, film stars and artistic compositions, perhaps in an attempt to rival television. The 16 October montage carried the headline 'MEN OF MAU MAU – IN KENYA IT MEANS "THE GREEDY EATERS"'. Underneath, two Mau Mau prisoners were shown standing between two African police askari.[24] Kenya dominated the *Mail's* montage section at least five times in October, with shots of terrorists being arrested or driven away by African soldiers, often supported by African and European police officers.[25]

In comparison with the *Mail*, the *Mirror* gave sparse coverage to Kenya – or anywhere in Africa – before October 1952. It had fewer column inches for news in general, especially with its large sports section. In any case the predicament of white settlers, with their aristocratic reputation, hardly made them a priority for a working-class daily. On 17 October, the *Mirror* mentioned Kenya for the first time that month in a small, inconspicuous, paragraph headed 'Government Backs the New Kenya laws'. The next week saw the beginning of sporadic but intensive coverage that lasted for over six months.

'All Quiet on the Kenyan Front – or is it?'

In the Emergency's first two months, the popular press across the board gave Kenya front- and back-page coverage, editorial comment and in-depth analysis. Only the royal family, with the death of Queen Mary and the young queen's coronation, rivalled the unfolding drama. The *Mail* and *Mirror* initially moved more into line with each other. Three aspects were common to their coverage: the arrival of British troops; horrific African violence; and photo-journalism. The one big difference was that one focused on the men giving the orders; the other on the men carrying them out.

The *Mirror*, like the *Mail*, liked a good story about the armed forces. They appealed to its male readership and informed families with conscript sons. Not surprisingly, Kenya commanded the front page on 21 and 22 October with the headlines: 'Emergency Decreed as Kenya Troops Land' and 'All Terrorist Leaders Arrested say Kenya Police'. The *Mirror* then refracted events through the experience of rank-and-file soldiers. The caption 'The Tommy and the Kikuyu' accompanied a large front-page photograph of a young soldier leaning on a wall watching a group of African women.[26] Here was British good humour in face of a tricky job. But there was more than a hint that this calm was an illusion. With language that evoked the first world war, the headline for 27 October asked, 'All Quiet on the Kenyan Front – or Is It?'[27]

A second theme in the *Mirror's* response soon appeared when events took a violent turn and demanded more explanation. This relied on sensationalizing the whites' terror and raiding popular stereotypes of Africa, the dangerous continent, and Africans, a pagan people. In late October a long piece appeared inside the front page entitled 'Suburbia in Darkest Africa Sits Tight on DYNAMITE'.[28] Kenya was an 'equatorial Ealing' by day, under which lurked 'a spiritual jungle as deep as the night'. Days later another feverish headline predicted: 'Full Moon May Bring New Crisis', followed by 'African Burns Down Church' and 'Mau Mau High Priest gets Twenty Years'.[29] The *Mirror*, in contrast to the *Mail*, gave more coverage of threats to Africans than to Europeans, even when highlighting the pagan and supernatural. Readers – now hooked, surely –

were told that moderate African politicians were at risk. Eliud Mathu had received a death warrant; Tom Mbotela had been murdered.

However, more in line with the *Mail* was the *Mirror*'s decision to lavish its Kenya coverage with illustrations. Photo splashes showed soldiers and police in action.[30] For the *Mail* itself, the Emergency recalled the spirit of wartime: 'Britain Blitzes the Terror: Troops Fly In – and Round-up Starts: ARRESTS BY THE HUNDRED – Kenya Emergency – Backed by Troops from Suez'. This was the multiple, front-page, headline-grabber of 21 October, followed by two more pages with another major heading: 'Terrorland'.[31] The initial stress was on the United Kingdom's rescue mission: the Lancashire Fusiliers, RAF bombers and a naval cruiser. They had to 'get tough' in response to 'months of terrorist outrages'. Reassuringly, there was no alternative 'in the face of growing lawlessness, violence and disorder'. The murder of 'one of the most revered African chiefs, Senior Chief Waruhiu ... in broad daylight' (the cheek of it) was proof enough. The *Mail* claimed that the arrests were a normal civil action, not that of a police state; even the detainees' compounds had been 'specially prepared'.

The *Mail* gave Kenya its silver-service treatment. A second article, also on 21 October's front page, combined two of its best techniques for audience engagement: bring on the ladies and play on our people's wartime pluck, under the heading 'WOMEN PUT GUNS IN THEIR HANDBAGS: Men Called for Home Guard'. The article itself barely mentioned either, but listed armoured car manoeuvres, police swoops, roadblocks, patrols and security clampdowns 'in the terror area'. Readers were now primed for thrilling action. How infuriating, then, it must have been to read of diplomatic threats to the United Kingdom's right to govern its colonies: 'Minister Tells the UN: Hands Off: THEY ARE OUR BUSINESS – The World Hears We Will not Tolerate Interference'. Readers were reminded that The United Kingdom aimed to develop its colonies and lead them to self-government. Henry Hopkinson, minister of state for the colonies, spelt this out to the UN's Trusteeship Committee. He added, 'Britain no longer seeks to hold dominion over palm and pine'. The *Mail* omitted to point out that his position contradicted that of Huggins.[32] Anyway, if proof were required of Kenya's – and Africa's – continuing need for white tutelage it was given in the next column, with the news: 'God of the tribe arrested: Kenya comb-out snares 98 leaders'.

Thereupon the *Mail* returned to what it did best: presenting situations as threats to law and order, and showing how the British authorities and security forces were pursuing fair and effective measures to restore the peace. Photos did the trick, with full-page montages under such headings as 'Navy Joins Mau Mau Fight'; 'Mau Mau Terrorist Is Charged' and – a *Mail* exclusive – photographs of 'The first major action against the Mau Mau'.[33]

Despite the gung-ho, hell-for-leather, potential of Tommies in the tropics, and the *Mail*'s exploitation of Kenya's echoes of British wartime heroism, the *Mirror* soon abandoned the sensational and barbaric aspects of the conflict. Hints of its displeasure with the government appeared as early as 30 October with 'a dilly-dally charge' on the back page. On 6 November a new voice appeared, to give readers an alternative view. This time, it was the 'Truth about Kenya', told by James Cameron. This article, outlined by drawn swords, bears out his reputation as one of the leading investigative journalists of the day. It also shows that the *Mirror* gave its readers serious, penetrating assessments of African news. Cameron complicated the picture in two ways. First, while he accepted that Mau Mau was a barbaric secret society, attractive to all the 'spivs and idlers of a troubled urban economy', he stressed that its causes ran deeper than 'mumbo jumbo'. Second, after sympathizing with Kenya's Europeans he warned that some of them were exploiting the trouble to impose 'even greater ascendancy over the African' and were guilty of 'racial arrogance'. For a while then, the *Mirror* had stood on the sidelines. But in less than a month after the start of the Emergency Cameron had taken the *Mirror* in the opposite direction to the *Mail.*

'Will Nobody Stop Mr Lyttelton?'

By late November, with ever more incidents of state violence against Africans, the *Daily Mirror* gave its readers a very different take on Kenya's Emergency. It now presented Kenya's news as a series of examples of excessive state repression: '15 Die as Police Fire on Kenya Mob'; 'Army Evicts 7,000 in Kenya Murder Zone' and 'Hang 25 Africans'.[34] Cameron led its assault on the official line, illustrating the potential of an individual journalist to shape press coverage. The *Mirror* launched five types of attack on the government in late November and early December, after which its Kenya coverage petered out. This short-winded punchiness was typical of the *Mirror,* with its limited space for news.

Cameron captained the first sortie, with the authority of the man on the spot. In 'Why Kenya Can't Wait' he argued that the colony was about to suffer 'a nuclear explosion of the human spirit'. Racial division had produced Mau Mau, a meaningless movement, 'like Sinn Fein' in its pure 'resentment'. So Cameron was disgusted by Baring's policy of rounding up all Kikuyu, innocent and guilty alike. 'All this by a Power that justifies itself in Africa by the claim that it did at least impose the British tradition of justice'. Cameron's line clearly swayed his editor. Perhaps, indeed, he wrote the subsequent editorials himself, the second form of attack. The editorial on the day of his report focused on 'KENYA CHAOS'. It accepted the need to restore order, but thought British methods would achieve the reverse. They invited more terrorism, they would lead to more arrests. The *Mirror* argued, instead, that 'THERE CANNOT POSSIBLY BE ANY SOLUTION WITHOUT ENLISTING THE COOPERATION OF RESPONSIBLE AFRICAN OPINION'. While it continued to report from Kenya the paper soon opened a third front by rounding on the government at home.[35] 'WILL NOBODY STOP MR LYTTELTON?' its front-page headline asked on

1 December 1952. Admittedly, it was not a great day for news. The two other headlines were 'The Icicles Hang Down Eight Feet', illustrated, and 'Ten Gassed in House – Two Die', not illustrated. Nevertheless, Kenya claimed both the front page and a robust editorial.

The *Mirror* then aimed a fourth shot at the government, in its favourite editorial style of question-and-answer. This technique drew in the audience and prompted an active response, a ploy perhaps especially necessary with a topic so distant from everyday life. 'What are we doing in Africa? What are we doing in Kenya? In our unhappy, furious, folly what are we doing to ourselves?' the *Mirror* asked. These were the editorial's remarkable, soul-searching, opening questions. The *Mirror* measured events in Kenya against British colonial policy in Africa as a whole. Race relations linked the particular to the general. In a 'tormented continent', Kenya was 'poised on the uneasy edge of racial hate'. The *Mirror* accepted that Mau Mau was evil, a 'revolting and dangerous thing', 'a vicious organisation'. But the editorial reiterated that still greater danger lay in the excessive use of British force. Kenyans were watching 'the disintegration of a country, the ruin of Colonial goodwill, and the strange, sad corruption of British rule'. What was at stake, ultimately, was 'our own morality as rulers'.

The editorial spelt out the *Mirror*'s two key criticisms of the Emergency. It had aroused the 'embittered hatred' of a million Kikuyu, Mau Mau's greatest victims and who must be deemed to be innocent until proven otherwise. The shootings, arrests and detention without trial; the rounding up of thousands behind barbed wire, 'with the gallows for company', had merely allowed Mau Mau to tighten 'its blackmail grip' and, moreover, had encouraged South Africa to emulate British methods. Secondly, the blame for disaster lay squarely with Lyttelton, secretary of state. A blistering personal attack on him incorporated the *Mirror*'s ultimate weapon, a comparison with pre-war appeasement. The paper had campaigned against this in the 1930s; it now seemed to imply that the settlers were today's Nazis. The editorial ended with the plea that, like the doctor who could not diagnose, Lyttelton must not be allowed to kill Kenya with his 'cure':

> To this hideous situation, Mr. Oliver Lyttelton reacts with the bluff and bland complacency of a company director. The impossibility and the smug assurances of his reasoning have not been matched since Neville Chamberlain brought home a piece of paper and called it Peace.
>
> He reaffirms the repellent principle of collective punishment, retribution on the guilty and innocent alike.
>
> He rejects the need for an all-Party inquiry.
>
> He rejects the offer of friendly Africans to go forth among their own people and denounce terrorism …
>
> He rejects the possibility of Mau Mau having an economic origin …
>
> He proposes a Royal Commission – that last life-belt of a barren administration – which is still, after six weeks of an emergency, not even recruited.

> He is committed to the sterile policy of brute force and barbed wire. This can have no meaning even to Mr. Lyttelton, until nearly every man and woman of the million Kikuyu is in gaol, the country paralysed, and British rule abhorred throughout all Africa.[36]

The political cavalry, in the shape of the Labour Party, now rode up to support this rhetorical onslaught. Next day, in what looks like a planned contrast to the previous day's coverage, the *Mirror*'s third front-page news item reported that 'Labour Prepares a Kenyan Plan'.[37] The 'special correspondent', a Labour insider, told readers that the party had prepared 'constructive' proposals to accompany their criticism of Lyttelton's 'disastrous handling of the situation'. Clearly the *Mirror* and the party were at one on this issue. For it was reported that the former Labour colonial secretary, James Griffiths, had long warned of the need for changes in racial land allocation, to alleviate African land hunger. 'To help them' Labour was tabling a motion to allow Africans to farm unused land in the White Highlands, to which the Tories had objected when it was first raised. Although keen to show that Labour was taking a critical and progressive stance in contrast to the Tories, what perhaps this report actually showed was Labour's earlier lack of a radical perspective on colonial policy in Kenya. For Labour MPs were merely asking why Lyttelton had been caught unprepared.

The link between the *Mirror* and Labour over Kenya grew closer by the day. In the Saturday edition of 6 December, the whole of the second page was given over to Griffiths, accompanied by his portrait and full title, with the heading in bold, in capitals and underlined: 'WHAT SHOULD WE DO IN KENYA'.[38] But, clearly, no reader was expected to know who Griffiths was. A short biography therefore established his working-class credentials (he had been a coalminer for 17 years) and his colonial expertise. On an earlier visit to Kenya he had achieved the apparently 'unique triumph' of being respected by both Africans and Europeans alike.

Here was a great opportunity to put the Labour view to the rank and file. The attempt is instructive. Griffiths' approach was scarcely radical. He agreed that Mau Mau was 'a throwback to barbarism'; that it must be eliminated; and that government must restore 'peace and order'. But he also roundly attacked the Conservatives' approach that was, in his view, setting back race relations in the multiracial colony. Like the *Mirror* (or Cameron), he wanted, instead, to enlist the support of African leaders. He urged that the ban on their public meetings be lifted: 'Let them hear Mr Mathu and other responsible leaders and they will I believe rally behind them'. He also called for 'bold and urgent measures to remove hardships and frustrations'. He listed these as land hunger, an absence of trades unions – vital, he revealingly insisted, not just to improve living standards but also to deliver 'cohesion and internal discipline' – the equal lack of producer co-operatives; and the colour bar. The tone was melodramatic, his final warning ominous. Using the image of natural elements out of control, he warned that 'All over Africa, there is a rising tide of

Nationalism': there was no time to lose.

Finally, the *Mirror*'s *pièce de résistance* was an open letter, purporting to be on behalf of the British people, addressed to an authority figure. Friday's edition for 12 December, inside the front page, carried an open letter 'To Sir Evelyn Baring, KCMG, Governor and Commander-in-Chief of Kenya' who was arriving in London the same day. It carried the big bold headline of 'OPEN LETTER to Sir Evelyn' beside a pensive photo of him. Cameron was the author, more evidence of his indignation at the excesses he had seen. He wrote on behalf of 'all the anxious and angry MPs' and for 'the thousands of British people who are horrified at what goes on in Kenya today'. He stated his purpose at the outset: Baring must change Lyttelton's mind 'QUICKLY' about his 'strong and forceful measures', before they 'sowed the final seeds of despair'. He told Baring, 'You are pretty well OUR last chance in Africa'.[39]

Cameron began by sympathizing with Baring. He had faced a 'hideous and deplorable situation' as a new governor, with 'a revolting pagan organisation' on one side, 'trigger happy settlers' on the other, and Lyttelton's 'rich layer of chaos and confusion' over all. But Cameron also barely disguised his contempt for one whose 'last administrative adventure', in southern Africa, had produced the 'sensational fiasco in human relations that resulted in the exile of Seretse Khama. For that you were promoted to handle the Mau Mau.' Ultimately, Cameron aimed to rally Labour anti-colonial activists, for he clearly had little faith in Baring's ability to deal with what the former thought they saw at the heart of Mau Mau, which was African nationalism. In melodramatic tones, again evoking the power of the elements and foreshadowing Harold Macmillan's rhetorical winds of change of 1960, Cameron reminded Baring of 'the terrifying fires that are smouldering right now from Cape Town to Casablanca. In the north the flames have broken out. In the south a dark neurotic cloud poisons the air. Nationalism – which you as a colonial servant are educated to respect – is being manipulated by evil opportunists. And right in the centre of it all – Kenya, and Your Excellency.'

Cameron was particularly angered by the white settlers' attack on the British left for its 'ignorance' of Kenya and lack of a stake 'in the country'. To the contrary, he replied, as if in Britain's name, 'WE HAVE ANOTHER STAKE IN THE COUNTRY; OUR GOOD NAME'. It was fatal to 'OUR REPUTATION' to impose collective punishment, detain without trial and destroy villages; it was also 'DISASTROUS, SELF-CORRUPTING and above all USELESS'. Repression was not achieving what everybody wanted – 'the crushing of terrorism and penalising of murder'. Cameron closed with a plea to Baring. He might well have the settlers behind him now. If, however, he did his duty 'BY YOUR HIGH OFFICE AND THE LIBERAL TRADITION OF YOUR SERVICE', he would have the 'British people' behind him in future.

Here was the moral crux of Kenya's real emergency, laid before a large slice of British public opinion. Even the left believed in the superiority of British colonial rule. They thought it to be liberal in purpose, and that officials – unlike settlers – aimed to nurture responsible African opinion. Paternal trusteeship for Africa's future remained acceptable. That made brute force unacceptable. This view reflected a long-standing British concern that absolute power overseas might corrupt individual officials, abuse native subjects and, ultimately, degrade Britain. The view that it was 'British' to avoid excess had been constructed in contrast to the spectre of other Europeans' brutality in Africa – King Leopold's outrages in the Congo. With the growth of a professional overseas civil service, it was possible to believe that white commercial greed and African fecklessness could be tempered by government vigilance. Kenya had been subject to the doctrine of the paramountcy of native interests since 1923. And after the second world war, a new generation of colonial civil servants had worked with London to reform the colonial state and redirect trusteeship towards development and training for self-government. But the superficial nature of that change could no longer be disguised, as the Emergency all too vividly revealed.[40] Scratch any colonial society, it seemed to the British left, and underneath one still found all the aggressions fomented by unequal racial rule. Guided by the pen of Cameron, a Celt bristling with working-class consciousness as well as macho-patriotism, *Mirror* readers had little cause to sentimentalize the notion of Britain and empire.

The Right thought Africans needed a much longer spell of white educational discipline. The *Daily Mail* showed little dismay at Kenya's Emergency, nor any anxiety about Britain's colonial reputation, in the following weeks. It published the Left's criticisms but countered by giving its readers more evidence of African brutality, good reason to doubt the Socialists. And their man on the spot reported differently, too. 'Full Moon Brings Theft Wave' was the Kenya news for 4 November; a month later '"If You Speak You Die", Mau Mau Tells African'.[41] These reports, which confirmed readers' prejudices, were flanked by smaller, quieter, headlines that offered an alternative perspective: 'Kenya Arrests Shock MP'; 'Pritt Complains a Second Time'. Such criticism would likely fall on stony ground, since readers had already been fed a critique of the critics – 'Starry-eyed Idealists Ignore Facts Behind Mau Mau'.[42] The *Mail* did not shield its readers from the growing Labour criticism of government policy. Under the headline 'Frustration of Mau Mau' they could read the Labour MP for Eton and Slough, Fenner Brockway's, declaration that Lyttelton was wrong to insist that Mau Mau owed nothing to social and economic grievance.[43] But how many would have read beyond the ambiguous headline and, had they done so, how many would have been concerned? For the piece was placed below another, much tastier, report: 'Dawn Swoop on Mau Mau Fanatics', cabled by Izzard from Nairobi.[44]

Similarly, the *Mail* gave little space to the escalating police and army violence. It saw this as of secondary importance or as a sad but inevitable consequence of the situation. For example, 'Dogs Whine in Dead Village of the Vultures: 2,000 Women Evicted'.[45] Moreover, the *Mail*'s reporters soon had the trial of Jomo Kenyatta with which to enthral and scare their readers. 'MAU MAU RITES REVEALED IN JOMO TRIAL – Name of Key Witness is Kept Secret to Save his Life' was headlined on 4 December. Two smaller items were placed at the side: 'Eight Kikuyu Shot in Raid', and '13,000 Arrests in Kenya' with the subtitle 'Knives Sharpened'. Any sense of a military over-reaction had little chance of surviving beyond the football results.[46] Moreover, reference to left-wing criticism was couched in partisan terms, such as 'Socialists After Lyttelton's Blood'.[47] Such an item, sandwiched between news that the Colonial Office intended to give the world a lead in co-operative race relations and a reminder that the 'Socialist government used collective punishment too', would cause irritation rather than concern. In any case, the *Mail*'s correspondent in Kenya, Izzard, like the *Mirror*'s Cameron, gave his readers the authoritative 'facts' with which to arm themselves against alternative voices. His own *coup de grâce* was delivered in late November, at the height of the left-wing barrage. Billed as the 'observer on the spot', Izzard identified the 'RED HAND BEHIND THE MAU MAU TROUBLES'.[48] Defying detection, Ethiopian Communist agents trained at the Russian mission in Addis Ababa and entering Kenya from Italian Somaliland, had allegedly disguised themselves as Kikuyu tribesmen in order to strengthen Mau Mau organization. A year later, would the right-wing popular press remain as unconvinced, as the left was convinced, that the Emergency besmirched the proud traditions of British colonial rule?

'Shoot Anyone you Like – if he is Black'

A year on from the declaration of the State of Emergency, Kenya was still hot news, thanks to allegations against a British officer, made public in November 1953. A 43-year-old company commander of the King's African Rifles' 5th (Kenya) Battalion, Captain Gerald Griffiths of the Durham Light Infantry, was alleged to have shot Mau Mau suspects in the back. At his court martial, details emerged of financial incentives offered to African troops for kills. A company score board (official kills on the front, unofficial kills on the back) was used in an inter-battalion killing competition. The story was front-page news for both papers, if in very different terms. The *Daily Mail* chose to print Griffiths' photo with only his name and rank, followed by 'pleads not guilty'. Elaboration came on page 3 under the headline 'Captain Paid 5sh. for Each Mau Death', swiftly followed by 'Shot Men Took Oath says Chief'. Thus readers were led gently to the sensational details, first via an image and title with an association of valour and rank; and then a self-justifying comment.[49]

The *Daily Mirror* showed no such care. It had led a day earlier with a bolder than bold heading that focused on the racial issue: '"SHOOT ANYONE YOU LIKE – IF HE IS BLACK": a British Officer is alleged to have given this order', and 'Barometer of "Kills"'.[50] The court martial took up most of the front page. Although there was no follow-up the next day, the paper nevertheless published a supportive, subliminal, message that, for the times, was remarkably harsh on white racism. The royal family – the queen indeed – acted as the *Mirror*'s messenger. Elizabeth and Philip had arrived in Kingston, Jamaica, on a royal tour, to be 'cheered by hundreds of thousands of the Queen's Negro subjects'. 'COLOURED CHILDREN RUSH TO CAR' was the headline, and 'Let them come, they are lovely, said the Queen'.[51] This shows perfectly how press manipulation could put the monarchy to a range of political uses. Two broadsides on Kenya followed. 'A TERRIBLE STATE OF AFFAIRS', the headline on 28 November, introduced a two-page, editorialized, account of the shoot-to-kill policy and its scoreboards. 'Ugly Picture' and 'What a Dreadful Plight Kenya Has Come To!' the *Mirror* exclaimed. Its characteristic rhetorical questions followed: 'Has the attack on Mau Mau turned into a British foxhunt? A tally was kept of "killed" as if they were grouse or partridge – not human beings and British subjects'.[52] The *Mirror* reckoned the public wanted an enquiry, under a high court judge. This surmise gave it authority for a self-styled '*DAILY MIRROR* CRUSADE'. The next edition – extraordinarily – carried a single extended news editorial to fill both the front and second pages. It opened with the question, 'What is Going On in our Colonies'.[53] The *Mirror* hammered the query home by linking events in Kenya and Bermuda, where a racial affront had been caused by the fact that 'no coloured guest' had been invited to dine with the queen. The paper reinforced its position on Kenya and the need for a public inquiry by again speaking for the people, and on behalf of colonial subjects, although it did not directly criticize Griffiths' acquittal. His case had nonetheless 'curdled millions of English folk'. It was parliament's duty to its '500,000,000 coloured subjects in the British Commonwealth ... to find out ... just what is being done in our name'.[54]

At first glance, the *Mail* seems to have reached a similarly critical stance. It produced a lengthy front-page editorial – under the dramatic heading 'CLOUD OVER AFRICA'.[55] But the commentary was different. For a start, the *Mail* had watched and waited an extra day. In the meantime the story had been covered through the words of the prosecuting officer '5s a head not wrong'. And then, on 1 December, a headline referred to an immediate, high-level, military reaction. General Erskine's deputy was reporting to the Home Office and Erskine himself would intervene: 'I am out to punish the unjust'.[56] Armed with such assurances, the *Mail*'s commentary warned its readers against being 'led into hysteria by those eager to denounce "ruthless imperialism" and its "brutal soldiering"'. The Griffiths revelations, it agreed, had 'shocked the British people'; and reprisals were 'not the answer'. However, Mau Mau was 'guilty of beastly atrocities' and could not be handled with 'kid gloves'. For the *Mail* it was enough that the most senior military officer had pledged himself to stamp out 'conduct which he "would be ashamed to wish against his own people"'.[57]

The papers then followed up the political repercussions. Their party connections tugged at editorial sympathies. The *Mail* soon found a way to present the colonial secretary, Lyttelton, as the hero of another colonial saga, the Kabaka's banishment from Buganda: 'Lyttelton Routs His Critics'. Next day the paper rubbished the Opposition: 'Socialist Party Split Over Africa Policy'.[58] It alleged there was about to be an 'explosion', since some Labour MPs 'broadly support the Government's policy in Africa'. The government's critics were a left-wing minority whose views were not shared by 'at least 20 influential backbenchers and ex-ministers'.[59]

Mirror readers, however, were oblivious to Labour's apparent disarray. The headline on 1 December 1953 saluted, instead, the opposition's courage in demanding a public inquiry into the five-bob-a-nob scandal: 'KENYA STORM BREAKS – MPs Told of General's Warning – Don't Just Beat Them Up Because They Live There!' The report cited Erskine's condemnation of beating up Kenyans, 'because they are the inhabitants'. It also quoted the minister for war, Anthony Head's, promise to order an immediate inquiry if the allegations proved true; and gave the overall verdict from Brockway, that the 'moral conscience of a large section of the people had been outraged'. In all, the *Mirror* implied that the Labour opposition held the initiative, in step with the generals.[60] A further instalment in the *Mirror*'s 'crusade' appeared on 6 December. The first item on the back-page 'World News Spotlight' reported the 'shock' of Kenya's Protestant church leaders. They were 'gravely concerned' and would continue to call for 'a radical change in attitude and action' from the Kenya authorities.[61]

The *Mail*, by contrast, responded to the Griffiths revelations with a tableau of government activity that suggested that official attitudes and action were appropriate and Lyttelton firmly in charge. It reported British funding for Kenya's development, over and above the counter-insurgent war: '£11,000,000 Lyttelton aid for Kenya Emergency. £6,000,000 to help fight Mau Mau war'. It also splashed the secretary of state's confident response to a 'fierce half hour' of Commons' questions. 'I WILL NOT TIE THE HANDS OF OUR TROOPS'; bombing had not been indiscriminate; troops were operating in 'thick jungle'; even under Labour there had been no less than eight colonial emergencies.[62]

However, the seriousness of this episode precluded any swift closure. To its credit, the *Mail* did not flinch from publishing the sequel. The minister for war announced Griffiths' suspension from duty, admitted the possibility of other such incidents and appointed a three-man board of inquiry, backed by Erskine, into rewards, scoreboards and inter-unit competitions. Neither the *Mail* nor its readers had enough of the context, or evidence, or the will, to interpret this outcome as a cover-up, or to worry too much about the possibility of abuse. But with even the war minister telling the Commons that 'the good name of the British army was at stake', and with yet further evidence of the abuse of power under the British flag, the right eventually had to concede what only the left had so far maintained. Where colonial rule had to confront a belligerent African nationalism was no place for an Englishman to be. Five years later both camps would share this view.

The British Popular Press and the Demoralization of Empire

'Another Mau Mau'?

In November 1959 the government announced the imminent end of Kenya's State of Emergency. In the history of decolonization, however, 1959 is not remembered for this. Two other events touched more seriously on the reputation of white colonial rule. Five years on, the press and its readers lived in a very different world against which to measure the actions of a post-Suez Tory government and the reactions of a reinvigorated Opposition. For *Daily Mail* readers in particular, the world was full of tension, its leaders angry. It was the Sputnik age of nuclear rivalry; and of growing preoccupation with China's 'yellow imperialism'.[63] The Gold Coast was independent Ghana; India's leaders had come in from the cold as they worried over Tibet. Yet some things never changed – from outrage that the Kabaka's brother had married a 17-year-old white girl to 'Sex Change GI to Wed'.[64]

Unsurprisingly, Kenya was no longer major news – not even a report, in early March, that 11 Mau Mau detainees had died in Hola detention camp. Ironically, at this very moment, the *Mail* ran a four-page publicity feature on the colony and its neighbours, designed to boost the confidence of investors and tourists. 'It's this striking success' was the verdict from Lennox-Boyd, the secretary of state, beside a map of Kenya showing the location of big game. Mau Mau was barely mentioned – 'a tragic diversion of both manpower and money', according to Baring. Instead, the governor pleaded that attention be directed to the 'agricultural revolution' and a three-point plan for progress. Other articles focused on 'the magic of Mombasa'; a thriving insecticide plant; and Tanganyika's reputation as 'the Crewe Junction of Africa'. The deaths at Hola attracted only a couple of lines in March; the inquest in April scarcely more.[65]

It was Nyasaland that commanded attention. The *Mail* showed familiar tendencies, at first portraying Hastings Banda as a fanatical megalomaniac. One headline read '"I'll Tell You What We Want" said Banda, the Black Messiah, "WE WANT THE LOT"'. Other descriptions followed suit: 'Banda is obsessed' and appeared 'flanked by two body guards called Caesar and Napoleon'.[66] The *Mail* also anticipated barbaric black bloodshed. The colony's capital was pictured waiting in a 'desperate stillness'; there were 'no men'; the 'quiet Sunday afternoon held something frightening and uncanny'. Readers were told on 4 March of a 'MASSACRE PLAN ... to kill black and white', like 'another Mau Mau'.[67] Never one to forget the ladies, the *Mail* headlined, 'We Fight to the End say British Wives', a couple of days later.[68]

Yet there were also signs that the *Mail* was less clear where it stood on news from Africa. Its special correspondent Noel Barber offered an in-depth analysis on the 'trouble and tension' that now spanned the continent. Photos of Banda showed him in sober suit and tie, accompanied by 'some of his African admirers'.[69] The *Mail* also gave more coverage now to left-wing opposition to white colonial rule. It reported the expulsion of the Labour MP John Stonehouse from Rhodesia; and used an interview with his wife to outline his career, under the sympathetic heading 'No Love for Johnnie in Africa'. Its parliamentary reporting featured the Opposition's criticisms of policy in Nyasaland.[70] Even a news item on Kenyatta's court appearance remarked on his flamboyance and 'hint of egoism' – no more evil genius, rather, eccentric celebrity.[71]

The *Daily Mirror*, which now claimed 'the biggest daily sale in the universe', allowed itself no such equivocation. Although it gave no space to Hola, its treatment of Nyasaland was bold and consistent. 'Cassandra' fulminated against the settlers. The paper was also sceptical of the 'massacre plot' and deplored the use of force in the colony. 'Who Speaks for Africans' was the headline of 10 March, supporting the paper's belief that African electoral representation was the only way forward.[72] By July, its stance was vindicated by the publication of an inquiry conducted by a high court judge, Lord Devlin, into the government's handling of the Nyasaland disturbances. On 24 July the front page was covered by a huge black map of Africa, with a triple headline: 'Macmillan's Day of Disgrace ... The Murder Plot That Never Was ... the Cabinet Minister He Refuses to Sack'.[73] Four days later, publication of the report into the Hola camp deaths lent more fuel to reignite the *Mirror*'s old crusade against Tory mishandling of the colonies. On 29 July, four pages into the paper, came the news that Labour MPs were demanding the resignation of both the colonial secretary and Kenya's governor.[74] A detailed account of the parliamentary debate then followed. This highlighted the observation by a Welsh Labour MP, George Thomas, that 'people regard it now as much a moral issue as a political issue and that somebody in authority should be man enough to take his punishment'. But the editorial of the day was reserved for Nyasaland, containing a three-point plan on 'HOW TO CLEAR UP THE MESS'. 'Nothing less', the editorial opened in familiar terms, 'can restore the good name and influence of Britain in Africa'. Next day it charged Lennox-Boyd and the government with neglecting the affair in order to concentrate on the forthcoming general election.[75]

The *Mail* also gave the Hola inquiry less space than the Devlin report. However, it gave more coverage to both than the *Mirror*, especially the controversy that broke out between the government and 'the Socialists'. The *Mail* stood by the Tories; in the paper's view, the barrage of left-wing criticism failed to find its mark. It reported, 'THE SOCIALISTS MISFIRE' and the 'jujube debate fizzles' – a reference to Nye Bevan's crossing the chamber to give Lennox-Boyd a throat pastille. The *Mail* was, nonetheless, pessimistic over the future of British rule in Africa.[76] Its charming cartoons provide the best evidence. 'Out on a limb' captioned a delightful sketch of a beleaguered Lennox-Boyd stuck up a tree and about to fall into the jaws of a pack of lions, representing the Labour front bench.[77] Four days later, the headline 'The Massacre Plan That Never Was' came with a cartoon that portrayed the colonial government's tragi-comic response to its fears of a second Mau Mau in Nyasaland. The giant shadow of a black man wielding a knife dripping blood was shown to be a silly nightmare, for the two white men with trembling knees in fact faced a smiling African sitting innocently by his cooking pot, what a contrast to the self-confident coverage of Mau Mau five years before.[78] Similarly, the *Mail* presented the Hola inquiry's criticisms without much indignation: 'Errors by Exemplary Officer Led to Mau Prison Disaster'.[79]

Overall, the *Mail*'s position by the end of the 1950s was that it was time to drop the burden of colonial rule. It had concluded that African nationalism was an aggressively masculine, even megalomaniac, force that dwarfed any well-meaning white colonial government that tried to protect ordinary Africans from the rapacious lust for immediate self-government. Again, it hammered the point home to readers with a cartoon image. The caption, 'Whitehall's Canutes CAN'T hold back this black tide', accompanied a giant of an African about to squash a scared and weedy white man leading 'his' African children to safety.[80] In similar vein, the editorial for 29 July began with the heading 'One Man's Burden' and concluded that the burden of colonial rule was now too heavy for one man, possibly a deliberate, if evasive, evocation of Rudyard Kipling's burdened 'white man'. It was, the *Mail* concluded, time to replace the Colonial Office with the Commonwealth Relations Office, 'the name alone being far more suitable'. What meaning was encoded here is hard to say. Commonwealth was self-evidently taking over from empire. But did the *Mail* also think it more acceptable to the United States, Kipling's own other white man?

When in November 1959 it was announced that Kenya's State of Emergency was to end, both *Mirror* and *Mail* showed little emotion; equally, both welcomed the new colonial secretary, Iain Macleod. For the *Mirror*, he offered a new approach. Unusually, it quoted a plea from Sir Patrick Renison, the new governor: 'let us put the darkness behind us'.[81] For the *Mail*, the news merited the front page with the headline, 'New Colonial Secretary Begins Chains-off Policy'. The paper supported this 'new thinking', this attempt to 'look bravely into the future'. Its editorial continued the theme under the heading 'KENYA FREED'. It invited its readers to see a British victory. Kenya would be free not only from Emergency restrictions but also from Mau Mau. Had it not been for the Emergency and its 'big programme of rehabilitation under the guidance of Lennox-Boyd the country would have been submerged into the primitive blood lust of Mau Mau'. Thousands of detainees had been 'transformed into normal Africans'; those 'perverted' by a beastly cult had been successfully 'recivilized'.

Conclusion

As this close re-reading of the two most influential British popular papers of the 1950s has shown, the declaration of Kenya's State of Emergency provoked great interest, while its most infamous debacle at Hola, and its ending, did not. The *Daily Mail* backed the Emergency regulations; supported the government; and sympathized with the settlers, often sharing their racial prejudice against African incapacity. The *Daily Mirror*, by contrast, became increasingly critical of the colonial government's response and attacked the very foundations of British policy in Africa. Although the *Mirror* was revolted by the barbarity of Mau Mau, it was equally revolted by strong-arm tactics in the face of a crisis that had political and economic roots. The *Mirror* was concerned that imperial force would both poison race relations and ruin the United Kingdom's reputation as a liberal, law-abiding, colonial power. By the end of the 1950s, even the *Mail* seems to have detached its readers from the cause of white settlerdom in Africa. It had come to recognize, instead, the unstoppable power of African nationalism.

The popular press did more than 'tickle the public' over the crises in colonial rule. It was informative, if also manipulative and provocative. As this chapter has shown, press coverage provided much news of empire. Since newspaper space was short, and readers' time shorter, coverage also had to be short and sharp. Journalists and editors had no choice but to inter-connect news reports, and find patterns in regional developments in ways that were beyond the politicians and the civil servants. Reporters on the spot offered what readers took to be authoritative accounts. Images were equally important, whether photographs or political cartoons, employed to back up one view of events. By the end of the 1950s, the Right had run out of positive images of empire – white minority rule of empire in particular – to display to its readers. African nationalists wore suits and ties. Colonial officials had wobbly knees and over-heated imaginations. For the Left, Africa was a solid black mass – its blackness being the shame of a colonial power that suppressed African self-determination.

This evidence suggests that the contribution of popular opinion to the politics of rapid decolonization has been unwisely neglected. The mass electorate read of Macmillan's 'winds of change', in the guise of 'tides' and 'fires' of African nationalism, years before 1960. Macleod's 'flying Scotsman' act followed in the wake of Cameron's critique of colonial policy. The sharp divergence within the popular press over the African colonies contrasts with the bipartisan consensus that the two major political parties tacitly upheld. As mediated by the press, Mau Mau, for all its tragic human cost, helped to prevent a much worse disaster – namely, a Conservative Party that might have resisted handing over power to African nationalists beyond the later 1950s. For the Tory government regained office in 1959 by appealing to the middle ground, and as far as keeping the empire went the middle ground, as represented by the *Mail*, was by now as demoralized as the Left was uninterested.[82]

Ultimately, and perversely, since this is a chapter on the coverage of imperial news in the British press, this study supports the view that the value of empire was by no means self-evident to the postwar public. Most people went along with empire. They could be cheered by a report of royalty extending the gloved hand of distant friendship to 'the native'; they could as well be angered by the Tory racket of empire, to which Mau Mau seemed to bear witness.[83] The Indian summer of empire's popular culture

– engendered in celluloid since the 1930s, fired by imperial wartime co-operation, regaled by royal tours overseas – may have actually shortened the shelf-life of empire after the second world war.[84] A ridicule of Colonel Blimps, caricatured in their imperial ornamentalism; a gratitude to colonial peoples for their sacrifices in battle; and a sense of being equal subjects under a single crown, whose young queen was happy to 'suffer the coloured children to come to me' – all these were powerful undercurrents that eroded a sentimental attachment to empire right or wrong. Far-off colonial affairs in any case mattered less than bread-and-butter loyalty to party. But for many working people, unionized and sympathetic to Labour, their class consciousness made them naturally more suspicious of colonial authority than has been supposed. Going along with empire co-existed with not going along with imperialism. By the 1950s, even the aristocracy of labour and the lower-middle-class reading and voting public had a complex understanding of colonial rule – that it must promote the evolution of a Commonwealth and shame South Africa in its race relations. The Celt, George Bernard Shaw, well knew the British gift for marrying high principle to self-interest. Empire was becoming costly; Commonwealth trade would doubtless continue. Colonial power-dressing had long lost its flair, and anti-imperialism had all the best tunes.

Notes

1. The archival research for this chapter was funded by the Department of History, Durham University. For the best treatment of the fetishization of Mau Mau in European minds see John M. Lonsdale, 'Mau Maus of the Mind: Making Mau Mau and Remaking Kenya', *Journal of African History* 31 (1990): 393-421; D. Kennedy, 'Constructing the Colonial Myth of Mau Mau', *International Journal of African Historical Studies* 25, 2 (1992): 241–60.
2. '"Rowdy Commons like Mau Mau", says MP', *Daily Mirror*, 8 Dec. 1952, p. 3; and family reminiscences over the years especially from my uncle, Andrew Lewis, Penclawdd, South Wales.
3. I am grateful to Professor Richard Rathbone for this. Sung to a popular tune, the lyrics, adulterated from the original 'Daddy wouldn't buy me a Bow-wow', are 'Daddy wouldn't buy me a Mau Mau (repeat). I've got a strangled cat, and I'm very fond of that, But I would rather have a Mau Mau Mau.'
4. See David Maughan Brown, *Land, Freedom and Fiction: History and Ideology in Kenya* (1985).
5. The late Richard Hennings, formerly of the Kenya administration, in conversation with John M. Lonsdale. For international relations in this period, see David Reynolds, *One World Divisible: A Global History Since 1945* (2000).
6. J. Tunstall, *The New National Press in Britain* (1996); J. Curran & J. Seaton, *Power Without Responsibility: The Press and Broadcasting in Britain* (1995); P. Catterall, C. Seymour-Ure and A. Smith (eds), *Northcliffe's Legacy: Aspects of the British Popular Press, 1896–1996*, (2000).
7. C. Seymour-Ure, 'Northcliffe's Legacy', in Catterall et al., *Northcliffe's Legacy*, p. 11.
8. Tunstall, *New National Press*, 223; *Annual Press Directory* (1952), British Library of Newspapers.
9. *Daily Mail*, 4 Sept. 1952, p. 4.
10. R. Negrine, *The Communication of Politics* (1996), especially Chap. 5, 'Public opinion, the

media and the democratic process', pp. 101–26.

11. Stephen Howe, *Anticolonialism in British Politics: The Left and the End of Empire, 1918-1964* (1993); Nicholas Owen, 'Critics of Empire in Britain', in Judith M. Brown & Wm. Roger Louis (eds), *The Oxford History of British Empire*, Vol. IV, *The Twentieth Century* (Hereafter *OHBE IV*) (1999), pp. 188–211.
12. For the broadsheets see Margery Perham, *Colonial Sequence 1949–69* (London, 1970); E.S. Atieno Odhiambo, 'The International Press and the Mau Mau War: A Diagnostic Note', Historical Association of Kenya Annual Conference paper (Aug. 1981); C. Shelton Nickens, 'British Newspaper Reaction to Mau Mau: The cases of the *Manchester Guardian*, *The Times* and the *Daily Telegraph*' (1970). On pamphleteering, see Joanna Lewis, 'Mau Mau's War of Words: The Battle of the Pamphlets', in James Raven (ed.), *Free Print and Non-Commercial Publishing since 1700* (London, 2000), Chap. 11, pp. 222–47. On Kenyan pampleteers, see Cristiana Pugliese's chapter in this volume.
13. Matthew Engels, *Tickle the Public* (1996).
14. Heather Jean Brooks, 'Suit, Tie, and a Touch of Juju – The Ideological Construction of Africa: A Critical Discourse Analysis of News on Africa in the British Press', *Discourse and Society* 6, 4 (1995): 461–94.
15. G. Ward Price, 'A New Dominion? Federation in Africa hinges on White Settlers' Opposition to Watch Committee Plan', *Daily Mail*, 4 Sept., 1952, p. 4.
16. 'The Women May Decide in New Dominion Polling: Africa's Great Experiment in Black and White', *Daily Mail*, (5 Sept 1952), p. 4.
17. *Ibid.*
18. *Daily Mail*, 13 Sept. 1952, p. 1.
19. 'How Recruits Join Mau Mau', *Daily Mail*, 15 Sept. 1952, p. 2.
20. 'Educated Men Organising the Pagan Terrorists: Threat of Death Keeps Mau Mau Secrets', from Ralph Izzard, *Daily Mail*, 16 Oct. 1952, p. 4.
21. We cannot know whom Izzard consulted. One of his informants may have been Dr Louis Leakey, anthropologist, self-styled Kikuyu and government adviser on Mau Mau, for Izzard had surprisingly acute ideas on the deviant sociology of Mau Mau oathing, and gave his readers a mini-lecture on Kikuyu animism. On Leakey in the Emergency see, Bruce J. Berman & John M. Lonsdale, 'Louis Leakey's Mau Mau: a study in the politics of knowledge', *History and Anthropology* 5, 2 (1991): 143–204.
22. 'Mau Mau: Kenya Chief to Clamp on Martial Law', *Daily Mail*, 13 Oct. 1952, p. 1.
23. 'God of the tribe arrested [above photo]: JOMO KENYATTA. He was once a farm worker in Sussex [below photo]'. Main headline: 'KENYA COMB-OUT SNARES 98 LEADERS: COLONY GREETS A "FIRM HAND"'. A small photo of Mrs Edna Grace Kenyatta (an Englishwoman), described as a 43-year-old preparatory-school teacher, accompanied the piece.
24. *Daily Mail*, 16 Oct. 1952, p. 8. Surrounding photos showed Nelson's column, recent Hollywood arrivals and an autumnal scene.
25. 'TOGETHER: MAU MAU TERRORIST IS CHARGED', *Daily Mail* 13 and 20 Oct. 1952.
26. *Daily Mirror*, 28 Nov. 1952, p. 1.
27. *Daily Mirror*, 27 Oct. 1952, p. 8. Supporting photos included African policemen, British soldiers in a control room reminiscent of the second world war, and two topless corporals.
28. *Daily Mirror*, 25 Oct. 1952, p. 2.
29. *Daily Mirror*, 3 Nov. 1952, p. 5; 11 Nov. 1952, p. 8; 12 Nov. 1952, p. 8.
30. 27 Oct. and 3 Nov. 1952, *Daily Mirror* editions.
31. *Daily Mail*, 21 Oct. 1952, pp. 1, 2, 8.
32. *Daily Mail*, 22 Oct. 1952, p. 1.
33. *Daily Mail*, 22, 25, 29 Oct. 1952, various pages.
34. *Daily Mirror*, 24, 26, 27 Nov, 1952, front and back pages.
35. *Daily Mirror*, 26, 27 Nov. 1952, front and back pages.
36. 'WILL NOBODY STOP MR LYTTELTON?' *Daily Mirror*, 1 Dec. 1952, p. 1.
37. 'Labour Prepares a Kenya Plan', *Daily Mirror*, 2 Dec. 1952, 1. The main headline was 'Russia's East German Army doubled'. Kenya also ranked below GI George who was now Christine: 'Dear Mum and Dad, son wrote, I've now become your daughter'. Sex

changes were tabloid favourites.

38. 'WHAT SHOULD WE DO IN KENYA BY THE RT. HON. JAMES GRIFFITHS, M.P.', *Daily Mirror,* 6 Dec. 1952, p. 2.
39. 'OPEN LETTER to Sir Evelyn', *Daily Mirror,* 12 Dec. 1952, p. 2. Compare Negley Farson, *Last Chance in Africa* (1947).
40. Joanna Lewis, 'The ruling compassions of the late colonial state in Kenya, 1945–52', *Journal of Colonial and Commonwealth History* 2, 2 (2001); Joanna Lewis, *Empire State-Building: War and Welfare in Kenya, 1925–1952* (Oxford, 2000), a view shared by Caroline Elkins' chapter in this volume.
41. *Daily Mail,* 4 Nov. 1952, p. 1; 2, 4 Dec. 1952, both p. 3.
42. *Daily Mail,* 29 Oct. 1952, p. 2.
43. *Daily Mail,* 14 Dec. 1952, p. 3.
44. *Ibid.*
45. *Daily Mail,* 27 Nov. 1952, p. 3.
46. *Daily Mail,* 4 Dec. 1952, p. 3.
47. *Daily Mail,* 16 Dec. 1952, p. 4.
48. *Daily Mail,* 1 Dec. 1952, back page.
49. *Daily Mail,* 27 Nov. 1953, pp. 1, 3.
50. *Daily Mirror,* 26 Nov. 1953.
51. *Daily Mirror,* 27 Nov. 1953, back page. John Walters reported how one 'withered and shabby' old woman cried, '"Lordie it's the Queen!" then she fell into the arms of a younger woman in a faint.'
52. *Daily Mirror,* 28 Nov. 1953, pp. 1–2 (with front-page photo of the queen).
53. *Daily Mirror,* 30 Nov. 1953, pp. 1–2.
54. *Ibid.*
55. *Daily Mail,* 1 Dec. 1953, p. 1.
56. *Daily Mail,* 28 Nov. 1953, p. 2; 1 Dec. 1953, p. 1.
57. Commentary, *Daily Mail,* 1 Dec. 1953, p. 1.
58. *Daily Mail,* 3 Dec. 1953, p. 1; 4 Dec. 1953, p. 2, subheaded 'Crisis Developing in the Socialist Party Over its Colonial Policy'.
59. *Daily Mail,* 4 Dec. 1953, p. 2.
60. Fenner Brockway, *Outside the Right* (1963). The first edition's cover carried an extract from a review by James Cameron.
61. *Daily Mirror,* 6 Dec. 1953, back page (16).
62. *Daily Mail,* 10 Dec. 1953, p. 2. There had been five emergencies so far under the Tories: Nigeria, British Guiana, Kenya, Buganda and Sarawak.
63. *Daily Mail,* 31 March 1959, p. 1.
64. *Daily Mail,* 12, 31 March 1959, front page stories.
65. 'They're falling like flies, said Mau Camp Man', *Daily Mail,* 7 April 1959, p. 2.
66. *Daily Mail,* 2, 6 March 1959, p. 1.
67. *Daily Mail,* 4 March 1959, p. 1.
68. *Daily Mail,* 6 March 1959, p. 1.
69. *Daily Mail,* 3 March 1959, p. 3.
70. *Daily Mail,* 4, 5 March 1959, pp. 4, 5 respectively.
71. *Daily Mail,* 3 March 1959.
72. *Daily Mirror,* 4, 19 March 1959, pp. 4, 1 respectively.
73. *Daily Mirror,* 24 July 1959, pp. 1, 3.
74. 'HOLA "GET OUT" CALL', *Daily Mirror,* 29 July 1959, p. 4.
75. 'You sacrifice Africans for the election', *Daily Mirror,* 29 July 1959, p. 14.
76. *Daily Mail,* 29 July 1959, pp. 1, 7.
77. *Daily Mail,* 20 July 1959, p. 4.
78. *Daily Mail,* 24 July 1959, p. 4.
79. *Daily Mail,* 24 July 1959, p. 6.
80. *Daily Mail,* 7 March 1959, p. 9.
81. *Daily Mirror,* 11 Nov. 1959, p. 4.
82. Ritchie Ovendale, 'Macmillan and the Wind of Change in Africa, 1957–1960', *Historical Journal* 38, 2 (1995): 455–77; Philip E. Hemming, 'Macmillan and the End of

the British Empire in Africa', in Richard Aldous & Sabine Lee (eds), *Harold Macmillan and Britain's World Role* (Basingstoke, 1995), pp. 97–121; Philip Murphy, *Alan Lennox-Boyd: a Biography* (1999); Wm. Roger Louis, 'The Dissolution of the British Empire', in Brown & Louis (eds), *OHBE IV*, Chap. 14, pp. 329–56; Nicholas Owen, 'Decolonisation and Post-War Consensus', in H. Jones & M.D. Kandiah (eds), *The Myth of Consensus. New Views on British History, 1945–64*, (1996), pp. 157–81.

83. Compare P. J. Marshall's review of David Cannadine, *Ornamentalism: How the British Saw their Empire* (London, 2001), at: <www.history.ac.uk>
84. John M. Mackenzie, 'The Popular Culture of Empire in Britain', in Brown & Louis (eds), *OHBE IV*, Chap. 9, p. 229.

Part V
Critical Modes

[17]

History and Imperialism:
A Century of Theory, from Marx to Postcolonialism

PATRICK WOLFE

IMPERIALISM RESEMBLES DARWINISM, in that many use the term but few can say what it really means. This imprecision is encouraged by a surfeit of synonyms. Two stand out: imperialism is taken to be interchangeable with colonialism and reducible to the word "empire." Add to these the compounding effects of elaborations such as hegemony, dependency, or globalization and the definitional space of imperialism becomes a vague, consensual gestalt.

In its stricter Marxist-Leninist applications, the word "imperialism" dates from the end of the nineteenth century and minimally connotes the use of state power to secure (or, at least, to attempt to secure) economic monopolies for national companies. On this basis, imperialism is not necessarily an extranational project, which would appear to distinguish it from colonialism. Moreover, the monopoly criterion excludes open-door policies, relegating "U.S. imperialism" and "cultural imperialism" to the realm of rhetoric but seeming to leave "Soviet imperialism" with at least a leg to stand on.[1] Since the term "imperialism" has been so closely associated with Left opposition to U.S. foreign policy, it is apparent that later usage of the term has not been too respectful of Marxist technicalities.

In what follows, I shall not presume to dispense a received definition of imperialism. Rather, the term will be used heuristically to group together a somewhat disparate set of theories of Western hegemony (including Marxism, dependency, postcolonialism, globalization, etc.).[2] Although these theories have most often been discussed in relative isolation from each other, taken together, as they will be here, they make up a multifaceted debate that continued for most of the

For their advice and criticism, I am very grateful to Tracey Banivanua Mar, Phillip Darby, Simon During, Leela Gandhi, and Stuart Macintyre. I would also like to thank Prasenjit Duara and the *AHR* staff for their helpful comments and Mike Grossberg for the opportunity.

[1] For informed and pointed comments on contemporary uses of the term "imperialism," see two of the contributions to *Radical History Review*'s (no. 57, 1993) forum, "Imperialism—A Useful Category of Historical Analysis?": Bruce Cumings, "Global Realm with No Limit, Global Realm with No Name," 46–59; and Carl P. Parrini, "The Age of Ultraimperialism," 7–20, esp. 13–14 and n. 16. For a thorough and somewhat skeptical account of the concept of cultural imperialism, see John Tomlinson, *Cultural Imperialism: A Critical Introduction* (London, 1991). For discourse analysis of a range of examples, see Amy Kaplan and Donald Pease, eds., *Cultures of United States Imperialism* (Durham, N.C., 1993).

[2] For reasons of space, Japanese imperialism will not be discussed. A good account that concludes with World War II is W. G. Beasley, *Japanese Imperialism 1894–1945* (Oxford, 1987). Though published in 1973, Jon Halliday and Gavan McCormack's remarks on 224–31 of their *Japanese Imperialism Today: "Co-Prosperity in Greater East Asia"* (New York) remain suggestive.

twentieth century. I shall attempt to characterize and criticize some of the more influential contributions to this debate. To give a sense of the theoretical contexts to which authors have been responding, the account will generally proceed in chronological order. This should not be taken to suggest a teleology in which theories of imperialism have progressively improved (or, even worse, approximated more closely to reality). As should become clear, these theories have varied so widely in terms of emphases and problematics that they are not necessarily even commensurable. Moreover, they have been enunciated under different historical conditions. This notwithstanding, a reasonable degree of coherence can be achieved by organizing discussion around two oppositions that, though misleading, have demonstrably structured debates about imperialism. The first of these is between the internal and the external, variously manifesting as European versus colonial, core versus periphery, developed versus developing, etc. Although this opposition is false because its two terms co-produce each other, accounts of imperialism are comparable on the basis of the ways in which they have distributed emphasis between the two. The second opposition is between the ideal and the material, whose alternatives include ideological versus practical, cultural versus economic, discursive versus instrumental, etc. Even though this opposition overlooks the obvious fact that consciousness is inseparable from practical activity, the majority of the theories that we will consider stress one at the expense of the other. These two oppositions are meant as implicit guides and should not be imposed too rigidly on the material. I intend to show that, at different times, in different political situations, and with different strategic intentions, they have been differently emphasized and configured. The interplay between theories of imperialism and the varied contexts within which they have been framed will, I hope, be more informative than an attempt to rank them on their merits. To this end, we will start with Marx.

ALTHOUGH KARL MARX PRECEDED THE DEBATE ON IMPERIALISM and did not use the term, the majority of theorists of imperialism have claimed to be furthering his ideas. While Marx saw capitalism's need for endless expansion as producing a Malthusian struggle for survival between an ever-dwindling group of monopolies, it is important to recognize that this vision was thoroughly positive, in the nineteenth-century sense. Rather than simply decrying capitalism, Marx admired its achievements, which were historically prerequisite to the transition to socialism. Moreover, the dialectical process ensured that, before a given mode of production was transcended, the class struggle would have scoured out its full historical potential. Historical development was, in short, as much qualitative as quantitative.

Although the "internal" dialectic of class conflict largely accounted for the historical preeminence of Europe, other societies were a different matter, for the simple reason that, unlike the European case, their historical development was not unprecedented. Rather, Europe was already there, a coexistent future whose impact was bound to be transformative.[3] Hence Marx's famous assertion—which

[3] In the case of the United States, this situation was reversed, since, unlike Europe, it lacked a

was to prove so embarrassing to Marxist liberation movements in the following century—that England had a double mission in India. While colonial intrusion and the reorganization of native society to serve the requirements of European capital had certainly occasioned untold destruction, the corollary was that capitalism itself—with its railroads, industrial infrastructure, and communication systems—had introduced a dynamic historical germ that would rouse Indian society from the timeless stagnation of the Asiatic mode of production and set it on its own course of historical development, a course that would eventually lead through capitalism to an Indian transition to socialism.[4]

In the decade following Marx's death in 1883, capitalist monopolization did indeed gain rapid momentum, only the consequences were not as he had foreseen. For, rather than carving up each other, monopolies began to carve up the market, with cooperative trusts, oil cartels, and, on the other side of the Atlantic, empire-wide closed shops becoming the order of the day.[5] Given the inconsistency between this trend and some of Marx's predictions,[6] it is not surprising that the most developed initial responses to it should have come not from within Marxism but from the world of liberal capitalism itself. Even though the English liberal J. A. Hobson's *Imperialism: A Study*, which appeared in 1902, was to shape subsequent debates about imperialism as a result of the formative influence it had on the thinking of V. I. Lenin, Hobson was not the first in the field. As Norman Etherington has shown, in the United States, with the possibilities of frontier expansion exhausted, the era that saw John D. Rockefeller's formation of the Standard Oil Trust, the recession of the 1890s, and the Spanish-American War produced a range of American proposals for exploiting the opportunities that imperialism held out. Not for the first time, description lagged behind prescription,

---

feudal past ("a country where bourgeois society did not develop on the foundation of the feudal system, but developed rather from itself; where this society appears not as the surviving result of a centuries-old movement, but rather as the starting-point of a new movement." Karl Marx, *Grundrisse: Foundations of the Critique of Political Economy*, Martin Nicolaus, trans. [New York, 1973], 884).

[4] Karl Marx, "The Future Results of the British Rule in India" (1853), rpt. in Marx and Friedrich Engels, *The First Indian War of Independence, 1857–1959* [*sic*] (Moscow, 1959), 29–35. For concise discussions of Marx's views on Asia (his attitude to colonized Ireland was different), see Anthony Brewer, *Marxist Theories of Imperialism: A Critical Survey*, 2d edn. (New York, 1990), 48–56; Hélène Carrère d'Encausse and Stuart R. Schram, *Marxism and Asia* (London, 1969), 7–10; A. James Gregor and M. H. Chang, "Marxism, Sun Yat-sen and the Concept of Imperialism," *Pacific Affairs* 55 (1982): 58–61.

[5] For U.S. trusts and the new economic thinking associated with them, see Carl Parrini and M. J. Sklar, "New Thinking about the Market, 1896–1904: Some American Economists on Investment and the Theory of Surplus Capital," *Journal of Economic History* 43 (1983): 559–78. For Chamberlain's "social imperialism," a radical departure from Victorian Britain's commitment to laissez faire in favor of a combination of tariffs and colonial trade compacts designed to strengthen the empire while assuaging unrest at home, a formula that rendered the weary imperial Titan ingloriously reliant on the good will of its dominions, see Peter J. Cain and Anthony G. Hopkins, *British Imperialism: Innovation and Expansion 1688–1914* (New York, 1993), 204–13; Bernard Semmel, *Imperialism and Social Reform: English Social-Imperial Thought, 1895–1914* (London, 1966); John Eddy and D. M. Schreuder, eds., *The Rise of Colonial Nationalism: Australia, New Zealand, Canada and South Africa First Assert Their Nationalities, 1880–1914* (Sydney, 1988), 19–20; compare Richard Jebb, *Studies in Colonial Nationalism* (London, 1905), 240.

[6] Though, in a corpus as tactically heterogeneous as that of Marx, it is often possible to find countervailing possibilities, as H. Gaylord Wilshire did in reaching the conclusion that Marx had anticipated the rise of trusts. See Norman Etherington, *Theories of Imperialism: War, Conquest and Capital* (London, 1984), 27.

or, as Etherington phrased it: "Hobson did not invent the idea that capitalism would benefit from imperialism. Capitalists invented that idea."[7]

For canonical purposes, though, the terms of the post-Marxian debate on imperialism were definitively set by Hobson, whose views were prompted by opposition to the Boer War.[8] Hobson's starting point, which was to become axiomatic to the entire debate on imperialism, was the problem of the economic surplus that capitalism generated. The downsizing and new technologies that an increasingly competitive domestic market generated boosted productivity beyond the market's capacity to consume its output, leaving a glut of both commodities and, since reinvestment was thus rendered pointless, of profits (the "underconsumptionist" thesis). The solution lay in immature markets overseas. Hence imperialism as an outlet for surplus. Since it only benefited a plutocratic few and directed national expenditure toward warfare and away from socially beneficial undertakings, Hobson recommended that imperialism be discontinued in favor of an income redistribution that would produce a more equitable and domestically viable form of capitalism.[9]

The details of Hobson's analysis need not concern us here. The crucial feature—which, apart from presaging World War I, distinguishes the "technical" imperialism that emerged at the end of the nineteenth century from earlier forms of colonial or imperial hegemony—is the element of compulsion that arose at the point where productivity exceeded the consumptive capacity of a metropolitan market conceived as finite and contained.[10] Co-conditioned by this imperative, monopoly trusts—which maintained domestic profits by fixing prices—and imperialism—which displaced the pressure of domestic limits—were two sides of the same coin.[11]

[7] Etherington, *Theories of Imperialism*, 7. For a different view, see James Sturgis, "Britain and the New Imperialism," in C. C. Eldridge, ed., *British Imperialism in the Nineteenth Century* (London, 1984), 85–105; compare A. M. Eckstein, "Is There a 'Hobson-Lenin Thesis' on Late Nineteenth Century Colonial Expansion?" *Economic History Review* 44 (1991): 297–318.

[8] He was also reacting more generally to Britain's post-1872 economic decline. Hobson's polemic on propaganda and the Boer War, *Psychology of Jingoism* (London, 1901), is a neglected gem that substantially anticipated cultural studies and amply rewards a contemporary reading. See also Hobson, *The War in South Africa: Its Causes and Effects* (London, 1900).

[9] Hobson's assessment was to receive laborious cliometric validation in Lance E. Davis and Robert A. Huttenback, *Mammon and the Pursuit of Empire: The Political Economy of British Imperialism, 1860–1912* (Cambridge, 1986), which concluded that, from 1880 on, empire did not provide the ordinary investor with better returns than the domestic economy.

[10] For obvious reasons, Hobson himself did not accept that domestic capitalism had no alternative. Within the Marxist tradition, N. I. Bukharin would systematically elaborate the element of compulsion in his influential 1917 work, *Imperialism and the World Economy* (London, 1972).

[11] In view of the constraint of space, I have decided not to discuss Karl Kautsky's "ultra-imperialism" (or Hobson's "inter-imperialism") thesis, important though it is for appreciating the implications of market-apportioning compacts between nation-states. Even though, as is well known, Kautsky had the misfortune to have an article explaining why wars between imperial powers were unlikely to happen published in *Die neue Zeit* on September 11, 1914, as the battle of the Marne was getting into full swing, his prediction that the capitalist states would cooperate rather than engage in internecine destruction has clearly had more purchase on the long term than it had on the immediate term. See Kautsky, "Ultra-imperialism" (original German title "Der Imperialismus"), *New Left Review* 59 (January–February 1970): 39–46, but ignore the introduction. For the same reason, I will not be discussing either Joseph Schumpeter or the Wisconsin school of Cold War revisionism associated with the name (and authority) of William Appleman Williams, which one might see as having much in common with Kautsky, especially insofar as it stressed the role of U.S. diplomacy in preventing political rivalries between the leading industrial democracies from hindering the international advancement of corporate

The classical Marxist debate on imperialism shuffled the foregoing concepts and derived varying strategic implications from them. Given the emancipatory aspirations of the Communist movement, however, it could hardly remain just a view from above. Initially surfacing at the Amsterdam and Stuttgart congresses of the Second International, in 1904 and 1907 respectively, but achieving full expression a decade of so later in the 1920 Comintern theses of M. N. Roy, founder of the Communist Party of India, the view was expressed that, rather than leading the rest of the world, the revolution in Europe was contingent on revolution in the colonies. Briefly, this conclusion followed from the observation that the bourgeoisie could buy off the metropolitan proletariat, and thus postpone the revolution in Europe, by intensifying exploitation in the colonies.[12] This consequence of imperialism was widely accepted, not only by prominent Marxist theoreticians such as Karl Kautsky,[13] Rudolf Hilferding,[14] and Rosa Luxemburg[15] but by arch-imperialists such as Cecil Rhodes[16] and Joseph Chamberlain.[17] Although the strategic implications that these varied figures derived from their common perception differed widely, for our purposes the perception itself is significant for its negation of a barrier between the metropolitan and the colonial, which emerged as integrated aspects of a systemic whole.[18] This theme would be considerably elaborated in later twentieth-century thinking on imperialism.

Of perhaps even greater significance for later—indeed, for some of the most recent—writing on imperialism is Roy's conclusion, which the classical theorists of imperialism rejected, that the colonized could be the subjects and authors of revolution. At the 1920 Comintern, Lenin made concessions to Roy's position, a gesture that was enabled by the accommodation to Asia that was built into his own theory of imperialism, an accommodation that a Russian revolutionary could hardly

---

interests (the open-door policy as more cost-effective than formal colonization). See Williams, *The Tragedy of American Diplomacy* (Cleveland, Ohio, 1959); and *Empire as a Way of Life* (New York, 1980). In this connection, I am grateful to my friend and departmental colleague (and one-time Williams student) Chips Sowerwine for showing me his illuminating unpublished paper, "A Revisionist's Historiography of the Cold War."

[12] Roy's perspective had been prefigured by Marx in 1853: "It may seem a very strange, and a very paradoxical assertion that the next uprising of the people of Europe, and their next movement for republican freedom and economy of government, may depend more probably on what is now passing in the Celestial Empire [China],—the very opposite of Europe,—than on any other political cause that now exists . . . But yet it is no paradox . . . [I]t may safely be augured that the Chinese revolution will throw the spark into the overloaded mine of the present industrial system and cause the explosion of the long-prepared general crisis [in England], which, spreading abroad, will be closely followed by political revolutions on the Continent." Karl Marx, *On Colonialism* (Moscow, n.d.), 15, 21.

[13] Karl Kautsky, *Sozialismus und Kolonialpolitik* (Berlin, 1907).

[14] Rudolf Hilferding, *Finance Capital: A Study of the Latest Phase of Capitalist Development*, Tom Bottomore, ed. (1910; London, 1981).

[15] Rosa Luxemburg, *The Accumulation of Capital* (1913; London, 1951).

[16] As Lenin recounted it, Rhodes said to his journalist friend Stead: "My dearest wish is to see the social problem solved: that is to say that in order to save the forty million inhabitants of the United Kingdom from bloody civil war, we colonial politicians must conquer new lands to take our excess population and to provide new outlets for the goods produced in our factories and mines. The Empire, as I have always said, is a question of bread and butter. If you do not want civil war, you must become imperialists." V. I. Lenin, *Imperialism, the Highest Stage of Capitalism* (1916; Moscow, 1970), 76.

[17] Semmel, *Imperialism and Social Reform*. See also E. J. Hobsbawm, *The Age of Empire 1875–1914* (London, 1987), 69.

[18] Marx and Engels had observed that the expansion of capitalism across the globe would result in a unified economic system; *Manifesto of the Communist Party* (1888 edn.; London, 1983), 18–19.

avoid. Even though Lenin's *Imperialism, the Highest* [or should it really be the latest?] *Stage of Capitalism* (1916) enjoys unrivaled status in the annals of theories of imperialism, apart from its Asian dimension, the work's originality was strategic rather than analytical. In arguing that the small but politically conscious Russian proletariat could sustain a revolutionary vanguard that would lead the feudal masses of Russia's Asian empire to skip over the capitalist mode of production and proceed straight to a socialist revolution, Lenin was not only revising the Eurocentric orthodoxy of classical Marxism.[19] Where the dialectic of history was concerned, his theory was also premised on the contention that, in extending the life of capitalism, imperialism enabled it to expand quantitatively but without the qualitative compensation. Lenin was an activist. In the lived exigencies of the practical struggle against imperialism, life had become too short to wait for Europe.

That Asia should figure at all was a fateful sign of things to come. Mao's peasants, agents and bearers of their own revolution, gathered just over the historical horizon, while, further on, Frantz Fanon would declare Europe to be so corrupting that the natives whom it touched could but betray the anticolonial movement. In the crucible of the struggle against imperialism, Eurocentrism would shift from program to problematic. This occurred in a world that had changed utterly since the late nineteenth century, when Marx had been fresh in his grave and the scramble for Africa was proceeding apace. In the post–World War II era of decolonization, neocolonialism, and development, dependency theory would insist that economic backwardness in the Third World resulted from the presence rather than the absence of capitalism, thus turning Marxism on its head. This was despite the fact that the theory's proponents (the *dependencistas*) either styled themselves as Marxists or closely aligned themselves with Marxism in theory and in practice. In turning to dependency theory, then, we turn to a new style of theory for a new style of imperialism, one that increasingly dispensed with the formality of colonial rule.[20]

A DUAL PROVENANCE is conventionally ascribed to *dependencia*, giving the doctrine a combined North and South American pedigree. In the United States, long-time collaborators Paul A. Baran and Paul M. Sweezy first formulated the contention that monopoly capitalism had stultifying rather than dynamic consequences for economic development. Third World markets were not so much profitable in their own right as on account of the massive state expenditure that safeguarding them triggered: "The loans and grants to so-called friendly governments of dependent countries, the outlays on the military establishment . . . all assume prodigious magnitudes."[21] In this early theorizing of the military-industrial complex, the Third World functioned as an alibi for ever-increasing levels of state patronage of domestic corporations. Since indigenous enterprise obstructed this arrangement, it

[19] Though it should perhaps be noted that, in a letter written toward the end of his life, Marx had referred to the Russian peasant commune as "the fulcrum of social regeneration in Russia." This letter was not, however, published until 1924. Karl Marx to Vera Zasulich, March 8, 1881, *Karl Marx, Frederick Engels: Collected Works* (London, 1992), 46: 71–72.

[20] In most of Latin America, neocolonialism had been prefigured, since this formality had not applied since the nineteenth century.

[21] Paul A. Baran, *The Political Economy of Growth* (New York, 1957), 118.

was either incorporated or disabled. Accordingly, the only areas outside the West where indigenous enterprise could be expected to flourish were those that had escaped Western domination. Hence Baran's famous contrast between the modernizing achievements of uncolonized Meiji Japan and India's abject failure to develop.[22] Somewhat later, and from the hemisphere below, Silvio Frondizi, Sergio Bagú, Luis Vitale, André Gunder Frank, Theotonio Dos Santos, and others asserted that underdevelopment in Latin America was not a frustration but an outcome of capitalist development.[23]

Though complementary, the two theories emerged in quite different contexts. Within European Marxism, Leon Trotsky notwithstanding, theories of imperialism had received little development since the death of Lenin. Not only had Stalinism constrained theoretical innovation within the Soviet Union, but, in the rest of Europe, the success of fascism had provided Marxists with a major distraction from external concerns. As U.S. dominance was consolidated in the wake of World War II, the Cold War, and McCarthyism, on the other hand, it was understandable that, in 1957, a beleaguered American Marxist such as Baran should recall the Great Depression and warn that all was not as it seemed, that monopoly capitalism was bound to produce stagnation in both the domestic and foreign economies. In contrast to Baran, the Latin American *dependencistas* of the 1960s and 1970s did not have the problem of explaining away the reality of a domestic boom. Rather, their immediate historical experience was dominated by an appalling mutuality between development programs and popular immiseration. As Arturo Escobar has recounted, the era of Third World development that was inaugurated along with the World Bank and the International Monetary Fund at Bretton Woods in 1944 produced and systematized a new regime of deprivation in Latin America, one that differed in quality and extent from the modes of exploitation that had characterized European domination of the subcontinent.[24] Dependency theory formalized its proponents' anger at the gap between the rhetoric of modernization and the reality of exploitation.

A basic premise of *dependencia* was that of historicity: European history was transcended and unrepeatable.[25] Ignoring this, the theory and ideology of modern-

[22] Baran, *Political Economy of Growth*, 149–50.

[23] Published in Buenos Aires in 1947 and 1949 respectively, Silvio Frondizi's *La integración mundial, ultima etapa del capitalismo (respuesta a una critica)* and Sergio Bagú's *Economia de la sociedad colonial* appeared well before Paul Baran's *Political Economy of Growth* (1957). All the same, Bagú and Frondizi were unrepresentatively (not to say presciently) early. In any event, Paul Sweezy, *The Theory of Capitalist Development: Principles of Marxian Political Economy* (New York, 1942), can be seen as a bridge between classical Marxism and later work, as Brewer does (*Marxist Theories of Imperialism*, 137). Latin American *dependencia* generally emerged in the mid to late 1960s, in the decade after Baran and generally after Paul A. Baran and Paul M. Sweezy, *Monopoly Capital: An Essay on the American Economic and Social Order* (New York, 1966).

[24] Arturo Escobar, *Encountering Development: The Making and Unmaking of the Third World* (Princeton, N.J., 1993), 70–94.

[25] The following is intended to express some of the central characteristics of dependency theory. Although individual theorists differed in matters of detail, it is contended that most would accept these basic premises. In view of his prominence, I have generally expressed them in the language of André Gunder Frank, though this should not be taken to imply endorsement of his oddly amateurish, nineteenth-century style of presentation, which involves tacking together extended verbatim quotations from a range of sources to an extent that can make it difficult to discern whether Frank himself has anything to add. For a judicially balanced collection on dependency theory as a whole, see Dudley

ization held out capitalist development as a process of catching up, forgetting that, when the West had been undergoing its own momentous development, there had not been another "West" already there. Rather, there had been colonies, whose exploitation had historically produced—and, in changing ways, continued to produce—the paramountcy of the West. In other words, the great global fact that modernization theory obscured in representing Western history as autochthonous and repeatable was that development and underdevelopment were not two distinct states but a *relationship*. Underdevelopment was not, as modernization theory's dual thesis would have it, external to capitalism, a condition that prevailed in backward regions that had yet to develop.[26] Rather, it was of the essence of capitalism, being both precondition to and corollary of the developed status of the dominant countries. In a fundamental break with Marxist temporality, therefore, underdevelopment did not figure as a residue or survival from a superseded mode of production—usually, from feudalism—but as an integral component of modernity. (In this respect, the theory prefigured a key feature of the thinking of the Subaltern Studies group.) Underdevelopment was, in short, a transitive condition (to put it in Foucauldian terms, a positivity)—something that capitalism produced.[27] If there were any areas of the globe that had yet to be touched by capitalism,[28] their independence of the international division of labor was *un*development, an intransitive historical separateness, rather than *under*development.[29]

Focusing primarily on unequal exchange, dependency theory provoked controversy in orthodox Marxist circles for seeming to privilege distribution over production.[30] Though employing geopolitical units of analysis (nation, colony,

Seers, ed., *Dependency Theory: A Critical Reassessment* (London, 1981). For particular viewpoints both critical and appreciative, see, for example, Theotonio Dos Santos, "The Structure of Dependence," *American Economic Review* 60 (May 1970): 231–36; Adrian Foster-Carter, "From Rostow to Gunder Frank: Conflicting Paradigms in the Analysis of Underdevelopment," *World Development* 4 (March 1976): 167–80; Colin Leys, "Conflict and Convergence in Development Theory," in Wolfgang Mommsen and Jürgen Osterhammel, eds., *Imperialism and After: Continuities and Discontinuities* (London, 1986), 315–24; Tony Smith, "Requiem on New Agenda for Third World Studies," *World Politics* 36 (1985): 532–61; John G. Taylor, *From Modernization to Modes of Production: A Critique of the Sociologies of Development and Underdevelopment* (London, 1979); and Charles K. Wilber's collection, *The Political Economy of Development and Underdevelopment* (New York, 1973), especially the two essays by Celso Furtado.

[26] The best-known example of modernization theory, and a prime target of *dependencia* critique, was Walt (W. W.) Rostow, *The Stages of Economic Growth: A Non-Communist Manifesto* (Cambridge, 1960). A comparably modernist optimism could still find Marxist expression in 1980, in Bill Warren's contention that capitalism would eventually develop the areas that it penetrated (eventually, the entire world). See Warren, *Imperialism: Pioneer of Capitalism* (London, 1980).

[27] This is not to say that capitalism simply modeled dependent societies at will, as if on some behaviorist tabula rasa. It means that, within a given country, a particular infrastructure of dependency was conditioned—encouraged, maintained, and modified in a delegated or indirect manner through the agency of the coopted national elite. See Baran, *Political Economy of Growth*, 194–98; Susanne Bodenheimer, "Dependency and Imperialism: The Roots of Latin American Underdevelopment," *Politics and Society* (May 1971): 337–38.

[28] *Dependencistas* had differing views as to the discreteness of the Second World.

[29] Despite the analytical centrality of this distinction, undevelopment received scant attention in *dependencia*, principally because areas that seemed to furnish good examples usually turned out to have been early mercantile growth centers of the colonial economy that had subsequently fallen into decline.

[30] Though attracting considerable attention for its critique of Frank, Ernesto Laclau's "Feudalism and Capitalism in Latin America," *New Left Review* 67 (May–June 1971): 19–38, principally confined itself to establishing a charge of heresy in relation to Marxist orthodoxy. Robert Brenner's aptly

country), the theory simultaneously problematized and, implicitly at least, subverted them (a feature to be elaborated in world-systems theory). A distinctive characteristic of dependency was a hierarchically replicated cyclopean structure whereby a metropolis (also known as "center," "core," etc.) dominated a number of (usually surrounding) satellites (the "periphery").[31] In addition to dominating its satellites, a metropolis was itself satellite to a higher-order metropolis further up the chain of dependency, say a state or regional capital, and so on up to the final metropolis, the colonial center. Apart from the very lowest and the very highest links in the chain, therefore, each level had a dual aspect, functioning both as metropolis and as satellite. A crucial difference was, however, that, as metropolis, it monopolized a number of satellites, whereas, as satellite, it served only one metropolis.

Though static, the model was not balanced. Rather, it was emphatically unidirectional. Power traveled downward: to depend was to subserve. In consequence, the theory was disappointingly undialectical. There was little sense of the metropolis' own dependence on the compliance of its satellites, little sense of the possibilities of contradiction. Above all, there was little sense of ideology, little evidence of Gramscian perspicacity concerning the crucial calculus of force and consent in the maintenance of hegemony, with the result that collaboration figured as crudely utilitarian. Yet it did not have to be thus. At various points, dependency theory was potently suggestive in regard to such matters, only to hurry back to economism as if questions of culture or consciousness were a frivolous indulgence. It has been suggested that Frank's theory was more influential than the sterner stuff that Baran dispensed because it fortuitously coincided with the Western radicalism of the 1960s.[32] While there may be some truth in this, we should not overlook the appeal of what lay between the lines, implicit but profound, in *dependencia*. This applies particularly to the client or *comprador* role of local elites, whom Frank deftly disparaged as *lumpenbourgeoisie*. They were the agential linchpin of the whole system, acquiescing in their own exploitation from above in return for the balance left over from what they had expropriated from below—including, of course, the military, political, and economic support that the metropolis committed to maintaining them in power. This deeply ambivalent condition confounds dualistic schemes of domination in a way that is particularly vulnerable to ideological critique. Indeed, Dos Santos seemed to lay some of the ground for Homi Bhabha's psychology of colonialism, though with greater economic and geopolitical substance, when he observed, "Domination is practicable only when it finds support

subtitled "The Origins of Capitalist Development: A Critique of Neo-Smithian Marxism," *New Left Review* 104 (July–August 1977): 25–92, offered a wider challenge. For an analogous critique emerging from a concrete empirical case-study, see N. S. Chinchilla, "Interpreting Social Change in Guatemala: Modernization, Dependency, and Articulation of Modes of Production," in Ronald H. Chilcote and Dale L. Johnson, eds., *Theories of Development: Mode of Production or Dependency?* (Beverly Hills, Calif., 1983), 139–78.

[31] Surprisingly perhaps, the terms "center" and "periphery" were coined by Raúl Prebisch, the first director of the Economic Commission for Latin America (CEPAL). See Ronald H. Chilcote, "Introduction: Dependency or Mode of Production? Theoretical Issues," in Chilcote and Johnson, *Theories of Development*, 12; and Escobar, *Encountering Development*, 90.

[32] Hamza Alavi, review of Wallerstein's *The Politics of the World-Economy*, *Race and Class* 27, no. 4 (1986): 87–88.

among those local groups which profit by it. Thus we see the irrelevance of the concept of alienation which claims that our elites are alienated because they look upon themselves with alien eyes."[33]

Shying away from its discursive dimension, however, the theory failed to account for the extent to which *lumpenbourgeois* leaderships could deploy the rhetoric of national independence to mobilize popular support for programs that actually intensified national dependency. Inattention to this paradox of liberalism rendered utopian the remedy (autocentric or independent development) that *dependencistas* advocated, a consequence that was exacerbated by the fact that, for all its radicalism, *dependencia* never questioned the concept or value of development per se.[34] Rather than imagining alternatives to development, it sought to orchestrate a takeover bid. Having so stressed the limits of local agency in the face of the enormous power of international capitalism, however, the theory subverted in advance its own commitment to enabling satellites to break free and keep their surpluses to themselves.[35]

As NOTED, DEPENDENCY WAS CONCEIVED AS UNIDIRECTIONAL—spreading out from Europe, it reduced the whole periphery (the singular is significant) to undifferentiated subordination.[36] Small wonder that other schools of thought have since stressed heterogeneity and particularity. In the 1970s and 1980s, Marxist anthropologists and economic historians influenced by Louis Althusser employed structuralist methods to map the complexities of social (including colonial) formations. A Western communist reacting against Stalinist iron laws, Althusser amended the teleology that had characterized much Marxist thought to that point, insisting that modes of production were ideal abstractions not to be found empirically. Actual social formations conjoined (articulated) a number of modes of production. (Even in Europe, feudalism persisted locally in subordinate relations to capitalism.) Rather than simply instantiating (however awkwardly) a predetermined stage of unilinear development, a given social formation comprised a particular configuration of modes of production, articulated together in unpredictable ways that had to be reconstructed anew in each particular case. Of these modes of production, one predominated—that is, it subordinated the others to the requirements of its own historical reproduction. In keeping with Marxist fundamentals, economic factors were determinant, but only in the last instance.[37] They were not necessarily

[33] Dos Santos, "Structure of Dependence," 78. Although he did not specify a particular target, Dos Santos must have had in mind Frantz Fanon, *The Wretched of the Earth*, Constance Farrington, trans. (New York, 1966, first French edn., Paris, 1961).

[34] Such questioning is the principal concern of Escobar's profoundly thought-provoking *Encountering Development*.

[35] Frederick Cooper has argued along comparable lines in relation to dependency theory's application to African contexts. See Cooper, "Conflict and Connection: Rethinking Colonial African History," *AHR* 99 (December 1994): 1524–25.

[36] Samuel P. Huntington, "The Goals of Development" in Myron Weiner and Huntington, eds., *Understanding Political Development* (Boston, 1987), 283–322, noted that the *dependencistas*' failure to acknowledge cultural differences prevented them from accounting for obvious counterexamples such as Korea and Taiwan.

[37] This premise is more clearly associated with Emmanuel Terray than with Althusser himself, whose

dominant as well, as in the case of capitalism, although they did determine which sphere was dominant (for instance, the political in the case of feudalism or kinship in the case of hunter-gatherer societies[38]).

The concept of social formation provided a powerful tool for analyzing the structural dynamics of complex societies in a manner that both preserved their historicity (inscribed in the power balance between the component modes of production) and identified points of tension around which historical transformations could occur. In the course of a long-running and celebrated French debate involving ethnographic and archival data from West Africa, for instance, Emmanuel Terray took issue with Claude Meillassoux's use of technological criteria to define the "lineage" mode of production, arguing that, since the same technologies occurred in different social systems, it was necessary to employ social criteria.[39] Terray instanced the Abron kingdom of Gyaman, in which the peasants (lineage mode of production agriculturalists) were dominated by slave-holding Abron aristocrats. Even though the peasants were only liable for the most token of agricultural tributes, they were obliged to be available constantly for the warfare that maintained the supply of slaves.[40] Thus the low level of tribute was explained on social criteria, the dominance of the slave mode of production, whose reproduction was the primary determinant of the social formation. On the basis of their account of Portuguese slave-trading on the west coast of Africa, Georges Dupré and Pierre Philippe Rey contended that Terray's model was too static. To account for historical change, it was necessary to bring out the tensions and contradictions between the articulated modes. According to Rey and Dupré, the slave trade had hooked into a chain of indigenous exchanges (slaves for prestige goods) that had obtained in the political sphere of indigenous society and predated the Portuguese. Since the political sphere had been the dominant sphere, and since the Portuguese trade had intensified rather than conflicted with it, indigenous society had remained intact. Upon the abolition of the European slave trade, however, the capitalist

---

commitment to structural causality rendered such formulations problematic. As elsewhere in this review, I am presenting an overview of the salient characteristics of the general approach.

[38] I use the term "societies" rather than "modes of production" to avoid controversy as to whether "hunter-gatherer," "lineage," "hoe," etc., constitute valid criteria for categorizing modes of production, a controversy that I cannot enter into here.

[39] See (in order of debate) Claude Meillassoux, "'The Economy' in Agricultural Self-Sustaining Societies: A Preliminary Analysis," and "The Social Organization of the Peasantry: The Economic Basis of Kinship," in David Seddons, ed., *Relations of Production: Marxist Approaches to Economic Anthropology* (Totowa, N.J., 1978), 127–69; Emmanuel Terray, "Classes and Class Consciousness in the Abron Kingdom of Gyaman," in Maurice Bloch, ed., *Marxist Analyses and Social Anthropology* (London, 1975), 85–135; Pierre Philippe Rey, *Colonialisme, néo-colonialisme et transition au capitalisme: Exemple de la Comilog du Congo-Brazzaville* (Paris, 1971); Georges Dupré and Pierre Phillipe Rey, "Reflections on the Pertinence of a Theory of the History of Exchange," in Harold Wolpe, ed., *The Articulation of Modes of Production* (London, 1980), 128–60; Claude Meillassoux, *Maidens, Meal, and Money: Capitalism and the Domestic Community* (Cambridge, 1981). See also the other articles in Seddons' and Wolpe's collections. For secondary accounts, see Adrian Foster-Carter, "The Modes of Production Controversy," *New Left Review* 107 (January–February 1978): 47–78; Bridget O'Laughlin, "Marxist Approaches in Anthropology," in *Annual Review of Anthropology* 4 (1975): 341–70: Janet Siskind, "Kinship and Mode of Production," *American Anthropologist* 80 (1978): 860–72.

[40] Slaves were emancipated into the peasantry in the second generation to prevent them from developing a potentially disruptive class solidarity on the basis of the shared language and culture that their parents, captured from a variety of different groups, had lacked.

mode of production had sought new sources of profit, penetrating the subsistence realm of indigenous society (that is, articulating to the economic rather than to the political sphere), which it rapidly dominated and subverted, engendering socioeconomic chaos and encouraging colonial occupation.[41]

For all its dated mechanicism, the social-formation model brought a welcome leaven of specificity to historical-materialist accounts of complex social structures. In contrast to dependency theory, it paid due heed to local determinations. It also conclusively invalidated the illusory but pervasive anthropological (functionalist/relativist) image of the contained and homogeneous culture, replacing it with a fissured, unstable composite that did justice to the fact that few if any human societies have developed in isolation. And yet, in suggesting that contingent features of a social formation could be inferred automatically once the dominant mode of production had been identified, the model failed to break with the predictive scientism that has so dogged the career of Marxism. By the same token, it failed to pay due attention to ideological and discursive factors, which were bypassed in the mechanical play of final determinations.[42] These deficiencies were not, however, essential to the model, whose deep structural strengths remain recuperable in an era preoccupied with rhetorical form. In particular, the concept of articulation enables us to distinguish between different modes of colonialism (settler, franchise, internal) and, accordingly, to gain insight into the different types of discursive regime that they respectively subtend.[43]

IF THE SOCIAL-FORMATION MODEL paid due heed to local determinations, Ronald Robinson and John Gallagher's distinctively British theory of "excentric" development, framed in the context of decolonization and the Nasserite revolution in Egypt, tended to make local determinations a law unto themselves. Although Robinson and Gallagher acknowledged that European imperialism had been partly motivated by economic and political factors internal to Europe, in their writings these factors were overwhelmed by the efficacy of local pressures that emanated from outside Europe and threatened imperial interests.[44] In this, their rejection of

[41] This aspect of Rey and Dupré's analysis shares ground with Peter J. Cain and Anthony G. Hopkins, "The Political Economy of British Expansion Overseas, 1750–1914," *Economic History Review* 33 (1980): 483–85. A number of other historians, usually reacting to Ronald Robinson and John Gallagher's theory (see below), have pointed to the consequences for West African society of the abolition of the slave trade, which led to the development of more "legitimate" commerce between Africans and Europeans—in particular, the vegetable oil trade—which favored groups of a lower status than the aristocratic ruling class that had benefited from trading slaves to Europeans. The rapid decline in vegetable oil prices after the 1860s is argued to have contributed to the circumstances that encouraged the scramble for Africa. See Perry Anderson, "The Figures of Descent," *New Left Review* 161 (January–February 1987): 42–44: Robin Law, "The Historiography of the Commercial Transaction in Nineteenth Century West Africa," in Toyin Falola, ed., *African Historiography: Essays in Honour of Jacob Ade Ajayi* (London, 1993), 91–115; but compare R. A. Austen, "The Abolition of the Overseas Slave Trade: A Distorted Theme in West African History," *Journal of the Historical Society of Nigeria* 5, no. 2 (1970): 16–28.

[42] In Althusser's original formulation, the ideological realm ("instance") had been co-determinate with the political and the economic. See Louis Althusser, *For Marx*, Ben Brewster, trans. (New York, 1970); and Althusser and Etienne Balibar, *Reading "Capital,"* Brewster, trans. (London, 1970).

[43] This point will be developed below.

[44] "Historically European imperialism might be defined as a political reflex action between one

the Marxist tradition was explicit, as was their privileging of political and diplomatic considerations over economic ones.[45] Their case was built on a rereading[46] of the scramble for (or partition of) Africa, a historical phenomenon that, in keeping with Marxist premises, had been represented as a contest between the major European powers for formal control of markets that capitalism had already, at least initially, opened up. Robinson and Gallagher reversed this schedule, placing colonial annexations before the development of markets: "It was not the businessmen or missionaries or empire-builders who launched the partition of Africa, but rather a set of diplomats who thought of that continent merely as a function of their concerns elsewhere . . . Only at the end of the process did the businessmen arrive . . . Imperialism was not the cause of the partition. It was the result."[47]

According to Robinson and Gallagher, throughout the nineteenth century, British imperial policy was consistently minimalist ("informal control if possible, formal rule if necessary"[48]), a strategy that relied crucially on the offices of native or (better still) white-settler collaborators.[49] The sudden rush of formal annexations in Africa during the 1880s and 1890s did not result from a change to this general policy but from a fear that nationalist successes in Egypt and South Africa might jeopardize wider imperial interests, specifically trade routes to India (the Suez Canal) and to Australasia (the Cape). Fears for the security of the Suez Canal led to the British occupation of Egypt, which, in turn, prompted France to annex large portions of West Africa so as to prevent the British from achieving cross-continental domination. Franco-British rivalry spiraled across the African interior, a situation that Bismarck was not slow to exploit. In this fracas, the strategic priorities that the contending parties displayed were not consistent with economic motivations. For instance, in order to keep the French out of Egypt, Lord Salisbury sacrificed West Africa, whose commercial potential was considerable, in favor of securing the Nile Valley, whose light soil was largely unproductive. Robinson and Gallagher concluded that the European powers had scrambled *in* rather than *for* Africa, their primary concern being to deny each other rather than aggrandize

non-European, and two European components. From Europe stemmed the economic drive to integrate newly colonised regions and ancient agrarian empires into the industrial economy, as markets and investments. From Europe also sprang the strategic imperative to secure them against rivals in world power politics. As the stock-in-trade of the old masters, these may be taken for granted, although of course they were indispensible to the process. Their role however has been exaggerated. They did not in themselves necessitate empire . . . There was nothing intrinsically imperialistic about foreign investment or great power rivalry." Ronald Robinson, "Non-European Foundations of European Imperialism: Sketch for a Theory of Collaboration" (1972), rpt. in Wm. Roger Louis, ed., *Imperialism—The Robinson and Gallagher Controversy* (New York, 1976), 128–51, quote p. 130.

[45] D. K. Fieldhouse significantly qualified Robinson and Gallagher's understatement of economic factors. See *The Theory of Capitalist Imperialism* (New York, 1967); and *Economics and Empire, 1830–1914* (London, 1973).

[46] The archives had only recently become available under the fifty-year rule.

[47] Ronald Robinson and John Gallagher, "The Partition of Africa" (1962), rpt. in Louis, *Imperialism*, quote p. 117.

[48] Ronald Robinson and John Gallagher, "The Imperialism of Free Trade," *Economic History Review* 6 (1953): 13. This much-cited article launched their theory.

[49] In Robinson's memorable phrase, the white settler was the "ideal prefabricated collaborator" ("Non-European Foundations," 134).

themselves. Once they had acquired their African possessions, however, they were obliged to make them pay their way. Hence trade followed the flag.[50]

Robinson and Gallagher's scheme, which they presented in some detail, attracted criticism on empirical and even documentary grounds.[51] For contemporary purposes, however, it is more revealing to consider its implications for subsequent scholarly alignments than to rehearse what are now ageing controversies. For instance, its emphasis on the significance of local collaborators was consistent not only with Baran's, Frank's, and Fanon's analyses of the role of *comprador* elites but also with Benedict Anderson's and Partha Chatterjee's more recent critiques of the derivativeness of colonial-nationalist discourse.[52] In this light, it is notable that Robinson and Gallagher's reversal of Eurocentrism, congenial as it now seems to postcolonialist sensibilities, should have been welcomed in conservative circles as providing a refutation of Marxism. Whether or not the theory did offer a challenge to Marxism is, however, another question. As Eric Stokes pointed out nearly quarter of a century ago, Lenin's definition of imperialism as dating from the point at which the capitalist powers had finally divided the world up between them is hardly affected by Robinson and Gallagher's thesis.[53] Indeed, when it is recalled that they were not denying either intra-European or economic factors but (ostensibly at least) were merely arguing about relative emphases, it is surprising how little they were actually saying. After all, no self-respecting Marxist dialectician would deny the relative determinacy of a wide range of factors.[54]

[50] See, in particular, Ronald Robinson and John Gallagher, *Africa and the Victorians: The Official Mind of Imperialism* (with A. Denny) (London, 1961); and "Partition of Africa." Numerous accounts of their theory have been published. The following are clear and reliable: A. E. Atmore, "The Extra-European Foundations of British Imperialism: Towards a Reassessment," in Eldridge, *British Imperialism in the Nineteenth Century*, 106–25; D. K. Fieldhouse, "Imperialism: An Historiographical Revision," *Economic History Review* 14 (1961): 187–209; Eric Stokes, "Imperialism and the Scramble for Africa: The New View" (1963), rpt. in Louis, *Imperialism*, 173–95. See also the articles in Andrew N. Porter and R. F. Holland, eds., *Theory and Practice in the History of European Expansion Overseas: Essays in Honour of Ronald Robinson* (London, 1988).

[51] For instance, C. W. Newbury and A. S. Kanya-Forstner contended that French policy in Africa had already shifted before British activities in Egypt could have occasioned the crisis that Robinson and Gallagher attributed to them. See "French Policy and the Origins of the Scramble for West Africa," *Journal of African History* 10 (1969): 253–76. See also A. Adu Boahen, *African Perspectives on Colonialism* (Baltimore, Md., 1987), esp. 28–57. Cain and Hopkins stressed how the post-1870 disparity between Britain's relative industrial weakness and the continuing financial strength of the City of London prompted a drive for new colonial markets. See Peter J. Cain and Anthony G. Hopkins, "Gentlemanly Capitalism and British Expansion Overseas, II: New Imperialism, 1850–1945," *Economic History Review* 40 (1987): 1–26; and *British Imperialism*, 181–99. Newbury, "Victorians, Republicans, and the Partition of West Africa," *Journal of African History* 3 (1962): 493–501, also asserted that French ministerial papers for the period made no connection between West Africa and Egypt. For a general survey, see John M. MacKenzie, *The Partition of Africa 1880–1900 and European Imperialism in the Nineteenth Century* (New York, 1983).

[52] Though their analyses are subtler, in that, by stressing the European provenance of the models of nationhood made available to colonial nationalists, they avoided problematizing the bona fides of committed nationalists. Benedict Anderson, *Imagined Communities: Reflections on the Origins and Spread of Nationalism* (London, 1983); Partha Chatterjee, *Nationalist Thought and the Colonial World: A Derivative Discourse?* (London, 1986); and *The Nation and Its Fragments: Colonial and Postcolonial Histories* (Princeton, N.J., 1993).

[53] Stokes, "Imperialism and the Scramble for Africa," 189.

[54] Various scholars have criticized Robinson and Gallagher on the grounds that their distinction between the political and the economic does not withstand scrutiny. See, for instance, Geoffrey Barraclough, *An Introduction to Contemporary History* (1964; Middlesex, 1967), 58; Ronald Hyam, *Britain's Imperial Century 1815–1914* (London, 1976), 373; Robin Law, "Imperialism and Partition,"

In view of its bearing on contemporary debates over postcolonialism, Robinson and Gallagher's emphasis on extra-European factors invites consideration. It should be noted that the enthusiasm with which some proclaimed their theory to be "Afrocentric" was misplaced.[55] The imperial interests that motivated British takeovers in Egypt and southern Africa were not internal to Africa, which merely functioned as an arena for the European powers to fight out wider imperial concerns. Moreover, Robinson and Gallagher's "collaborator" category grouped white settlers together with tribal federations, Muslim *mujahideen*, and other indigenous entities, a conflation achieved by treating those who resided in a sphere of colonial influence as undifferentiatedly belonging there.[56] In many cases, white settlers were not so much collaborators as delegates. In other words, Robinson and Gallagher's departure from Europe was merely geographical. In social, economic, and political terms, their purview remained resolutely Eurocentric, a quality reflected in their fondness for colonial boys'-club rhetoric.[57]

IN POSITING FOUNDATIONS that, though external to Europe, were not internal to anywhere in particular but were, rather, empire-wide and systemic, Robinson and Gallagher's theory begged the basic question of globalization: how are we to conceive of a system that lacks exteriority? This question grows ever more insistent in a decentered era that we might term virtual imperialism, when radically de-territorialized forms of capital flash around the globe at fiber-optic speed, seeking out low wages, tax and tariff advantages, currency disparities, and innumerable other opportunities that presuppose the very nation-state boundaries that their exploitation transcends. Although it would be unrealistic to deny the profound impact of cyberspace and satellite communications, we should resist the techno-

Journal of African History 24 (1983): 101–04; John Lonsdale, "The European Scramble and Conquest in African History," in Roland Oliver and G. N. Sanderson, eds., *The Cambridge History of Africa 1860–1905*, vol. 6 (Cambridge, 1985), 694. A number of historians both Western and African have argued that the scramble for Africa resulted from an interplay between African and European factors. See Cain and Hopkins, "Gentlemanly Capitalism"; Ian Phimister, "Africa Partitioned," *Review* (Fernand Braudel Center) 18 (1995): 355–81; G. N. Uzoigwe, "European Partition and the Conquest of Africa," in A. Adu Boahan, ed., *Africa under Colonial Domination 1880–1935*, UNESCO General History of Africa, vol. 7 (London, 1985), 19–44.

[55] For example, A. S. Kanya-Forstner judged their article "The Partition of Africa" to be "the most Afrocentric interpretation ever advanced." See "A Final Comment on the Value of Robinson and Gallagher," in Louis, *Imperialism*, 231. In Phimister's less generous assessment, Gallagher and Robinson "succeeded in combining anti-Marxist prejudice with the appearance of Africanist [*sic*] agency"; Phimister, "Africa Partitioned," 356. For a review of some subaltern theories of imperialism up to 1972 (but not Roy's), see Thomas Hodgkin, "Some African and Third World Theories of Imperialism," in Roger Owen and Bob Sutcliffe, eds., *Studies in the Theory of Imperialism* (London, 1972), 93–116.

[56] In contrast to "indigenes oscillating between collaboration and conflict," John Benyon has emphasized the significance of the proconsular "man on the spot." Benyon, "Overlords of Empire? British 'Proconsular Imperialism' in Comparative Perspective," *Journal of Imperial and Commonwealth History* 19 (1991): 164–202.

[57] Consider one example from scores: "the starveling colony of the Congo, the theocracies around Tchad, the petty Muslim oligarchies of Ubanghi-Shari, the wanderers in the marshes of the Bahr al-Ghazal, the Coptic state of Ethiopia, the stone-age men living around the sand-bank at Fashoda"; Robinson and Gallagher, "Partition of Africa," 107. A reading of their individual publications would suggest that this regrettable tendency was principally encouraged by Robinson.

logical determinism that credits them with effecting a wholesale historical rupture. Throughout the twentieth century, imperialism has been theorized as a global category cross-cut by the discontinuously intersecting dimensions of class, nation, race, and, more recently, gender. Moreover, Lenin's dating of imperialism from the end of the nineteenth century has by no means stood unchallenged, with writers such as Eric Wolf stressing the global significance of the late eighteenth century (the Industrial Revolution), ones such as Immanuel Wallerstein and Samir Amin stressing the late fifteenth century (Columbus) and the renovated Frank plumping (at the last count) for 2,500 B.C.[58] The choice of late fifteenth, late eighteenth, or late nineteenth century correlates, of course, with the emergence of mercantile, industrial, and monopoly/finance forms of capital respectively. Whichever one prefers, the point is that globality is not merely a postmodern condition.

A world system dating from the end of the fifteenth century had been prefigured in dependency theory, in which capitalism had rapidly and contagiously converted undevelopment into underdevelopment—for instance, in the Latin American case, had converted Amerindian economies into dependencies whose exploitation was subsequently to prove indispensible to the development of, first, Iberian (mercantile), then British (industrial), and, most recently, U.S. (monopoly/finance) capitalism. This scheme involved spatial and historical considerations that conflicted with the abstract concept of mode of production as theorized in the Marxist tradition. In particular, they were inconsistent with the definition of capitalism as being constituted on the basis of wage (that is, commodified) labor. The issue is similar to that noted in relation to Althusser: actual social formations do not manifest as pure theoretical types. In the case of world-systems theory, though, heterogeneity was (is) not conceived as obtaining *between* different modes of production as they were articulated together. Rather, it is conceived as obtaining *within* a single capitalist world-system. To cite two instances favored by Wallerstein, capitalism in urban northwestern Europe required as a concomitant condition of its development non-wage systems in eastern European wheat production (the so-called "second serfdom") and in American plantations.[59] Empirically, such considerations had been familiar to Marx.[60] As an inherent (as opposed to incidental) feature of capitalist expansion, however, non-wage labor lacked the flexible capacity for surplus production that "free" alienated labor alone enabled.[61] On the basis of this

[58] Samir Amin, *Accumulation on a World Scale: A Critique of the Theory of Underdevelopment*, Brian Pearce, trans. (New York, 1974); and *Imperialism and Unequal Development* (New York, 1977); Immanuel Wallerstein, *The Modern World-System* (New York, 1974–89). For André Gunder Frank, see "A Theoretical Introduction to 5,000 Years of World System History," *Review* (Fernand Braudel Center) 13 (1990): 155–248. On page 185, Frank states that "in his self-designated Marxist book, *Europe and the People Without History*, Eric Wolf (1982) takes a giant theoretical step backward by dating the beginning of the world capitalist system in 1800." For an account that breaks the barrier of the fifteenth century without going as far back as Frank would have us go, see Janet L. Abu-Lughod, *Before European Hegemony: The World System A.D. 1250–1350* (New York, 1989).

[59] Immanuel Wallerstein, *The Modern World-System*, Vol. 1: *Capitalist Agriculture and the Origins of the European World-Economy in the Sixteenth Century* (New York, 1974), 301–05; Vol. 2: *Mercantilism and the Consolidation of the European World-Economy, 1600–1750* (New York, 1980), 137–38, 174–75.

[60] "The veiled slavery of the wage-workers in Europe needed, for its pedestal, slavery pure and simple in the new world," Karl Marx, *Capital*, vol. 1 (Moscow, 1954), 711.

[61] To simplify a complex set of considerations, the proportion of the working day that labor takes up in ensuring its own reproduction is reducible by improvements to the efficiency of the means of production, which improvements require the reinvestment of accumulated surplus, one of the

and related questions, world-systems theory was driven by the force of its own logic to depart from orthodox Marxism to the extent of arguing that world capitalism had been shaped by the development of systems of distribution and accumulation as much as by the system of production.[62]

Defining capitalism as "the full development and economic predominance of market trade" and a world economy as "a single division of labor but multiple polities and cultures," Wallerstein held that the two were "obverse sides of the same coin," different ways of representing the same indivisible phenomenon, the capitalist world-economy.[63] On this basis, the unit of analysis ultimately becomes the world itself,[64] a level at which there is no separating internal from external factors, as in Robinson and Gallagher, since all factors are internal to the system. For Wallerstein, nation-states, which are crucial to the unequal exchanges whereby center ("core"), periphery, and "semi-periphery" relations are constituted, are cut across by the axial division of labor. Although the regional distribution of wealth and power shifts over time, the *dependencia*-style linkage between development at the core and underdevelopment in the periphery (uneven development) remains integral to the system and persists through alternating periods of growth and contraction.[65] The problem with taking the world as the unit of analysis is, of course, the dispersal of agency that almost inevitably follows. Lacking a stable location, "the core" is hard to track down and threatens to degenerate into a reified abstraction. This tendency is exaggerated in globalization theory, where the global system becomes so decentered that it can figure as a kind of disenchanted Gaia that looks for all the world like a hidden hand.[66]

Defined as a single division of labor with multiple polities, a world system need not, however, cover the whole globe. Nor need it be capitalist. Developing this aspect of the theory, Samir Amin has contended that the notion of a universal

hallmarks of capitalist development. See Marx's discussion of relative surplus value and the intensification of labor, *Capital*, 1: 380–92.

[62] Frank goes further: "I vote for replacing the focus on mode of production with a focus on the modes of accumulation in the world system"; "Theoretical Introduction to 5,000 Years," 177.

[63] Immanuel Wallerstein, "The Rise and Future Demise of the World Capitalist System: Concepts for Comparative Analysis" (1974), rpt. in Wallerstein, *The Capitalist World-Economy* (New York, 1979), 6.

[64] In this regard, histories of the world (e.g., Arnold Toynbee, Charles Tilly) should be distinguished from world-histories (e.g., Fernand Braudel, Christopher Chase-Dunn). To exemplify the latter, it seems fittingly ecumenical to cite the sentence with which the anthropologist Eric Wolf introduced his magisterial *Europe and the People without History* (Berkeley, Calif., 1982), 3: "The central assertion of this book is that the world of humankind constitutes a manifold, a totality of interconnected processes, and inquiries that disassemble this totality into bits and then fail to reassemble it falsify reality."

[65] Extending Wallerstein, Christopher Chase-Dunn has argued that military/political competition between states is as fundamental to the capitalist world-system as economic competition over markets. See Chase-Dunn, *Global Formation: Structures of the World-Economy* (Oxford, 1989). I cannot do justice here to the many modifications and elaborations that Wallerstein and others have added to the basic theory. For a good recent account of the current state of play in world-systems theory (one that evinces a promising sensitivity to the approach's shortcomings insofar as cultural issues are concerned), see W. G. Martin, "The World-Systems Perspective in Perspective: Assessing the Attempt to Move Beyond Nineteenth-Century Eurocentric Conceptions," *Review* (Fernand Braudel Center) 17 (1994): 145–85. See also Peter Worsley, "Models of the Modern World System," *Theory, Culture and Society* 7 (1990): 83–96.

[66] For Gaia, see Brett Fairbairn, "History from the Ecological Perspective," *AHR* 99 (October 1994): 1205.

history originating in European capitalism's unprecedented unification of the globe is misleading and Eurocentric.[67] Prior to the sixteenth century, groups of societies were linked by trade into regional and perhaps world systems. Of a number of proto-capitalist regional systems (Indian, Arab-Islamic or Mediterranean, Chinese, barbarian-Christian), all operating on a tributary basis (power was the source of wealth), barbarian Christendom was distinguished by its relative lack of administrative centralization.[68] In combination with the colonization of the Americas, this produced wage-labor based European capitalism (wealth became the source of power), which, though a qualitatively novel phenomenon, established itself on proto-capitalist foundations that were not unique to Europe. Once European capitalism had emerged, however, it stifled further development on the part of the other proto-capitalist systems.

Amin's analysis combines Marxist rigor in relation to wage labor with the postcolonial sensibility of an Egyptian scholar based in Paris. Compared to the dependency/world-systems tradition as a whole, his theory is refreshingly attuned to cultural and ideological questions, situating the discursive politics of the Western academy (as in the critique of Eurocentrism) in the context of the historical development of world systems. Observing that the philosophico-religious movements that culminated Antiquity and inaugurated universal history (Hellenism, Oriental Christianity, Islam, Zoroastrianism, Confucianism, Buddhism) emerged in concert with the consolidation of the great tributary societies, Amin locates the break between Antiquity and the Middle Ages, not, as the Eurocentric scheme of things would have it, at the end of the Roman Empire in the West but from the time of Alexander's unification of the Hellenic East. ("The choice of the conventional division at the end of the Roman Empire betrays a deeply rooted preconception that the Christian era marks a qualitative decisive break in world history, when in fact it does not."[69])

AT FIRST SIGHT, AMIN'S MARXIST BLENDING of cultural and material factors might seem to distinguish his approach from critiques of Eurocentrism that have been couched in the idiom of discourse analysis. Before dismissing poststructuralism as an idealist perspective that overlooks the material consequences of the international division of labor, however, we should recall that Marx himself was unfailingly attentive to questions of ideology and consciousness. Analogously, the fact that Michel Foucault appropriated the term "discourse" from linguistics should not lead us to forget that, in his hands, the concept encompassed institutional configurations

[67] A comparable polemic by a geographer recently attracted a withering *AHR* review. See J. M. Blant, *The Colonizer's Model of the World: Geographical Diffusionism and Eurocentric History* (New York, 1993), compare Dane Kennedy in *AHR* 101 (February 1996): 148–49.

[68] Samir Amin, *Class and Nation, Historically and in the Current Crisis*, Susan Kaplow, trans. (New York, 1980).

[69] Samir Amin, *Eurocentrism*, Russell Moore, trans. (New York, 1989), 58. It is instructive to compare Amin with Marshall Hodgson: "In sum, the whole Afro-Eurasian Oikumene was the stage on which was played all civilized history, including that of Islamicate civilization, and this stage was set largely by the contrasts and interrelations among the great regional cultural complexes"; Hodgson, *The Venture of Islam: Conscience and History in a World Civilization*, Vol. 1: *The Classical Age of Islam* (Chicago, 1977), 114.

as solid as the prison or the asylum. (As practices go, few can be more material than architecture.) Despite this, postcolonial writing has too often excluded historical, economic, and material factors. In terms of the second of our guiding oppositions, it is fair to state that, with the advent of poststructuralist methods, the dominant focus in scholarly discussions of imperialism shifted dramatically from material to representational phenomena. While it is easy enough to lament this development, as many have,[70] it should be noted that the introduction of a Saussurian concern with the operation of difference within fields of signification has produced an illuminating discussion of race, an issue that, bizarre as it may seem, had largely been left uninterrogated in traditional accounts of imperialism.[71] Thus it is worth considering the historical conditions under which issues of race and representation should have come to acquire a hold on scholarly debates.

One of the major determinants of contemporary global discourse is the significant (albeit limited) extent to which imperialism has been de-territorialized. This is, of course, an extremely complex and still emergent phenomenon. All the same, it is increasingly apparent that the escalating volume, speed, and intensity with which capital, information, commodities, technologies, and people move about the globe constitutes a situation that confounds stable categories of class and location, necessitating more labile, situational, and opportunistic modes of analysis than the repertoire of oppositional modernism makes available.[72] As imperialism came

[70] The charge that postcolonial criticism understates the materiality of imperialism and rarefies or aestheticizes oppression is a fairly common one. It is carefully put in Benita Parry, "Problems in Current Theories of Colonial Discourse," *Oxford Literary Review* 9 (1987): 27–58. See also Anne McClintock, "The Angel of Progress: Pitfalls of the Term 'Post-Colonialism,'" *Social Text* 31–32 (1992): 84–98, revised as the conclusion to her *Imperial Leather: Race, Gender, and Sexuality in the Colonial Contest* (New York, 1995); Elazar Barkan, "Post-Anti-Colonial Histories: Representing the Other in Imperial Britain," *Journal of British Studies* 33 (1994): 180–202; Ella Shohat, "Notes on the 'Post-Colonial,'" *Social Text* 31–32 (1992): 99–113; Aijaz Ahmad, *In Theory: Classes, Nations, Literatures* (London, 1992); and "The Politics of Literary Postcoloniality," *Race and Class* 36 (1994): 1–20. Anyone who has ever wished that he or she was Aijaz Ahmad might be glad not to be after reading Parry's measured and deadly response to Ahmad's *In Theory*, a sting that is all the crueler for Parry's own well-known reservations concerning Ahmad's targets. See Benita Parry's review in *History Workshop Journal* 36 (1993): 232–42.

[71] Phillip Darby and Christopher Fyfe have both made this point. See Darby, *Three Faces of Imperialism: British and American Approaches to Africa and Asia* (New Haven, Conn., 1987), 84–87; and Fyfe, "Race, Empire and the Historians," *Race and Class* 33, no. 4 (1992): 15–30.

[72] Such modes of analysis should accommodate—and, perhaps, be informed by—identitarian and social-movement politics, as distinct from, but not necessarily opposed to, traditional "organized" politics. I agree with Prasenjit Duara, though, that social movements need to move beyond the "politics of the wronged" to develop understandings of the historical conditions of their own emergence. See Duara, "The Displacement of Tension to the Tension of Displacement," *Radical History Review* 57 (1993): 60–64. A collection that offers a promising start in this direction is Arturo Escobar and Sonia E. Alvarez, eds., *The Making of Social Movements in Latin America: Identity, Strategy, and Democracy* (Boulder, Colo., 1992). See also Escobar, "Imagining a Post-Development Era? Critical Thought, Development and Social Movements," *Social Text* 31–32 (1992): 20–56; and "Reflections on 'Development': Grassroots Approaches and Alternative Politics in the Third World," *Futures* 24, no. 5 (1992): 411–36; compare Samir Amin, Giovanni Arrighi, André Gunder Frank, and Immanuel Wallerstein, eds., *Transforming the Revolution: Social Movements and the World-System* (New York, 1990). A comprehensive and accessible introduction to globalization theory is Frederick Buell's *National Culture and the New Global System* (Baltimore, Md., 1994). This endorsement should not be taken to extend to Buell's comments (252–54) on my "On Being Woken Up: The Dreamtime in Anthropology and in Australian Settler Culture," *Comparative Studies in Society and History* 33 (1991): 197–224, though this is not the place to argue the point, but see Patrick Wolfe, "Should the Subaltern Dream? 'Australian Aborigines' and the Problem of Ethnographic Ventriloquism," in S. Humphreys, ed., *Cultures of Scholarship* (Ann Arbor, Mich., forthcoming 1997), p. 90, n. 50. An entertaining overview that

home to roost in the form of labor, refugee, and other migrations, the metropolis followed in the demographic footsteps of the periphery, with major Western cities taking on the creolized, multi-ethnic look of a nineteenth-century colonial center.[73] Whereas, in traditional theories of imperialism, race had been redundant as an index of domination when that domination was most obviously constituted by spatial separation, in the post-imperial city the reverse has come to apply. Downtown, home addresses are not the main issue—people change neighborhoods more easily than they change races.

Space is not the only material casualty. Marxism's notorious color blindness is symptomatic of economic thinking as a whole, which simply lacks the categories to specify racial, ethnic, or cultural differences. When it comes to difference, the sovereign paradigm is phonology, which is exclusively given over to the refinement of discriminations. In poststructuralist hands, then, domination became a kind of language, with race figuring as an aestheticized construct that belied the physicality of its conventional signs. As we shall see, though, this did not need to be the case and has not always been the case. In turning to the controversial topic of postcolonialism, therefore, my argument is very simple. As noted at the outset, the distinction between the discursive and the instrumental is a false one; representations dialectically inform the (mis)understandings that permeate practical activity. Postcolonial theory offers suggestive ways for historians to open up some of the discursive and ideological dimensions of the complex field of imperialism, but this should not be allowed to suppress other dimensions.[74] Our goal should be a unified historical field.

The linkage of Marx and Foucault in this context is not accidental. Though appealing to kindred political instincts, their epistemologies are axiomatically incompatible. A consequence has been an uneasy division of radical loyalties in the Western academy. Within Europe, the circumstances of the late 1960s (in particular, the Soviet invasion of Czechoslovakia and the events of May 1968) undid the revolutionary credentials of a dour master-narrative of labor and class. In the Third World, on the other hand, Marxism's role in decolonization—and, above all, the

succinctly communicates a good feel for the discourse as a whole is Simon During, "Post-Colonialism," in K. K. Ruthven, ed., *Beyond the Disciplines* (Canberra, 1992), 88–100. Seminal articles in globalization theory include Roland Robertson, "Mapping the Global Condition: Globalization as the Central Concept," *Theory, Culture and Society* 7 (1990): 15–30; and Arjun Appadurai, "Disjuncture and Difference in the Global Cultural Economy," *Public Culture* 2 (1990): 1–24. A lively critique of traditional Marxism's incapacity to escape its own entrapment within the structuring logic of global capitalism is Arif Dirlik, *After the Revolution: Waking to Global Capitalism* (Hanover, N.H., 1994).

[73] "[T]he culture, society and space of early twentieth century Calcutta or Singapore pre-figured the future in a much more accurate way than did that of London or New York. 'Modernity' was not born in Paris but rather in Rio"; Anthony D. King, "Introduction," King, ed., *Culture, Globalization and the World-System: Contemporary Conditions for the Representation of Identity* (Binghamton, N.Y., 1991), 8.

[74] Thus I concur with the attitude recommended by Dane Kennedy, "Imperial History and Post-Colonial Theory," *Journal of Imperial and Commonwealth History* 24 (1996): 345–63. I also agree with Kennedy that postcolonialism's promise need not warrant impenetrable terminology: "Let us agree that the non-Western world remains in thrall to the discursive system of the West, to the system that Said identifies as Orientalism. How do the post-colonial theorists propose to liberate these hostages? By writing in a manner that is utterly inaccessible to most of them? By writing as the acolytes of Western theorists? By writing to mainly Western audiences from mainly Western academies about mainly Western literature? By writing? [!]" (p. 350).

triumph of the Viet Cong—gave it continuing vitality in oppositional discourse. Unlike many of their Western counterparts, therefore, Third World intellectuals who embraced poststructuralism were unlikely to see this as requiring them to renounce Marxism. This was the case even though most of those involved were based in the West.[75] Rather than viewing the incompatibility between Marxism and poststructuralism as necessitating a choice between them, diasporan postcolonialism has derived much of its disruptive energy from a strategically provisional juggling of the two.[76] Edward W. Said's *Orientalism* (which, along with Fanon, enjoys ironically foundational status in postcolonialism[77]) is a case in point. A prefatory quotation from *The Eighteenth Brumaire of Louis Bonaparte* dramatizes Marx's own complicity in Orientalism: "They cannot represent themselves; they must be represented." Yet no sooner has the introduction gotten under way than Foucault's concept of discourse is yoked to Antonio Gramsci's thoroughly Marxist concept of hegemony, as if the problem of the humanist subject did not present an

[75] The diasporan status of many (but by no means all—let us be fairer to Partha Chatterjee, Shahid Amin, Gyan Pandey, *et al.*) of these intellectuals has made them a soft target for critics such as Aijaz Ahmad (ex-Rutgers) and Arif Dirlik (Duke). Dirlik is wickedly effective: "'When exactly . . . does the "post-colonial" begin?' [he quotes Shohat, and answers] . . . When Third World intellectuals have arrived in First World academe"; Dirlik, "The Postcolonial Aura: Third World Criticism in the Age of Global Capitalism," *Critical Inquiry* 20 (1994): 328–29.

[76] Trained in Paris, Marxist to the core, Ranajit Guha prefigured this conjuncture, to which Bhabha is a notable exception, by some two decades. The conjuncture itself has been variously criticized on epistemological grounds. See, for example, Dennis Porter, "Orientalism and Its Problems," in Francis Barker, Peter Hulme, and Margaret Iversen, eds., *The Politics of Theory* (Colchester, 1983), 179–92 (in reference to Said); and Rosalind O'Hanlon and David Washbrook, "After Orientalism: Culture, Criticism, and Politics in the Third World," *Comparative Studies in Society and History* 34 (1992): 141–67 (in reference to Gyan Prakash). Various Western scholars have effected the same conjuncture. See, for example, Peter Hulme, *Colonial Encounters: Europe and the Native Caribbean, 1492–1797* (London, 1986), 7–8. See also Florencia E. Mallon, "The Promise and Dilemma of Subaltern Studies: Perspectives from Latin American History," *AHR* 99 (December 1994): 1515.

[77] From the point of view of the history of ideas, an epidemiology of Edward Said's *Orientalism* (New York, 1978) could cast light on the conditions of academic receptivity. Despite its extraordinary impact, Said's thesis was by no means unprecedented. In significant ways, it had been anticipated by, among others, Maxime Rodinson, "The Western Image and Western Studies of Islam," in Joseph Schacht, with C. E. Bosworth, ed., *The Legacy of Islam*, 2d edn. (Oxford, 1974), 9–62; Mohammed Arkoun, "L'islam vu par le professeur G. E. V. Grunebaum," *Arabica* 11 (1964): 113–26; and Hichem Djait, *L'Europe et l'Islam* (Paris, 1974). More is involved here than the fact that Said's book was in English or that it employed French theory. Consider, for instance, the following representative passage from a critique of the "neo-orientalism of western Europe" which appeared fifteen years before *Orientalism* in a journal (*Diogenes*) that is hardly obscure or lacking international credibility (excuse the length, but it is surely striking): "According to the traditional orientalists, an essence should exist—sometimes even clearly described in metaphysical terms—which constitutes the inalienable and common basis of all the beings considered; this essence is both 'historical,' since it goes back to the dawn of history, and fundamentally a-historical, since it transfixes the being, the 'object' of study, within its inalienable and non-evolutive specificity, instead of defining it as all other beings, states, nations, peoples and cultures—as a product, a resultant of the vection of the forces operating in the field of historical evolution. Thus one ends with a typology—based on a real specificity, but detached from history, and, consequently, conceived as being intangible, essential—which makes of the studied 'object' another being, with regard to whom the studying subject is transcendent: we will have a *homo Sinicus*, a *homo Arabicus* (and, why not, a *homo Aegypticus*, etc.), a *homo Africanus*, the man—the 'normal man' it is understood—being the European man of the historical period, that is, since Greek antiquity. One sees how much, from the eighteenth to the twentieth century, the hegemonism of possessing minorities, unveiled by Marx and Engels, and the anthropocentrism dismantled by Freud are accompanied by europeocentrism in the area of human and social sciences, and more particularly in those in direct relationship with non-European peoples"; Anouar Abdel-Malek, "Orientalism in Crisis," *Diogenes* 44 (1963): 108. Malek goes on to implicate one of Said's prime targets, Louis Massignon, who had died the previous year.

obstacle. In terms of scholarly outcomes, however, it seems safe to say that it has not presented an obstacle. Moreover, using Foucault without (say) Gramsci would have entailed an erasure of subjecthood that would have taken the colonizer out of colonialism. In this as in other respects, Said knew what he was doing.

In contrast to Marxist thought—which, with varying degrees of subtlety, posits a gap between reality and (mis)representation—Foucault's notion of discourse is constitutive (or, as he put it, "positive"). As opposed to a distortion put about by the powerful, discourse produces realities—regulating, ordering, and conditioning the possibilities of practical existence. Thus discourse is not simply ideational. Rather, it operates (though not homogeneously) through all the institutions and routines of social life. This basic distinction has crucial implications for postcolonialism.[78] In particular, it means that, when Said termed Orientalism a discourse, he meant much more than that the Western academy had disseminated misleading ideas about the Islamic Middle East: "Orientalism [is] a Western style for dominating, restructuring and having authority over the Orient . . . [an] enormously systematic discipline by which European culture was able to manage—and even produce—the Orient politically, sociologically, militarily, ideologically, scientifically and imaginatively during the post-Enlightenment period."[79] In underwriting Orientalism, the Western academy was, in a very wide sense, *making* the Middle East, a scenario that credited certain academics with extraordinary power. This consequence flowed from Said's harnessing Foucauldian positivity to a Marxist sense of hegemonic ideology. As a result, rather than a collaborative or dialogic process, discourse became unidirectional, something that the colonizers wielded. It would be hard to imagine a more fertile flaw.

In Said's account, Orientalism has a distinctly Cartesian quality. In producing its other as an object of thought and acting upon it, colonial discourse reproduces the familiar priority of mind over matter. The final object of colonial thought, a category that emerged in concert with Europe's encompassment of the rest of the globe, was the world itself (a historical achievement that Mary Louise Pratt termed "planetary consciousness"[80]). This dioramic purview was exemplified in cartography, a "projection" that reduced *terra incognita* to order, banishing the monsters and converting space into place.[81] As Paul Carter has observed, Captain Cook did not give New Island its name because it had only recently emerged from the Pacific

[78] In view of the constraints of space, I shall use the term postcolonialism loosely to refer to a generic body of work that brings poststructuralism to bear on colonial questions.

[79] Said, *Orientalism*, 3.

[80] Mary Louise Pratt, *Imperial Eyes: Travel Writing and Transculturation* (New York, 1992), 134.

[81] For Said's "imaginative geography," see *Orientalism*, 49–73. For suggestive discussions of the colonial functions of cartography, see, for example, Terry Cook, "A Reconstruction of the World: George R. Parkin's British Empire Map of 1893," *Cartographica* 21 (1984): 53–65; J. B. Harley, "Maps, Knowledge and Power," in Denis Cosgrove and Stephen Daniels, eds., *The Iconography of Landscape: Essays on the Symbolic Representation, Design and Use of Past Environments* (Cambridge, 1988), 277–312; Graham Huggan, "Decolonizing the Map: Post-Colonialism, Post-Structuralism, and the Cartographic Connection," in Ian Adam and Helen Tiffin, eds., *Past the Last Post: Theorizing Post-Colonialism and Post-Modernism* (New York, 1991), 125–38; Chandra Mukerji, "Visual Language in Science and the Exercise of Power: The Case of Cartography in Early Modern Europe," *Studies in Visual Communication* 10 (1984): 30–45. See also Michel Foucault, "Questions on Geography," in Colin Gordon, ed., *Power/Knowledge: Selected Interviews and Other Writings of Michel Foucault, 1922–1977* (Brighton, 1980), 63–77.

Ocean but because, as Cook noted in his journal, "it is not laid down in any chart."[82] In the discourse of discovery, to chart was to call into existence.

If mapping fixed the world for European statesmen, museology brought it home to the European masses. It also went beyond visuality, rendering the spectacle of empire a performative experience that democratically and pansensorily involved the whole body. One of the key features of museums (in common with imperial exhibitions, world fairs, and theme parks) is the fact that people walk through them; they are shaped and shaping experiences. Their immediacy makes them key sites of subject-construction, as evidenced in their openness to all classes and their incorporation into school pedagogies.[83] As various analyses have shown, the two most important discourses in which nineteenth-century museums involved their publics were those of citizenship and empire.[84] Moreover, the two were inseparable. Given evolutionary anthropology's all-encompassing phylogenetic hierarchy, any ethnological display was necessarily a statement about rank. For instance, commercial fairs that provided competing industrial nations with opportunities to demonstrate the superior efficiency of their products typically included anthropological displays that illustrated the world-historical development of the advanced technologies in question.[85] These displays conflated what we would today distinguish as archaeology and ethnography on the evolutionist premise that "their" present was "our" past—that non-European peoples differentially occupied the series of developmental niches through which European society had progressively raised itself. Thus space and time were collapsed; to travel beyond the bounds of European civilization was to travel back in time.[86] This global narrative was reenacted by the museum- or fair-going public when they moved between stands, pavilions, or model villages—a sensation that, at the larger fairs, was cemented by the provision of railways and other atmospheric devices designed to popularize imperial subjecthood.

In positioning the European spectator at the apex of universal history, "ethnological showbusiness" potently articulated nationalism and imperialism.[87] The

[82] Paul Carter, *The Road to Botany Bay* (London, 1987), 8.

[83] Tony Bennett, *The Birth of the Museum: History, Theory, Politics* (New York, 1995), 73–74; Annie E. Coombes, *Reinventing Africa: Museums, Material Culture, and Popular Imagination in Late Victorian and Edwardian England* (New Haven, Conn., 1994), 111.

[84] See Robert W. Rydell, *All the World's a Fair: Visions of Empire at American International Expositions 1876–1916* (Chicago, 1984). As Curtis M. Hinsley observed of the mesas and cliff-dweller sites of the American Southwest, a kind of archaeological outdoor museum, "Constructions of both the moundbuilders and the cliffdwellers suggest that the prehistory of America was inarticulately but intimately associated with the extension of national manhood: contact with the ancients' earthly ruins would serve as a medium of lineage from American fathers to sons." Hinsley, "The Promise of the Southwest," in Hinsley and David R. Wilcox, eds., *The Southwest in the American Imagination: The Writings of Sylvester Baxter, 1881–1889* (Tucson, Ariz., 1996), 185. See also Hinsley, "The World as Marketplace: Commodification of the Exotic at the World's Columbian Exposition, Chicago, 1893," in Ivan Karp and Steven D. Lavine, eds., *Exhibiting Cultures: The Poetics and Politics of Museum Display* (Washington, D.C., 1991), 344–65.

[85] The pattern was set by the Crystal Palace exhibition of 1851, evoked in the pen picture with which George W. Stocking, Jr., opens his definitive *Victorian Anthropology* (New York, 1987), 1–6.

[86] On temporality in colonial discourse, see particularly Johannes Fabian, *Time and the Other: How Anthropology Makes Its Object* (New York, 1983).

[87] The phrase comes from Bernth Lindfors, "Ethnological Show Business: Footlighting the Dark Continent," in Rosemarie G. Thomson, ed., *Freakery: Cultural Spectacles of the Extraordinary Body* (New York, 1996), 207–18. Lindfors deals with the limit of ethnological showbusiness attained in the

performative dimension, which is crucial here, eludes traditional approaches in which ideology figures as a species of misinformation that leaves reality continuing in parallel. Thus many recent analyses have turned to Foucault for ways to express the fuller discursive production of imperial subjects.[88] This is not to say that what Tony Bennett has called the "exhibitionary complex" was semantically monolithic. Display practice is inherently polyvocal and, accordingly, contested. To cite an obvious example, a skull in a museum might speak to an ethnologist of evolutionary taxonomy and to an Aboriginal person of grave robbery.[89] Even within ostensibly unitary paradigms, as Annie Coombes has noted of British images of Africa, heterogeneity and discontinuity prevail.[90] Coombes might have mentioned Timothy Mitchell's *Colonising Egypt*, which counterposed the European metaphysic of representation informing the "world-as-exhibition" to the differently framed cultural responses of Egyptian visitors to the Egyptian exhibit. Not only did the Egyptians confront simulacra of themselves within the exhibition; once back outside in the "real" world of nineteenth-century Paris, they found themselves immersed in

---

display of native peoples for the entertainment of European audiences. His subject is the infamous treatment of Saartjie Baartman, the San woman who was exhibited in London in 1810–1811 as the "Hottentot Venus," a topic he discusses without replicating the prurience of the gaze at which the display was directed (compare Sander Gilman, "Black Bodies, White Bodies," in *Critical Inquiry* 12 [1985]: 204–42). Barbara Kirshenblatt-Gimblett notes how, in the "tomb with a view," human exhibits, whether alive or dead, are subsumed into the economy of display objects: "The semiotic complexity of exhibits of people, particularly those of an ethnographic character, may be seen in reciprocities between exhibiting the dead as if they are alive and the living as if they are dead, reciprocities that hold as well for the art of the undertaker as they do for the art of the museum preparator"; Kirshenblatt-Gimblett, "Objects of Ethnography," in Karp and Lavine, *Exhibiting Cultures*, 398. On the display of human ethnological "specimens" generally, see Rydell, *All the World's a Fair*; Phillips Verner Bradford and Harvey Blume, *Ota: The Pygmy in the Zoo* (New York, 1992); Christian F. Feest, ed., *Indians and Europe: An Interdisciplinary Collection of Essays* (Aachen, 1987); C. A. Vaughan, "Ogling Igorots: The Politics and Commerce of Exhibiting Cultural Otherness, 1898–1913," in Thomson, *Freakery*, 219–33.

[88] A brilliant example is Tony Bennett's argument that nineteenth-century museums performed a function complementary to Foucault's carceral prisons and asylums, which only operated in cases where the museum's (and related civic institutions') production of a docile and self-regulating citizenry failed. In the museum, the crowd is not so much subject to a controlling view from above, à la Foucauldian panopticon, as exchanging looks between themselves, a "self-monitoring system of looks" that forms "a technology of vision which served not to atomize and disperse the crowd but to regulate it, and to do so by rendering it visible to itself, by making the crowd itself the ultimate spectacle"; Bennett, *Birth of the Museum*, 68. The possibilities of this approach for analyzing the construction of racial subjectivities in contexts like that of the museum, where anthropological displays incite glances across, between, and within "races," seem to me to be considerable.

[89] Bennett, *Birth of the Museum*, 59. A great deal has been written on the vexed topic of cultural property. A recent comparative discussion is Moira G. Simpson, *Making Representations: Museums in the Post-Colonial Era* (New York, 1996), which, despite the title's postmodernist resonance, is a conventional (albeit effective) work of reformist advocacy. For opposing views on the issue of the repatriation of Aboriginal skeletal remains in Australia, see Ros Langford, "Our Heritage, Your Playground," *Australian Archaeology* 16 (1983): 1–6: and D. J. Mulvaney, "Past Regained, Future Lost: The Kow Swamp Pleistocene Burials," *Antiquity* 65 (1991): 12–21. The issue is addressed internationally by "concerned" archaeologists in Robert Layton, ed., *Conflict in the Archaeology of Living Traditions* (London, 1989). For an evocative account of the world view of nineteenth-century amateur collectors, museums' principal source of supply, see Tom Griffiths, *Hunters and Collectors: The Antiquarian Imagination in Australia* (Cambridge, 1996), esp. 28–54. Lynette Russell has recently made an interesting attempt to counterpose European representations of Aborigines and Aboriginal self-representations within the museum context. See her "Focusing on the Past: Visual and Textual Images of Aboriginal Australia in Museums," in Brian L. Molyneaux, *The Cultural Life of Images: Visual Representation in Archaeology* (New York, 1997), 230–48.

[90] Coombes, *Reinventing Africa*, 2–3.

a sea of signification ("exotic" commodity displays[91] in shopping arcades, etc.) that was continuous with the self-consciously staged space of the exhibition. Reciprocally, when Europeans who had been to the exhibition visited the "real" Egypt, they found a disorderly confusion that challenged them to establish a commanding vantage point for themselves, to impose European form on the unruly oriental content.[92]

Mitchell's inclusion of the Egyptian visitors' reactions emphasizes the Eurocentrism of analyses that present the colonial encounter monologically, as a narcissistic projection of the Western will to power. As noted above, domination is a relationship. Europe became what it was through its unequal exchanges with the rest of the world; the Englishman's sweet tooth required the slave triangle.[93] Within the field of visuality itself, modernism's debt to colonial museology is well known.[94] Fifteen years after *Orientalism*, Said moved to remedy the book's one-sidedness by demonstrating that the development of European culture—right down to the genteel provincial reaches of Jane Austen's *Mansfield Park*—had presupposed imperialism as a condition of its possibility.[95] Whether or not an effective antidote

[91] The question of exotification in theme parks, shopping malls, department stores, etc., is, clearly, continuous with that of museology. Walter Benjamin's arcades project remains influential. See Susan Buck-Morss, *The Dialectics of Seeing: Walter Benjamin and the Arcades Project* (Cambridge, Mass., 1990). See also Marianna Torgovnik, *Gone Primitive: Savage Intellects, Modern Lives* (Chicago, 1990).

[92] Timothy Mitchell, *Colonising Egypt* (1988; rpt. edn., Berkeley, Calif., 1991), 1–33.

[93] As Benjamin put it, "There is no document of civilization that is not at the same time a document of barbarism"; Walter Benjamin, *Illuminations*, Harry Zohn, trans. (New York, 1968), 256.

[94] Primitivism and surrealism are obvious cases in point. See, in particular, James Clifford, "On Ethnographic Surrealism," in Clifford, *The Predicament of Culture: Twentieth-Century Ethnography, Literature and Art* (Cambridge, Mass., 1988), 117–51. Raymond Roussel's *Impressions d'Afrique* (Paris, 1910), English trans. by Lindy Foord and Rayner Heppenstall (1966; London, 1983), is a classic source in this regard. See also Hal Foster, "The 'Primitive' Unconscious of Modern Art, or White Skin Black Masks," in Foster, *Recodings: Art, Spectacle, Cultural Politics* (Port Townsend, Wash., 1985), 181–207.

[95] Edward W. Said, *Culture and Imperialism* (London, 1994). A growing number of studies have brought out metropolitan culture's indebtedness to colonialism. For instance, Vron Ware and Moira Ferguson have both argued that British feminist thought from Mary Wollstonecraft to John Stuart Mill borrowed language and imagery from the campaign to abolish slavery. See Ware, *Beyond the Pale: White Women, Racism, and History* (New York, 1992); Ferguson, *Colonialism and Gender Relations from Mary Wollstonecraft to Jamaica Kincaid: East Caribbean Connections* (New York, 1993). More subversively, Antoinette Burton argues that British feminism in the late nineteenth century was deeply complicit in the ideological work of empire, particularly in orientalizing Indian womanhood. See Burton, *The Burdens of History: British Feminists, Indian Women, and Imperial Culture, 1865–1915* (Chapel Hill, N.C., 1994). Javed Majeed, *Ungoverned Imaginings: James Mill's "The History of British India" and Orientalism* (New York, 1992), has shown how British Orientalism around the turn of the nineteenth century was concerned with British as much as with Asiatic society, providing a means for philosophical radicalism to fashion its critique. More generally, Linda Colley has argued, in "Britishness and Otherness: An Argument," *Journal of British Studies* 31 (1992): 309–29, that possession of the empire united British society, an argument that is more fully developed in John M. MacKenzie's work on empire and British popular culture. See MacKenzie, *Propaganda and Empire: The Manipulation of British Public Opinion, 1880–1960* (Manchester, 1984); and the introduction to his *Imperialism and Popular Culture* (Manchester, 1986), 1–16. See also Bill Schwarz's collection, *The Expansion of England: Race, Ethnicity, and Cultural History* (New York, 1996), in particular the articles by Couze Venn, "History Lessons: Formation of Subjects, (Post)colonialism, and an Other Project," 32–60; and Catherine Hall, "Imperial Man: Edward Eyre in Australasia and the West Indies, 1833–66," 130–70. The anthropologists Richard Handler and Daniel A. Segal have cogently argued that European nationalism was a product of the colonial project. See R. Handler and D. A. Segal, "How European Is Nationalism?" *Social Analysis* 32 (1992): 1–15; and Handler and Segal, "Introduction: Nations, Colonies and Metropoles," *Social Analysis* 33 (1993): 3–8 (this whole special edition is interesting). See also Shula Marks, "History, the Nation and Empire: Sniping from the Periphery," *History Workshop Journal* 29 (1990): 111–19.

to Eurocentrism is more Eurocentrism, Said's shift reflects the development, largely in response to *Orientalism*, of a widespread concern with Europe's reciprocal dependence on those whom it subordinated. Ideologically, the production of the European bourgeois self relied significantly on the colonized (savage or barbarian) not-self in a manner congruent with the way in which the productivity of Manchester cotton mills relied on the coercion of labor in Louisiana, India, and Egypt.[96] In one sense, this brings us back to M. N. Roy. When stressing Europe's dependence on colonialism, however, Roy had refused any dilution of its spatio-racial specificity. Colonial and metropolitan labor regimes were not homogeneous. On the contrary, colonialism had enabled the relative cossetting of a domestic aristocracy of labor, whose quiescence reflected its status as colonialism's beneficiary. Roy's view maintained the structure but reversed the value of Hobson's liberal fear "that the arts and crafts of tyranny, acquired and exercised in our unfree Empire, should be turned against our liberties at home."[97] The operative difference between Roy and Hobson was, of course, their antithetical positioning in relation to the colonial divide. The clarity of this distinction has regularly been called into question. It has already been observed, for instance, that imperialism could be conceived without reference to spatial separation. Hybridity also undermines colonial boundaries, as do synthetic analyses in which race, gender, and class figure as distinct but mutually encoding (in Anne McClintock's formula, as "neither separable from nor reducible to" each other[98]). In more direct relationship to Hobson's concern, the colonies have been seen as a laboratory in which ideological and disciplinary regimes have been developed before being brought back home to regulate metropolitan society.[99] Roy, however, remains provocative. After all, fingerprinting may have been pioneered in Bengal, but Englishmen were immeasurably more likely to be cautioned of their rights first.[100]

QUESTIONS OF BALANCE ASIDE, the fact remains that Europe and its others were co-produced in and through their unequal interactions. Discursively, this meant that, in constructing its other as an object of thought, Europe constructed itself as subject. From the Enlightenment on, this was a curiously unstated, transparent type

[96] This mutuality was expressed in the title of the 1984 Essex symposium "Europe and Its Others," whose published proceedings have had a major influence on postcolonial theorizing. See Francis Barker, Peter Hulme, and Margaret Iversen, eds., *Europe and Its Others: Proceedings of the Essex Conference on the Sociology of Literature, July 1984*, 2 vols. (Colchester, 1985). See also the same editors' *Colonial Discourse/Postcolonial Theory* (New York, 1994). Ann Laura Stoler recurrently addresses this issue in her *Race and the Education of Desire: Foucault's History of Sexuality and the Colonial Order of Things* (Durham, N.C., 1995).

[97] J. A. Hobson, *Imperialism: A Study* (New York, 1902), 160.

[98] McClintock, *Imperial Leather*, 361.

[99] Bernard S. Cohn has recently cited the development of fingerprinting in British India by the civil servant William Herschel. See Cohn, *Colonialism and Its Forms of Knowledge: The British in India* (Princeton, N.J., 1996), 11.

[100] To put it in Gramscian terms, the balance between civil and political hegemony (ideologically elicited consent and direct repression) shifted radically between the metropolis and the colonies. For a developed argument ("how professions of bourgeois democracy were violated in the practice of imperialism"), see Ranajit Guha, "Dominance without Hegemony and Its Historiography," *Subaltern Studies* 6 (1989): 210–309.

of subjectivity, a universal taken-for-grantedness in relation to which difference could only constitute default. In *Writing Degree Zero*, Roland Barthes provided a model for this elusive concept, associating the first cracks in bourgeois hegemony with the emergence of a concern with style—a concern which, in conceding that writing was not simply "white," a neutral medium for the copying of reality, conceded the disruptive possibility of alternatives.[101] Like nature itself, white writing is just there[102]; its power lies in its authorlessness (hence the embarrassing egotism of some postmodernist writing). To resist this kind of power—to tackle the Mercator behind the projection—it is first of all necessary to denaturalize it, to bring out the idiosyncracy of universal categories. Thus the concerted poststructuralist assault on Reason, Progress, the Nation, the Citizen, etc.

So far as historians are concerned, this assault would seem to have reached an end of sorts in Dipesh Chakrabarty's disconcerting conclusion that Europe is the subject of history—that the very historical project itself, regardless of its contents or emphases, is inherently and inescapably Eurocentric.[103] At first sight, Chakrabarty might seem to have mistaken history for geography. After all, as should be clear by now, Europe may occupy a fixed portion of the map, but its history is ubiquitous. But this (I think) is Chakrabarty's whole point—through inscribing its creole genealogy, we begin to undo Europe's arrogation of universal subjectivity.[104] In its positive or critical aspect, therefore, his ostensibly pessimistic thesis enjoins an invigorating politics, the project of provincializing Europe. Chakrabarty's position is informed by the Subaltern Studies collective's longstanding aversion to the prosopopoeia that replaces active consciousness with prefabricated scripts rehearsing the teleological Mission of the class or institution that historical actors are deemed to represent.[105] The other side of this coin is the problematic of exteriority: what can evade European discourse, and how to recover it?[106] Hence the labor of recovering subalternity from between the lines of colonial

[101] Roland Barthes, *Writing Degree Zero*, Annette Lavers and Colin Smith, trans. (London, 1976).

[102] In Jacques Derrida's influential variation on this theme, white mythology, "an invisible design covered over in the palimpsest," deftly combines race and the metaphysics of presence: "the white man takes his own mythology, Indo-European mythology, his own *logos*, that is, the *mythos* of his idiom, for the universal form that he must still wish to call Reason"; Derrida, *Margins of Philosophy*, Alan Bass, trans. (Chicago, 1982), 213. For a sustained and very stimulating series of analyses of the racial politics of the disinterested subject of judgment in Kant (the "Subject without properties"), see David Lloyd, "Analogies of the Aesthetic: The Politics of Culture and the Limits of Materialist Aesthetics," *New Formations* 10 (1990): 109–26; "Race under Representation," *Oxford Literary Review* 13 (1991): 62–94; and (for the prehistory of the argument) "Arnold, Ferguson, Schiller: Aesthetic Culture and the Politics of Aesthetics," *Cultural Critique* 2 (1986): 137–69. Analogously, Uday Mehta, "Liberal Strategies of Exclusion," *Politics and Society* 18 (1990): 427–54; and Etienne Balibar, *Masses, Classes and Ideas* (London, 1994), 194–96, have pointed to the racial coding of liberal universalism. Exegetically, Robert Young, *White Mythologies: Writing History and the West* (New York, 1990), provides a good author-by-author account of the key postulates of some of the more prominent postcolonial thinkers.

[103] Dipesh Chakrabarty, "Postcoloniality and the Artifice of History: Who Speaks for 'Indian' Pasts?" *Representations* 37 (1992): 1–26. For a radical precedent for this perspective, see Oliver Cromwell Cox, *The Foundations of Capitalism* (New York, 1959), 19.

[104] The term creole genealogy is taken from Handler and Segal, "Introduction," 4.

[105] "What, however, the practitioners of the gentle art of prosopography have not sufficiently emphasized in their writings on Indian history, is that the 'human ants' were also thinking animals"; Ranajit Guha, *A Rule of Property for Bengal: An Essay on the Idea of Permanent Settlement* (Paris, 1963), 19.

[106] Since well before *Orientalism*, scholars writing on India have been doing forms of discourse analysis on the modernity of tradition, generally focusing on the codifications of Hindu law that were

and nationalist discourse. Hence, too, Chatterjee's project of claiming "for us, the once-colonized, our freedom of imagination."[107]

The notion of exteriority is, of course, unsatisfactory here, since exteriority is not freestanding but is a determinate residue of interiority. Yet it is extremely difficult to find a better word. This difficulty itself illustrates the depth of the problem, which is one of the starting points of deconstruction. Subaltern discourse is not simply a mirroring negation of colonizing discourse. Hindu-Muslim communalism, for instance, is not some feudal survival, a transcendent essence that repetitively recruits human agents to frustrate postcolonial modernity. Rather, communalism is an integral component of modernity, concretely and specifically grounded in the complex modern consciences of those who participate in it. (The point recalls the distinction between undevelopment and underdevelopment.) To narrate the phenomenology of practical historical consciousness (in this case, of the subaltern), it is necessary to confound the essences and teleologies that colonial discourse ceaselessly disseminates; in Gyan Prakash's phrase, it is necessary to write "post-foundational" histories.[108]

To adopt Homi Bhabha's much-adopted terminology, the modern condition that includes but also exceeds colonialism's binomial categories can be expressed as hybridity. In Bhabha's theory, which represents a high point in the aestheticization of race, the concept of hybridity registers the (post)colonial co-production of Europe and its others, going beyond notions of colonial discourse as a unilateral projection to open up the reciprocal complexities of the colonial encounter. Hybridity confronts colonial discourse with the threat of recognition; the other is like, but only partially like, self—"almost the same but not quite/white."[109] With an unerring eye for contradiction, Bhabha repetitively points to the effort that colonial discourse was obliged to put into rehabilitating stereotypes that, though meant to be eternal, were constantly subject to historical change. In its anxious renovation of the racial essences that underpinned domination, colonial discourse betrayed a

drawn up by Orientalists in consultation with Brahmin pandits around the turn of the nineteenth century. See, for instance, J. D. M. Derrett, "The Administration of Hindu Law by the British," *Comparative Studies in Society and History* 4 (1961): 10–52; Lloyd I. Rudolph and Susanne Hoeber Rudolph, "Barristers and Brahmans in India: Legal Cultures and Social Change," *Comparative Studies in Society and History* 8 (1965): 24–49. With the benefit of Foucault, such studies have proliferated, though the essentialized notion of a "real" tradition that was distorted by the process of codification has proved resilient. It is certainly discernible in Bernard Cohn, "The Command of Language and the Language of Command," *Subaltern Studies* 4 (1985): 276–329. See also Lata Mani, "Contentious Traditions: The Debate on SATI in Colonial India," *Cultural Critique*, no. 7 (1987): 119–56; Ashis Nandy, "Shamans, Savages and the Wilderness: On the Audibility of Dissent and the Future of Civilizations," *Alternatives* 14 (1989): 263–77; David Ludden, "Orientalist Empiricism: Transformations of Colonial Knowledge," in Carol A. Breckenridge and Peter van der Veer, eds., *Orientalism and the Postcolonial Predicament: Perspectives on South Asia* (Philadelphia, 1993), 250–78.

[107] Chatterjee, *Nation and Its Fragments*, 13.

[108] Gyan Prakash, "Writing Post-Orientalist Histories of the Third World: Perspectives from Indian Historiography," *Comparative Studies in Society and History* 32 (1990): 383–408. Prakash has written a number of expositions of the Subaltern Studies collective's approach. See also his "Postcolonial Criticism and Indian Historiography," *Social Text* 31–32 (1992): 8–19, as well as his more recent contribution to the *AHR Forum* on subaltern studies, "Subaltern Studies as Postcolonial Criticism," *AHR* 99 (December 1994): 1475–90.

[109] Homi K. Bhabha, "Of Mimicry and Man: The Ambivalence of Colonial Discourse" (1984), rpt. in Bhabha, *The Location of Culture* (New York, 1994), 89.

profound ambivalence. On the one hand, it strove to domesticate—to assimilate—the native; on the other, it was undone—deauthorized, disavowed—by the partial resemblance, the "difference between being English and being Anglicized" that was thus produced.[110] Sincere or not, sly or not, imitation was a profoundly threatening form of flattery. The scornful stereotype of the Indian mimicking Englishness attested to the colonizer's fear of that which was held back in mimicry, of the recalcitrant brownness that mocked even as it mimicked. Recognizable in a brown skin, Englishness broke down.

IN ITS BASIC FORM, HYBRIDITY is, of course, a palpably material outcome of the primary subversion of the colonial divide. Wherever they have gone, male colonizers have impregnated native women.[111] This notwithstanding, issues of gender and sexuality (especially homosexuality) have until relatively recently been marginalized in scholarly discussions of imperialism.[112] Over the past decade or so, however, our understanding of the complexities of the colonial encounter has been enriched and transformed by an emergent body of work whose significance can hardly be overstated. To survey this work would require an article on its own. I shall merely indicate a few directions here.

As in so many areas, feminist scholars of imperialism have been obliged to labor the most elementary of points before being able to move on to more demanding questions. Thus they have had to remind us (or, at least, too many of us) that women were there too and that women have colonized and been colonized in different ways to men. Much of this work has been recuperative, rereading the imperial archive to disclose its female dimension.[113] White women in the colonies have emerged in all their variety, exploding the stereotypical opposition that James Buzard has characterized as "the Spinster Abroad and the Memsahib, the eccentric

[110] Bhahba, "Of Mimicry and Man," 89–90.

[111] The anthropologist Ann Laura Stoler's treatment of this and related topics is enlightening. See her "Making Empire Respectable: The Politics of Race and Sexual Morality in 20th-Century Colonial Cultures," *American Ethnologist* 16 (1990): 634–60; "Carnal Knowledge and Imperial Power: Gender, Race and Morality in Colonial Asia," in Micaela di Leonardo, ed., *Gender at the Crossroads of Knowledge: Feminist Anthropology in a Postmodern Era* (Berkeley, Calif., 1991), 55–101; and "Sexual Affronts and Racial Frontiers: European Identities and the Cultural Politics of Exclusion in Colonial Southeast Asia," *Comparative Studies in Society and History* 34 (1992): 514–51. By contrast, despite the title and suggestive cover illustration, Robert J. C. Young, *Colonial Desire: Hybridity in Theory, Culture and Race* (New York, 1995), is disappointingly thin, consisting mainly of literary criticism and hardly touching on the material processes of colonialism. (Chapter 6, for instance, "White Power, White Desire: The Political Economy of Miscegenation," has no economics and, if it can be called politics, only of the most genteel variety.)

[112] Ronald Hyam regularly broaches this topic, though not in any great depth, in *Empire and Sexuality: The British Experience* (Manchester, 1990). Richard C. Trexler, *Sex and Conquest: Gendered Violence, Political Order, and the European Conquest of the Americas* (Ithaca, N.Y., 1995), falls ironic victim to one of its own claims, since the repression of detailed reportage on homosexuality, even among the Amerindians of whom it was routinely and formulaically reported, repeatedly reduces the author to guesswork.

[113] This ever-growing literature is much too extensive for representative citation. Some of the many notable contributions not already mentioned include Napur Chaudhuri and Margaret Strobel, eds., *Western Women and Imperialism: Complicity and Resistance* (Bloomington, Ind., 1992); Cynthia Enloe, *Bananas, Beaches and Bases: Making Feminist Sense of International Politics* (London, 1989); Patricia Grimshaw, *Paths of Duty: American Missionary Wives in Nineteenth-Century Hawaii* (Honolulu, 1989); Margaret Strobel, *European Women and the Second Empire* (Bloomington, 1991).

traveler and the pampered Hill Station denizen."[114] Attempts by female scholars from the West to recover Third World women's experiences from against the grain of patriarchal discourse have, however, provoked controversy. A number of scholars, mainly from the Third World, have objected that the sharing of gender does not entitle Western women to claim a sharing of experience substantial enough to transcend the colonial divide from which they themselves have historically benefited.[115] Moreover, in taking up the cudgels on behalf of brown women against brown men, Western feminists have resuscitated a stock justification for colonialism. As Gayatri Spivak and, following her, Lata Mani have argued (their common example is *sati* in British India), the championing of native women's rights provided colonial authorities with a pretext for imposing their own order on native society.[116] Who, then, can speak for subaltern women who lack access to the academy? The very existence of an academic discourse on colonial discourse attests to the hazards of ethnographic ventriloquism.[117]

Gender is not, however, restricted to women. Rather, as Joan Scott so influentially stated, it is a way of encoding power relations.[118] Following up some hints in Said's *Orientalism*,[119] a number of scholars have analyzed the inherent genderedness of the colonial project. This has been most apparent when colonialism has functioned as a discourse on land, which, in settler colonies in particular, has

[114] James Buzard, "Victorian Women and the Implications of Empire," *Victorian Studies* 36 (1993): 443.

[115] See Valerie Amos and Pratibha Parmar, "Challenging Imperial Feminisms," *Feminist Review* 17 (1984): 3–19; Chandra T. Mohanti, "Under Western Eyes: Feminist Scholarship and Colonial Discourses," *Feminist Review* 30 (1988): 61–88; Marnia Lazreg, "Feminism and Difference: The Perils of Writing as a Woman on Women in Algeria," *Feminist Studies* 14 (1988): 81–107; Laura E. Donaldson, *Decolonizing Feminisms: Race, Gender and Empire Building* (London, 1992). See also Julie Stephens, "Feminist Fictions: A Critique of the Category 'Non-Western Woman' in Feminist Writings on India," *Subaltern Studies* 6 (1989): 92–125. Buzard, "Victorian Women," deals effectively with the problems posed for some feminist accounts by the fact that gender cuts across race—white women could be vigorous colonizers.

[116] An early version of Gayatri Chakravorty Spivak's well-known paper is "Can the Subaltern Speak? Speculations on Widow-Sacrifice," *Wedge* 7–8 (1985): 120–30. Mani, "Contentious Traditions." See also Anand Young, "Whose Sati? Widow-Burning in Early Nineteenth-Century India," in Cheryl Johnson-Odim and Margaret Strobel, eds., *Expanding the Boundaries of Women's History* (Bloomington, Ind., 1992), 74–98; Ania Loomba, "Dead Women Tell No Tales: Issues of Female Subjectivity, Subaltern Agency and Tradition in Colonial and Post-Colonial Writings on Widow Immolation in India," *History Workshop Journal* 36 (1993): 209–27. For a comparable and superbly constructed analysis of the ways in which discourse on the issue of female genital mutilation in between-the-wars Kenya cut across the colonial divide, see Susan Pedersen, "National Bodies, Unspeakable Acts: The Sexual Politics of Colonial Policy-making," *Journal of Modern History* 63 (1991): 647–80.

[117] "The subaltern cannot speak. There is no virtue in global laundry lists with 'woman' as a pious item. Representation has not withered away. The female intellectual as intellectual has a circumscribed task which she must not disown with a flourish"; Gayatri Chakravorty Spivak, "Can the Subaltern Speak?" in Cary Nelson and Lawrence Grossberg, eds., *Marxism and the Interpretation of Culture* (Chicago, 1988), 308 (from which article the brown women/brown men line is also adapted). Though acknowledging the problems, others have adopted more pragmatic approaches. See, for example, two of the contributions to the *AHR Forum* on subaltern studies; Cooper, "Conflict and Connection," 1528–30; Mallon, "Promise and Dilemma," 1507. The phrase "ethnographic ventriloquism" comes from my "Should the Subaltern Dream? 'Australian Aborigines' and the Problem of Ethnographic Ventriloquism."

[118] Joan W. Scott, "Gender: A Useful Category of Historical Analysis," *AHR* 91 (December 1986): 1053–75, rpt. in her *Gender and the Politics of History* (New York, 1988), 28–52. A powerful forerunner to this style of analysis was the anthropologist Sherry Ortner's "Is Female to Male as Nature Is to Culture?" in Michelle Zimbalist Rosaldo and Louise Lamphere, eds., *Woman, Culture and Society* (Stanford, Calif., 1984), 67–87.

[119] See, for instance, Said, *Orientalism*, 6.

figured as waiting to be penetrated, opened up, made fertile, and so on ("Guiana . . . ," as Walter Raleigh remarked, "hath yet her maydenhead").[120] As gender provides a model and precedent for the dominated, so, by the same logic, does it construct the dominator as male—or, in Catherine Hall's more complete formulation, which restores race as well as gender to the account, as white, male, and middle class.[121]

To begin to evoke the multifaceted fullness of imperialism, then, we not only have to bring it home, wherever that may be. We also have to trace its complex discursive intersections—not just around the triptych of race, class, and gender but, as noted, around (homo)sexualities and, it seems to me, the psychology of violence. Synecdoche—a cat massacre perhaps, or a Balinese cockfight—would seem to be favored. In her remarkable study of imperialism, which encompasses all these intersections, McClintock homes in on a filthy leather wrist-strap worn defiantly by Hannah Cullwick, working-class wife, servant, and cross-dressing partner in transgressive fantasy to a prominent Victorian lawyer. Cullwick's "slave-band," the imperial leather of McClintock's book title, functions as a fetish, a nodal point for the intersection of imperialist discourses: "The cross-cultural experiences marked by the fetish fuse in the slave-band: in the triangular relations among slavery as the basis of mercantile capitalism; wage labor as the basis of industrial capitalism; and domestic labor as the basis of patriarchy."[122]

A DIMENSION THAT DOES NOT SEEM TO CONVERGE on Cullwick's slave-band is that of territory, a precondition for any system of production. As a historian of European/indigenous relations in Australia, I find that, suggestive though recent writing on imperialism can be, much of it is irreducibly heterogeneous with Australian conditions, for the simple reason that, unlike Bhabha's India (though like Said's Palestine), Australia is a settler colony. For all the homage paid to difference, postcolonial theory in particular has largely failed to accommodate such basic structural distinctions.[123] To register them, and to trace their discursive ramifications, I suggest that Althusser provided a starting point, one that could be greatly

[120] See, for example, Louis Montrose, "The Work of Gender in the Discourse of Discovery," *Representations* 33 (1991): 1–41, quote p. 12. The well-known feminization of the Bengali was class-specific, applying to the Anglicized clerical *babu* but not, say, to Muslim plantation labor in East Bengal. Compare Mrinalini Sinha, *Colonial Masculinity: The "Manly Englishman" and the "Effeminate Bengali" in the Late Nineteenth Century* (Manchester, 1995). It is hard to resist the suspicion that contemporary resentment of clever-clever postcolonialist Bengalis in the Western academy is cognate with this deeply imperialist trope. For an insightful analysis of the gendering of the American colonial landscape, see Annette Kolodny, *The Lay of the Land: Metaphors as Experience and History in American Life and Letters* (Chapel Hill, N.C., 1975); and *The Land before Her: Fantasy and Experience of the American Frontiers, 1630–1860* (Chapel Hill, 1984). See also Ella Shohat, "Gender and the Culture of Empire: Toward a Feminist Ethnography of the Cinema," *Quarterly Review of Film and Video* 13, nos. i-iii (1991): 45–84. An early (but still suggestive) example of gender analysis is Clare Le Corbeiller, "Miss America and Her Sisters: Personifications of the Four Parts of the World," *Bulletin* (Metropolitan Museum of Art) 19 (1961): 209–23.

[121] Catherine Hall, *White, Male and Middle Class: Explorations in Feminism and History* (Cambridge, 1992).

[122] McClintock, *Imperial Leather*, 151.

[123] A recent, though hardly postcolonial, exception is Daiva Stasiulis and Nira Yuval-Davis, eds., *Unsettling Settler Societies: Articulations of Gender, Race, Ethnicity and Class* (London, 1995). See also

enhanced by bringing poststructuralist rigor to bear on materialist approaches to ideology. (Neo)structurally, the concept of social formation enables us to specify material conditions that favor the currency of particular colonial discourses. For instance, the narrative of the dying race, which harmonizes with the project of removing natives from the land, is congenial to settler colonization. It is incompatible with franchise colonization, where native labor is at a premium. Though black, therefore, Australian Aborigines have discursively figured as dying rather than as being endowed with a natural sense of rhythm. On the same basis, the colonization of Native Americans has been structurally distinct from the colonization of African Americans. In the main, Native (North) Americans were cleared from their land rather than exploited for their labor, their place being taken by displaced Africans, who provided labor to be mixed with the expropriated land, their own homelands having yet to become objects of colonial desire. Thus the two colonial relationships were (are) fundamentally opposed. The ramifications of this distinction extend to the present, particularly insofar as they affect the different constructions of "miscegenation" that have been applied to the two communities.[124] Briefly, while the "one-drop rule" has meant that the category "black" can withstand unlimited admixture, the category "red" has been highly vulnerable to dilution.[125] This is consistent with a situation in which, while black labor was commodified (so that white plantation owners fathered black children), red labor was not even acknowledged (so that white fathers generated "half-breeds" whose indigeneity was compromised). In Australia, the structural counterparts to African-American slaves were white convicts, which has meant that racial coding and questions of emanci-

---

Donald Denoon, *Settler Capitalism: The Dynamics of Dependent Development in the Southern Hemisphere* (Oxford, 1983).

[124] In other colonial situations, where native (as opposed to imported) labor is at a premium, people with combined ancestry can be counted as settler-become-native, as in the case of Latin American *mestizaje*. See, for example, Roger Bartra, *The Cage of Melancholy: Identity and Metamorphosis in the Mexican Character*, Christopher J. Hall, trans. (New Brunswick, N.J., 1992); Nicholas Canny and Anthony Pagden, eds., *Colonial Identity in the Atlantic World, 1500–1800* (Princeton, N.J., 1987): Magnus Mörner, *Race Mixture in the History of Latin America* (Boston, 1967): Mörner, ed., *Race and Class in Latin America* (New York, 1970); Jose Klor de Alva, "The Postcolonization of the (Latin) American Experience: A Reconsideration of 'Colonialism,' 'Postcolonialism' and 'Mestizaje,' " in Gyan Prakash, ed., *After Colonialism: Imperial Histories and Postcolonial Displacements* (Princeton, 1995), 241–75, or something separate from either native or settler, as in Colette Guillaumin's sharp specification of South African "coloreds" as a "class formed by people belonging in fact to one *and* the other group [which] is declared to belong to neither one nor the other but to itself"; "Race and Nature: The System of Marks; The Idea of a Natural Group and Social Relationships," *Feminist Issues* 8, no. ii (1988): 25–43.

[125] The most comprehensive and systematic account of the one-drop rule is F. James David, *Who Is Black? One Nation's Definition* (University Park, Pa., 1991). See also Virginia R. Dominguez, *White by Definition: Social Classification in Creole Louisiana* (New Brunswick, N.J., 1994); Joel Williamson, *The Crucible of Race: Black-White Relations in the American South since Emancipation* (New York, 1984). For official classifications of Native Americans, see M. A. Jaimes, "Federal Indian Identification Policy: A Usurpation of Indigenous Sovereignty in North America," in Fremont J. Lyden and Lyman H. Legters, eds., *Native Americans and Public Policy* (Pittsburgh, 1992), 113–35; Jack D. Forbes, *Black Africans and Native Americans: Color, Race, and Caste in the Evolution of Red-Black Peoples* (Oxford, 1988); Native American Consultants, Inc., *Indian Definition Study* (Contracted Pursuant to PL 95-561, Title IV, s. 1147, Submitted to the Office of the Assistant Secretary of Education, Department of Education, Washington, D.C., January 1980). For a remarkable example of the contingencies of these classifications in juridico-bureaucratic practice, see James Clifford, "Identity in Mashpee," in Clifford, *Predicament of Culture*, 277–346.

pation have operated quite differently between the two countries. Where the respective indigenous populations have been concerned, however, there are substantial similarities between the racial calculations on which official policies toward them have been predicated. Such discursive distinctions, which survive the de-territorialization of imperialism, are clearly of considerable historical significance. They only make sense in relation to the material conditions that historically shaped the different colonial relationships concerned.[126] If we wish to produce histories that tell us enough about imperialism to suggest ways of resisting it, we should start with these conditions.

[126] I have attempted a historical reconciliation of official discourses on Australian Aboriginal people on the basis of the settler-colonial relationship in my "Nation and MiscegeNation: Discursive Continuity in the Post-Mabo Era," *Social Analysis*, no. 34 (1994): 93–152. For official constructions of Aboriginality more generally, see Tom Clarke and Brian Galligan, "'Aboriginal Native' and the Institutional Construction of the Australian Citizen, 1901–48," *Australian Historical Studies* 26, no. 105 (1995): 523–43; Jeremy R. Beckett, "The Past in the Present, the Present in the Past: Constructing a National Aboriginality," in Beckett, ed., *Past and Present: The Construction of Aboriginality* (Canberra, 1988), 191–217. Gerald M. Sider has perceptively traced discursive continuities (in particular, the Indian as lone warrior/tracker) from seventeenth-century dispossessions of sedentary agriculturalists through to Native American enlistment patterns for the Vietnam War. See Sider, *Lumbee Indian Histories: Race, Ethnicity and Indian Identity in the Southern United States* (New York, 1993), 177–246. In *Colonialism's Culture: Anthropology, Travel and Government* (Cambridge, 1994), Nicholas Thomas stresses and illustrates the heterogeneity of colonialism.

Patrick Wolfe is an Australian Research Council Postdoctoral Research Fellow in the history department at the University of Melbourne, where he previously lectured on race and colonialism, historical theory, the history of ideas, and Aboriginal-European encounters. He is a council member and monograph series editor at the newly established Institute of Postcolonial Studies, 78–80 Curzon Street, North Melbourne, Victoria, 3051, Australia. Wolfe has published a number of articles on colonialism and the history of anthropology. His monograph, *White Man's Flour: Science, Colonialism and an Anthropological Soliloquy*, is being considered by a publisher. He is currently working on a book on the history of colonial discourse, to be titled *Deep Genealogies*.

Abbreviations for Fanon's Works

BS *Black Skin, White Masks* (New York: Grove Press, 1967), translation by Charles Lam Markmann of *Peau noire, masques blancs* (Paris: Éditions du Seuil, 1952).

DC *Studies in a Dying Colonialism* (New York: Monthly Review Press, 1967), translation by Haakon Chevalier of *L'An V de la révolution algérienne* (Paris: Maspero, 1959).

WE *The Wretched of the Earth*, preface by Jean-Paul Sartre (New York: Grove Press, 1968), translation by Constance Farrington of *Les Damnés de la terre* (Paris: Maspero, 1961).

AR *Toward the African Revolution: Political Essays* (New York: Grove Press, 1967), translation by Haakon Chevalier of *Pour la révolution africaine. Écrits politiques* (Paris: Maspero, 1964).

[18]

Nationalism and a New Humanism

Nigel Gibson

We must not voodoo the people.

Fanon, *The Wretched of the Earth*

An important part of my project has been to examine Fanon's cultural politics in a historical context. In my foregoing remarks on the veil and the radio, I emphasized the larger sociopolitical contexts and dynamics of Fanon's conception of national consciousness and nation-building. Here, still within the context of national consciousness, I argue that Fanon's cultural politics can lead to an understanding of his humanism. Further, if his humanism is predicated on anticolonial action, why then should it take a national form? We shall have to first discuss Fanon's conception of national liberation.

The Question of Nationalism

Fanon eschews an abstract populism which too narrowly stakes its claims in a racial reaction to White rule while too broadly taking the whole continent of Africa as its field of reference. Instead, he argues that a national culture, born in the anticolonial struggle, can provide a basis for success and lay the groundwork for a vibrant political society. It is also from this national basis that a genuine Pan-Africanism can develop. Colonialism created the national boundary, yet, Fanon maintains – though he resists an uncritical embrace of categories derived from colonialism – national liberation is the form that anticolonial struggles must take. Indeed, if the social struggle does not become a national endeavor it will inevitably degenerate along the retrograde, geographic, ethnic, and racial lines refashioned or simply created under colonial rule. He alludes to the threat of degeneration when he speculates on the likely consequences should the initial period of spontaneity not develop and the struggle remain within an elemental and local social consciousness where one group is unified in opposition to another group under the watchful eye of colonialism. If these struggles reach what Fanon calls "the stage of social consciousness before the stage of nationalism," fierce demands for social justice will be paradoxically allied with "tribalism" (*WE*, 204). Racial feeling, or a desire for revenge, might be good and cohesive enough reasons to join the struggle against colonialism, but the social consciousness it produces is rudimentary, local, and finally retrogressive.

During the Algerian war, the "nation" was, in practice, brought to life in the locality: the government is set up on the hillsides of Kabylia, for example, meting out justice in an immediate and authoritarian way, and the group is frequently held together by a "mystical body of belief" deriving in part from traditions of resistance as well as from democratic forms of local rule. This kind of local rule, which is inherently contradictory and fiercely independent, must develop into a richer and more inclusive concept of the nation. But here is where problems begin because other forces and other claims are involved in the nationalist project. With his critical insight Fanon foresaw the great potential for failure in the national movements, indicating that the test of a successful decolonization lay in the degree of human self-determination. By not making the national program explicit, by not deepening it "by a rapid transformation into a consciousness of social and political needs, in other words into humanism," he charged, it leads up a blind alley (*WE*, 204).

Some postcolonial critics claim that nationalism is alien to Africa, that it is a European idea that was adopted by anticolonial leaders to assert freedom from European domination. Certainly the nation-state in its geographical articulation was a European invention; but by the 1950s nationalism had much to do with the immediate promise that the chains of foreign rule would be shattered. Additionally, the sway of European intellectual authority continued virtually unchallenged partly because the critique of its authority lay within the Manichean thought that characterized European rule in Africa. To present an authentic African political form as *the* answer was a reaction to Manichean thinking but remained within its intellectual contours. Instead, there was a myriad of polities, some democratic and some not, and some more compromised with colonialism than others. It was necessary to see how variegated indigenous democratic forms provided a basis – while not being sufficient on their own – for nationalism to be successful. In short, Fanon's dialectic of anticolonialism is grounded in the local, but in order to defeat colonialism it moves of necessity to a centrally planned movement. This is where many nationalist movements stop. For Fanon this centralizing movement is further challenged by a return to the source, toward local decentralization enriched by the foregoing movement. Let us consider this move in more detail.

Fanon's Theory of Nationalism: Two Types of Nationalism or Three?

> Let us waste no time in sterile litanies and nauseating mimicry. (Fanon, *The Wretched of the Earth*)

It has often been argued that Fanon draws a distinction between two kinds of nationalist ideology in the context of anticolonialism. There was, on the one hand, a nationalism that wanted to take power but remain virtually subordinate to external powers; and, on the other, a nationalism that wanted a genuine independence represented by such groups as the FLN. I contend that Fanon adds a third, unique conception of nationalism, which is implicitly critical of the FLN and other national liberation organizations, and is grounded in what he calls a new humanism and an internationalism.

In many cases, the development of national consciousness on the African continent depended on the reaction of the colonialists, thus in part proving Fanon's point that the degree of resistance to decolonization determines the shape and depth of the nationalist movement. In some cases, the colonialists embraced the nationalist elite and negotiated withdrawal; in others, the colonialists' refusal to recognize the nationalist elite forced it into more radical politics. These positions can be summarily contrasted as a moderate and conformist nationalism ($nationalism_1$) as opposed to a militant nationalism ($nationalism_2$). The fundamental difference between these two forms of nationalism and a third which is Fanon's ($nationalism_3$) lies not only in their reaction to colonialism but in the people's perception and consciousness of nationalism. The more the victory over colonialism is seen as the work of the people, not some elite, the more it can become decentralized in the postcolonial period and thus be identified as $nationalism_3$. In Gramsci's pithy hypothesis, $nationalism_3$ can be thought of as optimism of the will and pessimism of the intellect, a celebration of human action and a critical attention to hazards of national consciousness. This antimony can only be solved in practice, a practice which includes the work of intellectuals. But it is easy for action to be subverted and for the human will, so delicate after the colonial experience, to be crushed. Because the postcolonial situation is problematic, Fanon argues that "there must be no waiting until the nation has produced new men; there must be no waiting until men are imperceptibly transformed by revolutionary processes in perpetual renewal. It is quite true that these two processes are essential, but consciousness must be helped" (*WE*, 304). Aided by constant criticism, "revolutionary theory, if it is to be completely liberating," has to painstakingly draw conclusions; for it is revolutionary theory that can help settle problems and signals "consciousness to take another step" (*WE*, 304–5).

In the following, Fanon's conception of nationalism is further addressed in terms of self-consciousness and how this relates to his revolutionary theory, and to his plea, at the close of *The Wretched*, to work out new concepts emerging from the African struggles. "To turn over a new leaf" suggests what the anticolonial struggle seeks to produce from itself without precedent. Because the disappearance of colonialism means both the disappearance of the colonizer and the colonized, it has to include a radical reordering of the social structure to forestall a neocolonial situation. It is the complex transformation of the colonized, not the simple departure of the colonizers, that will produce the new humanity. In short, to venture beyond Manicheanism is to transform the native into an active thinking historical subject: "to rise above this absurd drama that others have staged around me . . . to reach out to the universal" of reciprocal recognition (*BS*, 197). This is in part what Fanon means by a new humanism.

We should keep in mind that Fanon's concern to establish a radically democratic polity is posed as a problematic. For example, when he raises the issue of decentralization of the party into rural areas and the village councils as a model of decision making, these councils too have to undergo a radical mutation. Fanon asks some perennial questions and suggests ways to approach them.

To go beyond Manicheanism means to end the world of colonialism and racism and to inaugurate a new human reciprocity. The proposition is tautological. Authentic termination of the colonial condition requires a new humanism and a new humanism requires total decolonization. Fanon turns away from liberal European humanism, which he considers hypocritical, but seriously attempts to create a more human and fundamentally different future from the dehumanized and violent experience of colonial rule. In part, Fanon's is a practical or ethical humanism, because it is, after all, an issue of life. Previously we saw how the prefiguring of a new humanism is expressed culturally, in the radical mutation of consciousness taking place during the revolution. The fighting culture is thus one expression of the new humanism, though in *The Wretched* it is far from complete and does not exhaust Fanon's full intended meaning. To comprehend Fanon's intention we must rigorously trace how Fanon's cultural politics leads to, and is part of, a new humanism.

Revolutionary theory requires a "total" approach and Fanon announced the theoretical frame for his cultural politics in a speech before the First Conference of Black Writers. Given soon after his self-avowed participation in the Algerian revolution, this speech champions the struggle against all forms of alienation: "The logical end to this *will to struggle* is the total liberation of the national territory. In order to achieve this liberation, the inferiorized man brings all his resources into play, all his acquisitions, the old and the new, his own and those of the occupant" (*AR*, 43). Fanon construes the struggle as part of the process by which the native becomes a *social individual*, one who has "decided, 'with full knowledge of what is involved,' to fight all forms of exploitation and of alienation of man." The goal of this plunge into struggle is "total liberation." The new humanism is "prefigured in the struggle" (*WE*, 246). For the struggle of the oppressed to become "at once total, absolute," the "practical content" – which brings all the resources of the oppressed and of the colonizer into play – must be superseded or, in other words, undergo a radical mutation. Through this dialectical supersession, we encounter the free will in a new social order, a free will that realizes (and is conscious of) its own freedom of will. The *structure and rhythm of the people*, their radical mutation, provide the structure of the new society, already in evidence in the process of "total liberation."

It was one thing to propose such a framework for the "illogical maintenance of a subjective attitude in organized contradiction with reality" (*AR*, 53) in the dark days of the Battle of Algiers, and quite another to realize it. It is the gap between Fanon's theorization of absolute liberty and the "reality" of postcolonial Algeria that is a sticking point for many critics. How could the increasingly conscious and united masses, so forcefully projected by Fanon, so quickly dissipate in the years after independence? To further plumb this question and the content of Fanon's concept of national liberation and humanism, let us first turn back to his critique of nationalism$_1$.

For the colonialist, Fanon argues that the colonial idea of humanity is realized through its civilizing mission, with its "proclamation of an essential equality between men." Appearing logical to itself, colonialism invites a handful of the native elite "to become human and take as their prototype Western humanity as incarnated in the Western bourgeoisie" (*WE*, 163). This elite adopts Western tastes, while the rest of the colonial "subhumanity" are mired in poverty. In nationalism$_1$ it is this "caste," essentially an unproductive caricature of the Western bourgeoisie, that then assumes national leadership. In this scenario, independence does not lead to decolonization but to a curious self-recolonization where a native leadership simply mimics the privileges and postures of the Europeans and follows it on the path toward "decadence" – a jet-setting, Mercedes-driving, Martini-drinking elite – while the masses sink deeper into poverty. Fanon vociferates that if one's dream is to turn Africa into Europe, then it would be better to leave Africa under the control of the Europeans. Wearing the "mask of neocolonialism," the nation is not put on a new footing but stagnates. The ruling class flocks to the capital, the urban areas, and the regions marked out for privilege under colonialism, while the "rest of the colony [would] follow its path of underdevelopment and poverty" (*WE*, 159). Under the nationalist leadership the retrogression is on all fronts: economic, social, and political. Nationalism$_1$ reflects Europe's "balkanization" of Africa, with the elite of each "country" demanding its own privileges, its own civil service, and enormous government salaries, while resisting African unity. Fanon calls this type of nationalism "anti-national":

> The nationalist bourgeoisie with practically no economic power . . . not engaged in production, invention, construction or labor . . . enters, soul in peace, on the terrible anti-national path of a bourgeoisie, flatly, stupidly, cynically bourgeois. For them nationalization does not mean governing the state with regard to new social

> relations . . . [but] quite simply the transfer into native hands of those unfair advantages which are legacies of the colonial period . . . Enormous sums are spent on displays of ostentation, cars, houses . . . They will prove themselves incapable of triumphantly putting into practice a program with even a minimum humanist content, in spite of fine-sounding declarations . . . that come straight out of European treatises on moral and political philosophy. (*WE*, 149–63)[1]

This prescient analysis sums up the subsequent and saddening experience of a host of countries, including ones that had started along the track of a more militant nationalism.[2]

Even worse, not only have the nationalist leaders become Westernized in superficial though insidious ways, but they also accept European racial philosophy "in its most corrupt form." The rhetoric of bourgeois humanism is easily turned into a rhetoric of African uniqueness, and the "Africanization of the ruling class" heralds the culmination of a racist policy whose whole philosophy is really no more than the slogan "replace the foreigner."

The emptiness and danger of such nationalism is exposed as interracial and interethnic rivalries appear, created and recreated by colonial rule and classifications, and "African unity takes off its hollow mask"; soon, nationalist sentiment degenerates into racism. The rationalism that the masses had attained by confronting colonialism now dissipates, fierce old enmities are encouraged, and in place of a national consciousness religious identity and spiritual cults "show a new vitality." In short, the policies of nationalism_1 lead to stagnation, regression, fragmentation, and starvation. Sadly such xenophobia as the basis for politics has not diminished. Citizenship in many postcolonial African countries has become reduced to colonial classifications. Such politics, and the legacies of colonial rule, were found in the most extreme and tragic form in Rwanda, where "replace the foreigner" was used as a justification for genocide.

Nationalism_2: The Overworked Peasant and the Lazy Intellectual

> The unpreparedness of the educated classes, the lack of practical links between them and the mass of people, their laziness, and, let it be said, their cowardice at the decisive moment of the struggle will give rise to tragic mishaps. (Fanon, *The Wretched of the Earth*)

> Let us suppose that we would have produced as human beings... In the individual expression of my own life I would have brought about the immediate expression of your life, and so in my individual activity I would have directly *confirmed* and *realized* my authentic nature, my *human, communal* nature. Our productions would be as many mirrors from which our natures would shine forth. (Marx, "Excerpts from James Mill's *Elements of Political Economy*")

Fanon's singular critique of the more militant nationalism$_2$ gives us an insight into the dialectical character of his concept. Unlike nationalism$_1$, which is led by a kleptocratic, self-interested elite, nationalism$_2$ articulates a genuine desire to modernize and develop the nation. However, rather than developing new relations with the peasants and workers and genuinely involving them in the decision-making process, nationalism$_2$ regards them merely as the means to accumulate the capital needed for "modernization."

The colonial master's familiar complaint that the native is slow and lazy is repeated by the nationalist leaders with a new ideological twist: now they should sacrifice for the nation. "Development" by any means becomes the new fetish, which, with the lack of technology to increase surplus value, can only be accomplished by labor which is in plentiful supply.[3] This call by the nationalist$_2$ leaders to make "colossal efforts" for the nation accommodates various and often conflicting ideological determinations – negritude, African personality, or pan-Arabism, as well as various forms of "socialism," and "modernization." But among the variables, there is one constant: pressure on the peasantry to sacrifice *even more* than they did in the colonial period: "The exploitation of agricultural workers will be intensified and made legitimate. Using two or three slogans, these new colonists will demand an enormous amount of work from the agricultural laborers, in the name of the national effort of course" (*WE*, 154–5). The leader, in whose person the populace found a representative of national unity against colonial domination, inevitably becomes a new source of domination, overseeing the accumulation of capital. The term "leader" refers to a driver of animals, but Fanon reminds us, "the people are no longer a herd [and] do not need to be driven" (*WE*, 184).

Fanon's critique of nationalist bourgeoisie (as huckstering, greedy, and useless) is often associated with the underdevelopment school which sees colonialism as the expropriation and *under*-development of Africa by the West, with the unequal exchange in global capitalism determining and even undermining class relations. Yet unlike the dependency theorists' preoccupation with external relations, Fanon's dialectic enabled him to discern internal social conflicts. Choices can be made even in the vortex of the world market. This is a crucial consideration. The situation is far from perfect but for Fanon it is, in part, how and under what conditions people work that becomes a measure of independence and an important element in his critique of nationalism$_2$. Fanon compares the simple adoption of the productivist model and the colossal efforts demanded of the masses with his call for a new paradigm (*WE*, 100). Rather than a "developed" country, he argued, such exploitation created a devolved human being, a being turned animal because he or she is treated as such. Rather than worry about the withdrawal of capital, or primitive accumulation, Fanon voices concern in *The Wretched* about the withdrawal of the human being, the "very concrete question of not dragging [people] towards mutilation, of not imposing upon the brain rhythms which very quickly obliterate and wreck it" (*WE*, 187). Condemning forced labor in the name of the nation, he insists on the laborer's self-determination as an important step toward actualization. There are no stages of liberation, whereby the nation develops its economic basis first and then liberates the people second. Body is given to national consciousness only when "men and women are included on a vast scale in enlightened and fruitful work" (*WE*, 204). Other projects are fruitless.

Fanon's attention to the conditions of labor is reminiscent of Marx's contention that the realm of freedom is based on the transformation of alienated labor into a form of self-realization. "If conditions of work are not modified," Fanon warns, "centuries will be needed to humanize this world which has been forced down to animal level" (*WE*, 100). The necessary modifications can only be effected through people making decisions, experimenting at a local level, learning by mistakes and "starting a new history" (*WE*, 99, 188–9). Such a goal resides not in some utopian distance but in immediate development; thus he speaks of the Algerian experience as a "new beginning." Moreover, Fanon views work not as external compulsion but as an expression and act of creation of the social individual. From a psychological point of view, non-alienating labor is essential to the individual sense of self. The new social relations of work engender at the same time the reproduction of a newly created self who understands that "slavery is opposed to work, and that work presupposes liberty, responsibility, and consciousness." He claims that "in those districts where we have been able to carry out successfully these interesting experiments, we have watched man being created by revolutionary beginnings" (*WE*, 192). This is quite a different discourse of nationalist politics. In Fanon's mind national production actually rises rather than declines if the people take control. With the focus on the whole human being, not simply the immediate functioning of muscles, with meetings between producers and consumers during the Algerian war of liberation, the caloric intake in the liberated areas reached unheard of levels: "The fact is that the time taken up by explaining, the time 'lost' in treating the worker as a human being, will be caught up" (*WE*, 192). The problem remained, however, how to take this idealism of the war of liberation into the postindependence period.

Fanon can be considered a Marxist humanist in the sense that he is not championing a static notion of human nature, but a notion of human potential "created by revolutionary beginnings."[4] Rather than viewing Fanon's Marxism simply in terms of stretching class categories in the colonial context, what is especially provocative is the expression of the creativity of ideological intervention as a political act. In *The Wretched* he calls this intervention "political education," which he defines as opening the people's minds, "awakening them, and allowing the birth of their intelligence" (*WE*, 197). This birth is central to Fanon's conception of a national culture and is made possible by the transformation of consciousness catalyzed by the revolutionary struggle; and here that consciousness is created in a flash of common sense so straightforward that it seems extraordinary: "the peasants have very clearly caught hold of the idea that the more intelligence you bring to your work, the more pleasure you will have in it" (*WE*, 192).

In contrast, the nationalist$_2$ organization has an administrative attitude toward labor. They might eschew "technicians and planners coming from big Western universities" (*WE*, 192), but they have the same attitude to "human resources." What makes this so pernicious, in Fanon's mind, is the separation it introduces between organization and the revolutionary principles, and between organization and masses.

The division between the nationalist leaders and the masses, following so soon after independence and appearing so evident in retrospect, was neither automatic nor passive; it was the result of an intense class struggle where workers' organizations were banned and oppositions destroyed. It represents something of a counter-revolution. Stanching the free flow of ideas that had given impetus to the independence process, the party disintegrates into a "trade union of individual interests" and an "empty shell," used by the nationalist leadership to form a "screen" between it and the masses. Unwilling to expand democracy, the party becomes authoritarian and systematically eliminates all opposition: "The embryo opposition parties are liquidated by beatings and stonings. The opposition candidates see their houses set on fire. . . . All the opposition parties . . . have been, by dint of baton charges and prisons, condemned first to silence and then to clandestine existence" (*WE*, 182). Fanon's prediction would soon be seen in Algeria, where political dissidents were silenced, radicals purged, and strikes were termed labor "indiscipline" and declared not to be in the national interest.[5]

The question of organization provides a powerful lens for focusing the degeneration of nationalism$_2$. Again Fanon presciently describes the postcolonial African situation. Though helping to fulfill the "historical mission" of ridding the nation of the colonialists, the organization all too frequently metamorphoses into a bureaucratic dictatorship. Invariably centered in the urban areas, where it becomes increasingly corrupt, it degenerates into a dictatorship of party officials. Embracing a military model, it frequently acts like a "common sergeant-major," ruling from the top. It demands of the people "silence in the ranks," predicts Fanon: increasingly separated from all decision-making, the masses are sent back, intellectually and physically, "to the caves."

Fanon's project of deepening the anticolonial revolution into humanism is reminiscent of Marx's point in the *Eighteenth Brumaire* that proletarian revolutions move forward through a process of constant criticism. For national consciousness to be "deepened" into a humanism, there needs to be a different conception of time and development. It is no use importing capitalist notions; rather production needs to be considered in terms of human development. People must understand that a new social agenda will follow a novel timetable, often improvised, tempered by patience and fortitude, especially since "the spirit of discouragement, which has been rooted in people's minds by colonial domination, is still very near the surface" (*WE*, 194). Such discouragement can, and Fanon fears will, lead to an all-too-quick retrogression.

The profundity of Fanon's critique of the separation between leaders and ranks, and the lack of practical connections between them, has been borne out by the early years of African independence. Genuine commitments to agricultural cooperatives have failed. Often targeted from the urban center, the peasantry has been permitted no voice, no representation, being placed at the receiving end of "collectivization." The emphasis on cash crops rather than food crops has often led to food shortages and increased dependence on imported foods, and has been tacitly determined by a characterization of the peasants not as valuable in themselves but as mere producers of value. The authoritarian character of the implementation of the plan led "to the triumph of a dictatorship of civil servants" (*WE*, 180). Even attempts to reduce the growing government bureaucracy through decentralization, as in Nyerere's Tanzania, did not halt "the process of its own contradictions" (*WE*, 165) but only increased the regional bureaucracy. Politics were directed at the symptoms rather than the underlying causes. Part of the problem resulted from the assertion that the capitalist, or the landed exploiter, was unknown to traditional African society.[6] This perspective led to a rather naive and uncritical attitude toward incipient class divisions emerging most profoundly in the organization. In many cases, harking back to "traditions" became part of an ideology used to mask new divisions between leaders and masses, and put an end to dialogue, discussion, and the "free exchange of ideas" (*WE*, 170). While nationalization transferred to the elite the unfair advantages which are legacies of the colonial period, privatization has not challenged this legacy but only helped produce more inequality and poverty. Projects of "African socialism" were genuine if bureaucratic; neoliberal capitalistic "structural adjustment," on the other hand, is nothing but systematic exploitation.

Humanism and Ideology

> [The] clarity of ideas must be profoundly dialectical. The awakening of the whole people will not come about all at once; the people's work in the building of the nation will not immediately take on its full dimensions. (Fanon, *The Wretched of the Earth*)

Reluctant to produce an abstract "treatise on the universal," Fanon's attention to the centrality of labor in the independence context attempts to create meaning for lived experience and gain insight into African processes of national reconfiguration. Fanon's dialectic can perhaps be approached by remembering his engagement with Hegel. Axel Honneth argues that *The Wretched* "is an anticolonialist manifesto that attempted to explicate the experience of the oppressed Black Africa by drawing directly on Hegel's doctrine of recognition."[7] Honneth grasps a truth, but in almost too simple a fashion, ellipsing Fanon's sharp critique of Hegel and thereby reducing Fanon's innovative recreation of the Hegelian dialectic of recognition to the experience of oppression. For Fanon the paradigmatic development of reciprocity that Hegel develops has to be remapped in the colonies. When the slave is also colonized the development of recognition through labor is blocked off. Fanon offers another route through the development of national consciousness. In other words, rather than equate reciprocity with identity which inevitably annulled the Other, Fanon grounded mutual recognition in the moment of alterity, and called for recognition from the Other while demanding it not be reduced to the same. This dialectic of reciprocity, made concrete in terms of a national liberation movement against colonialism, is not reducible to the dialectic of labor. Fanon is not simply replacing one dialectic (the anticolonial) for another (the class struggle) but, through a system of interpenetration, deepening each. The result is, as we saw in his critique of Sartre, a much more open-ended or, as Fanon would put it, "untidy" dialectic, which can be best understood in the social context. At least that is where Fanon saw the possibility of freedom. For such a possibility is never automatically realized; indeed, "philosophical thought teaches us," Fanon observed in *The Wretched*, that "the consciousness of the self is not the closing of the door to communication, but guarantees it" (*WE*, 247). This "self" which does not close the door to communication develops by undergoing mediation (and therefore self-negation) and only then embraces the other in mutual recognition.

The movement of the dialectic in *The Wretched* is first expressed by Fanon's profound retelling of the *experience* of anticolonial political activity. It is an experience that destroys old colonial truths and a hermeneutic that reveals contradictions that have been hidden by colonialism. Spontaneous activity, as we saw earlier, reaches for a self-understanding based on action not hemmed in by Manicheanism. In fact, Fanon argues that it is "the rebellion" itself that "gives proof of its rational basis" (*WE*, 146). The power of this drive to self-understanding is, however, impeded by the "laziness" of the intellectuals, who continue to insist on a Manichean analysis when "shades of meaning" are needed. Optimism in the possibility of African freedom is a result of revolutionary action based on a vital transformation in the character of subjectivity. But, and here he marks a new theoretical warning, "colonialism and its derivatives do not, as a matter of fact, constitute the present enemies of

Africa . . . [T]he deeper I enter into the culture and political circles the surer I am that the great danger that threatens Africa is the absence of ideology" (*AR*, 186).[8] What is of overriding importance to Fanon's conception of ideology was its relation to revolution. That was exactly why the young Fanon criticized Bantu Philosophy as a closed epistemology which placed disproportionate value on the externals of culture (*WE*, 234); summing up the dialectic of culture and liberation in *The Wretched*, he noted, "The struggle for freedom does not give back to the national culture its former values and shapes."

One important turning point of *The Wretched* is when he charts the challenge to theory, schematically mapping the development of a small group of revolutionary intellectuals who help the development of "new meanings" inherent in the spontaneous activity. Hounded by the authorities in the town and isolated in the nationalist party, this group of what we have called "honest intellectuals" (who have begun to learn a new ethics in prison), are forced underground. Their estrangement and distrust of the mainstream nationalist party drives them to the countryside. Whereas earlier contacts between the urban militant and the peasantry had resulted in mutual distrust, this second meeting results in a "radical mutation." The intellectual, who had previously seen the peasant as backward, sees them as spontaneously anticolonialist. The peasant, on the other hand, who hates the colonial police machine, welcomes with open arms these militants on the run. Fanon looks for a solution to this pressing problem of the relationship between urban and rural and mental and manual labor, to express the Marxian problematic, by considering the *experience* that the handful of intellectuals have in the small illegal party as it makes contact and develops a working relationship with the rural masses. It is these relationships that he thinks can be pressed by demanding a process of organizational decentralization, and that can create the atmosphere for developing the revolutionary ideology that has been so sorely absent. The intellectual's "instinctive distrust of the race for positions" (*WE*, 177) provides the basis for a new type of organization and is key to the postcolonial situation.

Nevertheless there still remains the question: what is the place of the intellectual in the discovery of what constitutes the national? It is a question that returns to the problematic of the absence of ideology. For Fanon, ideology is the development of a new humanism built around and promoting the people's self-reliance and creative potential. An important indicator of this relationship, nevertheless, is the language of politics. His concern for a common language turns on the way in which the politicos speak to the masses, and the type of language they use, which is quite different from the liberal discourse of "individual rights" spoken by the nationalist elite. Fanon is mapping out new terrain in which the narrative of the honest intellectual's development is seen in the very method of *The Wretched*. Honesty produces commitment but it does not, of itself, produce the exploration of social relationships, and the practical-critical activity that Fanon is asking for.

It needs to be stressed that Fanon's concern that the intellectual be aware of *what happens after* decolonization leads him to criticize the very Manicheanism that had first motivated the mass movement. Thus Fanon does not support any and every peasant–intellectual interaction. First, he is critical of the intellectual's elitism toward the masses (inculcated by Western culture), and thus the intellectual's first rule should be to emphasize that the whole political project is based on the masses coming to realize that the future of the nation depends on themselves. Second, he is critical of the intellectual's rejection of their Western experiences, which leads them to make sacred, almost uncritically, any manifestation of native culture, which has been seriously compromised during the period of colonialism. Such a valorization can lead to reactionary consequences. Fanon's claim that *The Wretched* is directed to his African comrades, not to the West, should be taken seriously. Certainly "The Pitfalls of National Consciousness" and "On National Culture" are pointedly addressed to that small group of committed intellectuals; they are also critiques of a Manichean "Africanist" bootstrap ideology which says no to foreign influences but hounds the peasantry to work harder, to make "colossal efforts" for the nation (*WE*, 154–5). The "optimism of the will and pessimism of the intellect" of this small band of revolutionaries is not equivalent to Che Guevara's focoism, or to Plato's "philosopher Kings,"[9] but rather they are a group willing to tip the scales of destiny through painstaking work. A philosophy born of struggle also means that philosophy has a role to play in the struggle.

For Fanon the appellation *nation* was not a strategic move to intervene in metropolitan debates. The importance of the rural in Fanon's conception of national consciousness problematizes such intellectual discourse. Indeed, for Fanon national consciousness was a unifier, it crossed urban and rural and tribal and ethnic barriers and racial and religious categories, either invented or reinforced by colonialism, and it was the only possible political form that could successfully challenge colonialism. He attacked those leftists who thought that the stage of national liberation could be bypassed in the colonies,[10] as though it was a "phase that humanity has left behind." National liberation met a need of people long denied such recognition, and without it, social and political demands would tend toward racism. This is no better seen than by the passion with which the native intellectual defends the existence of a national culture in the face of being "swamped" by "Western culture." This reaction, which is a response to the colonialist theory of precolonial barbarism, represents a psychological need. Fanon maintained that national liberation, which was not nationalism, was more than a necessary moment, but he was also perceptively aware of the problematic. While he was ready to concede on the factual plane that the glories of past African civilizations do not help the starving peasant today, he regarded their existence in other times as both rehabilitating and a justification for the future. This work of discovery is of "dialectical significance," opening up space for a new national culture to be reconstituted through new connections between cultural historians and the new cultural voices emerging in the liberation struggle. These new relations are essential to Fanon's project and, inverting the familiar complaint about the laziness of the peasant, Fanon placed blame for the "tragic mishaps" of the liberation struggle on the laziness of the nationalist intellectual.

Political Education: How National Consciousness can Deepen into a Humanism

> Now, political education means . . . to teach the masses that everything depends on them; that if we stagnate it is their responsibility, and if we go forward it is due to them too, that there is no such thing as a demiurge, that there is no famous man who will take responsibility for everything, but that the demiurge is the people themselves. (Fanon, *The Wretched of the Earth*)

Looking at Europe, its styles and techniques, Fanon argues that he sees only "a succession of negations of man, and an avalanche of murders," and a bourgeoisie which proclaims the "essential equality between men" (*WE*, 163) while murdering everywhere (*WE*, 311). However, even though its Enlightenment claims to universalism specifically excluded Africa, Fanon does not reject the positive project of human equality:

> All the elements of a solution to the great problems of humanity have, at different times, existed in European thought. But the action of European men has not carried out the mission which fell to them . . . [i.e.] bringing the problem of mankind to an infinitely higher plane. (*WE*, 314)

Europe must be rejected not because it speaks of humanism, and not only because it speaks hypocritically, but because its promise, its intellectuals and its workers, on whose shoulders the task has rested of breaking with its narcissism and its imperialist spirit, have also failed. Europe must be forsworn because there the dialectic of liberation has become "the logic of equilibrium." The dialectic, which never belonged exclusively to the Europeans anyway, has to be delinked from a Europe which has become antidialectical.[11] The European is no longer the site for ideas of liberation. Hitler's concentration camps gave notice that the idea of Europe as the site for the human project had come to an end, but the anticolonial movements had uncovered the real source of its barbarity. Fanon's conceptual new leaf, his new humanism, is intimately connected to conscious action and critical of any action that "does not serve to reconstruct the consciousness of the individual."[12] This is the challenge to Africa and to Africana philosophy.

When Fanon writes that his philosophy is "an untidy affirmation of an original idea propounded as an absolute" (*WE*, 41), he is not making claims about universal human development. He is insisting that it is only through conscious, reflective activity that the "question of mankind," and indeed the "rehumanization" of humanity, can be discussed (*WE*, 314). He does believe that it is the human's essence to be free, but his idea of humanism is not based on uncovering an essentialist idea of the human being. The *creation* of the liberated human being must be fabricated by conscious work.

While Fanon argued that not experiencing a nationalist period represented a serious deprivation, an unwise shortcut, with perhaps dire consequences, he clearly differentiated between a narrow, racially defined nationalism and a national (antiracist) consciousness that wanted to "open out" to the "truth of the world." It claims "universality" only because he locates it in a "decision to recognize and accept the reciprocal relativism of different cultures, *once* the colonial status is irreversibly excluded" (*DC*, 44). The road to this universality is through national consciousness. The irreversible exclusion of colonial ideology, including any movement toward establishing a neocolonial social structure, means for Fanon that the ultimate goal cannot reside in taking over existing institutions with their exploitative practices (*WE*, 144–5). Fanon's new humanism develops during the struggle for freedom, beginning as a reaction to the Manichean status quo, with the native "vomiting up" the Western values force-fed by the colonialists. This development results not from the cognitive persuasiveness of some humanist treatise; rather, it is compelled by a visceral reaction to colonialism's actual dehumanization. If not exhausted by Manichean agitation, the native's energies can lead to the reconstruction of the consciousness of self. Independence and reciprocity are the necessary conditions for freedom. It is only when the native gets beyond Manichean action, an action determined by the Other, that he or she can truly be considered self-acting.

When Fanon argues that "national consciousness, which is not nationalism, is the only way to give us an international dimension" (*WE*, 247), he is not merely communicating the need for national recognition on the international stage. He is also declaring that the native's struggle for freedom could start a new world history. Though this new history might find some use for Europe's "prodigious theses," Fanon's proclaimed intention to enlighten the world and create a basis for a new human reciprocity represents a new beginning. At the same time, his internationalism is revolutionary, for his idea of national liberation was explicitly continental: he wanted to "carry Algeria to the four corners of Africa," assembling revolutionary Africa across the desert and thereby creating a continent (*AR*, 180).

While the concept of radical mutation is bound up with the development of indigenous intellect, the philosophic basis, on which the intellectual makes a "reasoned analysis" and aids the indigenous intellect, needs to be further explored. The principal aim of a national culture is to encourage and assist self-understanding, which cannot come all at once. Because self-understanding is a "profoundly dialectical" process, Fanon stresses its development through facing contradictions. Still, some notion of where one is going – what sort of society one is trying to create – has to be spelled out in some conceptual form. This is what Fanon means when he says, "we must work out new concepts, and try to set afoot a new man" (*WE*, 316).

Taken out of context, Fanon's assertion that "Africa will not be freed through the mechanical development of material forces," and his concentration on a mental and cultural revolution, seem to wash out a concern about material conditions. Profoundly concerned with life, he is not antidevelopment. Instead of addressing change as a machine, he insists on the human aspect and in a Marxian way stresses the ideal unity of mental and manual labor: "It is the hand of the African and his brain that will set into motion and implement the dialectics of liberation of the continent" (*AR*, 173). The "practice of action" affects the mind and also is a product of the mind. The radical mutation in consciousness which is a result of the revolutionary struggle is not only an act directed at the externality of objective conditions, but it also supplies the impetus for the revolutionary subject to seek self-development.

Implicit in Fanon's conception of national culture is its organization, especially in the sense of creating "practical links" between intellectuals and the masses. The masses seek self-clarification and understanding of the workings of the objective world. They seek this self-clarification from an organization that can analyze the contradictions in the revolution from *within* the revolution. In Fanon's mind, this working relationship between the intellectuals and the masses is crucial to the survival, self-determination, and development of a truly independent society.[13] The extent to which the masses continue to play a central role in the postcolonial society determines the success of – indeed defines – Fanon's new humanism. And the part played by revolutionary intellectuals, insofar as it bolsters and sustains the masses' efforts, performs a crucial function.

The process whereby colonized people come to understand that "everything depends on them" involves a degree of spontaneity and a process of enlightenment. As we have already seen, to transcend the limitations of Manicheanism created by colonialism depends on what Fanon calls political education. Yet understanding is still grounded in action. What is required, Fanon suggests, is a real working relationship between the dissident intellectuals who bring their "knowledge of the practice of action" and the masses who have decided to "embody history." This does not necessarily mean that intellectuals do the thinking. Fanon challenges both the colonial idea that the masses have no thoughts of their own, and the intellectual's uncritical celebration of any subjugated idea.

Intellectuals must undergo a profound sense of alienation from themselves as products of the colonial civilizing mission. Without this experience, the intellectual, in one way or another, will tend to be set apart and antagonistic to the people's aspirations. This process is not a straightforward one. Most obviously, the eyes of the first type of nationalist intellectual (nationalist$_1$) are focused more on the "mother country" than on their own people. They are the enfranchised slaves of *Black Skin* who never fought for their freedom and remain indebted to their colonial masters. This type of nationalism is merely the empty sentiment of flag waving. More interesting is the plight of the $nationalist_2$ who, while hoping to make the nation matter on the world stage of nations, wants more than juridical recognition. Here the organization plays a centralizing role, bringing together all the fragmented and diverse anticolonial struggles. Under the banner of liberation, this centralizing role is a "natural" one for the $nationalist_2$ intellectual, who is wont to speak *for* the masses and to suppress differences for the sake of unity. Disagreements are submerged to buoy up the national cause. Both the vanguard party and nationalism are homogenizing forms. While this strategy is an important one for the success of the anticolonial struggle, it creates a "sclerosis" (*DC*, 66). It can lead to the rights of different groups being trampled on and an exaggerated importance being placed on the ethnicity of the leaders. In the name of the "nation," one ethnic or religious group can come to dominate.

The tricky problem is to judge the differences and how to allow them expression. When Fanon speaks of deepening national consciousness into a new humanism, it is precisely this problem he is addressing, because he wants the most democratic and pluralistic culture – where "minorities" and genuine differences are allowed full expression – to emerge. This problem is not worked out, but he claims that individual liberation does not automatically follow as a consequence of national liberation; rather, individual liberation emerges as part of a process: "The liberation of the individual does not follow national liberation. An authentic national liberation exists only to the precise degree to which the individual has irreversibly begun his own liberation" (*AR*, 103).

National culture takes as its point of departure the "fighting culture" developed during the anticolonial period and thus Fanon does not pretend that a national culture is innocent of suppressing those differences that hinder the development of the national cause. Nor does he look uncritically at the indigenous culture that had survived under colonialism. Tribal, racial, and ethnic identifications, often encouraged or even fabricated by colonialism, pose barriers to national and individual self-determination. Instead of uncritically embracing either traditions or modernity as external unifiers, Fanon turns to the revolutionary movement as the source for creating an entirely new context. If national struggle makes possible the development of a social consciousness, then culture is simply "a whole body of efforts made by a people in the sphere of thought to describe, justify, and praise *the action which the people has created itself*," because it "takes its place at the very heart of the struggle for freedom" (*WE*, 233). Dehumanized by colonialism, the native is newly individualized, Fanon argues, by the experience of being part of the struggle for freedom. It is through the activity of self-creation that the social individual comes into being:

> Individual experience, because it is national and because it is a link in the chain of national existence, ceases to be individual, limited, and shrunken . . . during the period of national construction each citizen ought to continue in his real, everyday activity to associate himself with the whole of the nation, to incarnate the continuous dialectical truth of the nation and to will the triumph of man in his completeness here and now. (*WE*, 200)

Far from reflecting an a priori, the dialectic of self-determination of the individual and self-determination of the nation is, in Fanon's view, not something put off for the future but is a constantly developing process. This process is expressed through the individual's experience in building up the nation. Fanon uses the example of building a bridge. He says that if it does not enrich the awareness of those who work on it, then it ought not to be built (*WE*, 200–1). Successfully carrying out a program is by no means the proof of the program's worth or merit. In Fanon's ethos, financial or utilitarian standards of value count for little: human activity must first and foremost enrich human awareness. Fanon's liberatory ideology is a practical matter, it fulfills the task of criticizing other ideologies (colonial and nationalist) and gives meaning to events. This latter process does not come from the intellectual's head but from a back and forth between people and militants in a working group. Liberatory ideology seeks to uncover the mystifications that block the people's self-activity. Fanon's example of the building of a bridge is also a metaphor for the practical matter, of the building of bridges between the organization and the people.

Liberation is an ongoing project. No plan, no leaders, no temporary strategic necessity can take its place: "If we stagnate it is [the people's] responsibility, and if we go forward it is due to them too." The individual's self-understanding becomes inseparable from their quest for liberation. There is also, for Fanon, an important concomitant process between the activity of individual liberation and the release of a people's inherent intelligence which needs further clarification.

If the emphasis on the people's self-creation leaves room for individual self-determination, there still remains the question: what is the place of the intellectual in the discovery of what constitutes the national? In fact, the intellectual's interpretation of the "national" can lead to confusion and obfuscation if it does not take into account a "conception . . . of the future of humanity" (*WE*, 234–5).

It seems at first glance that Fanon assumes as given, or at least as unproblematic, the value of the expertise or knowledge that the intellectual has "snatched" from the West. Nevertheless, we have seen that Fanon does not intend intellectuals to educate in the same fashion as they have been educated; the educator becomes newly educated by challenging preconceived ideas about the backwardness of the masses. It is only in this context that a mutual education can take place.

Fanon introduces the question of political education to criticize how the nationalization of the economy benefited an oligarchical government of privileges. Instead "public business should be the business of the public," carried out on a "democratic basis," with the mass of people taking part in its running. The greatest challenge to Fanon's fundamental humanist belief that "everything can be explained to the people, on the single condition that you really want them to understand" (*WE*, 189) is to ensure that the lines of communication are open, and that new ears are found to listen to the so recently voiceless and dehumanized. The task of political education is not the practical administration of things but enlightenment. It involves a fundamental questioning and rethinking of every aspect of life, beginning "everything all over again" (*WE*, 100). Far from proposing a return to an idyllic past, Fanon is speaking of a thorough reexamination of production and human relations, questioning the environment which has been detrimentally used by the "economic channels created by colonialism." Because its central credo is the self-activity and self-determination of the masses, "political education" must be profoundly democratic, encouraging meetings and discussion where the people are "able to speak, to express themselves, and to put forward new ideas" (*WE*, 195). It requires a new patience on the part of the intellectual, whose "return to the source" is also a turn to an oral culture and history not judged as the past but in the making.

The move toward an engaged intellectual is seen from the shift from the abstractions of the "poet's Africa" to the concrete of revolutionary Africa. Fanon's change in attitude can be seen in the different approaches taken in *Black Skin* and in his Mali notebooks ("This Africa to Come," in *AR*, 177–90). In *Black Skin* he writes that "The discovery of the existence of a Black civilization in the fifteenth century confers no patent of humanity on me. Like it or not, the past can in no way guide me in the present moment" (*BS*, 225). In the midst of his revolutionary reconnoitre of the Southern Front Fanon changes his focus. The issue now is not the meaning of African civilizations for Fanon's own sense of self, but the need to know the histories of the peoples of Africa to work out postcolonial problems: "In Kidal I plunge into some books on the history of the Sudan. I relive, with the intensity that circumstances and the place confer upon them, the old empires of Ghana, of Mali, and Gao, and the impressive Odyssey of the Moroccan troops with the famous Djouder. *Things are not simple*" (*AR*, 185).

Because things are not simple, Fanon does not operate under romantic illusions that there will be an immediate understanding of the most complicated problems. This is why he emphasizes a dialectical process, a deepening spiral rather than a straight line, a working through contradictions rather than a static subject/object identity. Because self-consciousness does not come about all at once, the intellectual's role is to destroy the ideology that characterizes the masses as backward and incapable of governing themselves. Fanon's faith in the ability of the masses to understand everything does not imply a withdrawal of the intellectual and the advocacy of the type of autarkic economy where specialist knowledge and technology is shunned and the regime is based on "miserable resources" (*WE*, 103). Fanon is neither a voluntarist[14] nor an anti-intellectual. Nor is he suggesting that the division between the intellectuals and the masses is bridged by the intellectual performing manual labor. The point is not that the masses' thoughts are more relevant than those of the intellectual, but because of the masses' lack of esteem for their own ideas, the intellectual is crucial in eliciting and explaining their subjugated knowledge. This is what Fanon means when he says that the intellectuals should put themselves "to school with the people."

The intellectual's job is to make the *social* individual's own self-understanding the basis for understanding the world: "Political education is the . . . birth of their intelligence" (*WE*, 197); it is not about applying knowledge, but helps the immanent development of the indigenous reason. In other words, it helps the reason that is born in the decolonization struggle to test itself out, raise itself to truth, and set about learning about the world and acquiring genuine content. By helping reason reflect on its (Manichean) certainty, political education helps develop the truth of the anticolonial struggle. This is the intellectual's main role. "The nation does not exist in a program which has been worked out by revolutionary leaders"; it is created by "the muscles and brains of the citizens" (*WE*, 203, 201). Implicit here is that the intellectual's theoretical work will foster national liberation.

What Type of Organization for the Postcolonial Future?

> For the people, the party is not an authority but an organism through which they as the people exercise the authority and express their will. (Fanon, *The Wretched of the Earth*)

In contradistinction to the formal questions of organization, Fanon was concerned with its nature and the relations of power that it expresses. For Fanon the political organization is a "living party," an *organism* that encourages an exchange of ideas elaborated by the needs of the people. This new type of organization is quite different from the imported Western model. Fanon criticizes the nationalist elite's "fetish of organization" that often takes precedence over "a reasoned study of colonial society" (*WE*, 108), which is of much greater consequence than the existence of a formal organization. The problem, then, is how to give an organizational form to a "reasoned study." Such a study should not be confined to a strategic interpretation of alienated conditions of the moment; it should seek to understand and explain the epoch of decolonization. Where Fanon had previously postulated a "time lag" between the rural masses and the urban nationalists, he now speaks of a different register of time needed to make a reasoned analysis – to take stock and think critically of the situation.

Despite the centrality of the intellectual, Fanon's dialectic of organization does not grant a privileged site to ideas *per se*. In fact, Fanon implies that the intellectual is not necessarily the bearer of the intellect since the *practice of action* itself is the source of a new way of knowing. It is through reflection on such action that unexpected details and new meanings are discovered, and it is through this self-reflected knowledge that the colonized come to be freed from the colonial condition and conditioning. Although the activity of the revolutionary intellectuals makes it possible for the masses to "understand social truths," the development of the indigenous intellect requires constant dialogue.

Fanon presents a number of practical ways for the form of organization to foster indigenous intellect and stymie intellectual elitism. His conception of organization is highly democratic and encourages the free exchange of ideas. In its first appearance during the early stages of revolt, the organization necessarily assumes a centralizing character in order to unify the colonized to counter the tactics of the colonialists, but in the postcolonial period it is desirable for the organization to be "decentralized in the extreme." It is from below "that forces mount up which supply the summit with its dynamic, and make it possible dialectically for it to leap ahead" (*WE*, 198). Whereas the town-based nationalist parties had "show[n] a deep distrust towards the people of the rural areas" (*WE*, 109), the Fanonian organization bends the stick the other way as it avoids the capital "like the plague" and is headquartered, or decentralized into the countryside. Regionalism and tribalism need to be confronted, but Fanon does not believe that they can be tackled from above by a centralized and an urbanized organization which would tend to disregard the real concerns of the people. It is at the local level that the new society is created and the "decentralized despotism"[15] of the colonial legacy confronted.

The problem is that, like colonial forms of governance, old ideas and cultures – along age and gender lines – have been challenged but not completely uprooted. It is a ticklish problem because in many cases these forms have been a bulwark against colonialism during the early period of resistance. In the most practical sense the Manicheanism that exists after liberation can only be addressed with great patience. In part this is often one of the legacies of "late colonial rule" where urban civil society is deracialized but where "despotic" customary rule is kept in place in rural areas. By considering the peasant as the central protagonist of national liberation, Fanon has in part approached the problematic of postcolonial Africa, making land and labor central to the rights of the nation's citizens. It is in the rural areas that the success of national liberation can really be judged by the challenge to "customary rule."

Fanon's call for a breaking down of the distinction between town and country, and for the extreme decentralization of the organization, echoes his belief (albeit undeveloped) that the degenerating communal form might be reinvigorated during the independence struggle and become an element on which a future decentralized state and nation might be based. Fanon understands that, though there is no going back, the democratic polities that existed in many African societies should be regenerated. However, Fanon's fundamental point is to identify the "enlightened action" of the people with the "nation":

> The flag and the palace where the government sits cease to be the symbols of the nation. The nation deserts these brightly-lit, empty shells and takes shelter in the country, where it is given life and dynamic power. The living expression of the nation is the moving consciousness of the whole of the people; it is the coherent, enlightened action of men and women. (*WE*, 204)

On an individual level, Fanon deplores madness as a loss of liberty; on the social level, colonialism has created a form of madness and enforced a loss of liberty. The conclusions to *Black Skin* and *The Wretched* are remarkably similar. The question of human reciprocity that dominates *Black Skin* is approached in *The Wretched* from the perspective of a historicized consciousness, which becomes responsible for its own action. Throughout, Fanon remained committed "to educate man to be actional, preserving in all his relations his respect for the basic values that constitute the human world" (*WE*, 200). Thus the organization must not block this historical and social self-consciousness. The organization, he says, should "not [be] an authority but an organism through which . . . a people exercise their authority and express their will" (*WE*, 185). Fanon argues for a separation of organization and administrative body. The party leaders should not have any administrative powers: "The party should be a direct expression of the masses. The party is not an administration responsible for transmitting government orders . . . we must rid ourselves of the very Western, very bourgeois and therefore contemptuous attitude that the masses are incapable of governing themselves" (*WE*, 187–8).

Once again we return to the proposition that the people can and should govern themselves. This principle battles the "spirit of discouragement" drummed into the colonized during the period of colonialism. It is on this basis that the organization can remain an "incorruptible defender of the masses." The reasoned analysis and rethinking of social conditions and political exigencies must be worked out through a dialogue, and at the same time this working out of what to do immediately and practically must be informed by "an idea of man and the future of humanity" (*WE*, 203). It is the activity from below that makes possible the "dialectical leap," but it depends on a free flow of ideas between the rank and file and the leadership. Each side, on its own "would split apart in incoherence and anarchy."

Fanon's approach to nationalism is dialectical. Nationalism is both an imported European idea and a product of opposition to the colonial regime. As such, it can undergo a dialectical development and be taken over and used against the colonialists. Moreover, for Fanon, a national consciousness, which he argues is not nationalism, signifies the form, not the goal, of postcolonial society. The struggle for independence looks forward but also backward, and part of its goal is to invent a history and a tradition. Fanon's concept of national liberation is an attempt to transcend this Manichean problematic where the backward-looking tendency of nationalism can easily degenerate into racism. It is not possible to return to a precolonial standpoint (often promoted to a separatist and authoritarian nationalism that looks to the past and seeks cultural regeneration),[16] and nor is it desirable to approach the future in mimicry of the West (nationalism$_1$ often unites both these tendencies, with the mimicry of the colonialist administration often also echoing attitudes to the "customary"). The decolonized society has to find its own way. Such self-consciousness provides a form which can open out to other cultures and becomes continental. Fanon is perhaps a perceptive critic of the rhetoric of the "essential African" that cloaks its racist paradigms, and its politics of ethnic cleansing, behind a mask. There is nothing essentially progressive, therefore, about African essentialism.[17] The point was not only to uncover a neocolonialist conspiracy behind the "African" mask, but to highlight the internal problematic of African decolonization.

In Place of a Conclusion

Part of Fanon's dilemma is a result of the important role he reserves for the intellectual, who is potentially the most unstable element in the Fanonian scheme. Yet in helping create a national consciousness through a new cultural politics and in encouraging the masses' self-certainty, intellectuals contribute greatly to stability. They play a central role in either the development or the failure of a new humanism. If a new humanism is to develop and succeed, then the intellectuals themselves must also develop, discarding the universals inculcated through colonial training; their development is both a practical rather than theoretical matter, a physical and a cerebral experience. In the new movement, the liberated voice of the radical intellectual "gives rise to a new rhythm of life and to forgotten muscular tensions, and develops the imagination" (*WE*, 177).

The African movements for freedom opened up a new dialectic and page in history. Today, Fanon's ideas might seem overly idealist, but he was, in fact, a consummate realist. Sadly his predictions about postcolonial Africa have often proved correct: Africa is worse off than it was over 40 years ago. On the other hand, the revolutionary pressures in Africa have not ceased. It is the unfinished nature of decolonization that continues to haunt Africa in this present moment of decomposition. Fanon's conceptualization of development, with its focus on labor (more often female in contemporary Africa), is no more "idealist" than it was 40 years ago. The hard facts of twenty-first century Africa tell a different story. The last 25 years have seen life expectancy fall, the health care and education systems in crisis and food production decline. There is a growing gap between rich and poor. There has been hardly a positive from structural adjustment. Who but the ideologues believe that Africa can now "develop" along capitalist lines? Fanon's prognosis, however incomplete, remains eerily concrete. His point was not merely to foretell the crisis in Africa and the degeneration of the independence movements, but to intervene and affect the process. To tap into the vast reservoir of popular resistance and to try and "put Africa in motion . . . behind revolutionary principles" – that was his self-assignment.

Yet perhaps Fanon's most enduring legacy today is to have formulated a series of problematics rather than answers. Thus when Fanon asks in the middle of *The Wretched*, "Do I exist?" "In reality, who am I?" (*WE*, 250), the question touches both ontological and epistemological issues; the fragmentation of identity as well as the uncertainty of binary concepts that are to be employed to understand the postcolonial social situation. Rather than celebrate their certainty or ambiguity, or back away to a "neutral" standpoint, Fanon engages these categories, understanding that they are products of power. Human freedom remained central to Fanon's dialectic. Humanity is also yes-saying, he says in *Black Skin*, and thus he rejected the idea that the individual is powerless to change reality or to construct a self. But it is never enough to dismiss a way of thought without engaging the social condition that produces it. Fanon's postcolonial imagination is a challenge; an insistence that one confronts the here and now. Rather than a technological solution, his idea of the future Africa rested on the hand and brain of the African. Imagination may seem a sorry answer to the powerful forces of neoliberal globalization that attempt to discipline Africa today, yet Fanon's insistence on bringing "invention into existence" and to imagine a future is in fact a concrete response to the threadbare technical economic authoritarianism of structural adjustment, the grim reaper which continues to haunt the continent.

Notes

1 Fanon's idea of premature senility of the nationalist bourgeoisie is brilliantly rescribed by Ayi Kwei Armah in *The Beautyful Ones Are Not Yet Born* (London: Heinemann, 1981) when he describes birth to death in seven years, mirroring the short time between Ghana's independence from the British and its degeneration under Nkrumah and the coup against him.
2 Ngugi wa Thiongo has quite aptly characterized the literature about postcolonial Africa as a "series of imaginative footnotes" to Fanon's "Pitfalls" chapter (see Ngugi's "The Writer in the Neo-colonial State," in *Moving the Centre* (London: Heinemann, 1993), p. 66).
3 A theory propounded by W. A. Lewis, "Economic Development with Unlimited Supplies of Labour," *The Manchester School of Economics and Social Studies*, 36, no. 1 (Jan. 1958).
4 I am using the term "potential" guardedly, but I think it gestures to a more dialectical rather than a static view of an unchanging human essence merely being uncovered by revolution. A material reordering (to use Fanon's words) releases human potential. Fanon, like Marx, called his philosophy a "new humanism." Tony Martin argues that Marx's *Eighteenth Brumaire*, especially Marx's idea that people make history but not in the circumstances of their own choosing, "had a special attraction for Fanon . . . [and] provided him with the *leitmotif*

of his philosophy" (Martin, "Rescuing Fanon from the Critics," in Nigel C. Gibson (ed.), *Rethinking Fanon: The Continuing Legacy* (Amherst: Humanity Books, 1999).

5 Likewise in Nkrumah's Ghana, the right of workers to strike against the new government was disallowed.

6 For example see Julius Nyerere, "Les Frondements du socialisme africain," reprinted in *Freedom and Unity: A Selection from Writings and Speeches, 1952–1965* (Dar es Salaam: Oxford University Press, 1966).

7 Axel Honneth, *The Struggle for Recognition: The Moral Grammar of Social Conflict* (Cambridge: MIT Press, 1996), p. 160. Of course, the experience was limited to the racial designation "Black Africa."

8 Fanon does not think that there are simply no ideologies; there are plenty of "morbid symptoms," as Gramsci put it, to choose from, but these are all retrogressive. The problem is a lack of revolutionary ideology (or perhaps more appropriately revolutionary theory) grounded in the anticolonial social movements and with a vision of the future. "Ideology" is needed to counteract the hollow rhetoric of the nationalist middle class and the romanticized, and potentially retrograde, negritude ideology, which includes appeals to "traditions," including religion.

9 See L. Adele Jinadu, *Fanon* (London: Kegan Paul International, 1983).

10 Lenin also emphasized the importance of national liberation in his conception of social revolution: "To imagine that social revolution is possible without revolts by small nations in the colonies . . . is to repudiate social revolution. So one army lines up in one place and says, 'We are for socialism,' and another, somewhere else says, 'We are for imperialism,' and that will be a social revolution! . . . Whoever expects a 'pure' social revolution will never live to see it. Such a person pays lip service to revolution without understanding what it is" (V. I. Lenin, "The Discussion of Self-Determination Summed Up," in *Collected Works*, Vol. 22 (London: Lawrence and Wishart, 1964), p. 355).

11 Cf. Jean-Paul Sartre, *Critique of Dialectical Reason* (London: Verso, 1991), pp. 726–7. Nevertheless, Fanon had not totally given up on the Europeans. If they want to be involved in "reintroducing mankind to the world . . . [they] must first wake and shake themselves" out of their stupor (*WE*, 106). Europeans might disagree though it was the anticolonial revolts in Luso-Africa that shook Portugal out of its stupor.

12 Found in Fanon's "Blida notes" (1955), quoted in Peter Geismar, *Frantz Fanon* (New York: Grove Press, 1969), p. 197.

13 Fanon defines "intellectual resources" as "engineers and technicians" (*WE*, 152) but includes poets, some of whom became political leaders.

14 Fanon perceptively notes that "men and women, young and old, undertake enthusiastically what is in fact forced labor, and proclaim themselves slaves of the nation," but he adds perceptively that "we

238

cannot believe that such an effort can be kept up at the same pace for very long."

15 See Mahmood Mamdani, *Citizen and Subject: Contemporary Africa and the Legacy of Late Colonialism* (Princeton: Princeton University Press, 1996).

16 Christopher Miller's view that Fanon's attitude is "massively ethnocentric," because he views precolonial society as having no history, is based on several misquotations. The idea of precolonial traditions can also be "massively ethnocentric." Rather than talked about in generalities, each "tradition" and its history needs to be discussed. Miller, who consistently wants to find some African essence, ends up privileging "ethnicity" over "nation." But he fails to understand how ethnicity is also manipulated by colonialism (Miller, "Ethnicity and Ethics," *South Atlantic Quarterly*, 87, no. 1 (1989)). In Fanon's time, it was clearly the ethnic entrepreneurs who were used to destroy Lumumba.

17 His penetrating critique of Leopold Senghor, the President of Senegal, who heralded African humanism while supporting the French in Algeria, pointed to the problematic of negritude in power.

[19]

Ngugi's Concept of History and the Post-Colonial Discourses in Kenya

James A. Ogude

Résumé

L'article cherche à démontrer que les sens de l'histoire chez Ngugi est étroitement lié à sa politique d'interprétation et que ses textes post-coloniaux peuvent être mieux compris si on les place dans le contexte des discours contradictoires post-coloniaux au Kenya. Ses romans expressent la quête d'un ordre socio-politique nouveau et critiquent l'élite africaine qui s'est comparée du pouvoir à l'indépendance pour devenir simple gardien du capitalisme occidental. Une lecture des textes de Ngugi lie son concept de l'histoire aux discours sur la théorie de la dépendance au Kenya et à la conceptualisation de la révolution post-coloniale en Afrique de Fanon. L'article déclare que les histoires supprimées dans les textes de Ngugi sont invariablement liées à la tendance à supprimer les contradictions à la fois au niveau local et à un niveau plus spécifique dans la perspective de la dépendance.

Introduction

In his essays, Ngugi wa Thiong'o argues for a "radical" reinterpretation of Kenya's history. The thrust of his argument is that Kenya's history has been distorted by the colonial writers and by Kenya's professional or guild historians, trained and schooled in Western critical modes of thought.[1] At the heart of Ngugi's thesis is his contention that Kenya's working people, the workers and peasants, are marginalized, if not totally ignored, in the country's narrative history. Ngugi, therefore, seeks to intervene and salvage the history of the subaltern[2] from the ruins of colonial plunder.

And yet, can one safely argue that Ngugi has a monopoly over what constitutes Kenya's history simply because he privileges history of the subaltern? Does not the privileging of one form of history also entail the suppression of the other? To raise these questions is to ask questions of theoretical approaches to historical meaning; they are questions about the politics of historical interpretation. But they are also questions about the complexity of a theoretical perspective a writer adopts and how that choice enhances or limits his/her grasp of the subject she/he may be handling.

The view taken in this article is that one can best understand history by exploring the politics of interpretation that inform a specific historical subject or phenomenon. Here, I lean on Hayden White's thesis that the significance of any historical narrative lies squarely on the politics that inform the interpretation of that subject and that, "interpretation presupposes politics as one of the conditions of its possibility as a social activity" (1987, 59). White's point is that historical apprehension is guided by specific interests that a given historical interpretation ultimately serves: "Everyone recognizes that the way one makes sense of history is important in determining what politics one will credit as realistic, practicable, and socially responsible" (1987, 73). In other words, no interpretation is value free and, indeed, there can never be one interpretation of an historical subject. This does not mean, however, that every interpretation is adequate once the politics behind it has been established; one needs to explore the possibilities and limits a given interpretation or framework offers in exploring complex layers of knowledge.

This article is both a critique and a demonstration of Ngugi's sense of history as a major voice in the struggle for socio-political change in the post-colonial state in Kenya.[3] It seeks to demonstrate that Ngugi's sense of history is closely linked to his politics of interpretation — to his political project vis-à-vis the post-colonial body politic in Kenya — and that his texts depicting post-colonial Kenya are best understood if placed against the contradictory flux of post-colonial discourses in Kenya. The article also seeks to demonstrate that although Ngugi's novels have been perceived largely as discourses on cultural decolonization, they involve the quest for a new socio-political order. In this quest, Ngugi foregrounds land as a recurring economic and political metaphor in the decolonization process in Kenya; he critiques the African elite that captured state power at independence as mere watchdogs of Western capitalism, and, indeed, he raises his pet theme of cultural imperialism and strategies for the African revolution. A dialogical reading of Ngugi's texts, as this article will show, links his concept of history to dependency theory discourses in Kenya and Frantz Fanon's conceptualization of the post-colonial revolution in Africa.[4] The article will argue that the silences — the suppressed histories in Ngugi's texts — are invariably linked to the tendency to suppress local and the more specific contradictions within a dependency perspective.

Ngugi's Narrative and the Post-Colonial State

Fiction is a representation of history. And to the extent that both history and fiction deploy narrative structure, O. Louis Mink writes, they can both be seen as "a primary and irreducible form of human comprehension, an article in the constitution of common sense" (1978, 132). For this reason, narrative has increasingly come to be regarded as a type of explanation and form of knowledge as forceful as "scientific knowledge" (White 1987, xi; Mink 1978, 133). White makes much the same point when he argues that the historical text is necessarily a literary artefact because the process of creative imagination involves the writer of fiction as much as it does the historian.[5]

The point is that both fiction and history, while having marked differences, also share vast similarities. Both history and literature invoke the principle of selection and derive their material from specific cultures and historical experiences. According to Tony Bennet, "History does not supply a key with which to unlock the meaning of the literary text, nor does the latter function merely as a particular route into the study of a history conceived as a set of realities outside its own boundaries" (1990, 71), but rather, the literary text should be seen as part of the wider historiography in its own right. Most critics desist from treating Ngugi's text as part of Kenya's historiography. I am hoping that this article will reassert Ngugi's narrative within the contested terrain of Kenya's historiography.

Ngugi recognizes the link between history and fiction. Indeed, for Ngugi, the narrative is a tool for shaping, ordering, and reinterpreting history. As Carol Sichermann puts it, "Ngugi blurs the lines between history and literature and that, perhaps as a consequence of this blurring of the two genres, the distinction between Ngugi and his narrators and certain characters also becomes blurred" (1989, 348).[6] Sichermann's point is that Ngugi's narrative is steeped in Kenya's historical landscape and, indeed, at times borders close to direct allusion on actual historical personages and events. In the act of historical recovery, Ngugi is both selective and creative.

Four basic thematic strands tend to characterize Ngugi's recreation of Kenyan history. Most of his works are marked by the portrayal of a peaceful African past until the coming of whites, a documentation of the injustices of colonialism, a portrayal of the glorious struggle for Uhuru, the betrayal of the common people in the post-independence period, and the resilience of the people. Since I am not interested in a chronological account of Ngugi's sense of history, but rather in the recurrent factors in his narrative, such as the Mau Mau war and also in the more recent radical shifts and discourses in the novels that deal directly with the period after independence, I will not focus on his early works such as *Weep Not Child* (1964), *The River Between* (1965), and *A Grain of Wheat* (1967).

Although the latter remains a prophetic novel that casts doubts on the positive claims associated with independence by the African nationalists, it is nonetheless a novel of renewal: a novel of new beginnings in which individuals, loyalists, and fighters alike have to come to terms with their past and forge a sense of community. Nevertheless, Ngugi's uncertainty with the period following independence is left in no doubt through a forceful ironic structure and, at times, overt references to the betrayal of the masses by the African elite. But that is as far as his critique of the post-colonial state goes in *A Grain*. In his subsequent publications, *Petals of Blood* (1977), *Devil on the Cross* (1982), *Matigari* (1987), and in his critical essays published in the period from 1972 to 1993,[7] Ngugi, with a passionate rendering, revisits some of the issues raised obliquely in *A Grain of Wheat*.

The theme of a glorious past manifests itself clearly in Ngugi's novels that deal directly with the colonial presence in Kenya (*Weep Not Child* [1964] and *The River Between* [1965]) and need not concern us directly here. But to the extent that this theme of a glorious past lingers on as a sub-text in the novels whose main project is the post-colonial period, it remains an important element.

According to Ngugi, the single most important virtue in traditional African society was common ownership of land which was worked by all, for the common good. When the white colonialist appropriated the land, conflict and general suffering ensued. Ngugi's treatment of these issues suggests that Kenya's pre-colonial history was devoid of any turmoil and conflict until the advent of colonialism. Thus, one might deduce that, for Ngugi, the history of conflict in Africa is the history of colonialism and how it affected the African populace. Ngugi is therefore at pains to document colonial injustices in most of his works. Those that deal with the post-colonial experience, the colonial context always serves as a major backdrop against which the post-colonial experiences (read neo-colonial) are examined.

The colonial state, for Ngugi, is always allegorical of the post-colonial state. The most outstanding image in his recreation of the colonial and post-colonial experience is land. Land, for Ngugi, is an important metaphor for explicating Kenya's past and present history. Land is depicted as a metaphor for life; it is a source of livelihood. Land is both a metaphor for struggle and the physical space for political contestation in virtually all Ngugi's works. A metaphor for flux, land is the agent for social change and economic mobility — the agent for social transformation within society. Indeed, the themes of resistance to, and collaboration with, colonial institutions are all linked to this metaphor. Thus, the nature of the colonial and the neo-colonial experience in Kenya can only be understood through the contradictory and multiple functions and conflicts that land generates for Ngugi. The solution to social conflict is, by implication, only possible when land is shared and worked by all.

Ngugi's interest in land clearly points to his concern with the plight of the peasants. His involvement with the plight of the peasantry as a dispossessed lot seems to echo Fanon's (1967, 85-118) understanding of the peasantry as both the most exploited group and those with the potential to provide revolutionary change in the post-colonial state. It is significant that Ilmorog, which is both a symbol of land in its most ideal state — land as a communal property — and a home of the peasantry, is one of the major settings of the two novels, *Petals* and *Devil.* And with the advent of colonialism and capital investment in Ilmorog, we witness economic deprivation of peasants and workers. They are forced to live off the slave wages of African landowners and businessmen in partnership with multinational companies that have recently taken over Ilmorog. The deprivation of the peasants of Ilmorog contrasts sharply with the wealth of colonial settlers and African farmers. Independence does not usher in any comfort or economic gains for peasants and workers; it is the same group of loyalists, otherwise called "homeguards" by Ngugi, that emerge as the beneficiaries of Uhuru. Ilmorog is, therefore, a physical manifestation of the contradictory presence of poverty and capital in Kenya. Thus the ills of the colonial state are simply reproduced in the post-colonial state.

The "mutilation" of land by both the colonial and the post-colonial oppressor is done with the aid of religious, cultural, and educational institutions which instill and perpetuate the mental slavery of the oppressed and buttress the interest of the oppressor (Ngugi 1972, 31). The Christian religion is used to inflict what Ngugi calls a "psychological wound ... on the whole generation" (1973, xii). Ngugi's maintains that religion is a tool for oppressing workers. In *Petals,* Waweru is portrayed as a man who propagates Christianity because it is rewarding to him and his family. Reverend Waweru is said to have taken refuge in religion at the time of Kenya's struggle for independence, denouncing all such anti-colonial activities as Mau Mau oathing rituals as the devil's work.

In addition, Ngugi sees cultural and educational institutions as tools for mental slavery; they are used to perpetuate mental captivity in the post-colonial state. Criticism of the naked imitation of Western values is chiefly represented by the native bourgeoisie in *Devil.* Kihaahu in *Devil* is a typical example of the alienated black who aspires to be white in all respects. He changes his name to a white one. Indeed, Ngugi's (1982, 113) satire on Kenyan bourgeois attitudes is best expressed by Kihaahu's nursery school scheme whose success is associated with everything white.

The love for Western goods reaches a level of absurdity when Gitutu suggests that they should import air (Ngugi 1982, 107). Thus, for the African elite, goods only acquire their true value if and when they are imported. In a way, the writer is providing a salient critique of the post-colonial economy in which the raw materials are exported from the colonies, manufactured in the West, and brought back as finished products. Ngugi's assessment of the national bourgeoisie is much worse than Fanon's of them as entrepreneurial, because they are mere consumers helping to entrench trade imbalance between the poor and the rich Western countries, while perpetuating the poverty of their own people. In *Petals,* Ngugi depicts the displacement of Abdullah and Wanja of Thengeta breweries as a conspiracy between rich African financiers and their foreign allies. Ngugi seems to point to a conspiracy between the African leadership in the post-colonial state and international capital as the major cause of this cultural and economic impoverishment. They are a decadent class that perpetuates contempt for African values.

To recapitulate, Ngugi seems to be suggesting that the churches, the African leadership, the local media, and foreign capital are in an undeclared pact to exploit Kenya's resources, thereby depriving the black masses of what is left of colonialism. Ngugi seems to be echoing Fanon's critique of the national bourgeoisie as shallow and uncreative, a class which works at naked imitation of its European counterpart without helping the African masses because it cannot simply sever its links with the Western bourgeoisie, which it serves. In *Devil,* Ngugi is apparently dramatizing the fate of this class through his use of the fantastic and the unbelievable by putting on show characters who boast about their cleverness and their cunning in how they steal from the people and serve their foreign masters.

But as a response to this deplorable state of affairs in the post-colonial state in Kenya, Ngugi suggests that workers do resist the post-colonial leadership's naked robbery. He does not just create the possibility of revolt and a revolution, but demonstrates that Kenya's history has never been a one-sided story of the victorious oppressor and has instead been characterized by the heroic resistance of ordinary people. As Karega, the main protagonist in *Petals,* says:

> The true lesson of history was this: that the so-called victims, the poor, the downtrodden, the masses, had always struggled with their spears and arrows, with their hands and songs of courage and hope, to end their oppression and exploitation (Ngugi 1977, 303).

Ngugi reinforces the possibilities of revolt in creating characters who are positively disposed to revolutionary transformation within the society.

But Ngugi's position regarding the revolutionary force in Kenya remains blurred. It is not consistent as he seems to shift his opinion in all the three novels from the peasants' political consciousness to the proletariat as the custodians of the political future. At times, Ngugi seems to be espousing Fanon's theory on the role of the peasants as a decisive force in Ilmorog, exemplified by the march of the Ilmorog peasants to the city in *Petals.* And yet, he shifts to the alternative of the trade union as a vehicle for change. Karega, the brewery worker and trade union leader, embodies Ngugi's shift. After having organized with the peasants the march to Nairobi, he moves to the building of a union and the organization of strikes in the industrial world, for better wages and working conditions.

Ngugi seems to anticipate a socialist revolution through organized labour. In his description of the desperate conditions of the workers, Ngugi moves from Fanon's (1967, 86) theory of the urban proletariat as a pampered lot. He does not, however, create a distinction between the urban working class and the poorer peasantry. In *Petals,* neither the poor peasantry nor the factory workers own the means of production, and those who own some form of business, like Wanja and Abdulla, are displaced by big capital.

Ngugi's message would seem to be a revolutionary movement consisting of committed intellectuals such as Karega and the people, whether they are peasants or workers in factories. It is this same vision that we find in *Devil,* where Muturi rallies the Ilmorog workers to invade the Devil's feast. Muturi also tries to create awareness by organizing the workers for higher pay in Boss Kihara's company. The role of trade unionism as a tool to build a socialist state appeals to Ngugi. This would seem to be Ngugi's primary discourse on resistance in *Petals* and *Devil,* as reflected in his portrayal of Karega and Muturi.

And yet, even in *Petals* and *Devil,* the possibility of violent resistance is an undeveloped sub-text. We have the constant reference to Mau Mau as the ultimate symbol of national liberation in Kenya. Resistance through armed struggle is pushed further through a symbolic gesture in the action of Wariinga in killing Gitahi, "to save many other people, whose lives will not be ruined by words of honey and perfume" (Ngugi 1982, 253).

But the theme of violence in Kenya's history is best dramatized in *Matigari.* According to the hero, Matigari, the oppressor cannot be rooted out without violence (Ngugi 1987, 131). Indeed, Ngugi seems to be suggesting that armed struggle ought to supplement trade union resistance. What Ngaruro wa Kiriro, the worker leader in *Matigari,* is doing in organizing workers only finds its concrete expression in the violent attempt by Matigari to win back his house and land that had been taken by Settler Williams and later passed on to John Boy and family.

Ngugi is implying that the history of the post-colonial state in Kenya is one in which peasants and workers grow poorer, where women are exploited, and where the national cultures of the people are trampled upon by a powerless bourgeoisie — alienated to the extent of thinking in terms of, and serving blindly, European values. The answer to all these problems is the concerted struggle of peasant workers through mass mobilization, trade union movements, and violent resistance aimed at defeating, as Ngugi himself puts it, "imperialism and creat[ing] a higher system of democracy and socialism in alliance with all the other peoples of the world" (1986, 29-30).

What, then, is the nature of the politics behind Ngugi's interpretation of Kenyan history? How do we account for Ngugi's radical shift in his representation of Kenyan history in his post-colonial novels?[8] We can begin to account for Ngugi's ideological shift in terms of his biographical development. His exposure to the works of Marx and Fanon and the influence of a cohort group of African scholars while he was at Leeds University has been well documented.[9] Reading Fanon, in particular, must have transformed Ngugi's views on a number of issues, ranging from violence for liberation to the nature of neo-colonialism. Fanon's criticism of the national bourgeoisie and his prediction of their neo-colonial mentality find echoes in the post-colonial novels of Ngugi, as does Fanon's embracing of violence as a cardinal imperative in the decolonization process. Fanon's notion of the "native poet" as the custodian of national culture and educator is frequently echoed in Ngugi's (1972, 1981) essays.

But Ngugi was also influenced by the changes that were taking place in the Kenyan body politic since independence. The political scenario after independence was fraught with fears and frustrations, as well as disillusionment with Uhuru. As early as 1966, Ngugi's bitterness was beginning to show. In a note to *A Grain of Wheat*, he observes:

> But the situation and the problems are real — sometimes too painfully real for peasants who fought the British yet who now see all that they fought for being put to one side.

That Ngugi was increasingly frustrated by the new African government that could not deliver became abundantly clear

(Ngugi 1981). Like many of his contemporaries, Ngugi was beginning to suspect that for the national bourgeoisie (used loosely here to mean the African ruling class), independence did not entail fulfilling the fundamental promises the nationalist elite had made at the height of nationalism. As the historian Fredrick Cooper observes,

> African novelists were the first intellectuals to bring before a wide public inside and outside the African continent profound questions about the corruption within postcolonial governments and the extent to which external domination persisted. Growing disillusionment made increasingly attractive the theories of "underdevelopment," which located the poverty and weaknesses of "peripheral" societies not in the colonial situation but in the more long-term process of domination within a capitalist world system (1994, 1524).

Besides, the 1970s were marked by major debates on the nature of Kenya's political economy, and these were primarily within the related theoretical frameworks of dependency and underdevelopment. These debates sought to explain Kenya's political and economic predicament by linking colonial transformations and the post-colonial development strategies.

Two major studies set the tone for the debate. E.A. Brett's *Colonialism and Underdevelopment in East Africa* (1973) and Colin Leys's *Underdevelopment in Kenya* (1974) spelt out the broad outlines of the underdevelopment and dependency perspectives, as well as their empirical manifestations in the context of Kenya's development processes. Focusing on the effects of colonial rule on economic change in Kenya, Brett (1974, 302-09) noted how colonialism catalysed Kenya's absorption into the world capitalist system, while fostering economic measures that resulted in an imbalanced development.

Leys characterized Kenya's emergent economy as a neo-colonial one with numerous structural constraints. He argued that Kenya's blend of neo-colonialism was rooted in the transition from colonialism to independence, a transition which resulted in the transfer of political power to a regime based on the support of social classes closely linked to foreign capital. On the question of the evolution of an indigenous social class capable of spearheading national development, Leys noted that a middle class of educated Africans and new property owners became the core of the nationalist movement during the later phase of the colonial period. Yet this emerging class was unable to lead the socioeconomic transformation after independence because of its subordination to settler and international interests (Leys 1974).

The influence of Brett's and Leys's analyses of Kenya's political economy is evident in Ngugi's texts. For one, they reinforced Fanon's thesis on "the pitfalls of national consciousness," whose reading Ngugi (1986, 63) argued, was central to the understanding of African literature. Besides, Fanon's *The Wretched of the Earth*, Lenin's *Imperialism, The Highest Stage of Capitalism*, and Walter Rodney's *How Europe Underdeveloped Africa* were compulsory readings in the Literature Department at Nairobi University on the recommendation of Ngugi.[10] All these books point to underdevelopment and dependency perspectives which Ngugi has passionately embraced since his days in Leeds. These perspectives continue to inform his texts, whether in Gikuyu or English.[11]

Finally, I need to add that the continued existence of poverty and inequalities in post-colonial Kenyan society forced Ngugi to look back into history for a radical tradition, particularly after the banning of the Kenya Peoples Union (KPU), the only popular voice of the marginalized group in Kenya at the time (Furedi 1989, 211-13). Fired by his admiration for Fanon's theory of "revolutionary violence," Mau Mau was a sure source of instant inspiration for Ngugi; it became the central link in the tradition of struggle among the subaltern that seems to be at the heart of Ngugi's sense of history and all his narratives.

Supression and Silences in Ngugi's Sense of History

The thrust of Ngugi's narrative concerns over the last two decades has been the struggle for *Matunda ya Uhuru* — the "Fruits of Freedom." It has been a project directed at that decolonization process which embodied the varied processes of political independence, national liberation, and people's revolution and one which focused on the making of democracy — the struggle for social change in the post-colonial state — and therefore a useful intervention in the post-colonial discourses in Kenya. And yet, Ngugi's understanding of the historical processes in Kenya is too deeply imbedded in dependency theory to allow for a nuanced understanding of the complex colonial and post-colonial experience in Kenya. Ngugi's articulation of Kenyan history from a dependency theory perspective cannot allow him to deal with specific contradictions and local divisions within Kenya, and Ngugi is therefore forced to suppress certain histories.

What are these ellipses in Ngugi's narrative? One of the major gaps has to do with Ngugi's linear representation of the Mau Mau as a monolithic nationalist movement devoid of any contradictions. If the colonialists gave an extremely one-sided and perhaps an entirely biased historical version of the Mau Mau war, it would seem to me that Ngugi, in his anxiety to counter this, has tended to provide a wholly romantic picture of the Mau Mau war. In Ngugi's post-colonial novels, Mau Mau is appropriated to legitimize the anti-imperialist struggle in post-colonial Kenyan political economy. In the process, Ngugi gives Mau Mau "new" ideological attributes: it was class-based in both its aims and goals to eradicate capitalism and establish a socialist Kenya; it united all Kenyan peasants and workers; it was not just a regional revolt, but a nationalist revolution with a clear vision for the post-colonial state.

In his invention of the Mau Mau, Ngugi presupposes the existence of a collective consciousness amongst the peasantry and the working class in Kenya, the kind of consciousness that engendered their struggle against colonialism (Ngugi and Mugo 1976, Preface). Thus, for Ngugi, all Kenyan peasants and workers had the same nationalist goals in their resistance to colonial rule, and the same interests continue to inspire their resistance in the post-colonial state. What we have is a situation in which the intellectual writer subsumes what may be local or regional interests of the peasants into national or class issues.

For Ngugi, the Mau Mau war was not just a localized anti-colonial resistance waged by a section of the Gikuyu, but a national phenomenon and a point at which the schismatic segments of Kenyan history are summoned and ordered to a coherent centre. Thus, the ethnic interests and dimensions are suppressed, and the Mau Mau fighters are given a class vision. Ngugi is therefore silent on the diverse and often conflicting layers of consciousness that might have informed the historic Mau Mau. For example, the Mau Mau songs testify to their simultaneous commitment to the house of Mumbi, to the Gods of Mount Kerenyaga, to liberating the land, and to a future Kenya ruled by Kenyatta (Maina wa Kinyatti 1980; Wanjiku Kabira and Karega wa Mutahi 1988). The songs point to layers of consciousness and complex layers of knowledge about the Mau Mau that cannot be conflated into a monolithic narrative of the Mau Mau as Ngugi attempts to do in most of his works.

The view here is that the production of Mau Mau history has always fallen within the terrain of power contestation (Odhiambo 1991, 300-07; Cohen 1986, 48), and as long as the contestants continue to appropriate Mau Mau to either subvert or legitimize the politics of the day, the image of Mau Mau can never be as absolute as Ngugi attempts to present in his narrative. Over the years, the Mau Mau war has survived as an ambivalent phenomenon in colonial and post-colonial Kenyan politics. It is a symbol to be appropriated, and at times negated, for political gains.

In this game of political manipulation, the Mau Mau war veterans have tended to serve sectarian, conservative, and ethnic interests. Kenyatta suppressed the role of Mau Mau fighters on the eve of independence and declared that all Kenyans fought for UHURU. In 1966, when Oginga Odinga broke ranks with Kenyatta and formed an opposition party, Kenyatta deemed it fit to rally Mau Mau veterans, as the custodians of the Gikuyu interest, against the perceived threat from Odinga's Luo dominated Kenya Peoples Union (Furedi 1989, 208). When Bildad Kaggia, a former Mau Mau detainee, joined KPU to help Odinga to articulate the interests of the Mau Mau guerrillas, especially on the question of land, he received no support from former guerrillas. Ethnic interest took precedence (Maloba 1993, 175). As recently as 1992, the current President of Kenya, Daniel Toroitich Arap Moi, rallied an estimated three thousand former Mau Mau fighters against the main opposition parties fighting for the restoration of democracy. Ironically, in this shrewd and opportunistic political ploy, Moi, who was the lackey of the colonial regime, reaped the spoils of Mau Mau heroism in order to subvert democracy. In the typical language of Ngugi and wa Kinyatti, the former guerrillas dismissed certain members of the opposition as "collaborators" and "sons of homeguards" (*The Weekly Review* [Nairobi] 24 July 1992: 18).

Another major gap in Ngugi's narrative is his attempt to link the conditions of the colonial state with those of the post-colonial state. Ngugi assumes a linear tradition and continuity in the anti-imperialist struggle. He contends that the fight against colonialism and capitalism in the post-independent Kenya is a continuation of Kenyan people's struggle which stretches back to the primary resistance against colonialism. We are given a glorified picture of heroic resistance by Kenyan peasants to foreign invasion. Indeed, this linear approach to historical interpretation also overlooks the possibility that there may be no link between the militant nationalist struggles of 1950s and the anti-imperialist forces in the post-independence Kenya. And yet, Ngugi seems to suggest that the same continuity persists in the camp of collaborators who seem to reproduce themselves in a geometrical manner right from the colonial period into the post-colonial Kenya.

It seems to me that Ngugi does not succeed in capturing the ambivalent relationship between the colonial state and the loyalists. In Ngugi's texts, there seems to be no tension between the loyalists, on the one hand, and the colonial state, on the other. He depicts the relationship as one of mutual trust and dependence. A good example of this relationship is Ngugi's portrayal of Waweru and Nditika in *Petals* and his treatment of John Boy in *Matigari*. All the characters seem to have a linear and unproblematic relationship with the colonial regime, their loyalty to the colonial state absolute. This relationship of absolute dependence is best dramatized in Wariinga's nightmare in which the colonizing devil is crucified upon the cross, and he ends up being rescued by the local comprador — symbolically signalling the emergence of neocolonialism (Ngugi 1982, 13-14).

The story of resistance and collaboration, as portrayed by Ngugi, has a certain unity of view which lacks precision when one is searching for a complex interpretation of history. First, this approach tends to oversimplify the real nature of the colonial and imperialist context within which the initiatives of resistance and collaboration by Africans were undertaken. The impression Ngugi creates is that the choice between collaboration was always a simple one in which the loyalists were always motivated by sheer economic greed, while the resisters were motivated by their love for humanity. Second, Ngugi gives the impression that once one was in the loyalists' camp, he/she remained there and ensured that his progeny continued to prosper. There are no grey areas in Ngugi's colonial and post-colonial world. One is either a patriot or a traitor. But as Bruce Berman argues,

> The development and character of the African petit-bourgeoisie in Kenya, and elsewhere in colonial Africa, cannot be understood

> outside its deeply ambivalent relationship with the colonial state. This ambivalence, expressed in sharply contrasting and often alternating patterns of collaboration and conflict, encouragement and constraint, attraction and rejection, was felt both by African and the colonial authorities and was grounded in some of the most fundamental contradictions of colonialism (1992a, 197).

Evidently, the dialectic of collaboration and struggle which characterized the relationship between the emergent African petit-bourgeoisie and the colonial state was a complex one in which grounds were ever shifting, positions were never permanent, and relationships were never free of conflict and contradictions. For example, Marshall Clough (1990) has demonstrated that the position of the African chiefs, particulary in the Kiambu district of Kenya, kept on shifting, depending on whether or not their interests and those of their subjects were threatened. Paradoxically, Kiambu, which was regarded by the colonial officials as a soft and loyal district, was also home to such key political leaders as Harry Thuku, Koinange wa Mbiyu, and Jomo Kenyatta. It is also the district that lost most land to settlers in spite of their protests (Clough 1990, 65-67).

William Ochien'g has also questioned the popular assumption that all loyalists were motivated by personal economic greed. He writes that the so-called Mau Mau loyalists were neither stooges nor self-seekers, but an integral part of Africans' struggle for progress and dignity in the face of acute political and economic difficulties (Ochien'g 1972, 46-70). Ochien'g's position is also supported by M. Tamarkin, who sees the Mau Mau loyalists "as having entered in the political struggle to defend legitimate group interests, to promote their political ideals and even to fight for what they regarded as the interests of their fellow Africans" (1978, 247-61).[12] The relationship between the loyalists and the colonial state was never a linear one.

Ngugi's portrayal of workers and the emergent African petit-bourgeoisie robs them of initiative in the context of decolonization. The workers and peasants are doomed to a vicious circle of poverty which renders all their struggles irrelevant because there are no gains — no democratic scores in the post-colonial state after many years of anti-colonial struggle. They cannot manipulate spaces that are open for them, and when they do, like Wanja in *Petals*, all efforts are brought to naught by big capital. The native bourgeoisie, on the other hand, are mere "watchdogs" of foreign capital. They are not innovative, but reckless, apists of Western values — their masters that they serve dutifully. The Kenyan petit-bourgeoisie are portrayed as if they have no desire to be their own masters, but want simply to limp after the image of the Western bourgeoisie.

The picture of the national bourgeoisie as mere puppets or watchdogs of the white imperialists who are totally powerless without their masters is hard to sustain since it tends to oversimplify a rather complex class dynamic in Africa. The problem is inherent in dependency theory in that it tends to divert attention from the national struggles within Africa by "underplaying the growth of real local divisions" (Brenda Cooper 1992, 38) and by implying that the local bourgeoisie may not be as dangerous as the international capital that it serves. Dependency theory seeks to explain the problems of Africa and indeed those of the "Third World" as ones of global imperialism, "depicted as part of a self-reproducing global system in which the perverse underdevelopment of the periphery was the necessary mirror of genuine capitalist development at the centre" (Berman and Lonsdale 1992a, 197).

Ngugi is a prisoner of the broad perspective of dependency. In most of his works, he creates a simplistic binary opposition between the oppressor and the oppressed, which precludes any possibility of conflicting interests within these broad social categories. Apart from conflating workers and peasants into one group without any social content or specific defining features, Ngugi's construction of "the people" in these broad categories of the leaders and the led, the oppressor and the oppressed, constitutes the people as lacking initiative — a passive group who are acted upon.[13] And although Ngugi attempts to create a picture of a heroic collective of workers and peasants, they come through as faceless. The so-called power of the working people is not visible beyond the slogans of the workers' undefined strikes and mass demonstrations (Ngugi 1977, 4). The workers do not seem to have any visible conflicts of interest other than the politics of ethnic divisiveness Ngugi which presents as primarily a construction of the elite. Wanja seems to be speaking for Ngugi when she insinuates that it is the rich — "the Mercedes family" — who are preoccupied with ethnic divisions to delude the workers into believing that there is no divide between the rich and the poor within one ethnic community.

> For to us what did it matter who drove a Mercedes Benz? They were all one tribe; the Mercedes family: whether they came from the coast or from Kisumu. One family. We were another tribe: another family (1977, 98).

Ngugi tends to dismiss ethnicity as an invention of colonialism and the ruling elite in Kenya. Moi and his cohort group are therefore responsible for generating ethnic consciousness and manipulate, to their advantage, what was invented by the colonialists.

Ngugi's thesis that modern ethnicity is a product of the colonial history of divide and rule, which helped to give the "tribe" its real identity by "specifying `tribes' culturally within the context of a uniquely colonial sociology," to use Vail's words, may have some strength (Vail 1989, 3).[14] His pet argument — that ethnicity is an ideological mask employed by ambitious and crafty members of the petty-bourgeoisie to secure their own interests against the ever growing class divisions within their own ethnic groups — may also contain certain elements of truth. However, Ngugi's twin stance, while having some validity, does not answer the question of why ethnic consciousness and its close relative, regionalism, remain attractive to ordinary Kenyans well beyond the colonial period. Why was it possible to revitalize ethnicity well beyond the colonial period and, in as recent a event as the 1992 multiparty elections in Kenya, to mobilize popular opinion around ethnicity?[15]

The position taken in this article is that "ethnicity is not a natural cultural residue but a consciously crafted ideological creation" (Vail 1989, 7). The construction of ethnicity, however, is not always from above, but quite often, it is also given impetus by the practical needs of those from below and the actual persistence of "ethnic moments of identity" (Piper *et al.* 1992, 13). The theory that the African masses are gullible pawns — easily manipulated by colonialists and the crafty African elite into ethnic consciousness — is ripe for debunking. Ethnicity, when seen as a mechanism for political and economic control, ceases to be the often abhorred return to primordial values, or a monopoly of the ruling elite in which they manipulate the ignorant masses in the struggle for power in the modern state.

Ethnicity, on the contrary, should be seen as an important

instrument of control steeped in ethnic ideologies and in group interests that are constantly changing. In the words of Berman and Lonsdale, ethnicity is "a vehicle of unquestioning sectional ambition" (1992b, 317). In this struggle to realize sectarian ambitions, ordinary people have found ethnicity useful in protecting internal rights and a defense against threats whether real or perceived. Of course, in the invention of ethnicity and its appropriation into competitive politics, the elite have emerged as the most eloquent articulators of the cultural characteristics of their ethnic identities through written histories, accounts of traditional ways of the tribe, and written ethnic literatures.

In this sense, it might be argued that even Ngugi has, in modern Kenya, contributed to the reinvention of Gikuyu ethnic consciousness by resorting to the use of Gikuyu in his recent creative works and essays.[16] But ultimately, it is competitive politics and the fear of economic exclusion that has made ethnicity, with its appeal to common heritage of the group and its land, so attractive in modern times. As Gerhard Mare has observed, material (and ultimately political) factors provide the impetus for ethnic moments of identity to be transformed into politicized ethnicity: "Political ethnicity (ethnic nationalism) moves social identity to political agency, provides the means for political mobilisation, and submits the ethnic identity and group to another set of rules — those of competition for power" (1992, 43).

Evidently, if Mare's argument carries some weight, then ethnicity cannot be dismissed as an invention of colonialism and the intellectual elite in Africa, as scholars like Ngugi are wont to do. Neither is it useful to dismiss ethnicity as false consciousness. It is, in my view, an effective instrument in the political power game in which the ordinary people are as much active agents as the ruling elite are in Africa. There is "nothing wicked," to use Lonsdale's phrase, in ethnicity's "modern persistence" (Berman and Lonsdale 1992b, 329). Instead, in a society such as Kenya, which is still groping for a sense of nationhood, and, indeed, striving to build a modern state, one should expect a coexistence of multiple identities, often in a continous and dynamic tension. The Mau Mau songs, for example, were used by ordinary men and women to constitute their identity both as belonging to the house of Mumbi (meaning the Gikuyu community), but also as desiring the broader Kenyan nation in the face of colonial oppression. Here was a classic case of two layers of identity coexisting within the consciousness of a specific ethnic community in Kenya. The construction of a specifically Gikuyu identity did not preclude the imagination of a wider Kenyan identity.

Lastly, Ngugi's narrative seems to be silent on the role of dissenting voices within the church. His presentation of religion is one-dimensional. For Ngugi, religion is a tool of oppression — a vehicle for lulling the poor and turning them away from the material reality of this world. No one doubts that religion in Kenya has, in certain instances, served to entrench and justify exploitation in both colonial and post-colonial contexts. But it is doubtful, as past and recent histories of religious groups have proved in Kenya, that they are mute tools of exploitation.[17] At the height of intertribal (ethnic) tension in 1969, when a section of the Gikuyu took to oathing, which Ngugi refers to as the "tea party" (Ngugi 1977, 84), it was the National Christian Council of Kenya (NCCK)[18] that condemned its ethnic parochialism. In the run-up to multi-party elections in 1992, the church, under the NCCK umbrella, played a crucial role in calling on the government to democratize the levers of governance and appealed to the opposition to forge unity in the interest of the nation. A leading Kenyan weekly wrote:

> After leading the way for the opposition, the NCCK was now shepherding the opposition itself. Indeed the NCCK and some of the opposition figures have fought parallel battles against the government in the past six years. Some of the clerics ... have, over the years tended to be more critical of the government than many of the radical politicians (*The Weekly Review* [Nairobi] 19 June 1992: 4).

Ngugi's classical understanding of religion cannot allow him to appreciate the role played by the church in contemporary politics; but more importantly, he fails to accept the church as an enduring form of popular organization in which the "the people" take the initiative in interpreting and integrating their world to gain some control over it. A complex reading of religion should see it as a vehicle for cognition — as the space for relating the self to the material and the spiritual being.

Conclusion

It seems fair to argue that the weaknesses inherent in Ngugi's sense of history are, in fact, attributable in a large measure to the weaknesses of dependency perspective which are manifested in the suppression of specific and local contradictions and the privileging of the centre-periphery approach.[19] Thus, a single-track theory which seeks to explain Kenya's underdevelopment only in terms of the centre as a block exploiting the periphery fails to grasp the specific character of capitalist development in Kenya and, subsequently, to lay down proper political strategies for meaningful change. The point to reiterate is that Ngugi's ideological framework, underpinned by Fanon's prediction and dependency perspective, tends to obscure the way in which classes reproduce themselves and derive any relative autonomy of politics within these class formations. It therefore obscures the particularities of different social formations. Ngugi is clearly imprisoned within a static evaluation of classes, and his framework tends to be rigidly deterministic in locating connections of state and capital, depicting the national bourgeoisie as mere puppets or watchdogs of Western capital, and insisting that there is continuity between the resistance to the colonial state and resistance to the post-colonial state. Indeed, Ngugi's framework is deterministic in its espousal of a linear reproduction of the colonial class formations in the post-colonial state.

The path to meaningful social change in Africa cannot ignore the internal contradictions and the specific social dynamics of the post-colonial state. And yet the fundamental pre-condition for democratic transformation is the unrelenting struggle to create space for political dialogue and change. In this act of social transformation, Ngugi has played his part precisely because his narrative discourse, whatever its limitations, "is dominated by its transformative 'text' in which the captive nation, overcome in recent history, awaits its desired redemption" (Gurnah 1993, 142).

Notes

[1] Ngugi argues that the colonialist writers (Ruark 1955, 1962; Huxley 1961) have tended to give a very biased account of Kenya's nationalist history, particularly in their portrayal of the Mau Mau war. The suppression of Mau Mau history and the marginalization of workers and peasants, Ngugi asserts, has also been a major feature of works written by Kenyan historians like Ogot (1972, 1977), Ochien'g (1972), and Muriuki (1974). Maughan-Brown (1985, 206-29) and Maina wa Kinyatti (1977,

1987) seem to agree with Ngugi that many Kenyan scholars followed a definite line of interpretation aimed at discrediting Mau Mau as a nationalist movement.

[2] The subaltern is used here in a double sense. First, it means the dominated and the marginalized groups such as peasants, workers, and women in the post-colonial state. Second, it is also used as an analytical category to embrace the colonized subjects, defined solely by their commmon surbodination to the colonizer. In its conception of colonialism, subalternity assumes colonialism's ability to coerce, co-opt, and categorize challenges into its own structure of power and ideology. Although not Ngugi's terminology, I use it because it best describes the dyad of resistor/oppressor which is central to Ngugi's discourses in Kenya, as well as his tendency to evoke a simple binary opposition between the oppressed and the oppressor, and to isolate it from its context.

[3] It is important to point out that Ngugi sees his fictional works as part of Kenya's historiography. And although this article was teased out of a broader project dealing with the impact of Ngugi's concept of history on his narrative strategies and characterization, the study of Ngugi's concept of history is quite justified in its own right, given Ngugi's critical position within the competing versions of Kenya's history.

[4] The debate on Kenya's underdevelopment has been raging since the 1970s. Brett (1973) and Leys (1974) underscore the manifestations of basic features of underdevelopment and dependency perspectives in Kenya's development processes. Kitching (1977, 1980) and Langdon (1975, 1977, 1981) have reasserted some of the basic tenets of the dependency and underdevelopment frameworks in Kenya, which seek to argue that Kenya is an integral part of international capital, where the development of an indigenous bourgeoisie was impossible. Ngugi seems to share this dependency perspective and Fanon's critique of the African national middle class as both decadent and parasitic (Fanon 1967, 119-65).

[5] Recently, Arthur Marwick (1995) has forcefully challenged White's position. Although Marwick argues correctly that history is not a branch of literature, his casual dismissal of narrative elements in history is hardly convincing. It seems to me that Marwick's otherwise brilliant article is nothing but a return to the empiricist conception of the past — history as "the study of human past, through the systematic analysis of the primary sources, and the bodies of knowledge arising from that study" (1995, 12). This article takes the view of the past as a discursive construct which does not preclude Marwick's principal methods of retrieving the past, but throws open the past as an arena for competing versions of historical recovery. In this sense, the place accorded literary texts in relation to

other components of the historical record within, on the one hand, the procedures of literary scholarship and, on the other, those of historical inquiry need not be seen as privileging one discipline over the other, but as part of the total project of historical recovery.

[6] In an earlier version of this article, Carol Sicherman puts it even more poignantly that: "In Ngugi's hand, the pen has written not only story but history, sometimes with deliberate intermixture of the two" (1-2). The quote is from an earlier version of the article under the same title: "Ngugi wa Thiong'o and the Writing of Kenyan History," presented at Nairobi University, 1988. A shorter version of the article was later published in *Research in African Literatures* 20, no. 3 (1989): 347-70.

[7] I have in mind the following works of Ngugi: *Homecoming* (1972), *Writers in Politics* (1981), *Barrel of a Pen* (1983), *Decolonising the Mind* (1986), and *Moving the Centre* (1993).

[8] The radical shift is best captured more poignantly in his portrayal of the Mau Mau war. In the early novels before *A Grain of Wheat*, Ngugi gives a more complex picture of the moral dilemma that faced both the loyalists and the fighters during the violent period of the 1950s, while in his post-colonial novels, one gets a fairly linear history of the movement in which we have neat camps of the abhored collaborators, on the one hand, and the patriotic fighters, on the other.

[9] For Ngugi's biographical details, see, Gikandi 1989, 148-56; Cook and Okenimpke 1983, 205-08.

[10] Ngugi (1986, 63) himself acknowledges the centrality of these books in the understanding of African literature.

[11] Although, in my view, the dependency perspective remains a fundamental influence on Ngugi's texts, it is also possible to account, in part, for Ngugi's tendency towards a linear history in terms of his use of allegory in the more recent texts. It is not difficult to see why Ngugi resorts to allegory in his post-colonial narratives in Kenya. As a writer of praxis, whose freedom of expression has constantly been suppressed by the successive regimes in Kenya, he is always dogged by conditions of fragmentation. Indeed, his most obvious example of allegorical narrative, *Devil on the Cross*, was written in dentention. According to Walter Benjamin (1977), in periods of fragmentation and displacement, allegory is often the mode best suited for piecing together history out of the ruins of the past. This is because allegory's tendency towards a lineary typology provides the writer, in a situation of fragmentation and marginality, with a coherent framework within which to rewrite history.

[12] B.A. Ogot (1972, 134-48) has also dealt with the moral complexity of the

Mau Mau.

[13] For Ngugi's elaboration of this binary opposition, see his seminal work (1972, 22-25); for the more comprehensive treatment, see Ngugi (1981, 123-38).

[14] Terence Ranger's study of the invention of a Manyika identity in Zimbabwe demonstrates a major role by "three different missionary churches, each appealing most to different areas and to different classes or proto-classes" (1989, 145). Ranger also shows how both the Rhodesian regime, during the war, and the petty-bourgeois African nationalists exploited the notion of traditional ethnic divisions among the Manyika (1989, 118-49).

[15] Whatever the merits and demerits of the 1992 general elections in Kenya, the results showed a clear pattern of voting on ethnic lines (*The Weekly Review* [Nairobi] 1 January 1993).

[16] The importance of language in defining ethnicity has received attention recently (Hofmeyr 1987, 95-123; Fabian 1983, 165-87).

[17] The independent church movements, which became the pillars for independent school movements, attempted to offer alternative education to missionary education and, therefore, became major vehicles for political mobilization among the Gikuyus in the period from 1920 to 1960. Incidentally, Ngugi has tended to suppress the role of independent church movements in Kenya's political struggle, even in his works that are set in the colonial period. For information on the independent school movement, see Anderson (1970) and Ranger (1965).

[18] The NCCK, the National Christian Council of Kenya, is an umbrella body which represents the mainstream Protestant churches in Kenya, such as the Anglican among others.

[19] Writers like Leys (1978, 1982), Cowen (1979, 1982), and Swainson (1980) have cast a great deal of doubt on dependency theories that sought to explain Kenya's underdevelopment purely in terms of a weak periphery solely dependent on a dominant centre. Thus, the theory that the national bourgeoisie is almost non-existent and that even the small comprador bourgeoisie that there is only works for, and in tandem with, international capital can no longer hold sway in the face of increasing evidence of a long history of an indigenous bourgeoisie that enjoys the support of the state.

Bibliography

Anderson, J. 1970. *The Struggle for the School*. London: Longmans.

Berman, Bruce J. and John Lonsdale. 1992a. *Unhappy Valley (Book One: State and Class).* London: James Currey.

——. 1992b. *Unhappy Valley (Book Two: Violence and Ethnicity).* London: James Currey.

Benjamin, Walter. 1977. *The Origin of German Tragic Drama.* London: New Left Books.

Bennet, Tony. 1990. *Outside Literature.* London: Routledge.

Brett, E.A. 1973. *Colonialism and Underdevelopment in East Africa.* New York: NOK Publishers.

Clough, Marshall S. 1990. *Fighting Two Sides: Kenyan Chiefs and Politicians, 1918-1940.* Niwot: University Press of Colorado.

Cohen, David. 1986. "Position Paper." *Fifth International Roundtable in Anthropology and History.* Paris: Maison des Sciences de l'Homme, July.

Cook, David and Michael Okenimpke. 1983. *Ngugi wa Thiong'o: An Exploration of His Writings.* London: Heinemann.

Cooper, Brenda. 1992. *To Lay These Secrets Open: Evaluating African Writing.* Cape Town: David Phillip.

Cooper, Fredrick. 1994. "Conflict and Connection: Rethinking Colonial African History." *The American Historical Review* 99, no.5: 1516-45.

Cowen, M.P. 1979. "Capital and Household Production: The Case of Wattle in Kenya's Central Province, 1903-1964." PhD thesis, Cambridge University.

——. 1982. "The British State and Agrarian Accumulation in Kenya." In *Industry and Accumulation in Africa,* edited by Martin Fransmann. London: Heinemann.

Fabian, J. 1983. "Missions and the Colonization of African Languages: Developments in the Former Belgian Congo." *Canadian Journal of African Studies* 17, no. 2: 165-87.

Fanon, Frantz. 1967. *The Wretched of the Earth.* Harmondsworth: Penguin Books Ltd.

Furedi, Frank. 1989. *Mau Mau in Perspective.* London: James Currey.

Gikandi, Simon. 1989. "On Culture and the State: The Writings of Ngugi wa Thiong'o." *Third World Quarterly* 11, no. 1: 148-56.

Gurnah, Abdulrazak. 1993. *Essays on African Writing.* London: Heinemann.

Hofmeyr, Isabel. 1987. "Building a Nation from Words: Afrikaans Language, Literature and Ethnic Identity, 1902-1924." In *The Politics of Race, Class and Nationalism in Twentieth-Century South Africa*, edited by Shula Marks and Stanley Trapido. London: Longman Group.

Huxley, Elspeth. 1961. *A Thing to Love*. London: Chatto and Windus.

Kabira, M. Wanjiku and wa Mutahi, Karega. 1988. *Gikuyu Oral Literature*. Nairobi: Heinemann.

Kinyatti, Maina wa. 1977. "Mau Mau: The Peak of African Political Organization in Colonial Kenya." *Kenya Historical Review* 5, no. 2: 287-391.

——, ed. 1987. *Kenya's Freedom Struggle: The Dedan Kimathi Papers*. London: Zed Press.

——, ed. 1980. *Thunder from the Mountains: Mau Mau Patriotic Songs*. London: Zed Press.

Kitching, Gavin. 1977. "Modes of Production and Kenyan Dependency." *Review of African Political Economy* 8: 56-74.

——. 1980. *Class and Economic Change in Kenya: The Making of an African Petite Bourgeoisie*. New Haven, Connecticut: Yale University Press.

Langdon, Steven. 1975. "Multinational Corporations, Taste, Transfer and Underdevelopment: A Case Study from Kenya." *Review of African Political Economy* 2: 12-35.

——. 1977. "The State and Capitalism in Kenya." *Review of African Political Economy* 8: 90-98.

——. 1981. *Multinational Corporations in the Political Economy of Kenya*. London: Macmillan.

Lenin, V.I. 1968. "Imperialism, the Highest Stage of Capitalism." In *Selected Works*, 169-262. Moscow: Progress Publishers.

Leys, Colin. 1974. *Underdevelopment in Kenya: The Political Economy of Neo-Colonialism 1964-1971*. London: Heinemann.

——. 1978. "Capital Accumulation, Class Formation and Dependency: The Significance of the Kenyan Case." In *Socialist Register*, edited by Ralph Miliband and John Savile. London: Merlin Press.

——. 1982. "Accumulation, Class Formation, and Dependency: Kenya." In *Industry and Accumulation in Africa*, edited by Martin Fransman. London: Heinemann.

Maloba O. Wunyabari. 1993. *Mau Mau and Kenya: An Analysis of a Peasant Revolt.* Bloomington: Indiana University Press.

Mare, Gerhard. 1992. *Brothers Born of Warrior Blood: Politics and Ethnicity in South Africa.* Johannesburg: Ravan Press.

Marwick, Arthur. 1995. "Two Approaches to Historical Study: The Metaphysical (Including 'Postmodernism') and the Historical." In *Journal of Contemporary History* 30: 5-34.

Maughan-Brown, David. 1985. *Land Freedom and Fiction: History and Ideology in Kenya.* London: Zed Press.

Mink, O. Louis. 1978. "Narrative Form as a Cognitive Instrument." In *The Writing of History and Historical Understanding,* edited by Robert H. Canary and Henry Kozicki. Madison: Wisconsin Press.

Muriuki, G. 1974. *A History of the Kikuyu, 1500-1900.* Nairobi: Oxford University Press.

Ngugi wa Thiong'o. 1964. *Weep Not Child.* London: Heinemann.

——. 1965. *The River Between.* London: Heinemann.

——. 1967. *A Grain of Wheat.* London: Heinemann.

——. 1972. *Homecoming.* London: Heinemann.

——. 1973. "Introduction." In *Africa's Cultural Revolution,* edited by Okot P'Bitek, i-xiii. Nairobi: EAPH.

——. 1976. *The Trial of Dedan Kimathi* (with Micere Mugo). London: Heinemann.

——. 1977. *Petals of Blood.* London: Heinemann.

——. 1981. *Writers in Politics.* London: Heinemann.

——. 1982. *Devil on the Cross.* London: Heinemann.

——. 1983. *Barrel of A Pen.* Trenton: African World Press.

——. 1986. *Decolonising the Mind.* Nairobi: Heinemann.

——. 1987. *Matigari.* London: Heinemann.

——. 1993. *Moving the Centre: The Struggle For Cultural Freedoms.* Nairobi: East African Educational Publishers.

Ochien'g, W.R. 1972. "Colonial African Chiefs — Were They Primarily Self-Seeking Scoundrels?" In *Politics and Nationalism in Colonial Kenya,* edited by B.A. Ogot, 46-70. Nairobi: EAPH.

Odhiambo, E.S. Atieno. 1991. "The Production of History in Kenya: The Mau Mau Debate." *Canadian Journal of African Studies* 25, no. 2: 115-23.

Ogot, Bethwell A. 1972. "Revolt of the Elders: An Anatomy of the Loyalist Crowd in the Mau Mau Uprising." In *Politics and Nationalism in Colonial Kenya*, edited by Ogot, 134-48. Nairobi: East African Publishing House.

——. 1977. "Introduction." In *Kenya Historical Review* 5, no.2: 169-72.

Piper, Laurence, Sihle Shange and Volker Wedekind. 1992. "Ethnicity and the Contest over Meaning: Considerations on Ethnicity Based on a Case Study of School-Going Youth in the Greater Pietremaitzburg Area." University of Natal.

Ranger, Terence. 1965. "African Attempts to Control Education in East and Central Africa 1900-1939." In *Past and Present* 32: 56-85.

——. 1989. "Missionaries, Migrants and the Manyika: The Invention of Ethnicity in Zimbabwe." In *The Creation of Tribalism in Southern Africa*, edited by Leroy Vail. London: James Currey.

Rodney, Walter. 1976. *How Europe Underdeveloped Africa*. Dar-es-Salaam: Tanzania Publishing House.

Ruark, R. 1955. *Something of Value*. London: Hamish Hamilton.

——. 1962. *Uhuru*. London: Hamish Hamilton.

Sichermann, Carol M. 1989. "Ngugi wa Thiong'o and the Writing of Kenyan History." In *Research in African Literature* 20, no.3: 347-70.

Swainson, N. 1980. *The Development of Corporate Capitalism in Kenya*. London: Heinemann.

Tamarkin, M. 1978. "The Loyalists in Nakuru During the Mau Mau Revolt and Its Aftermath, 1953-1963." *Asian and African Studies* 12, no.2: 247-61.

Vail, Leroy. 1989. "Introduction: Ethnicity in Southern African History." In *The Creation of Tribalism in Southern Africa*, edited by Leroy Vail. London: James Currey.

White, Hayden. 1987. *The Content of the Form: Narrative Discourse and Historical Representation*. London: The John Hopkins Press.

Part VI
Modes of Remembering

[20]

Savage wars? Codes of violence in Algeria, 1830s–1990s

JAMES MCDOUGALL

ABSTRACT *Political violence in Algeria has often been accounted for only by recourse to caricatures of a society supposedly 'intensely violent' by nature, or else rationalised as the product of a peculiar political culture and national historical experience. Departing from both approaches, this article suggests that different occurrences of both state and non-state violence must be understood as particular, distinct moments in both the recomposition and breakdown of inherently conflictual social relations. While Algerian history (including colonial history) provides many examples of the non-violent negotiation of social and political tensions, the social production and experience of violence have been written into dominant historiographies and public culture in complex ways. These complexities of the successive ways in which different moments of violence have been encoded belie both theories of the inescapable reproduction of cyclical violence as a pattern of political behaviour, and less sophisticated, but enduring, clichés of 'Algerian savagery'.*

On a trip into the Algerian Sahara my friends and I gave a lift in our car to a blind man who had been stranded with his stick, a small bag and a huge terracotta serving-dish at a petrol station in an isolated village. He had been waiting all day in a gusting light sandstorm for a bus to his home town, but every one that had passed was crowded to its seams. Si el-Haj, as we all automatically referred to the older gentleman, rode beside me in the back seat and, perceiving that I was the only European in the party, quizzed me intently for a while in the usual amalgam of Arabic and French about the war in Iraq, my knowledge of Islam, what I thought constituted democracy, etc. He chatted to my friends about life in the area and the forthcoming saints' festivals, led their prayer by the side of the road, and when we dropped him off at his home, insisted that we come in for tea and the local dried dates that taste like thick, dark chocolate. We sat on the floor in a clean, spartan reception room whose only furniture was a long, low table, a huge, chiselled French-style dresser and a recent, wide-screen television. Si el-Haj told a story about a local theft and complained about corruption in local bureaucracy; we stayed a respectable length of time and, after being warmly embraced, thanked and duly offered a fare for the lift, which we duly refused, we left. It was all

James McDougall is in the Department of History, Princeton University, 129 Dickinson Hall, Princeton, NJ 08544-1017, USA. Email: jmcdouga@princeton.edu.

perfectly pleasant and conventional. We learned shortly afterwards that Si el-Haj, who had been a locally prominent Islamist militant, had spent much of the past decade in prison. When he was arrested, we were told, a cache of arms had been found at his house along with a list of local dignitaries marked for assassination. It was in prison that he had lost his sight.

The purpose of the anecdote is not soothingly to suggest that Algeria's Islamist insurgents, whose campaigns of violence in the mid-1990s led simultaneously to the isolation of the country and to the internationalisation of a particularly horrific image of its internal politics, are basically decent, hospitable and ordinary people 'underneath', any more than it is sensationally to 'prove' that even the most apparently pleasant and benign individual encountered in this part of the world can turn out to be a 'terrorist' 'underneath'. Both readings of the story miss the point.

'If an Algerian says: "I'll kill you"—he really will kill you':[1] violence as caricature

Algeria has experienced so distressing a degree of violence in the course of its recent history that images and accounts of the country routinely reiterate two perceptions. First, a supposed ubiquity of violence, endured and inflicted, in Algerian society and its history—so that the infliction and suffering of violence becomes an explanatory factor in Algerian history and social organisation, rather than a problem to be explained. Second, the exceptional intensity of this apparently pathological fact. Nor is it only observers inclined to neo-Orientalist clichés or post-imperial nostalgia who acquiesce in this imagery. Other people from places in Africa and the Middle East which have their own terrible histories, from Iraq, Palestine, Sudan, can be heard (anecdotally) to say much the same thing. The image of endemic, ubiquitous and unusually extreme violence as a constitutive element of Algeria, whether in media clichés or in the spontaneous ethnography of casually informed observers as close by as Morocco and Tunisia or as far away the USA, or in the more ostensibly sophisticated garb of academic analysis, is a first and most readily apparent aspect of the problem of naming violence in this context, from the colonial conquest to the present. It should also be immediately apparent that this representation of a society so 'plagued', as Algeria's incumbent president, Abdelaziz Bouteflika, himself put it in a re-election speech of early 2004, that all the other people of the world must keep a safe distance, itself does much violence to a country and a people who can only be caricatured, and who cannot begin to be understood, in these terms. The point of departure for an examination of violence in Algeria must be to acknowledge, but recuse, not reiterate, the caricature of 'savagery' with which Algerian history has been burdened, and which has generally debilitated understanding of this experience, rather than enlightening it.

Some understanding of the meanings of violence in Algeria, then, needs first of all to escape from this very old stereotype, in all its more or less elaborate forms. Conflictual social relations are as constitutive of this society as of any other; extreme forms of overt violence are not, by some particularly perverse streak of 'national character', nor by inculcation through a long colonial oppression, themselves characteristic of Algerians. Any explanation—and I do not presume to offer one here—of those particular forms which physical violence has taken, in the war of independence and again in the 1990s, would have to begin with the social and political conditions in which such practices arose. And it would have to account for the choices made in resorting to a violence that is no more instinctive to Algerians than to anyone else.

To do this, however, would not mean *rationalising* violence, either (at the crudest extreme) as the expression of a peculiar culture, history and social organisation, or (at the most sophisticated) as 'a virtue' in a peculiarly Algerian political imaginary, constructed across several centuries in which violence served as the most effective means of accumulating symbolic capital.[2] Such rationalisations in fact offer only another form of that naturalisation which we began by recusing. On the contrary, any more adequate account will have to find ways to address the very irrational, unimaginable unnaturalness of a violence which is, precisely, 'foreign' to most ordinary Algerians, to their self-conceptions, world-view and morality.[3] At the same time it should be recognised that certain narratives which have 'naturalised' a vision of the past as constituted by permanent and reciprocal violences—in official history, public commemoration and political discourse—have had their own effective force in shaping decisions and behaviour in the present.[4] If it is true, however, that the echoes of past violence, remembered and narrated, do indeed constitute an important part of the symbolic universe of Algerian culture, history and politics, it is crucial to understand the particular formulation, deployment and reproduction of such symbols in terms of their specific historicity.

This article examines three distinct moments of the social production and cultural encoding of the various forms of violence, physical or euphemised, which have entered into the constitution of social relations in Algeria, as well as playing a part in their crisis and breakdown. These three narratives move from the colonial obsession with an imagined 'native' savagery, which both produced and exonerated the spectacular exercise of colonialism's own violence, through the institution of a legal system of inflexible repression which came to dominate the nationalist imaginary of the colonial period and of its own history, to the complex afterlife of the war of independence and the emergence of new codes of legitimate warfare in the 1990s. The links between each moment are neither direct nor determining. Rather, each obeys a specific logic of its own, reflecting a particular constellation of circumstances. Si el-Haj, our Saharan fellow traveller and sometime alleged terrorist, is not a cipher for either the banality or the exoticism of violence in Algeria, but rather a man in a particular place and time with his own history, and his own view of history.

Piracy, banditry, fanaticism: the alterity of violence

Imperial depictions of an empire's subject populations and territories are adept at externalising the violence of the empire's own exercise of power, projecting it onto its victims as inherent to *them*. Rather than a specifically situated practice, with its own social and cultural logic, arising at a particular moment, 'native' violence is, in imperial eyes, necessarily irrational, instinctive, 'savage'. Imperial power projection, on the other hand, is only ever conceived of as the necessary policy response to a specific situation: as deliberated, calculated (and now, of course, 'precision targeted'). While modern Europe led the world in the practice of organised violence—economic, symbolic and physical, and on an increasingly apocalyptic scale—from the early 16th century onwards its accounts of the world simultaneously became increasingly effective at portraying, not the effects of the vertiginous expansion of its own capacity to produce and direct coercive force, but the mortal danger faced by its legitimate interests and civilising works among the anarchic, despotic or barbaric zones of disorder in Africa, Asia and the Americas.

One of the first theatres of this developing conception of civilised selfhood and barbarian otherness was the western Mediterranean, where long-standing patterns of trade and warfare underwent significant changes of meaning in correlation with both the developing structures of early modern European states and these same states' expansion of colonial plantation slave economies across the Atlantic.[5] The original European stereotype of Algeria, as a fleshpot haven of renegade villains, a nest of pirates whose infamous depredations not only harried legitimate commerce but also enslaved white (and, by the early modern period, free-born) Christian subjects and citizens of Europe, is one of the earliest and most tenacious modern images of the alterity of violence.[6] The blanket bombardment of Algiers in 1816 by the British navy, which fired some 34 000 shells into the city in nine hours, and the French invasion and conquest in 1830 found their justification in the Algerines' limited, and economically almost insignificant, return to a moribund corsairing which had in any case been forced upon them at the end of the 18th century when the European fleets effectively closed off to them any less overtly rapacious commerce.[7] This fact, of course, like the death and destruction inflicted by Lord Exmouth's cannon and the 'pacifying' armies of de Bourmont, Lamoricière and Bugeaud,[8] was erased from the imperial narrative.

The point here is not simply to highlight the selective and self-serving automystification of imperial fantasies of power; it is, rather, to suggest that a fundamental psychological and ideological mechanism of colonial rule—one of the several ways in which Europeans not only produced imperialism, but contrived to live with it in perfectly good conscience, indeed in the conviction of its 'greater good'—has been the externalisation of imperialism's own violence onto its victim. This does not mean, of course, that the colonised internalised this projection, that they did in fact *become* 'the sneering face of [Europe's] own evil shadow' which early colonial observers thought they recognised on the Mediterranean's southern shore.[9] On the contrary, colonised populations were and remained, in this respect, the entirely innocent objects of a developing European world-view, one to which African and Asian peoples remained external precisely as their bodies and territories were incorporated into the domain of European power projection. The efficacy of this operation lay not in the minds and practices of Algerians, but in those of Europeans.

Colonial violence was encoded, in Algeria as elsewhere, as defensive, preventive—even, already, as pre-emptive—a necessary response to the putative, and very really feared, instinctive, unpredictable and unlimited violence that the 'native' supposedly bore always within his breast, and of which his occasional self-assertion in rebellion was simply proof. All the early colonial typologies of Algerian violence—pirate at sea, bandit on land, religiously inspired fanatic, unremittingly suspicious xenophobe—are variations on this same obsessive theme, and the apologetics of the conquest's war criminals are perfectly clear and, one imagines, of perfectly good conscience, on the subject:

> Little does it matter if France in her political conduct goes beyond the limits of common morality at times. The essential thing is that she shall establish a lasting colony and that as a consequence she will bring European civilisation to these barbaric countries. When a project which is of advantage to all humanity is to be carried out, the shortest path is the best. Now, it is certain that the shortest path is terror; without violating the laws of morality, or international jurisprudence, we can fight our African enemies with powder and fire, joined by famine, internal division, war.[10]

Nor was this basic ideological operation limited in scope or efficacy to the period of conquest and the wars of pacification from 1830 to 1870. The alterity of violence underpinned a crucial, constitutive reflex common among the European population. While never simply collectively shared by all—one cannot speak of a monolithic and undifferentiated 'settler psyche'—it was a powerful presence in widespread socialisation processes and in the consensus of the colony's internal politics. It remains present, even if only in the form of a cipher, in Camus' *L'Etranger*, and reached its suicidal acme in the ultra-colonialist terrorism of the Organisation de l'Armée Secrète (OAS).[11] The conviction of quotidian colonial racism—'the Arabs are cut-throats'—which so effectively held Algerians as invisible to settler society and, when visible, as intolerably threatening,[12] was itself an acute form of symbolic and psychological violence, simultaneously inflicted and endured (as an hysterically internalised fear of the 'native') by Algeria's Europeans. It also served as the unspoken, since self-evident, ground of justification for the spectacular exercise of physical violence against Algerians by both regular armed forces and the settlers' own militia. This is most obviously visible on a large scale in the reprisal massacres at Sétif and Guelma in May 1945[13] and later in the OAS death-squad murders of 1961–62. In these cases colonial violence was a massively and demonstratively disproportionate reaction to Algerian resistance. Not so much the suppression of the actual acts of violent resistance which Algerians had carried out, these spectacles of force were ferociously self-assertive pre-emptions of any conceivable resistance, a terrified exorcism of the latent 'savagery' of the 'native'. As a divisional army commander after Sétif reported, the repression exacted was intended to bring 'peace for ten years'.[14] The poet and playwright Kateb Yacine, who witnessed the events of Sétif at first hand at the age of 16, and later located the emergence of his own nationalist commitment in that experience, set the European settlers' response in a striking fictional dialogue, published in 1956, as the war of independence gathered pace:

> F: This time they've understood.
>
> N: You think so? I'm telling you, they'll have another go. We didn't do it properly.
>
> Mme N: My God, if France doesn't deal with them ... we can't defend ourselves alone!
>
> F: France has had it. They should give us arms, and let us get on with it. There's no need for law here. They only understand force. They need a Hitler.
>
> Mme F, caressing [a schoolboy] R: And to think they go to school with you, dear [...]
>
> R: Oh, things will change. We were scared before. There are lots of them in my class—there are only five of us who are French, not counting the Italians and the Jews.
>
> Mme F: Take care, dear, they're savages![15]

The massacres of May 1945 and the indiscriminate serial assassinations of the OAS were seen by their perpetrators as *defensive* actions, prompted as they were by the same fear (the same simultaneously internalised and externalised, endured and inflicted, violence) that Fanon, in one of his most astute passages, puts in the mouth of a metropolitan French child: '*Regarde le nègre!...Maman, un nègre!...maman, le nègre va me manger*'![16]

'Order' and armed struggle: the law of violence

Underlying these occasional conflagrations there was a more euphemised, everyday and insidious means of assuring imperial rule and of keeping Algerian 'anarchy' in check, through the juridical 'incarnation of the violence of the coloniser'[17] in special native-status legislation, the *indigénat*. Enacted in 1881 as a transitional, emergency measure, it remained in force in various forms until 1944. Overtly a wartime law, a set of emergency regulations for the suppression of revolt, but maintained thereafter in what was notionally a time of peace, the *indigénat* both symbolised and, in the exactions it entailed, made manifest that aspect of the colonial state which constituted an apparatus of permanent, routinised low-intensity warfare.[18] This, alongside the generalised extrajudicial regime of daily indignity suffered by a non-citizen, mostly disenfranchised and expropriated subject population, was a crucial pillar of the colonial order and constituted a major aspect of ordinary Algerians' experiences of colonialism. In the nationalist historical vulgate, this aspect is indeed the *only* face of colonial history, and it is this century-long story of inflexible, unreformable,[19] total oppression which leads, inexorably and as if by an equally iron law of historical evolution, to the taking up of arms and the ultimate, supposedly military, defeat of the occupier by a corresponding, and obligatory, revolutionary violence.

This 'law of violence' in the unfolding of a collective Algerian destiny, a homogenising meta-narrative in which total, reciprocal conflict is understood as the determining law of history, has done much to obscure the intense complexities and contradictions of both colonial relations of power and the emergence of nationalism and armed struggle. The entirety of the colonial period, in the 'official' national history and its rhetorical commemoration, is seen in flat monochrome. As Jacques Berque, the eminent (and entirely sympathetic) historian and sociologist of Islam who grew up in colonial Algeria, observed: 'the violence of the liberation struggle nourished a bitter, sometimes frenzied, literature denouncing the wounds inflicted by colonialism. In short, the literature retained from the colonial dialectic only the outer layer, and of that only what was destructive.'[20] The many deeper 'layers' of the long and viciously intimate colonial dialectic are as invisible to the nationalist orthodoxy as was the injustice of its domination to colonialist self-justification.

Principal among the crucial factors written out of this account is the long and impassioned search of Algerians for a workable reform of the colonial system, for a *peaceful* solution to the intolerable condition of their subject status within the free and egalitarian republic. Or for one which would liberate both communities in the colony ('Algerians of long date'—presumably including the ancient local Jewish population—and 'Algerians of recent date', as one leading nationalist and Islamic scholar expressed the difference between the indigenous and settler societies as late as 1951[21]) from the mutually destructive relationship of violence which would ultimately consume them both. The francophone intellectuals who sought accommodation with and emancipation within *la mère patrie* from around 1908 up to the end of the 1930s are dismissed as at best misguided, at worst treacherous, 'assimilationists',[22] or grudgingly rehabilitated (and miscast) as precursors of the ultimate revolt in a preparatory phase of 'political resistance'. This very notion is manifestly tributary to the later, and more worthy, 'mature' phase of armed struggle whose centrality determines, in this teleological re-reading, the meaning of all previous history since the conquest. In this interpretive dynamic, which seems to have emerged in the mid-1940s can be traced the deeply ingrained suspicion of its own intellectuals prevalent in Algerian political culture. The arabophone scholars and teachers of Islam, whose political programme was similarly reformist, gradualist and opposed to the use of violence, and who saw themselves as the 'awakeners', guides and spokesmen of the nation (whose 'self-awareness' they considered to be of their own making) are similarly drafted after the fact into the unifying teleology of 'the national movement' as the spiritual fathers of a revolution whose paternity was decidedly not theirs.[23] Read backwards from the exhilarating vantage point of victory, through an intensely divisive and traumatic war which could, nonetheless, be quickly enough re-imagined as the triumphant climax of one long, unending struggle over 132 years, the whole history of colonial Algeria appears to conform exclusively, unremittingly, to the law of violence.[24] A violence to which no alternative was *ever* possible, against which no possible political victory (including that which in fact eventually occurred[25]) could be won, but which could only be overcome by a corresponding recourse to violence.

Reducing the complex totality of this history to the simplicity of total conflict, the 'law of violence' underpins an important post-independence political myth of the war of national liberation, as the divinely guided act of the People (in the singular) arising *en bloc* against the monolithic force of oppression. In the words of Algeria's leading nationalist poet, in an epic text officially commissioned to celebrate the writing of Algeria's national(ised) history, the voluntarist insurrection launched by a small fraction of radical nationalists on the night of 31 October – 1 November 1954 becomes an act of the entire people under God, telescoped into Islamic religious history:

> Your Lord announced the Night of Destiny/ And cast a veil over a thousand months/ The people said: Your command, Lord!/ And the Lord replied: Your enterprise is mine!/ ...November...you changed the course of life/ And you were, November, the rising dawn/ You recalled to us, in Algeria, the battle of Badr/ And we arose, as the Companions of Badr.[26]

The official history of the revolution is that of a glorious epic in which only extremes of purity or corruption are possible, in which 'men were snatched from their mediocrity to become the "sublime heroes" or the "absolute traitors" of the unfolding tragedy'.[27] For Algerian historian Mahfoud Kaddache, 1 November was 'the beginning of a new and glorious page of the history of Algeria'.[28] The constitution of 1976 asserted in its opening paragraphs that the war of national liberation 'will remain in history as one of the great epics marking the resurrection of the peoples of the Third World' and that 'Algeria today holds a place of the first order in the international arena thanks to the worldwide influence of the Revolution of 1 November 1954'. It further asserts 'the continuity and reaffirmation of the noble ideals which have animated, from its beginnings, the great Revolution of 1 November 1954'.[29] As the original point of reference for the independent state, its supplier of legitimacy and principal symbolic resource, the revolutionary epic was instituted at the very centre of Algeria's political imaginary, the founding aporia of the nation's forgetful memory.[30]

This social memory of the seven years' war of decolonisation as the founding experience of modern political community, of the single myth of origin for contemporary Algeria and Algerians has had an important series of consequences. The first is the erasure from official history and social memory of the actual divisions and conflicts of the revolution, of the means by which an activist fringe of the radical nationalist movement, having launched the insurrection on its own initiative in order to transcend the factional crisis of its party,[31] thereafter inspired, persuaded and coerced the loyalty of the masses, and eliminated or absorbed their rivals along the way.[32] As everyone is perfectly aware but as it is perfectly impossible to admit, the Front de Libération Nationale (FLN)'s revolution, whose slogan remains 'by the people and for the people', in fact was made 'by the FLN for the

Nation...with the support of the People whenever possible and against the opposition of the People whenever necessary'.[33] The role of the active minority of revolutionary militants who in fact sparked the war is, of course, recognised. Indeed, the 'men of November' are particularly celebrated,[34] but they, and the counter-state institution of the FLN which succeeded them and eventually assumed power, are imagined as the expression of 'the People' (in the singular), not as their own, wilful, emancipatory–coercive selves, sometimes followed, sometimes opposed, and who certainly did not naturally subsume the whole of 'Algeria'.[35]

A second effect is the apparent converse of this—the actual expropriation of Algeria's people (in the plural) from the revolution and from the emancipation and self-determination it was supposed to bring. While the armed struggle is said to have mobilised *le peuple tout entier*, simultaneously a military elite issued from the revolutionary army, while proclaiming that the 'sole hero' was indeed the people, lost no time in asserting its right to rule over the people, a right which it considered had been earned in the prosecution of the war. While the war was said to have been the act of the unanimous nation, it in fact constituted a unanimist state out of the conflicts which split Algerians (Europeans from Muslims, and each community against itself), under the aegis of a postcolonial authoritarianism, alienating the state from 'its' people and eventually, in the eyes of many of the people themselves, considering them only with *hogra,* 'contempt'.[36] The doctrine of the historical necessity and inevitability, the supremely uncompromising virtue, of armed struggle (as against the necessarily compromising practice of politics) in the overthrow of colonial domination, and the legitimacy gained by engagement in that struggle—especially late in the war, after the early heroes of the guerrilla were mostly dead, and men flocked from the French army and from civilian life suddenly to swell the ranks of the ALN on the brink of victory[37]—required that all 'the People' be implicated in it, but only in the person of those who themselves incarnated the people's destiny, not through *any* destiny that the people themselves might, eventually, choose.

Terrorists, patriots, victims and martyrs: the inheritance of violence

This complex underside of the foundational political culture of revolutionary legitimacy begins to explain the strange ambivalence of the social memory of the war of independence as, outside the political field, it is actually experienced in Algerian life. There is a tension, tangible in private and in certain public expressions (the press, cinema, literature), between the war remembered as enactment, the epically memorialised active prosecution of the guerrilla in the maquis, and the reality of the war as the endurance of massive counter-insurrectionary violence at the hands of the French army. Of these two aspects, the latter is, if anything (and unsurprisingly, given the numbers of people involved), more prevalent, more acutely felt and more generally remembered. The FLN maquisard (*mujahid*) remains a ubiquitous summarising symbol of national virtue and honour, expression of Algeria's greatest trials and triumph, and repository of society's values and commitments. The kind of poster one can see on the walls of a youth association office—with the text of the national anthem, *Qassaman* (written by the same poet mentioned earlier), unfurled above an artist's impression of a company of uniformed *mujahidin* running into battle amid the explosions of French bombs—and the imagery of schoolbooks and popular histories, as well street names and their commemorative portraits and plaques, exude this message. At the same time, however, there is, at a deeper level of popular imagination, the predominant image of a war fought against, rather than by, Algerians, of the people of Algeria, as a whole, as having endured the war fought against their emancipation rather than having actively fought a war for it. Fifty years after the outbreak of the insurrection many small towns and villages, or distinct quarters of towns, are still easily identified as having been established by the colonial army as 'regroupment centres', forced-relocation camps where the rural population, driven away from their homes and off their lands (which were razed, napalmed and cordoned off as free-fire zones) were resettled in squat, cramped shelters under the observation of a local garrison. The memory of the cordons and *ratissages* ('raking-over', the systematic, intrusive searches of urban districts, or combing of whole rural zones), the uncounted disappearances, internments, summary executions, torture and rape, involved, of course, far more people as objects of a violence visited upon them than were ever under arms (or engaged in any other active capacity) as agents of revolutionary war.

These two sides of the conflict are in a sense complementary, and the figure of the *mujahid*, marching victoriously under the national flag across the frontier at independence, is the obverse image of the 'one and half million martyrs' which the war is routinely said to have cost Algeria.[38] The dead, both the civilian victims of colonialism and the actively fighting martyrs fallen 'on the field of honour' in the maquis, are perhaps the strongest of all postwar national symbols. Beyond the structural symbolic complementarity of these aspects of Algeria's social memory, however, there remains a certain malaise, an unspoken recognition of the horrific tragedy of the war, below the 'glorious' rhetoric of its celebratory myth. In Merzak Allouache's 1976 masterpiece, *Omar Gatlato*, internationally recognised as one of the first Algerian films to break the mould of postwar heroic epic and portray a deeper, more intimate and multifaceted reality of Algeria, the revolution is an acknowledged but distant backdrop. It is referred to explicitly, almost as pre-history, in Omar's opening speech but then more subtly in the guise of an occasional tattoo-drumming soundtrack cut with views over the Algiers rooftops, a neat reference to Gillo Pontecorvo's *The Battle of Algiers*, shot in the city a decade earlier. In *Omar Gatlato* there is a remarkable sequence where the hero is assailed, one imagines for the *n*th time, by his braggart uncle evidently fabricated tales of heroism during the revolution, and does his best to pay no attention. Throughout the scene the main character's elderly relative, a man who has himself quite obviously witnessed and lived through colonialism and the war, sits unmoved in the corner of the shot, his eyes fixed on the television—and says nothing.

The figure of the 'fake *mujahid*' *(faux mujahid)*, a scammer who, in independent Algeria, has forged testimony of his wartime service so as to receive the substantial benefits available to a recognised, card-carrying ex-maquisard, is the grotesque complement of the torch-bearing freedom fighter whose lofty statue adorns the base of the colossal martyrs' monument on the Algiers skyline. The question of the numbers of *faux mujahidin* (and of whether, in fact, there are any) is hotly disputed and occasionally the scandal gives rise to exasperated ire in the press. The country's favourite and most infamous caricaturist, Ali Dilem, portrays a card-wielding loafer in conversation with his signature female figure (who stands in all his work as a cipher for Algeria): 'That's it, I've got my card.'—'You fought in the war?'—'No, I filled in the form!'[39] Another Saharan anecdote may also contribute something in this regard. On our return trip from the desert, a distinguished gentleman with spectacular white whiskers hitched a short ride with us. He was, he said, a former maquisard himself (he exhibited his card, to our great curiosity), and was now engaged in a local self-defence group, one of the militia units armed by the state during the 1990s to fight Islamist guerrillas and, reportedly, not infrequently constituted by FLN veterans. Most of these *patriotes*, the generic term applied to all such militia, have since been stood down and (at least officially) disarmed, but his group had continued to exist as an auxiliary arm of the customs service, tracking contraband traffickers across the desert. When the man had left us, one of my friends remarked speculatively that the story, in this case, might actually have been true. In his own experience genuine former *mujahidin* generally do not introduce themselves as such, rarely have the famous card, and are intensely reluctant to talk about it.

The societal inheritance, then, of this history which is said to be 'inhabited by violence' is, at the personal, familial, local level, and at that of national political culture, the rhetoric and monuments of commemoration and the narratives of official history, a most ambiguous one. In this context, the notion of violence, in any one of a series of historical guises (Ottoman corsairs, anti-colonial *mahdi*s, nationalist revolutionaries) as having simply provided a generic model of political behaviour for replication in all subsequent moments of Algerian history, is clearly too simple. There are, undoubtedly, aspects of the insurgency and repression of the 1990s which explicitly echo, in the language and self-view of the actors involved, the codes of earlier violence. Islamist militants are *mujahidin* fighting a holy war for the recovery of Algeria's 'authentic values' and the popular sovereignty of the *mustad'afin* (the oppressed, the new 'wretched of the earth') against the corruption and tyranny of those who have 'betrayed' the promise of the revolution, against the traitors of the 'party of France' *(hizb fransa)* who have compromised Algeria's true destiny. The army and its auxiliaries are *patriotes* fighting the alien and un-Algerian terror of 'sons of *harki*s',[40] who have betrayed the nation through their allegiance to the 'Islamist international' and seek to destroy the republican state created by the revolution, condemning Algeria through 'programmatic regression' to a barbaric medieval theocracy. Some, at least, among the Islamist insurgents in the early 1990s explained their strategy of terror—the murders of low-level state functionaries, police officers, artists and intellectuals—with reference to the war of liberation. In a contemporary documentary film, a woman recalls the explanation given her by a family acquaintance and member of an armed group, after his colleagues have murdered one of her relatives, a woman police officer: 'It's just like in the war of independence'.[41] And, correspondingly, the senior army officers behind the suspension of elections in January 1992, and the subsequent repression of the Islamist opposition, explain their move as a 'patriotic act' and a 'Novembrist' engagement for the salvation of the state and nation.[42]

But this has not been simply the instinctive reiteration of culturally entrenched patterns of political behaviour. Rather, such expressions reflect a continuous, deliberate reinvention, and struggle for the appropriation, of the strongly valorised and widely diffused inheritance of the war of independence and the nationalist register of legitimacy in a situation of political implosion where the symbolic order has been fragmented, and where symbolic goods are up for repossession. The necessity and legitimacy of armed struggle, inherited by the army as 'shield of the revolution'[43] or by Islamist maquisards as new *mujahidin*, and of Islam as the core component of national belonging (despite the opposition to this doctrine in the councils of the wartime FLN[44]), find new significance in the entirely altered circumstances of the new political and social struggles emerging in the 1980s and 1990s. To these already established registers are added new, previously unthought elements, introduced from elsewhere. Doctrinal imports from the Middle East include a reinvented notion of the 'Islamic state' influenced by the Taliban emirate in Afghanistan, the practice of *takfir* (declaring 'nominally' Muslim rulers and regimes to be apostates) as theorised by Egyptian Islamist radicals, and the sacralisation of redemptive *jihad* even against Muslim civilians who are reluctant follow the Islamist 'call'. (Omar Carlier, in this regard, points to the contrast with the peasant insurgents of early 20th century colonial Algeria, who, even amid the frantic bloodletting of millenarian revolt, allowed Europeans to live who consented to utter the *shahada*, the formulaic expression of testimony to Islam.[45]) The emergence of this reinvented lexicon, pressed into the service of a radical, transnationalist, utopian and chiliastic Islamism, is part of the new conflict's geopolitical context, just as Bandung, self-determination, socialism and Third Worldism were in a previous time.

The comparison most often drawn between the forms of violence enacted during the war of independence and those of the 1990s—the mutilation of bodies, the extreme, exhibitionist atrocity against one's physical adversary which leaves 'the body of the victim without even the value of a sacrifice, [being] ostensibly dehumanised'[46]—also requires more subtle reading than that furnished by the label of 'Algerian savagery'.[47] A beginning might be made in the decryption of 'the accumulation of tensions occasioned by the unravelling of each and every mechanism of social solidarity'which Algerian society has endured in its multifaceted (urban, rural, demographic, economic, educational, linguistic, political) crises since the early 1980s.[48] The most recent reproduction and recoding of the recourse to political violence in

Algeria is the product of its own, specific context of crisis, and of the ways in which this crisis has been managed, or mismanaged, exploited and exacerbated, by particular actors.[49] Such conditions of crisis, with which Algeria has been particularly terribly afflicted, have nonetheless been shared, in varying degrees, with other parts of Asia and Africa. They are not intrinsic to Algeria, its social organisation, cultural values or political ideas, and no more are the forms of terribly extreme overt conflict which, in this case, have arisen out of it. Each moment of the breakdown or recomposition of social order presents its own possibilities within its own context of constraints, but no ingrained societal or political structure of violence, as an innate characteristic or determining law of history, inherently precludes the creation of alternatives. However difficult such choices are and however unlikely such alternatives may appear given the circumstances of the past decade,[50] they undoubtedly remain possible. However many savage wars Algeria may have suffered, Algerians have not thereby been collectively brutalised into thinking with savage minds.

Notes

1 Tunisian saying (reported in personal communication, 1999).

2 L Martinez, *La Guerre civile en Algérie*, Paris: Karthala, 1998, p 9.

3 Thus the early actions of armed Islamists in the 1990s were initially attributed in public opinion to 'foreigners'.

4 H Remaoun, 'La Question de l'histoire dans le débat sur la violence en Algérie', *Insaniyat*, 10, 2000, pp 31–43; A Moussaoui, 'Du danger et du terrain en Algérie', *Ethnologie française*, 31, 2001, pp 51–59; and J McDougall, 'Martyrdom and destiny: the inscription and imagination of Algerian history', in U Makdisi & P Silverstein (eds), *Memory and Violence in the Middle East and North Africa*, Bloomington, IN: Indiana University Press, forthcoming 2005, ch 8.

5 G Weiss, 'Mediterranean captivity and the language of slavery in early modern France', paper presented to the Society for French Historical Studies, Paris, June 2004; and Weiss, 'Barbary captivity and the French idea of freedom', *French Historical Studies*, forthcoming 2005.

6 For a recent restatement of the theme, see RC Davis, *Christian Slaves, Muslim Masters. White Slavery in the Mediterranean, the Barbary Coast and Italy, 1500–1800*, Basingstoke: Palgrave, 2003. For an incisive analysis of the relationship between imperial vulnerability and imperial power, see L Colley, *Captives. Britain, Empire and the World, 1600–1850*, London: Jonathan Cape, 2002.

7 D Panzac, *Les Corsaires barbaresques. La fin d'une épopée, 1800–1820*, Paris: CNRS, 1999; and L Valensi, *On the Eve of Colonialism. North Africa before the French Conquest, 1790–1830*, New York: Africana, 1977, ch 5.

8 Respectively, the commander of the Anglo-Dutch naval expedition of 1816 and the early generals of the French army of Africa.

9 Valensi, *On the Eve of Colonialism*, p xiii.

10 Quoted in M Bennoune, *The Making of Contemporary Algeria. Colonial Upheavals and Post-Independence Development*, Cambridge: Cambridge University Press, 1988, p 40.

11 The 'ultra' terror group formed in 1961 by militant European settlers to resist the abandonment of 'Algérie française'.

12 While individually an Algerian could be *mon pôte Ali* ('my mate Ali'), visible, collective self-assertion was intolerable, as is evidenced, for example, by the fact that, before independence, organised (and authorised) demonstrations by Algerians in the city of Oran which dared to leave the so-called *village nègre* and descend the main boulevard toward the Place d'Armes in the European *centre-ville* were met with police repression. On both of the only two occasions that such marches occurred before 1962, there were deaths among the demonstrators.

13 On 8 May 1945, and for several days following, an abortive insurrection in these districts of eastern Algeria was followed by massive retaliation by military, naval and air forces, and (especially in Guelma) by local militia armed and supervised by the local sub-Prefect (who had been a wartime hero of the anti-Nazi resistance). Around 200 Europeans were killed in the initial rioting; the most reliable estimates of Algerian casualties seem to range between 15 000 and 20 000 (the official nationalist figure

being 45 000). See J-P Peyroulou, 'La milice, le commissaire et le témoin: le récit de la répression de mai 1945 à Guelma', *Bulletin de l'Institut d'histoire du temps présent*, 83, 2004, pp 9–22; and J-L Planche, 'La répression civile du soulèvement nord-constantinois, mai-juin 1945' in D Rivet *et al*, *La Guerre d'Algérie au miroir des décolonisations françaises*, Paris: Société Française d'Histoire d'Outre-Mer, 2000, pp 111–128.

[14] Quoted in A Horne, *A Savage War of Peace: Algeria, 1954–1962*, Basingstoke: Macmillan, 1996, p 28.

[15] K Yacine, *Nedjma*, Paris: Seuil, 1996, p 220.

[16] F Fanon, *Peau noire, masques blancs*, Paris: Seuil, 1971, pp 91–92.

[17] C Collot, *Les Institutions de l'Algérie durant la période coloniale (1830–1962)*, Paris: CNRS/Algiers: OPU, 1987, pp 190–200 (quote at p 200).

[18] A simultaneously unyielding and highly flexible system (since almost anything—from travelling to gathering firewood to pasturing one's flocks—could be constituted, in particular circumstances, as an infraction), the *indigénat* was based on the (constitutionally illegal) premise that certain acts not normally punishable under French criminal law were in fact crimes if committed by persons of 'native personal status' (ie after 1870 and until 1944, most Algerian Muslims).

[19] The (only partially enacted) new dispensations of 1944–47, which finally removed the *indigénat*, established parity of elected representation for the European and Muslim communities, bracketing the Muslim vote in a second college, where 1 300 000 electors, voting on behalf of a population of eight million, voted for the same number (60) of Algerian representatives as the 532 000 voters of the first (overwhelmingly European) college. J-C Vatin, *L'Algérie politique. Histoire et société*, Paris: FNSP, 1983, pp 260–261. Subsequent elections, most notoriously those held under Marcel-Edmond Naegelen (Governor-general from 1948 to 1951—a socialist and anti-fascist resister during World War II), were notable for the blatant fraud deployed by the administration.

[20] Berque, *Dépossession du monde*, quoted in Valensi, *On the Eve of Colonialism*, p xiii.

[21] Interview with shaykh Larbi Tebessi, *Alger républicain*, 10 November 1951.

[22] The classic formulation of their position was made in a newspaper article of 1936 by the liberal leader, Ferhat Abbas, whose stand was considered 'treachery to the national cause' by the radical nationalists.

[23] J McDougall, 'S'écrire un destin: l'association des 'ulama dans la révolution algérienne', *Bulletin de l'Institut d'histoire du temps présent*, 83, 2004, pp 38–52. For more detail on the '*ulama* (Islamic scholars), see McDougall, *History and the Culture of Nationalism in Algeria*, Cambridge: Cambridge University Press, forthcoming.

[24] In the words of Houari Boumédienne (Algeria's iconic president from 1965 to 1978): 'This generation has not only fought colonialism, but has known the signal honour of achieving victory. There resides the difference between ourselves and our ancestors.' Speech made in 1976, quoted in H Remaoun, 'Pratiques historiographiques et mythes de fondation', in Ch-R Ageron (ed), *La Guerre d'Algérie et les Algériens, 1954–1962*, Paris: Armand Colin, 1997, p 317. Evoking the leader of 'primary resistance' in the 1830s to1840s, an Algerian historian asserts what became conventional truth: 'The revolution in Algeria began with 'Abd al-Qadir, and never ceased since his time'. Muhammad al-Tammar, *Ta'rīkh al-adab al-jazâ'irî*, Algiers: SNED, nd (1969) , p 278.

[25] Independent Algerian official memory cultivated a myth of victory by arms, but the revolution was, in fact, ultimately successful not on the battlefield (which remained dominated at the end of the war by the French), but through its international political efforts and the creation of a situation of critical instability to which the only solution, for the French, had to be political and not military (as de Gaulle eventually understood, although his rebellious generals did not).

[26] M Zakarya, *Ilyadhat al-jaza'ir*, Algiers: Ministry of Original Education and Religious Affairs, 1972, p 45 (p 23 in accompanying French translation). The 'Night of Destiny', *laylat al-qadr*, celebrated on 26–27 Ramadan, is the night on which the first of the Qur'anic revelations is held to have been vouchsafed to the Prophet (Q97). The battle of Badr, fought in 2 AH (623–24 CE), was a crucial battle of the Prophet's campaigns in the Arabian peninsula.

[27] B Stora, 'La Guerre d'Algérie quarante ans après: connaissances et reconnaissance', *Modern and Contemporary France*, 2 (2), 1994, pp 131–139 (quote at 131).

[28] M Kaddache & D Sari, *L'Algérie dans l'histoire. (t5) La Résistance politique (1900–1954; Bouleversements socioéconomiques*, Algiers: OPU, 1989, p 127.

[29] *Journal officiel de la République algérienne*, 15(94), 1976, p 1042.

[30] B Anderson, *Imagined Communities*, London: Verso, 1991, ch 11.

[31] The Parti du Peuple Algérien (Algerian People's Party—PPA), founded in 1937 and clandestine since 1939, and its (legal) electoral cover, the Mouvement pour le Triomphe des Libertés Démocratiques (MTLD), established in 1946.

[32] The most violent confrontations, both in the maquis and, especially, in the emigrant community in France, occurred between the FLN and the rival Mouvement National Algérien which was formed by dissident ex-militants of the PPA/MTLD.

33 H Roberts, *The Battlefield: Algeria, 1988–2002. Studies in a Broken Polity*, London: Verso, 2003, p 211, n 1.

34 The original leader of the Front Islamique du Salut (FIS), Abassi Madani, derived his own legitimacy from having been one of this select band. The prevention of the FIS's victory by the interruption of the electoral process in January 1992 was correspondingly declared a 'Novembrist' act by its architects in the military.

35 M Harbi, *Le FLN, mirage et réalité, des origines à la prise du pouvoir (1945–62)*, Paris: Jeune Afrique, 1980; and Harbi, *L'Algérie et son destin: croyants ou citoyens*, Paris: Arcantère, 1992.

36 '*Hogra barakat*', an end to the disdain of the powerful for the powerless, is a leitmotiv slogan of recent protests against the political status quo in Algeria.

37 The ALN, the FLN's revolutionary armed forces, were constituted as such at the Soummam conference in 1956. The late flood of adherents to the struggle at the moment of the ceasefire in March 1962 gave rise to the term *marsiens* (a laconic pun on the homonymous *martiens*, Martians).

38 The official '*milyun shahid*', an enduring repetition whose value is not historical but symbolic, is generally recognised as an ideologically inflated figure. While calculations are hotly disputed, the likely true figure of Algerian war dead appears to be around 300 000. See Ch-R Ageron, 'Pour une histoire critique de l'Algérie', in Ageron (ed), *L'Algérie des Français*, pp 7–13; and X Yacono, 'Les pertes Algériennes de 1954 à 1962', *Revue de l'Occident musulman et de la Méditerranée*, 34, 1982, pp 119–134.

39 Cartoon appearing in *Liberté*, 17 November 2002. The original reads: 'Ça y est, j'ai eu ma carte'. 'T'as fait la guerre?' 'Non, j'ai fait la *demande*'.

40 The *harkis* were auxiliary counter-insurgency and 'self-defence' troops recruited among the Algerian population. The term has come to signify any Algerian held to have collaborated, in any capacity, with the French army during the war.

41 J-P Lledo (dir), *Chroniques algériennes*, 52 mins, Algiers–Paris: Audience productions/Planète, 1994.

42 K Nezzar (Minister of Defence in 1992), *Algérie: Échec à une régression programmée*, Paris: Publisud, 2001, and his various interventions in the press, especially *Le Soir d'Algérie*, 11 October 2003, 3 February 2004; and interview with Nezzar by A Shatz, 'Algeria's ashes', *New York Review of Books*, 18 July 2003.

43 According to the 1976 constitution, art 82.

44 Particularly in the various Algerian student unions (UGEMA, UNEA, UEAP), where membership contingent on adherence to Islam was a point of contention, and most importantly in the drafting of the Tripoli programme, the unfulfilled constitutional document of 1962, most of whose artisans were in favour of a secular republic and opposed to the designation of Islam as religion of state.

45 O Carlier, 'D'une guerre à l'autre, le redéploiement de la violence entre soi', *Confluences Méditerrannée*, 25 (1998), pp 123–137.

46 *Ibid*, p 136.

47 R Delphard, *Vingt ans pendant la guerre d'Algérie. Générations sacrifiées* (a memorial account of the war as seen by young French conscripts), Paris: Michel Lafon, 2001, ch 11.

48 Carlier, D'une guerre à l'autre', p 136.

49 H Roberts, 'Doctrinaire economics and political opportunism in the strategy of Algerian Islamism', in J Ruedy (ed), *Islamism and Secularism in North Africa*, Basingstoke: Macmillan, 1994, ch 8.

50 Possibilities included the short-lived presidency of Mohamed Boudiaf in 1992; the Sant'Egidio (Rome) reconciliation platform in 1995; and the civil concord of 1999. Each of these episodes is, of course, controversial (on the latter, see especially International Crisis Group, Africa Report 31, *The Civil Concord: A Peace Initiative Wasted*, Brussels, 9 July 2001). The possible outcomes of the second presidential mandate gained by Abdelaziz Bouteflika in April 2004, on a platform of 'national concord', peace and stability, remain to be seen.

[21]

Antiracist memories: the case of 17 October 1961 in historical perspective

JIM HOUSE
University of Leeds

Abstract

This article examines the causes and subsequent cover-up of the massacre of Algerians by French security forces on 17 October 1961, and assesses the place and symbolic importance the memory of this massacre has come to occupy within Algerian immigrant communities and antiracist groups since the 1970s. These groups have actively campaigned for official recognition of the extent of and responsibility for the massacre. Finally, the article reflects on the way in which the 17 October massacre is often discussed in relation to Vichy, and the ambivalent conclusions which can be drawn from this in relation to France's coming-to-terms with its colonial past.

The idea of a *devoir de mémoire* is commonly heard in contemporary France, most frequently evoked in relation to Holocaust memory.[1] However, antiracist groups have, over the past 20 years in particular, also called on French society to come to terms with its colonial past. The pivotal event which, for campaigning groups, links previous forms of racism to present hostility towards Maghrebi migrants and their descendants in particular,[2] is the massacre of between 50 and 200 Algerians by French police and *gendarmes* on and around 17 October 1961, during and after a demonstration by the main Algerian nationalist organisation, the Front de libération nationale (FLN).[3] The Algerians were protesting on 17 October against a night curfew placed on them by the Paris prefect of police, Maurice Papon—Papon's idea being to stop both FLN attacks on security forces, and undermine fund-raising in the cafés. Police tactics against this peaceful demonstration of around 25,000 men, women and children, were to arrest 11,538 people. Those killed that evening and over the following days were shot, beaten, tortured or drowned in the Seine or canals, in both central Paris and the outskirts, their corpses dumped or placed in anonymous graves. The other protestors detained were eventually released, or 'repatriated' to detention centres in Algeria.

This article does not seek to offer a detailed history of the massacre, nor of the state cover-up, already amply covered elsewhere.[4] Rather, while studying aspects of the causes of the massacre, it concentrates on how the initially successful state cover-up slowly gave way to greater visibility from the late 1970s onwards, due to the campaigning by antiracist and immigrant-based groups focusing on the memory of 17 October. Illustrating Richard Terdiman's definition of memory as 'the modality of our relation to the past',[5] these groups' counter-memories denounce the past and present forms of physical and symbolic racial violence, be that from the police, judicial system or general public—all implicated, in albeit different ways, in the 17 October massacre and its subsequent cover-up. The history of this specific memory therefore offers an interesting perspective on historical remanence, on the modes of transmission of social memory within migrant and solidarity groups, and the politically marginal place such groups have occupied. By historicising memory, it is possible to see the changing social and political significance of the same event within antiracist discourses over a 40-year period, an event which, it will be argued, remains overshadowed in many respects by the legacy of Vichy.

How was such a massacre possible?

Any explanation for the Paris massacre has to come to terms with several overlapping time scales in order to understand how the effects of colonial ideology were reworked into the French decolonising context. From this perspective, the exceptionality of the Paris massacre was simply that it took place in metropolitan France. The wide-scale killing of French colonial subjects and citizens in the colonies and dependent territories (often in the context of political opposition to French rule) was a well-established feature of French colonial governance, as attested by Sétif (1945)[6] and Madagascar (1947),[7] to name only postwar examples. From the 1920s onwards, French fears that the growing numbers of Algerian migrants would be attracted to Algerian nationalism and/or Communism, had given rise to police surveillance, political repression involving mass round-ups, and, in the press, a discourse of criminalisation.[8] From 1947 onwards in particular, police, army and (apparently) more benign social welfare measures reflected tactics prevalent within Algeria,[9] and there was a considerable transfer of key colonial personnel between Algeria and France. Therefore, the colonial functionaries who came and went across the Mediterranean brought prejudices with them in addition to the policies they implemented. As a police report as early as May 1947 succinctly put it, '[...] le problème nord-africain dans la Métropole est devenu non plus une question de prévention mais une question de répression'.[10] Furthermore, security forces opened fire on the Algerian section of the Paris 14-July march in 1953, thus providing an eloquent example of the violence inflicted on Algerians *before* the outbreak of the war. This resulted in seven dead, six of whom were Algerian, guilty of holding aloft Algerian nationalist banners. During the ensuing parliamentary debate, Algerian *député* Abdelkader Cadi asked: 'Pourquoi la police perd-elle son sang-froid en présence d'Algériens? [...] pourquoi cette différence de traitement?'[11] These already high levels of hostility and security-force violence towards Algerians would be exacerbated from 1954 onwards.[12]

Public indifference to such developments was not total. The French organisation that was most consistent in its denunciation of policing methods was the Mouvement contre le racisme, l'antisémitisme et pour la paix, or MRAP, founded in 1949 as an extension of communist-affiliated Jewish Resistance groups.[13] MRAP activists highlighted the continuity of state racism from Vichy to the Fourth and Fifth Republics. For the MRAP, while it may have been easier for police officers to 'spot' an 'Algerian' in 1958 than a 'Jew' in 1943,

> [...] les erreurs sont toujours possibles : un de nos amis, instituteur, israélite, nous signalait l'autre jour qu'il avait été arrêté à la sortie du métro dans une rafle d'Algériens. La forme de son visage l'avait rendu 'suspect': l'inspecteur sans doute s'était trompé de quelques années.[14]

The parallels the MRAP established with previous forms of racism would become a central theme of subsequent memory activism, as we shall see. The Mouvement pour le triomphe des libertés démocratiques (MTLD), the FLN and other Algerian-based organisations also mobilised against police violence and official and media stereotyping,[15] as did the Secours populaire français, Trotskyist and anarchist groups, *porteurs/porteuses de valise*, anticolonial collectives and the Parti socialiste unifié.[16] However, these groups—which would show solidarity with Algerians after the massacre—were very marginal within the Left, divided among themselves, and had little mass appeal. Social relations outside the workplace between French and Algerian workers were limited.[17] The FLN decision to undertake military operations in mainland France in August 1958 brought a further deterioration of the situation, as did the continuing internecine conflict between rival nationalist factions. In response, Papon was installed as *préfet de police*. Papon brought over the *harki* police units in 1960, and used his extensive experience of *pacification* in Constantine (1956–1958). The inability (or reluctance) of senior police officers to control the anger of their uniformed officers faced with armed FLN attacks, was also a major factor.[18] In moving to demonstrate against a curfew, which was severely disruptive of its organisation and fundraising, and to recapture the symbolic space of the capital, the FLN drew a terrible official response.[19] De Gaulle was wary of appearing weak in order to placate the pro-*Algérie française* lobbies, and also wanted to maintain a strong bargaining position when negotiations would eventually resume with the Gouvernement provisoire de la République algérienne.[20] The massacre was therefore the result of long-term and seemingly 'normalised' repressive governance, public indifference and antipathy, and short-term conjunctural factors linked to the late war period.

The immediate aftermath

Maurice Halbwachs suggested that if an event were accorded wide importance at the time and could 'constitute an event' ('faire événement'), only then would that event thereafter be inscribed within a group's collective memory.[21] In fact, the massacre constituted an event in this Halbwachsian sense only for the Algerian communities and those solidarity groups previously described (and in different ways), rather than throughout French society. This helps to comprehend how and why the massacre was to disappear from the memory of many political parties and individuals within the space of only a few months, and how it would require the deliberate, campaigning cultivation of memory for it then to be transmitted more widely throughout society.

Many reasons explain the difficulty of ensuring that the memory of 17 October remained alive. The main sites where the killings took place were dispersed in the suburbs as well as in central Paris, some in closed spaces such as the Palais des sports. In addition, many bodies were thrown into the Seine or canals, thus rendering problematic the choice of a particular memory site on which to focus commemorations. One refers to a date—17 October (although the killings were spread over several days)—rather than a specific place, as is the case for the Charonne massacre. The official removal of bodies to unmarked graves further complicated any possible commemoration.[22] There was a well-established security force policy of 'anonymising' those Algerians it had killed, removing all distinguishing papers and belongings. [23] As David Le Breton suggests, 'il est socialement absurde de concevoir des hommes sans visage dont on puisse se souvenir'.[24]

Various other tactics were successfully deployed in the cover-up. First, the official narrative was that violence had been started by Algerians, that the security forces had acted in self-defence, and that there were three victims, not more. Second, through censorship and repression, the state prevented the widespread dissemination of testimonies that compromised the official version.[25] Third, even those high-ranking civil servants critical of police tactics, such as Michel Massenet, head of 'social services' for Algerians, refused to publicise their unease.[26] Fourth, Papon managed to block the judicial enquiry into the deaths by opening criminal investigations.[27] Longer-term factors include the unanimously voted amnesty legislation and selective access granted to archives.[28] This deliberate occultation should also be seen within the wider process of organised forgetting that covers the War in its entirety, a process no doubt aided by the lack of many of the memory frameworks (*cadres sociaux de la mémoire*) that form the essential structural, conceptual elements of space, time and language shaping predispositions to remember or forget.[29] Jean-Pierre Rioux has underlined the absence of a single memorial site either in France or Algeria, or of any clearly definable dates with which historical actors could identify, the result being a fragmented memory of the Algerian War across and within a whole range of social groups.[30] It is only since the law of 10 June 1999 that the Algerian War has been officially qualified as such.[31]

However, the need for active state intervention to cover up the massacre stemmed from protests that did occur. Broadly speaking, most dissent came from far-left and anticolonial groups. The mainstream Left was experiencing endemic disunity due to the Cold War, over what attitude to adopt regarding de Gaulle, and the linked question of how best to support French withdrawal from Algeria. Well aware that the official death toll was false, but in line with the broader mainstream consensus which de Gaulle was building on Algeria, the Groupe parlementaire socialiste decided not to protest forcefully, and the *Bureau national* of the PSU of 18 October regretted the 'quasi impossibilité de faire un véritable meeting commun' owing to disunity on the Left.[32] Relatively small-scale demonstrations did take place in Paris and elsewhere, the largest, on 20 October, comprising 1500 Algerian women and children.[33] Of the

32 protests linked to 17 October, 20 were composed entirely of Algerians.[34] Anticolonial and antiracist student and teacher groups protested where possible, but lacked the 'relais organisationnels susceptibles de soutenir un grand mouvement de masse'.[35] Some everyday forms of solidarity—so rare on 17 October itself—did therefore subsequently occur, both in the workplace and outside.[36]

Opposition groups used two main discursive themes. The first of these—that repression in Algeria had been transported to France—was already in wide circulation within anticolonial and antiwar groups.[37] For example, *Les Temps modernes* wrote: 'née à Alger, la "ratonnande" s'installe à Paris'.[38] As the MRAP had been doing for a decade, a second, more controversial theme highlighted the similarities between police tactics during the Vichy period and those now being used against Algerians. A petition published in *Les Temps modernes* drew a direct parallel between the Algerians held in the Palais des sports after 17 October and those Jews imprisoned at Drancy prior to deportation: 'entre les Algeriens entassés au Palais des sports en attendant d'être "refoulés" et les Juifs parqués à Drancy avant la Déportation, nous nous refusons de faire la différence'.[39] *Esprit* disagreed, declaring it 'inutile [...] de pratiquer des assimilations historiques'.[40]

The growing historiography of the late period of the Algerian War contrasts these low-key reactions to 17 October with reactions to the killing by police of nine protestors (eight of whom were PCF members) at the Charonne metro station on 8 February 1962.[41] However, the undeniable 'discriminatory sympathy' in operation does not explain everything: the political context in February 1962 was different from that of October 1961. During the intervening period, the mainstream Left had unified temporarily around opposition to the OAS, campaigned for an end to the War and against repressive police tactics at anti-OAS demonstrations; however, the massacre may well have acted as a catalyst in the widening of a revolt against what the state was doing in the name of its citizens.[42] The general strike of 13 February 1962 to mark the burial of the Charonne protestors constituted the largest political demonstration in Paris since February 1934. Charonne clearly did 'constitute an event' *à la* Halbwachs. After Charonne, the Left could refer to both the 1930s and the recent anti-Poujadist antifascism. In addition to being a well-known métro station, Charonne was at the heart of the Left's symbolic space, between *République* and *Nation*.[43] In contrast, there was no well-established tradition of republican antiracist campaigning against colonial racism, with easily identifiable dates, themes or well-known key figures that could have provided an ideological anchorage for moral protest after 17 October. The PCF was to subsume the memory of 17 October within the memory of Charonne, and socialist groups did not challenge such a representation. Jacques Panigel's underground film *Octobre à Paris*, shot in 1962, was a rare example of Vichy, 17 October and Charonne being brought together, closing with the narrator saying: 'La porte se ferme sur l'Algérien. Mais ne partez pas! Le 17 octobre continue! La porte va se rouvrir/C'est sur nous qu'elle rouvre! Sur nous qui ne sommes pas des bicots, qui n'étions pas des youpins, il y a vingt ans!'[44]

How and why the underground memory resurfaced

Before examining how and why the massacre's memory would invest the public domain, it is necessary to consider both the question of memory transmission, and the socio-political factors explaining the receptivity of individuals and groups to a given memory and the messages this carries.[45] In the case of the Paris massacre, two main aspects of memory transmission are studied. First, transmission within Algerian communities in France since 1961 across the generations. Second, the groups' ability to transmit this memory 'horizontally' to other, non-experiential groups, in order to create solidarity through what Halbwachs called a 'mémoire empruntée'.[46] The term 'memory vectors'[47] will be used to refer, for example, to immigrant rights groups, antiracist groups, far-left groups and their mobilisations and publications which, in the absence of any official memory vectors, have spread these 'oppositional' forms of memory.[48]

In Algeria, 17 October is the *Journée nationale à l'Émigration*. However, the massacre's importance in post-independence Algeria has fluctuated. The decimation the repression brought to FLN structures, the rapid resumption of negotiations, and the fact that over the war period this massacre was one of many examples of repression, have, at times, ensured little visibility for the massacre.[49] Similarly, the FLN single-party state held an ambivalent attitude to Algerian migrants in France, and wrote out from the history of Algerian nationalism the Messalist current (Mouvement national algérien) to which many Algerians in France were attached until the late 1950s. A more pluralist history of the war has been tolerated since the 1980s.[50] The pro-FLN Amicale des Algériens en France marked the 25th anniversary of 1961 by calling for a 'mémoire solidaire [et] conviviale' between the French and Algerian peoples.[51] The memory of 17 October as carried by the Algerian migrant communities and antiracist and immigrant-rights associations has therefore had to negotiate a space between the negation of the French state, and those dominant memories provided by the Algerian state (evoking the memory partially and inconsistently) and the mainstream French Left, which subsumed the memory within antifascism.[52]

For Algerians in France during the period until the mid-1970s, the major vector of memory transmission was the family. The survival of this private, familial memory is all the more remarkable, given the many factors proper to emigration that have affected memory transmission across the generations: geographical mobility and uprootedness; rehousing away from *bidonvilles, cités de transit* and inner-city districts which could have constituted memory sites; the return of migrants to Algeria due to labour rotation, redundancy, retirement or deportation; intense socio-economic disadvantage; and lack of access to cultural resources in the French context. More generally, Algerian migrants sometimes do not speak openly of the hardships endured.[53] Some parents probably deliberately shielded their descendants from knowing the full horrors of the massacre.[54] Silence is, of course, not the same as forgetting. As for many migrant communities, it was often the most politicised Algerian parents who transmitted the memory to their descendants.[55] Those familial memories are not homogeneous. While the massacre is usually remembered for the severe physical, emotional and economic consequences the repression brought, for some 17 October is remembered more positively, as an example of self-affirmation in the public sphere of a previously marginalised community; or, for some Algerian women, of a spatial and political visibility from which they were often excluded.[56]

Neither formalised, closed or institutionalised, the memory of 17 October was available to be used by Algerians and other racialised groups as a strategic resource in their opposition to racism in France from the early 1970s onwards, first by the pro-Maoist Mouvement des travailleurs arabes (MTA), which brought together manual workers and students from Morocco, Tunisia and Algeria in particular. The MTA campaigned against the racially motivated killings of Algerians in Paris and Marseille from 1971 onwards.[57] The MTA's protest against the killing in police custody in Versailles of Algerian Mohamed Diab, led the MTA organisers to route their (banned) protest demonstration of 16 December 1972 along that area of the Grands Boulevards where the police had fired on protestors on 17 October 1961.[58] Aware of the different political context since 1961, the organisers nevertheless drew a parallel with the continuing high levels of racism and socio-economic precariousness faced by Algerians. The march on the Justice Ministry started from '*Bonne nouvelle = le cinéma Rex*—où les Algériens avaient rougi les pavés de leur sang en octobre 1961. [...] Cet appel permettait de faire pleins feux sur les horreurs que connaissent aujourd'hui aussi les immigrés'.[59] Campaigners refused to allow the victims of racial attacks to sink into anonymity, contrary to what had happened in previous decades.[60] However, it was in the early 1980s that antiracist and immigrant-based associations attempted more systematically to invest the public domain with the memory of the massacre.

Some former MTA activists, along with the descendants of Algerian migrants raised in France, formed the autonomous counter-cultural Sans frontière (SF) media project (1979–1985) which, through its publication of the same name, was the first main vector of 1980s memory activism.[61] SF brought together the two closely linked themes within which memory of the massacre remains inscribed today. First, within calls to re-evaluate the memory of past and present migrations to France and, second, within campaigns against racial violence. With the official ending of primary migration in the post-1974 period, and the fading 'myth of return' once harboured by many migrant parents, most of the descendants of Algerian migrants conceived of their futures in France rather than elsewhere and therefore sought to understand better their parents' trajectories. These factors helped explain both the significance of, and the increased receptivity to, the theme of memory among Algerian migrant communities and other racialised groups.

Sans frontière sought to remind all young people active within the autonomous antiracist movements of the period 1980–1985, that their action should be situated within a long-established tradition of political activism and defence of rights of racialised groups. Unlike many of their parents, however, SF activists possessed the cultural capital to express demands in the French public sphere.[62] SF challenged media images (but also the views of some younger participants in the 1983 *Marche pour l'égalité et contre le racisme*) that the parents' generations had been submissive and fatalistic.[63] SF therefore looked to create intergenerational solidarity between migrant parents and their descendants. In 1984, SF activist Farid Aïchoune, after a spate of racist murders of young people of Maghrebi origin, declared: 'de la tuerie du 14 juillet 1953 au massacre du 17 octobre, en passant par les assassinats de Maghrébins ces dernières années, la même haine semble traverser les générations, à travers certaines couches de la population'.[64] Memory was thereby used as a 'narrative of resistance' to racism, and a focal point of the search for an identity politics in the face of an increasingly hostile media and political discourse on the theme of 'immigration' from the late 1970s.[65]

The relevance of the massacre to groups outside as well as within the Algerian communities is arguably explained by the fact that its memory fulfils a metonymic function, representing, in condensed form, many of the aspects of racism in contemporary France. These include the daily manifestation of the racist gaze in the 'picking out' by police of racialised groups for identity checks.[66] This, in turn, has led to the denunciation by these young people of their being considered as a 'corps-cible'.[67] Furthermore, when there is a racially motivated killing or attack, the police officer or other perpetrator usually escapes what the victims consider to be full justice, or the police or courts fail to recognise the racial intent behind the crime.[68] Rather as the cause of *L'Algérie française* had done during the Algerian War, the emergence of the Front national (FN) has crystallised and given greater confidence to the various racist constituencies within French society. SF's antiracist counter-memories articulate the composite nature of contemporary racism which blends both novel and long-standing ideologies and practises reworked in a new historical context.[69] These memories of racism help to bring together diverse racialised groups configured as sharing a 'community of suffering'[70] in relation to racism, and who demand equality, social justice, and increased citizenship. Memory thus has a 'transversal' function,[71] creating solidarity across national, ethnic and class identities, especially where the massacre is evoked as but one of a range of instances of state violence to have affected different groups. For example, SF insisted on the need for the massacre to be remembered alongside Charonne: both were part of a colonial history with which French society had yet to come to terms. As Aïchoune write: 'le sang des uns ne peut laver celui des autres, nos racines sont sanguinolentes—et la mémoire ne peut faire son choix [between 17 October and Charonne]'.[72] The Mouvement des droits civiques (MDC) held its 17 October commemoration at Charonne in 1990.[73] A collective linked to the 1984 antiracist social movement Convergence '84 pour l'Égalité advocated mobilising 'autour de l'histoire et des commémorations de dates permettant de reconstituer une mémoire collective. Exemples: 8 mai 1945 (massacre de Sétif), 17 octobre 1961 (massacre des Algériens à Paris), 16 juillet 1942 (rafle des juifs au Vél d'Hiv), date de proclamation de la commune et d'autres dates à trouver qui permettent l'ouverture à d'autres communautés [...]'[74] These examples illustrate Tzvetan Todorov's call for memory to be used to comprehend the sufferings of other groups, rather than simply to reflect inwardly the preoccupations of one's own group(s).[75] Crime writer Didier Daeninckx draws out these links in *Meurtres pour mémoire*, where Vichy is figured alongside 17 October, the linking chain being a thinly disguised equivalent of Papon.[76]

These developments within antiracist campaigning in the decade 1980–1990 were contemporaneous with the growth in unofficial public memories of the Algerian War, helped by the democratisation of access to media resources.[77] Another significant factor was the growing openness on the mainstream Left to (re-)examine 17 October. Many former far-left activists rejoined the Parti socialiste (PS) and re-infused the PS with the memory of 17 October, and 1981 saw the end of three decades of Gaullist-inspired rule.[78] SOS-Racisme was arguably representative of such a development on the mainstream Left; for the then president Harlem Désir, 17 October 'fait partie de notre culture politique', due to the founding activists' (former) far-left and student politics, and the numerous descendants of Algerian migrants in the association.[79] Yet it is ironic that the mainstream media interest in 17 October, which is noticeable from 1980–1981 onwards, was probably prompted more by these developments on the mainstream Left than by SF campaigning.[80] Indeed, in 1985, one year after the first commemoration in Paris of 17 October organised by (among others) SF, MDC and Radio-Beur, the same organisations held a ceremony separate from SOS-Racisme's commemoration. Notable also was Jean-Louis Péninou's article in *Libération* on 17 October 1980, which triggered much of this new media interest.[81] Péninou denounced what he saw as the Left's different value systems: universal condemnation after the racist bomb attack on the rue Copernic synagogue (3 October 1980), and the Left's comparative indifference to forms of racism linked to France's colonial and post-colonial history. The links and differences between attitudes to anti-Semitism under Vichy, and postcolonial racism are therefore a constant in any militant consideration of the memory of 17 October.

The 1990s—'Pour le droit à la mémoire?'

The 1990s witnessed a continuation of the theme of 17 October within the memory of migration and the construction of solidarity between racialised groups in their opposition to racism, while, at the same time, seeing the development of more demands addressed to governments. The 30th anniversary in 1991 saw some 10,000 demonstrators follow the symbolic route from the Canal Saint-Martin to the Rex cinema, marching under the banner 'Non au racisme, non à l'oubli. Pour le droit à la mémoire'.[82] This march and its extensive media coverage, a colloquium at the Sorbonne, the publication of Einaudi's *La Bataille de Paris* and Anne Tristan's *Le Silence du fleuve* (based on Mehdi Lallaoui and Agnès Denis' film of the same name),[83] all ensured that the massacre resurfaced as an important theme in the 1992 commemorations of the 30th anniversary of the end of the Algerian War. This renewal of interest—journalistic, academic and militant—helped to reveal the historical complexity of the massacre and its legacy. It also finally brought about a recognition from the PCF of the symbolism of 17 October, as affirmed by Claude Billard: 'cet hommage aux martyres d'hier, victimes du colonialisme, et l'action d'aujourd'hui pour la défense des droits et le respect de la dignité sont intimement liés.'[84]

The association Au nom de la mémoire (ANM; 1990–) has been one of the key vectors of this memory activism. It sets out to 'faire que la mémoire ne soit pas une matière figée, mais toujours en mouvement, impliquant un travail de fond rassemblant beaucoup de partenaires'.[85] Both the MRAP and ANM share a similar framework in relation to the memory of colonial massacres and the Algerian War, namely that: 'L'amnésie collective et le non-dit qui recouvrent cette période douloureuse, entretiennent le racisme anti-maghrébin'.[86] Official recognition of past atrocities is a necessary first step towards a more respectful attitude towards those groups still incurring hostility. For MRAP president Mouloud Aounit, 'Il faut une réparation symbolique à ce qui s'est passé. Il faut que la mémoire soit partagée par tous, que toutes les victimes soient reconnues comme telles, et que cela soit accepté par toutes les composantes de la société'.[87] Similarly, the ANM's Mehdi Lalloui argues that '[...] une histoire partagée par tous contribuera au respect de l'autre et, d'une certaine façon, à une réconciliation des peoples des deux rives de la Méditerranée'.[88] Such a 'mémoire critique'[89] stresses that any future project for French society can only be realised once the plurality of visions of France's colonial legacy has been officially recognised.

Since the early 1990s, both the MRAP and ANM have insisted that historians be allowed access to essential archives. With the added stimulus of the Papon trial (October 1997–April 1998), which publicised his role as *préfet* in 1961, this access is now beginning to be granted for certain researchers.[90] Although the numbers and identity of the dead are still unclear, Papon's claim of three deaths on 17 October has been refuted both by the conservative Mandelkern report of 1998 on the police archives, and the bolder Géronimi report of 1999 on the judicial archives, the latter report estimating the death toll at 48.[91] During Papon's failed attempt in February 1999 to prove defamation by Jean-Luc Einaudi,[92] the deputy public prosecutor Vincent Lesclou used the term 'massacre', and, in an official indictment of police behaviour, stigmatised the security forces on 17 October as 'jouets de la haine qui les a aveuglés'.[93]

Thus in the late 1990s, the 17 October massacre once again returned to the political agenda via a link with Vichy. As previously, this has attracted controversy. Several voices were critical of any comparison between Vichy and massacres during the Algerian War as evoked at Papon's trial, with Rousso in particular asking: 'Peut-on (ainsi) faire l'équation entre les rafles anti-juives de 1942–1944 et les massacres d'Algériens de 1961, et donc entre Pétain et de Gaulle? Absurde!'[94] However, none of the memory activism analysed in this article (perhaps with the exception of *Les Temps modernes* in November 1961 referred to above) has ever sought to equate 17 October within the logic of genocide. The parallels established by activists highlight the police techniques involved, the singling-out of a social group—very often racialised—for violent treatment, the impunity of those responsible and subsequent official reluctance to disclose information, and the messages this sends out to racialised groups (and their persecutors). One of the lawyers for the civil parties in the Papon trial expressly praised the 'solidarité dans le malheur' which Einaudi's testimony of 16 October 1997 had created between the descendants of those deported under Vichy and the descendants of the dead on 17 October.[95] If properly contextualised, historically speaking such parallels can help to strengthen awareness of past crimes committed in the name of the state, and to increase citizenship through reaffirming the importance of official accountability of state agencies, their policies and employees.[96] Such parallels also question any over-reductive vision of racism that sees it merely as an emanation of the extreme Right.

Conclusion

Over the past few decades, memory activism concerning the Paris massacre has contained an important 'vertical' function, by addressing demands to successive governments for the symbolic recognition of the extent of and responsibilities for the massacre, and for the opening of archives. Such activism has continued the well-established horizontal, transversal function of memory activism within antiracism, and which works to solidify internal bonds within social groups, to form collective identities, and to transmit memories to other groups. The memory of 17 October is a good example of the 'revenge' of post-1968 civil society on the state described by Pierre Nora.[97] It also provides an example of 'revenge' within civil society, of the hearing of newer voices and assertions of agency in relation to the established Left, as the result of autonomous social movements campaigning against racism. This article has situated the causes, nature, occultation and recovery of memory of 17 October within the *longue durée* of colonial and postcolonial history. Very often, we have seen the figure of Vichy haunt and complicate these separate but interrelated histories, providing a vital comparative link to other forms of racism. And yet the evocation of Vichy within antiracist discourses is not devoid of ambivalence, for, on the rare occasions where the 'tabou de l'objet'[98] of colonial and postcolonial racism is lifted, it is as if this can only be by means of reference to the Vichy period, with which French society is coming to terms more readily. This reminds us that what James Clifford calls the 'discrepant temporalities'[99] of racialised postcolonial migrant groups—for whom the key dates and events of national history do not, will not and cannot tell the whole story—are only beginning to force recognition by French society at large.

Notes and references

1. WIEVIORKA, A., *L'Ère du témoin* (Plon, 1998).
2. *See* BALIBAR, É., *Les Frontières de la démocratie* (La Découverte, 1992); GIUDICE, F., *Arabicides. Une chronique française 1970–1991* (La Découverte, 1992); STORA, B., *Le Transfert d'une mémoire. De l''Algérie française' au racisme anti-arabe* (La Découverte, 1999).
3. *See* BRUNET, J.-P., *Police contre FLN. Le drame d'octobre 1961* (Flammarion, 1999); EINAUDI, J.-L., *La Bataille de Paris: 17 octobre 1961* (Seuil, 1991); GAÏTI, B., 'Les ratés de l'histoire. Une manifestation sans suites: le 17 octobre à Paris', *Sociétés contemporaines* (nos. 18–19, 1994), pp. 11–37; TRISTAN, A., *Le Silence du fleuve. Ce crime que nous n'avons toujours pas nommé* (Au nom de la mémoire, 1991).
4. *See* note 3 above, and HOUSE, J. and MACMASTER, N., '*Une journée portée disparue*: the Paris massacre of 1961 and memory', in M.S. ALEXANDER and K. MOURÉ (eds), *Twentieth Century France: Crisis and Renewal* (Berghahn, forthcoming).
5. TERDIMAN, R., *Past Present. Modernity and the Memory Crisis* (Cornell University Press, 1993), p. 7.
6. *See* MEKHALED, B., *Chroniques d'un massacre, 8 mai 1945, Sétif, Guelma, Kherrata* (Au nom de la mémoire/Syros, 1995).

7. *See* BENOT, Y., *Les Massacres coloniaux 1944–1950: la IVe République et la mise au pas des colonies françaises* (La Découverte, 1994).
8. MACMASTER, N., *Colonial Migrants and Racism. Algerians in France, 1900–1962* (Macmillan, 1997), pp. 153–71 *passim*.
9. *See* Archives nationales (hereafter AN), F1a 5010; F1a 5054; *see* also VIET, V., *La France immigrée. Construction d'une politique 1914–1997* (Fayard, 1998), pp. 184–220 *passim*.
10. AN F1a 5061, *Directeur général de la Sûreté générale* to *Directeur des Affaires générales, Sous-Direction de l'Algérie*, 10 mai 1947.
11. *Journal officiel. Débats parlementaires* (17 juillet 1953), p. 3505.
12. MANCERON, G. and REMAOUN, H., *D'une rive à l'autre. La guerre d'Algérie de la mémoire à l'histoire* (Syros, 1993), p. 161.
13. In 1987 MRAP was renamed Mouvement contre le racisme et pour l'amitié entre les peuples. *See* HOUSE, J., 'Antiracism and antiracist discourse in France from 1900 to the present day', unpublished PhD dissertation (University of Leeds, 1997); LLOYD, C., *Discourses of Antiracism in France* (Ashgate, 1998).
14. 'Au faciès' (anonymous article), *Droit et Liberté*, 169 (janvier 1958), p. 2.
15. AN F1a 5061, *Situation des Nord-Africains en France: synthèse 29 septembre–18 octobre 1949.*
16. *See* EVANS, M., *The Memory of Resistance. French Opposition to the Algerian War (1954–1962)*, (Berg, 1997); HEURGON, M., *Histoire du PSU. 1. La fondation et la guerre d'Algérie (1958–1962)*, (La Découverte, 1994).
17. *See* AN F1a 5014, *Synthèse des rapports trimestriels établis par les conseillers techniques pour les affaires musulmanes*, rapport du 3e trimestre 1958, p. 37.
18. AN (Fontainebleau) 770391, Article 8, Dossier *Divers-événements-SAT*. *See* also VIET, *La France immigrée*, pp. 215–17.
19. *See* HAROUN, A., *La 7e Wilaya. La Guerre du FLN en France* (Seuil, 1986).
20. GAÏTI, 'Les ratés de l'histoire'.
21. HALBWACHS, M., *La Mémoire collective* (PUF, 1950—first published 1939), p. 48.
22. *See* HALBWACHS, M., *Les Cadres sociaux de la mémoire* (Albin Michel, 1994—first published 1925), p. 126.
23. EINAUDI, *La Bataille de Paris*, pp. 230–2; BRUNET, *Police contre FLN*, pp. 127–62.
24. LE BRETON, D., *Des Visages. Essai d'anthropologie* (Métalié, 1992), p. 201.
25. EINAUDI, *La Bataille de Paris*, pp. 239–42.
26. AN (Fontainebleau) 770391, Article 8 Dossier *Divers-événements-SAT*. *See* also EINAUDI, *La Bataille de Paris*, p. 253, note 1.
27. THÉNAULT, S., 'Le 17 octobre en question', *Jean Jaurès Cahiers semestriels*, 148 (juillet–septembre 1998), pp. 89–104.
28. MANCERON and REMAOUN, *D'une rive à l'autre*, pp. 35–6. LIAUZU, C., 'Le 17 octobre: guerres de mémoires, archives réservées et questions d'histoire', *Cahiers d'histoire immédiate*, 15 (printemps 1999), pp. 11–24.
29. HALBWACHS, *Les Cadres sociaux.*
30. RIOUX, J.-P., 'La flamme et les bûchers', in J.-P. RIOUX (ed.), *La Guerre d'Algérie et les Français* (Fayard, 1993), pp. 497–508. *See* also STORA, B., *La Gangrène et l'oubli. La mémoire de la guerre d'Algérie* (La Découverte, 1992).
31. *See* GROSJEAN, B., 'La France reconnaît qu'elle a fait la "guerre" en Algérie', *Libération* (10 juin 1999).
32. Fondation nationale des sciences politiques, Archives contemporaines (FNSPAC), Archives du Groupe parlementaire socialiste, minutes of meetings held 18 October and 7 November 1961; FNSPAC, Archives Daniel et Cletta Mayer 2M 1.1, *Compte-rendu de la réunion du bureau national du PSU*, 25 octobre 1961.
33. TRISTAN, *Le Silence du fleuve*, pp. 80–1.
34. TARTAKOWSKY, D., 'Les manifestations de rue', in RIOUX (ed.), *La Guerre d'Algérie*, p. 132, note 4.
35. MANN, P., 'Les manifestations dans la dynamique des conflits', in P. FAVRE (ed.), *La Manifestation* (Presses de la FNSP, 1990), p. 299.

36. SECOURS POPULAIRE, *Le Secours populaire français répond à des questions qui vous préoccupent. Les manifestations algériennes, pourquoi?* (Secours populaire français, 1961).
37. *See* SAUZAY, L., 'La Revue "Vérité–Liberté"; un exemple de la lutte contre la censure pendant la Guerre d'Algérie', unpublished DEA dissertation (Sciences Po, 1992).
38. 'La "Bataille de Paris"', *Les Temps modernes*, 186 (novembre 1961), pp. 618–20, p. 618.
39. 'Appel', *Les Temps modernes*, 186 (novembre 1961), pp. 624–8, p. 624.
40. 'Contre la barbarie', *Esprit* (novembre 1961), pp. 667–70, p. 668.
41. GAÏTI, 'Les ratés de l'histoire', p. 28; HEURGON, *Histoire du PSU*, p. 340; MANN, 'Les manifestations', p. 300.
42. HEURGON, *Histoire du PSU*, pp. 334–54 *passim*; RANCIÈRE, J., 'The cause of the other', *Parallax*, 4, 2 (1998), pp. 25–33, p. 28.
43. *See* TARTAKOWSKY, D., *Le Pouvoir est dans la rue. Crises politiques et manifestations en France* (Aubier, 1998).
44. Scenario reproduced in *Image et son*, 160 (mars 1963), pp. 2–23, p. 22.
45. WIEVIORKA, *L'Ère du témoin*, pp. 79–81 *passim*.
46. HALBWACHS, *La Mémoire collective*, p. 37.
47. ROUSSO, H., *Le Syndrome de Vichy de 1944 à nos jours* (Seuil, 1990), p. 253.
48. FENTRESS, J. and WICKHAM, C., *Social memory* (Blackwell, 1992), p. 135.
49. *See* HOUSE and MACMASTER, '*Une journée portée disparue*'.
50. REMAOUN, H., 'Pratiques historiographiques et mythes de fondation: le cas de la Guerre de libération à travers les institutions algériennes d'éducation et de recherche', in AGERON, C.-R. (ed.), *La Guerre d'Algérie et les Algériens*, pp. 305–22.
51. DJEGHOUL, A., 'Pour une mémoire conviviale', *Actualité de l'émigration*, 59 (15 octobre 1986), pp. 10–11, p. 10.
52. On 'dominant memory', *see* ROUSSO, *Le Syndrome de Vichy*, p. 12.
53. SAYAD, A., *L'Immigration ou les paradoxes de l'altérité* (De Boeck Wesmael, 1991), p. 141.
54. LEVINE, M., *Les Ratonnades d'octobre. Un meurtre collectif à Paris* (Ramsay, 1985), p. 220.
55. BAÊTA NEVES FLORES, L. F., 'Mémoires migrantes. Migration et idéologie de la mémoire sociale', *Ethnologie française*, XXV, 1 (1995), pp. 43–50.
56. TRISTAN, *Le Silence du fleuve*, pp. 80–1.
57. *See* GIUDICE, *Arabicides*, pp. 55–153 *passim*.
58. *Ibid.*, pp. 83–92 *passim*.
59. Bibliothèque de documentation internationale et contemporaine (BDIC), Nanterre, Fonds Saïd Bouziri, microfiche 214/4, *Lettre à un camarade en prison* (anonymous).
60. STORA, *Le Transfert d'une mémoire*, p. 92.
61. *See* POLAC, C., 'Quand "les immigrés" prennent la parole: histoire sociale du journal *Sans Frontière* 1979–1985', in P. PERRINEAU (ed.), *L'Engagement politique. Déclin ou mutation?* (Presses de la FNSP, 1994), pp. 359–86.
62. POLAC, 'Quand "les immigrés" prennent la parole'.
63. BOUAMAMA, S., *Dix ans de marche des Beurs. Chronique d'un mouvement avorté* (Desclée de Brouwer, 1994), p. 26.
64. 'La mémoire et l'oubli', *Sans frontière*, 88–89 (undated [late 1984]), p. 27.
65. On the idea of a 'narrative of resistance' to racism, *see* FENTRESS and WICKHAM, *Social Memory*, p. 117. *See* also BALIBAR, *Les Frontières*; BOUAMAMA, S., SAD-SAOUD, H. and DJERDOUBI, M., *Contribution à la mémoire des banlieues* (Volga, 1994).
66. *See* BAÊTA NEVES FLORES, 'Mémoires migrantes'.
67. ALLOUCHE, A., 'Les jeunes des banlieues et la mémoire des crimes sécuritaires', *Hommes et migrations*, 1158 (octobre 1992), pp. 6–9, p. 8.
68. *See* GIUDICE, *Arabicides*, and 'L'État assassine, meurtres racistes et sécuritaires', *Réflexes*, Hors série no. 1 (1992).
69. SILVERMAN, M., *Facing Postmodernity. Contemporary French thought on culture and society* (Routledge, 1999), ch. 2, pp. 40–65 *passim*.
70. WERBNER, P., 'Essentialising essentialism, essentialising silence: ambivalence and multiplicity in the constructions of racism and ethnicity', in P. WERBNER and T. MODOOD (eds), *Debating*

Cultural Hybridity. Multi-cultural Identities and the Politics of Antiracism (Zed Books, 1997), pp. 226–54, p. 243.
71. YUVAL-DAVIS, N., 'Ethnicity, gender relations and multiculturalism', in WERBNER and MODOOD, *Debating Cultural Hybridity*, pp. 193–208, pp. 203–6 *passim*.
72. 'Le temps des charognes', *Sans Frontière*, 49 (12–18 février 1982), p. 5.
73. EINAUDI, *La Bataille de Paris*, p. 295.
74. RODRIGUES, N., CHAPELLE, J., NAJBEGORN, O. and VIEIRA, J., *Convergence '84 pour l'Égalité. La ruée vers l'égalité* (Mélanges, 1985), p. 86.
75. TODOROV, T., *Les Abus de la mémoire* (Arléa, 1995).
76. *Meurtres pour mémoire* (Gallimard, 1984).
77. CITRON, S., 'La "nationalisation" des mémoires', in Collectif, *Mémoire et intégration* (Syros, 1993), pp. 65–71, p. 69.
78. *See* EINAUDI, *La Bataille de Paris*, pp. 227–9 *passim*.
79. Author's interview with Harlem Désir, Paris, 25 August 1995.
80. THÉNAULT, 'Le 17 octobre en question', p. 98.
81. EINAUDI, *La Bataille de Paris*, pp. 278–9.
82. *Le Monde* (19 octobre 1991).
83. Vidéothèque de Paris, code VDP6237.
84. *L'Humanité* (17 octobre 1991).
85. MESSAOUDI, S. 'Au nom de la mémoire', *Hommes et migrations*, 1175 (avril 1994), p. 4.
86. MRAP flyer, March 1993.
87. 'Sortir de l'oubli', *Différences*, 190 (novembre 1997), p. 1.
88. 'Sétif, 8 mai 1945, le devoir de mémoire', *Libération* (8 mai 1995).
89. CITRON, S., *Le Mythe national. L'histoire de France en question* (Éditions ouvrières, 1987), p. 287.
90. *See* LIAUZU, 'Le 17 octobre: guerres de mémoires'.
91. *Cf. Libération* (22 octobre 1997); MANDELKERN, D., *Rapport sur les archives de la Préfecture de Police relatives à la manifestation organisée par le FLN le 17 octobre 1961* (6 janvier 1998); *Libération* (5 mai 1998). For the Géronimi report, *see Le Monde* (13 août 1999).
92. *See Le Monde* (7–8, 13 février 1999); *Libération* (12 février 1999).
93. Quoted in STORA, *Le Transfert d'une mémoire*, p. 110.
94. ROUSSO, H., *La Hantise du passé. Entretien avec Philippe Petit* (Textuel, 1998), p. 121; GOLSAN, R.J., 'Memory's *bombes à retardement*: Maurice Papon, crimes against humanity, and 17 October 1961', *Journal of European Studies*, 28, 109–110 (March–June 1998), pp. 153–72.
95. For Einaudi's testimony, *see Le Procès de Maurice Papon. Compte rendu sténographique*, vol. 1 (Albin Michel, 1998), pp. 225–44. *See* also the statement by Maître Boulanger in *Le Procès de Maurice Papon*, vol. 2, p. 661.
96. *See* BALIBAR, É., *Droit de cité. Culture et politique en démocratie* (L'Aube, 1998).
97. 'L'ère de la commémoration', in NORA, P. (ed.), *Les Lieux de mémoire: Les France*, 3 (Gallimard, 1992), pp. 977–1012.
98. FOUCAULT, M., *L'Ordre du discours* (Gallimard, 1971), p. 11.
99. Clifford, J., *Routes. Travel and Translation in the Late Twentieth Century* (Harvard University Press, 1997), p. 263.

Name Index